Collective Security Law

The Library of Essays in International Law

General Editor: *Robert McCorquodale*

Titles in the Series

International Human Rights Law
Michael Addo

International Law and Indigenous Peoples
S. James Anaya

Law of the Sea
Hugo Caminos

Humanitarian Law
Judith Gardam

International Economic Regulation
Jane Kelsey

Sources of International Law
Martti Koskenniemi

Self-Determination in International Law
Robert McCorquodale

International Dispute Settlement
Mary Ellen O'Connell

International Crimes
Nikos Passas

International Environmental Law, Volumes I and II
Paula M. Pevato

State Responsibility in International Law
René Provost

Jurisdiction in International Law
W. Michael Reisman

Title to Territory
Malcolm Shaw

The Nature of International Law
Gerry Simpson

Collective Security Law
Nigel D. White

Collective Security Law

Edited by .

Nigel D. White

University of Nottingham, UK

ASHGATE
DARTMOUTH

Published by
Dartmouth Publishing Company
Ashgate Publishing Limited
Gower House
Croft Road
Aldershot
Hants GU11 3HR
England

Ashgate Publishing Company
Suite 420
101 Cherry Street
Burlington, VT 05401-4405 USA

Ashgate website: http://www.ashgate.com

British Library Cataloguing in Publication Data
Collective security law. – (The library of essays in
   international law)
   1. Security, International – Law and legislation
   I. White, N. D., 1961–
   341.7'2

Library of Congress Control Number: 2001099644

ISBN 0 7546 2235 5

Printed in Great Britain by The Cromwell Press, Trowbridge, Wiltshire

Contents

PART III UN COLLECTIVE SECURITY MEASURES

PART IV COLLECTIVE SECURITY OUTSIDE THE UN

Acknowledgements

The editor and publishers wish to thank the following for permission to use copyright material.

American Society of International Law for the essays: David D. Caron (1993), 'The Legitimacy of the Collective Authority of the Security Council', *American Journal of International Law*, **87**, pp. 552–88; Jose E. Alvarez (1996), 'Judging the Security Council', *American Journal of International Law*, **90**, pp. 1–39; Oscar Schachter (1991), 'United Nations Law in the Gulf Conflict', *American Journal of International Law*, **85**, pp. 452–73; Jules Lobel and Michael Ratner (1999), 'Bypassing the Security Council: Ambiguous Authorizations to Use Force, Cease-Fires and the Iraqi Inspection Regime', *American Journal of International Law*, **93**, pp. 124–54. Reproduced with permission from 87 *AJIL*, 552–88 (1993); 90 *AJIL*, 1–39 (1996); 85 *AJIL*, 452–73 (1991), 93 *AJIL*, 124–54 (1999), Copyright © The American Society of International Law.

Frank Cass Publishers for the essays: David M. Malone and Karin Wermester (2000), 'Boom and Bust? The Changing Nature of UN Peacekeeping', *International Peacekeeping*, **7**, pp. 37–54; David O'Brien (2000), 'The Search for Subsidiarity: The UN, African Regional Organizations and Humanitarian Action', *International Peacekeeping*, **7**, pp. 57–83.

Indian Society of International Law for the essay: V.S. Mani (1995), 'The Role of Law and Legal Considerations in the Functioning of the United Nations', *Indian Journal of International Law*, **35**, pp. 91–118.

Journal of International Law and Politics for the essay: Keith Harper (1994), 'Does the United Nations Security Council have the Competence to Act as Court and Legislature?', *New York University Journal of International Law and Politics*, **27**, pp. 103–57.

Kluwer Law International for the essay: Christian Walter (1997), 'Security Council Control over Regional Action', *Max Planck Yearbook of United Nations Law*, **1**, pp. 129–93.

Michigan Journal of International Law for the essay: Martti Koskenniemi (1996), 'The Place of Law in Collective Security', *Michigan Journal of International Law*, **17**, pp. 455–90.

Oxford University Press for the essays: N.D. White (2000), 'The Legality of Bombing in the Name of Humanity', *Journal of Conflict and Security Law*, **5**, pp. 27–43. Copyright © 2000 Oxford University Press; Martti Koskenniemi (1995), 'The Police in the Temple: Order, Justice and the UN: A Dialectical View', *European Journal of International Law*, **6**, pp. 325–48; W. Michael Reisman and Douglas L. Stevick (1998), 'The Applicability of International Law Standards to United Nations Economic Sanctions Programmes', *European Journal of International Law*, **9**, pp. 86–141; Bruno Simma (1999), 'NATO, the UN and the Use of Force: Legal Aspects', *European Journal of International Law*, **10**, pp. 1–22. Copyright © 1999 EJIL.

Royal Institute of International Affairs for the essay: J.L. Brierly (1946), 'The Covenant and the Charter', *British Yearbook of International Law*, **23**, pp. 83–94.

T M C Asser Press for the essay: Roberto Lavalle (1990), 'The "Inherent" Powers of the UN Secretary- General in the Political Sphere: A Legal Analysis', *Netherlands International Law Review*, **37**, pp. 22–36.

Transnational Law & Contemporary Problems for the essay: Colin Warbrick (1995), 'The United Nations System: A Place for Criminal Courts?', *Transnational Law and Contemporary Problems*, **5**, pp. 237–61.

Yale Law Journal for the essay: Hans J. Morgenthau (1946), 'Diplomacy', *Yale Law Journal*, **55**, pp. 1067–80. Reprinted by permission of The Yale Law Journal Company and William S. Hein Company from *The Yale Law Journal*, Vol. 55, pp. 1067–80.

Every effort has been made to trace all the copyright holders, but if any have been inadvertently overlooked the publishers will be pleased to make the necessary arrangement at the first opportunity.

Series Preface

Open a newspaper, listen to the radio or watch television any day of the week and you will read or hear of some matter concerning international law. The range of matters include the extent to which issues of trade and human rights should be linked, concerns about refugees and labour conditions, negotiations of treaties and the settlement of disputes, and decisions by the United Nations Security Council concerning actions to ensure compliance with international law. International legal issues have impact on governments, corporations, organisations and people around the world and the process of globalisation has increased this impact. In the global legal environment, knowledge of international law is an indispensable tool for all scholars, legal practitioners, decision-makers and citizens of the 21st century.

The Library of Essays in International Law is designed to provide the essential elements for the development of this knowledge. Each volume contains essays of central importance in the development of international law in a subject area. The proliferation of legal and other specialist journals, the increase in international materials and the use of the internet, has meant that it is increasingly difficult for legal scholars to have access to all the relevant articles on international law and many valuable older articles are now unable to be obtained readily. These problems are addressed by this series, which makes available an extensive range of materials in a manner that is of immeasurable value for both teaching and research at all levels.

Each volume is written by a leading authority in the subject area who selects the articles and provides an informative introduction, which analyses the context of the articles and comments on their significance within the developments in that area. The volumes complement each other to give a clear view of the burgeoning area of international law. It is not an easy task to select, order and place in context essays from the enormous quantity of academic legal writing prublished in journals – in many languages – throughout the world. This task requires professional scholarly judgment and difficult choices. The editors in this series have done an excellent job, for which I thank and congratulate them. It has been a pleasure working with them.

ROBERT McCORQUODALE
General Series Editor
School of Law
University of Nottingham

Introduction

The Concept of Collective Security Law

There are many definitions and discussions of what is meant by 'collective security' (Downs, 1994). Very generally we can delineate this area of international relations as any collective action designed to defuse situations that endanger the peace and combat threats to, and breaches of, (international) peace. Using United Nations (UN) Charter terminology, collective security can both promote the peaceful settlement of situations that endanger peace (Chapter VI) and take action with respect to threats to the peace, breaches of the peace or acts of aggression (Chapter VII). Much debate, mostly legal, then centres around the meaning of terms such as 'threat to the peace', 'breach of the peace', and the more judgemental concept of 'aggression' (see Article 39). Many different explanations and applications will be found in the essays in this volume. The greater the lack of consistency and certainty in the development and application of these terms will tend to suggest that the delicate balance between law and politics inherent in the area of collective security leans heavily towards the political. As Martti Koskenniemi states in the first essay of this volume: '[i]f everything depends on the particular facts and circumstances, the rule-governed character of the procedure will disappear and, with it, the system's deterrent force. It will start to seem like just another context for politics' (p. 12). If the keys that unlock the collective security procedures and machinery are simply political tools, then law does not play a profound role in this area.

Law at this primary constitutional level is under the greatest political pressure. Relatively clear terms such as 'breach of the peace', while retaining their core certainty, may be applied selectively, while other terms, such as 'threat to the peace', have an inherent ambiguity, deliberately chosen so as to allow a significant amount of discretion. The amount of discretion, however, is debated,[1] with there being strong contentions that even determinations of threats to the peace by the Security Council are subject to law. It has been suggested that legal principles applicable include the concept of *bona fides* (Franck, 1993), the principle of due process,[2] the norms of *jus cogens*, as well as the purposes and principles of the United Nations Charter (Cryer, 1996). Such issues are debated in several of the essays in this volume, particularly in relation to the Security Council's coercive action against Libya, and Libya's attempt to question the legality of this action before the International Court of Justice.[3] Although the case has not yet proceeded to the merits, and may never do so given the trial of the two Libyan agents suspected of the Lockerbie bombing of 1988,[4] the issue is of profound significance for collective security law. An assertion of legal review over the most jealously guarded element of Security Council discretion would indeed establish the idea and reality of collective security *law*. The existence of discretion is not inconsistent with the idea of the rule of law. It is perfectly possible to state that discretion must be exercised in accordance with the law – a proposition found in most municipal public law systems.

Beneath this level of primary constitutional norms, we can evaluate the application of collective security mechanisms in legal terms, tracing them back to their source, normally within the provisions of constituent treaties of international organizations. As many of the essays in this volume show, law is more secure at this secondary level since it is not as pressured by political considerations. Collective security action may take the form of peaceful settlement (or Chapter VI action in UN Charter terms) or coercive action in the form of economic or military measures (Chapter VII action). Furthermore, institutional development within the UN and other entities operating in the field has led to the implication and assertion of other powers. These include the creation of a consensual military option in the form of a peacekeeping force (sometimes labelled 'Chapter VI^1/$_2$' action) as well as the more controversial use of international criminal tribunals in a collective security context. Fierce debate is still to be found at this level of legal analysis – for example, in the discussion of whether international criminal tribunals can actually contribute to international peace and whether the Security Council has the power to create such tribunals.

Since the focus of this volume is on collective security *law*, discussions on what constitutes collective security have not been allowed to dominate but will emerge during the course of the essays. Each essay has its own particular view on this issue as a prerequisite, or sometimes a presumption, upon which the author then builds her or his vision of the role of law in collective security. The diversity of views on what is collective security is interesting in itself since it reflects the profound uncertainty in this crucial field. In a sense, this is partly a product of the sense that collective security is a voyage into the unknown in that it transcends the view that international society is essentially horizontal and consensual and can have no effective system of regulation or governance. We may have seen the erosion of this in certain areas – in economics and even human rights – but to argue that such regulation has evolved, or can evolve, in relation to the ultimate expression of high politics – the use of military power – automatically attracts accusations of 'idealism' or 'utopianism'.

Indeed, to talk about collective security – and more so when talking about a collective security *system* – we are already assuming some sort of order, some sort of regulation perhaps. Law is presumed to exist, although it is not necessarily inherent in a collective security system, given that it is entirely feasible to build a system or order on political foundations. However, it can be contended that such an order is limited, allowing a tremendous amount of change, often violent, as political considerations alter. Maybe it is too much to expect law and mechanisms created by legal means to *govern* or *regulate* the use of military (and perhaps economic) force in international relations. In opposition, the vision offered by the pragmatic or realist view of international relations as a brutal interplay of political interests and power, sometimes disguised in normative language, seems unrealistic given the time and energy that states devote to justifying their actions, and even their transgressions, not simply politically but legally. In Chapter 2 Hans Morgenthau propounds his realist arguments that international law applied by international organizations will lead to the failure of collective security. According to Morgenthau, peace and order cannot be based on law but on a real understanding of the 'rules of the political art', by which he means that 'what is at stake in conflicts . . . is not who is right and who is wrong but what ought to be done to reconcile the particular interests of individual nations with the general interest in peace and order' (p. 51). Is the Middle East crisis better settled by the old diplomacy based on balancing political interests or on the new diplomacy based on law embodied in the United Nations?

Both visions – realist and institutionalist (legalist) – are offered in the literature. Indeed, the global collective security system embodied in the UN can be analysed as an (unholy?) alliance of realist balance-of-power considerations (the permanent five of the Security Council with their veto power) within an institutionalist legal framework. J.L. Brierly in 'The Covenant and the Charter' (Chapter 3) points out, with his usual prescience, that the presence of the veto is a significant, perhaps fatal, flaw in the constitutional edifice of the Charter. He further argues that the much derided League system may have been an honest attempt to shape a collective security mechanism more suited to a society of states, based as it was on principles of unanimity and voluntarism: '. . . before international institutions can be raised from the co-operative to the organic type . . . we need a society far more closely integrated than the society of states is to-day' (p. 64). The League failed, according to Brierly, not because of weaknesses in the design of the organization, but in the failure of states to fulfil their obligations under the Covenant.

Nevertheless, the United Nations has survived, although it was largely ineffective during the Cold War. Although a minority of member states breached the fundamental Charter provision prohibiting the use of force (Article 2(4)), and the permanent members ignored the restraints that do exist on their right of veto (Article 27(3)) (White, 1997, pp. 8–11), the Charter has survived, albeit modified in certain respects by practice that has been accepted as normative.[5] Furthermore, although powerful states have chosen to ignore the Charter in many instances, the idea of the United Nations as a mechanism for collective security has survived and its activities in the field have increased dramatically since the beginning of the 1990s. Powerful states cannot afford to be outside the United Nations. This is illustrated by the temporary Soviet absence from the Security Council in 1950 – an absence that enabled the Security Council to authorize military action against North Korea. Weaker states, too, find a certain sanctuary within the UN, although this is as much a product of economic factors and the fact that they, at least in the General Assembly, can make their voice heard, as it is about receiving protection under the collective security umbrella.

The essay by V.S. Mani on 'The Role of Law and Legal Considerations in the Functioning of the United Nations' (Chapter 4), picks up the question of the legal character of the United Nations, positing the Charter as somewhere between a simple treaty and a constitution. His analysis recognizes the value of the law-making functions of the UN, particularly for developing states, as a method of countering the power politics of developed states. Nevertheless, he also points to the Janus-faced character of the Charter, in that it both seeks to regulate the conduct of states and, at the same time, permits a huge measure of discretion for powerful states. Mani's essay points to many issues in collective security law that are confronted more fully in later essays. One such issue is the relationship between customary international law and the treaty-dominated collective security structures. Another is the debate that exists between those who argue that collective security mechanisms are governed by law and those who deny this. Both these issues go to the heart of the existence and nature of collective security law. Were the actions taken by the US-led armies against North Korea in 1950 and against Iraq in 1991 misuses of the Security Council by powerful states or were they lawful exercises of power by that organ? Mani's essay sets up the debate, but no one can ignore his post-Cold War clarion call to developing states 'to awake from their dazed state and assert themselves, or at least vociferously remind the Big Powers of the legal and moral limits of political action' (p. 89).

Martti Koskenniemi in 'The Place of Law in Collective Security' (Chapter 1) offers us a different vision of the place of law in collective security. The distance between the formalistic utopian vision of law regulating powerful states and the 'flesh and blood of the application of power by states to fulfill their interests' (p. 3) leads him to put forward an alternative analysis of the role of law in collective security. He states in relation to the realist approach that '[a]rguing that normative factors are either irrelevant or only marginally relevant to Security Council action undermines the degree to which any social action, including international activity, makes constant reference to normative codes, rules, or principles' (p. 16). Although there may be great debate and controversy about the content of these rules and principles, their presence and usage signifies that the 'controversy is therefore normative . . . and not empirical' (p. 17). Powerful states may choose to step outside the normative framework on occasions (the Cuban Missile Crisis in 1962 and the NATO bombings of the Federal Republic of Yugoslavia (FRY) in 1999 are arguably two examples). However, those states normally try to justify their actions either as actually coming within the institutional legal framework, or they try to stretch the framework, or they claim a customary basis for their action, or sometimes they simply have to admit that, in all honesty, this is an exceptional circumstance that does not create a precedent for the future. Nevertheless, Koskenniemi does not subscribe to the formalistic application of law to the facts. However, that is not to say we cannot engage in such exercises, as the student of law knows all too well. Koskenniemi's argument is that this approach hides the 'truth about international law as a cultural instead of an instrumental phenomenon, highlighting the engaged aspect of the law, its being "inside" social practices instead of "outside" them as an objective language or a formal procedure' (p. 37). He concludes that, for him, it is clear that 'law has a place in collective security as a working culture of the "gentle civilizer" by opening conceptions and practices of "security" to public debate, and by enhancing the accountability of governmental and international institutions for what goes on under the label of "security policy"' (p. 38). Whether the reader agrees with him or not, there is a case to be answered, and practically for the purposes of this volume, his account does provide us with the alternative approaches – the realist and the institutionalist (legalist) – threads of each being found in the other essays in this volume.

This is a volume of essays about collective security law, as outlined above. It is not directly a volume about the customary and treaty rules governing the use of force in international relations. Of course, the two areas of international law are interrelated, since the main function of a collective security system is to control the use of violence in the international system. The UN Charter provides for the prohibition of the threat or use of force in international relations (Article 2(4)). It provides that the Security Council can undertake or authorize military action to maintain or restore international peace and security (Articles 42 and 53). It also preserves the right of states to defend themselves either individually or collectively, but only 'until the Security Council has taken measures necessary to maintain international peace and security' (Article 51). Inevitably such a scheme, relying as it does on a very active, non-selective and powerful Security Council, has been subject to criticisms that are often combined with arguments that there are much wider customary rights belonging to states. Thus there are claims to a much wider right of self-defence than that embodied in the Charter, that military intervention is permitted with consent, that customary law allows for the protection of nationals and that international law has embraced a doctrine of humanitarian intervention (Gray, 2000). The presence of additional customary rights is not necessarily an anathema to the idea of collective security, although it may be argued that if these rights are recognized as wide-ranging and subjective, then it is no longer possible to talk about collective security. If this is the case, while not completely returning to the pre-1919 period of a virtually unlimited right to go to war, international relations will have reached a point where force is permitted in so many instances that the prohibition of it no longer makes any sense. All the essays in this volume are written against the background of the rules governing the use of force. However, those rules are not the main focus. The volume looks at the issue from the angle of the collective security systems and mechanisms put in place, although the reader must be aware of the relationship between these systems and the types of activity they attempt to regulate.[6]

Actors within the United Nations: Powers and Legitimacy

The UN is the main actor in the field of collective security. Although there are many other organizations in the field – regional (for example, the Organization of American States (OAS)), defence (for example, the North Atlantic Treaty Organization (NATO)) and security (for example, the Organization on Security and Cooperation in Europe (OSCE)) – the UN is the only global actor. Regional organizations may contribute to dealing with local threats to, or breaches of, the peace but can they deal with threats to international peace? Such issues will be discussed in Part IV. Part II, however, considers the principal actors within the UN system – the Security Council (by far the most powerful body), the General Assembly, the Secretary-General and the International Court of Justice. While the Security Council has 'primary responsibility' for international peace and security (Article 24(1)), the other organs have subsidiary competence, often overlooked in the cascade of activity emerging from the Security Council with the end of the Cold War. This activity has caused international lawyers great concern: while applauding increased effectiveness and enforcement, they have been concerned with issues of legality and legitimacy (Franck, 1990).

David Caron (Chapter 5) examines the legitimacy of the most powerful actor in the field of collective security: the Security Council. With the end of the Cold War in the late 1980s, the Security Council has flexed its muscles in a variety of ways. Sometimes, as the essays in this volume will show, this has been legally problematic; more often than not there have been question marks over the legitimacy of individual actions, and more fundamentally over the legitimacy of a 15-member organ (with a built-in 'pentarchy') 'dictating' to the membership of 191 states. Caron looks at the reform debate that has been rumbling on within the UN throughout the 1990s and into the new century, focusing on the veto and making many practical suggestions including the removal of the 'reverse veto' that allows a permanent member to block attempts to amend previous Security Council decisions. Caron's 1993 analysis is still pertinent today. The reform debate has progressed but is not, by any stretch of the imagination, reaching a conclusion (Winkelmann, 1997). Furthermore, the use of the reverse veto by the USA and the UK, which has prevented the lifting of the sanctions regime against Iraq first imposed in 1990, constitutes one of the most serious crises facing the UN today. Whatever the justifications for the continuation of this punitive regime, the USA and the UK seem to have missed Caron's basic point: 'if the target state and its citizenry conclude that, no matter what they do, the sanctions will remain in place because of the wishes of one or two permanent members, they may simply stiffen their resistance and reject further efforts to satisfy what they see as an undemocratic and unresponsive Council' (p. 130).

Caron's analysis and proposals represent an attempt at balancing two competing considerations – legitimacy and effectiveness. An expanded Security Council may be more legitimate but would it be effective? 'To be effective, international governance must be concentrated in some body other than the whole. The question is how to design this body so that the governed as a whole, both in fact and in perception, are served rather than oppressed' (p. 131). Changes to the most powerful organ must be considered carefully (Murphy, 1994). However, there is no doubt that recent events in Somalia, Rwanda, Bosnia and Kosovo, where the Council has either failed to act effectively or failed to act at all, have put increased pressure on the UN for reform of its executive body. Without permanent member agreement, however, reform is impossible (Article 108).

The concentration of governance in the hands of the Security Council is of direct concern to Keith Harper (Chapter 6). Like Caron, he is concerned with the increased activity of the Security Council. While this should have a 'positive effect on the international landscape', Harper points out that this causes problems for both legality and legitimacy: '. . . the Council must protect its institutional legitimacy by acting in ways which most states deem appropriate and within its competence' (p. 135). A serious issue discussed by Harper is the extremely broad powers granted either explicitly or implicitly to the Council. While being conceived primarily as an executive body 'bestowed with policing power and the capacity to use coercive force in the form of military and economic sanctions' (p. 137), the Security Council has also acted in judicial and legislative capacities. In liberal democratic theory, the failure to separate these powers in different organs (executive, judicial and legislative) is seen as a recipe for abuse of power, given that this may lead to one organ, or indeed one person, making, applying and enforcing the law. Harper also considers the Security Council's actions as regards Iraq, Libya and Israel and indicates that there may be a problem with the Council usurping the functions of the General Assembly and the International Court of Justice. He states that in ignoring the 'clear separation of function and power set forth in the Charter, the Security Council diminishes the legitimacy of the entire U.N. system' (p. 172). However, he concludes that the legitimacy of the Council's actions will be improved if the Council, when acting legislatively acts 'appropriately as a legislature', and when it acts in a judicial manner then the focus should be on whether 'it acted appropriately as a court' (p. 186). When acting as a legislator, Harper suggests that consultation with the Assembly is in order, while when acting as a Court he suggests that rules of due process be adopted.

Martti Koskenniemi's second essay, 'The Police in the Temple' (Chapter 7), also considers the separation of powers between the Security Council and the General Assembly but from a more contextual, and perhaps more fundamental, angle. He considers that, although the Great Powers (or the Permanent Five (P5)) may have wanted to create an organization based on order or power, they failed to eradicate all references to justice and authority in the Charter. More importantly those powers made minor concessions to the smaller powers, which wanted the General Assembly to have some competence to deal with economic, social and humanitarian matters. These matters had the potential, within a developing constitutional order, to spill into the Security Council's main area of competence. The result is that '[t]he Organization is neither simply a policeman nor a Temple of Justice' (p. 192). During the Cold War, with the Council (the police) largely unemployed, matters were dealt with in the Assembly (the Temple), not simply in terms of order but in terms of the injustices felt by the majority of members. The result was that '[t]he "tyranny" of the Great Powers was overruled by the "tyranny" of the majority' (p. 201). The Assembly, although much weaker in terms of powers, did occasionally try to maintain order in the absence of an effective Security Council, by recognizing that it had recommendatory enforcement powers in the (in)famous Uniting for Peace Resolution of 1950 and by creating the first peacekeeping force to help resolve the Suez crisis in 1956. However, with the end of the Cold War the position has been changed: '[i]t is not the Assembly that is trying to deal with the problem of order; the Security Council is attempting to deal with the problem of international justice' (p. 205). Koskenniemi argues against this development in essence by stating that considerations of justice and the good life (embodied in wide conceptions of peace and security) are not the concern of the police but of the Temple: 'the peace of the police is not the calm of the temple but the silence of the tomb' (p. 212).

The legality of the Uniting for Peace Resolution is regarded by many as a theoretical problem given that, as Koskenniemi points out, issues of order (and, increasingly, justice) are now in the hands of the Council. However, there are arguments that, in exceptional cases, it should be revived. In 'The Legality of Bombing in the Name of Humanity' (Chapter 8), N.D. White considers these arguments in relation to the Kosovo crisis, where the Security Council again appeared to be deadlocked. The arguments in favour of NATO bombing of the FRY in 1999 seemed to be predicated on the need to uphold human rights and to prevent grave injustices – ideal issues to be considered by the General Assembly. The fact that General Assembly approval was not sought is considered in terms of its impact on the collective security apparatus and the future of collective security. Rhetorical claims to be acting on behalf of the 'international community', without grounding those actions within concrete manifestations of that community, constitute a serious erosion of the fragile foundations of peace.

Of considerable importance in the day-to-day diplomacy and peacemaking efforts of the UN is the role of the Secretary-General (Murthy, 1995). Although the impact of this office does depend to a large extent on the personality of the Secretary-General (contrast the largely administrative approach of Kurt Waldheim with the dynamism of Dag Hammarskjöld), there are legal issues to be considered here. A glance at the UN Charter reveals that the Secretary-General is not granted much by way of 'autonomous' powers, independent of mandates given to him by other political organs (Articles 97–99). Yet the Secretary-General has developed a significant array of functions such as good offices, fact-finding, and even arbitration. The question is whether these are compatible with the UN Charter, whether they can be implied or inherent powers, or whether they are, as Roberto Lavalle suggests in 'The "Inherent Powers" of the UN Secretary-General in the Political Sphere' (Chapter 9), the product of a 'permissive rule of customary international law' (p. 238).

While recognizing the legality of certain autonomous powers, and the practical limitations upon their further development, Lavalle is right to point out that it is the lawyer's job 'to determine the purely legal limits of the autonomous powers' (p. 240). However, it is one thing to recognize the existence of a doctrine of *ultra vires* in international institutional law, but it is a different matter as to whether there exists mechanisms of accountability and review. Koskenniemi in 'The Police in the Temple' (Chapter 7) argues that the General Assembly performs a function of political review of the Security Council and, to a certain extent, it did this during the Cold War. But, for international lawyers, the crucial issue is whether the International Court of Justice has the competence and the confidence to judicially review the actions of the political organs. The issue has emerged in the field of collective security, in particular with Libya's application to the World Court in the *Lockerbie* cases, starting in 1992. Part of Libya's claim is that the Security Council did not have the competence to find a threat to the peace in the case of Libya's activities and therefore its sanctions regime was illegal (White, 1999a). The divisions that this case has caused amongst international lawyers justifies the reintroduction into this volume, in the essay 'Judging the Security Council' by Jose Alvarez

(Chapter 10), of the debate between the realist and legalist approaches. The former places politics above law, while the latter, conceding that political factors are predominant in Security Council decision making, still sees that there are legal parameters within which the Council should act. Alvarez considers this dispute and suggests that the way forward is not as black and white as either of these schools suggest: '"Judicial review" often does not arrive fully formed, heralded and portentous; aspects of review are more likely to emerge incrementally, unannounced and, sometimes, unnoticed' (p. 253). If the Court is faced with the issue, whether in advisory or contentious cases, of giving its views on the meaning of crucial Charter provisions, whether on the jurisdiction of particular organs (for example, Article 39), or the division of competence between organs of the UN (for example, Articles 11(2) and 12), or the division of competence between organs of the UN and member states (see Article 2(7)), then it will normally respond. Although the Court is highly unlikely to declare a current Security Council resolution null and void, its legal opinion will shape future Security Council action, unless the Council wishes to lose credibility by taking what are clearly (after the Court's opinion) *ultra vires* decisions.

Of course, the role of the International Court in the realms of collective security is not simply as a possible court of review; it also contributes in more direct ways to the idea of peace through law. Bearing in mind the realist position advocated by Morgenthau that disputes are best settled by political means, the essay by Dapo Akande, 'The Role of the International Court of Justice in the Maintenance of International Peace' (Chapter 11), puts forward the legalist position. Akande considers that the International Court has contributed more generally to international peace and security by its decisions and its procedures in contentious cases on matters that have caused, or are likely to cause, hostilities among states. Its advisory opinions have also had a role in this regard. Furthermore, he argues that settlement by judicial means is an effective way of resolving disputes: 'Recourse to the Court allows for an authoritative and more palatable vindication of the position of one side over the other' (p. 305). Fundamentally, he considers the Court's jurisprudence on the so-called dichotomy between legal and political disputes and finds that the Court generally assumes jurisdiction in highly politicized cases because they almost always involve legal issues. Of course, one would expect the World Court to assert the supremacy of law over politics – after all, it is a legal forum – but this would disregard the tremendous political pressure that the Court was under in, for example, the *Nicaragua*[7] and *Lockerbie* cases, as well as *Legality of Nuclear Weapons* opinions.[8]

UN Collective Security Measures

Part III is concerned with legal issues arising from the adoption and application of the most significant collective security measures. Focus here will be on Chapter VI^1/$_2$ (peacekeeping) and Chapter VII measures (sanctions, military measures and international criminal tribunals). Pure Chapter VI activities will not be considered here, although they are discussed in many of the essays in this volume (see also Merrills, 1998).

Of course, all such measures are (or should be) adopted within the normative framework of the UN Charter as developed by practice that is considered as normative. Although no direct Charter base for peacekeeping operations can be discerned, it is true that consensual peacekeeping operations are framed by a much more sophisticated set of institutional rules than enforcement operations, despite the presence of greater formal provisions in the Charter for the latter (White,

1996). The much looser control exercised over enforcement operations may be argued (by pragmatists) to be essential for those operations to be effective, given that they generally have much more ambitious mandates (to restore peace as opposed to keeping an existing one) than their blue-helmeted counterparts. However, as later essays in this volume show, the less control the Security Council has over military operations, the greater the legitimacy deficit. Furthermore, the infusion of such looseness in control into peacekeeping operations, particularly those with more belligerent mandates,[9] may be said to undermine the very essence of peacekeeping, leading to host states suspecting that a peacekeeping force may operate in accordance with the wishes of the major contributing states, rather than with the principles of peacekeeping crafted within the UN. Such issues are discussed by David Malone and Karin Wermester in 'Boom and Bust? The Changing Nature of UN Peacekeeping' (Chapter 12), an essay which also provides a useful overview of the changes that have occurred in UN collective security actions. The authors point in particular to the 'strikingly intrusive nature' of Security Council decisions (p. 329), a development that has certainly led to the reduction in the impact of the principle of non-intervention (Article 2(7)) (Blokker and Kleiboer, 1996).

In addition to acting within the institutional legal framework, UN peacekeeping operations are bound by fundamental principles of international law, although the issue of the direct application of international humanitarian law has been debated (Rowe, 2000). The arguments over whether international legal standards apply to the application of economic sanctions by the Security Council is discussed by Michael Reisman and Douglas Stevick in 'The Applicability of International Law Standards to United Nations Economic Sanctions Programmes' (Chapter 13). They argue that legal principles drawn from international humanitarian law are applicable to UN economic sanctions programmes. Considerations of 'necessity, proportionality and the capacity for discrimination of the technique to be used' (p. 388) have certainly not been internalized within the Security Council when considering or monitoring its sanctions regimes to date, although the greater recent emphasis on 'smart' sanctions tailored to meet the perceived threat to or breach of the peace seem to be a recognition that such standards are applicable (Cortright and Lopez, 2000, pp. 239–45). Of interest, though, is the question of whether the applicable legal standards are solely those of international humanitarian law. The Committee on Economic, Social and Cultural Rights opined in December 1997 that sanctions programmes should take full account of the provisions in the Covenant on Economic, Social and Cultural Rights (General Comment No. 8). The Committee stated that sanctions regimes 'often cause significant disruption in the distribution of food, pharmaceuticals and sanitation supplies, jeopardize the quality of food and the availability of clean drinking water, severely interfere with the functioning of basic health and education systems and undermine the right to work'. The humanitarian exceptions often built into the sanctions regimes by the UN do not necessarily alleviate these problems and so the Committee strongly recommended that basic human rights 'must be taken into account when designing an appropriate sanctions regime'. The premise behind the Committee's approach is that 'lawlessness of one kind must not be met with lawlessness of another kind which pays no heed to the fundamental rights that underlie and give legitimacy to any such collective action'.

Article 41 of the UN Charter is the legal basis upon which non-military sanctions have been put in place by the Security Council. Such measures are clearly authorized by the provision. However, as part of its post-Cold War strategy in dealing with interethnic conflicts in the former Yugoslavia and Rwanda, the Security Council created a very different kind of non-military measure – ad hoc international criminal tribunals. The Appeals Chamber of the International Criminal Tribunal for the Former Yugoslavia (ICTY) has stated in the *Tadic* case that the legal basis for such measures is also Article 41.[10] The case raised the issue of the legality of the creation of such tribunals by the Council, and wider issues of the place of such tribunals in the UN system. Colin Warbrick in 'The United Nations System: A Place for Criminal Courts' (Chapter 14), addresses such issues in his essay. He is of the opinion that 'the *one* place for criminal courts in the U.N. system is in support of the U.N. Security Council's function of preserving and maintaining international peace and security' (p. 412). He views the early jurisprudence of the tribunals as supporting this, although he recognizes that the tribunals are an 'experiment . . . to see *if* the Tribunals can make an effective contribution to the discharge of the U.N. Security Council's responsibilities' (p. 413). The possible creation of further ad hoc, though mixed tribunals, in Sierra Leone and Cambodia (Frulli, 2000) seem to indicate that the Council appears to want to continue with the experiment. Warbrick, writing in 1995, is also doubtful about the place of a permanent international criminal court, stating that '[i]t remains to be seen if there exists a community based on the cooperation of States which feels the need for the facility that a permanent court will provide' (p. 413). However, the Court's Statute was adopted at Rome in 1998.[11]

Although largely complementary to national jurisdictions, the Court is not entirely based on a consensual model. Despite not being founded on universal jurisdiction, it does have the competence to try individuals of states not parties to the Statute (Article 12(2)(a) of the Statute), and, furthermore, the Security Council is recognized as being able to refer cases to the Court (Article 13(b) of the Statute). The International Criminal Court may thus also contribute to the maintenance of international peace and security in a similar fashion to the tribunals, a possibility recognized by the Preamble of the Rome Statute that states, *inter alia*, that 'grave crimes threaten the peace, security and well-being of the world'.

The most serious coercive powers belonging to the Security Council are contained in Article 42 which provides that the Council 'may take such action by air, sea, or land forces as may be necessary to maintain or restore international peace and security'. However, the military option developed by the Security Council since the Korean war in the 1950s has taken on a much looser shape than that intended by the framers of the Charter in 1945. There are no special agreements under Article 43 of the Charter whereby troops are to be provided, and there is no command and control by the Military Staff Committee and, ultimately, the Security Council, as provided by Articles 44–48. In the face of the unwillingness of powerful states to place their forces at the disposal of the United Nations, the Security Council has authorized a state or group of states to carry out military actions. Such a system of volunteers gives the maximum amount of discretion to states as to whether (and to a great extent how) they carry out the mandate granted by the Security Council. Oscar Schachter in 'United Nations Law in the Gulf Conflict' (Chapter 15) doubts whether the UN authorization of the Coalition in the Gulf Conflict of 1991 actually derived from Article 42. He is of the opinion that Article 51, which preserves the right of individual and collective self-defence, is a much sounder legal basis.

There is a lack of clarity as to the legal basis of Operation Desert Storm against Iraq and this adds to the confusion about the legality of continued military actions by the dwindling Coalition after the conflict had ended in March 1991 (White, 1999b). This started with the protective measures taken by Western forces in Kurdish northern Iraq in April 1991, although there was no clear Security Council authority for such an operation.[12] The claiming of such authority by those states using force has become part of the diplomatic and legal exchanges in the UN. This has not only been the case with continued military action (mainly by the USA and the UK) as regards Iraq but also the action taken by NATO against the FRY in 1999. Action taken 'in support' of Security Council resolutions has become a controversial legal claim to the extent that it is sometimes combined with claims of customary rights allegedly belonging to the states taking the action such as self-defence or, much more controversially, humanitarian intervention. Jules Lobel and Michael Ratner in 'Bypassing the Security Council' (Chapter 16) consider the system of authorizations that has emerged from the Charter and suggest that there are certain limitations on them (see also Blokker, 2000). Furthermore, they are very critical of the trend towards interpreting Chapter VII resolutions, that contain no clear authority, as permitting the use of force. They write of the 'grave dangers attendant on a regime of law permitting individual nations or even regional organizations to use nondefensive force without explicit Security Council authority' (p. 466). It is clear that these authors, writing before the NATO bombing of the FRY in 1999, would not have changed their minds in the light of that action. Indeed, they seem to anticipate the dilemma for international law posed by the Kosovo intervention when they write that 'in the extreme case of an ongoing genocide for which the Security Council will not authorize force, perhaps the formal law ought to be violated to achieve the higher goal of saving thousands or millions of lives' (p. 449).

Collective Security Outside the UN

From a scrutiny of the law relating to the UN and collective security, the volume then moves on to look at the legal nature and powers of other international organizations active in the field. These may be generally termed 'non-universal' or 'closed organizations', although more conceptually they may be called 'regional entities'. However, whatever label is used, we may identify several different types – defence, security, sub-regional, regional – each of which is conceptually and legally different from the other.

In considering the relationship between the UN and these entities it is pertinent to ask whether we have a collective security system in which universal and regional entities act in harmony to contribute to greater collective security, or whether we have competition between them. A related issue is whether we can have a system based solely on regional bodies or whether they are dependent to a greater or lesser extent on the universal organization. There are necessarily two levels of constitutional analysis here. First, we must consider the universal rules applicable to all such organizations. These are contained in the UN Charter, principally Chapter VIII. At the next level we must assess the constitutional provisions governing the operations of the non-universal organizations themselves – the NATO treaty is very different from the Charter of the OAS, for instance. In assessing the legal basis of a particular action taken by an international organization in the field of collective security we must assess its compatibility with the UN Charter and then assess its legal competence within the parameters of its own legal regime. Beyond this, there are residual claims made by regional bodies to be able to act under rules of customary international law, either embodied in the UN Charter and other treaties, or uncodified. The most controversial of these claims is the right of humanitarian intervention (Chesterman, 2001).

The Kosovo question raises the issue of the use of force by regional agencies. The UN Charter seems quite clear on these matters. While collective defence is preserved for such organizations under Article 51, any enforcement action beyond the purely defensive – for example, to deal with a threat to the peace – requires the authorization of the Security Council (Article 53(1)). Bruno Simma in 'NATO, the UN and the Use of Force' (Chapter 17), writing immediately before the NATO campaign against the FRY commenced in March 1999 but after the legal framework had been set, undertakes an assessment of the legality of NATO threats of force, and therefore its subsequent use of force, since both are covered equally by Article 2(4) of the UN Charter. His analysis follows from that of Lobel and Ratner in relation to Iraq in the post-1991 era, in that, in both instances, the Security Council, while finding a threat to the peace, did not go as far as to authorize the use of force. In the case of Kosovo, though, we have an international organization (NATO) consisting of 19 member states, which acted throughout on the basis of consensus. Should such an organization be limited by the use or threat of the veto in the Security Council, particularly when its intent is to prevent crimes against humanity being committed? The belief that regional organizations should not be so limited is not confined to NATO, but is also evident in the case of the Economic Community of West African States (ECOWAS), a subregional organization. ECOWAS has intervened in civil wars in Liberia and Sierra Leone without clear Security Council authority and has adopted a Protocol that purports to allow it to do this (Abass, 2000).[13]

Such claims to collective regional intervention are sometimes bolstered by additional assertions of a customary right to humanitarian intervention, or as Christian Walter states in his comprehensive essay on regional action, 'Security Council Control Over Regional Action' (Chapter 18), on the consent of the government (if this can be obtained). The fact that regional organizations feel the need to base their interventions on (controversial) customary grounds rather than solely on the basis of their own constituent treaties or documents is perhaps a sign of the weaknesses that exist in the legal basis of these actions. However, when taking account of the motives of these organizations – principally, but not exclusively, the desire to prevent human rights atrocities – should not collective security law reflect their demands? Walter shows that there are possible avenues to explore within the context of the UN Charter, which may allow for such practice. He accepts the legitimacy of retrospective authorizations by the Security Council for instance. Further, he suggests that just as Article 51 of the Charter was inserted to ensure that regional organizations had the right to defend themselves in emergency situations when confronted with an armed attack, so should such organizations be allowed an emergency right to defend human rights from serious violations (see p. 531). However, such a recognition would have to be built into the legal framework of the UN, not necessarily by formal amendment but perhaps by an Assembly resolution adopted by consensus.

Without universal recognition, regional humanitarian military actions will lack legitimacy as well as legality. Furthermore, the General Assembly would have to set precise prerequisites for regional humanitarian intervention, otherwise, to paraphrase Simma (Chapter 17) the genie of regional self-authorization will be let out of the bottle (see p. 490). Nevertheless, the increasing need to utilize regional mechanisms to achieve a better system of collective security is pointed out by David O'Brien in 'The Search for Subsidiarity: The UN, African Regional Organizations and Humanitarian Action' (Chapter 19). O'Brien shows that, in the African context, there is considerable practice towards 'subsidiary' – that is, regional or subregional – humanitarian action, which has, to a certain extent, been encouraged by the UN. The challenge for the UN and regional actors is to produce an acceptable legal framework that allows for regional initiatives and actions but at the same time regulates them.

Conclusion

The challenge faced by collective security law in attempting to regulate violent actions by states is encapsulated by the view of Dean Acheson, former US Secretary of State, when he considered the legal objections to the US quarantine of Cuba in 1962. Acheson stated '[t]he power, position and prestige of the United States had been challenged by another state; and law simply does not deal with such questions of ultimate power – power that comes close to the sources of sovereignty' (Acheson, 1963, pp. 14–15). The United Nations system protects such power to a great extent by elevating the P5 to a position where they cannot normally be subject to enforcement action. However, with such power comes responsibility. If the P5, acting within the Security Council, disable that body, preventing it from carrying out its responsibility for peace and security, then the UN system loses its credibility. Pressure from regional bodies, ad hoc coalitions, and single states then mounts to allow them greater freedom of action in the sphere of collective security. In a sense, the essays in this volume share a focus on the tensions between universal and regional action, between collective and unilateral action, as well as those that exist between institutional legal frameworks and customary international law, and above all, as Acheson's statement shows, between politics and law. The structures and rules that form the corpus of collective security law are inevitably rudimentary in a field of international relations that is still dominated by sovereign states. Their weaknesses contribute greatly to the impression that many of us have that the world, or at least a significant part of it, is continually balancing on the brink of disaster. With the horrific attacks launched against the USA on 11 September 2001, when three hijacked civilian airliners were flown into the World Trade Center and the Pentagon, we seem to have moved closer again to that edge of lawlessness. It is to be hoped that the essays in this volume show that there are lawful and legitimate solutions to such crises that can be sought and achieved, predicated – as many (but not all) of them are – on the idea that peace *can* be achieved through law.

Notes

1   See Kelsen (1951). He argues for maximum discretion.
2   *Prosecutor* v. *Tadic*, Case No. IT-94-1-AR72, 2 October 1995, para.18 (Judge Sidhwa dissenting).
3   *Lockerbie* cases (provisional measures), 1992 ICJ Rep.3; (preliminary objections), 1998 ICJ Rep. 9.
4   (2001), *International Legal Materials*, **40**, p. 582.
5   For example, the practice that does not equate an abstention with a veto under Article 27(3) of the Charter, see the *Namibia* case, 1971 ICJ Rep. 22.
6   In addition, the collection does not consider the highly relevant, but very specialized, area of arms control law. See Myjer (2001).
7   1986 ICJ Rep. 14.
8   1996 ICJ Rep. 26 and 66.
9   For recent reform proposals in this area see *Report* (2000).
10 Case No. IT-94-I-T-AR72, para. 36.
11 (1998), *International Legal Materials*, **37**, p. 999.

12   SC Res. 688, 5 April 1991 in (1991), *International Legal Materials*, **30**, p. 858.
13   For developments in European regional security see Wouters and Naert (2001).

References

Abass, A. (2000), 'The New Collective Security Mechanism of ECOWAS: Innovation and Problems', *Journal of Conflict and Security Law*, **5**, p. 211.

Acheson, D. (1963), 'Response to Panel: The Cuban Quarantine – Implications for the Future', *American Society of International Law Proceedings*, **14**, pp. 14–15.

Blokker, N.M. (2000), 'Is Authorization Authorized? Powers and Practice of the UN Security Council to Authorize the Use of Force by Coalitions of the Able and Willing', *European Journal of International Law*, **11**, pp. 541–68.

Blokker, N.M. and Kleiboer, M. (1996), 'The Internationalization of Domestic Conflict: The Role of the Security Council', *Leiden Journal of International Law*, **9**, pp. 7–35.

Chesterman, S. (2001), *Just War or Just Peace? Humanitarian Intervention and International Law*, Oxford: Oxford University Press.

Cortwright, D. and Lopez, A. (2000), *The Sanctions Decade: Assessing UN Strategies in the 1990s*, Boulder, CO: Lynne Rienner.

Cryer, R. (1996), 'The Security Council and Article 39: A Threat to Coherence?', *Journal of Armed Conflict Law*, **1**, pp. 161–95.

Downs, G.W. (ed.) (1994), *Collective Security Beyond the Cold War*, Ann Arbor: Michigan University Press.

Franck, T.M. (1990), *The Power of Legitimacy Among Nations*, Oxford: Oxford University Press.

Franck, T.M. (1993), 'The Bona Fides of Power: Security Council and Threats to the Peace', *Hague Recueil*, **240**, pp. 189–221.

Frulli, M. (2000), 'The Special Court for Sierra Leone: Some Preliminary Comments', *European Journal of International Law*, **11**, pp. 857–69.

Gray, C. (2000), *International Law and the Use of Force*, Oxford: Oxford University Press.

Kelsen, H. (1951), *The Law of the United Nations*, London: Stevens.

Merrills, J.G. (1996), *International Dispute Settlement*, Cambridge: Cambridge University Press.

Murphy, S.D. (1994), 'The Security Council, Legitimacy and the Concept of Collective Security After the Cold War', *Columbia Journal of Transnational Law*, **32**, pp. 201–88.

Murthy, C.S.R. (1995), 'The Role of the UN Secretary General Since the End of the Cold War', *Indian Journal of International Law*, **35**, pp. 181–96.

Myjer, E.P.J. (2001), 'The Law of Arms Control, Military Security and the Issues: An Introduction', in E.P.J. Myjer (ed.), *Issues of Arms Control and the Chemical Weapons Convention*, The Hague: Martinus Nijhoff, pp. 1–10.

Rowe, P. (2000), 'Maintaining Discipline in United Nations Peace Support Operations: The Legal Quagmire for Military Contingents', *Journal of Conflict and Security Law*, **5**, pp. 45–62.

Report of the Panel on United Nations Peace Operations ('Brahimi Report') (2000), UN docs A/55/305/ S/2000/809, 17 August.

White, N.D. (1996), 'The United Nations Charter and Peacekeeping Forces: Constitutional Issues', *International Peacekeeping*, **3**, pp. 43–63.

White, N.D. (1997), *Keeping the Peace: The United Nations and the Maintenance of International Peace and Security*, Manchester: Manchester University Press.

White, N.D. (1999a), 'To Review or Not to Review? The *Lockerbie* Cases Before the World Court', *Leiden Journal of International Law*, **12**, pp. 401–23.

White, N.D. (1999b), 'The Legality of the Threat of Force Against Iraq', *Security Dialogue*, **30**, pp. 75–86.

Winkelmann, I. (1997), 'Bringing the Security Council into a New Era', *Max Planck Yearbook of UN Law*, **1**, pp. 35–90.

Wouters, J. and Naert, F. (2001), 'How Effective is the European Security Architecture? Lessons from Bosnia and Kosovo', *International and Comparative Law Quarterly*, **50**, pp. 540–76.

Further Reading

Conforti, B. (2000), *The Law and Practice of the United Nations*, The Hague: Kluwer Law International.

Cot, J.P. and Pellet, A. (eds) (1991), *La Charte des Nations Unies*, Paris: Economica.

Fassbender, B. (1998), *The UN Security Council Reform and the Right of Veto: A Constitutional Perspective*, The Hague: Kluwer Law International.

Goodrich, L.M., Hambro, E. and Simons, A.P. (1969), *Charter of the United Nations: Commentary and Documents*, New York: Columbia University Press.

Higgins, R. (1963), *The Development of International Law Through the Political Organs of the United Nations*, Oxford: Oxford University Press.

Kelsen, H. (1951), *The Law of the United Nations*, London: Stevens.

McCoubrey, H. and Morris, J. (2000), *Regional Peacekeeping in the Post-Cold War Era*, The Hague: Kluwer Law International.

Müllerson, R. (2000), *Ordering Anarchy: International Law in International Society*, The Hague, Martinus Nijhoff.

Ratner, S. (1995), *The New UN Peacekeeping: Building Peace in Lands of Conflict after the Cold War*, Basingstoke: Macmillan.

Sarooshi, D. (2000), *The United Nations and the Development of Collective Security*, Oxford: Oxford University Press.

Simma, B. (ed.) (2002), *The Charter of the United Nations: A Commentary*, Oxford: Oxford University Press.

White, N.D. (1997), *Keeping the Peace: The United Nations and the Maintenance of International Peace and Security*, Manchester: Manchester University Press.

Part I
The Concept of Collective Security Law

[1]

THE PLACE OF LAW IN COLLECTIVE SECURITY

*Martti Koskenniemi**

It may seem anachronistic to suggest that law might have something to do with the high politics of international security. The period between the two world wars has, of course, been credited precisely by a mistaken reliance on such an idea. Confidence in the League of Nations' ability to deter aggression did not only, we are told by Realists of the post-war order, prove an academic error, it was positively harmful in directing attention away from the need to prepare for the inevitable aggression when it came.

This is the understanding that most of us, as diplomats, political theorists, or lawyers, have cultivated through most of the past five decades. We have labelled belief in the ability of rules and institutions to deter aggression "formalism," or even worse, "legalism," highlighting its abstract, utopian character, its distance from the flesh and blood of the application of power by states to fulfill their interests. Only ten years ago, Stanley Hoffmann commented on the state of world order studies:

> Nobody seems to believe anymore in the chances of collective security; because of its constraining character, it is too contrary to the freedom of judgement and action implied by sovereignty; and . . . it is in conflict with the imperatives of prudence in the nuclear

---

* Professor of International Law at the University of Helsinki, Finland. LL.D. (Turku, Finland). Served with the Finnish Ministry for Foreign Affairs from 1978 to 1995; Legal Advisor to Finland's Permanent Mission to the United Nations from 1989 to 1990.
This is a substantially revised version of a paper presented at the Conference "The United Nations: Between Sovereignty and Global Governance," held at the University of La Trobe, Melbourne, in July, 1995.

age, in which the localization or insulation of conflicts appears far preferable to their generalization.[1]

In this article I want to examine the place of law in our thinking about and sometimes participation in decisionmaking regarding international security. After the end of the Cold War, and particularly since the United Nations' reaction to Iraq's occupation of Kuwait in 1990–91, an academic debate concerning the possibility of collective security has arisen anew.[2] My intention is not to take a definite view in that controversy. Instead, I shall suggest that this debate has been framed so as to obscure the role of normative considerations, including law, in the production or construction of collective security. A theoretical-instrumental bias produces competing descriptions of the conditions of international "security," but it fails to provide an understanding of the actual contexts of decisionmaking on "security." For an internal, or cultural examination of collective security, a distinctly legal approach seems not only useful, but unavoidable.

I. REBIRTH OF COLLECTIVE SECURITY?

The collective security system of the Charter is based on two elements. First, there is the prohibition against inter-state threat or use of force under Article 2(4). The second element is the Council's "primary responsibility for the maintenance of international peace and security, . . . [expressed in both the members' agreement] that in carrying out its duties under this responsibility the Security Council acts on their behalf"[3] and in those Charter provisions which establish a legal obligation on member states to carry out the Council's decisions.[4]

Collective security, often academically distinguished from balance of power politics, is seen as invoking an "automatic" reaction against any

---

1. STANLEY HOFFMANN, *Is There an International Order?*, in JANUS AND MINERVA: ESSAYS IN THE THEORY AND PRACTICE OF INTERNATIONAL POLITICS 85, 117 (1987). The essay was originally published in French in 1985.

2. *See, e.g.,* Richard K. Betts, *Systems for Peace or Causes of War? Collective Security, Arms Control, and the New Europe,* INT'L SECURITY, Summer 1992, at 5; Helmut Freudenschuß, *Between Unilateralism and Collective Security: Authorizations to Use Force by the Security Council,* 5 EUR. J. INT'L L. 492 (1994); Andrew Hurrell, *Collective Security and International Order Revisited,* 11 INT'L REL. 37 (1992).

3. U.N. CHARTER art. 24, ¶ 1.

4. *Id.* arts. 25, 48. Also relevant in this context is Article 2(5), which requires member states to "give the United Nations every assistance in any action it takes in accordance with the present Charter," and requires that no assistance be given to any state against which preventive or enforcement action is being taken pursuant to the terms of the Charter. *Id.* art. 2, ¶ 5.

potential aggressor.[5] Collective security under the U.N. Charter system, however, involves little automation. Under the Charter, the decision of whether and how to react is vested with the Council, which itself has broad discretion. Whether this makes the Charter system something other than collective security under some definition is uninteresting. No system of rule-application is "automatic" as envisioned by the academic distinction between collective security and balance of power. The point is that under the Charter, member states have renounced some of their freedom of action by vesting the Council with competence to decide on collective action on their behalf and are (legally) bound by the decisions the Council has made. The United Nations system has a strong bias against unilateralism and broad directives to guide the Council as it exercises its competence.

That the Cold War made it impossible to apply the security system embedded in Chapter VII of the Charter is, of course, well-known.[6] The procedure for collective reaction in Articles 39 through 42 was set aside in favor of the balance of power strategies employed by the great powers outside the United Nations. The little enforcement activity that remained with the Security Council was limited to decolonization issues that did not bear upon great power relations. Appeals by the General Assembly to activate collective security under the Charter system came to nought.[7]

Judged against the Council's historical record, its reaction to Iraq's invasion of Kuwait from August 1990 onwards was clearly something new, even though paradoxically described as a "return" to the original concept of Chapter VII of the Charter. In his 1992 *Agenda for Peace*, the Secretary-General made several references to "collective security." He explained:

> an opportunity has been regained to achieve the great objectives of the Charter — a United Nations capable of maintaining international peace and security, of securing justice and human rights and of promoting, in the words of the Charter, "social progress and better standards of life in larger freedom." This opportunity must not be

---

5. *See, e.g.*, Betts, *supra* note 2, at 16; John J. Mearsheimer, *The False Promise of International Institutions*, INT'L SECURITY, Winter 1994/95, at 5, 29–32.

6. For analyses, see, e.g., N.D. WHITE, THE UNITED NATIONS AND THE MAINTENANCE OF INTERNATIONAL PEACE AND SECURITY (1990).

7. *See* G.A. Res. 159, U.N. GAOR, 40th Sess., 117th plen. mtg., Agenda Item 73, U.N. Doc. A/RES/40/159 (1986); G.A. Res. 119, U.N. GAOR, 37th Sess., 108th plen. mtg., Agenda Item 137, U.N. Doc. A/RES/37/119 (1983).

458　　　　*Michigan Journal of International Law*　　　　[Vol. 17:455]

squandered. The Organization must never again be crippled as it was in the era that has now passed.[8]

During the first forty years of the United Nations (1946–86), the Council made only two determinations of "breach of the peace" under Article 39.[9] In that same time span, only two states (Israel and South Africa) had their acts labelled "aggression" while the Council recognized the existence of a "threat to international peace and security" seven times.[10] During the first forty-five years of the United Nations' history, the Council had resorted to military force three times,[11] and to binding non-military sanctions twice.[12] In light of the perhaps seventy-three inter-state wars that broke out during this same period,[13] the data clearly shows the dramatic extent of the Council's paralysis.

Since 1990, the situation looks altogether different. Collective measures have been taken in eight situations — Iraq, Liberia, former Yugo-slavia, Somalia, Libya, Angola, Haiti, and Rwanda. The Council has authorized the use of military force five times through a total of nine-teen resolutions.[14] In each of the eight situations, the Council had re-course to binding, non-military sanctions. For comparison, consider the following statistics: in 1988, there were five peacekeeping operations, by 1994, the number was seventeen; in 1988, the Council adopted fifteen

---

8. Boutros Boutros-Ghali, *An Agenda for Peace: Preventive Diplomacy, Peacemaking and Peace-Keeping: Report of the Secretary-General*, U.N. GAOR, 47th Sess., Agenda Item 10, ¶ 3, U.N. Doc. A/47/277 (1992).

9. S.C. Res. 502, U.N. SCOR, 37th Sess., 2350th mtg., U.N. Doc. S/RES/502 (1982) (Falklands); S.C. Res. 82, U.N. SCOR, 5th Sess., 473d mtg., U.N. Doc. S/1501 (1950) (Korea).

10. S.C. Res. 573, U.N. SCOR, 40th Sess., 2615th mtg., U.N. Doc. S/RES/573 (1985) (Israel's attack on PLO headquarters in Tunis); S.C. Res. 418, U.N. SCOR, 32d Sess., 2046th mtg., U.N. Doc. S/RES/418 (1977) (South Africa); S.C. Res. 353, U.N. SCOR, 29th Sess., 1781st mtg., U.N. Doc. S/RES/353 (1974) (Cyprus); S.C. Res. 307, U.N. SCOR, 26th Sess., 1621st mtg., U.N. Doc. S/RES/307 (1971) (Pakistan); S.C. Res. 232, U.N. SCOR, 21st Sess., 1340th mtg., U.N. Doc. S/RES/232 (1966) (South Rhodesia); S.C. Res. 161, U.N. SCOR, 16th Sess., 942d mtg., U.N. Doc. S/4741 (1961) (Congo); S.C. Res. 54, U.N. SCOR, 3d Sess., 338th mtg., U.N. Doc. S/902 (1948) (Palestine).

11. Korea, The Congo, South Rhodesia. The last was an authorization for Britain to patrol Beira harbour in Mozambique to prevent oil from reaching Rhodesia. S.C. Res. 221, U.N. SCOR, 21st Sess., 1277th mtg., U.N. Doc. S/RES/221 (1966).

12. The economic blockade of Southern Rhodesia (1966–79) and the arms embargo of South Africa (1977–94).

13. WHITE, *supra* note 6, at 47.

14. S.C. Res. 940, U.N. SCOR, 49th Sess., 3413th mtg., U.N. Doc. S/RES/940 (1994) (Haiti); S.C. Res. 929, U.N. SCOR, 49th Sess., 3392d mtg., U.N. Doc. S/RES/929 (1994) (Rwanda); S.C. Res. 836, U.N. SCOR, 48th Sess., 3228th mtg., U.N. Doc. S/RES/836 (1993) (former Yugoslavia); S.C. Res. 814, U.N. SCOR, 47th Sess., 3188th mtg., U.N. Doc. S/RES/814 (1993) (Somalia); S.C. Res. 794, U.N. SCOR, 47th Sess., 3145th mtg., U.N. Doc. S/RES/794 (1992); S.C. Res. 678, U.N. SCOR, 45th Sess., 2963d mtg., U.N. Doc. S/RES/678 (1990) (Iraq). For a full analysis of the resolutions, see Freudenschuß, *supra* note 2, at 493–522.

resolutions, in 1994, the Council adopted seventy-eight. From 1988 to 1994, the number of annual informal consultations among Council members rose from forty to 240.[15]

A qualitative development has likewise taken place in the Council's understanding of its task of "maintaining international peace and security." Traditionally, collective security — and with it, the Council's competence — was seen as a military matter, concerned with the prevention of inter-state violence and, in particular, the transboundary use of force. However, most modern large-scale violence does not involve formal armies marching across boundaries. As *Agenda for Peace* never tires to remind us, and countless reviews of post-Cold War peacekeeping keep repeating, the greatest proportion of large-scale violence that presents a threat to international peace and security is home-brewn violence — civil war. Whatever conceptual difficulties tackling with non-international conflicts might pose for traditional applications of collective security,[16] the limitation of violence within one state has not prevented the Security Council from using its mandate to intervene during recent years.

> Of the five peace-keeping operations that existed in early 1988, four related to inter-state wars and only one (20 per cent of the total) to an intra-state conflict. Of the 21 operations established since then, only 8 have related to inter-state wars, whereas 13 (62 per cent) have related to intra-state conflicts . . . . Of the 11 operations established since January 1992 all but 2 (82 per cent) relate to intra-state conflicts.[17]

Moreover, it has long been argued that war can effectively be prevented only by tackling its root causes, that war is merely the external manifestation of the violence of the social institutions, that peace follows only from domestic enlightenment and justice.[18] Modern liberals have continued to make the same case. Peace starts at home with the eradication of poverty, social injustice, and the violation of human rights.[19] Today, "non-military threats to security" and the "comprehensive concept of

---

15. *See Report of the Secretary-General on the Work of the Organization*, U.N. GAOR, 49th Sess., at 5, U.N. Doc. A/49/1 (1994); *Supplement to An Agenda for Peace: Position-Paper of the Secretary-General on the Occasion of the Fiftieth Anniversary of the United Nations*, U.N. GAOR, 50th Sess., ¶ 11, U.N. Doc. A/50/60 (1995).

16. *Cf.* Hurrell, *supra* note 2, at 38–39.

17. *Supplement to An Agenda for Peace: Position-Paper of the Secretary-General on the Occasion of the Fiftieth Anniversary of the United Nations*, *supra* note 15, ¶ 11.

18. *See* IMMANUEL KANT, *To Perpetual Peace: A Philosophical Sketch*, in PERPETUAL PEACE AND OTHER ESSAYS ON POLITICS, HISTORY, AND MORALS 107 (Ted Humphrey trans., Hackett Publishing Co. 1983) (1795), especially the "First Definitive Article of Perpetual Peace: The Civil Constitution of Every Nation Should Be Republican[,]" *id.* at 112–15.

19. For a programmatic discussion, see Fernando R. Tesón, *The Kantian Theory of International Law*, 92 COLUM. L. REV. 53 (1992).

460   *Michigan Journal of International Law*   [Vol. 17:455

security" are rooted in the vocabulary of diplomats and politicians throughout the political spectrum. At one euphoric moment in 1992, the Security Council, in its first meeting at the level of Heads of State and Government, stressed that "[t]he non-military sources of instability in the economic, social, humanitarian and ecological fields have become threats to peace and security."[20] It is not yet clear whether this much-quoted sentence should be taken at face value; that is, as an indication of the Council's readiness to use its collective security powers under Chapter VII of the Charter to deal with economic, social, humanitarian, or ecological developments which, in its opinion, are sufficiently grave to warrant such treatment. But the statement invokes the language of Article 39 of the Charter that triggers the Council's reactive competence and does suggest an image of the Council as a post-Cold War Leviathan; not only as police but as judge,[21] or perhaps as priest,[22] of a new world order.

II. COLLECTIVE ACTION OR POWER POLICY?

However, there is controversy about the correct understanding of these developments. While many agree with the Secretary-General that the Council's newly found activism should be seen as a "return" to the "original" Charter conception, others have been more doubtful. Several factors complicate a reading of the Council's recent activity as an application of collective security.

The first problem relates to the Council's notorious selectiveness.[23] Why Libya, but not Israel? Why the Council's passivity during most of the eight-year Iran-Iraq war? Why has the Council's reaction in Africa been markedly less vigorous and effective than in the Gulf? Why the discrepancy between the Council's forceful attack on Iraq (an Islamic country) and its timidity to defend the Muslims of Bosnia-Herzegovina? The choice of targets, as well as the manner of reacting, has certainly not been automatic. The argument is made that the Council has not reflected the collective interests of United Nations members as a whole, but only

---

20. *Note by the President of the Security Council*, U.N. SCOR, 47th Sess., 3046th mtg. at 3, U.N. Doc. S/23500 (1992).

21. *See* Jean-Marc Sorel, *Rapport général L'élargissement de la notion de menace contre la paix, in* SOCIÉTÉ FRANÇAISE POUR LE DROIT INTERNATIONAL, COLLOQUE DE RENNES, LE CHAPITRE VII DE LA CHARTE DES NATIONS UNIES 3, 52 (1995); Keith Harper, Note, *Does the United Nations Security Council Have the Competence to Act as Court and Legislature?*, 27 N.Y.U. J. INT'L L. & POL'Y 103 (1994).

22. *Cf.* Martti Koskenniemi, *The Police in the Temple: Order, Justice and the UN: A Dialectical View*, 6 EUR. J. INT'L L. 325 (1995).

23. *See* OLIVIER RUSSBACH, ONU CONTRE ONU: LE DROIT INTERNATIONAL CONFISQUÉ (1994).

the special interests and factual predominance of the United States and its Western allies within the Council.

This point seems particularly potent in relation to the form of the Council's recourse to military force. The Kuwait crisis presented a unique opportunity to activate the integrity of the Charter's collective reaction machinery. This would have included not only a decision on military action against Iraq, but also the conclusion of "special agreements" under Article 43 between the Council and member states for the submission of national military contingents to the Council as well as the activation of the military staff committee as envisioned in Article 47. However, none of this was done. The Council merely gave its "authorization" for a coalition led by the United States to attack Iraq while absolving itself from the operational command and control of the coalition action.[24]

Lawyers have been at pains to find a plausible legal basis for this novel formulation: collective security or unilateral action in (collective) self-defence — or *excès de pouvoir*?[25] The debate has been largely inconsequential. Since Operation Desert Storm, the same formulation has been used in each of the four other situations (Somalia, former Yugoslavia, Rwanda, and Haiti) in which the Council has decided to use military force. In each, the acting party has been a powerful member or a coalition led by a powerful member (usually the United States, except for "Operation Turquoise" in Rwanda, which was carried out by France).[26]

It is equally difficult to interpret the "new generation peacekeeping" as a collective security device. True, the appearance of blue helmets with increasing frequency in the context of actual fighting, and sometimes with a mandate to use limited force, has seemed a step toward collective enforcement of pre-established standards of behavior. However, a closer study of the relevant cases (particularly those of UNPROFOR in Krajina and Bosnia and UNOSOM II in Somalia) shows that the use of force is

---

24. S.C. Res. 678, U.N. SCOR, 45th Sess., 2963d mtg. at 1, U.N. Doc. S/RES/678 (1990).

25. There is a great deal of literature on the subject. *See, e.g.*, Robert Lavalle, *The Law of the United Nations and the Use of Force, Under the Security Council Resolutions of 1990 and 1991, to Resolve the Persian Gulf Crisis*, 23 NETH. Y.B. INT'L L. 3, 33–46 (1992); Oscar Schachter, *United Nations Law in the Gulf Conflict*, 85 AM. J. INT'L L. 452 (1991); Colin Warbrick, *The Invasion of Kuwait by Iraq*, 40 INT'L & COMP. L.Q. 482, 486–87 (1991); Michel-Cyr Djiena Wembou, *Réflexions sur la validité et la portée de la résolution 678 du Conseil de Sécurité*, 5 AFR. J. INT'L & COMP. L. 34, 44–49 (1993); Ralph Zacklin, *Les nations unies et la crise du Golfe, in* LES ASPECTS JURIDIQUES DE LA CRISE ET DE LA GUERRE DU GOLFE 57, 69 (Brigitte Stern ed., 1991).

26. S.C. Res. 940, *supra* note 14 (U.S.-led military intervention in Haiti "to facilitate the departure from Haiti of the military leadership"); S.C. Res. 929, *supra* note 14 (French action to "achieve . . . humanitarian objectives" in Rwanda); S.C. Res. 836, *supra* note 14 (NATO air strikes to support peacekeepers); S.C. Res. 794, *supra* note 14 (Operation "Restore Hope" in Somalia).

462   *Michigan Journal of International Law*   [Vol. 17:455

not directed at keeping aggression at bay, but at carrying out humanitarian assignments during armed conflict for pupuses similar to those of the
Red Cross.[27] A careful examination of the nineteen resolutions in which
the Council has either authorized member states to take military action or
otherwise expanded the mandate of peacekeeping forces has prompted
one observer to conclude that "a new instrument has been created out of
the need to fill the gap between the invocation of an inapplicable or
inopportune right to collective self-defence and the unwanted application
of the system of collective security."[28]

In addition, the application of economic sanctions by the Council in
the eight Chapter VII situations has not been automatic in a way that
would have clearly distinguished it from an interest-governed exercise of
economic power. True, most states implemented the Iraqi sanctions
diligently, transforming the Council's decisions into acts of national
law.[29] Yet the Council's failure to manage its economic statecraft in a
rational way has made it doubtful whether member states should continue
to take its use of sanctions seriously. There has been no antecedent planning of the measures nor an evaluation of their effects on the target
states' economy or political decisionmaking. The objectives of sanctions
have sometimes been very unclear. The sanctions have been managed by
five separate committees consisting of diplomats of the member states of
the Council who have neither the interest, time, or resources to do the
job properly. These five committees work in secret, not even reporting to
the Council. They follow partly differing procedures resulting in differing
interpretative decisions on, for example, the application of the humanitarian exemptions.[30] The Council has failed to react to widely publicized
violations of sanctions by individual states, for example, the Islamic
states' non-application of the Libyan boycott in force since 1992. The
Council has also failed to take action to alleviate the problems of vulnerable third states.[31]

---

27. *Cf.* S.C. Res. 836, *supra* note 14 (limited use of force to protect the "safe areas"); S.C.
Res. 814, *supra* note 14 (limited use of force mandate for UNOSOM II).

28. Freudenschuß, *supra* note 2, at 522.

29. *Cf.* THE KUWAIT CRISIS: SANCTIONS AND THEIR ECONOMIC CONSEQUENCES (D.L.
Bethlehem ed., 1991).

30. *See* Koskenniemi, *supra* note 22, at 345–46; *infra* note 92.

31. Some of these difficulties were taken up by the Secretary-General in early 1995. *See
Supplement to An Agenda for Peace: Position-Paper of the Secretary-General on the Occasion
of the Fiftieth Anniversary of the United Nations, supra* note 15, ¶¶ 66–76. The Council
responded by indicating certain measures to "make the procedures of the Sanctions Committees
more transparent[.]" *Note by the President of the Security Council,* U.N. SCOR, 50th Sess.,
U.N. Doc. S/1995/234 (1995).

III. The Realist Critique of Collective Security

These various critiques suggest the foundation for two conclusions usually associated with the doctrine of international Realism. First, they imply that the Council's activity should not be understood in terms of a functioning collective security system. It does not involve rule-application in the way that would differentiate it from "normal" hegemonic or balance of power policy. All aggressors are not, in fact, being hit by the system. Some states that are not aggressors are being hit by it because that seems to be in the interests of the hegemonic powers. I call this critique the *interpretative thesis*. Its point is that we cannot interpret or understand the recent United Nations actions as applications of collective security.

Second, the critiques also support the more general Realist position according to which collective security is impossible — that it simply cannot work (the case of the Cold War) or works only as a camouflage for power policy. Whether peace exists is not dependent upon the presence or absence of rules about collective reaction, but upon the application of power by those states in a position to do so in the advancement of their interests. I call this critique the *causal thesis*.[32]

The two theses rely on a clear differentiation between legal "rules" and political "interests" and on the priority of the latter over the former. Since the great powers' interests are protected by Articles 24 and 27 of the Charter, the mechanism seems already defined so as to defer to them. Nor are other interests irrelevant. It is not difficult to conceive of cases in which the interests of a member state that has a special relationship with the target state or which is vulnerable to retaliation seem so important as to override conventional obligations.[33] Jordan's continuous and widely accepted breach of sanctions against Iraq is one example. A variation of this theme links it to the logic of state behavior. Whatever rationally calculable long-term advantage there might be for a state to abide by a collective measures norm will not offset the more immediate harm that it will seem to suffer as a result of obedience. So even if a purely rational calculation of interests might speak in favor of obedience, considerations relating to, for example, the unwillingness of political elites to make "hard decisions" will overrule such calculations. This is a variant of the argument from the "tragedy of the commons" — that even

---

32. For a forceful reformulation, see Mearsheimer, *supra* note 5, at 28–33.

33. The doubts about the reality of the American nuclear umbrella in case of an attack on Western Europe, and its consequent readiness to set itself as a target for a similar attack, illustrate this point. So does the hypothesis of a Russian attack on the Ukraine. It is not plausible to believe that small European states will risk their safety by joining in a campaign to support Ukraine's independence.

464   *Michigan Journal of International Law*   [Vol. 17:455

if it were rational for all participants in a common good ("security" in this case) to take action to safeguard it against danger, there are always some who choose to become free riders — with the effect that it will appear rational for others to choose a similar policy as well.[34] Collective security, Realists have insisted, relies upon trust between the partners. In the absence of trust (a fact that defines the condition of international "anarchy"), it seems both rational and responsible to place immediate self-interest before an uncertain and fragile common interest.[35]

Moreover, procedural difficulties may seem daunting. Within an agreement to react to aggression some members will receive more protection than others. Selectivity is unavoidable. Much may depend on whether the aggressor is able to invoke the support of a permanent member. Even if members of a security pact had parallel interests, a collective reaction procedure could still not be applied consistently. Political choices will have to be taken when interpreting, for example, who the aggressor is, or whether there has been a "threat to the peace." We are not entitled to assume that the historic, ethnic, or political, affiliations or hostilities between particular members of such a pact are irrelevant when making those choices. But even if there were no divergent affiliations, we may hardly hold as irrelevant factors such as the likelihood that retaliatory action against one aggressor would expose pact members to attack by another aggressor or drive the aggressors into each others' arms, a fear that hampered the League's sanctions policy against Italy in 1935–36. Who decides when to react and how? Who pays for reaction or the costs of preparation? Who will command the collective force or decide on the objectives of common action and when they have been attained?[36] If everything depends on the particular facts and circumstances, the rule-governed character of the procedure will disappear and, with it, the system's deterrent force. It will start to seem like just another context for politics.[37]

IV. The Limits of Realism: Theory v. Engagement

The above theses are powerful. They show that decisionmaking within the Security Council cannot be described as rule-application in the

---

34. *See* Josef Joffe, *Collective Security and the Future of Europe: Failed Dreams and Dead Ends*, Survival, Spring 1992, at 36, 42.

35. See the discussion in Justin Rosenberg, The Empire of Civil Society: A Critique of the Realist Theory of International Relations 27 (1994).

36. *See* Adam Roberts, *The United Nations and International Security*, Survival, Summer 1993, at 3, 23–26.

37. These questions reflect the different position in which members to a collective security pact are *vis-á-vis* each other. Some will have to lead, others will have to follow. It is not self-evident that parties will be ready to accept the assessment of the largest potential contributor — but if they do not, will the contributor contribute?

abstract fashion in which "collective security" has often been portrayed. However, the theses are also limited. They operate with a very narrow notion of "rule-application" and fail to see to what extent their determining concepts such as "interest," "power," or "security" are themselves defined and operative within a normative context.

Realism receives its strength from its focus on empirical-instrumental questions such as "what happened?" or "what can be made to happen?" But it avoids posing normative questions such as "what should happen?" or "what should have happened?" Or more accurately, Realism deals with the latter set of questions on the basis of its responses to the former. Having committed itself to a descriptive sociology of the international world characterized by the struggle for "power" by "states" in the pursuit of "national interests," Realism marginalizes normative questions into issues of "ethics," oscillating between the private (and thus inscrutable) morality of individual statesmen and the public morality of states in which it seems necessary sometimes to dirty one's hands in order to prevent the system's collapse into anarchy. Realism is avowedly instrumentalist, that is, concerned with the effects of particular policies on the world. However, its instrumentalism is not that of the situated participant but that of the external observer, the rational calculator, the theory-builder. To the external observer, the statesmen and states are atomistic subjects, equipped with a predetermined bag of interests or "values," standing outside the international polity on which they seek to employ various diplomatic, economic, and military management techniques. However, since the basic tenents of its sociology turn out to be normatively loaded, Realism seems compelled to defend itself on normative terms: one's "security" will appear as another's domination, one's "intervention" as another's "protection of sovereignty."[38] In this debate, there is no privileged realm of pure description.

A. *The Normative in the Empirical*

The *interpretative thesis* argued that legal or political principles "are not sufficient to explain either the past history of collective security or the course of events in the Gulf."[39] The determinant factors in recent Council actions were not Charter provisions or international law, but the new rapport between the United States and the Soviet Union/Russia, the strategic and economic significance of Kuwait to the Western allies, and

---

38. For this latter theme, see Cynthia Weber's collapsing of the two apparent opposites into a single term she refers to as "sovereignty-intervention," a term which can characterize any conceivable inter-state relationship. CYNTHIA WEBER, SIMULATING SOVEREIGNTY: INTERVENTION, THE STATE AND SYMBOLIC EXCHANGE 123–27 (Cambridge Stud. Int'l Rel. No. 37, 1995).

39. Hurrell, *supra* note 2, at 49.

so on. I have no great problem with this thesis. It opens a critical perspective that refuses to take at face value the suggestion that United
Nations action represents communal interests merely because it has been
decided by the Security Council. Nonetheless, the thesis' usefulness remains limited precisely because its hermeneutic suggestion excludes
reference to international norms.

During the past years, the foundational character of the hard facts of
state power and interest to our understanding of international politics has
been questioned from a wide variety of perspectives. The "level of analysis" approach already modified Realism's strong reliance on *states* as the
basic units by which international acts should be explained.[40] Structural
constraints and non-state actors seemed to create effects as well. Yet,
even structural Realism's analytical priority for states may seem like an
ideological move, justifying conservative policy and failing to account
for the determining agency of class, economic system, or religious faith
in the geopolitical, just as in the national, space.[41] Perhaps less controversially, liberal Internationalists have long insisted that the "globalization
of politics" has formed interest groups and lines of battle that cannot be
reduced to the application of power by states.[42] To "explain" the United
Nations action in Somalia, for instance, in terms of a power play between
members of the Security Council would undermine the extent to which
humanitarian perceptions, institutional programs and ambitions, the
legacy of East African colonialism, and the character of the Siad Barre
regime account for the relevant events. Aside from states, we see both
metropolitan (United Nations) and peripheral (Somali) actors, ideas, and
interests as relevant.[43] To argue that things went so bad because there
was no clear national interest to protect is a *non sequitur*: things went as
they did because the events showed factors other than a "national interest" as relevant.

The concept of "power" is likewise famously contested. Realists'
over-identification of power with military power was undermined by the
end of the Cold War. Inasmuch as "power" is seen in larger terms of

---

40. For the classic neo-Realist work which introduced the "level of analysis" concept, see
KENNETH N. WALTZ, MAN, THE STATE AND WAR (1959). The level of analysis approach,
however, is only a temporary resolution of the problem of adjusting theory to observable facts.
A more fundamental problem relates to the constructive aspects of observation itself: whether
we tend to see individual states, economic systems, ideologies, individuals, or transnational
communities as the relevant actors seems dependent on our prior choice of the relevant "level"
(matrix). The choice of the level, however, must be independent from the thing to be explained, i.e., on a pre-empirical evaluation of significance.

41. *See generally* ROSENBERG, *supra* note 35.

42. The ideas of "common security" and "comprehensive security" seeks to capture this
image. For one recent reformulation, see COMMISSION ON GLOBAL GOVERNANCE, OUR GLOBAL
NEIGHBORHOOD 78–84 (1995).

43. The argument draws inspiration from MICHAEL W. DOYLE, EMPIRES 22–30 (1986).

structure and knowledge, its embedment in other *explicanda* becomes evident.[44] Power is a matter of perspective. It receives meaning as threat or support depending on how we relate to it. It is applied as a means to an end different from itself. A study of ends, however, introduces normative elements into the explanatory matrix that cannot be grasped by the sort of empiricism that Realists espouse.[45] The establishment of economic sanctions on Libya by the Security Council in 1992 as a result of Qaddafi's unwillingness to extradite the suspects for the 1988 Lockerbie terrorist attack can clearly be seen as an application of power by the Western allies. But this is more the starting point than the end of the analysis. It would be difficult to understand the action without further reference to the role "terrorism" plays in Western political discourse, enabling the taking of extraordinary means — in this case the non-application of a valid treaty (the 1971 Montreal Convention against aerial terrorism) and the overrunning of the International Court of Justice. It is the normative construct of a specific "terrorism discourse" that makes possible the organization and application of physical power against Libya.[46]

Nor is "national interest" any more transparent. Whose interest is that? States, just like individuals, live in a network of partly overlapping, partly incompatible interests. Choosing an interest to base a policy is, as feminists have always argued, a normative act, and not something one automatically discovers after one has decided to further national interests. In any case, the assumption of a unitary national interest fails to account for, and even less articulate, the contrasting interest of a local population, minority, or women, for instance.[47] To say that Yemen supported Iraq in the Council during 1989–90 because that was in its interests is not only questionable insofar as Yemen's economic or diplomatic position was concerned (and undermines the effect of the ideological and religious links involved), but lifts the policy of the Yemeni male elite to a representational position inimical to other Yemeni interests.[48] In fact, a refer-

---

44. Alexander Wendt, *Constructing International Politics*, INT'L SECURITY, Summer 1995, at 71, 73–75.

45. For the expanding literature challenging the empiricist/positivist bias of international relations studies and stressing the need to undertake normatively focused analyses, see generally CHRIS BROWN, INTERNATIONAL RELATIONS THEORY: NEW NORMATIVE APPROACHES (1992); MERVYN FROST, TOWARDS A NORMATIVE THEORY OF INTERNATIONAL RELATIONS (1986); MARK A. NEUFELD, THE RESTRUCTURING OF INTERNATIONAL RELATIONS THEORY (1995).

46. *See* Ileana Porras, *On Terrorism: Reflections on Violence and the Outlaw*, 1994 UTAH L. REV. 119.

47. Anne Orford, *The Politics of Collective Security*, 17 MICH. J. INT'L L. 373 (1996); *see generally* AMERICAN SOC'Y INT'L L., STUDIES IN TRANSNATIONAL LEGAL POLICY No. 25, RECONCEIVING REALITY: WOMEN AND INTERNATIONAL LAW (Dorinda G. Dallmayer ed., 1993) [hereinafter RECONCEIVING REALITY].

48. The point is strikingly illustrated by the fact that in the first post-Gulf War elections in Kuwait in October 1992, only 14% of the country's 600,000 citizens were eligible to vote.

ence to "interests" is often no more than a sweeping gesture toward the truism, present since Vattel, that states act in accordance with their self-interest. However, the important point is that even "[s]elf-interest cannot be an unproblematic concept if the self is conceived as a set of constructed identities that need not be stable over time."[49]

Arguing that normative factors are either irrelevant or only marginally relevant to Security Council action undermines the degree to which any social action, including international activity, makes constant reference to normative codes, rules, or principles. Political events are never simply physical acts or people behaving empirically in this way or that.[50] They exist in relation to a shared normative code of meaning. Sending troops into another country is not a full description of an event: normative terms such as "aggression," "self-defence," "counter-measure," "territorial sovereignty," or "peacekeeping" are not solely disinterested descriptions of the events. They refer back to more general, systemic theories, assumptions, world-views, and prejudices that provide the implicit matrix that makes description possible. An account of the Gulf War that makes no reference to such notions but is content to refer to United States military or economic interests would be no understanding at all. It would fail to grasp the difference between that sequence of military moves and those to which they were a response, or between Kuwait and Panama, or Kuwait and the Soviet attack on Finland in 1939. The distinctions are normative and characterized as such by the various participants involved.

Let me illustrate these remarks by reference to the comprehensive conception of security. That an understanding of "security" should not be limited to military security, but should also encompass non-military threats to states and people, has become a commonplace of post-Cold War diplomatic language.[51] This expansion of the operating concept of "security" highlights the fact that explaining international action by reference to "security needs" remains an empty phrase unless "security" is first given a meaning. This involves an appreciation of what is signifi-

---

Orford, *supra* note 47, at 390 & n.71.

49. Richard Price, *A Genealogy of the Chemical Weapons Taboo*, 49 INT'L ORG. 73, 88 (1995).

50. See PETER WINCH, THE IDEA OF SOCIAL SCIENCE AND ITS RELATION TO PHILOSOPHY 108–11 (1958), and more recently, with special reference to modern international theory, NEUFELD, *supra* note 45, at 70–94.

51. See GARETH EVANS, COOPERATING FOR PEACE: THE GLOBAL AGENDA FOR THE 1990s AND BEYOND 15–16 (1993); OUR GLOBAL NEIGHBOURHOOD: THE REPORT OF THE COMMISSION ON GLOBAL GOVERNANCE, *supra* note 42, at 80–82; Barry Buzan, *New Patterns of Global Security in the Twenty-First Century*, 67 INT'L AFF. 431, 439–51 (1991).

cant to the identity of political communities called "states."[52] Again, an answer to that question depends on whether we see a state's identity in territorial, economic, institutional, ideological, gendered, religious, or constitutional terms.[53] Besides, the links between security and statehood are increasingly questioned, and diplomatic rhetoric has resorted to notions such as "common security," "comprehensive security," or even "human security" to describe the objectives of international policy. A reference to "security needs" as an explaining factor or an agreed principle of policy encounters, on the Realist side, the same difficulties that the attempt to define "aggression" has always (and famously) met on the Idealist side: the notions remain both overdetermining and underdetermining. On the one hand, every event that modifies the state's external environment poses a threat to the state, and may therefore be deemed to constitute "aggression" or "intervention." On the other hand, no event can permanently remain within these categories since the principle of inclusion may always be challenged by constructing the state's identity or its sphere of sovereignty in a novel fashion. The controversy is therefore normative — "what is significant for the identity of this state or for the furtherance of this type of policy?" — and not empirical.[54]

The matrix that describes the international world in terms of statal power policy has been challenged by interdependence theory and more recent research into the roles of culture, class, gender, and tradition for international affairs.[55] Nonetheless, as R.B.J. Walker notes, "a large proportion of research in the field of international relations remains content to draw attention to contemporary innovations while simply taking a modernist framing of all spatiotemporal options as an unques-

---

52. *See, e.g.,* J. Ann Tickner, *Re-visioning Security, in* INTERNATIONAL RELATIONS THEORY TODAY 175 (Ken Booth & Steven Smith eds., 1995); Ole Waever, *Identity, Integration and Security: Solving the Sovereignty Puzzle in E.U. Studies,* 48 J. INT'L AFF. 389 (1995).

53. BARRY BUZAN, PEOPLE, STATES & FEAR 57–107 (2d ed. 1991).

54. The same point may be made by highlighting the degree to which the debate about the United Nations' or individual states' competence to intervene in internal crises constantly redefines the basis of sovereign statehood. Whether we believe "sovereignty" to be located in the "people," in the Head of State, or in the state's institutions will provide us with different, and often contradictory, justifications for or against intervention. From this perspective, statehood provides no limit for intervention. On the contrary, it is an effect of our assumptions about the right form of government. *See* WEBER, *supra* note 38. The resuscitated "constitutivist" approach to the recognition of states, which conditions statehood on domestic democracy and guarantees for minority protection, works, of course, in the same direction. *See European Community: Declaration on Yugoslavia and on the Guidelines on the Recognition of New States,* 31 I.L.M. 1485 (1992).

55. For a particularly strong anti-statal matrix using the "deep-structure" of the capitalist world-system in which nationalism and universalism appear as historical or local instances, see IMMANUEL WALLERSTEIN, GEOPOLITICS AND GEOCULTURE: ESSAYS ON THE CHANGING WORLD-SYSTEM 139–237 (1991) (discussing the role of "culture" and "civilization" as the "intellectual battlegrounds" of post-Cold War policy).

470 *Michigan Journal of International Law* [Vol. 17:455

tionable given."[56] This is partly a result of the fact that Realism encapsulates deeply entrenched commonsense assumptions. In part, it also follows from a real difficulty to see how the "innovations" would inform political practices. After all, as I have argued elsewhere, one can reimagine the structures of the international world only now and then. For the rest of the time we seem compelled to act within an actual political community.[57]

For present purposes, it suffices to note that the need to choose the matrix highlights the normative element hidden in Realist premises, an element sometimes revealed in private positions Realists have taken on moral or political issues.[58] By failing to take its normative commitments seriously (even at best marginalizing them into a problem of "ethics and international relations"), Realism opens itself to a political criticism which alleges that Realism lacks the instruments to defend itself. Moreover, lack of sensitivity for the non-descriptive undermines the instrumentalism upon Realism bases its claim for superiority. The kind of tragic heroism embedded in Realism's attempt to confront power and vice directly, without the mediating vessels of ethics/ideology, is undermined by the equally ideological character of that posture itself; the posture being equally a role within the drama of international diplomacy that it pretends to "describe," a role that, however logically compatible with fighting the noble fight (for a lost cause), too easily becomes a justification for complacency.

B. *The Engaged Perspective*

For Realists, reference to norms, such as the obligation to participate in common action under Articles 2(5) or 48 of the Charter, in an explanation of international politics appears as it appeared to the American legal Realists of the 1930s; namely, as transcendental nonsense, an "attempt to exorcise social evils by the indefatigable repetition of magic formulae."[59] Obligations are both causally ineffectual and unamenable to scientific inquiry. By contrast, the process whereby states apply power to advance their interests seems more firmly linked with observable reality

---

56. R.B.J. WALKER, INSIDE/OUTSIDE: INTERNATIONAL RELATIONS AS POLITICAL THEORY 7 (1993).

57. Martti Koskenniemi, Book Review, 89 AM. J. INT'L L. 227, 230 (1995) (reviewing RECONCEIVING REALITY, *supra* note 47).

58. The two standard examples are Morgenthau's opposition to the Vietnam War and Martin Wight's private pacifism. For a discussion, see Jim George, *Realist "Ethics," International Relations, and Post-Modernism: Thinking Beyond the Egoism-Anarchy Thematic*, 24 MILLENNIUM J. INT'L STUD. 195, 205–07 (1995).

59. Hans J. Morgenthau, *Positivism, Functionalism, and International Law*, 34 AM. J. INT'L L. 260, 260 (1940).

and may therefore appear amenable to causal hypotheses whose verity can always be checked by experience.[60]

That Realism is the *genre* of theory, and not engagement, is clear from its emphasis on causality. The acting subject is the external observer, the policy-scientist, possibly employed by a government office to "predict" the future course of international policy in order to formulate scenarios for appropriate response. In the previous section, I argued that Realism's causal models were dependent on, or could not be applied in abstraction from, normative choices regarding desirable courses of action. Here I make the point that causal description fails to grasp the ("internal") perspective of diplomats or lawyers working within an institutional environment such as the Security Council. For them, the argument that the Council's policy is caused by interests well-represented in the Council is as relevant or interesting a point to make as the argument to government officials that governments tend to propose legislation that advances the interests represented by the governmental coalition. Such statements, whatever their status otherwise, raise at least three points. First, neither statement has a necessary bearing on whether the proposed legislation or policy is *justified*. That the United Nations has dealt with the humanitarian crisis in Bosnia in an insufficiently effective manner because the resources, interests, or policies of the great powers have militated against full-scale involvement may or may not be true. But its truth or falsity is not a sufficient response to the question of whether the United Nations has been justified in acting in the way it has, or what might be the right course of action to proceed in the future.

Second, neither statement is helpful when it is precisely what those interests are or what kind of action best serves them that needs examination. To some extent, at least, the United Nations' hesitation at the outset of the crisis in the former Yugoslavia during 1991 reflects this problem. Was it in the Western allies' interests to prevent or to facilitate dissolution? This is not only a technical question. Often interests cannot even be identified without a prior political choice. Will participation in a Common European Defense be in the interests of traditional military neutrals such as Austria, Finland, or Ireland? An answer to this question depends on an earlier choice regarding whether the "natural home" of these countries is within or without a Western political community.

Third, and most fundamental, Realism's theoretical-empirical bias compels it to treat justification as a process of "façade legitimation," the dressing of the technically necessary policy in the garb of generally acceptable norms. This leads Realism into supporting manipulative

---

60. *Id.* at 260–84; *see also* J.S. Watson, *A Realistic Jurisprudence of International Law*, 1980 Y.B. WORLD AFF. 265, 266–67, *reprinted in* INTERNATIONAL LAW 3, 4–5 (Martti Koskenniemi ed., 1992).

diplomatic practices, approaches to negotiation that presume the primacy of the hegemonic powers. This is not simply ethically questionable, but also bad policy. For, inasmuch as "interests" or "security" are not facts of nature but social constructions, the effects of language and political preference, they cannot be distinguished from the justifications that seek to realize them. Whether or not dealing with an internal humanitarian crisis (such as Liberia in 1992 or Rwanda in 1994) should be seen as a matter of collective security, and thus the object of concerted action, cannot be adequately discussed by invoking a presumed causal chain from the crisis to the security of other states (through the resulting refugee problem, for instance), but involves a prior redefinition of the community itself — who are "we" as subjects of security?

In order to grasp the "internal" or engaged perspective on collective security, let me discuss the Security Council's reaction to the Iraqi attack on Kuwait in the fall of 1990 in the light of personal recollections of the role that legal argument seemed to play in the process.

During 1989–90, Finland was one of the elected members of the Security Council. I was posted at the Finnish Permanent Mission in New York at the time and assigned to serve as legal advisor to the Finnish Council team. The nine-member team was headed by the Permanent Representative who was not only Ambassador and Under-Secretary of State, but also a former professor of Political Science in Finland. Most of the team came from the political department of the foreign service. My position in the delegation was relatively humble, somewhere around the middle of the list. This corresponded closely to the place of my opposite numbers, the lawyers in the other fourteen delegations. We were neither among the leading policy-makers nor among the youngest rapporteurs.

I had no formal instructions to obey as the lawyer of the team. Of course, there were general guidelines applicable to all the members regarding the direction of Finnish United Nations policy, plus some more specific instructions in particular crises. But while it seemed evident to everyone that there had to be one lawyer (indeed, one was certainly enough) among the nine, there was no articulated explanation for this certainty. The same applied, I believe, to my colleagues, at least in the WEOG ("Western European and Others' Group") delegations. None of us had any specific "legal" instructions. The place of law in the Security Council was in this respect obscure. It was perhaps assumed that since we had done quite a bit of international law previously, we would know what to do at the right moments. Our role arose from a shared professional background, not from conscious planning.

Much of the lawyer's work was identical with that of others: sitting at informal and formal meetings, participating in recurring consultations headed by the month's president, and reporting home on a daily basis. The lawyer concentrated on textual aspects of resolutions, on those aspects of particular crises that involved legal status (such as the situation in the Palestinian occupied territories) and on the negotiation of generally formulated, "legislative" resolutions (such as a resolution on plastic explosives and on terrorism[61]). From a policy perspective, these issues were neither quite central, nor fully marginal: my diplomatic placing corresponded to the level of my tasks.

In routine matters, the law's (lawyer's) role in the Council during 1989–90 arose from two informal considerations embedded in the working culture of the Council. First, the jurist was expected to assess the domestic and constitutional implications of particular resolutions. Second, particular geographically limited disputes that had been on the Council's agenda for a long time were allocated to political officials experts on the region or on the dispute itself. Contrary to received wisdom, law's role seemed the most limited in routine issues on which everyone had fixed positions and no dramatic moves were or could reasonably be expected. Where the political framework was stable, the lawyer was the handmaid of the politician, helping out if new language for negotiation and consensus was needed. That role depended on pragmatic considerations, not on any shared or articulated theory regarding the delimitation of legal and political matters.

However, things looked different when a non-routine issue emerged. On the night of August 2, 1990, Iraqi troops invaded Kuwait. I was on holiday in Finland on that day but returned to New York very soon thereafter. By the time of my return, the Council had demanded immediate withdrawal of Iraqi troops, established the obligation of non-recognition on member states, and implemented the first full-scale economic embargo on any state since the League of Nations' action against Italy in 1935–36.[62]

I have been trained as a Finnish career diplomat in the belief that in matters concerning the existence of states — such as the Kuwait crisis — Finland's vital interests, as determined by the political leadership, become the basis for our diplomatic action. Trained in the spirit of post-war Realism, I had little difficulty accepting that legal norms should in such cases defer to political requirements. Indeed, Finland's own experience with the League in 1939 seemed the best argument for this necessity.

As I returned to New York in the middle of August 1990, however, I was struck by the enthusiasm with which my "political" colleagues in the delegation had immersed themselves in a controversy about the legal status of the various courses of action taken by or available to the Council and to my own delegation. How should sanctions be administered? What about the blocking of Iraq's ports? What was the status of

---

61. S.C. Res. 638, U.N. SCOR, 44th Sess., 2872d mtg., U.N. Doc. S/RES/638 (1989); S.C. Res. 635, U.N. SCOR, 44th Sess., 2869th mtg., U.N. Doc. S/RES/635 (1989).

62. S.C. Res. 661, U.N. SCOR, 45th Sess., 2933d mtg., U.N. Doc. S/RES/661 (1990); S.C. Res. 660, U.N. SCOR, 45th Sess., 2932d mtg., U.N. Doc. S/RES/660 (1990).

Western troop concentrations in Saudi Arabia? What law applied to the Embassies in Kuwait City or in Baghdad? The delegation, as well as Helsinki, clearly believed that legal viewpoints were not only somewhat relevant, but in some respects central to devising a national position.

The headquarters acted in a similar way. I found permanent representatives and political colleagues grouping in the corridors with the little blue book — the U.N. Charter — in their hands, quarreling about the meaning of the various parts of Chapter VII of the Charter, giving contrasting interpretations about the extent of the right of self-defense under Article 51, and disagreeing about whether Article 42 (military sanctions) needed to be applied in conjunction with Articles 43 and 47 on the provision of national contingents and the role of the military staff committee respectively. Even Prime Minister Thatcher at one point took pains to argue that the concentration of coalition troops in Saudi Arabia before the Council had authorized the use of military force had been a perfectly legitimate application of the right of collective self-defense under Article 51.

How should we understand the fact that in the midst of one of the most serious cases of aggression in the post-war order, diplomats at the United Nations started invoking legal norms and arguing as if whatever action the United Nations or its member states could take was dependent on rules of law? A first point to make is that I do not think anyone saw the Council's role akin to a penal court, acting in Montesquieu's image as *"la bouche qui prononce les paroles de la loi."* Though necessary, nobody thought it sufficient to establish what the law said. Of course, this would also have been bad law. The Council is not a court. It is not obliged to react in any predetermined way to any "breach of the peace, threat to the peace or act of aggression." Nor do these concepts spell out an "international crime" akin to "theft" under national law that would require the Council to order a "sanction."[63] The Council may react even in the absence of unlawfulness; and a violation of the law does not by itself trigger Council competence. Besides, as every national judge knows, Montesquieu's image is pure fiction. There is always choice and policy involved in law application, the relevant norms being open-textured and open to exceptions. This was a fact that was easy to agree upon in the Council.

A second possibility is to think that the delegations agonized over international law in the fall of 1990 not because they felt they had to find the "one right answer," but because they needed to determine what limits were imposed by the law upon Council "discretion." This would

---

63. For the juristic discussion about the nature of Chapter VII "sanctions" as police measures, see, e.g., HANS KELSEN, THE LAW OF THE UNITED NATIONS: A CRITICAL ANALYSIS OF ITS FUNDAMENTAL PROBLEMS 732–37 (1951).

be a liberal and a realistic response, imagining Charter provisions as a neutral framework leaving ample room for political maneuver. But this is not really psychologically plausible. "Law" and "discretion" did not exist in separate pigeon-holes in our minds. The legal debate did not "stop" at any point to leave room for a separate political choice; political choices were posed the moment the legal debate started.

A better metaphor than pigeon-holing for the law/politics relationship might refer to the contemplation of a landscape. In the morning, we see the colors of the trees and the reflection of the leaves on the water; in the evening, we notice the outline of the cliffs against the grey sky, and the shadow of the forest stretches far into the sea. The landscape is the same, the messages it conveys are different. The images are equally self-contained and full. We can reproduce both separately, but we cannot mix them. Likewise, law and politics seemed coherent and separate, yet related to one single reality.

And yet reality has a temporal dimension: morning turns into day and the evening begins sooner than we had noticed. In the Security Council, law and politics developed analogously into each other. As the debate progressed each successive moment added something to our understanding, until the original image had turned into its counterpart. We saw the landscape first in the brightness of legal language: aggression, sanctions, blockade, non-recognition. This language was used to give expression to the contrasting positions of the delegations. These were positions of the evening, visible only in an obscure, shadowy form, impossible to reach in description. The further the debate progressed, the clearer became the interdependence of light and shadow, law and politics, and the focus was increasingly on the boundary. The amount of time available determined the point at which debate had to finish and action had to be taken. Thereafter, that action, and its justifications, turned into precedent, calling for formal consistency in future behavior. Legal and political simultaneously, the long line of resolutions in the fall of 1990 sought to give effect to the ambitions of their drafters as well as to the Charter. In retrospect, we interpret them from both perspectives, yet we can do this fully only from one perspective at a time, by keeping the other outside our gaze.

There is, of course, a third possible understanding about the sense of these debates; namely, that they served only to camouflage the play of ideologies, power, and interests that were "really determining" behind a *legalistic façade*. What may appear as the brightest day is in truth the darkest night! There are two versions of this understanding. First, it may be assumed that part of diplomatic training is to learn to lie about one's true aims. Under this version, the debate in New York was a fraud. It is difficult to prove or disprove this suggestion which speaks about the real, though hidden, intentions of diplomats at the United Nations. Although I have to make allowance for the odd exception, I find this psychologically implausible. Most of the diplomats "honestly" felt that arguments about the Council's competence to order a blockade of Iraq's ports, for instance,[64] had intrinsic relevance. In any case, this criticism misses the point. These are arguments whose validity in no way presupposes honesty in making them. The legality of the blockade has nothing to do with the state of mind of the person invoking it. A day is a day if it looks like one. There is no deeper reality that might prove it otherwise; even our watches provide only a conventional temporal interpretation.

The same is true of the second version which provides that, notwithstanding the states of mind of delegation members, the legal debate was intrinsically without a consequence. Under this view, the diplomats were acting under a false consciousness, a legalistic ideology which camouflaged the fact that what was going on was use of power to further national interests. This kind of "Realism" is very common and presents an extremely critical picture about the United Nations assuming that diplomats do not really understand their job but act under a legalistic spell. I find it hard to support this understanding on an intuitive basis. The Finnish delegation, for instance, was *en bloc* trained as hard-headed Realists. If there had been indoctrination, it was surely not of the legalist sort. The architect of post-war Finnish foreign policy, President Paasikivi, once remarked famously that the Kremlin is no Court of Law, meaning (among other things) that sound legal arguments are a poor substitute for clever policy when it comes to Finland's relations with its Eastern neighbor. Though the historic background is of course different, I believe that this applied to the non-lawyers in the other delegations as well.

More important, however, is that this criticism presents an exclusively external perspective on the events. Legal arguments camouflage the determining force of political or economic power. That is their very point. In the morning we see light. But we know it is inevitable that darkness will fall, and we can examine it later, but not at the same time. However determining political power may be, it is irrelevant for delegations struggling to find public justification for Council action. It may be true that "international government is, in effect, government by that state which supplies the power necessary for the purpose of governing."[65] But such a causal assumption provides nothing to those examining the justifiability of proposed courses of action within an institutional structure.

This is my point about the role of law in the Kuwait crisis. In 1990, the traditional patterns of Council decisionmaking had become irrelevant

---

64. For the Council's actions regarding the blockade, see S.C. Res. 665, U.N. SCOR, 44th Sess., 2938th mtg., U.N. Doc. S/RES/665 (1990).

65. EDWARD H. CARR, THE TWENTY YEARS' CRISIS 1919–1939: AN INTRODUCTION TO THE STUDY OF INTERNATIONAL RELATIONS 107 (Harper & Row 1964) (1939).

and inapplicable. There was no anterior political agreement, no long-standing negotiation with fixed positions, and no routine language to cover the events. The situation was canvassed nowhere but in the Charter itself. As the debate took on a legal style and an engaged aspect, the rest of formalism followed suit: the search for precedent (Southern Rhodesia for the management of economic sanctions) and consistency (in the formulation of the resolutions during the autumn of 1990), the concern for human rights, diplomatic inviolability, and humanitarian law were all strikingly central to the resolutions. Placing the argument in the context of law, there seemed to be no halfway house. The Council could not just apply some law in the Kuwait crisis, leaving the rest unapplied. Long shadows would have been inconsistent with the place of the sun in our landscape. After all, this was the same time as the signing of the "Charter of Paris" by the Conference on Security and Cooperation in Europe (CSCE) which stressed the need for the rule of law in the management of political societies.

It is an uninteresting truism that delegations couch decisions in legal garb to make them look more respectable. That is the point of law. Clearly both the United States and the Yemeni delegations, like those of Finland, Canada, and Romania, sought interpretations that would be in line with their (partly differing) policies. No delegation wishes to report to its capital that it cannot pursue the instructed policy because it cannot defend it in legal terms. Those terms will be found. But though this may appear to support the Realist critique about "façade legitimation," it fails to appreciate how legitimation or justification always has a "façade" aspect to it without this making it any less necessary. Justification is only more complex, tentative, and fragile than the Realist straw-man image of "rule application" would suggest. Newton may have come up with the theory of gravity by sitting under an apple tree and being struck by a falling apple. This causal account of the events, however accurate, is no explanation of his genius nor even a beginning of a theory of gravitation defensible in the scientific community. Newton's genius was in the act of justifying his intuition to his fellow scientists in the form of a coherent theory in accordance with the rules of scientific discourse, not in the process which causally produced it.

The engaged perspective that looks for justification differs from the construction of theories about determining causes by assuming the existence of and invoking an inter-individual, international, political community in which the speaker is situated. Saying that "I believe this is aggression because it suits me to think so" emerges from a solipsism in which others exist only as objects of want-satisfaction. By contrast, saying that this is "aggression" under Article 39 of the Charter invokes a 1945 agreement and a polity in which the speaker situates herself and every person to whom the statement is directed. The road to an undistorted communal life is of course not thereby created. Much more would

478   *Michigan Journal of International Law*   [Vol. 17:455

be needed for that purpose. Without justifying discourse, however, social life would be reduced to manipulative relationships: security will be the security of the king while no problem will seem too small for the intervention of the security force!

Law's contribution to security is not in the substantive responses it gives, but in the process of justification that it imports into institutional policy and in its assumption of responsibility for the policies chosen. Entering the legal culture compels a move away from one's idiosyncratic interests and preferences by insisting on their justification in terms of the historical practices and proclaimed standards of the community. Even if it does not, as both Formalists and Realists may have thought, lift the burden of substantive choice, it implies a recognition of the existence of a world beyond the speaker's immediate subjectivity. Only in this way can "security" maintain its beneficial, altruistic orientation, instead of invoking the somber association with the security police — arrests after midnight, featureless officials, and insulated cellars. As opposed to technical-instrumental rationality, a legal culture involves a "situational ethics,"[66] encompassing not only rules and principles (after all Realists were right in stressing their indeterminacy) but a fairness of process, an attitude of openness, and a spirit of responsibility that implicitly or expressly means submission to critique and dialogue with others about the proper understanding of the community's principles and purposes — in a word, its identity.[67] Law is what lawyers do, said Max Weber in one of the most adept definitions of it. He was of course thinking about national societies with a high degree of professional specialization. In the international context, law is what diplomats do when they debate the meaning of the U.N. Charter, the competence of the Security Council, or Libya's duties under particular Council resolutions. There is nothing *substantive* that would distinguish those debates from political *Diktat*. An enlightened despot or a monkey might sometimes succeed in reciting the right Charter article. What makes these debates *legal* is the manner in which they are conducted: by open reference to rules and principles instead of in secret and without adequate documentation; by aiming toward coherence and consistency, instead of a selective bargaining between "old boys"; by an openness to revision in light of new information and accountability for choices made, instead of counting on getting away with it.

---

66. Robert H. Jackson, *The Political Theory of International Society*, *in* INTERNATIONAL RELATIONS THEORY TODAY, *supra* note 52, at 110, 124–27.

67. For a useful redefinition of Weber's "ethics of responsibility" so as to involve a dialogical relationship between the responsible agent and the person *to whom* the agent is responsible, see DANIEL WARNER, AN ETHIC OF RESPONSIBILITY IN INTERNATIONAL RELATIONS 104–16 (1991).

Realism's theoretical-empirical bias would not be too serious if Realism remained content with its status as expert knowledge. But it does not. Realists stress the practical character of their information, its role in the formation of policy and statecraft. Thereby Realism itself becomes a sociological problem. Even as it readily concedes the (theoretical) separation of "is" and "ought" as a matter of practical consequences, it answers the latter by reference to the former. It thinks about peace, security, and social order in terms of "jobs" to be carried out, or a series of "problems" to be resolved. It hopes to do this by employing resources in accordance with advice from technical, intelligence, and military experts whose expertise is limited to the narrowest possible range of relevant "issues": nuclear deterrence, arms control, peacekeeping, diplomacy. The tricky and eminently political question of the meaning of "peace" in particular circumstances, indeed, the delimitation of the circumstance itself, is never raised and *cannot be raised without immediately posing the question of the qualifications of the experts charged to deal with it.* Was the "issue" in the Gulf War the old boundary disagreement between Iraq and Kuwait? The internal regime of these countries? Peace in the Middle East? Or was the "issue" access to strategic resources? It was treated as an "aggression" of one United Nations member state against another because that is the language of the Security Council, but it was managed through a military operation because "hard" issues of sovereignty are deemed to fall ultimately under the soldiers' realm of competence. In contrast, genocide in Rwanda would trigger principally the competence of relief workers and refugee organizations.

Difficulties in reaching political agreement at the global scale (which is the United Nations' scale) on the right characterization of local political events (do they implicate "security?") and priorities for action has led to an international culture of functional specialization and compartmentalization. This is nowhere more visible than in the separation of the United Nations' hard core political activities from its economic and social activities, with each body and each department in the Secretariat jealously guarding its individual allotment of problems to solve. The justification for a particular action is always given by the non-political, technical competence of the body dealing with it. Indeed, it often seems that the crucial decision about some particular policy is which organ or department is empowered to deal with it (or succeeds in monopolizing it). Once we know the organ or department, we already have a good idea about what sort of action will be taken.

In contrast, a legal culture is never only about *how* to get there. It also poses the question of what there is to get to. The lawyers' anxiety about the proper legal basis of a Security Council resolution always implicitly refers to the institutional teleology of the United Nations. It has two aspects which a purely instrumental debate lacks. First, it implies recognition of situatedness in a political community and openness to dialogue with other members of the community. To put one's argument in terms of Articles 42, 43, and 47 of the Charter is to reaffirm the institutional character of the problem, a readiness to bind oneself to a policy *vis-à-vis* the others, and an assumption of the responsibility for so doing. Second, it entails a redefinition of the community's (the United Nations') constitutive principles and objectives. Legal argument is never deduction from self-evident rules. It always adds to our understanding of the law, and thus to the identity, objective, and principles of the community. The periodic fluctuations of the United Nations' image between that of an economic and social development organization and that of the guarantor of "peace and security" reflect a constant redefinition of the organization's identity as a result of its institutional policies.

There is in fact not much difference between standard Realism and its traditional rival, Institutionalism. Both are concerned about cause and effect in a description of the international world juxtaposing uniform agents (states) within a structure of international policy in which "power" is deployed for the attainment of "interests" and in which the aggregate result is characterized in terms of "peace/war." Where Realists assume that the best causal model reproduces the structure of the balance of power, and that any institutional policy must defer to this, Institutionalists agree, but argue that the best way for the balance to operate is to defer to institutions.[68] Accordingly, any description of the international world is capable of supporting both positions: the absence of peace may always be explained either as the absence of the balance or power, or as the absence of adequate institutions through which the balance could realize itself![69]

This indeterminacy of the Realist/Institutionalist debate is one result of their theoretical-instrumental bias. The anterior choice of the determining structures in a causal description of the international world is left unaddressed in both theories and the conclusions are hidden in their premises. Realist descriptions win if one already believes in the superiority of an understanding of the world in terms of atomistic and egoistic states obsessed by a power-maximizing urge. Institutionalist portrayals seem more compelling if one sees the world in terms of an underlying structural causation that views states as instruments for an underlying histori-

---

68. Charles A. Kupchan & Clifford A. Kupchan, *The Promise of Collective Security*, INT'L SECURITY, Summer 1995, at 52 (a response to the criticism by Mearsheimer, cited *supra* note 5).

69. The same applies to international lawyers' standard response to the Realist challenge. To argue that most states do follow most of the rules most of the time may seem to rescue international law's "relevance" by showing the wide scope of application of its rules — but it does this only at the cost of their normative nature. The result is a description of international reality that underwrites both politics *and* law — obscuring the normative aspects of both in the process. MARTTI KOSKENNIEMI, FROM APOLOGY TO UTOPIA: THE STRUCTURE OF INTERNATIONAL LEGAL ARGUMENT 143–53 (1989).

cal, economic, or military logic. To repeat: any fact situation can always be described in terms of either matrix while the choice of the matrix — indeed, the question whether the choice is more apparent than real — seldom enters the picture.

V. THE WORK OF THE SECURITY COUNCIL

The European Congress system that was set up after the Napoleonic wars during 1814–15 is usually regarded as the first attempt at collective security. It was based on a statist ideology that held all threats against the *status quo* as security threats to be counteracted as necessary by collective force. Even Castlereagh was able to defend Austrian intervention against the revolution in Naples in 1820, which evoked much sympathy in Britain, by reference to Austrian security interests that had been sanctioned by the Alliance. The main interest was an undefined "security" to which other normative concerns had to defer. The fundamental problem of that system was clearly explained in an early British memorandum:

> The idea of an "Alliance Solidaire," by which each State shall be bound to support . . . all other States from violence and attack, upon condition of receiving for itself a similar guarantee, must be understood as morally implying the previous establishment of such a system of general government as may secure and enforce upon all kings and nations an internal system of peace and justice. Till the mode of constructing such a system shall be devised the consequence is inadmissible, as nothing would be more immoral or more prejudicial to the character of government generally than the idea that their force was collectively to be prostituted to the support of established power without any consideration of the extent to which it was abused.[70]

During the Cold War, issues of legitimacy and justifiability such as those raised in this memorandum could not arise as it was clear that there was no such "system of general government" to which they could be dealt with by reference. Now, however, the situation may have changed. The vocabulary of the CSCE Paris Charter of 1990[71] or of the Security Council summit declaration of 1992 suggests that at least governmental rhetoric has moved to a level that has prompted observers to speak about

---

70. THE CONCERT OF EUROPE 42 (René Albrecht-Carrié ed., 1968) (quoting a memorandum on the Treaties of 1814 and 1815, submitted by the British Plenipotentiaries at the Conference of Aix-la-Chapelle, October 1818).

71. *Conference on Security and Co-operation in Europe: Charter of Paris for a New Europe*, 30 I.L.M. 190, 193–208 (1991).

an "emerging right to democratic governance."[72] It may appear that the Security Council is now in a position to enforce the public morals of a new order.

Many of the Council's recent actions have been seen in this light, especially its readiness to intervene in civil wars[73] and its increasing resort to statements about the illegality of particular forms of state behavior.[74] Closely related are the Council's decisions to set up two war crimes tribunals[75] and a war reparations procedure,[76] as well as the authorization to use force to apprehend criminals.[77] The Council has demarcated and guaranteed boundaries,[78] enforced its own decisions by recourse to economic sanctions,[79] and authorized the use of force to ensure the departure of a military regime.[80] All of this seems justified through a redefinition of "security" by reference to a background conception of an international law, or of a public morality that has become the Council's business to enforce.

The most remarkable action in this respect has been, of course, the Council's much belabored economic boycott to force Libya to extradite

---

72. Thomas M. Franck, *The Emerging Right to Democratic Governance*, 86 Am. J. Int'l L. 46 (1992).

73. *See, e.g.*, S.C. Res. 929, *supra* note 14, at pmbl. para. 10 ("[d]etermining that the magnitude of the humanitarian crisis in Rwanda constitutes a threat to peace and security in the region"); S.C. Res. 794, *supra* note 14, at pmbl. para. 3 ("[d]etermining that the magnitude of the human tragedy caused by the conflict in Somalia, further exacerbated by the obstacles being created to the distribution of humanitarian assistance, constitutes a threat to international peace and security"); S.C. Res. 788, U.N. SCOR, 47th Sess., 3138th mtg. at pmbl. para. 5, U.N. Doc. S/RES/788 (1992) ("[d]etermining that the deterioration of the situation in Liberia constitutes a threat to international peace and security").

74. On the illegality of forcible territorial acquisitions and on the violation of the 1949 Geneva Conventions, see, e.g., S.C. Res. 836, *supra* note 14; S.C. Res. 780, U.N. SCOR, 47th Sess., 3119th mtg., U.N. Doc. S/RES/780 (1992); *see also* S.C. Res. 941, U.N. SCOR, 49th Sess., 3428th mtg., U.N. Doc. S/RES/941 (1994) (all declarations concerning property made under duress are void). For an extensive overview of the Council's practice in condemning violations of international humanitarian law, see Sidney D. Bailey, The UN Security Council and Human Rights 59–89 (1994); *cf. supra* note 21.

75. S.C. Res. 955, U.N. SCOR, 49th Sess., 3453d mtg. at 2, U.N. Doc. S/RES/955 (1994); S.C. Res. 827, U.N. SCOR, 48th Sess., 3217th mtg. at 2, U.N. Doc. S/RES/827 (1993). It is particularly noteworthy that these resolutions also contain the statutes of the two tribunals (on former Yugoslavia and Rwanda) that *define* what law should be applied — a real legislative power.

76. S.C. Res. 692, U.N. SCOR, 46th Sess., 2987th mtg. at 2, U.N. Doc. S/RES/692 (1991); S.C. Res. 687, U.N. SCOR, 46th Sess., 2981st mtg. at 7, U.N. Doc. S/RES/687 (1991); S.C. Res. 674, U.N. SCOR, 45th Sess., 2951st mtg. at 3, U.N. Doc. S/RES/674 (1990).

77. S.C. Res. 837, U.N. SCOR, 48th Sess., 3229th mtg. at 2, U.N. Doc. S/RES/837 (1993); *see also* S.C. Res. 978, U.N. SCOR, 50th Sess., 3504th mtg. at 2, U.N. Doc. S/RES/978 (1995) (call for all states to apprehend suspects accused of participating in the Rwandan massacres).

78. S.C. Res. 833, U.N. SCOR, 48th Sess., 3224th mtg., U.N. Doc. S/RES/833 (1993).

79. S.C. Res. 687, *supra* note 76.

80. S.C. Res. 940, *supra* note 14.

two Libyan citizens suspected of the terrorist attacks on the Pan Am flight over Lockerbie in December 1988 and the French UTA flight over Niger in September 1989.[81] The Council defined Libya's refusal to extradite the two men "as a threat to international peace and security."[82] There was no threat or use of force by Libya against any state. Libya's policy was simply too unacceptable, and therefore definable as a security threat, a position that overruled the provisions of an international convention in force between all the parties that would have allowed Libya to refuse extradition.[83]

For the Realists, these developments are just more power policy in disguise. Because the world remains as it was in Castlereagh's day, it would be illusory to think that the Council is acting to enforce some new code of morals or law. But, as I argued in the foregoing section, this is certainly not so from an engaged perspective. Whatever the Council does appears as an institutional activity and calls for an institutional justification. However, as recent debates on the concept of "threat to international peace and security" (and hence of the Council's competence) have shown, how such justification should be construed is by no means clear. Lawyers have sought normative limits to Council authority from an interpretation of Articles 1, 2, 24(1), and 39 of the Charter, laying down the purposes and principles of the organization and the formal competence of the Council to try to create a link between them.[84] But the principles and purposes of the Charter are many, ambiguous, and conflicting. In particular, they are no less indeterminate than the original concept of "threat to the peace" that they pretend to clarify. If the Security Council takes action, does that not, by *fiat*, suffice to determine the issue? What more is there to say? For this reason, some have em-

---

81. *See* S.C. Res. 731, U.N. SCOR, 47th Sess., 3033d mtg., U.N. Doc. S/RES/731 (1992).

82. S.C. Res. 748, U.N. SCOR, 47th Sess., 3063d mtg. at pmbl. para. 7, U.N. Doc. S/RES/748 (1992).

83. Questions of Interpretation and Application of the 1971 Montreal Convention Arising from the Aerial Incident at Lockerbie (Libya v. U.S.), 1992 I.C.J. 114, 126–27 (Apr. 14) [hereinafter Lockerbie Case]. For background and comment, see Fiona Beveridge, *The Lockerbie Affair*, 41 INT'L & COMP. L.Q. 907, 907–09 (1992).

84. Lockerbie Case, 1992 I.C.J. at 155–56 (Judge Bedjaoui, dissenting); *id.* at 170–75 (Judge Weeramantry, dissenting). Of the large commentary on the Lockerbie case, see, e.g., Jean Chappez, *Questions d'interprétation et d'application de la Convention de Montréal de 1971 résultant de l'incident aérien de Lockerbie*, 1992 ANNUAIRE FRANÇAIS DE DROIT INTERNATIONAL [A.F.D.I.] (Centre National de la Recherche Scientifique) 468, 477–79; Bernhard Graefrath, *Leave to the Court What Belongs to the Court: The Libyan Case*, 4 EUR. J. INT'L L. 184, 186–87 (1993); *see generally* OSCAR SCHACHTER, INTERNATIONAL LAW IN THEORY AND PRACTICE 399–400 (1991); HAGUE ACAD. INT'L L., THE DEVELOPMENT OF THE ROLE OF THE SECURITY COUNCIL: PEACE-KEEPING AND PEACE-BUILDING (René-Jean Dupuy ed., 1992).

484   *Michigan Journal of International Law*   [Vol. 17:455

braced the Kelsenian point that "[i]t is completely within the discretion of the Security Council to decide what constitutes a 'threat to the peace.' "[85] However, others have pointed out in impeccable legal logic that "the United Nations is the creature of a treaty and, as such, it exercises authority legitimately only in so far as it deploys powers which the treaty parties have assigned to it."[86]

In this controversy, law and politics keep deferring to each other in an endless search for authority and normative closure: texts constrain (law) — but need to be interpreted (politics); interpretative principles need to be applied (law) — but they are conflicting and ambiguous (politics); the International Court of Justice could perhaps decide the matter (law) — but the Court has no jurisdiction in "political" matters (politics); but is not the possibility for such judicial control implied in the Charter (law) — well, that depends on how it is interpreted, and so on.[87]

Yet the question about the justifiability of Council action under Chapter VII does not really pose itself in the abstract tone of whether or not the Council is "bound" by legal principles. It is much more concretely linked to the Council's handling of particular problems. If there is a problem about the legitimacy of Council action, as many argue,[88] it

---

85. KELSEN, *supra* note 63, at 727; *see also* MICHAEL AKEHURST, A MODERN INTRODUCTION TO INTERNATIONAL LAW 219 (6th ed. 1992) ("[A] threat to the peace is whatever the Security Council says is a threat to the peace.").

86. Thomas M. Franck, *The Security Council and 'Threats to the Peace': Some Remarks of Remarkable Recent Developments*, *in* THE DEVELOPMENT OF THE ROLE OF THE SECURITY COUNCIL: PEACE-KEEPING AND PEACE-BUILDING, *supra* note 84, at 83.

87. It is interesting how *all* the parties in the Lockerbie Case subscribed both to the view that law and politics were part of the same hierarchical structure as well as to their being hermetically isolated from each other. *Libya* claimed that the Council's resolutions "infringe . . . the enjoyment and the exercise of the rights conferred on Libya[,]" Lockerbie Case, 1992 I.C.J. at 125, and that there is "no competition or hierarchy between the Court and the Security Council, each exercising its own competence[,]" *id.* at 126. The former argument assumes that law and politics are part of the same structure, and that law (namely the law of the Montreal Convention) predominates — the second argument assumes that law and politics are separate, and that the Court should only be concerned with the former. The *United States* claimed that protecting Libya's rights "would run a serious risk of conflicting with the work of the Security Council[,]" *id.*, and that "Libya has a Charter-based duty to accept and carry out the decisions in the resolution," *id.* The former argument assumes again that law and politics are separate and that it is precisely because they are separate that they may conflict — and it is the Court's business to avoid such conflict. The latter argument links both into a hierarchical structure where law predominates — this time the law of the Charter (instead of that of the Montreal Convention). Neither party answers its opponent directly: If law should prevail, should it be the law of the Charter or that of the Montreal Convention? If law and politics are distinct, does this mean that the Court should ignore the possibility of conflict or prevent it?

88. *See, e.g.*, Legal Consequences for States of the Continued Presence of South Africa in Namibia (South West Africa) Notwithstanding Security Council Resolution 276, 1971 I.C.J. 16, 293–94 (June 21) (Judge Fitzmaurice, dissenting); David D. Caron, *The Legitimacy of the Collective Authority of the Security Council*, 87 AM. J. INT'L L. 552 (1993).

is precisely in its practical approach to its task. There are at least five broad groups of problems in this respect.[89]

The first problem is secrecy. Since the late 1980s the Council's practice of holding informal consultations has expanded rapidly.[90] Today, practically all the Council's substantive discussions take place outside the official meetings. Council delegations meet at the horseshoe table in front of the public only when substantive agreement has already been attained or proved impossible. There is in general no access to the *travaux préparatoires* of particular resolutions.

Secrecy is, of course, a general problem of the political activities of the United Nations. One example concerns the work of the Sanctions Committees, established for the management of the sanctions regimes (at the moment altogether six).[91] The Committees do not publish their records or even their interpretative decisions. With the insignificant exception of the Iraqi sanctions committee, and only with respect to the Iraqi arms embargo, the Committees do not report to the Council. As a result, there is no access for member states or the public to data that is crucial for an evaluation of the success of the economic measures, with the further implication that they will continue to be used as an article of faith, not as a rational policy measure.[92]

A second problem concerns the lack of procedural safeguards when the Council is acting in a judicial or quasi-judicial role. For example, its determination of Libya's guilt for complicity in the Lockerbie terrorist attack and its liability in resolution 731 in January 1992 fell below all standards of procedural fairness.[93] Nor did the Council take into account Iraq's claims when in 1993 it determined the place of the long-disputed Iraq-Kuwait boundary.[94] And the basis on which the Iraqi Compensation Commission distributes compensation is far from clear.[95] In fact, the Council has so far been unable to put its provisional rules of procedure

---

89. *See also* Koskenniemi, *supra* note 22, at 345–47.

90. *See* G.R. BERRIDGE, RETURN TO THE UN: UN DIPLOMACY IN REGIONAL CONFLICTS 3–11 (1991); *cf.* W. Michael Reisman, *The Constitutional Crisis in the United Nations*, 95 AM. J. INT'L L. 83, 86 (1993).

91. For descriptive overviews, see *Report of the Secretary-General on the Work of the Organization*, U.N. GAOR, 49th Sess., at 5, U.N. Doc. A/49/1 (1994); Nico Schrijver, *The Use of Economic Sanctions by the UN Security Council: An International Law Perspective*, in INTERNATIONAL ECONOMIC LAW AND ARMED CONFLICT 123 (Harry H.G. Post ed., 1994).

92. For descriptions and criticisms, see Paul Conlon, *Legal Problems at the Centre of United Nations Sanctions*, 64 NORDIC J. INT'L L. (forthcoming 1995); Martti Koskenniemi, *Le comité des sanctions (crée par la résolution 661 (1990) du Conseil de Sécurité)*, 1991 A.F.D.I. 119; Michael P. Scharf & Joshua L. Dorosin, *Interpreting UN Sanctions: The Rulings and Role of the Yugoslavia Sanctions Committee*, 19 BROOK. J. INT'L L. 771 (1993).

93. *See* Graefrath, *supra* note 84, at 187–91, 196, 204.

94. S.C. Res. 833, *supra* note 78.

95. *See Report of the Secretary-General Pursuant to Paragraph 19 of the Security Council Resolution 687 (1991)*, U.N. SCOR, 46th Sess., at 7, U.N. Doc. S/22559 (1991).

into a definite form. However, since most of its activity takes place in informal consultations, a mere formalization of its public procedures would be of little avail. It has traditionally been argued that it is not the Council's business to engage in the material settlement of disputes. Practice has shown, however, that in cases where an argument can be found based upon the Council's primary responsibility to uphold or restore peace and security, even the imposition of a binding settlement does not fall outside the Council's competence.

A third group of problems relates to the Council's lack of account-ability both within the United Nations system and beyond. Much discus-sion has centered on the possibility of judicial control over the Council's actions by the International Court of Justice. It may be more relevant for the General Assembly to use its powers, for instance its budgetary powers, to seek to influence or override the policy of the Council.[96] In addition, a revitalization of the "right of last resort" of member states might be a non-negligible means to enhance the Council's accounta-bility.[97] However, none of these means answers the need to enhance the Council's accountability to the groups of individuals and populations that are affected by its actions.[98] It is not easy to see how this might take place, aside from increasing the transparency of the Council's activity. The suggestion to reserve a right of participation in the Council's debates for the representatives of local and other special interests would be a step in a positive direction, although its impact would of course be much di-minished by the practices of secrecy.

A fourth set of problems is related to the Council's lack of commit-ment to the policies it has chosen. The weakness of its reaction to the crisis in the former Yugoslavia is a famous example. The practice of authorizing member states to take military action on the Council's behalf is another abdication of its responsibility; however, many delegations explain it as a lack of resources on the United Nations' part. The same explanation is given for the Council's lack of adequate political and material support to the two war crimes tribunals. Much publicity has concentrated on the situation of the Yugoslavian war crimes tribunal. The Rwandan case seems even worse. By the end of August 1995, some sixteen months after the genocide, the work of the war crimes tribunal had not even commenced, while 51,000 prisoners were being held in

---

96. For a skeptical view in this respect, however, compare Francis Delon, *L'Assemblée générale peut-elle contrôler le Conseil de sécurité?*, *in* LE CHAPITRE VII DE LA CHARTE DES NATIONS UNIES, *supra* note 21, at 239.

97. *See* DAN CIOBANU, PRELIMINARY OBJECTIONS RELATED TO THE JURISDICTION OF THE UNITED NATIONS POLITICAL ORGANS 173–79 (1975) (discussing a state's right of last resort under the laws of the United Nations).

98. *See* Orford, *supra* note 47.

Rwandese prisons in facilities meant for 12,500.[99] A technical reason, such as lack of resources, cannot function as a justification here. The resources do exist in member states but are not allocated for a purpose that might seem marginal or risky to potential contributors.

Finally, there is the much belabored question of the representativeness of the Council as reflected in its composition. Most member states and many observers view this as the Council's main problem, and suggest amending the Charter so as to enhance its democratic legitimacy. Aside from the diplomatic impossibility to agree on the amendment, I am uncertain about the suggestion itself. As I have argued more fully else-where, the Council's role is to co-opt military power for the service of the organization. Enhancing its democratic image supports even more expanded powers for it, a consequence which I find objectionable.[100] Inasmuch as it makes sense to speak of democracy in a statist interna-tional political system (which is by no means self-evidently beneficial rhetorical strategy), it is surely the job of the General Assembly to imagine the political community whose boundaries are then to be policed by the Council. A number of suggestions to review the Council's working patterns have been dealt with recently by United Nations bodies. The Council itself initiated a number of minor, but still beneficial, amend-ments to its procedures.[101] The Secretary-General has suggested reviewing the practices that relate to the management of economic sanctions.[102] In 1994, the General Assembly stressed the need to increase the trans-parency of the Council's activity and requested more detailed information from the Council for this purpose.[103] A working group was set up to look into the composition of the Council and its working practices. While the democracy problem has, in the course of 1994 and 1995, proved as intractable as in the past, without any agreement emerging on how the Council's composition could be amended, a number of proposals have

---

99. *Letter Dated 29 August 1995 from the Secretary-General Addressed to the President of the Security Council*, U.N. SCOR, 50th Sess., U.N. Doc. S/1995/762 (1995); *see also Third Report of the Secretary-General Pursuant to Paragraph 5 of Security Council Resolution 955 (1994)*, U.N. SCOR, 50th Sess., U.N. Doc. S/1995/741 (1995).

100. Koskenniemi, *supra* note 22.

101. These include regular briefings by the president of the Council to the president of the Assembly and the chairmen of regional groups, consultations with troop-contributing and other "interested" countries, daily publication of the agendas of the Council's informal consultations, monthly circulation among the permanent missions of its program of work, "orientation debates" open to all members as the Council begins the consideration of new items, and the reconsideration of the format of its reports to the Assembly. *Question of Equitable Represen-tation on and Increase in the Membership of the Security Council*, U.N. GAOR, 49th Sess., Agenda Item 33, U.N. Doc. A/49/965 (1995). Not all of these, however, have yet been implemented.

102. *Supplement to An Agenda for Peace: Position-Paper of the Secretary-General on the Occasion of the Fiftieth Anniversary of the United Nations*, *supra* note 15, ¶¶ 66–76.

103. G.A. Res. 264, U.N. GAOR, 48th Sess., 102d plen. mtg., Agenda Item 53, U.N. Doc. A/RES/264 (1994).

been presented to the working group on the secrecy issue.[104] The thrust of the proposals is to increase the transparency of the Council's activity with regard to non-members and especially "interested states." While many proposals repeat the minor modifications already introduced by the Council itself, other proposals underline the need to clarify the division of competence among the Council and other United Nations bodies, to review the practice of economic sanctions, and to update and make permanent the Council's provisional rules of procedure.[105] The proposals do not seek to modify the statist image of collective security, but they do go some way toward strengthening legal culture within the Council.

VI. Security and Law as Institutional Cultures

If there is any single point on which Realism agrees with Institutional formalism, it is expressed in this one sentence by the most paradigmatic of the formalists, Hans Kelsen: "By its very nature, collective security is a legal principle, while the balance of power is a principle of political convenience."[106] Realists embraced this definition and rejected collective security precisely as the kind of legalistic Utopianism whose failure seemed the single most important lesson from the League of Nations experiment. *De maximis non curat praetor.* Today, most lawyers have accepted that if law has a role to play in matters of security, it is as a handmaid to state power and interest, a facilitator for politics to take its natural course "by rationalizing and stabilizing the existing and improvised means of collaboration between [the] Powers."[107] The favorite metaphor invokes traffic regulation: the law's role is based on its usefulness for states in the same way as rules of the road are useful to motorists. "But it is precisely in the vital realm of power relations that it is at its weakest."[108]

The assumed primacy of policy over law implies both the existence of fixed and verifiable state security interests and the presence of reliable information on the causal chains that allow their realization. In this image, shared by Realists and Institutionalists alike, law is purely external and instrumental, something that decisionmakers choose to ignore or apply at their will when seeking to fulfill interests and values. This is the modern image of the "gardening state," the image of public policy in the

---

104. *Question of Equitable Representation on and Increase in the Membership of the Security Council, supra* note 101, Annex.

105. *Id.*

106. Hans Kelsen, Collective Security Under International Law 42 (Naval War College Int'l L. Series No. 49, 1954).

107. George W. Keeton & Georg Schwarzenberger, Making International Law Work 96 (1946) (making this point about the United Nations' role).

108. Hoffmann, *supra* note 1, at 89.

service of human betterment.[109] In this image, international security appears as a function of bureaucratic management skills in the combination of unilateral with institutional policies.

However, much of our late modern experience suggests skepticism about the ability of public decision processes to reach their goals. In the first place, there is uncertainty about those goals — whether their familiar rhetorical forms actually encapsulate shared values or interests. The present consensus about a new "world order" is not immune from the observation by E.H. Carr that "as soon as the attempt is made to apply these supposedly abstract principles to a concrete political situation, they are revealed as the transparent disguises of selfish vested interests."[110] Second, even if there were agreement on such values or interests, we seem to lack information about how they can be reached. Our science and technology no longer seem reliable guides for action. Sometimes the solution of problems creates new, unforeseen, and often more serious problems, making the very process of policy as "problem-solution" inherently suspect.

For such general reasons, there is room for skepticism about the instrumental nature of law, its ability to express and to realize values, interests, or indeed, "security."[111] This skepticism is in no way diminished by a reason specific to the law, such as the indeterminacy of its rules and principles. Instead of being an external, objective instrument for policy, law is enmeshed with the same uncertainties as policy — its application remaining simultaneously a political act.

Realism and Institutionalism both imagine the law as an instrument for political purposes. This, I argued earlier, is an offshoot of their theoretical-empirical bias, that bias itself being inseparable from the modern image of the "gardening state" and supporting an international culture of technical expertise in the manipulation of "power" for the enhancement of "interests." I want to contrast that with my favorite quote from George Kennan who once depicted international law as having "the unobtrusive, almost feminine, function of the gentle civilizer of national self-interest[.]"[112] Despite the intended irony, the quote reveals an important truth about international law as a cultural instead of an instrumental phenomenon, highlighting the engaged aspect of the law, its being "inside" social practices instead of "outside" them as an objective language or a formal procedure. From that aspect, law acts as a spirit or an attitude that involves recognizing the communal situatedness of the speaker: hence its

---

109. ZYGMUNT BAUMAN, MODERNITY AND AMBIVALENCE 20, 26–39 (1991).

110. CARR, *supra* note 65, at 87–88.

111. For one useful discussion of the significance of such (and other) anti-instrumental themes for legal practice, see Guyora Binder, *Beyond Criticism*, 55 U. CHI. L. REV. 888 (1988).

112. GEORGE F. KENNAN, AMERICAN DIPLOMACY 1900–1950, at 54 (1951).

curious, yet typical, ability to engage the practitioner in political action while seeking distance from anyone's idiosyncratic interests. Engaging in the formalism of the legal argument inevitably makes public the normative basis and objectives of one's actions and assumes the actor's communal accountability for what it is that one is justifying. It is the antithesis of a culture of secrecy, hegemony, dogmatism, and unaccountability.

For a brief moment in the autumn of 1990, the political context within the Security Council seemed open and institutional culture might have been revised. By early 1991, that momentum was gone. The Council met only once during Operation Desert Storm, and even then in a closed session. There is no longer much debate around the meaning of collective self-defense, or the relationship among Articles 42, 43, and 47. The long list of procedural problems, however, that remain under discussion in the General Assembly as well as, to some extent, in the Council itself, remain relevant for the development of a legal culture within the Council. Many factors work against such development. The background of diplomats at the United Nations who serve in the Council has traditionally focused on the hard realities of power politics — one does not get into a Council delegation by having served in development assistance! The routines and composition of the political secretariat of the United Nations are equally resistant to legal culture, as are its administrative inertia, lack of resources, recruitment policies, and the relative isolation of the office of legal affairs from the political centre.

For me, it seems clear that law has a place in collective security as a working culture of the "gentle civilizer" by opening conceptions and practices of "security" to public debate, and by enhancing the accountability of governmental and international institutions for what goes on under the label of "security policy." That security has expanded beyond its military and statist component highlights its political and constructive aspects and the inadequacy of the practices within the United Nations (and elsewhere in international organizations) through which "security matters" have been handled. Security can no longer be seen in terms of expert knowledge managed through secret bureaucratic routines, but as one theme among others that seeks to articulate the political values on which we claim to base our communal identities.

[2]

DIPLOMACY

HANS J. MORGENTHAU†

WHEN Metternich was informed of the death of the Russian ambassador at the Congress of Vienna, he is supposed to have exclaimed, "Ah, is that true? What can have been his motive?" The great diplomatist of the post-Napoleonic era was not alone in this moral depreciation of diplomacy. From the anti-Machiavellian writers to our time, the diplomat has been held in low esteem, and while his professional competence and even his ordinary intelligence have frequently been questioned, his moral qualities have always been under a cloud.

It is, however, one thing to have a low opinion of the intellectual and moral qualities of a group of professional men, and it is quite another to believe that they and their work fulfill no useful function, that they have become obsolete, and that their days are numbered. While the former opinion is as old as the profession of diplomacy itself, the latter belief has its roots in the liberal philosophy of the nineteenth century. In the Wilsonian conception of foreign affairs and the philosophy of the League of Nations it bursts forth in full bloom, and today we witness in the theory and practice of the United Nations and the movement for world government a second flowering of the same thought.

While the spokesmen of public opinion seem to be unanimous in opposition to traditional diplomacy, they split into two schools of thought on the question, what, if anything, shall replace the discarded method of conducting foreign affairs. There are those who believe that foreign policy itself is a relic of a pre-scientific past which will not survive the coming of the age of reason and good will; when foreign policy disappears, diplomacy as the technique by which foreign policy is effectuated will disappear, too. There are others who would substitute for power politics another type of foreign policy based on international law and consequently would replace the "old" diplomacy by a "new" one, the diplomat of national power by the advocate of international law.

The former school, which one might call perfectionist in contradistinction to the legalistic one, has found its typical representatives among nineteenth-century liberals, some Wilsonians, and contempo-

---

† Associate Professor of Political Science, University of Chicago; Instructor in Public Law, University of Geneva, 1932–5; Professor of International Law, Institute of International and Economic Studies, Madrid, 1935–6; member of the Executive Council of the American Society of International Law; member of the American Bar Association; editor of Peace, Security and the United Nations, 1945; author of numerous works, including The International Jurisdiction, Its Nature and Its Limits, 1929; The Concept of Politics and the Theory of International Disputes, 1933; Scientific Man vs. Power Politics (to be published in October, 1946, by the Chicago University Press).

raneous adherents of world government. The liberals of the nineteenth century saw in foreign policy a residue of the feudal age, an aristocratic pastime bound to disappear with the application of liberal principles to international affairs. According to Bentham,[1] "Nations are associates and not rivals in the grand social enterprise." "At some future election," said Cobden,[2] "we may probably see the test of 'no foreign politics' applied to those who offer to become the representatives of free constituencies." "The idea of conscious planning," says Paul S. Reinsch,[3] "or striving to subject national and economic facts and all historic development to the conscious political will—that conception of diplomacy is synonymous with the essence of *politics* and will stand and fall with the continuance of the purely political state. Manipulative, and hence secret, diplomacy is in fact the most complete expression of the purely political factor in human affairs. To many, it will seem only a survival of a hyper-political era, as human society now tends to outgrow and transcend politics for more comprehensive, pervasive and essential principles of action. . . . But if it should be achieved, then plainly the old special functions of diplomacy will fall away and administrative conferences will take the place of diplomatic conversations. When Portugal became a republic, the proposal was made to abolish all diplomatic posts and have the international business of Portugal administered by consuls. That would eliminate politics from foreign relations."

Here, the disappearance of foreign policy and, with it, of diplomacy is expected as a by-product of the ascendancy of liberal principles over the feudal state, and this expectation is indeed in harmony with the laissez-faire philosophy of nineteenth-century liberalism. The twentieth-century opponents of any foreign policy and any kind of diplomacy have found in the conception of world government a positive instrumentality which will make foreign policy and diplomacy superfluous. "The United Nations," declares a group of distinguished members of the American Bar Association,[4] "cannot be saved by the process of shunting all the major controversies between its members back for solution by diplomacy. It can only be saved . . . by transforming the present league structure into a general government to regulate and promote the common interests of the people of the States. The American Bar can dedicate itself to no greater responsibility nor higher aim than that of world government to make world laws for the control of world affairs so as to assure world peace."

The adherents of the legalistic school, too, believe in law as the

---

1. BENTHAM, *Principles of Penal Law* in 1 WORKS (1843) 563.
2. Quoted in BLEASE, A SHORT HISTORY OF ENGLISH LIBERALISM (1913) 195.
3. REINSCH, SECRET DIPLOMACY (1922) 13, 15.
4. (1946) 32 A. B. A. J. 270.

alternative to power politics. They expect, however, the preservation of peace not from a world law enacted by a world government, but from international law agreed upon by sovereign nations organized in a Holy Alliance, a League of Nations, or the United Nations. Traditional foreign policy pursuing the national interest is superseded by a new conception of international affairs, the essence of which is respect for international law as embodied in the fundamental law of an international organization. According to this school, the League of Nations and the United Nations supersede the methods by which foreign policy has been conducted in the past. The period of power politics, spheres of influence, alliances, and secret diplomacy has come to an end; a new conception of international affairs, recognizing the solidarity of all nations, based upon the respect for international law and operating through the instrumentality of the new organization, has come into being. Consequently, traditional diplomacy, too, must give way to a new conception of diplomatic intercourse appropriate to the new relations established between nations. If the end of the state is power, the character of its diplomacy will be adapted to that end. If the end of the state is the defense of international law, a different type of diplomacy will serve that end.

Woodrow Wilson is the most eloquent apostle of the new diplomacy of the League of Nations. It is true that sometimes Wilson seemed to join hands with the opponents of any diplomacy whatsoever, as when he wrote in his letter to Senator Hitchcock of March 8, 1920, "For my own part, I am not willing to trust to the council of diplomats the working out of any salvation of the world from the things which it has suffered." However, he saw more clearly than anybody else the intimate connection between the new conception of international affairs as embodied in the League of Nations and a new diplomatic technique by which that new conception was to be realized. The preamble to, and the first of, the Fourteen Points are still the most persuasive statement of the new philosophy of international affairs.[5]

The philosophy of the United Nations has added nothing to Wilson's program. While it equals the Wilsonian philosophy in its opposition

---

5. The Preamble to the Fourteen Points states, "It will be our wish and purpose that the processes of peace, when they are begun, shall be absolutely open, and that they shall involve and permit henceforth no secret understandings of any kind. The day of conquest and aggrandizement is gone by; so is also the day of secret covenants entered into in the interest of particular governments, and likely at some unlooked-for moment to upset the peace of the world. It is this happy fact, now clear to the view of every public man whose thoughts do not still linger in an age that is dead and gone, which makes it possible for every nation whose purposes are consistent with justice and the peace of the world to avow, now or at any other time, the objects it has in view." The first point reads, "Open covenants of peace, openly arrived at, after which there shall be no private international understandings of any kind, but diplomacy shall proceed always frankly and in the public view." HART, SELECTED ADDRESSES AND PUBLIC PAPERS OF WOODROW WILSON (1918) 247–8.

THE YALE LAW JOURNAL

to traditional diplomacy, it is much less outspoken as to the alternative. Thus, the former Secretary of State, Cordell Hull, said on his return from the Moscow Conference [6] that the new international organization would mean the end of power politics and usher in a new era of international collaboration. Mr. Philip Noel-Baker, British Minister of State, declared in the House of Commons [7] that the British government was "determined to use the institutions of the United Nations to kill power politics, in order that, by the methods of democracy, the will of the people shall prevail." Mr. Ernest Bevin, the British Secretary of Foreign Affairs, in his speech of March 30, 1946,[8] expressed in somewhat more cautious language the expectation that while "you cannot change a policy that has been pertaining for three or four hundred years among different powers in a moment," the United Nations would put an end to the imperialistic methods of the past. Secretary of State Byrnes declared in his address of February 28, 1946,[9] that "we have pinned our hopes to the banner of the United Nations. . . . We have joined with our allies in the United Nations to put an end to war. We have covenanted not to use force except in the defense of law as embodied in the Purposes and Principles of the Charter. We intend to live up to that covenant."

Since the philosophy underlying these statements proclaims respect for international law and, more particularly, for the Charter of the United Nations as the alternative to traditional power politics, it is safe to assume that it favors a diplomacy commensurate with the new foreign policy. Indeed we have already seen this new legalistic diplomacy in action when the Security Council of the United Nations dealt on the basis of international law with the Greek, Syrian, Indonesian, Iranian, and Spanish situations.

Even those, however, who, like Mr. Noel-Baker, are out "to kill power politics" through the instrumentality of the United Nations must by implication admit that power politics, as of today, is still alive. Even those who, like the nineteenth-century liberals and their twentieth-century heirs, see in power politics nothing but an irrational atavism, cannot deny that the end of power politics is yet to come. They welcome the new legalistic diplomacy of the United Nations as a step toward the ultimate victory of law over politics. They expect that the persisting dualism between traditional and legalistic diplomacy will gradually transform itself into the monism of the latter. Though the heads of state still meet in secret conferences and the foreign ministers discuss the most important post-war problems accord-

---

6. N. Y. Times, Nov. 19, 1943, p. 1, col. 6.
7. 419 H. C. DEB. (5th ser. 1946) 1262.
8. N. Y. Times, March 31, 1946, p. 22, col. 1.
9. N. Y. Times, March 1, 1946, p. 10, col. 1.

ing to the procedures of traditional diplomacy, future negotiations of this kind will be carried out within the United Nations and according to the procedures of the new diplomacy. President Truman gave voice to this expectation when he told his press conference of March 21, 1946 [10] that "The United Nations Organization is supposed to take over the questions formerly discussed in Big Three meetings, and it was time it assumed that responsibility if there was to be peace in the world. . . ." The same philosophy, aiming to superimpose the new legalistic diplomacy of the United Nations upon the traditional diplomatic methods, is at the foundation of the proposal advanced by Secretary of State Byrnes to charge the Assembly of the United Nations with the task of writing the peace treaties with the powers defeated in the Second World War.[11]

This philosophy of legalistic monism is, however, contradicted by the Charter of the United Nations itself which, explicitly and implicitly, recognizes a dualism between the methods of traditional diplomacy and the new diplomacy of the United Nations.

It should be noted in passing that this dualism between the old and the new methods of settling international disputes was expressly recognized in Article 13 of the Covenant of the League of Nations, which provides that certain disputes "which cannot be satisfactorily settled by diplomacy" shall be submitted to arbitration. This dualism was likewise recognized in the debates of the League of Nations. Thus, in the face of certain Iranian complaints submitted to the Sixth Committee of the Assembly of 1928, its president declared,[12] "Every country had diplomatic difficulties. If all these difficulties were discussed before the League of Nations, it would be overwhelmed with work. Each Government must try to solve its own difficulties by direct negotiations, and not refer them to the League unless the negotiations failed."

The dualism between the procedures of the League and those of traditional diplomacy became a manifest problem, however, mainly in the interpretation of Article 11, Paragraph 2, of the Covenant. Article 11, Paragraph 2, stipulated "the friendly right of each Member of the League to bring to the attention of the Assembly or of the Council any circumstance whatever affecting international relations which threatens to disturb international peace or the good understanding between nations upon which peace depends." Its function within the system of the Covenant was similar to that which Article 35, Paragraph 1, fulfills in the Charter of the United Nations.

The non-exclusive and supplementary character of the procedures

10. N. Y. Times, March 22, 1946, p. 1, col. 5.

11. N. Y. Times, May 21, 1946, p. 1, col. 8.

12. (1928) LEAGUE OF NATIONS OFFICIAL JOURNAL, Spec. Supp., No. 70, at 29.

under Article 11, and hence the dualism between the latter and the traditional procedures of diplomacy, was stressed in theory [13] and practice.[14] With an incisiveness and maturity of political judgment justifying extensive quotation, Mr. Jean Ray, the leading commentator of the Covenant of the League, pointed out under the heading of "Possible Abuses of Article 11," [15]

> "There are in international relations a great number of delicate or irritating questions: it is the function of diplomacy to resolve them. Any document which organizes an international agency creates a risk: the one of accentuating differences of opinion. This risk is increased when the document is very vague, and that is exactly the case of the second paragraph of Article 11. What is the circumstance which is not, more or less indirectly, of such a nature as to 'affect international relations' and which does not threaten therefore to 'disturb,' one day or another, the good understanding between the nations? One must therefore wish that this provision be applied with great zeal perhaps in certain exceptional cases but with great moderation in ordinary ones.
>
> "Let us say, first of all, that it is not very fortunate that the eventual recourse to the League of Nations be presented, in the course of a negotiation, as a kind of threat. It is natural and excellent that this supreme remedy be envisaged, that it be taken into account beforehand, that it be raised in diplomatic conversations; but it seems to us a practice which ill prepares the League for its conciliatory function to mention the eventual appeal to the League in an official step in order to exert pressure upon the other side. . . . But in a certain number of cases states have submitted to the Council secondary questions which without doubt could have been settled by diplomatic means; in such cases the Council has adopted the wise policy of inviting the parties to come to an understanding outside the League."

---

13. See, *e.g.*, the Rutgers Memorandum on Articles 10, 11 and 16 of the Covenant, submitted in 1928 to the League's Committee of Arbitration and Security. The Memorandum declared, ". . . in certain cases it may be expedient to resort to all possible means of direct conciliation, and to the good offices of third Powers, before bringing a dispute before the Council.

". . . if efforts of conciliation are to be successful, it may be essential that the question should be discussed by a very small number of Powers . . . [with] full latitude to decide whether the Council should be kept informed. . . ." 9 LEAGUE OF NATIONS OFFICIAL JOURNAL (1928) 670, 675–6.

14. See, *e.g.*, Politis' objection that Albania's bringing a complaint against Greece before the Council while direct diplomatic negotiations were in progress constituted "pressure" and "abuse" of Council procedure. *Id.* at 873. The Zaleski report on this dispute endorsed "friendly agreement" by "direct negotiation." *Id.* at 942. And see the debates on the applicability of Article 11, Paragraph 2 to the Swiss war claims and Finnish ships cases, 15 *id.* (1934) 1436 *et seq.*, 1454.

15. RAY, COMMENTAIRE DU PACTE DE LA SOCIÉTÉ DES NATIONS (1930) 380–1.

The theory and practice of the League of Nations had to develop this general dualism between the procedures of the League and of traditional diplomacy out of the interpretation of Article 11, Paragraph 2, of the Covenant and the explicit formulation of Article 13 which allowed, however, of only limited application. The over-all importance of this dualism is implicit in the structure of the Covenant and only the decay of the League of Nations in the 'thirties made it fully obvious. The Charter of the United Nations, on the contrary, makes this dualism explicit from the very outset in the words of its provisions. On the one hand, Article 24 establishes as a matter of principle the Security Council's "primary responsibility for the maintenance of international peace and security." On the other hand, in the specific provisions of Chapter VI the Charter makes explicit not only the general character of this dualism but also, as a matter of practical application, the primary importance of the traditional methods of diplomacy. At the very beginning Chapter VI stipulates in Article 33 that the parties shall "first of all" try to settle their disputes "by negotiation, enquiry, mediation, conciliation, arbitration, judicial settlement, resort to regional agencies or arrangements, or other peaceful means of their own choice." Paragraph 2 gives the Security Council the right at its discretion to refer the parties to such traditional means of diplomatic and judicial settlement. Article 36 elaborates this right by empowering the Security Council to make recommendations, and stresses, in Paragraph 2, the primary importance of the traditional procedures of diplomacy by stipulating that "the Security Council should take into consideration any procedures for the settlement of the dispute which have already been adopted by the parties." While Articles 34 and 35 establish the discretionary competency of the United Nations, concurrent with the traditional methods of peaceful settlement, Article 37 reaffirms the primary character of the traditional methods and at the same time establishes the supplementary character of the procedure under the Security Council by obligating the parties who have failed to settle a dispute by the traditional means enumerated in Article 33 to refer it to the Security Council.

The same dualism is again explicitly recognized in Articles 51 and 52. Article 51 is in this respect important, as it stipulates "the inherent right of . . . collective self-defense." Collective self-defense, especially under the conditions of modern warfare, is impossible without political and military understandings anticipating military eventualities which might make collective military measures desirable. In other words, "the inherent right of . . . collective self-defense" involves the inherent right to conclude political and military alliances against a prospective aggressor.

The qualifications of this right in the remainder of Article 51 are of a verbal rather than of a substantive nature. These qualifications are three-fold. First, the right of collective self-defense shall remain unimpaired only "until the Security Council has taken the measures necessary to maintain international peace and security." Yet the Security Council can act only through its member states, and when, as will be regularly the case, one of the permanent members of the Council is a party to collective self-defense, the requirement of the unanimity of the permanent members according to Article 27 will vouchsafe the identity of any measures taken by the Security Council with the measures taken in collective self-defense. Second, measures taken in collective self-defense have to be reported immediately to the Security Council, whose information through press, radio, and ordinary diplomatic channels will thus be duplicated. Finally, such measures shall not affect the authority and responsibility of the Security Council to take appropriate action itself. Here again, however, the Security Council is but another name for the five permanent members acting in unison, and the measures which one or the other of these members has taken by virtue of the right of self-defense will of necessity be in harmony with the measures to which these members are willing to agree by virtue of the Charter of the United Nations. Thus, while the wording of Article 51 seems to subordinate the traditional methods of international intercourse to the new diplomacy of the United Nations, its actual effect reverses this relationship.

It is in the light of this structure of Article 51 that one must read Articles 52 and 53. Article 52 stipulates not only the right but also the obligation of member states to use regional arrangements or agencies for the settlement of regional matters before they are referred to the Security Council. The latter, in turn, is charged with encouraging regional settlements and, in Article 53, with utilizing regional arrangements and agencies for enforcement actions. Such arrangements and agencies, however, must be created and maintained by the traditional methods of diplomacy. Since it is difficult to visualize an international dispute or situation which would not have a geographical focus, and therefore a regional character, Articles 52 and 53 not only reaffirm for practically all international situations and disputes the dualism between traditional and United Nations diplomacy but also establish the precedence of the former over the latter as both a right and a duty of all concerned. It is true that according to Article 52, Paragraph 4, Article 52 must be read in the light of Articles 34 and 35. But it is no less true, even though it is not expressly stated, that, in point of practical application, Articles 34 and 35 must be read in the light of Articles 51, 52, and 53.

This dualism between traditional diplomacy, conceived in terms of regionalism, and the new diplomacy of the United Nations suffers only one exception provided for in Article 53. Enforcement actions under regional arrangements or by regional agencies are subordinated to the United Nations; they can be taken only with the authorization of the Security Council. Here again, however, the subordination is verbal rather than actual, for the likelihood that one of the nations instrumental in regional enforcement will be identical with one of the nations without whose consent the Security Council cannot act, will make it unlikely that the action which the Security Council is willing to authorize will diverge from the regional enforcement upon which that particular nation has decided.

Even this exception is, however, limited, at least for the time being, to enforcement actions which would be taken on a regional basis against states which have not been enemies of any signatory of the Charter. According to Articles 53, 106, and 107, any action, regional or otherwise, taken or to be taken against an enemy power as a result of the war or for the purpose of forestalling renewed aggression on the part of such power, is for the time being not subject to the limitations of the Charter. Here the dualism between traditional and United Nations procedures is replaced, at least temporarily, by the monism of the traditional methods of international intercourse. Traditional methods become here a substitute for United Nations procedures until the latter are available for the purpose of preventing aggression by an enemy state.[16] Article 106 in particular establishes for the five big powers, as well as for other members of the United Nations, the obligation to consult outside the framework of the new organization, and reference to Paragraph 5 of the Moscow Declaration,[17] whose purport is identical with that of Article 106, only serves to underline the monistic conception of this provision.

The dualism between traditional and United Nations diplomacy, explicitly stated or implicitly contained in the individual provisions of the Charter, reveals itself also in the over-all structure of the new organization. The United Nations, in the performance of its functions according to the purposes of its Charter, is predicated upon the continuing unity of the permanent members of the Security Council. In the scheme of the Charter these members are, as it were, the nucleus of a world federation, a Holy Alliance within a Holy Alliance, without whose consent the Security Council can make no binding

---

16. It might be mentioned in passing that the same dualism is also made explicit in Article 79 of the Charter, where the agreement on the terms of trusteeship is referred to the states directly concerned and where the agencies of the United Nations are only called upon for approval of the agreements arrived at in traditional diplomatic negotiations.

17. Paragraph 5 of the Moscow Declaration reads as follows: "That for the purpose of maintaining international peace and security pending the re-establishment of law and order and the inauguration of a system of general security, they will consult with one another and as occasion requires with other members of the United Nations with a view to joint action on behalf of the community of nations." *Official Documents* (1944) 38 AM. J. INT. L. (Supp.) 5.

decision in substantive matters. Under Article 27, Paragraph 3, the United Nations cannot exist as a functioning organization without the consent of all permanent members to decisions in substantive matters. This general rule is inapplicable only to the pacific settlement of disputes to which permanent members are party, their consent in this case not being required to make the decision of the Security Council legally binding. Yet their consent is required to enable the Security Council to enforce the pacific settlement through sanctions under Chapter VII. If the Security Council should try to enforce its decision despite the dissent of one or the other of its permanent members, the United Nations would lose its function for "the maintenance of international peace and security," and at the same time its legal identity; it would at best become a political and military coalition against the dissenting permanent member or members. The United Nations would break up into warring camps, and only through total victory in war would the Nations be re-United.

The consent of the permanent members, which is but the outward manifestation of their continuing political unity, the Charter does not create but presupposes. How is this unity to be created and maintained? The Charter does not say. Its silence refers by implication to those methods by which traditionally political unity among nations has been established and maintained, that is, the traditional methods of diplomacy. As the continuing political unity of the great powers (who are permanent members of the Security Council) is the foundation upon which the edifice of the United Nations rests, so is the successful operation of traditional diplomacy the cement which keeps that foundation together. The successful operation of the old methods gives the new diplomacy of the United Nations a chance to operate.

This dualism between old and new diplomacy and the dependence of the latter upon the success of the former are implicit in the structure of the United Nations. This dualism, however, if not the fundamental importance of the successful operation of traditional diplomacy, is expressly recognized by the Report of the Crimea Conference.[18] Under the heading "Meetings of Foreign Secretaries" this report states:

> "These meetings have proved of the utmost value and the Conference agreed that permanent machinery should be set up for regular consultation between the three Foreign Secretaries [of the United States, Great Britain, and the Soviet Union]. They will, therefore, meet as often as may be necessary, probably about every three or four months. These meetings will be held in rotation in the three capitals, the first meeting being held in London, after the United Nations Conference on World Organization."

---

18.   (1945) 12 DEP'T OF STATE BULL. 213.

Here we are in the presence of a legal understanding establishing a concert of the great powers not for a limited purpose as envisaged in Article 106 of the Charter but, in view of its proved usefulness, on a permanent basis. In order to realize fully the import and the potentialities of this provision, it is useful to compare it with the text of Article 6 of the Treaty of Paris of November 20, 1815, which established the "diplomacy by conference" of the Holy Alliance:

> "To facilitate and to secure the execution of the present Treaty, and to consolidate the connections which at the present moment so closely unite the Four Sovereigns for the happiness of the world, the High Contracting Parties have agreed to renew their Meetings at fixed periods, either under the immediate auspices of the Sovereigns themselves, or by their respective Ministers, for the purpose of consulting upon their common interests, and for the consideration of the measures which at each of those periods shall be considered the most salutary for the repose and prosperity of Nations, and for the maintenance of the Peace of Europe." [19]

Since it is not likely that the authors of the Report of the Crimea Conference had this article of the Treaty of Paris in mind when they phrased their document, the coincidence between the two provisions reveals a striking similarity in the underlying political situations.

The provision that this permanent machinery of traditional diplomacy should operate for the first time after the permanent machinery of the new diplomacy of the United Nations had been established makes the dualism between the two methods of international intercourse most emphatic. The quoted paragraph from the Report of the Crimea Conference has the same fundamental importance for traditional diplomacy which Article 24 of the Charter has for the new diplomacy of the United Nations. The organic link between both is provided by the structure of the United Nations, which presupposes the continuing political unity of the great powers without being able to create and maintain it. It is for the achievement of the latter task that the Crimea Conference has called upon the traditional diplomacy of the foreign offices.

The monism of the new diplomacy of the United Nations, proclaimed by the spokesmen of public opinion, finds no support in the Charter and structure of the new organization. Since the latter's inception, diplomatic procedure has been dualistic in practice. On the one hand, the chief executives and foreign ministers of the great powers have tried to solve by the traditional methods of diplomacy the fundamental political issues of the post-war world. On the other hand, the

---

19. Anderson, Constitutions and Documents Illustrative of the History of France, 1789–1901 (1904) 484–5.

Security Council of the United Nations has attacked by the new methods of legalistic diplomacy certain secondary issues, such as the Greek, Syrian, Indonesian, Iranian, and Spanish situations. The question arises as to which of the two methods is more appropriate to the problems dealt with and therefore more promising of success. For while it is obvious that the monism of United Nations diplomacy does not exist in actuality, it might be that it ought to exist by virtue of the superiority of United Nations diplomacy over the traditional diplomatic methods, and that therefore an ever greater number of ever more important international issues ought to be dealt with by the former rather than by the latter. Conversely, it is also possible that the legalistic approach to essentially political problems is but an aberration from the true laws of politics and that, far from increasing the scope of the new diplomacy, our statesmen ought to return to the traditional principles of diplomacy which, truly understood, reflect the nature of man, the nature of politics, and the conditions for successful political action. I shall try to prove that this latter conception is indeed correct.

The legal decision, by its very nature, is concerned with an isolated case. The facts of life to be dealt with by the legal decision are artificially separated from the facts which precede, accompany, and follow them and are thus transformed into a "case" of which the law disposes "on its merits." In the domestic field this procedure is not necessarily harmful, for here executive and legislative decisions, supposedly taking into account all the ramifications of a problem, together with the "spirit of the law" manifesting itself in a judicial tradition of long standing, give the isolated legal decisions a coherence which they cannot have standing alone.

On the international scene, however, these regulating and integrating factors are absent; for that reason the social forces operate on each other with particular directness and spontaneity, and the legal decision of isolated cases is particularly inadequate. A political situation presenting itself for a decision according to international law is always one particular phase of a much larger situation, rooted in the historic past and extending far beyond the issue under legal consideration. There is no doubt that the League of Nations was right, according to international law, in expelling Russia in 1939 because of her attack upon Finland. But the political and military problems with which Russia confronted the world did not begin with her attack on Finland and did not end there, and it was unwise to pretend that such was the case and to decide the issue on that pretense. History has proved this, for only Sweden's refusal to allow British and French troops to pass through Swedish territory in order to come to the aid of Finland saved Great Britain and France from being at war with Germany and Russia at the same time. Whenever the League of Nations endeavored to deal with political situations presented as legal issues, it could deal with them only as isolated cases according to the applicable rules of international law and not as particular phases of an over-all political situation which required an over-all solution according to political principles. Hence, political problems were never solved but only tossed about and finally shelved according to the rules of the legal game.

What was true of the League of Nations has already proved to be true of the United Nations. In its approach to the Greek, Syrian, Indonesian, Iranian, and Spanish situations, the Security Council has remained faithful to the legalistic tradition established by the Council of the League of Nations. These cases have provided opportunities for exercise in parliamentary procedure and for just that chicanery for which traditional diplomacy has so often been reproached, but on no occasion has even an attempt been made to face the political issues of which these situations are the surface manifestations. What would have happened to Europe and to the world if the very similar conflicts which separated Great Britain and Russia in the 'seventies of the last century had been handled in 1878 by the Congress of Berlin in a similar manner?

Conflicts of this kind cannot be settled on the basis of established rules of law, for it is not the established law, its interpretation and application that is in doubt. The parties to the conflict were well aware of the law in the Ethiopian case of 1935, in the case of the Sudetenland in 1938, of Danzig in 1939, and of Iran in 1946. What they wanted to know was whether and how the law ought to be changed. Hence, what is at stake in conflicts of this kind is not who is right and who is wrong but what ought to be done to reconcile the particular interests of individual nations with the general interest in peace and order. The question to be answered is not what the law is but what it ought to be, and this question cannot be answered by the lawyer but only by the statesman. The choice is not between legality and illegality but between political wisdom and political stupidity. "The question with me," said Edmund Burke, "is not whether you have a right to render your people miserable, but whether it is not your interest to make them happy. It is not what a lawyer tells me I *may* do, but what humanity, reason and justice tell me I ought to do." [20] "Lawyers, I know," the same author said, [21] "cannot make the distinction for which I contend, because they have their strict rule to go by. But legislators ought to do what lawyers cannot; for they have no other rules to bind them, but the great principles of reason and equity, and the general sense of mankind."

---

20. BURKE, *Speech on Conciliation with the Colonies* (1775) in 2 THE WORKS OF EDMUND BURKE (1920) 202.
21. BURKE, *Letter to the Sheriffs of Bristol* (1777) in *id.* at 247.

1080   *THE YALE LAW JOURNAL*   [Vol. 55 : 1067

Law and political wisdom may or may not be on the same side. If they are not, the insistence upon the letter of the law will be inexpedient and may be immoral. The defense of the limited interest protected by the particular rule of law will injure the larger good which the legal system as a whole is supposed to serve. Therefore, when basic issues, on the national scene, in the form of economic, social, or constitutional conflicts demand a solution, we do not as a rule appeal to the legal acumen of the judge but to the political wisdom of the legislator and of the chief executive. Here we know that peace and order do not depend primarily upon the victory of the law with the aid of the sheriff and of the police but upon that approximation to justice which true statecraft discovers in, and imposes upon, the clash of hostile interests. If sometimes in our domestic affairs we are oblivious to this basic truth of statesmanship, we pay with social unrest, lawlessness, civil war, and revolution.

On the international scene we have not stopped paying for our forgetfulness since 1914, and we seem to be resolved to pay with all we have for the privilege of continuing to disregard the lessons of history. For here our first appeal is always to the law and to the lawyer, and since the questions which the law and the lawyer can answer are largely irrelevant to the fundamental issues upon which the peace and welfare of nations depend, our last appeal is always to the soldier. *Fiat justitia, pereat mundus* becomes the motto of a decadent legalistic statecraft. But this alternative to our legalism we do not dare face as long as we still can choose. Thus, an age which seems to be unable to meet the intellectual and moral challenge of true statesmanship, or to face in time the cruel alternative to its political failure, takes refuge in the illusion of a new diplomacy. The old diplomacy has failed, it is true, but so has the new one. The new diplomacy has failed and was bound to fail, for its legalistic tools have no access to the political problems to be solved. The old diplomacy has failed because the men who used it had forgotten the rules by which it operates. Blending misplaced idealism with misunderstood power politics, our statesmen vacillate between the old and the new, and each failure calls forth an ever stronger dose of an illusory remedy. Whether they swear by Wilson or follow Machiavelli,[22] they are always Utopians pursuing either nothing but power or nothing but justice, yet never pausing to search for the rules of the political art which, in foreign affairs, is but another name for the traditional methods of diplomacy well understood.

---

22. Compare Morgenthau, *The Machiavellian Utopia* (1945) 55 ETHICS 145; for the philosophy underlying this article, see the author's forthcoming SCIENTIFIC MAN VS. POWER POLITICS (to be published by the University of Chicago Press).

[3]

THE COVENANT AND THE CHARTER[1]

By J. L. BRIERLY, D.C.L., LL.M.

Chichele Professor of International Law in the University of Oxford

IN these early days of the United Nations there is a risk that a comparison between the Covenant and the Charter may not be altogether fair. We know now most of what we shall ever know about the Covenant, because the history of the League is now a closed chapter, and it tells us how the Covenant worked in practice. But in a sense we do not yet know much about the Charter, because the text of a document is never a very safe guide to an understanding of the institution to which it relates. Constitutions always have to be interpreted and applied, and in the process they are over-laid with precedents and conventions which change them after a time into something very different from what anyone, with only the original text before him, could possibly have foreseen. The Covenant underwent a process of this kind, and we must expect the Charter to do the same. Apart from the text of the Charter itself we have a few months' rather confused and inconclusive experience of its working to go on. Most of us feel, I know, that that experience has so far been disappointing and even alarming, but it is too early yet to be discouraged. Even if the start has been unpropitious we must never forget that for the time being, and probably for a long time to come, our only hope of a better international order is somehow to make the Charter work in its present form. Criticism of it therefore should be tentative and provisional, and it should try to be constructive.

It would be impossible in a single lecture to examine in any detail the points of similarity and of difference in the Covenant and the Charter. The similarities were inevitable, because the purposes of the League and of the United Nations are fundamentally the same. The Covenant stated the purposes of the League with its usual economy of words as being 'to promote international co-operation and to achieve international peace and security'; and the Charter says much the same at greater length. The draftsmen had no real choice, for these are the two great purposes to which any general international organization whatsoever is bound to be directed. But the differences are very numerous too. The Charter makes an obvious and rather childish attempt to get away from the associations of the Covenant even in small points of terminology, such as the substitution of the Security Council for the Council, of the General Assembly for the Assembly, and of the Trusteeship system for the system of Mandates.

[1] The Henry Sidgwick Memorial Lecture delivered at Newnham College, Cambridge, on 30 November 1946. (The Editorial Committee wish to acknowledge their indebtedness to the Cambridge University Press for permission to reprint this lecture. H. L.)

I intend, however, in this lecture to confine myself to differences which seem to me to be based on important differences of principle. I shall have very little to say, therefore, about the social and economic side of the two organizations. It is generally recognized that in this field the League had a large measure of success, and that the methods that it used were not open to serious criticism. It is evidently intended that in the main the United Nations should carry on the work with perhaps some improvements of organization, such as the establishment of the Economic and Social Council, but without any change of principle.

The important innovations which the Charter has introduced begin to appear as soon as we remind ourselves of the reasons which were thought to make it necessary to create a new organization instead of reviving and continuing the League. I know that there were political causes which would have made that difficult in any case, but there was also a general feeling that the League had failed because it was not strong enough for its task. It was to correct the supposed weakness of the League as a system of security that a new and stronger body had to be created, and in a sense the feeling was justified. The League had not been strong enough to deal with the aggressions, first of Japan, then of Italy, and finally of Germany. But most of the critics did not inquire very deeply into the causes of the League's weakness, though they were not far to seek. When a great experiment has failed it is easy to salve our consciences by attributing the failure to some defect in the original design for which others, and not we, were responsible, rather than to the manner in which we ourselves have carried out our obligations to make it succeed. I think that is what the critics did. For there is no need to look for an explanation beyond the plain fact that of the seven Great Powers upon whose support the League necessarily depended for success one stood aside from the first, one was in a state of chaos and was left out in the cold, three repudiated everything for which the League stood, and the other two, whose burden had thus been made unexpectedly heavy, were, not without some excuse, never more than half-hearted in the support which they gave to it. That the League failed to deal with the aggressions of the inter-war period cannot, therefore, fairly be held to prove anything one way or the other about the merits of the Covenant, for, if the circumstances had been the same, it would have failed just as certainly if the Covenant had been the most perfect document ever drafted.

But of course that only proves that as events turned out it was not any weakness in the Covenant that led to the failure. It may still be true, as the founders of the United Nations evidently thought, that the League was based on a wrong principle which would have made it fail even if the circumstances had been more favourable. The principle of the Covenant is very simple. It was intended that it should create a system of co-operation between States, which were to retain their sovereignty but to agree to do and not to do certain things in the exercise of their sovereign rights. The Covenant did not contain even the beginnings of a system of international government in the proper sense of the word 'government'. I remember in the early days of the League meeting a Member of Parliament who had just returned from a first visit to Geneva. He said he had discovered that the League was not 'it' but 'they', and he was perfectly right. As a corporate body there was hardly anything that the League could do; in fact, there is, I think, only one Article in the Covenant which envisages action by the League as such at all, and I suspect that this provision was a mere slip of drafting. Article XI does say that in the event of war or any threat of war 'the League shall take any action that may be deemed wise and effectual to safeguard the peace of nations', but elsewhere throughout the Covenant it is normally 'the members of the League' who undertake to act in some particular way in a certain event, and so far as I know the departure from the usual terminology in Article XI had no special significance in the practice of the League.

Now it is clear that an association, whether of individuals or of states, which is nothing but a name for the members collectively, cannot, as an association, be otherwise than weak. It may be effective for its purposes, but that will depend on the conduct of the members individually, upon their ability and willingness to honour the obligations they may have under-taken; they cannot be made to act together, and a majority of them cannot decide or act for the whole body. Hence, if we want an association to be strong, it is a right instinct which urges us to exchange the co-operative basis of the association for one that is organic. But that cannot be done merely by giving the association a new constitution, just as you cannot turn a nation into a democracy merely by giving it democratic institutions to work. In both cases you need also certain other conditions which cannot be hastily improvised, and the most vital question which the Charter seems to me to raise is whether we yet have in the international field the conditions which are needed in order to make an organic international institution work. I do not think we have.

If you compare the Preamble of the Covenant with the 'Purposes' of the United Nations in Article I of the Charter, you will see how the Charter has taken a first step, a rather hesitating first step it is true, away from the purely co-operative basis of international organization. All the emphasis in the Covenant is on what the High Contracting Parties, that is to say the Members of the League, are to do; they are to accept obligations not to resort to war, to follow prescriptions of open, just, and honourable relations between nations, to respect treaty obligations, and so on. In the Charter on the other hand the 'Purposes' are those of the United Nations, and the context shows that this means the Organization as a whole and not its Members severally. The same contrast runs all through the two documents. It is, I think, one of the reasons why the Charter had to be a much longer document than the Covenant—it has 111 Articles against the Covenant's 26—though the greater length is also partly due to mere prolixity. The Covenant did not need to cramp the future activities of its organs by minute definitions of their respective functions; it could say quite generally that either the Assembly or the Council was to be able to 'deal with any matter within the sphere of action of the League or affecting the peace of the world', and leave them to adjust their relations with one another, as they did, as experience accumulated. Thus for the organization as a body it contained the mere outlines of a constitution, and its prescriptions only became precise and detailed when it proceeded to define the obligations which the members were undertaking. The scheme of the Charter had to be exactly the reverse of this. It strictly defines the respective spheres of the Security Council and of the General Assembly, for there had to be no overlapping, and it makes the distinction turn on the separation of matters relating to security from those relating to social and economic problems. That, unfortunately, disregards the important fact that these problems are often the causes of international friction and so are not really separable from questions of security, and it also makes it more difficult than it need have been for the Security Council, with little or no work of a constructive character to do, to develop that corporate spirit which was found so valuable in the League. The obligations of the Members on the other hand are stated in very general terms. They are merely to observe the 'Principles' which are contained in Article II; to fulfil their obligations in good faith, to settle their disputes peacefully, to refrain from the threat or use of force, and so on. The Members, in fact, are given little more than a string of platitudes to guide their conduct.

The contrast is especially striking and, I think, unfortunate in the Articles which deal with the settlement of disputes and with enforcement action. Articles XII–XV of the Covenant prescribe clearly and in detail the procedures which the Members of the League are to follow in order to reach a peaceful settlement, and they contain a valuable safeguard against any attempt by the Council to sacrifice the just claims of a weak power to political expediency by requiring it to publish a statement of the facts and the terms of the settlement if one is reached, or its recommendations if one is not. Chapter VI of the Charter merely says that the parties are to seek a solution by some peaceful means of their own choice, and then goes on to specify in detail what the Security Council is to do in different events. So again in Article XVI of the Covenant the event upon which sanctions are to become applicable is precisely defined—resort to war by a member state in disregard of its covenants—and so are the obligations which then fall due from the other members. Whether in any particular case the event has occurred, and therefore whether the obligation has fallen due, is left to each Member to decide for itself, and it is this provision, perhaps more than any other, which has been thought to point to the weakness of the whole Covenant plan of security. Certainly it does involve the risk that the members may not all decide alike, but since sanctions would never be seriously contemplated except in a very clear case it is practically certain, provided only that states act honestly, that their decisions would be the same. Of course, if they refuse to honour their obligations the case would be different, but then in that case no system would work. At any rate on the only occasion in the League's history when the sanctions Article was applied, all the Members except a few small states which were entirely under the influence of Italy did reach identical decisions, and the failure to enforce the Covenant had nothing whatever to do with the fact that the League Council had no power to make a decision on behalf of the League as a body. In Chapter VII of the Charter, on the other hand, the event upon which enforcement action is to be taken by the United Nations is left entirely undefined; the Security Council has only to determine that a threat to the peace or a breach of it exists or that an act of aggression has been committed, and it may then decide on behalf of the whole Organiza-tion what measures shall be taken to maintain or to restore the peace. It has been argued, I know, that it is unwise to define too clearly the occasion on which sanctions will be applied—Sir Austen Chamberlain once said that to define aggression was more likely to provide an intending aggressor with a signpost than with a warning—but the Covenant plan seems to me to avoid any such risk as that. It does not define aggression; what it does is to make a definition unnecessary by making the question turn simply upon the acceptance or the refusal of a prescribed procedure of peaceful settle-ment. There seems to me to be a very serious danger in leaving the matter wholly to the determination of the Security Council, as the Charter does, with nothing to ensure that the determination will be just except its general obligation to act in accordance with the Purposes and Principles of the United Nations. For it has been quite justly pointed out that there is nothing in the Charter to preclude the Security Council from deciding that a threat to the peace would most conveniently be met by another Hoare–Laval or Munich solution at the expense of a weak Power.

A necessary corollary of the co-operative principle on which the Cove-nant was founded was the so-called 'rule of unanimity', and many not always well-informed critics have seized on this as a capital instance of a weakness in the Covenant which it was essential to remove. Generally the argument has proceeded on *a priori* lines. Since Article V had declared that 'except where otherwise provided . . . decisions at any meeting of the Assembly or of the Council shall require the agreement of all the members of the League represented at the meeting', this *must* have paralysed the League; therefore it did paralyse it. At San Francisco the Great Powers in a formal declaration even went so far as to claim that in this matter the Covenant was more stringent than the Charter, inasmuch as the Security Council, which was to be subject to the veto of only the Great Powers, would be less subject to obstruction than the League Council was with its requirement of complete unanimity. This was an astonishing statement, for the comparison was wholly fallacious, and I think it may help to an understanding of the real nature of the League and of the difference between the principles on which it and the United Nations are based, if we ask why it was that the rule of unanimity did not in fact paralyse the League.

There was more than one reason. In the first place there were important exceptions to its operation, especially the provision in Article XV that the votes of the parties were not to be counted for the purpose of unanimity when the Council made its report and recommendations on a dispute. Secondly, the practice of the League developed certain conventions which mitigated the operation of the rule in important respects. But the really fundamental reason was that the effectiveness of the League as a going concern did not depend upon its organs being able to reach decisions, but on the observance by the individual Members of their obligations under the Covenant. It is true that decisions of the Assembly or the Council did often lead to the Members taking joint action of various kinds, but no decision could alter or add to the obligations of a Member against that Member's will. The real effect of the rule was to prevent a Member being forced to accept some addition to the obligations by which it was already bound under the Covenant. There were very few cases in which it was used as a veto to hold up action. I think the only one of serious consequence was when Japan used the rule to block a resolution on her own conduct in Manchuria in 1931, and this was only possible because of an unexpected and doubtfully correct ruling by the lawyers that under Article XI there was nothing to exclude the vote of an interested party. If the ruling was correct it was almost certainly due to an error of drafting, and it would not have been acquiesced in if the Council had not been glad to be thus provided with an excuse for inaction.

But decisions under the Charter have a wholly different function from decisions under the Covenant; they are necessary in order to make the Security Council work at all. Hence it was absolutely necessary to provide against the possibility of deadlocks, and this could only be done by introducing some form of majority voting. That had become inevitable once it had been decided to abandon, as a weakening factor, the Covenant system

THE COVENANT AND THE CHARTER   89

of states binding themselves individually to act in certain specified ways and instead to confer a power of directing how they should act upon an organ of the collective body. Thus the crucial Article is Article XXIV: 'In order to ensure prompt and effective action by the United Nations, its Members confer on the Security Council primary responsibility for the maintenance of international peace and security, and agree that in carrying out its duties under this responsibility the Security Council acts on their behalf.'

Now undoubtedly, so long as we are considering principles of political organization in the abstract and not the context in which a particular political organization will have to work, this change is the first and necessary step towards the formation of what the American Constitution calls 'a more perfect union'. If, indeed, a corporate body is to act, it is the only way, as the Charter says, 'to ensure prompt and effective action'. But for this advance there has been a price to pay, and the question is whether it has not been too heavy. The price is the veto of the Permanent Members of the Security Council.

In speaking of the veto I shall not dwell on the uses to which it has been put in the short experience that we have of the working of the United Nations. Most of us, I suppose, would say that it has been gravely abused by the Soviet Government on numerous occasions, but that is a matter which is not relevant to my argument. If we have patience we may eventually get an arrangement, such as that which Mr. Bevin recently proposed without success, which will prevent its use in a manner which violates both the spirit and the letter of the declaration which the Great Powers, including Soviet Russia, made at San Francisco. But the important question seems to me to be whether, even assuming an arrangement to limit the use of the veto, in accordance with the San Francisco declaration, to decisions which 'may have major political consequences and require enforcement measures', we shall not, even so, find that the price has been too high, and that the union which the Charter has given us is in the result even less perfect than that which we had under the Covenant.

It is certain and, I think, it is now generally understood, that the veto has made it impossible that enforcement measures should ever be taken against a Great Power. That means that in 1935, if the Covenant had contained a similar provision, Italy could, and of course would, have vetoed the taking of sanctions against herself, and she would have been free, so far as the Covenant was concerned, to proceed undisturbed with her aggression against Ethiopia. But to-day the only event which can seriously endanger the peace of the world is the aggression of a Great Power, and a system which solemnly declares, as the Charter does, that its purpose is 'to take effective collective measures for the prevention and removal of threats to the peace and for the suppression of acts of aggression', and yet does not propose to deal with aggression by a Great Power, is, I venture to say, not a system of collective security at all. Of course it may be that no system can deal with that case, and this seems to be the view taken by the official British Commentary on the Charter.

'It is imperative', it says, 'that the consent of the Great Powers should be necessary to action in cases in which they are not a party, since they will have the main responsibility for action. It is also clear that no enforcement action by the Organization can be taken against a Great Power itself without a major war. If such a situation arises the United Nations will have failed in its purpose and all members will have to act as seems best in the circumstances. . . . The creation of the United Nations is designed to prevent such a situation from arising by free acceptance by the Great Powers of restraints upon themselves.'

All that may be true. But if it is, it seems hardly fair that the Preamble of the Charter should declare that the peoples of the United Nations have 'determined to unite their strength to maintain international peace and security'. What they have done, according to the Commentary, is something quite different.

Perhaps after all, however, the explanation of the Commentary is an afterthought. For if there never was any idea that the procedure of the Charter might, if necessary, be used against a Great Power, why do we need all those elaborate provisions which are contained in Chapter VII on 'Action with Respect to Threats to the Peace'? It really does not make sense to suppose that all the Members are to make armed forces available to the Security Council on its call, that they are to hold air-force contingents immediately available for combined international action, that a Military Staff Committee is to advise the Security Council on all questions relating to its military requirements, and so on, if the only purpose of all these carefully thought out preparations is to deal with a Small Power when it misbehaves. Small Power aggression has never been, and cannot be, a serious problem if the Great Powers are agreed among themselves, and if they are not, then this machinery cannot be used.

Much the most probable explanation of the impasse at which we have arrived seems to me to be historical. I suspect it has resulted from the mood which prevailed at the moment when the Charter was made. Both the Covenant and the Charter reflect conditions which were existing at the time of their drafting; it was inevitable that they should, but the authors of the Covenant, by concentrating on the bare essentials, and leaving ample room for the League to grow, made this limitation of their outlook a less serious handicap than it is in the Charter. Still the weak points in both become more intelligible when we remember the contemporary circumstances. The Covenant was made after the First World War had ended, but when its lessons, or what then seemed to be its lessons, were still

THE COVENANT AND THE CHARTER 91

vividly present to the minds of its authors. There was a case for thinking that in 1914 the world had stumbled into a war which no one had really desired or intended; most men everywhere were peacefully inclined, but there had been obstacles which had prevented their desires from finding expression, and if these could be removed peace might be made secure. Hence there should be open diplomacy and publicity for the engagements to which statesmen committed their nations; provision for delaying the outbreak of a threatened war in the belief that war delayed would probably be war averted; reduction of armaments because sooner or later the piling up of armaments must lead to their being used; and if war should come in spite of all these precautions, then it would probably be enough to rely on the economic weapon, whose decisive effects the recent war seemed to have proved, and the use of military sanctions might be relegated to the hazy background.

The Charter, on the other hand, was shaped at Dumbarton Oaks in the autumn of 1944, when the issue of the Second World War was still uncertain, and to outward appearance at least Germany and Japan still seemed immensely strong. It sought to forge a weapon which could be used against just such a danger as then existed if history should ever repeat itself, a security system of irresistible power, and ready, as the Allies in 1939 had not been, for immediate action, and every other consideration was subordinated to this overriding purpose. No one believed that we had merely stumbled into the War of 1939; it had obviously been deliberately planned, and against a planned war the palliatives of the Covenant seemed a puny defence. Unfortunately, the weapon which was fashioned has turned out to be a highly specialized instrument, useful only against a particular danger for which we now no longer need it, and only on the assumption that the war-time unity of purpose among the Great Powers would be a permanent feature of their relations. In the circumstances then it seems a little odd that the one danger which the Charter system does seem well fitted to deal with, a revival of aggressive tendencies in Germany or Japan, should have been excluded from the sphere of the Security Council and left, by Article LIII, to be dealt with by regional arrangements. Thus the desire for a system of security ready always for immediate action, which was the leading motive behind the substitution of the Charter for the Covenant, has resulted in a system that can be jammed by the opposition of a single Great Power. Under the Covenant the League might be unable to act as a League, but at least the Members of the League could act together if the occasion demanded joint action. The Members of the United Nations cannot even do that; a Great Power can forbid it. The Covenant scheme had weaknesses, as I have already admitted, and perhaps it might not have worked even if it had been given a fair trial; if so no doubt it is better that we should know where we stand, as I think we do to-day. But we must realize that what we have done is to exchange a scheme which might or might not have worked for one which cannot work, and that instead of limiting the sovereignty of states we have actually extended the sovereignty of the Great Powers, the only states whose sovereignty is still a formidable reality in the modern world.

This is a depressing conclusion, and I do not want to end my comparison on a purely destructive note. For I think there is a moral to be drawn. It is common ground, I think, among all of us who recognize the urgency of a better international order that a condition of the stabilization of peace is some limitation of the sovereignty of states. We may not all use that phrase in quite the same sense, but at least there is a large measure of agreement about the ultimate aim. But there are differences amongst us as to methods, and I think the choice lies between the method of a frontal attack on sovereignty and what I may call the method of erosion. The Charter has tried to proceed by the former of these, and it has found the road barred. It insisted that to act effectively an international organization must have the power to make decisions, which means that a majority must be able to overrule a minority. But the Great Powers have refused to be outvoted. I know that the Charter has introduced majority voting into the General Assembly as well as into the Security Council, and that the Great Powers have not insisted on a veto over the decisions of the former. But this only reinforces the lesson which I think we have to learn. The General Assembly cannot act for all its Members as the Security Council can, and this makes all the difference. Its decisions are not directions issued by the Organization to the member states to tell them what they are to do. Apart from its control of the Budget, all that the General Assembly can do is to discuss and recommend and initiate studies and consider reports from other bodies. In principle its functions are similar to those of the Assembly of the League; it must rely on co-operation among the Members and not on power, for it has no powers. Hence the rule allowing it to take its decisions by majority voting was no very serious innovation in international organization. The case is entirely different when it has been decided that an international body shall exercise power, as the Security Council is to do. Then you are departing from the co-operative principle which has hitherto been the basis of international institutions; you are introducing a genuinely governmental element into them, converting the organization from a 'they' into an 'it'. To my mind the moral of the veto is that it teaches us that before international institutions can be raised from the co-operative to the organic type, which in itself is a desirable aim for which we have to work, we need a society far more closely integrated than the society of states is to-day; we need a society whose members have the same sort of confidence

THE COVENANT AND THE CHARTER 93

in one another's intentions and policies and the same absence of fundamental diversity of interests that the states of a federation must have if
their union is to endure. I do not myself feel that in present world conditions the insistence of the Great Powers on their veto, however much we
may deplore it, is altogether unreasonable, and I do not think that any
system of weighted majority voting will induce them, or at any rate induce
all of them, to change their attitude. I think we have been led into a cul-de-
sac by the over-hasty pursuit of a perfectionist policy, and by a too shallow
diagnosis of the causes of failure of the League. By insisting that only an
institution which has power to decide can act effectively we have created
one that can neither decide nor act.

What I have called the method of attacking sovereignty by erosion is less
spectacular, but, I think, more likely to give results. It means doing everything we can to make it easy for states to work together and so gradually
develop a sense of community which will make it psychologically more
difficult to press the claims of sovereignty in ways that are anti-social. This
was the method of the League, and for a time at least it did seem to be
leading to results. The Charter has made it more difficult by making the
sessions of the Security Council continuous and excluding all but questions
of security from its sphere. Many of the causes of embitterment of recent
months would never have been raised if the Security Council had not
provided a too tempting sounding board for ideological invective; to raise
them in diplomatic notes would not have been worth while. For our hopes
for the United Nations we must look, I think, to the General Assembly, and
more especially to the Economic and Social Council which in effect is one
of its committees.

More obviously to-day, though not more certainly, than ever before,
peace depends on the ability of the Great Powers to work together. In
a sense I think we have returned, as I have seen it somewhere suggested,
to the idea which underlay the Concert of Europe in the nineteenth century.
We have failed to institutionalize the preservation of peace, and perhaps
we have to recognize that that cannot be done. But it is something that we
should face the future, as I think we now do, with a fairly general realization of where we stand. A generation ago the number of those who both
believed that the League was tremendously important and also saw that
the difficulties in its way were immensely formidable was not very large;
too many of those who thought it important underrated the difficulties,
and too many of those who saw the difficulties had no particular wish to see
it make good. I think the present attitude of public opinion is more
healthy. There is no disposition to look upon the United Nations as a
beneficent power which will usher in the millennium without any effort on
our part, and the pseudo-realism of those who thought that we had had to

94   THE COVENANT AND THE CHARTER

accept the League in order to humour President Wilson has also disappeared. It is true, as Lord Cecil has somewhere pointed out, that
whereas the League was imposed on the governments from the outside,
the United Nations is the work of the governments themselves. The only
realist to-day is the man who knows that somehow we have got to use it to
create a more civilized international order, and that probably we may not
have very long in which to do it.

[4]

THE ROLE OF LAW AND LEGAL CONSIDERATIONS IN THE FUNCTIONING OF THE UNITED NATIONS

V.S. Mani*

The role of law in the functioning of the United Nations is, in a sense, a beaten track, as there is a plethora of literature, including writings by eminent international jurists and practitioners of international law and organization. The present endeavour does not pretend to examine in any detail this mountain of literature, nor does it claim to be a comprehensive treatment of all aspects of the interface between law and the United Nations. It is a modest effort to look at a few selected aspects of the latter, largely from the looking-glass of a post-Soviet, emerging international system, and seeks to suggest a possibly revised "Third World" perception of the principal normative issues of law.

I. THE RELATIONSHIP BETWEEN LAW AND INSTITUTIONS - A PERCEPTION

The function of law in a community, whether national or international, is two-fold. At the level of minimum order in the community, it seeks to provide and promote conditions to enhance peace. At the level of the optimum order, it seeks to identify, integrate, and promote community goal values with a view the enhancing the quality of human life, and in that sense it seeks to provide a viable legal framework for community action. Indeed, the boundary line between the minimum order and the optimum order is not as clear-cut as one would like it to be: there is considerable overlap at the interface.

The relationship between law and community institutions is close. In fact, the legal process is an intrinsic part of the process of organization in a community. Both share the community goal values which both seek to promote. Both are subject to the forces in the community. Both in their own respective subtle ways seek to moderate upon, if not influence these forces to an acceptable pattern of behaviour.

---

*   Professor of International Space Law, School of International Studies, Jawaharlal Nehru University, New Delhi - 110 067, India.

Their capacity to do so would, however, depend upon the nature and the extent of power these forces wield *inter se* and, *vis-a-vis* the members of the community in general. In the result, quite paradoxically at times, law and institutions at once become both the handmaids as well as moderators of social conduct in the community. Law and institutions acquire the role of moderators corresponding to the 'authority' or 'the capacity to hold the stamp of legitimacy on behalf of the community, with which they may be conferred, by the generality of members of the community. In view of all this, the effectiveness, success, or failure of law or an institution is a function of the forces that set the pattern of the social process in the community at a given point of time.

The international legal process and the process of international organization have shared a common historical development. They owe their origins to the evolution of the sovereign state system. They have evolved in response to the needs of the international community. The process of their evolution has closely reflected the 'changes', 'breakdowns' and 'progress' that the structure and the nature of the international community have undergone over time. They respond to the inexorable logic of history. Their 'successes' or 'failures' must be so evaluated.

Unlike the national community the international community is largely decentralized. The decentralised nature of the community mirrors itself through international law and international organization, which makes many aspects of the national community and the international community incomparable. The *sine qua non* of the decentralised state of international community is the absence of centralised (and perhaps impartial) institutions with constitutional authority to legislate laws, to execute them, and to adjudicate disputes by applying them in a manner readily binding on all members of the community. In fact these functions are performed by the sovereign states, which results in unfair situations where in the state, instead of performing the impartial role of an agent of the international community seeks to promote its individual interests. Thus, international law and international organization are typified by their checkered development through the continual interaction of mutually adversary attitudes and conduct of states. As luck would have it, however, state attitudes and conduct many a time coincide, albeit for diverse reasons and in diverse circumstances. These points of coincidence undoubtedly form the building blocks of international law and international organization.

It is fashionable these days to talk about a 'new world order', now that one of the super powers, the Soviet Union, has suddenly disappeared from the world scene. However, it is important to remind oneself that to characterize an era soon after an historical upheaval is usually most tempting. People and nations might have, with equal facility designated the years immediately following the Peace of Westphalia of 1648, the Congress of Vienna of 1815, the Treaty of Versailles of 1919 and the end of the Second World War in 1945 all dawns of a new world order. The Third World countries, as they came out of the trauma of colonialism, clamoured for a New International Economic Order and a New International Information Order. While the clamours for a new world order are welcome, because each of them reflects the hopes and aspirations of the international community for the future and its frustrations with the past, they convey an unhistorical feeling that things have so fundamentally, and even perhaps irreversibly, changed. This should be taken with a large chunk of salt. Since the emergence of the sovereign state system after the Peace of Westphalia, actors and their names may have changed, but the characters have largely remained the same. The course of international affairs continues to determined by the currents and cross-currents of politics among nations. Yet, on this Westphalian model a new world order model seems being slowly superimposed.[1] The emergence of international law and international institutions even with revolutionary concepts, and the expansion of international community over time are two major factors that evidence the dawn of a new world order with international organizations and international law being called up at least to be the instruments for harmonisation of national action, even if this task may not amount to that of a world government. The identification, clarification, integration and promotion of the goal values of this new world order are indeed the coordinate functions of the contemporary international law and organization.

It is against this perception of the linkage between international law and international organization that a few principal aspects of the role of law in the functioning of the United Nations are considered herein.

II. THE FUNCTION OF LAW IN THE UNITED NATIONS

Five principal aspects of the functional relationship between international law and the United Nations, and indeed between the law and the international organization in general are considered here. They relate to the constituent instrument of the Organisation, i.e. the legal status of the Charter of the United Nations, the internal law of the Organisation, law-making by the United Nations, disputes settlement by the United Nations, and ramifications of illegality of acts of the United Nations.[2]

A. The Legal Status of the UN Charter

Is the UN Charter merely a treaty? Or is it more than a treaty, say a constitution of the world community?[3] Positivists would argue that the Charter is merely a treaty reflecting reservation of rights and undertaking of obligations by states parties to it. As a treaty it is binding only as between member states; it regulates admission of new members to the exclusive club; it lays down the rules of admission, continuation and extinction of membership; it in no way abrogates the sovereign right of a state to withdraw from it; it recognises the need for the sovereign consent for its amendment or revision; it creates an international organization and it also lays down the ground rules for the powers and functions of the various organs of this organization which are not permitted to stray beyond these ground rules, and at any rate the principles and purposes of the Charter—in other words, a limited 'government'. The argument specifically points to the limitations on the functioning of the United Nations, namely domestic jurisdiction, self-defence and action in relation to former enemy states.

As against this, a neo-naturalist/functional argument is that the Charter is not a treaty but a constitutional instrument - a fundamental law - of the evolving international community. The Organisation created by the Charter represents the aims and aspirations of the international community, and is entitled and empowered to perform its functions in terms of the Purposes and Principles laid down in the Charter as interpreted by the generality of the membership of the Organisation. This was clear at the 1945 San Francisco Conference itself, as the argument would proceed, when the makers of the Charter adopted provisions relating to the Purposes and Principles of the Charter, those concerning the powers and functions of the various organs of the United Nations, the special provisions such as, those of Article 103 (supremacy of Charter obligations) and Article 2(5) the Organisation's competence to seek compliance of non-members with its decisions, the absence of a specific provision for withdrawal of a member from the Organisation, and indeed, in the very name "United Nations".

Given the basis of international law and organization being the points of co-incidence of wills of states, the ground situation appears to be dictated by the identification of these points of co-existence, or at least an indication of toleration of a legal position evidenced by the absence of strong objections emanating from significant groups of states. This 'unsatisfactory' position results from the dual role of the international organization in international relations: One, it represents a stage in the evolution of identification and integration of international community values, and hence the justification for its claims to autonomy and legitimacy and to function on behalf of the international community. Two, it is still an instrument of foreign policies of its member states, given the existing nature and structure of international community. Small wonder, each of these rule inhibits the other. Added to this, is the variability of the perception of the Organisation's objective and principles, and of state attitudes on them, over time. Yet, the fact remains that there have been numerous occasions when the generality of membership has tolerated or acquiesced in, a neo-naturalist/functional interpretation and application of the provisions of the UN Charter favouring organizational action. This perspective on the evolving nature of the UN Charter is crucial in the appreciation of the interface between law and the United Nations.

The International Court of Justice has, however, been pro-international organization and as such belongs to the neo-naturalist/functional school. In the *Reparations* case in 1949, the Court expounded its perception of the United Nations thus:-

> The Charter has not been content to make the Organisation created by it merely a centre "for harmonizing the actions of nations in the attainment of these common ends" (Article 1, para 4). It has equipped that centre with organs, and has given it special tasks. It has defined the position of its members in relation to the Organisation.

> In the opinion of the Court, the Organisation was intended to exercise and enjoy and, is in fact exercising and enjoying, functions and rights which can only be explained on the basis of the possession of a large measure of international personality and the capacity to operate upon an international plane. It is at present the supreme type of international organization and it could not carry out the intentions of its founders if it was devoid of international personality. It must be acknowledged that its Members of entrusting certain functions to it, with the attendant duties and

responsibilities, have clothed it with the competence required to enable those functions to be effectively discharged.[4]

As Brownlie points out, "judicial interpretation may lead to expansion of the competence of an organization if resort be had to the teleological principle according to which action in accordance with the stated purposes of an organization is *intra vires* or at least is presumed to be". However, he rightly warns, "The process of interpretation cannot be subordinated to arbitrary devices".[5]

For, the United Nations and its constitution are both creatures of international law and are as such bound by it both directly and indirectly - directly because the Charter and the organization owe their validity to their conformity with the fundamental principles of international law, and indirectly because states participants in both are obliged not to conduct themselves either inside or outside the United Nations in contravention of the fundamental principles of international law.[6] As an international person the organization, has the most direct responsibility to conduct itself as a subject of law.

It is true that the UN Charter has immensely contributed to the development of contemporary international law. However, to say this is not to accept that international law and the Principles of the Charter are identical and hence the latter must be held to "supervene" or "subsume" the principles of general international law, whatever else be the import of Articles 1 (2), 25, 48 and 103 of the Charter. This question squarely arose before the International Court in the case concerning *Military and Paramilitary Activities in and against Nicaragua.*[6a] In that case the Court recognised three categories of legal situations covered by the UN Charter and international customary law, namely (1) where areas covered by both are identical; (2) where they are not so identical, and (3) where they do not overlap. While noting these situations, the Court also noted the relationship of the Charter with the pre-existing international law as well as the role of the Charter in the subsequent development of international law which still had an existence independent of the Charter. By way of illustration, the Court referred to the term "inherent right" in Article 51 of the Charter ("*droit naturel*" in the French text). In the Court's view, "Article 51 is only meaningful on the basis that there is a "natural" or "inherent" right of self-defence, and it is hard to see how this can be other than of a customary nature, even if its present content has been confirmed and influenced by the Charter. Moreover the Charter, having itself recognised the existence of this right, does not go on to regulate directly all aspects of its content". The Court by way of examples referred to the non-mention in Article 51 of some of the conditions for exercise of the right of self-defence such as the principle of proportionality and determination of "armed attack". Thus, the Court ruled: "It cannot therefore be held that Article 51 is a provision which "subsumes and supervenes" customary international law. It rather demonstrates that in the field in question, . . . customary international law continues to exist alongside treaty law".[7]

In order to demonstrate that the Charter is not co-extensive or co-terminous with the entire body juridic of international law, the Court remarked, in the context of its discussion of the principle of non-intervention:

Of course, statements whereby states vow their recognition of the principles of international law set forth in the United Nations Charter cannot strictly be interpreted as applying to the principle of non-intervention by States in the internal and external affairs of other states, since this principle is not as such, spelt out in the Charter. But it was never intended that the Charter should embody written confirmation of every essential principle of international law in force.[8]

On the basis of the Court's rulings in the *Nicaragua* case referred to above, at least three propositions may be made. First, even if the content of a principle is identical both under the Charter and under the existing international law, both the legal realms may co-exist for a number of reasons, the chief difference between the two being the organisational linkage in the former. Second, where both the realms overlap and are yet not co-extensive (such as in regard to the right of self-defence), the Charter law does not subsume or supervene general international law. Third, the Charter does not embody all principles of international law, not even all fundamental principles.

Finally, as already pointed out, being themselves the creations of international law, both the Charter and the organization established thereunder are expected to operate in conformity with *jus gocens*, the fundamental principles of international law. Articles 53 and 64 of the Vienna Convention on the Law of Treaties proclaim the invalidity or nullity of a treaty inconsistent with *jus cogens*, whether pre-existing or emerging subsequent to the treaty. The operation of the Charter as well as of the United Nations will undoubtedly be inhibited by the considerations of harmony with the peremptory norms of international law. These norms determine the field of application of obligations undertaken under the Charter (including Article 103) and the operational interpretations of the powers and functions of the Organisation, as may be seen later.

It would appear, therefore, that the answer to the question whether the UN Charter is merely a treaty or whether it is the constitution of the international community, is that the Charter is more than a mere treaty, but it would still be a tall claim for it to be the constitution of the international community. This is not to deny the global importance of the Charter principles and objectives which have indeed helped the international community to identify and integrate many of its goal values, and encourage the organization to pursue them. Yet in terms of the degree of integration of these goal values and the level of state commitment to achieve them by individual, collective and organizational action, the UN Charter falls far short of being the 'constitution of the international community'.

b) The Internal Legal Regime of the United Nations

Three principal categories of internal legal norms, principles and rules may be identified in respect of the UN Charter. They are (1) the law regulating the relationship between the member states and the functioning of the organization; (2) the law regulating the powers and functions of the organs of the United Nations, and (3) the law regulating the procedure for the decisional processes of these organs. While the first two categories may be referred to as the substantive law of the United Nations, the third is essentially the procedural law, although one should readily enter a caveat here - that in international law, the distinction between the substantive law and the procedural law is rather blurred,[9] and that states may often totally ignore such a distinction and insist on their rights, whether substantive or procedural, even at the risk of causing serious distortions in the functioning of the international organization.[10]

The main provisions of the Charter that determine the relationship between the members and the Organisation are Articles 1, 2, 4, 5, 6, 25, 48, 55, 56 and 103. According to these provisions, the relationship between the organization and its members is governed by the principles of sovereign equality, good faith fulfilment of Charter obligations, peaceful settlement of disputes, prohibition of force, assistance to enforcement action by the United Nations, domestic jurisdiction, compliance with the decisions of the UN Security Council taken "in accordance with the Charter", obligation to take measures for achievement of the objectives laid down in Article 55, and supremacy of Chater obligations over obligations undertaken under other international agreements. These lay down the ground rules for the functioning of the Organisation *vis-a-vis* its member states. Yet at least two factors have led to the "expanding jurisdiction" of the United Nations.[11] First, the above principles *per se* do not establish precise criteria for application *vis-a-vis* the Organisation, and instead look to the Organisation to take care of the operational conditions with reference to specific contexts. Indeed, some of them are overlapping, e.g. the principles of sovereign equality and domestic jurisdiction, and the principle of good faith which encompasses all principles of the Charter. Secondly, the Charter makers have deliberately left open the question of authentic interpretation of the provisions of the Charter to be determined by the relevant organs of the United Nations.[12] In this sense the first two categories of 'internal' law is closely interlinked. Boundaries of one would depend on those of the other. While the approach of the Charter makers has proved to be pro-organization, it does not help resolve the claims of members as to the jurisdiction of an organ, competitive or overlapping claims to jurisdiction by two or more organs, or the question of importance attributable to an interpretation expounded by the "principal judicial organ", the International Court of Justice. The latter aspect of the question seems to assume increasing significance in the context of allegations of "abuse" of the Organisation by the only super power left in the international arena after the demise of the Soviet Union in 1991. The issue turns out to be one of competence of the International Court to be the arbiter of the legitimacy of organizational action *vis-a-vis* the Members of the United Nations.[13]

It may be recalled that in the *Namibia* advisory opinion, the International Court observed:

Undoubtedly, the Court does not possess *powers of judicial review or appeal* in respect of the decisions taken by the United Nations Organs concerned.

The question of "the validity or conformity with the Charter of the General Assembly resolution 2145 (XXVI) or of related Security Council resolutions" did not form the subject of the request for advisory opinion. Yet the Court did not appear to shirk from its judicial responsibility and hence its statement:

However, in the exercise of its judicial function and since objections have been advanced, the Court, in the course of its reasoning, will consider these objections before determining any legal consequences arising from these resolutions.[14]

That was indeed a curious bundle of logic. On the one hand, the Court was inhibited by an acute awareness of the limitations on its own jurisdiction. Yet on the other, it had a prick of judicial conscience, as it were, and hence its willingness to examine the South African challenges to the validity of the relevant UN decisions! In fact, in order to determine the legality of the continued presence of South African administration in Namibia, the crucial aspect of the request for the Court's opinion, an examination of the validity of the relevant UN decisions was a condition precedent. The Court did not have to feel so sensitive, if not hesitant, about "exercise of its judicial function". Whether or not the Court recognizes its power of judicial function", to examine the challenges to the validity of the relevant organizational decisions "in the course of its reasoning",[15] which no doubt amounts to admitting that the Court's power of judicial review is part of its judicial function.[16]

The above problem of authentic interpretation of the Charter with reference to the function of an organ of the United Nations has always existed ever since the inception of the organization.[17] The International Court has, in the advisory proceedings, consistently taken a pro-organization, functional approach in view of its role as "the principal judicial organ" of the United Nations. The *Certain Expenses* case is illustrative of this approach. In that case, the Court, for the first time, came close to considering the question of jurisdictional competence of the General Assembly *vis-a-vis* the Security Council. The Court held:

> Save as they [the Charter makers] entrusted the Organisation with the attainment of these common ends, the member states retain their freedom of action. But when the Organisation takes action which warrants the assertion that it was appropriate for the fulfilment of one of the stated purposes of the United Nations, the presumption is that such action is not *ultra vires* the Organisation . . . If the action was taken by the wrong organ, it was irregular as a matter of internal structure, but this would not necessarily mean that the expense incurred was not an expense of the Organisation. Both national and international law contemplate cases in which the body corporate or politic may be bound, as to third parties, by an *ultra vires* act of an agent.[18]

The above exposition of the powers and functions of the United Nations *vis-a-vis* its Members, and the powers and functions of the UN organs *inter se* yields three propositions. First, states retain their freedom of action beyond what they have mandated the organization. Second, there is a presumption of validity of every action taken by the United Nations, if the action "warrants the assertion that it was appropriate for the fulfilment of one of the stated purposes of the United Nations". Third, even if an action is taken by "the wrong organ", it does not cease to be an action by the United Nations, even if "it was irregular as a matter of internal structure".[19] One does not have any problems with the first two propositions, so long as the second proposition recognises only a *presumption* in favour of the validity of organizational action. Because such a presumption may be questioned in suitable cases on grounds of *mala fide*, violation of principles of natural justice, violation of the basic structure and the principles of the UN Charter - grounds analogous to those under the constitutional laws of states. The final proposition does not appear tenable for at least two reasons. One, the analogy of the body corporate or politic in municipal law *vis-a-vis* third parties does not apply when a member of the United Nations questions the validity of an action authorised by the wrong organ, since that member is itself part of the "internal regime" of the United Nations. Nor is it a question of agency, because an organ of the United Nations is the principal itself. It is doubtful if the excuse of procedural irregularity[20] is good enough to save an organizational action from a legal challenge by a member state on grounds of either the principles of the Charter or the principles of general international law.

The functional argument, as expounded by the Court, may provide some legitimacy for organizational action in appropriate cases in the context of the internal legal regime of the Charter. But it would be difficult for it to legitimise all actions of the Organisation in all contexts at all times. Also, it cannot insulate the organizational action from challenges based on states rights under international law. In the *Case Concerning Certain Phosphate Lands in Nauru*, the Court rejected an Australian argument that the UN General Assembly, by its resolution terminating the Trusteeship over Nauru, had extinguished Nauru's claims relating to rehabilitation of lands mined out during the Mandate and Trusteeship periods. It held, on the basis of evidence external to the resolution, that at the time when the General Assembly adopted the resolution in question, Nauru's claim was well known and that it was outstanding, awaiting solution, even though the resolution itself did not specifically say so.[21] Had the Court not so interpreted the resolution, the Court would, as a necessary next step, have had to face the formidable question whether the General Assembly was competent to extinguish a right founded on general international law. No amount of supervisory powers over a "sacred trust of civilization" would have justified the Assembly extinguishing an international legal right of the indigenous people of that sacred trust: It is of interest to note in this context that Nauru is not a member of the United Nations, and this would inhibit unrestrained application of the functional argument in favour of an expansive field of organizational action.

At any rate, at least in respect of two advisory opinions, namely the *Admissions case* and the *Certain Expenses* case, the member states have not evinced "general acceptance" of the Court's expositions *in toto*. The United Nations practice has shown that both the proof of the objective criteria for membership and the desirability of admitting a state continue to be subject to the *subjective judgment* of the Organisation despite the universality principle, and that regardless of the legality of peace keeping operations and their being acts of the Organisation, member states insist on the principle of voluntarism in their participation in them as well as in sharing the expenses incurred in the mounting of such operations. Such attitudes of members also indicate the need to put a break on the functional approach, pure and simple.

The apprehensions of smaller states expressed at the San Francisso Conference in 1945 about the concentration of power in a body like the Security Council "so dominated by the great powers", and its possible arbitrary use, have been well recorded by commentators on the UN Charter.[22] Although most of the proposals made by the smaller states to amend the Dumbarton Oaks Draft were "successfully resisted" by the great powers, there were at least three significant concessions made by the latter. First, they agreed to revise the Dumbarton Oaks text to eliminate a provision seeking expressly to authorize the Security Council to determine that a failure to settle a dispute under Chapter VI of the Charter amounted to a threat to international peace and security. Second, the big powers gave the assurance that recommendations for settlement of disputes under Chapter VI were not binding. Finally, "It was also emphasized that the Council should not be expected to discharge its responsibilities in an arbitrary manner since under the terms of Article 24 it was required to act "in accordance with the Charter".[23]

In the *Lockerbie (Provisional Measures) cases*, Judge Weeramantry, after an in-depth study of the San Francisco Documents of 1945, observed in his dissent that although the Security Council was clothed with "enormous power", it had an "imperative duty" under Article 24(2) of the Charter to act in accordance with the Purposes and Principles of the United Nations, which included "respect for the obligations arising from treaties and other sources of international law". According to him,

> The history of the United Nations Charter . . . corroborates the view that a clear limitation on the plenitude of the Security Council's powers is that those powers must be exercised in accordance with the well-established principles of international law.[24]

In the same cases, the dissent of Judge Bedjaoui (as he then was) was equally forthcoming. On the question of validity of the resolutions of the principal UN organs with respect to the Charter and/or international law, the judge referred to the observations of Judges Gros and Sir Gerald Fitzmaurice in the *Namibia* case noted above. He quoted Judge Gros as saying:

> To assert that a matter may have a distant repercussion on the maintenance of peace is not enough to turn the Security Council into world government.[25]

Judge Bedjaoui also referred to the following remarkable observations of Judge Sir Gerald Fitzmaurice in the same case:

> Limitations on the powers of the Security Council are necessary because of the all too great ease with which any acutely controversial international situation can be represented as involving a latent threat to peace and security, even where it is really too remote genuinely to constitute one. Without these limitations, the functions of the Security Council could be used for purposes never originally intended . . .[There was] no threat to peace and security other than such as might be artificially created as a pretext for the realization of ulterior purposes.[26]

Against the background of these observations of Judges Gros and Sir Fitzmaurice in the *Namibia* case, Judge Bedjaoui noted that the *Lockerbie* cases involved the question of validity of certain resolutions of the Security Council. According to him:

> This question of validity is liable to raise two major problems, at once serious and complex, namely whether the Security Council should, in its action, firstly respect the United Nations Charter and secondly respect general international law.[27]

Answering the first question, Judge Bedjaoui said: "the Security Council must respect the Charter" and "the spirit of the Charter [as emerging from its *travaux preparatoires*] is indeed to prevent the Security Council from diverging in any way at all from the Charter".[28] Apart from its "spirit", the actual text of the Charter also points to the same conclusion, he said, specifically relying on Article 24(2) of the Charter.

In this context Judge Bedjaoui raised the question of harmony of functioning of the different principal organs of the United Nations. He remarked that Article 24(2) would raise the question "whether one organ can act in a way which renders the role of the other impossible. And this applies as much to the Security Council as to the Court itself, in as much as it is true that the Charter lays down that each of the United Nations organs should carry out its task fully, and not abdicate any part of it, in order to assist in the accomplishment of the purposes and principles of the United Nations".[29] Pondering over the object or effect of the Council resolution 748 (1992), he remarked:

> It would, indeed, be manifestly incompatible with the Charter for an organ of the United Nations to prevent the Court from accomplishing its mission, or for it actually to place the Court in a state of subordination which would be contrary to the principle of separation and independence of the judicial from the executive power within the United Nations.[30]

On the second problem too, his answer was in the affirmative on the basis of the same provision of the Charter. Here again, he referred with approval to another of Judge Sir Fitzmaurice's observations in the *Namibia* case:

> There is a principle of international law that is well-established as any there can be, and the Security Council is as much subject to it (for the United Nations is itself a subject of international law) as any of its individual member states are.[31]

and asserted that this was the principle that "the Council is bound to respect 'the principles of international law', an expression that holds a more precise meaning for international lawyers".[32]

There is an argument, the diplomats' favourite, which insists that international organization is essentially a political body, that its decisions are dictated by the logic (or illogic?) of political factors, that its decisional processes are political in nature, that even its interpretation of its own constitutional objectives are bound to be political in essence, and that, therefore, the lawyers' insistence on the organizational activities to conform to legal tests contrived from the United Nations Charter is totally opposed to the realism of international politics. While expounding the diverse interpretations of the provisions of the UN Charter, Kelsen often refers to an interpretation highlighting the 'political' nature of the Security Council and the total freedom of decision-making and action on its part.[33] One is familiar with the centuries-old debate about "political" and "legal" disputes[34] and the validity of the above argument of 'realists' depends upon their perceptions of international relations, their assessment of the relevance and role of international law in world affairs, and indeed of the role of law in human affairs. What in fact the 'political' argument suggests is that the international organization deals with situations not amenable to solution by application of international law and that therefore, the justification of an organizational action lies in resolving the problem, whatever be the means of doing so.

The principal aspects of the procedural law of the Organization are the power to appoint subsidiary organs and the rules of procedure adopted by each of the principal organs. The general power of each of the six principal organs of the United Nations is granted under Article 7, paragraph 2 of the Charter, whereby each of these organs may establish "such subsidiary organs as may be found necessary". Evidently, this power has to be exercised in accordance with the Charter. Article 22 relates this power specifically to the UN General Assembly, Article 29 to the Security Council (this is quite different from the power under Article 47 to establish a Military Staff Committee whose special responsibilities have been stipulated in the Charter itself) and Article 68 to the Economic and Social Council (whereby the ECOSOC may set up various commissions). The test of legitimate exercise of this power is indeed the need for creation of a subsidiary organ to enable the relevant principal organ to perform its functions. Questions can, however, arise concerning a) the compatibility of the functions of a subsidiary organ with those of its principal organ, and (b) scope and extent of delegation of powers permissible on the part of the principal organ in favour of its subsidiary organ.

Similarly, the power of a principal organ to make rules is akin to the power to make subordinate legislation under the domestic administrative law and questions that arise in the day-to-day functioning of the latter may arise in the context of the former as well. It is axiomatic that the rule-making power is co-extensive with the constitutional mandate of the relevant organ in the absence of any inhibiting stipulation. It cannot be exercised either inconsistent with or exceeding the mandated powers of the organ merely on grounds of 'political expediency'. In the name of autonomy of rule-making power, the organ cannot claim more powers than mandated, or powers inconsistent with its mandate, or exercise mandated powers wrongly or *mala fide*, without reasonable proof of nexus between the exercise of power and the object to be achieved.

As an arena for free play of conflict of interests among member states, the United Nations finds itself confronted with the constant use of the rules of its internal legal regime as the rules of the 'game'. To the extent that they are used in furtherance of the objectives of the Organisation, they promote 'parliamentary diplomacy' and international co-operation through it. To the extent that they are used dysfunctionally, they may thwart, a legitimate organizational action which may even be consistent with objectives of the United Nations. Kauffmann cites an outstanding example of a historic opportunity for organizational action having been lost owing to procedural wrangles in the UN General Assembly. In the wake of the collapse of the super power Summit in 1960 as a consequence of the U-2 incident, a draft resolution jointly sponsored by Ghana, India, Indonesia, the UAR and Yugoslavia was orally moved by Jawaharlal Nehru, the Prime Minister of India. The resolution appealed to both the President of the United States and the Chairman of the Council of Ministers of the USSR to meet "as a first urgent step" to ease world tension and renew their contacts. Australia moved another draft resolution seeking a five-Power summit, which was voted down by 5 votes in favour, 45 against and 43 abstentions. Argentina, pursuant to relevant rules, asked for separate votes on the phrases of the operative part of the 5-Power resolution. A lengthy procedural debate followed, culminating in a decision of 41 votes in favour, 37 against and 17 abstentions, but it failed to secure the required two-thirds majority. The debate over the words "The President of" and "the Chairman of the Council of Ministers of" left most delegations bitter. Thus,

> An idealistic initiative had been lost in a procedural morass. The importance attached to certain words is illustrated by this case, in which the United Nations as an institution was unable to provide a framework of securing agreement on an issue which was considered important and to which many delegations attached great urgency.[35]

Such instances make what President Winiarsky of the World Court said in his dissent in *Certain Expenses* case, look realistic, even if with a tingle of cynicism:

> The intention of those who drafted it [the Charter] was clearly to abandon the possibility of useful action rather than to sacrifice the balance of carefully established fields of competence, as can be seen, for example, in this case of voting in the Security Council. It is only by such procedures, which were clearly defined, that the United Nations can seek to achieve its purposes. It may be that the United Nations is sometimes not in a position to undertake action which would be useful for the maintenance of international peace and security or for one or another purpose indicated in Article 1 of the Charter, but that is the way in which the Organization was conceived and brought into existence.[36]

c) Peaceful Settlement of International Disputes

Article 1 of the Charter stipulates that the principal objective of the United Nations is to maintain international peace and security and to this end "to take effective collective measures for the prevention and removal of threats to the peace, and for the suppression of acts of aggression or other breaches of the peace, and to bring about by peaceful means, and in conformity with the principles of justice and international law, adjustment or settlement of international disputes or situations which might lead to a breach of the peace". This provision clearly points to the close linkage between the principles of prohibition of force (Article 2(4) and of peaceful

104   LEGAL CONSIDERATIONS IN THE FUNCTIONING OF THE UN

settlement of international disputes (Article 2(3)) on the normative plane, and the functions of promotion of peaceful adjustment or settlement of international disputes or situations on the institutional plane; the linkage is both normative as well as institutional.

At the normative level, one of the immediate implications of the principle of prohibition of force is the principle of peaceful settlement of international disputes. A number of legal issues have arisen in connection with the operationality of the principle of peaceful settlement of disputes.

First, does the principle apply to all types of disputes? The Friendly Relations debates witnessed a minority view that the preoccupation of the United Nations being the maintenance of international peace and security, the obligation under this principle arose only in respect of disputes "the continuance of which is likely to endanger the maintenance of international peace and security", *a la* Article 33(1) of the Charter, and not other disputes. This view came to be rejected and consensus could eventually be reached in favour of the stipulation embodied in the 1970 Friendly Relations Declaration that the obligation of peaceful settlement applies to all disputes.[37]

A second set of issues relates to the relationship between peaceful settlement and the principles of justice. This arises from Article 1(1) of the Charter itself. Hans Kelsen makes the point that the Security Council and the General Assembly have an option to choose between the principles of justice and those of international law, when in their opinion, the principles of justice are in conflict with those of international law.[38] This interpretation, however, is based on the assumption that international law does not envelope all principles of justice, an assumption whose validity depends on one's perspective of the role of international law in international community.

Also, the term "justice" lends itself to abuse by a state, or even by an organ of the United Nations. While states have a wide choice of disputes settlement means as indicated in Article 33 of the Charter, once they have exercised their option and a solution has been arrived at through a peaceful means so selected, the parties to a dispute are required to comply with it. It is not open to any of them to avoid compliance by arguing that the solution was not in conformity with the principles of justice.[39]

A third set of issues relates to Article 33 of the Charter. Voluntarism and the principle of consent are the hallmarks of the means of dispute settlement enumerated in that provision. They cannot be abridged in any way either by the General Assembly or by the Security Council.

Two other normative aspects need to be emphasised here. One is that the obligation to settle a dispute through peaceful means, to be effective, includes an obligation to continue to seek a peace settlement, in the event of failure to reach a solution by any one peaceful means. Second, the obligation of peaceful settlement also implies an obligation to refrain from aggravating the situation so as to endanger the maintenance of international peace and security. Without such an obligation a party to a dispute, having opted for a peaceful settlement means, may seek to frustrate the process.[40]

At the institutional level, there are questions of the difference, if any, between a "dispute" and a "situation"; the overlap of jurisdictions of the General Assembly and the Security Council, and possibly of the Secretary-General, and between one or the other political organ and the International Court of Justice; transfer of competence from one to another organ; the nature and timing of inter-position by an organ, relationship between peaceful settlement and peace-keeping ("peaceful adjustment *a la* Article 14) the sequence between peaceful settlement under Chapter VI and enforcement action under Chapter VII, and the role of regional organizations.

Article 36, paragraph 3, of the Charter commends to the Security Council that "legal disputes should as a general rule be referred by the parties to the International Court of Justice in accordance with the provisions of the Statute of the Court". Only once has this provision been pressed into service by the Council and that was in connection with the *Corfu Channel* case.[41] The distinction between "legal" and "political" disputes is often unclear. The traditional school believes in such dichotomy. According to Goodrich and Hambro, "legal" disputes involve conflicting claims of legal rights whose solution is based on international law, whereas "political" disputes involve claims arising from "dissatisfaction with the applicable rules of law". The factors of "justice" and "expediency", rather than law, govern the search for solution.[42] It is in this sense that J.L. Brierly said that "when a state claims . . . something which is not its legal right, something even which it knows it can have only by alteration of the legal position, it is useless to suggest that it should submit the determination of its claim to legal decision. It knows beforehand that the answer of the law will be adverse; and that answer is precisely what it claims to have altered".[43]

The US statement of 18 January 1995 on its withdrawal from the then on-going proceedings of the *Nicaragua* case[44] ran thus:-

> It is inherently a political problem that is not appropriate for judicial solution. The conflict will be solved only by political and diplomatic means - not through a judicial tribunal. The International Court of Justice was never intended to resolve issues of collective security and self-defense and is patently unsuited for such a role.[45]

In other words, the United States argument was that "issues of collective security and self-defense" were "patently" political questions. The Court's reply was quite emphatic. It said:

> It is true that the jurisdiction of the Court under that provision [i.e. Article 36(2) of its Statute] is limited to "legal disputes" concerning any of the matters enumerated in the text. The question whether a given dispute between two states is or is not a "legal dispute" for the purposes of this provision may itself be a matter of dispute between those two states and if so, that dispute is to be settled by the decision of the Court in accordance with paragraph 6 of Article 36.[46]

The Court emphasized that the question of non-justiciability of the dispute was never raised by the United States before the Court's decision on preliminary objections. The Court had in that decision already rejected US contention that the

Nicaraguan claims must be reserved for the political organs of the United Nations.[47] But such contentions did not mean that the dispute was not a "legal dispute". Indeed, the Court noted, the United States did at that time emphasize before the Court that when it argued that the Court should not exercise its judicial function in this case, "this did not mean that it was arguing that international law was not relevant or controlling in a dispute of this kind".[48]

Judge Lachs in the same case remarked that "the dividing line between justiciable and non-justiciable disputes is one that can be drawn only with great difficulty".[49] He then quoted Sir Hersch Lauterpacht:-

> There is no fixed limit to the possibilities of judicial settlement. All conflicts in the sphere of international politics can be reduced to contests of a legal nature. The only decisive text of the justiciability of the dispute is the willingness of the disputants to submit the conflict to the arbitrament of law.[50]

Finally, in the words of Sir Robert Jennings, the President of the Court,

> The former tendency of commentators to distinguish between legal and political disputes, as if they fell into quite distinct categories, had a dangerous artificiality ... The important distinction, therefore, is not between legal and political disputes so much as between legal and political methods of dealing with disputes and indeed also with situations.[51]

This proposition flows also from the logic of Article 33. If the principles of voluntarism and state consent are the hallmarks of the obligation to choose a means of disputes settlement, the decision to select one rather than the other means would bear upon the choice exclusively of states parties to the dispute in favour of either the political or the legal *method* of settlement, and within each category, a particular means of settlement. Nay, a state choosing negotiation as a method, may even insist on bilateral rather than multilateral negotiation.

This would also imply that a solution found through an agreed method of settlement is binding on the parties thereto. At the same time, neither the General Assembly pursuant to Chapter IV nor the Security Council pursuant to Chapter VI, has power to force either a dispute settlement means or a solution of a dispute upon the parties.

Further, even the Security Council does not have an unqualified mandate to interfere with any procedures for the settlement of a dispute which have already been adopted by the parties thereto. While discussing what came to be Article 36, paragraph 2, of the Charter, Turkey had proposed the following sentence at the San Francisco Conference: "Nevertheless, recommendations made by the Security Council must not interfere with legal procedures in the case of a dispute which has already been submitted for legal settlement". At the tenth meeting of Committee III/2, the delegate of Turkey explained that the purpose of this amendment was to ensure that the Security Council would not intervene in a case which was being heard by the International Court of Justice. If the dispute developed into a threat to the peace in the meantime, then the Council could intervene, but otherwise there should be no interference in the judicial proceedings. Peru supported Turkey's proposal. South

Africa, the United Kingdom and the United States took the position that the Security Council would only interfere, if the dispute amounted to a threat to the peace, or was likely to endanger international peace and security. The US delegate added that the Turkish amendment did not purport to place any restrictions on the action of the Council in such a case, but that "it meant that if a dispute were being satisfactorily handled by the Court and there was no threat to peace, then there should be no interference by the Council". The Turkish delegate agreed with this interpretation. The result was Article 36(2) of the Charter. Explaining this provision, the Summary Report of the Committee III/2 stated: "According to this Article, the Security Council, in making recommendations in accordance with the first sentence, must determine whether or not the parties had already adopted pacific procedures. If so, the Council would not ordinarilly call upon them to adopt such procedures or make recommendations for employment of other designated procedures".[52]

d) Law-Making by the United Nations

Article 38, paragraph 1, of the Statute of the International Court of Justice provides an acceptable point of reference for an international lawyer in search of legal rules applicable to a situation in hand. Although it was drafted in 1920 in the wake of the establishment of two world organizations, namely the League of Nations and the ILO, the draftsmen of the Statute, the eminent jurists who constituted the Advisory Committee of Jurists, did not include the decisions of international organizations among the sources they chose to recognise in Article 38(1). They had enough trouble drafting the existing provision itself.[53] The only explanation for such an omission is perhaps that in 1920 the law-making potential of the international organization was clearly underestimated, if not unestimated, for want of an adequate perception of or experience with organizations with global functions.

The International Court has recently shown that so long as the law-making decisions of international organizations can be subsumed under one or the other of the sources of Article 38(1) of the Statute, one need not worry about the legal significance of these decisions. In the *Nicaragua* case, the Court found evidence of international customary law principles of prohibition of force and non-intervention in consensual resolutions of the UN General Assembly such as Resolution 2625(XXV), the 1970 Declaration of Friendly Relations.[54] It would seem that the same tests of state practice and *opinio juris cive necessitatis* as evidence of customary law could *a priori* apply to all the seven principles embodied in that resolution, namely, prohibition of force, non-intervention, peaceful settlement of disputes, good faith, international co-operation, sovereign equality, and self-determination, since the resolution itself declares them to be "basic principles of international law".[55]

In this context, it is important to recall the definition of a peremptory norm (*jus cogens*) of international law contained in Article 53 of the Vienna Convention on the Law of Treaties 1969:-

[A] peremptory norm of general international law is a norm acceptable and recognized by the international community of states as a whole as a norm from which no derogation is permitted and which can be modified only by a subsequent norm of general international law having the same character.

The question is not through what procedural modality a peremptory norm emerges, but whether a norm is (1) accepted and recognised (2) by the international community of states *as a whole* (3) as a peremptory norm. It is submitted that the same test of acceptance and recognition by the international community of states as a whole applies equally to every legal norm, principle or rule applies equally to every legal norm, principle or rule embodied in every consensual resolution. The legal significance of a norm-setting resolution of a UN organ, or for that matter, of any international body rests on (a) whether the norm embodied in it is accepted and recognised as a legal norm, and (b) whether this acceptance and recognition is performed by "the international community of states *as a whole*". States are indeed free to perform this act of acceptance and recognition of a legal norm in any arena, whether inside an international organization or outside it.[56] Such law-making competence of the United Nations shall continue to exist so long as it provides an arena for state interactions.

The United Nations General Assembly thus performs its law-making functions not only within the framework of Article 13 of the Charter but outside it as well. Every decision it takes in performance of its functions implies an interpretation of the relevant provisions of the Charter in respect of the competence of an organ, it may involve an elaboration of the norms contained in the Charter provisions,[57] it may involve a statement, re-statement or a new formulation of principles of international law. Often it is difficult to draw a dividing line between the elaboration of the principles of the Charter and that of the principles of international law in view of their mutual interfaces. The norm setting resolutions of the General Assembly are numerous -- the 1946 resolution on the Nuremberg Principles, the Universal Declaration of Human Rights 1948, the Declaration on the Granting of Independence to Colonial Peoples and Territories 1960, the Declaration on the Permanent Sovereignty over Natural Resources 1963, the Declaration on Principles of Peaceful Uses of Outer Space 1963, the Friendly Relations Declaration 1970, the Declaration Defining Aggression 1974, and so on. Where these declarations are based on consensus, it has been pointed out by some scholars of positivist orientation, they lack in clarity and precision and instead of resolving problem areas (i.e. divergence of views of states), the diplomatic mechanism of consensus hides them under the carpet and carries them forward.[58] However, three points may be noted in favour of consensual decisions. First, human language can never be perfect, and there can aways be more than one interpretation to any postulation of law.[59] Second, consensus mechanism reflects diplomacy, i.e. multilateral diplomacy, being the art of the possible. It is more important to ensure commitment, or at least absence of any serious objection, on the part of all significant segments of the international community. Third, the United Nations has furnished the Third World countries with ample opportunities for serious participation in law-making as borne out by the strenuous negotiations often stretching over long years, like those which preceded the 1970 Friendly Relations Declaration and consensus ensures their participation.

The norm-setting function of the UN General Assembly through resolutions in new areas of international law has been extremely significant. In the field of outer space, the General Assembly adopted in 1982 a resolution on Principles of Direct Broadcast Satellites, in 1986 on Principles of Remote Sensing, and in 1992 on

Principles of Use of Nuclear Power Sources in Launching of Space Objects.

Pursuant to Article 13, the General Assembly promotes the "traditional" method of law-making in two ways, one by directly evolving international agreements and commending them for signature and ratification through the normal treaty making practices of states. The Genocide Convention 1949, the International Covenants on Human Rights 1966, the International Convention on the Rights of the Child 1989, and many of the international disarmament treaties are some of the numerous examples of this method of treaty-making. A second "traditional" method is to promote treaty-making through specialised subsidiary law-making bodies like the International Law Commission and the UN Commission on International Trade Law. These treaty-drafting bodies report yearly to the General Assembly in making known the responses of states not only on the specific drafts, but also on the agendas of these bodies and even on the approach being adopted by them.

The International Law Commission, conceived during the heydays of "jurisconsults" as McWhinney would call them, and charged with the dual task of "progressive development of international law and its codification" has contributed substantially over the years by drafting a number of international conventions, some codifying existing law, and many both codifying as well as simultaneously developing the law. The fifties saw considerable tension between the Commission and the General Assembly and the former was reminded time and again that it was a subsidiary body of the Assembly. It was also criticised for being Eurocentric or pro-Western in its composition as well as its approach. As the "geography of international law" had changed by 1960, the General Assembly decided to expand the membership to 25 in 1961 and 34 in 1981. Additionally, the General Assembly took upon itself the task of law-making in regard to the substantive questions of international relations, particularly in view of the argument of the Third World countries that most of the traditional international law was Eurocentric, in the making of which these countries played little or no role, and that therefore the Assembly should itself directly play an active role.[60] This was the reason why the General Assembly engaged itself in the development of a wide variety of aspects of international law bearing upon substantive areas of international relations such as the law of outer space (since 1958), the law of friendly relations (since 1961), the law of the sea (since 1967), the principles of equitable economic relations (since 1974), defining aggression, the strengthening of the Charter, the peaceful settlement of international disputes and so on. Also, the Assembly took a firmer hold on the agenda of the Commission than before, directing the latter to work on specific areas of international law.

The importance of the role of the Commission, according to some scholars, has considerably reduced since the days of the "jurisconsults" of the first generation, with the "[l]ater generations of lawyers within the General Assembly legally less well formed and disciplined" as Edward McWhinney finds. Reviewing the composition and the work of the Commission from the vantage point of the eighties, McWhinney asks:

> How could such a body, whose membership was so fiercely centested in the quinquennial elections and with such a degree of attention to "regional" factors, which as a result was now stocked with "foreign office lawyers" sophisticated

in United Nations internal politics and lobbying, be content to remain at the periphery of great events of contemporary international law-making, and to be bypassed or excluded when great new issues of the progressive development of international law should arise?[61]

McWhinney's lament on the passing of the era of jurisconsults is at best a show of nostalgia, but at worst an expression of a subsconscious taint of bias in favour of the traditional Eurocentric legal thought - and it is surprising to see this coming from McWhinney whose writings have shown much greater sensitivity to, and reception of the factors leading to the expansion and the need for reorientation of international law in the post-war world. However, it is submitted that his major point on the Commission allowing itself to be sidelined in the United Nations law-making process is well taken. The problem with the "foreign office" lawyers is not necessarily their alleged lack of expertise or legal technique, but the limits of time. Since their primary callings do not allow them to have full time focus on the Commission's work, the "foreign office" lawyers, particularly those from the developing countries, are unable to do full justice to their membership of the Commission. Indeed in many developing countries there continues to be a serious paucity of expert assistance in their Foreign Offices. Often Foreign Offices are run by three to five officers, most of them of junior rank and lacking in the knowledge of international law. Indeed, the type and range of resources and research back-ups and facilities which the international lawyers of the developed world enjoy are vast and those of the lawyers from the developing countries are not comparable. Perhaps one or two suggestions may be made in this regard. First, there must be some pooling of resources and expertise among the developing countries. Second, like the developed countries, the developing countries too - at least the larger ones amongst them - should utilise non-governmental (including academic) expertise, if locally available.

While one does not find anything wrong with "regional factors" in the election of members to the Commission, one does feel that a 34-member Commission (if all the members were to attend its sessions regularly, which they do not) is too unmanageable a drafting Committee: it is a mini-Assembly. Even following the "regional" factors, the membership could be reduced to 15 or 20, with the Sixth Committee closely monitoring its work.

e) **The Implications of Illegal Acts of the United Nations**

As pointed out by the International Court in the *Anglo-Norwegian Fisheries* case, where a unilateral act of a state has international implications, its validity "with regard to other states depends upon international law".[62] There is a burden on the shoulders of the state concerned to explain its conduct, if called upon, and to prove that its conduct is in conformity with international law.[63] What is true of the legality of unilateral acts of states is also true of the acts of international organizations. Indeed, "The correlative of legal personality and a capacity to present international claims", as Brownlie rightly says, "is responsibility".

Moreover, when creating institutions states cannot always hide behind the organization when its activities cause damage to the interests of states or other organizations. General international law provides criteria according to which an organization may be held to be unlawful in conception and objects, and, apart from this, particular acts in the law may be void if they are contrary to a principle of the *jus cogens*.[64]

At the doctrinal level five principal points may be made in respect of the concept of illegality of acts of international organizations. First, the law of international responsibility imposes an obligation on states not to use or allow the use of an international organization for commission of an act that is illegal under international law. What a state is itself forbidden to do, it cannot get done through one of its devices. Second, as pointed out above, international organization is itself a subject of international law and its responsibility commensurate with its legal personality. Third, illegality is a concept which has different levels and range of ramifications corresponding to the nature of the breach of the law to which an organization is subject.[65] Illegality may result from an act contrary to a principle of the *jus cogens*,[66] an act contrary to its own constitution, or an act contrary to specific undertakings which the organization may have committed itself with other organization(s) on states in performance of its functions. In the case of the first category, illegality may operate absolutely with no scope for rectification even through reparation. In the case of the other two categories, perhaps it could prove due dilligence. In any case it could not, however, make a self-exculpatory argument that it was a victim of international diplomacy, for the decisions of an international organization are based on deliberations. And the failure on the part of the member states to prevent the commission of illegality would raise its own questions of international responsibility of states.

Fourth, pursuant to its constitution a distinction needs to be made between a palpably illegal conduct and the general practice of the organization (whether the practice of the organization amounts to state conduct under its constituent treaty, even to the extent of modifying the trreaty, is a question to examined in terms of the treaty provisions as also general international treaty law). The Vienna Convention on the Law of Treaties 1969, under Article 60, recognizes "a material breach of a bilateral treaty", empowering the non-breaching party to seek unilateral termination of the treaty. Similarly, the sanction of expulsion is envisaged under Article 7 of the UN Charter against a member state "which has persistently violated" the Principles of the Charter. Whether a material breach of a Charter provision would entitle a member state to 'unilateral termination' of the Charter is not clear under international law. Indeed, a member may withdraw from the organization. However, an illegal act of the United Nations may raise questions of reparations to the aggrieved party. The general practice of the United Nations, on the other hand comprise decisions/acts made or performed by its organs pursuant to their respective mandates. Their interpretation of their mandate stands, unless it fails the test of "general acceptance". There exists no third party mechanism to be the arbiter in case of a challenge to the legality of an act of the organization, or of a claim of reparation based on such a challenge.[67] This indeed is an unjust situation.

Finally, in the functioning of the United Nations legal considerations are but one set of considerations that move an organ to a decision/action. Hence Leo Gros' counsel of realism:

Resolutions of both the General Assembly and the Security Council need not legally be binding in order to be effective; they may be effective even though their legality is doubtful.[68]

Yet it is equally useful to remember that an argument of illegality comes handy as a good defence against any claim of non-compliance with an organizational decision. In certain cases, such as the recent Gulf Crisis (the manner in which the Security Council took decisions, abdicating its constitutional powers, ratifying (*ex post facto*) the action taken by some of the members individually, and imposing and maintaining sanctions against Iraq, largely by way of retribution even violating the basic norms of human rights), the organizational action may provoke adverse international public opinion.

One example where international public opinion, even if alongside the forces of international politics, played a role was the question of Chinese representation. Through the Rumanian-inspired Resolution 2728 (XXVI) of 25 October 1971, the General Assembly had to swallow the bitter pill and recognize implicitly that it was responsible for allowing "the representatives of Chiang Kai-skek" to "unlawfully occupy" the place of the "legitimate representatives of China to the United Nations". It also thereby "restored" "all the rights to the People's Republic of China" as the only legitimate representative of China.[69]

It may be recalled that at the fifth session of the Assembly in 1950, India had asserted that the Central Government of the People's Republic of China was entitled to represent China in the Assembly and this proposal was voted down in the Assembly.[70] Similarly, a Soviet proposal made in the Security Council in January 1950 that the Security Council decide "not to recognise the credentials of the representative" of the Nationalist Government, was rejected by the Council.[71] An implication of the 1971 General Assembly resolution would be that those early decisions of the Assembly and the Council were illegal which would mean that the organizational decisions relating to the 'UN action' in Korea were also illegal on the grounds that the relevant organs of the United Nations were illegally composed and that the state of China acting through its legitimate representative, i.e. the Central Government of the People's Republic of China, was denied the right to be heard in respect of the Korean situation, a serious violation of the principles of natural justice!

In the recent Gulf Crisis, the sole surviving super power demonstrated how it could so easily manipulate the decisional process of the UN Security Council to be an instrument of its foreign policy giving scant regard for the explicit provisions of the Charter. R.P. Anand, on an in-depth examination of the decisions of the Security Council in the Gulf Crisis and action taken by the multilateral armed forces presumably thereunder, questions the validity of Resolution 678 of 30 November 1990, (which, *inter alia*, authorized "member states co-operating with the Government of Kuwait", "to use all necessary means to uphold and implement" a 1990 resolution of the Security Council) for its non-conformity with Article 27(3) of the Charter (in respect of China's interpretation of its abstention).[72] He also argues that the military action taken admittedly pursuant to that resolution was illegal as it did not conform to the scheme of enforcement action pursuant to Chapter VII of the UN Charter. He points out further that the military action was not under the control of the Council. The action was further legally unsustainable because even assuming it took a variant form of a Council-blessed enforcement action, or by an outside chance, the form of collective self-defence, it violated the principles of reasonableness and proportionality in the use of weapons and incidence of violence unleashed - the Gulf War was indeed a blatant exhibition of high-technology weapons and their devastating potential. Added to these, are the questions of violations of humanitarian laws applicable in armed conflict by the multinational forces fighting pursuant to the Council's 'authorization'.[73]

To the above formidable list of aspects of illegality of the roles of the Council and the multinational forces in the Gulf Crisis, one may add two more. First, in the event of inoperability of Article 42 of the Charter, the only other course left open by the Charter for organizational armed action is under Article 106 whereby, pending the coming into force of the Article 43 special agreements, the Big Five are required to consult with one another, and if necessary with other members, "with a view to such joint action on *behalf of the Organization* as may be necessary for the purpose of maintaining international peace and security" (emphasis added). Second, the sanctions imposed on Iraq amounted to retribution, resembling the cumulative effect of the stringent provisions of the Treaty of Versailles 1919 which John Maynard Keynes had castigated as a "Carthagenian Peace". And in actual operation, they violated the basic principles of humanity as they were instrumental in denying life-saving drugs to sick children and other weaker sections of the Iraq population, and essential goods and services for the entire population.

Some other recent instances of UN involvement in troubled situations, such as in Somalia, Rwanda and the former Yugoslavia, have also caused the raising of some legal eyebrows on the legality of acts of the Organization. Peacekeeping operations have traditionally been based on the consent of the parties concerned. This time-honoured principle was not observed by the Security Council in Somalia. Since there was no effective Government in that country, the United Nations thought it unnecessary to have prior consultations with the parties to the internal conflict thre. In the cases of the former Yugoslavia and Rwanda, the Security Council thought it proper to establish UN War crimes Tribunals for the trial and punishment of persons accused of war crimes and crimes against humanity. Apart from the questions of the 'Victor's Justice,'[74] other legal questions also arise concerning these actions. Can the Council, a political organ, establish a judicial tribunal as its subsidiary organ? Is it competent to do it in exercise of its powers relating to mounting of an enforcement action or even a peacekeeping operation? Can it be eclectic, in this regard (i.e. it decides to institute such a tribunal in one case, but not in another). For instance, it failed to play any role at all during the two decades of Vietnam War?? Incidents of disregard for the humanitarian laws applicable to armed conflict on the part of the armed forces participating in some of these operations have also come to light, be they in the form of the Pakistani troops' retaliation against civilians in Somalia, or of failure of the NATO military to distinguish between military and civilian targets in the former Yugoslavia. The Organization and the participating Governments (where the command is not with the Organization) will ultimately be answerable to the international community for these illegalities.

V. CONCLUDING REMARKS

In 1995 we celebrate the Golden Jubilee of the United Nations without much euphoria. The absence of euphoria is due to our feeling that many of the expectations of the world community inspired by the establishment of the organization have been belied. For this, the nations of the world are as much to blame as the organization itself. We relied on too much of "idealism", as the nations wantonly practised too much of self-centred 'realism' real-politik.

The purpose of this paper has not been to oversell the role of either international law or the organization. One is aware that the Charter makers - at least two prominent powers among them, i.e. the United States and the Soviet Union - had hated, for different reasons though, the label of the League of Nations and anything that it represented. One of the 'constitutional defects' of the League was its excessive reliance on international law and legal methods for resolution of world problems. Added to this, was the new clarion call from the likes of Hans Morganthau and George Kennan for nations to launch upon a relentless pursuit of power politics as the sole panacea for the solution of international problems. To them, neither international law nor international organization was relevant except as instruments of power. These two factors oversaw a certain demotion of the role of law in the Organisation (quite symbolically, if the First Committee of the League Assembly was the Legal Committee, the UN General Assembly relegated the Legal Committee to the sixth position). The role of law in international relations of the post-war has certainly not been crucial; so has been the role of the international organization!

Yet, an area where the United Nations has made one of the greatest contributions has been that of norm-setting. The contribution of the United Nations in the field of law-making has been phenomenal. And indeed, the Third World countries have had ample opportunities to participate in it and thereby to play a role in partly modifying the classical, Eurocentric international law in the framing of which they had no say. The 1970 Friendly Relations Declaration adopted by consensus by the General Assembly on the Silver Jubilee Day of the United Nations was, for instance, a crowning achievement.

The law, as part of the political process in, and of, the United Nations, also seeks to streamline and rationalise the sphere of action of the Organization. As was held by the International Court in the *Admissions case* in 1948:

> The political character of an organ cannot release it from the observance of the treaty provisions established by the Charter when they constitute limitations on its powers or criteria for its judgment. To ascertain whether an organ has freedom of choice for its decisions, reference must be made to the terms of its constitution.[75]

The Third World countries still appear to remain stupefied by the changes that overtook the world since 1990, with the sudden disappearance of one of the super powers from the world scence. The world is dominated by the sole super power (the United States) left in the arena. At the hands of this super power, the United Nations is being manipulated to respond to situations it would never have had in the past, to adopt methods which have little harmony with the Charter framework, the objectives of the Organization. It is important for the smaller Powers to awake from their dazed state and assert themselves, or at least vociferously remind the Big Powers of the legal and moral limits of political action. Law would come as a handy tool for this purpose.

International law offers a range of institutions, methods, arenas, norms and principles to be pressed into service for resolution of international problems. Failure to utilise these facilities and avenues reflects on the nations constituting the world community rather than on the law itself.

The consensual Declaration, adopted by the whole membership of the United Nations, represented for the first time at the highest political level of the General Assembly, to mark the 50th anniversary of the Organization on 24 October 1995 affirmed, *inter alia*, the determination of this community of nations to:

-   Build and maintain justice among all States in accordance with the principles of the sovereign equality and territorial integrity of States:

-   Promote full respect for all implementation of international law;

-   Settle international disputes by peaceful means;

-   Encourage the widest possible ratification of international treaties and to ensure compliance with the obligations arising from them;

-   Promote respect for and the implementation of international humanitarian law;

-   Promote the progressive development of international law in the field of development, including that which would foster economic and social progress;

-   Promote respect for and implementation of international law in the field of human rights and fundamental freedoms and to encourage ratification of or accession to international human rights instruments;

-   Promote the further codification and progressive development of international law.[76]

The members of the international community have the responsibility to live upto this determination without allowing themselves to be 'clients' or 'satellites'. The big powers (of course including the sole Super Power) have a special responsibility to uphold the law, and pursue the Purposes and Principles of the United Nations, impartially and fairly, "with charity for all and malice towards none".

Notes and References

1. Antonio Cassese identifies the overlapping of the traditional "Westphalia model" with the "UN Charter Model", but he finds that "international law possesses two souls, and the second seems to be incapable of supplanting the first". See Antonio Cassese, *International Law in A Divided World* (Oxford, 1986), p. 4.

2. These are illustrative areas of relevance of law to the functioning of international law, Paucity, of space has restricted this choice of areas. Outside this list, are a number of legal issues like the law of employment contracts with the United Nations, the legal capacity of the Organization under Article 104 of the Charter treaty-making powers of the United Nations, privileges and immunities of the United Nations and its personnel, the "public law" and the "private law" governing specific activities of the United Nations relating to property, contracts etc. with outside entities, the United Nations and the problems of succession to the League of Nations, and the proper law of the organization. On these see generally D.W. Bowett, *The Law of International Institutions* (London, 3rd ed., 1975). Nor does this paper examine the UN in terms of each of the Charter principles.

3. On these questions, see Alf Ross, *The Constitution of the United Nations* (New York, 1950), pp. 30-40, Norman Bentwich and Andrew Martin, *A Commentary on the Charter of the United Nations* (London, 1950), p. 26.

4. *ICJ Reports 1949*, pp. 178-179. For an extensive treatment of the case, see Rahmatullah Khan, *Implied Powers of the United Nations* (Delhi, 1970).

5. Ian Brownlie, *Principles of Public International Law* (Oxford, 3rd edn., 1985 reprint), p. 687.

6. For a study of the relationship between the UN and the *Jus cogens*, See R.St. J. Macdonald, "The Charter of the United Nations and the Development of Fundamental Principles of International Law, in Bin Cheng and E.D. Brown, ed., *Contemporary Problems of International Law* (London, 1988), pp. 196-215.

6a. *ICJ Reports 1986*, p. 14.

7. *Ibid.*, p. 94, para 176.

8. *Ibid.*, p. 106, para 202.

9. On this point see Shabtai Rosenne, *The Law and Practice of the International Court* (Dordrecht, 2nd ed., 1985), pp. 541-44; V.S. Mani, *International Adjudication: Procedural Aspects* (The Hague, 1980), pp. XIII-XIV.

10. The debate over the distinction between 'substantive' and 'procedural' matters in the context of Article 27 of the Charter is quite notorious in this regard. See Hans Kelsen, *The Law of the United Nations*, (New York, 5th print, 1966), pp. 239-44.

11. On the 'expanding' jurisdiction of the UN, See M.S. Rajan, *The Expanding Jurisdiction of the United Nations* (Bombay, 1982), which is a follow-up of his earlier, seminal work, *The United Nations and Domestic Jurisdiction* (Bombay, 2nd ed., 1961).

12. See Leland Goodrich, Edvard Hambro and A.P. Simmons, *Charter of the United Nations, Commentary and Documents* (New York, 3rd edn., 1969), pp. 63-64. The San Francisco statement on the interpretation of the Charter provisions stipulated that each organ of the United Nations "will interpret such parts of the Charter as are applicable to its particular functions. It further said:

    > It is to be understood, of course, that if an interpretation made by any organ of the Organization or by a Committee of Jurists is *not generally acceptable* it will be *without binding force*. In such circumstances, or in cases where it is desired to establish an authoritative interpretation as a precedent for the future, it may be necessary to embody the interpretation in an amendment to the Charter. (Emphasis supplied). See also, the Report of the Rapporteur of Cmtee. IV/2 (Judicial Organisation, Legal Problems) to Commn. IV (Judicial Organization), Doc. 933, 12 June, 1945, *Documents of the UNCIO*, 1945, vol. 13, p. 710.

13. Behold, for example, the fate of the Court's advisory opinions in the *Admission* case *ICJ Reports 1948*, p. 57 and the *Certain Expenses* case, *ICJ Reports, 1962*, p. 151, before the General Assembly.

14. *ICJ Reports 1971*, p. 45. For a comment on the case, see V.S. Mani, "The Advisory Opinion in Namibia Case : A Critique", *IJIL*, vol. 11 (1971), pp. 467-80.

15. The Court's ambivalence in this respect did provoke strong views from at least five members of the Court, including three supporting the majority opinion: See Judge Petren's separate opinion, ibid., at pp. 130-1; Judge Oneyama's separate opinion, at pp. 141-5; Judge Dillard's separate opinion at pp. 151-2; Judge Fitzmaurice's dissent at pp. 301-4) and Judge Gros' dissent at pp. 331-2. They argued that any relevant issue of law must be a matter for the Court to decide. For a treatment of this case, see Brownlie, note 5, pp. 703-704.

16. The issue of the role of the Court in interpreting the provisions of the Charter for a determination of the *vires* also an organizational action, as will be seen later, has also figured prominently

in the recent *Lockerbie (Provisional Measures of Protection)* cases, and is still pending disposal by the Court. One is not sure, however, of the fate of the proceedings in these cases. See *ICJ Reports 1992*, pp. 3 ff and pp. 114ff.

17. See, for the instance of claims of domestic jurisdiction, noted by M.S. Rajan, *The United Nations and Domestic Jurisdiction*, Note 1; See also Rosalyn Higgings, *The Development of International Law Through the Political Organs of the United Nations* (London, 1963), pp. 58-130.

18. *ICJ Reports 1962*, p. 168, For an elaborate comment on the case, see Rahmatullah Khan, note 4, especially at pp. 27-30. The first two sentences quoted above from the Court's advisory opinion, according to Rahmatullah Khan, constitute "a statement which is destined to become a landmark in the jurisprudence of the Court and the evolution of the UN"; See *Id.*, pp. 28-29.

19. At *ICJ Reports 1962*, p. 163, the Court did clarify that in the case before it, the General Assembly was exercising a "special power" of organizing peace-keeping operations, as part of its functions in the field of international peace and security.

20. Even under municipal legal systems, not all procedural irregularities are treated lightly. They distinguish between "curable" and "incurable" irregularities.

21. *ICJ Reports 1992*, p. 240, at pp. 252-253.

22. E.g. Goodrich, Hambro and Simmons, note 12, pp. 291-293.

23. *Id.*, pp. 291-292. These concessions were also reflected in stipulating in Article 2(7) of the Charter, pursuant to an Australian proposal, that the principle of domestic jurisdiction "shall not prejudice the *application of enforcement measures* under Chapter VII. See *ibid.*,. pp. 60-63.

24. See *ICJ Reports*, 1992, p. 3, at pp. 61-65; See also *ICJ Reports 1992*, p. 114, at pp. 171, 175.

25. *ICJ Reports 1971*, at p. 340, quoted by Judge Bedjaoui, *in ICJ Reports 1992*, p. 42 and p. 153.

26. *ICJ Reports 1971*, p. 294, quoted by Judge Bedjaoui, *in ICJ Reports 1992,* p. 43 and p. 153. Judge Bedjaoui agrees with the proposition that there are limits to the Security Council's powers, not necessarily with the application of these limits by Judges Gros and Sir Gerald to the *Namibia* case.

27. *ICJ Reports 1992*, p. 45, and p. 155.

28. *Id.*

29. *ICJ Reports 1992*, p. 45, and p. 155.

30. *ICJ Reports 1992,* p. 46 and p. 156, footnote.

31. *ICJ Reports 1971*, p. 294.

32. *ICJ Reports 1992*, p. 46, and p. 156.

33. Hans Kelsen, note 10, pp. 732-35.

34. On this, see R.P. Anand, *International Courts and Contemporary Conflicts* (Bombay, 1974), pp. 222-238.

35. John Kauffmann, *United Nations Decision-Making* (Alphen Aanden Rijn, 1980), p. 172.

36. *ICJ Reports 1969*, p. 151.

37. See V.S. Mani, *Basic Principles of Modern International Law* (New Delhi, 1993), pp. 99-100.

38. Kelson, note 10, p. 366.

39. Mani, note 37, pp. 101-102.

40. Both of these obligations have found expression in the formulation of the principle of peaceful settlement of international disputes embodied in the 1970 Friendly Relations Declaration - Resolution 2625 (XXV) of 24 October 1970. For more on this, see Mani, note 37, pp. 128-130.

41. *ICJ Reports 1949*, p. 4.

42. Goodrich, Hambro, Simmons, note 12, p. 182.

43. Quoted in Lincoln Bloomfield, "Law Politics and International Disputes", *International Conciliation* (Washington, D.C.) No. 516, January 1958, p. 284.

44. *ICJ Reports 1986*, p. 14.

45. *ILM*, vol. 25 (1985), p. 246.

46. *ICJ Reports 1986*, pp. 26-27.

47. *ICJ Reports 1984*, pp. 431-36.

48. *ICJ Reports 1986*, p. 27.

49. *Ibid.*, p. 158, at p. 168.

50. Hersch Lauterpacht, *Function of Law in the International Community*, (Oxford, 1933), p. 389; *ICJ Reports 1986*, p. 169. But for a contrary view that the Nicaragua case was not a "legal dispute", see Judge Oda, *ICJ Reports* 1986, pp. 219-236; Judge Schwebel, *ibid*, pp. 284-296.

51. Address by Sir Robert Y. Jennings, President of ICJ reporting on the work of the Court, before the UN General Assembly, 46th Session, 44th mtg., 8 November 1991, *ICJ Yearbook 1991-1992*, pp. 205-212, at p. 209. For the political role of the Court see *id.*, and Shabtai Rosenne, note 9, pp. 1-6. On 'legal' as opposed to 'political' questions in advisory proceedings, see Rosenne, *ibid.*, pp. 702-8.

52. Hans Kelsen, note 10, pp. 405-7, footnote 1, relying on UNCIO Documents.

53. For more on this, see R.P. Anand, note 34, pp. 346-435.

54. *ICJ Reports 1986*, pp. 100, 107.

55. For a study of the *travaux preparatoires* of resolution 2625 (xxv) of 1970, see V.S. Mani, note 37.

56. The basis of legality of all law is its acceptance by its subjects. For more on this see Harold J. Laski, *A Grammar of Politics* (London, 4th edn., 1960 Reprint), pp. 248-263. Formal law-making institutions are just the upper surface of an iceberg, the whole law-making process being part of the social process in a given society.

57. See for example the Declaration on Decolonisation 1960 (Resolution 1514 (xv) of 15 December 1960), and comments thereon by Professor Manfred Lachs (as he then was) in his "The Law in and the The United Nations", *Indian Journal of International Law*, vol. 1, (1960-61), pp. 429-442.

58. See, e.g., Julius Stone's critique of the Declaration on Defining Aggression, in his *Conflict through Consensus: UN Approaches to Aggression* (London, 1977).

59. Kelsen, note 10, pp. (xiii) - xvii), his Preface "On Interpretation".

60. See Mani, note 37, pp. 1-2.

61. Edward McWhinney, *United Nations Law-Making* (UNESCO, Paris 1984), p. 160.

62. *ICJ Reports 1951*, p. 132.

63. This greatly modifies the traditional *Lotus* dictum (P.C.I.J. Seriee A.No. 10), p. 28 that "Restrictions on independence of States cannot be presumed".

64. Brownlie, note 5, pp. 698-699.

65. See Brownlie, *ibid.*, p. 509.

66. In the *Barcelona Traction Case* (Second Phase), the International Court spokeof State obligations "towards international community as a whole". Such obligations derive, for example, in contemporary international law, "from the outlawing of acts of aggression, and of genocide, as also from the principles and rules concerning the basic rights of the human person, including protection from slavery of the human person, including protection from slavery and racial discrimination". *ICJ Reports 1970*, p. 3 at p. 32.

67. For the juristic debate on this, see Dan Ciabanu, *Preliminary Objections Related to the Jurisdiction of the United Nations Organs* (The Hague, 1975), pp. 193-201.

68. Leo Gros, "The United Nations and the Role of Law", *International Organisation* vol. 19 (1965), pp. 537-561, at p. 539.

69. One this question, see M.K. Nawaz, "Chinese Representation in the United Nations", *IJIL*, vol. 11 (1971), pp. 459-66.

70. Goodrich, Hambro and Simons, note 12, pp. 109-10.

71. Reacting to this the Soviet representative withdrew in protest from the Council, *ibid.*, pp. 200-201.

72. R.P. Anand, *United Nations and the Gulf Crisis*, (New Delhi, 1994), pp. 17-20.

73. *Ibid.*, Parts III and IV.

74. For more on such questions see, Radha Binod Pal, *Crime in International Relations* (Calcutta, 1951).

75. *ICJ Reports 1948*, p. 4, at p. 64.

76. Paragraph 13 (unlucky number, again?), of the UN Declaration.

Part II
Actors within the United Nations: Powers and Legitimacy

[5]

THE LEGITIMACY OF THE COLLECTIVE AUTHORITY OF THE SECURITY COUNCIL

By David D. Caron*

> The ideal, once it is embodied in an institution, ceases to be an ideal and becomes the expression of a selfish interest, which must be destroyed in the name of a new ideal. This constant interaction of irreconcilable forces is the stuff of politics. Every political situation contains mutually incompatible elements of utopia and reality, of morality and power.
>
> *E. H. Carr*[1]

> [T]he crucial question is not *what* principle is acknowledged but *who* is accepted as the authoritative interpreter of the principle or, to put it in institutional terms, *how* the process of legitimization works.
>
> *Inis Claude, Jr.*[2]

INTRODUCTION

At this pivotal point in history, a fundamental and oft-raised issue is "international governance." Means of effective governance are seen as necessary to more complex arrangements of world order. But achieving effective governance *ultimately* will mean the existence of institutions that legislate, that is, institutions that make decisions binding on the whole. As a general matter, states have been skeptical of, if not hostile toward and consequently unwilling to accept, such governance. The United Nations Security Council is a notable exception; in the sometimes broad, sometimes narrow, area of international peace and security, the Security Council has taken decisions in the name of, and binding upon, the entire international community.[3]

---

* Of the Board of Editors. Earlier drafts of this article were presented at the Institute of International Studies, the University of California at Berkeley, on November 9, 1992; at a joint United Nations Association/Russian Foreign Policy Association/American Society of International Law Conference in Moscow on December 7, 1992; before the U.S. Commission on Improving the Effectiveness of the United Nations on February 2, 1993; at the Annual Meeting of The American Society of International Law in Washington, D.C., on April 2, 1993; and at a meeting of government and UN lawyers who work with the Sixth Committee of the General Assembly in New York on May 6, 1993. The article benefited greatly from the discussions at these meetings and from the comments of many colleagues and officials.

[1] EDWARD HALLETT CARR, THE TWENTY YEARS' CRISIS: 1919–1939, at 94 (2d ed. 1945).

[2] Inis Claude, Jr., *Collective Legitimization as a Political Function of the United Nations*, 20 INT'L ORG. 367, 369–70 (1966).

[3] Article 39(1) of the Charter provides that the trigger for action under Articles 41 and 42 shall be the determination by the Council of "the existence of any threat to the peace, breach of the peace or act of aggression." On the meaning of "threat to the peace," see LELAND GOODRICH, EDVARD HAMBRO & ANNE PATRICIA SIMONS, CHARTER OF THE UNITED NATIONS: COMMENTARY AND DOCUMENTS 295–97 (3d rev. ed. 1969).

For examples of a recent trend to interpret "threat to the peace" more broadly than previously, see SC Res. 688 (Apr. 5, 1991), *reprinted in* 30 ILM 858 (1991) (determining that Iraqi actions in the Kurdish areas of Iraq were a threat to regional peace and security); and SC Res. 794 (Dec. 3, 1992) (determining that the "magnitude of the human tragedy caused by the conflict in Somalia" constituted a threat to international peace and security).

Collective Security Law

With the end of the Cold War, the most apparent ideological distinctions between East and West, political and economic, ended. As the "First" and "Second" worlds merged, the Iraqi invasion of Kuwait swept the world up in an endeavor that breathed new life into a United Nations long hobbled by the East-West conflict. The Security Council acted in utterly unprecedented ways: ordering economic sanctions and, ultimately, authorizing the use of force by "Member States co-operating with the Government of Kuwait" so as to implement the resolutions of the Council and "restore international peace and security in the area."[4] This vitality has continued in the United Nations with the imposition of economic sanctions against Libya,[5] Serbia[6] and, most recently, Haiti.[7]

It is thus with no small measure of irony that, as the international community finally achieved what quite a few of its members at least officially had sought—a functioning UN Security Council—many of them began to have second thoughts about the legitimacy of that body's use of its collective authority. For some, this irony has yielded to cynicism regarding the Council. However, in view of the central role of the Security Council, both now and in the future, this irony must also give rise to determination to renew the Council and lay the basis for models of governance generally. This article explores the roots and relevance of chal-

---

A particularly interesting recent issue involves the competence of the Security Council to establish, by binding decision, an ad hoc criminal court. *See* Letter from the Permanent Representative of France to the Secretary-General, UN Doc. S/25266 (1993). "[T]he establishment of a [ad hoc] Tribunal would be an appropriate measure if . . . it seems likely to attain or facilitate the objective of restoring international peace and security." *Id.* at 13. The Council ultimately established an ad hoc tribunal in Resolution 827 (May 25, 1993).

[4] SC Res. 678, para. 2 (Nov. 29, 1990), *reprinted in* 29 ILM 1565 (1990).

[5] In response to the destruction of Pan Am Flight 103 and UTA Flight 772, the Security Council unanimously passed Resolution 731, inter alia, urging the Libyan Government to comply with requests for the surrender of the bombing suspects for trial in the United States or the United Kingdom, the disclosure of all relevant information and the payment of appropriate compensation. SC Res. 731 (Jan. 21, 1992), *reprinted in* 31 ILM 732 (1992). When Libya failed to comply, the Security Council, acting under chapter VII, passed by a vote of 10 for, 0 against and 5 abstentions (Cape Verde, China, India, Morocco, Zimbabwe), Resolution 748 imposing diplomatic and economic sanctions upon Libya if Libya failed to comply with the demands in Resolution 731 and to take concrete steps toward ceasing all terrorist actions by April 15, 1992. SC Res. 748 (Mar. 31, 1992), *reprinted in* 31 ILM at 750.

[6] In response to the violence in Bosnia and Hercegovina, the Security Council adopted Resolution 752 (May 15, 1992), *reprinted in* 31 ILM at 1451, setting forth various demands aimed at ending the fighting. On May 30, 1992, the Security Council, acting under chapter VII, passed by 13 votes for, 0 against and 2 abstentions (China, Zimbabwe), Resolution 757, *reprinted in* 31 ILM at 1453, imposing economic and diplomatic sanctions against the Federal Republic of Yugoslavia (Serbia and Montenegro) until such time as the Council found that Serbia and Montenegro had complied with Resolution 752. These sanctions were expanded upon in several Security Council resolutions over the next year.

[7] For recent UN actions, see Howard French, *U.N. Approves Ban on Shipments of Oil to Haitian Military,* N.Y. TIMES, June 17, 1993, at A1; and Paul Lewis, *U.N. Council Plans to Order Full Ban on Oil for Haiti,* N.Y. TIMES, June 10, 1993, at A1.

Earlier, the Organization of American States had authorized more limited sanctions against Haiti. On September 30, 1991, the OAS Permanent Council, established only recently under Resolution AG/RES.1080 (XXI–0/91) and acting pursuant to its authority under Article 64 of the OAS Charter, as amended by the Protocol of Cartagena de Indias in 1985 (Doc. OEA/Ser.A/41), convened an ad hoc Meeting of Consultation of Ministers of Foreign Affairs. That body, without veto, adopted by consensus Resolutions MRE/RES.1/91 and MRE/RES.2/91 on October 3 and 8, 1991, respectively. Those resolutions are nonbinding appeals by the regional body for its 34 members and other governments to halt all commercial and financial transactions with Haiti until President Jean-Bertrand Aristide is restored to office.

lenges to the legitimacy of the Council's use of its authority, and suggests some ways that the forces motivating such challenges may be addressed.[8]

A basic assumption often made in discussions regarding allegations of illegitimacy is that those allegations make a practical difference. Whether this assumption is warranted is touched upon in part I. Accepting this assumption for the moment, however, the conclusion reached in the case of the Security Council is that the likelihood of continued collective action depends in part on the perceived legitimacy of the decision maker, the Council itself. But, as Andrew Boyd observed of the Council twenty years ago, "the first time the tool is used there are almost bound to be complaints, from one quarter or another, that it is bent sinisterly."[9] Even amid the virtually universal agreement that the Iraqi invasion should be reversed, some were uneasy about specific aspects of the Security Council's decision.[10] Like concerns have been voiced in the months since, both generally,[11] and particularly when the Council acted in regard to Libya.[12]

---

[8] I gain the impression from individuals involved with the Security Council that the cutting edge of their concerns about the Council is shifting. Two years ago, even one year ago, the concern of a substantial group of states was, as noted in the text, the legitimacy of the Council's use of its authority. Against the background of the difficult situations in Serbia, Somalia and Cambodia and the hard task of finding resources to match both rhetoric and aspiration, the concern of many now is with the reality of the Council's "power." *See, e.g.,* Paul Lewis, *U.N. is in Arrears on Peace Efforts: Increased Costs Raise Doubts About Ability to Finance Its Future Operations,* N.Y. TIMES, May 16, 1993, §1, at 9; Richard Bernstein, *Sniping is Growing at U.N.'s Weakness as a Peacekeeper,* N.Y. TIMES, June 21, 1993, at A1; *The United Nations: Heart of gold, limbs of clay,* ECONOMIST, June 12, 1993, at 21. If the United States does not assume the burden of making real the orders of the Council, as in the case of Iraq's invasion of Kuwait, is the Council revealed as a paper tiger mostly roaring condemnations and occasionally establishing regimes of economic sanctions of questionable efficacy? "There isn't any concert of powers out there to join. If there is to be collective action, it will happen only if the U.S. not only participates, but plays a leading constructive role." Jeane Kirkpatrick, *Facing a World Without Threats,* NEW PERSPECTIVES Q., Summer 1992, at 10, 12. *See also* Michael Gordon, *New Strength for U.N. Peacekeepers: U.S. Might,* N.Y. TIMES, June 13, 1993, §1, at 11. Although serious indeed, this more recent concern about power does not moot the earlier concern about legitimacy. The more recent concern may increasingly preoccupy those on the front line, but ultimately we will need to address the first.

[9] ANDREW BOYD, FIFTEEN MEN ON A POWDER KEG: A HISTORY OF THE U.N. SECURITY COUNCIL 222 (1971).

[10] For example, the Colombian representative stated just prior to the adoption of Resolution 665, the resolution authorizing the use of maritime forces to implement provisions of the economic sanctions against Iraq:

> We are under no illusion that when the Council comes to vote on this draft resolution it will be establishing a naval blockade . . . .
>
> That neither worries nor frightens us, but we wish to be candid: We feel concern . . . over the fact that in this draft resolution the Security Council is delegating authority without specifying to whom. Nor do we know where that authority is to be exercised or who receives it. Indeed, whoever does receive it is not accountable to anyone.

UN Doc. S/PV.2938, at 21 (1990).

Many more, and much stronger, statements can be found by persons who do not represent a government. *See, e.g.,* Erskine Childers, *Gulf Crisis Lessons for the UN,* 23 BULL. PEACE PROPOSALS 129 (1992).

[11] See, e.g., the statements of various states during the UN debate on the Agenda for Peace, *infra* note 16, summarized in Peter J. Fromuth, *The Making of a Security Community: The United Nations After the Cold War,* 46 J. INT'L AFF. 341, 363 (1993). *See also* Charley Reese, *The U.N.: Just a Front,* OAKLAND TRIB., Dec. 15, 1992, at A13.

[12] *See, e.g.,* Badi M. Ali, *White House Plays the Libya Card,* N.Y. TIMES, May 5, 1992, at A18 (letter to the editor). *The Economist* expressed the general sense of these concerns, observing: "The council,

Thus, as the ideological obstacles to collective action that characterized the Cold War appear to have receded (or at least greatly diminished, since China—or any permanent member for that matter—with its veto could end the activism of the Security Council), the international community faces the perennial core questions of how to decide that a threat to international peace and security exists and that collective action is required. There are at least two aspects to these questions: the first concerns the acceptability to various states of the process of decision in the Security Council; and the second inquires into principled justifications for collective action. Although I focus here on the process of decision, consideration of both aspects is essential to the rejuvenation of the Council. Consequently, this article should be viewed in combination with the work of other groups exploring the substantive bases of collective action.[13]

These fundamental questions regarding the Council reassert themselves at a time when change seems both possible and overdue. It is a time when many question whether the correct states hold the veto.[14] It is a time when the Soviet Union dissolved and succession to its seat and veto became an issue.[15] Finally, it is a time when fundamental change in the United Nations seems possible as a result of both the renewal of interest in the Organization since the gulf war and the upcoming fiftieth anniversary of the Charter.[16]

In examining the Security Council's exercise of collective authority, I found my research and conversations with colleagues continually returning to basic questions as to what it means to speak of an institution's use of authority as illegitimate. Part I briefly considers these basic questions.[17] Part II identifies and discusses five particular circumstances that underpin two broad perceptions of illegitimacy regarding the collective authority of the Security Council.[18] In part III I evaluate whether proposals for reform of the Council are addressed to these five circumstances. The proposals include reforming the veto, increasing the Council's membership and opening up its proceedings so as to engender a sense of greater participation in the Council by UN members generally. The first route, reforming the veto, does not appear likely to occur any time in the near future. The second, increasing the size of the Council, indirectly might increase the perception of

---

exult northerners, has been reborn to keep the peace in a manner that fits with modern times. No, grumble southerners, the council is becoming a flag of convenience for old-time neo-imperialists." *Open the Club*, ECONOMIST, Aug. 29, 1992, at 14.

[13] Such an inquiry is currently under way in several forums, including the American Academy of Arts and Sciences, the Council on Foreign Relations and the Henry L. Stimson Center. *See, e.g.*, EMERGING NORMS OF JUSTIFIED INTERVENTION (Laura W. Reed & Carl Kaysen eds., 1993); W. J. DURCH & B. M. BLECHMAN, KEEPING THE PEACE: THE UNITED NATIONS IN THE EMERGING WORLD ORDER (1992); and LAW AND FORCE IN THE NEW INTERNATIONAL ORDER (Lori F. Damrosch & David J. Scheffer eds., 1991). *See also* PETER MALANCZUK, HUMANITARIAN INTERVENTION AND THE LEGITIMACY OF THE USE OF FORCE (1993).

[14] *See, e.g., Open the Club, supra* note 12, at 14 ("The council is an anachronism.").

[15] *See, e.g.*, Yehuda Z. Blum, *Russia Takes Over the Soviet Union's Seat at the United Nations*, 3 EUR. J. INT'L L. 354 (1992); Richard Gardner & Toby Trister Gati, *Russia Deserves the Soviet Seat*, N.Y. TIMES, Dec. 19, 1991, at A31; and Stefan A. Riesenfeld & Frederick Abbott, *A UN Dilemma: Who Gets the Soviet Seat on the Security Council?*, CHRISTIAN SCI. MONITOR, Oct. 4, 1991, at 19.

[16] *See, e.g.*, An Agenda for Peace, Preventive diplomacy, peacemaking and peace-keeping—Report of the Secretary-General, UN Doc. A/47/277–S/24111, para. 85 (1992), *reprinted in* 31 ILM 953 (1992) ("the present phase in the renewal of this Organization should be complete by 1995 . . .").

[17] For a related discussion, see David D. Caron, *Governance and Collective Legitimation in the New World Order*, HAGUE Y.B. INT'L L. (forthcoming).

[18] For a summary listing of these circumstances, see p. 566 *infra*.

legitimacy, but risks weakening the Council's ability to function. The third, opening up the proceedings, holds the most promise of minimizing perceptions of
illegitimacy, but likely will not suffice.

Since the veto will probably last for some time, part IV suggests practical means
to deal in part with the legitimacy concerns expressed. Specifically, I identify and
explore a new use of the veto—which I term the "reverse veto"—that tends to
undercut the legitimacy of the Security Council's collective authority. In particular, I point to the importance of distinguishing between the authority to initiate
an action and the authority to modify an action already initiated. Recommendations are put forward for dealing with this use of the veto that, unlike proposals
generally involving the veto, do not require amendment of the Charter.

The structure of the Security Council was and will be a political decision mixing
"elements of utopia and reality, of morality and power." But the wisdom of the
initial political decision may diminish over time and structural changes are not
easily gained in international organization. Yet, although aspects of the Council
are indeed anachronistic, it is functioning and, overall, functioning well in difficult circumstances. The challenge is to refashion the ideal without losing the
reality.

I. "LEGITIMACY" IN THE CONTEXT OF INTERNATIONAL GOVERNANCE

If this study in part seeks to understand and respond to questions regarding the
legitimacy of the Council's use of its authority, then it is essential that we understand what motivates and influences such questions. In recent years there has
been substantial discussion of the notion of "legitimacy" by the legal community
in general, and the academic international legal community in particular.[19] The
extent of this discussion, however, is quite small in comparison to the degree to
which this rather nebulous term is loosely employed. It is not the purpose of this

---

[19] A central part of the recent international law discussion is THOMAS M. FRANCK, THE POWER OF
LEGITIMACY AMONG NATIONS (1990). As to associated commentary, see, e.g., Jose E. Alvarez, *The
Quest for Legitimacy: An Examination of "The Power of Legitimacy Among Nations" by Thomas M.
Franck*, 24 N.Y.U. J. INT'L L. & POL. 199 (1991); Dencho Georgiev, Letter to the Editor, 83 AJIL 554
(1989); and Martti Koskenniemi, Book Review, 86 AJIL 175 (1992).

See generally ERNST B. HAAS, WHEN KNOWLEDGE IS POWER: THREE MODELS OF CHANGE IN INTERNA-
TIONAL ORGANIZATIONS (1990); TOM TYLER, WHY PEOPLE OBEY THE LAW (1990); Margherita Ciacci,
Legitimacy and the Problems of Governance, in LEGITIMACY/LÉGITIMITÉ 20 (Athanasios Moulakis ed.,
1986); Claude, *supra* note 2; Maurice Cranston, *From Legitimism to Legitimacy, in* LEGITIMACY/
LÉGITIMITÉ, *supra*, at 36; JÜRGEN HABERMAS, *Legitimationsprobleme in modernen Staat, in* ZUR RE-
KONSTRUKTION DES HISTORISCHEN MATERIALISMUS (1976), *translated in* JÜRGEN HABERMAS, COMMU-
NICATION AND THE EVOLUTION OF SOCIETY 178 (T. McCarthy trans., 1979) [hereinafter *Legitimation*];
Alan Hyde, *The Concept of Legitimation in the Sociology of Law*, 1983 WIS. L. REV. 379; Tilo Schabert,
*Power, Legitimacy and Truth: Reflections on the Impossibility to Legitimise Legitimations of Political
Order, in* LEGITIMACY/LÉGITIMITÉ, *supra*, at 96; Jerome Slater, *The Limits of Legitimization in Inter-
national Organizations: The Organization of American States and the Dominican Crisis*, 23 INT'L ORG.
48 (1969); Joseph H. Weiler, *Parlement européen, intégration européenne, démocratie et légitimité, in*
LE PARLEMENT EUROPÉEN 325 (1988), *in English in part in The Transformation of Europe*, 100 YALE
L.J. 2403, 2466–74 (1991) [hereinafter *Transformation*]. The relationship between ethics and power,
a central part of the discussion of legitimacy, is examined in literature not specifically concerned with
legitimacy. *See, e.g.*, HEDLEY BULL, THE ANARCHICAL SOCIETY: A STUDY OF ORDER IN WORLD POLI-
TICS (1977); and CARR, *supra* note 1. Despite the rather curious statement by Koskenniemi, *supra*, at
175, that "legitimacy" is "a recent innovation. . . . Hobbes . . . had no use for it," the basic questions implicit in the notion of "legitimacy" have deep roots in the literature. *See, e.g.*, Cranston, *supra*
(discussing conceptions of legitimacy "well before the French Revolution").

article to set forth a general account of the notion of legitimacy in international governance; rather, in this section I present some basic observations so as to situate the inquiry and analysis that follow.

Legitimacy is approached here primarily in social and political terms; I focus specifically on the political and social dynamic that accompanies allegations of illegitimacy.[20] As an occasional feature of political discourse, perceptions that a process is "illegitimate" are difficult to describe because they reflect subjective conclusions, perhaps based on unarticulated notions about what is fair and just, or perhaps on a conscious utilitarian assessment of what the process means for oneself.[21] At a minimum, allegations of illegitimacy manifest dissatisfaction with an organization.[22]

If this study also suggests that attention be given to perceptions of illegitimacy, then it is important that we understand whether and when such perceptions in a practical sense warrant attention. Although I think it clear that perceptions of illegitimacy can matter, precisely when and how they matter is hard to say because the determinants of their significance in practice remain unclear.[23] Is an organization perceived as legitimate more likely to be used and thus more likely to operate

---

[20] This perspective parallels Habermas's view in *Legitimation, supra* note 19, at 178, that "[l]egitimacy means a political order's worthiness to be recognized." It is, however, both very difficult and simplistic to characterize one's task as simply to observe the phenomenon of legitimacy. In part, emphasis on understanding the social and political dynamic of legitimacy, rather than the philosophical inquiry into what forms of governance are "just," reflects the lack of consensus on the latter and the potentially persuasive allegations implicit in the former.

An ironic consequence of this normative ambiguity is that the process by which concerns about illegitimacy are addressed may become the best substitute for consensus about what is legitimate. This observation also explains why my attempt here to provide an account of a dynamic shades into process serving as a strategy for reconciliation, which perhaps could lead to consensus at least as to what is illegitimate. *See, e.g.,* HAAS, *supra* note 19, at 193 ("Moral progress, if it is to be attained by means associated with international organizations, must be defined in procedural terms.").

[21] In an approach focusing on the social phenomenon of legitimacy, "[t]he legitimacy of an order of domination is measured against the *belief* in its legitimacy on the part of those subject to the domination." Habermas, *Legitimation, supra* note 19, at 199. For HAAS, *supra* note 19, at 87, legitimacy similarly, but perhaps with more calculation by those accepting it, "exists when the membership values the organization and generally implements collective decisions because they are seen to serve the members' values."

[22] In this sense, statements voicing mistrust or suspicion of the motives of the permanent members of the Council represent related manifestations of negative assessments of the Council.

[23] Both Franck's and Haas's comments on legitimacy, as indeed my own, are based on a theoretical, nonempirical inquiry. None of us, except on rare occasions, ask states or persons independent of states whether they view an international organization as legitimate or not, why they do so, and whether and how such a perception may influence their future relation with the organization. Professor Tyler's *Why People Obey the Law* is of particular interest to the present inquiry because it is based on empirical research, the questioning of 1,575 citizens in the Chicago area. To the surprise of the domestic realists who tend to speak in terms of greater and more certain punishment as the prime determinant of compliance, Professor Tyler concludes:

> People obey the law because they believe that it is proper to do so, they react to their experiences by evaluating their justice or injustice, and in evaluating the justice of their experiences they consider factors unrelated to outcome, such as whether they have had a chance to state their case and been treated with dignity and respect.

TYLER, *supra* note 19, at 178. Some of Tyler's conclusions arguably stem from human psychology generally, and others—perhaps most—seem deeply rooted in the social values of the study group. Thus, among the lessons to take from his work are the importance of the empirical approach and the conclusion that the perception of legitimacy was influenced significantly by whether there was procedural justice.

within the full scope of its agenda?[24] Or is the concern with illegitimacy over-stated? Is the truth of the matter that the effectiveness of an institution such as the Security Council can withstand occasional perceptions of illegitimacy? As Haas observes, "States may grudgingly meet the organization's expectations with-out at the same time appreciating or valuing them."[25]

Although a general account of the determinants of the significance of percep-tions of illegitimacy is not available, one can hypothesize how such perceptions may bear on the effectiveness of an organization. Let me suggest five examples of how perceptions of illegitimacy may work against the effectiveness of the Security Council. First, they may lead to failure to pass a resolution—not necessarily be-cause the underlying objective is questioned, but because of suspicion about the details and where it will lead. Second and more likely, such perceptions may lead to a refusal to adopt as strong a resolution. Third, they may make it difficult for states to build the domestic support necessary to act under a resolution. For example, because of such perceptions, a state may have trouble convincing its citizenry that granting landing rights to aircraft en route to a UN-authorized action is supportive of community concerns rather than the thinly veiled imperial-ism of the Council's permanent members. Fourth, such perceptions may lead states to move more slowly in supporting a resolution, in terms of the sending of troops, the provision of financial support, or the enforcement of embargoes. Fifth and last, such perceptions may lead either intentionally or accidentally to actions and strategies that weaken the Council.[26]

These possible scenarios are most likely if the perception of illegitimacy is held by a particularly influential actor or shared by a larger group of actors that in the aggregate are influential. Correspondingly, isolated allegations of illegitimacy by actors at the margin of an organization would likely have little significance for the

---

[24] Broadly speaking, a perception of illegitimacy might be said to affect the effectiveness of an institution in two ways. First, it might undercut the perceived legitimacy of the rules that emanate from the institution. Second, it might threaten the future effectiveness of the institution. Thus, the perceived legitimacy of the Security Council may influence both the willingness of states to obey and support particular decisions of the Council and its future use generally. This is particularly so when, as in the case of the Council, the *organizational agenda* itself is controlled primarily by the members and their disposition toward the setting of that agenda may be greatly affected by their perception of the legitimacy of the organization.

[25] HAAS, *supra* note 19, at 87. For a critical view of the practical significance of legitimacy, see generally Hyde, *supra* note 19.

[26] As to the last possibility, it is worth recalling Claude's observation, *supra* note 2, at 368, that "[p]olitics is not merely a struggle for power but also a contest over legitimacy, a competition in which the conferment or denial, the confirmation or revocation, of legitimacy is an important stake." Over what alternatives, then, is there a "contest" in the case of the Security Council? One might conclude that if there is no viable alternative, an allegation of illegitimacy cannot be of much practical signifi-cance. *See* Habermas, *Legitimation, supra* note 19, at 178–79. But the lack of alternatives also may mean that the contest regarding legitimacy involves higher stakes for the organization involved and the issues before it. With no alternate route to promote, the contest ultimately may reduce to the rejection of contemplated action or pressure for reforms by the dissatisfied, not because they have an alternate order to propose, but because they simply desire to move away from the status quo. For their part, states now working through the Council, such as the United States and the United King-dom, in turn may view the refusal of an ineffective Council as not being legitimate and, as a conse-quence, may return to the unilateral imposition of force or sanctions upon the allegedly offending state. *See, e.g.,* Peter Wilenski, *Reforming the United Nations for the Post–Cold War Era, in* WHOSE NEW WORLD ORDER: WHAT ROLE FOR THE UNITED NATIONS? 122, 126 (Mara R. Bustelo & Philip Alston eds., 1991). In both reactions—inaction at the multilateral level or action at the unilateral level—community objectives and tools are lost.

organization as a whole. Assuming that there will always be some actor at the margin who calculatingly alleges that a certain means or act of governance is illegitimate, the issue becomes what influences whether such an allegation resonates with others more influential and thus may lead the allegation to take on greater significance. If actors at the margin often are the "root" of the allegation of illegitimacy, then the "echo" is how other actors, more central and influential, react upon hearing such an allegation. Given the existence of the root, the challenge for governance is to address the likelihood of substantial resonance with others. Given also that the identity of the speaker at the margin, for example, a terrorist state, likely is already discounted by the listener, the task is not to discredit the speaker, but rather to address what gives rise to the receptivity of the listener.[27]

From this perspective, an important question is: what circumstances influence the formation and course of such perceptions?[28] Although the perception of illegitimacy with which we are concerned can spring from the taking of an illegal act, it often seems to arise from a deeper criticism of the organization.[29] Even if an organization acts in accordance with its rules, it nonetheless may be viewed as illegitimate against some broader frame of reference.[30]

In one such frame of reference, allegations of illegitimacy appear to manifest a sense of betrayal of what is believed to be the promise and spirit of the organization.[31] It is this promise and spirit that allows the organization collectively to

---

[27] A difficult aspect of the perception of illegitimacy is the difference in "sophistication" of the different actors. On the one hand, officials with foreign ministries close to and involved with the Council might be thought to be the most sophisticated and tactical. That is, it might be thought that they would accept that the structure and operation of the Council is a matter of power, and indeed it is in that light that they quite consciously would frame their objections to such structure and operation in the language of legitimacy. But at whom is this initiative targeted? If this image of calculating actors is correct, then would not other actors close to the Council see through this ploy or simply discount it? Inasmuch as a substantial part of the critique of the Council turns on domination by the Permanent Five, and alludes to the closed nature of their deliberations and their imperialist pasts, perhaps the answer in the case of the Council, as in most cases, is that even the government representatives are a mix of the insider and the outsider simultaneously both discounting the language of legitimacy and being drawn to the values implicit in such phrasing.

[28] These questions form the core of the inquiry by FRANCK, *supra* note 19, which focuses on the legitimacy of rules. Interestingly, the inquiry appears to change slightly if one's focus is not on increasing the legitimacy of a rule, but rather on countering or anticipating an allegation of illegitimacy. Professor Franck's search for indicators of legitimacy is presumably motivated by a desire to increase the pull toward compliance of rules. However, because an allegation of illegitimacy may be merely a means to oppose an institution or rule, the dominant order does not seek so much to strengthen the pull toward compliance as to preserve the quantum of "belief" it already has.

[29] Weiler, *Transformation*, *supra* note 19, at 2468–69. "The notion of formal legitimacy . . . implies that all requirements of the law are observed . . . . 'Social legitimacy,' on the other hand, connotes a broad, empirically determined societal acceptance of the system." *Id.*

[30] *See* Claude, *supra* note 2, at 368–69 ("Lawyers tend simply to translate legitimacy as *legality* . . . . [But] the legitimacy of the positive law . . . is sometimes the precise issue at stake in a political controversy.").

[31] Although it often can be heard that the United Nations is only a collection of governments, a statement of the majority of the United Nations is for some reason taken as more than a statement of that same majority operating outside the United Nations. Turning that around, we seem to expect the United Nations to act differently than the same nations acting separately. We expect the United Nations, and other organizations of a universal character, to act consistently with the aura we give it.

For example, when the contributors to the International Monetary Fund require that borrowers undertake austerity measures before new loans are made, there is for some a concern regarding the legitimacy of the organization. On the other hand, if such conditions are requested in direct negotia-

legitimate ideas or actions. Such collective legitimation at its worst masks, but in some cases perhaps limits, the extent to which particular actors pursue their own agenda under the banner of collective action. The loss of the perception of legitimacy is tied to loss of the ability to legitimate and consequently results in a reexamination of motives. "If the U.N. loses its credibility, the Security Council would still be able to order governments about, but its orders would have lost their international sheen and look more like big-power bullying."[32] All of these considerations suggest that, although international organizations are not world government and a realist's recognition of power is built into their constitutive documents, these organizations hold the promise of something more than politics as usual.[33] Thus, I would argue that an important area within which perceptions of illegitimacy resonate in the case of international organizations is exemplified by that space between the promises of the preamble to the charter of the organization and the realities of the compromises in the text that follows, a space in which there is discretion regarding the use of authority. In this sense, the belief that there is too great a discrepancy between what the organization promises and what it delivers would be at least one major circumstance permitting the resonance of allegations of illegitimacy. Sometimes—and I would assert this is the case with the veto—the potential to betray the promise is built directly and tragically into the organization.

Similarly, the perception of illegitimacy may spring as easily from not acting as from acting. The critique of the Security Council at present focuses on the legitimacy of its use of authority. However, restricting its use of authority is not necessarily an answer because an ineffective institution in all likelihood would also be perceived—albeit perhaps by different states—as illegitimate. An institution is created for a purpose. To serve that purpose effectively, it is provided a measure of authority.[34] The failure of an institution to govern out of inability to use its

---

tions between one lender and one borrower, then that situation seems subject to at least a different legitimacy critique. The critique used for the international organization seems less applicable in the bilateral case because the power of the lender has not been clothed with the symbols of authority; there is no or little pretense of legitimacy to critique. In the bilateral case, we do not critique the cloak of legitimacy, but rather the motives of power.

[32] *Open the Club, supra* note 12, at 14.

[33] In particular, there is a promise of good faith and honest dealings with one another and in joint undertakings. As Leland Goodrich wrote:

> [T]here is perhaps an excessive tendency today to view the United.Nations simply as a set of organs and procedures made available to its Members in much the same way that various mechanical gadgets are offered to the public as means of making life easier. . . . Of much greater importance than the machinery itself are the basic commitments of Members, the purposes to which the machinery is put, and the spirit which governs its use.

LELAND GOODRICH, KOREA: A STUDY OF U.S. POLICY IN THE UNITED NATIONS 2 (1956).

[34] For Professor HAAS, *supra* note 19, at 87, "authority consists of the ability of the organization to have its decisions implemented irrespective of the goodwill of the members concerned." Professor Weston asserts that Franck's notion of legitimacy "appears to be close to, if not identical with, the meaning of 'authority' as defined by Professors McDougal and Lasswell." Burns H. Weston, *Security Council Resolution 678 and Persian Gulf Decision Making: Precarious Legitimacy*, 85 AJIL 516, 516 n.1 (1991) (citing Myres S. McDougal & Harold Lasswell, *The Identification and Appraisal of Diverse Systems of Public Order*, 53 AJIL 1, 9 (1959)). The many different ways in which these terms are employed in scholarly writings need be approached with care. Professors Haas and Franck apparently agree that "authority" signifies the ability of the organization to coerce compliance, while "legiti-

authority, particularly an institution that represents or aspires to represent a system of order, has long been a basis for alleging that the order is illegitimate because it fails to perform its basic mission. The Council was created to be an effective mechanism for the maintenance of international peace and security, and to that end was granted substantial authority. At the same time, other values such as representation and cohesion of the international community informed the design of the institution that would use that authority. The perceptions of illegitimacy may thus arise from both the failure to use authority effectively and the abuse of authority. Consequently, one must seek an institution that simultaneously can employ its authority effectively and employs it in a manner that is regarded generally as legitimate.

These observations suggest that a basic challenge for international governance is to seek designs that promote institutional integrity, and that consequently address in the ordinary course of business the circumstances that make possible the resonance of allegations of illegitimacy. What are the characteristics of a process of decision with integrity, that may be trusted? How does one ensure that an institution is faithful to the promise of the organization, that is, that it acts with integrity? I would suggest that there are at least four ways.

First, in some instances integrity is promoted by entrusting operation of the organization to persons who can claim to be independent of those governed and to have no interest in a particular outcome. This approach is used to a degree, for example, with the International Court of Justice and the International Law Commission. It is not an option for the Security Council, where the member states are those governed. Second, states entrusted with the operation of the organization may be held accountable for the consequences of their actions. In particular, they may be politically accountable through elections; perhaps past failure to represent the members of the Assembly generally should be or has been a factor in the election of nonpermanent members of the Council. Third, an institution may also be accountable in that a court, an entity whose integrity is assured via independence, reviews the institution's decisions. But here, the competence of the International Court of Justice to review the performance of the Council appears to be quite circumscribed.[35] Fourth, integrity may be promoted by providing the opportunity for representative participation and fostering an ongoing dialogue as to the legitimacy of any action. In other words, the discussion regarding legitimacy moves into the decision-making process itself.

These observations also suggest methodologically that an organization confronted with allegations of illegitimacy that strike a responsive chord in some quarters needs to identify what circumstances give rise to that resonance and how those circumstances might be addressed. Consequently, parts II and III respectively consider (1) what circumstances concerning the Council appear to provide the basis for resonance of questions regarding legitimacy, and (2) whether the proposed reforms address those circumstances. Part IV, in considering the reverse veto, seeks to promote integrity in the decision-making process by suggest-

---

macy" is evidenced at least in part by the willingness of those governed to comply or, I would assume, by the willingness of those governed to coerce compliance by their peers.

[35] *See* W. Michael Reisman, *The Constitutional Crisis in the United Nations*, 87 AJIL 83 (1993). *But see* Thomas M. Franck, *The "Powers of Appreciation": Who Is the Ultimate Guardian of UN Legality?*, 86 AJIL 519 (1992); and Geoffrey R. Watson, *Constitutionalism, Judicial Review, and the World Court*, 34 HARV. INT'L L.J. 1 (1993).

ing practices that may further an ongoing dialogue as to the legitimacy of any particular action.

As it is both difficult and simplistic to characterize one's task as observation alone, so also is it simplistic to focus on the relation of process to perceptions of illegitimacy without considering the substance of what is being discussed in relation to those perceptions. As noted above, there is substantial work in progress on elaborating principled bases for intervention, and I believe that work on both the principles at play and the process of decision needs to be undertaken. I emphasize process in this article, however, because even in the face of agreement on the principles to be applied—and in many cases substantial agreement already exists—legitimacy concerns often arise in relation to the details of their application to a particular case.[36] Successful outcomes will go far in painting over perceived defects in the process of decision. It is ultimately the process, however, that may allow participants who are somewhat distrustful of one another to believe in and support the organization.

II. CHALLENGES TO THE LEGITIMACY OF THE SECURITY COUNCIL

The Security Council through its decisions can both legitimate and legislate. It can legitimate the actions of others because it can purport to authorize those actions on behalf of the United Nations. It legislates in that its decisions potentially bind all states—both members of the United Nations that are not then sitting on the Security Council and states that do not belong to the United Nations at all. In short, the Council has substantial authority.

The current challenge to the legitimacy of the Security Council's use of that authority may be seen to have at least two major dimensions. Giving rise to each of these dimensions are a number of circumstances. Some of these circumstances are often discussed, others rarely mentioned, and one—crucially important in my view—has gone virtually unnoted. Although not wholly separate, the two broad dimensions of the challenge to the legitimacy of the Security Council's use of its authority reflect the perceptions (1) that the Council is dominated by a few states, and (2) that the veto held by the permanent members is unfair. The next two sections examine these two dimensions, ultimately identifying five circumstances that give rise to them. In considering these dimensions and circumstances, one should bear in mind the potential perception in the background referred to in part I; namely, a Council that fails to employ its authority effectively will also be viewed as illegitimate.

The Perception of Dominance of the Council by a Few States

A major charge against the Security Council is that it is dominated by several of the permanent members.[37] Interestingly, although the Council's voting rules require that at least nine of the fifteen members must vote in favor of an action potentially binding all the members of the United Nations, it nonetheless suffers from the allegation of dominance by a subgroup of two, possibly three, or sometimes all five permanent members.[38] At least ten, but most often thirteen or

---

[36] *Accord* Claude, *supra* note 2, at 369–70.

[37] "America, Britain and France dominate decision-making; Russia is out of things and China intent on its own affairs." *Open the Club, supra* note 12, at 14.

[38] Childers, *supra* note 10, at 133 ("No longer is it morally possible for democratic people to accept that 5 out of 165 member governments can have such deadly power in the name of a peace-dedicated world organization.").

fourteen, members of the Council voted in favor of all its recent decisions, but the legitimacy concerns expressed tend to focus on the United States, France and the United Kingdom. The assumption appears to be that, although Third World countries such as Colombia and Malaysia also voted in favor of the resolutions authorizing force against Iraq and were, with others, necessary to the passage of those resolutions, the Council is in fact dominated by certain members that, if motivated, can get a resolution adopted.

Thus, on the Libyan sanctions, Badi M. Ali, Chairman of the Islamic Committee for Palestine–North Carolina, wrote that "the United Nations has been brought in to do the dirty work of the British-American alliance against the Muslim world and third world countries."[39] As pointed out above, there will always be dissenting voices to the use of collective authority. What is important is whether such challenges to legitimacy, for whatever reason they are voiced, echo in the concerns of others. For example, the recent concerns of three U.S. political scientists do not conflict with, and could be said to support, the charge made by Mr. Ali: "The real problem was that leadership turned into headship, where decisions for the group are arrived at unilaterally by a leader whose overweening power ensures that subordinates will have few other options than to comply."[40] Or as Burns Weston observed, "the process by which Security Council Resolution 678 was won, while perhaps legally correct *stricto sensu*, confirms how complete the power of the United States over the UN policing mechanism had become in the absence of Cold War opposition."[41]

At first blush, it might seem that the need to have nonpermanent members, in a significant number of cases from the developing world, join the permanent members in voting for a particular measure would block dominance of the Council by one, two, or even five states. This statement presumes, however, that each member's decision about its vote is independent. Thus, one can imagine a member asserting that, even though its vote formally was needed for passage, the actual process of voting was dominated by a subgroup. Less extreme, and probably closer to the mark, would be the assertion that these nonpermanent members were broadly in agreement with the need to act, but not necessarily with all the particulars of the draft resolution. In this situation, dominance consists of the ability to push a *certain* proposal through to adoption.

Although not articulated by those concerned, this dominance can be seen as arising in three ways that should be carefully distinguished.

First, dominance can result from the power of the permanent members in international affairs generally. The power of the permanent members generally in the world potentially allows them outside the Council to influence the behavior of states within the Council. Professor Weston recounted, for example, various reports of U.S. promises of rewards and threats of punishment outside the Council so as to influence the vote on Resolution 678 authorizing the use of force against Iraq.[42] Importantly, just as it is alleged that the United States in essence bought

---

[39] Ali, *supra* note 12.

[40] Andrew F. Cooper, Richard A. Higgott & Kim R. Nossal, *Bound to Follow? Leadership and Fellowship in the Gulf Conflict*, 106 POL. SCI. Q. 391, 407 (1991).

[41] Weston, *supra* note 34, at 525.

[42] *Id.* at 523–25. His list includes the promise of financial help to Colombia, Côte d'Ivoire, Ethiopia and Zaire; agreement with the Soviet Union "to help keep Estonia, Latvia, and Lithuania out of the November 1990 Paris summit conference"; a pledge to the Soviet Union to persuade Kuwait and Saudi Arabia to provide it with desperately needed hard currency; and, to secure Chinese abstention

votes, so is it as possible that some states demanded that their votes be bought. In any event, allegations of influence or demands outside the Council have not resurfaced in regard to the proceedings that followed the adoption of Resolution 678. In this sense, Resolution 678, and the urgency attached by the United States to its passage, may be the exception rather than the rule. However, the wielding of such power in international affairs need not be overt. It is generally in the interest of small states not to alienate the permanent members.

Second, dominance can result from the capabilities of the permanent members within the Council. The staffing capabilities of the permanent members within the Council allows them disproportionately to influence the outcome of its proceedings. The delegations of the nonpermanent members can simply be overwhelmed by delegations of members such as the United States. As in litigation where one side can afford what is relatively a vast amount of assistance, the initiative resides with those with the greatest capabilities. The other side is reduced to trying to respond to the initiatives of the more capable. Thus, the drafts under discussion are offered by permanent members, and the scheduling of meetings and informal discussions is quite naturally dominated by those most able to attend. The situation is aggravated substantially by the permanent members' practice of working out most decisions in informal consultations among themselves.[43]

This is not to say that the capabilities of certain states within the Council should be curbed dramatically. Indeed, given the hesitancy, if not passivity, of others, it can be strongly argued that if certain states did not draft and then push resolutions, nothing would be passed, and the organization would be ineffective. It is to suggest, however, that we need to look to how institutional structures may ensure that all the members of the Council play a role in its task of governance despite differences in capabilities.

Moreover, the relatively much stronger capabilities of the Permanent Five within the Council are accentuated even further when a sense of urgency focuses the Council's efforts on quick passage of a resolution. As has been apparent in the Council's action regarding the conflict in the former Yugoslavia, the longer a response is considered, the greater the influence of nonpermanent members can become.[44] Also accentuating this aspect of dominance is the historical weakness of the Secretary-General as a referee in the Council acting to redress imbalances in capability.[45]

Third, dominance by a group of states can result from disproportionate representation of that group on the Council. Representatives of states other than permanent

---

in the Council, agreement to lift trade sanctions in place since the Tiananmen Square massacre and to support a World Bank loan of $114.3 million to China. Finally, Weston cites the report that, as a result of Yemen's negative vote on Resolution 678, the United States said it would cut off its $70 million in annual aid to that state.

[43] *See* Reisman, *supra* note 35. *See also* Loie Feuerle, Note, *Informal Consultation: A Mechanism in Security Council Decision-Making*, 18 N.Y.U. J. INT'L L. & POL. 267 (1985).

[44] *See, e.g.,* Paul Lewis, *U.N., With Abstention by Russia, Tightens Its Sanctions on Belgrade*, N.Y. TIMES, Apr. 18, 1993, §1, at 1 (referring to the important role of Venezuela, Cape Verde, Morocco, Djibouti and Pakistan). However, in the case of the former Yugoslavia, the nonpermanent members not only had more time to develop their position, but also had greater room to maneuver since the permanent members were reluctant to take forceful action against Serbia.

[45] But the role of the Secretary-General is certainly evolving in a more active direction. See the range of discussion and proposals in THE CHALLENGING ROLE OF THE UN SECRETARY-GENERAL: MAKING "THE MOST IMPOSSIBLE JOB IN THE WORLD" POSSIBLE (Benjamin Rivlin & Leon Gordenker eds., 1993).

members sometimes maintain that the Council does not hold its authority legitimately because its composition is "not representative." This conclusion is reached often by a logic that one hopes is confined to the United Nations. Simply put, the argument runs that, since there are more states now than there used to be, there should be a corresponding proportional increase in the size of the Council.[46] The more satisfying explanation is that, although a Council of fifteen could be "representative," the Council as currently constituted is not representative. Moreover, because it is very hard to redistribute the present membership pie, initiatives necessarily seek to regain representativeness through a remedial increase in the pie. Interestingly, representatives who express this view focus far more on "representation" than "dominance" even within the present scheme of representation, a circumstance likely explained by the fact that their prime motive is to increase the opportunity for membership on the Council.

Despite the possibility of such other motives for this position, the dominance of a group of states over the Council's proceedings certainly could be possible because of their disproportionate representation in the Council's membership. However, I do not think this possibility explains the dynamic now at work in the Council. As discussed more fully below, when present proposals for increasing the size of the Council are evaluated, they do not appear either to mitigate significantly the permanent members' dominance or to alter significantly the current distribution of representation.

The Perception of Unfairness Surrounding the Veto

Concern over the veto has dominated discussion of the Council since its birth. The essential insight to be sought is how concern over the veto has been transformed by the end of the Cold War. Previously, the primary concern centered on how the veto prevented the Council from doing anything. The concern in the currently more active times has not been fully articulated, but I suggest that it has two aspects.

First, the five holders of the veto, and whatever states any of the five is willing to shield, potentially are free from the governance of the Council. Since for almost all of the Council's existence it did not act, the freedom from governance of some was not a significant problem because few states, if any, were governed by it.[47] But as the Council begins to function, the question becomes: are there states that will be governed and states that will not? The ability of the Security Council to take decisions binding on the community as a whole in the area of peace and security is a strong form of governance. The veto means, however, that certain members of the community potentially are not governed. In the context of the Council's actions in response to Iraq's invasion of Kuwait, the question for many became: is there a double standard—will the Council be as assertive with Israel as it was with

---

[46] Another argument raised is that, inasmuch as the Council has more work to do, it should have more members. To the contrary, more members might only generate more work in terms of coordination, and more work seems to suggest a need for an increase in staff rather than membership.

[47] It is of course a simplification to say there was no governance or no concern with double standards prior to the recent activity of the Council. Previously, the charge of a double standard generally involved the willingness of UN members to criticize the West and Israel, but not socialist or other Third World states. *See* Thomas M. Franck, *Of Gnats and Camels: Is There a Double Standard at the United Nations?*, 78 AJIL 811 (1984); Theo van Boven, Letter to the Editor, 79 AJIL 714 (1985).

Iraq?[48] When the Council acted against Libya, the question became: is it only the Arab world that is so governed? There is no simple answer to these questions, but the permanent presence of some members, with vetoes, clearly gives a privileged position to a few.

Second, the veto distorts any governance undertaken because it severely limits the basis of possible discourse. Such distortion is discussed in detail in part IV. What is important to see here is that this impact of the veto reinforces the perception and reality of dominance of the Council by the permanent members.

The Five Challenges

There are thus five challenges to the legitimacy of the Council's use of its authority:

- The perception of dominance of the Security Council by a few states

  1. Dominance because of the power of those states in international affairs generally
  2. Dominance because of the capabilities of those states within the Council
  3. Dominance because of the disproportionate representation of those states on the Council

- The perception of unfairness surrounding the veto

  4. Unfairness because of the possibility of a double standard in governance
  5. Unfairness and dominance because of the disabling effect of the veto on the sense of participatory governance

III. EVALUATING PROPOSALS FOR REFORM

Having sketched the circumstances that give rise to perceptions of illegitimacy, I consider in this section the degree to which suggested reforms might rectify the problem. This task is particularly important because the motives behind some of the reform proposals have little to do with remedying the circumstances underlying concerns about legitimacy.

Ideally, reform should promote the international community's objective in the Council: an effective mechanism for the maintenance of international peace and security.[49] And, as asserted in part I, the perception of legitimacy regarding the authority necessary for such a mechanism is desirable for both short- and long-term effectiveness. Now that the Council is acting, legitimacy arguably is essential

---

[48] *See, e.g.*, Youssef M. Ibrahim, *Many Arabs See "Double Standard,"* N.Y. TIMES, Jan. 15, 1993, at A8; Clyde Haberman, *And Even Some Israelis Agree With Them, id. See also* Childers, *supra* note 10, at 136 ("[I]t has been the blatant use of double standards in the invocation of UN principles against Iraq that has so eroded the confidence of the Southern majority of humankind in the world organization."). A more diplomatic and positive phrasing of the question can be found in the statement of the Colombian representative before the Council as Resolution 678 authorizing the use of force against Iraq was adopted: "We hope that this climate of understanding will be maintained and will serve as a basis for the decisions that the Security Council may have to take in the future so as not to have its credibility and effectiveness tarnished through use of a double standard . . . ." UN Doc. S/PV.2963, at 38 (1990).

[49] This objective is evident in the language and drafting history of the UN Charter. *See, e.g.*, UN CHARTER Art. 24 ("primary responsibility for the maintenance of international peace and security, and . . . carrying out its duties [on behalf of the members]").

to ensuring its long-term effectiveness. But just as it seems wrong to gain effectiveness at too great an expense to legitimacy, so does it not make sense to increase legitimacy at the expense of a significant loss in effectiveness. Thus, I will argue, for example, that we should take care in rushing to increase the size of the Council. That states individually desire the status of membership and propose expansion does not mean it makes sense collectively. The Council could probably expand somewhat without significantly decreasing its effectiveness. The issue, however, is: how much could it expand without such a loss? Would a Council of twenty-five members remain effective or would we see the emergence of the unending procedural spirals seemingly endemic to the Second Committee of the General Assembly? As calls for increased membership and other proposals are considered, the relationship of power and legitimacy to effectiveness must be kept in mind.

The fundamental question is: how should the decision-making authority of the Security Council be allocated so as to maximize the effective use of its authority and the perceived legitimacy of that use? The powerful presence of the veto, however, has tended to capture attention in a way that misplaces the focus of both the academic and the diplomatic worlds. Simultaneously, the driving force behind diplomatic concerns often seems to be more the preservation and attainment of status than the efficacy and legitimacy of collective decision. It is the latter concern that falls to the academy. The proposed reforms tend to fall into three broad categories, which will be considered in turn.

Reform of the Veto

Practically speaking, it is quite unlikely that the veto can be eliminated or even significantly limited. Moreover, if one's goal in reforming the veto is to mitigate the possibility of a double standard in governance, any substitute voting procedure will in all likelihood allow some sort of double standard to continue.

The voluminous literature on the Security Council has several branches. A review of these branches helps one to understand why the permanent members of the Council possess a veto and why they probably will continue to do so.

The first branch: the debate over the wisdom of granting vetoes to some states. Much of the early literature focused on the decision to grant a veto to some members of the Council. Initially, this branch revisited the negotiation of the relevant Charter provisions. The negotiation was a matter of politics and, as E. H. Carr would say, consequently involved a confrontation between utopia and reality, morality and power.[50] The permanence of membership of a few and, even more, the veto of those permanent members were perceived *from the outset* by some states as a threat to the legitimacy of the Council's authority.

The significance of membership and voting procedures in international organizations depends directly on the powers of the body and the importance of the issues that will come before it. The importance attached to the structure of the Security Council during the preparation and drafting of the Charter flowed from the recognition that the Council would have both "primary responsibility for the maintenance of international peace and security" and the authority to carry out that responsibility. Agreement among the Allies at Dumbarton Oaks in 1945 on the number of members and the permanent membership of the five major Allied powers did not resolve the question of voting, and the issue in particular became

[50] CARR, text at and note 1 *supra*.

"how to balance what might be called 'democratic' procedures with the realities of the concentration of power among the five permanent members."[51] There was a range of possibilities:

> the inclusion in any affirmative vote of a stated majority of the permanent members, such as three-fifths or four-fifths; the inclusion of two or three of the strongest powers indicated by name; the stipulation of a majority made up of a certain proportion of both the permanent and the non-permanent members; the requirement of unanimity among the great powers plus enough votes of the smaller powers to prevent "dictation" by either group over the other.[52]

The Dumbarton Oaks Conference settled on the last option, requiring a majority of seven of the eleven members (today nine of fifteen), the seven to include the permanent members except with regard to procedural matters.[53]

The work of the Dumbarton Oaks Conference, as elaborated on at Yalta in February 1945, was the starting point for negotiations at the United Nations Conference on International Organization held in San Francisco in May and June of 1945. The proposed voting procedure of the Council was the subject of extensive negotiation, as seventeen of the forty-four states present offered amendments to it. Faced ultimately with the belief that the conference would fail if any other voting procedure was chosen, the participants adopted the Yalta formula.[54]

The debate over the wisdom of this initial decision can be found in much of the literature. At its core, the debate sets "internationalists," who in essence opposed the veto as a superpower obstacle to a truly functioning United Nations, against "realists," who viewed the agreement of each of the major powers as politically wise and necessary to the undertaking of action by the Security Council.

The second branch: the veto in practice. The existence and likely continuation of the veto produced an offshoot of the first branch, the study of the use of the veto. At first, this was an extension of the internationalists' literature, focusing on what many regarded as the abusive obstructionary use of the veto and possible mechanisms for limiting that use. Indeed, the veto quickly proved to be much more of a problem than even the more pessimistic of the delegations at the San Francisco Conference had probably foreseen.[55] One abusive phenomenon particularly stud-

---

[51] Dwight E. Lee, *The Genesis of the Veto*, 1 INT'L ORG. 33, 35 (1947).

[52] *Id.*

[53] Left unresolved at Dumbarton Oaks and preventing agreement generally on voting at that time was whether a member, particularly a permanent member, of the Council could vote when it was a party to the dispute under consideration. The recent experience of the League of Nations, particularly the vote of Italy blocking action against it under Article 11 of the Covenant, loomed large. In February 1945 at Yalta, a compromise formula was agreed upon by the United States, the United Kingdom and the Soviet Union: a member of the Council that was a party to the dispute under consideration would abstain from voting in efforts at peaceful settlement (what came to fall under chapter VI of the Charter) or efforts to encourage such settlement by regional arrangements or agencies (Article 52(3) of the Charter). This meant, however, that the member need not abstain from voting when stronger measures aimed at peace enforcement were contemplated (what came to be governed by chapter VII of the Charter).

[54] The fight during the negotiations, however, did yield the oft-cited and much-debated Statement by the Delegations of the Four Sponsoring Governments on Voting Procedure in the Security Council, explaining their understanding of the Yalta formula. *See, e.g.,* Leo Gross, *Double Veto and the Four-Power Statement on Voting in the Security Council,* 67 HARV. L. REV. 251 (1953).

[55] Although Sydney Bailey asserts that "the United Nations has been hamstrung by the veto neither as frequently nor as decisively as has sometimes been suggested." SYDNEY BAILEY, VOTING IN THE SECURITY COUNCIL 62 (1969).

ied was the "double veto." Article 27 of the Charter establishes two voting procedures, one for procedural matters and one for "all other matters." The existence of two voting procedures necessarily engenders a "border" question, that is, which of the procedures applies in a given situation and which voting procedure is to be used to decide that preliminary question. The double veto was the term coined for the employment of the veto to block the characterization of any question as "procedural."[56]

The main limitations on the scope of the veto involved the decision in practice to regard abstentions or the failure of a permanent member to vote as a "concurring vote,"[57] and the effort by the General Assembly in the early years of the Organization to limit the range of subject matter to which the veto was applicable.[58]

More recently, the study of the veto in practice has seen an increase in empirical examination of its use,[59] a trend that in all likelihood reflects the ultimately discouraging recognition that the veto is essentially immune from reform.

The third branch: the difficulty of amending the Charter. The difficulty of amending the Charter, and hence reforming the veto, can be taken to explain the evolution of the literature. This difficulty also may explain why this third branch of the literature is comparatively a trickle,[60] although it should not justify the absence of scholarly attention.

Basically, the internationalists, in seeking to alter the veto practice, needed to call for an amendment to the Charter, and the unlikelihood of success in this regard ultimately led their debate with the realists to recede to the margins of discourse. The debate became dormant largely because there appeared to be little chance that the permanent members would ever relinquish the veto. To call for

[56] *See* Alexander W. Rudzinski, *The So-Called Double Veto,* 45 AJIL 443 (1951); Marion K. Kellogg, *The Laos Question: Double What Veto?,* 45 VA. L. REV. 1352 (1959); Leo Gross, *Question of Laos and the Double Veto in the Security Council,* 54 AJIL 118 (1960) (Editorial Comment); Alan R. Feldstein, Comment, *The Double Veto in the Security Council: A New Approach,* 18 BUFF. L. REV. 550 (1968–69); and Franciszek Przetacznik, *The Double Veto of the Security Council of the United Nations: A New Appraisal,* 58 REVUE DE DROIT INTERNATIONAL DE SCIENCES DIPLOMATIQUES, POLITIQUES ET SOCIALES 153 (1980).

[57] *See* Yuen-li Liang, *Abstention and Absence of a Permanent Member in Relation to the Voting Procedure in the Security Council,* 44 AJIL 694 (1950); Myres S. McDougal & Richard Gardner, *The Veto and the Charter: An Interpretation for Survival,* 60 YALE L.J. 258 (1951); Leo Gross, *Voting in the Security Council: Abstention from Voting and Absence from Meetings, id.* at 209; Constantin A. Stavropoulos, *The Practice of Voluntary Abstentions by Permanent Members of the Security Council Under Article 27(3),* 61 AJIL 737 (1967); Sydney Bailey, *New Light on Abstentions in the UN Security Council,* 50 INT'L AFF. 554 (1974); and Charles G. Nelson, *Revisionism and the Security Council Veto,* 28 INT'L ORG. 539 (1974).

[58] *See* FRANCIS O. WILCOX & CARL M. MARCY, PROPOSALS FOR CHANGES IN THE UNITED NATIONS 317–19 (1955); BAILEY, *supra* note 55, at 48–52, 112–35.

[59] *See, e.g.,* ANJALI V. PATIL, THE UN VETO IN WORLD AFFAIRS 1946–1990 (1992); James E. Todd, *An Analysis of Security Council Voting Behavior,* 22 W. POL. Q. 61 (1969); and Robert S. Junn & Tong-Whan Park, *Calculus for Voting Power in the UN Security Council,* 58 SOC. SCI. Q. 104 (1977).

[60] *See, e.g.,* Egon Schwelb, *Amendments to Articles 23, 27 and 61 of the Charter of the United Nations,* 59 AJIL 834 (1965); *idem., The 1963–1965 Amendments to the Charter of the United Nations: An Addendum,* 60 AJIL 371 (1966); *idem., The Amending Procedure of Constitutions of International Organizations,* 31 BRIT. Y.B. INT'L L. 89 (1954); *idem., Charter Review and Charter Amendment: Recent Developments,* 7 INT'L & COMP. L.Q. 303 (1958); *idem., The Question of a Time Limit for the Ratification of Amendments to the Charter of the United Nations,* 4 INT'L & COMP. L.Q. 475 (1955); Emile Giraud, *La Revision de la Charte des Nations Unies,* 90 RECUEIL DES COURS 311 (1956 II); Jyrki Kivisto, Amendments to the Charter of the United Nations (1968) (unpublished LL.M. thesis, University of California at Berkeley).

amending the Charter on the subject of the veto came to be viewed as naive. To some degree, it would still be regarded as naive. Indeed, Sydney Bailey, a leading authority on the Council, wrote in 1992 that "I know of no evidence that any of the five permanent members is at present willing to give up the right of veto."[61] Thus, it is not surprising that empirical studies in recent years came to prevail in the literature on the veto.

Ernst Haas has emphasized, however, that many events that until quite recently were thought highly unlikely—such as the fall of the Berlin Wall and the breakup of the Soviet Union—have come about and so, too, may the permanent members be convinced in the not-so-distant future to relinquish the veto.[62] Moreover, he stated, it is the place of the academy to prepare for this possibility, to devise the alternative arrangement of voting that will both facilitate such a change and make it successful. His return to the basic issues is welcome and appropriate, although he probably would agree that how the willingness of the permanent members to relinquish the veto might arise is as yet unclear.

Procedurally, the permanent members have a veto over any effort to take away their right of veto.[63] Thus, both the foreign ministries and the entities involved in the domestic ratification process of all the permanent members must concur in an amendment to do away with or limit the veto. In some ways, this provision was objected to even more than the veto itself at the San Francisco Conference in 1945.[64]

Let us, despite the difficulty of amendment, assume for a moment that the new U.S. administration asked for an assessment of whether the United States should seek to eliminate the veto. What would that assessment be? What would the United States gain by relinquishing the veto? The primary gain would be the relinquishment of the veto by all the other permanent members and thus assurance that the Council would not fall back into the paralysis that gripped it during the Cold War. How much gain is that? If the Council were once again to be paralyzed, could not the United States simply return to the unilateral imposition of sanctions or force? The United States, for example, reportedly wrote in December 1992 to President Slobodan Milošević of Serbia that, "[i]n the event of conflict in Kosovo caused by Serbian action, the United States will be prepared to employ military force against the Serbs in Kosovo and in Serbia proper."[65] De-

---

[61] Sydney Bailey, *The Security Council, in* THE UNITED NATIONS AND HUMAN RIGHTS 304, 324 (Philip Alston ed., 1992).

[62] Ernst Haas, Will the New UN Lead Us to a New World Order?, lecture delivered at the Institute of International Studies, University of California at Berkeley (Nov. 2, 1992).

[63] Article 108 of the Charter provides:

> Amendments to the present Charter shall come into force for all Members of the United Nations when they have been adopted by a vote of two thirds of the members of the General Assembly and ratified in accordance with their respective constitutional processes by two thirds of the Members of the United Nations, *including all the permanent members* of the Security Council. (Emphasis added)

To the same effect, see UN CHARTER Art. 109(2).

[64] *See* GOODRICH, HAMBRO & SIMONS, *supra* note 3, at 638–39.

[65] David Binder, *Bush Warns Serbs Not to Widen War*, N.Y. TIMES, Dec. 28, 1992, at A6; *see also* Elaine Sciolino, *Aides Give Clinton Bosnia Peace Plan*, N.Y. TIMES, Feb. 9, 1993, at A14 (reiteration by Clinton administration of warning to Serbia by Bush administration). This warning, however, although forceful, is not without ambiguity as to whether UN authorization for such a use of force would be sought. *See also* Douglas Jehl, *U.S. Turns Bosnia Threat Into a Near Ultimatum*, N.Y. TIMES, Aug. 4, 1993, at A1.

spite the fact that it could return to unilateral action, the assistance the United States gains through the Security Council's collective legitimation of an action should not be minimized. Authorization to board ships so as to enforce a regime of sanctions, for example, was an important aid in both the Iraqi and the Serbian cases—and a provision whose loss at the last moment was particularly noted in the Haitian case.[66] Similarly, the request that all states aid those states acting in concert with Kuwait during the Persian Gulf war reportedly eased the way for the United States in several instances.[67]

What is lost by relinquishing the veto? The United States becomes subject, like everyone else, to the governance of the Security Council. But we must bear in mind that an alternate, and probably quite complicated, voting arrangement would replace the present one; the United States, while lacking a veto, would likely need only a few other votes to protect itself. Yet we might ask why the United States might feel the need to shield itself absolutely from such governance, i.e., do we anticipate acting in such a manner that even our closest allies would not vote with us? This brings us to the one advantage that probably would be lost, namely, the ability to shield Israel from the governance of the Council. Here, hope for relinquishment of the veto resides in the possibility that a general settlement in the Middle East may not be far off.

Assuming that the United States would be convinced by analysis along the lines stated above, could the international community induce the United Kingdom, France, Russia and China to make similar moves? China, absorbed with maintaining internal order, would likely oppose relinquishing its veto (although, here too, fundamental change may not be that far off). Moreover, if Russia recalls its desire to shield Serbia from stronger Council actions in the spring of 1993[68] and China recalls its opposition during the same period to Council sanctions against North Korea because of likely nuclear proliferation,[69] both may oppose relinquishment of the veto.

Yet even if elimination of the veto altogether is not possible, it may be possible to limit its use. Significant limitations likely would run into the obstacles posed above. Perhaps a feasible limitation would be to eliminate the veto in the election of the Secretary-General.

In sum, despite the calls for change, it must be recognized that it will be difficult to amend the Charter, particularly if the amendment seeks to eliminate the veto or restrict it in any significant way. Consequently, the pressures for change in

---

[66] French, *supra* note 7. Such authorization was also of concern in the case of Southern Rhodesian sanctions. *See* Vera Gowlland-Debbas, Commentary on the Report on the Use of Economic Sanctions by the UN Security Council (presented at the Second Verzijl Symposium, Feb. 19, 1993).

[67] Paragraph 3 of SC Res. 678, *supra* note 14, "[r]equest[ed] all States to provide appropriate support for the actions undertaken in pursuance of paragraph 2." Officials involved with Operations Desert Shield and Desert Storm indicated to the author that this provision was helpful in gaining rights of overflight and permission for landing and refueling of aircraft.

[68] *See* Paul Lewis, *U.S. Seeks Tougher Sanctions on Yugoslavia*, N.Y. TIMES, Apr. 7, 1993, at A6; Paul Lewis, *Security Council Delays Action Against Serbs*, N.Y. TIMES, Apr. 13, 1993, at A8; Elaine Sciolino, *U.S. Agrees to Delay in Voting on Serbia Sanctions*, N.Y. TIMES, Apr. 13, 1993, at A9; Paul Lewis, *Russians Resisting Tighter Sanctions Against Belgrade: May Thwart Vote at U.N.*, N.Y. TIMES, Apr. 9, 1993, at A1; Paul Lewis, *Russia Seeks to Delay Vote on Belgrade Sanctions*, N.Y. TIMES, Apr. 12, 1993, at A8; Michael Gordon, *Russia Declines to Support Tighter Sanctions on Serbia*, N.Y. TIMES, Apr. 18, 1993, §1, at 8.

[69] *See* Nicholas D. Kristof, *China Opposes Sanctions in North Korea Dispute*, N.Y. TIMES, Mar. 24, 1993, at A8; and Nicholas D. Kristof, *China and North Korea: Not-So-Best Friends*, N.Y. TIMES, Apr. 11, 1993, §4, at 4.

the decision-making process in the Security Council will likely focus on other proposals, in particular expansion of its membership.

Increasing the Membership of the Security Council

Most of the proposals for reform have been directed at dealing with the perceived imbalance in control of the Council, in particular its alleged domination by the West. In the main, however, these proposals do not seek to curb the strength of the West in the process but, rather, somehow to increase the strength of others.

Thus, one line of proposals calls for an increase in the size of the Council, in many cases with permanent status being given to the major regional powers in the developing world. Former Soviet President Mikhail S. Gorbachev, in his 1992 address at Westminster College, the site of Winston Churchill's "Iron Curtain" speech, advocated expanding the Security Council to include such states as India, Japan, Poland, Mexico, Germany, Brazil, Canada, Indonesia and Egypt.[70] Shortly after taking office, the Clinton administration indicated that "it favors allowing Germany and Japan to have permanent seats,"[71] and this past June informed them that it would soon start a campaign to that end.[72] Numerous other calls for similar expansions of the membership have been made,[73] some of them over a decade ago.[74] The General Assembly is expected to hold a major debate on increasing the Council's size in the fall of 1993.[75]

With the purpose of the Security Council and the memory of the League's experience in mind, the delegates to the United Nations Conference on International Organization generally accepted that the Council's membership should be representative of the entire membership, yet also able to summon up the concerted military power of the international community.[76] Ultimately, the Charter as agreed upon in San Francisco provided that the six nonpermanent members of the eleven-member Council would be elected for a term of two years by the

[70] Francis X. Clines, *At Site of "Iron Curtain" Speech, Gorbachev Buries the Cold War,* N.Y. TIMES, May 7, 1992, at A1.

[71] Paul Lewis, *U.S. Backs Council Seats for Bonn and Tokyo,* N.Y. TIMES, Jan. 30, 1993, at 4.

[72] Paul Lewis, *U.S. to Push Germany and Japan for U.N. Council,* N.Y. TIMES, June 13, 1993, §1, at 7.

[73] *See, e.g.,* Martín C. Ortega Carcelén, *La Reforma de la Carta de Naciones Unidas: Algunas Propuestas Institucionales,* 43 REVISTA ESPAÑOLA DE DERECHO INTERNACIONAL 389, 400 (1991) (recommending the addition of India, Germany and Japan).

[74] As Australia's Permanent Representative to the United Nations wrote:

[D]uring the 1979 General Assembly India proposed that the non-permanent members be expanded from ten to fourteen, with the four extra to come from the African Group (up from two to five), and the Asian and Latin American Groups (both up by one to three). All the Permanent Five except China were opposed to any expansion.

Wilenski, *supra* note 26, at 126.

[75] Lewis, *supra* note 72.

[76] At the Dumbarton Oaks Conference in 1945, the memory of the inability of the League of Nations to act decisively against Italy impressed upon the delegates that the Council must be small enough as not to be unwieldy and that the requirement of unanimity—even in such a small group—would likely render the Council ineffective. As to the drafting history of the membership and voting structure of the Security Council, see Francis O. Wilcox, *The Rule of Unanimity in the Security Council,* 40 ASIL PROC. 51 (1946); James B. Reston, *Votes and Vetoes,* 25 FOREIGN AFF. 13 (1946); B. A. Wortley, *The Veto and the Security Provisions of the Charter,* 23 BRIT. Y.B. INT'L L. 95 (1946); Hans Kelsen, *Organization and Procedure of the Security Council of the United Nations,* 59 HARV. L. REV. 1087 (1946); Yuen-li Liang, *The Settlement of Disputes in the Security Council: The Yalta Voting Formula,* 24 BRIT. Y.B. INT'L L. 330 (1947); and Lee, *supra* note 51.

General Assembly, with "due regard being specially paid, in the first instance to the contribution of Members of the United Nations to the maintenance of international peace and security . . . and also to equitable geographical representation."[77] The membership of the Council was increased to its present level of fifteen in 1963 by raising the number of nonpermanent members from six to ten.[78]

The new proposals seek to increase the Council again, this time perhaps quite substantially. Often a total of twenty members is sought; occasionally, as many as twenty-five. But how do such proposals further the objective of maximizing both the effectiveness and the legitimacy of the Council?

Would an increase in membership lead to a stronger perception of legitimacy? Why should we think that having more states would lead to less domination? One way that increased membership results in less domination of the process is by reducing the frequency of turns for the permanent members to fill the rotating presidency of the Council. This effect concerned the permanent members at the time of the last increase in the Council's size.[79] But increased membership otherwise might not increase perceptions of legitimacy. If Colombia and Malaysia cannot at present be said to represent the developing world, would the addition of three more representatives of the developing world do so? Or would it simply increase the number of countries the United States would need to convince to go along with a resolution? What is it that makes a nonpermanent member of the Council also a representative of the remaining members of the Assembly?

Moreover, as mentioned, many of the proposals to increase the membership are aimed at bringing particular states into the Council. The permanent addition of Germany and Japan would only seem to strengthen the ability of the permanent members to dominate the Council: Germany and Japan presumably would participate in informal consultations; they would bring their power in international affairs with them, which could influence the disposition of the nonpermanent members; and they would add their staffing capabilities to those of the present permanent members. In addition, if the other new members are regional powers, then representation, at least in terms of representing the perspective of small states, would not be increased. Indeed, such representation would, by dilution, be decreased.

Will an increase in membership lead to a loss in effectiveness? Referring to the several increases in membership of the Council of the League of Nations, E. H. Carr wrote: "The Council, in becoming more 'representative', lost much of its effectiveness as a political instrument. Reality was sacrificed to an abstract principle."[80] Echoing this concern, the Permanent Representative of Australia to the United Nations recently wrote that "[p]erhaps the greatest drawback in making the Council more representative is the practical risk that a significantly enlarged Council would make decision-making more difficult."[81] Several close observers of the United Nations consider this "practical risk" to be quite high. Michael Reisman recently wrote that "expansion of the Council would be unlikely to satisfy those agitating for change, yet it would make the Council more unwieldy

---

[77] UN Charter Art. 23(1).

[78] As to the amendment, see Leo Gross, *Voting in the Security Council: Abstention in the Post-1965 Amendment Phase and Its Impact on Article 25 of the Charter*, 62 AJIL 315 (1968).

[79] *See* Davidson Nichol, The United Nations Security Council: Towards Greater Effectiveness 16–17 (1982).

[80] Carr, *supra* note 1, at 29.   [81] Wilenski, *supra* note 26, at 127.

and less efficient."[82] Similarly, Brian Urquhart observed that an increase in the membership of the Council would reduce its effectiveness.[83]

Is it possible that this concern about effectiveness is overstated? Could the entire image of impending doom in the form of a loss of effectiveness itself be a result of dominance? Does the language of the dominant influence even the way we talk about and analyze the situation? This possibility, intriguing as it is, seems misplaced at least in the sense that at some point an increase in the size of the Council would inevitably reduce its effectiveness. Thus, the question becomes the point at which this limit is reached. Moreover, one must recall that some states desire an increase in membership not because they necessarily seek an effective Council but because they understandably seek the status of membership. As importantly, those few rogue states that fear the Council may threaten the continuance of their rule may support increased membership precisely because they believe it will reduce the Council's effectiveness.

All of these considerations point to the importance of thinking through the need for strengthening the relationship of the Council to the Assembly generally and adding members as appropriate to solidify that relationship without also weakening either the effectiveness or the legitimacy of the Council. Since there are reasons why it may not be wise to increase the membership, we would do well to recall the precedent for informal mechanisms that do not require amendment of the Charter and may go far toward satisfying demands for fundamental change. An example of how such informal changes work can be found in the United Nations budgetary process. The Charter provides that the budget shall be approved by the General Assembly by a two-thirds majority vote.[84] However, in response primarily to a U.S. demand for change, the operational, though informal, budgetary process now is one of consensus.[85] This process is not legally guaranteed through enshrinement in the Charter. But its operation, however temporary, eliminated a major objection to the United Nations and took the wind out of extremists' arguments in the United States that it should withdraw from the Organization. Similarly, the pressure for fundamental change in the Security Council could be diminished by satisfying some of the demands of the states in question. The desire of Germany and Japan for more influence on the Council could be met in part by informally granting them a significant role in decision making or by informally ensuring that one or both of them are placed on special Council committees. For example, Japan has wielded great influence, if not a veto, in the United Nations Transitional Authority in Cambodia because its involvement is essential to the financial viability of the effort; it is maintaining this influence through membership on the International Committee on the Reconstruction of Cambodia.[86] Similarly, the Council could offer the promise of increased consultations with regional powers such as India, Nigeria, Brazil and Egypt.

---

[82] Reisman, *supra* note 35, at 96.

[83] Brian Urquhart, Remarks, 87 ASIL PROC. (1993) (forthcoming). *See also* Rochelle Stanfield, *Worldly Visions*, NAT'L J., Oct. 27, 1990, at 2597, 2600 (reporting many experts to believe the Council would be rendered unwieldy).

[84] UN CHARTER Arts. 17(1), 18(2).

[85] As to the meaning of consensus in this context, see Erik Suy, *Consensus, in* [Installment] 7 ENCYCLOPEDIA OF PUBLIC INTERNATIONAL LAW 49 (1984).

[86] *See* Yuli Ismartono, *Cambodia: Continued Factional Rivalry Impedes Peacekeeping Mission,* Inter Press Service (Apr. 15, 1992), *available in* LEXIS, Nexis Library.

Increasing the Involvement of the General Assembly

The final line of reform proposals seeks to open up Council proceedings to the General Assembly and thus increase the sense of participatory governance and in some measure create political accountability for members of the Council. The premise motivating these proposals is that the decision making of the Security Council takes place in informal consultations that increasingly involve only a subgroup of its membership and that consequently exclude not only the nonpermanent members but the membership generally. Thus, it has been proposed:

- that the Assembly acquire its own "watch and alert" capacities by increasing the size of the office of its President;[87]

- that the Assembly be permitted to evaluate and criticize the efforts of the Security Council to maintain international peace and security;[88]

- that the prohibition in the Charter on the immediate reelection of nonpermanent members be lifted;[89]

- that the Secretary-General be authorized to notify the Assembly of disputes and situations "being dealt with" by the Security Council;[90] and

- that a "Chapter VII Consultation Committee" be created, to be composed of twenty-one members of the Assembly representing a range of regions and interests, and to be notified by the Council whenever it contemplates action under chapter VII.[91]

Some of these proposals tend to be "top down" efforts to involve the broader membership, e.g., the creation of a consultation committee. Others assume that efforts to ensure greater participation will bubble up from the bottom and thus seek to remove barriers to participation, e.g., removal of the ban on immediate reelection. To the extent that the legitimacy concerns described above are indeed widespread, we should encounter increased bottom-up demands on the nonpermanent members by those outside the Council at any given time. For example, in electing nonpermanent members to the Council, the General Assembly may come to place greater value on the willingness and ability of the candidate state to consult with members of the United Nations generally or with a specific subgroup they might be said to represent.

Do the Proposals Remedy the Circumstances Underlying Legitimacy Concerns?

Unfortunately, the proposals often suggested have only a modest effect on the circumstances giving rise to legitimacy concerns about the collective authority of the Council. As far as the potential double standard in governance engendered by

---

[87] Childers, *supra* note 10, at 134.   [88] Ortega Carcelén, *supra* note 73, at 400–02.

[89] *See, e.g.*, Ramesh Thakur, *The United Nations in a Changing World*, 24 SECURITY DIALOGUE 7, 13 (1993).

[90] The Secretary-General under Article 12(2) of the Charter currently needs the consent of the Council to so notify the Assembly. *See* Childers, *supra* note 10, at 134; *see also* Reisman, *supra* note 35, at 98.

[91] Reisman, *supra* note 35, at 98–99.

the veto is concerned, it is unlikely that the veto will be eliminated in the near future. Moreover, any voting procedure that would replace the present one would be complex and involve some form of weighted voting. Thus, a weaker form of double standard in governance would likely persist. However, since the trigger of this weaker double standard would not be within the discretion of a single state and its use would in any event be less obvious, the perception of illegitimacy would probably be reduced. Consequently, although reform could reduce the perception somewhat, the sense of unfairness that now surrounds the veto can be expected to continue for the foreseeable future.

As for the sense of western domination of the Council, the proposal for increasing the Council's membership would not affect the power of the West in international affairs generally, and would only marginally diminish the capabilities of the West in the Council. Rather, the main benefit appears to be that it may increase the strength of the nonpermanent members by increasing their number. This causal link between strength and number will presumably occur because more nonpermanent members will increase the linkage to the UN membership generally and will make each nonpermanent member individually more resistant to domination by the West. These results are possible, but a danger is that increased membership may interfere with the ability of the Council to operate effectively. Overall, it appears that because the present Council membership may not be reshuffled easily, the simplest thing for members to do is to call upon what appears to be a free good—increased membership. The issue, however, is the actual cost of additional membership.

Because of the uncertainty concerning the effect of increased membership and because any changes in membership will probably not be implemented until the turn of the century, the proposals to increase participation in the Council as currently constituted are especially valuable. They are valuable because they do not run the risk of undermining the Council's ability to operate owing to an unwieldy size. They are needed because the Council is being challenged now and the legitimacy of its collective authority should be strengthened. Finally, such reform would aid our understanding of precisely what changes in membership are necessary to deal with the perception of dominance of the Council by the West.

As with the proposal to increase membership, the proposals to open up Council proceedings so that members of the General Assembly would enjoy a greater sense of participation would not affect the power of the West in international affairs generally, and would only marginally diminish the capabilities of the West in the Council. Their benefit is that they would directly increase participation in the Council.

The difficulty with even this last avenue of proposals is that increased consultation with members of the Assembly and an increased sense of participation by the Assembly in Council proceedings will not alter the dominance of the few if there is a sense of urgency. This is a fundamental challenge because much of the Council's agenda is "urgent," or can be argued to be urgent. In such moments, consultation and caucuses will be slow and unwieldy in comparison with the speed with which draft resolutions will be offered by the permanent members. Here, in my view, is where the real root of dominance lies: Council proceedings often focus on a moment in time and all efforts converge on a single vote, which, when coupled with a sense of urgency, provides the greatest leverage to those with greater capabilities, the permanent members. It is to this aspect that I now turn.

IV. Towards Mooting Dominance and Restoring Participation Through the Elimination of the Reverse Veto

What has been virtually overlooked over the past two years is that states have threatened to use the veto in a fundamentally different context.[92] Moreover, this new use is part and parcel of the charge that the Council's authority is illegitimate, because this threat to employ the veto reduces the need to maintain consensus on a policy and thus is emblematic and supportive of dominance. This new use, which I term the "reverse veto," does not block the Security Council from authorizing or ordering an action but, rather, blocks it from terminating or otherwise altering an action it has already authorized or ordered. The recent surge in Council activity requires that we distinguish between the authority to initiate an action and the authority to modify an action already initiated. If this distinction is made, it is argued below, both internationalists and realists should agree that the reverse veto is not desirable. Most importantly, this use of the veto, unlike its other uses, can be addressed without amending the Charter.

The U.S. and UK Threats to Use the Veto in the Gulf Crisis

The reverse veto was threatened in the closing days of the gulf war. In that instance it would not have blocked the United Nations from undertaking an action; rather, it would have kept the United Nations from backing off from something it had already authorized. The Security Council in Resolution 678 had authorized "Member States co-operating with the Government of Kuwait . . . to use all necessary means to uphold and implement [the Security Council's resolutions regarding the Iraqi invasion] and to restore international peace and security in the area."[93] As Iraq withered beneath the air attacks of the coalition, peace initiatives were actively pursued by various countries.[94] In response, particularly to the Soviet peace efforts, both the United States and the United Kingdom reportedly stated that they had the power to maintain the UN sanctions and to continue the use of force authorized by the Council because any alteration of the sanctions or the authorization to use force would require a new resolution that they, as permanent members, could veto.[95]

Since then, other references to this use of the veto have been made. Prime Minister John Major reportedly stated on May 11, 1991, in a speech to the Congress of the Conservative Party, that the United Kingdom would veto any resolution aimed at easing the sanctions against Iraq as long as Iraqi President Saddam Hussein remained in power.[96]

---

[92] A brief reference to this use of the veto can be found in Richard Gardner, *Practical Internationalism: The United States and Collective Security*, SAIS Rev., Summer–Fall 1992, at 35, 43.

[93] SC Res. 678, *supra* note 4, para. 2.

[94] *See, e.g., Excerpts From the Statement By Gorbachev on Gulf War*, N.Y. Times, Feb. 10, 1991, §1, at 12; *New Peace Plan at U.N.*, N.Y. Times, Feb. 15, 1991, at A6.

[95] Paul Lewis, *U.S. and Britain Assert U.N. Power: They Say They Can Continue Sanctions and the War*, N.Y. Times, Feb. 22, 1991, at A4.

[96] The UK position was particularly troubling to some states because none of the Security Council's resolutions call for the removal of President Hussein. In his letter of May 13, 1991, to the President of the Security Council, the Iraqi Minister for Foreign Affairs used Major's statement to invoke the underlying question of the legitimacy of a Council arrangement that could allow Britain to take such an action:

The critical point here is that these threatened uses turn the realists' justification for the veto completely on its head. In the realist argument, a properly assigned veto is justified because all of the major players should be in agreement on any peace-enforcing effort. Here, however, the veto now means that any one of the major players, having jointly authorized the use of force or the imposition of sanctions, may force the authorization or imposition to continue.

To illustrate, let us assume that during the spring of 1993 the Clinton administration was successful in convincing a vast majority of Council members to support the adoption of more aggressive steps to stop "ethnic cleansing" in Bosnia, one of these steps being the lifting of the arms embargo. However, one—possibly two—of the permanent members then vetoed the effort to end the arms embargo. With such widespread division among states, the embargo, as a practical matter, would likely have fallen apart. But this division probably also would have placed a great strain on both the authority and the legitimacy of the Council. If the realists' justification for the veto was to prevent precisely such a division, the reverse veto should not be desirable in their view.

Must the Council Terminate Its Actions? The Charter and Rhodesia

The Charter is silent on the means of termination or, more generally, modification of actions taken by the Security Council. Nonetheless, interpreting the Charter so as to ensure its effectiveness leads quite clearly to the position that it is for the Council itself to end or modify its actions. The United States and the United Kingdom, in supporting this interpretation of the Charter in the context of the gulf war, cited the fact that the sanctions against Rhodesia were terminated by Security Council resolution. It is ironic that the United States and the United Kingdom should so refer to the Rhodesian sanctions because, although the handling of that incident does support this interpretation of the Charter, these two states were at best weak supporters of that conclusion at the time.

The Rhodesian situation first came before the Council in 1963, but the Council's extended consideration of it began with the Unilateral Declaration of Inde-

---

Does this not mean that the United Kingdom, as a permanent member of the Security Council, seems fully prepared to violate its obligations and responsibilities under the Charter and do so in a premeditated way, without any valid legal reason and in blatant contradiction to those responsibilities?

. . . .

We warn against this dangerous precedent in international relations, which, if sanctioned, will destroy the entire basis on which the Charter of the United Nations rests . . . .

UN Doc. S/22591, at 2–3 (1991).

The United States maintained a similar view on removing President Hussein, although both Britain and the Clinton administration in 1993 backed off from this position. Paul Lewis, *U.S. and Britain Softening Emphasis on Ousting Iraqi,* N.Y. TIMES, Mar. 30, 1993, at A3:

Both President George Bush and Prime Minister John Major had said on several occasions that the sanctions must remain until President Hussein has been toppled . . . .

Their insistence . . . has become increasingly unpopular with other Arab countries because it clearly exceeds the Council's decisions . . . .

Neither the United States nor Britain mentioned this condition today when the Security Council reviewed the embargo.

See also Elaine Sciolino, *Clinton to Scale Down Program to Oust Iraqi Leader,* N.Y. TIMES, Apr. 11, 1993, §1, at 3.

pendence by the Ian Smith Government in 1965.[97] The Council condemned this act and called upon states not to recognize or assist the illegal regime.[98] Ultimately, the Security Council, on May 29, 1968, unanimously adopted Resolution 253 establishing comprehensive and mandatory sanctions by all member states against the illegal government of Southern Rhodesia.[99]

The first time the Security Council considered lifting the sanctions occurred in connection with bilateral negotiations in 1971 between the Smith government and the United Kingdom, which had resulted in the Home-Smith Proposal. The United Kingdom had developed "five principles," which, if met and if agreeable to the Rhodesian people, would permit the British granting of independence to Southern Rhodesia.[100] In November of that year, the United Kingdom requested a Council meeting to discuss an agreement on ending the Southern Rhodesian problem.[101]

The Security Council proceeded to discuss the UK proposal on February 16, 1972. A week later, the Soviet representative to the Council asserted that "certain States are openly attempting to throw aside the Security Council decisions on sanctions, to forget them themselves and to try to make others forget them."[102]

---

[97] Between 1963 and 1980, the Security Council met 128 times on the Southern Rhodesian problem. Bailey, *supra* note 61, at 308. *See generally* VERA GOWLLAND-DEBBAS, COLLECTIVE RESPONSES TO ILLEGAL ACTS IN INTERNATIONAL LAW: UNITED NATIONS ACTION IN THE QUESTION OF SOUTHERN RHODESIA (1990); PATIL, *supra* note 59, at 170–89; HARRY R. STACK, SANCTIONS: THE CASE OF RHODESIA (1978).

[98] SC Res. 216, UN SCOR, 20th Sess., Res. & Dec., at 8, UN Doc. S/INF/20/Rev.1 (1965).

[99] Acting under chapter VII of the Charter, the Council decided that "all States Members of the United Nations shall prevent" the import into their territories of all commodities and products originating in Southern Rhodesia, the sale or supply of any commodities or products to Southern Rhodesia, and any activity by nations that would promote the movement of such commodities. In addition, each member state was required to prevent entry into its territory of any person traveling on a Rhodesian passport and prohibit airline service to or from Southern Rhodesia. A committee on implementation was formed and the United Kingdom was asked to provide "maximum assistance." Although further efforts to strengthen these sanctions would be made and in some cases taken, the essential system of sanctions was contained in Resolution 253, UN SCOR, 23d Sess., Res. & Dec., at 5, 6, UN Doc. S/INF/23/Rev.1 (1968).

In June 1969, a draft resolution that would have widened and strengthened the sanctions failed by a vote of 8-0-7. 1969 UN Y.B. 115. During the same period, the General Assembly passed Resolution 2508 (XXIV), UN GAOR, 24th Sess., Supp. No. 30, at 67, UN Doc. A/7630 (1969), which condemned the intervention of South Africa into Rhodesia and "[r]eaffirm[ed] its conviction that the sanctions will not put an end to the illegal racist minority régime in Southern Rhodesia unless they are comprehensive, mandatory, effectively supervised, enforced, and complied with." *Id.*, para. 13.

Two draft resolutions failed to be approved by the Security Council early in 1970. The United Kingdom put forward a resolution that would have prevented recognition of the newly proclaimed Rhodesian Republic. The African and Asian representatives felt this was a diversionary measure and attempted to pass a resolution that would have authorized the use of force to implement Resolution 253. The African-Asian resolution failed by only 7-0-8. 1970 UN Y.B. 158. Finland then introduced a compromise resolution, which was adopted quickly as Resolution 277. This resolution introduced very little that had not already been resolved. SC Res. 277, UN SCOR, 25th Sess., Res. & Dec., at 5, UN Doc. S/INF/25 (1970). Resolution 288 was likewise a holding resolution, deciding "that the present sanctions against Southern Rhodesia shall remain in force." SC Res. 288, *id.* at 7.

[100] Letter from the representative of the United Kingdom of Great Britain and Northern Ireland to the President of the Security Council (Dec. 1, 1971), UN SCOR, 26th Sess., Supp. for Oct.–Dec. 1971, at 60.

[101] In December 1971, Somalia introduced a draft resolution before the Security Council that would have rejected the British proposal. The United Kingdom exercised its veto to prevent passage of the resolution. 1971 UN Y.B. 100–01.

[102] UN SCOR, 27th Sess., 1642d mtg., at 2, UN Doc. S/PV.1642 (1972).

He continued, "[T]he sanctions introduced by the Security Council are not only mandatory, but fundamentally imperative" under chapter VII. "[N]o single State has the right to violate them unilaterally."[103] Speaker after speaker from African and other developing states condemned the UK proposal.

Somalia, Guinea and Sudan introduced a draft resolution providing that the present sanctions would remain in effect until the aims and objectives of Resolution 253 were met, urging all states to comply, and holding domestic statutes in violation of Resolution 253, such as the Byrd Amendment in the United States, "contrary to the obligations of States."[104] Somewhat plaintively, the British representative asked "the Council [to] suspend judgment on the proposals until we know the results" of the Peace Commission's investigation of Rhodesian public opinion.[105] The African draft was adopted as Resolution 314 by a vote of thirteen in favor, none against, and two—the United Kingdom and the United States—abstaining.[106] Shortly thereafter, the United Kingdom informed the Council that the Peace Commission had found "that the people of Rhodesia as a whole did not regard the Proposals as an acceptable basis for independence."[107] "We feel," he continued, "that the best atmosphere for constructive discussion and advance will be provided if we maintain the situation as it is today, including sanctions, until we can judge whether or not an opportunity for a satisfactory settlement will occur."[108]

The second instance accompanied the end of the crisis in 1979. In that year, several initiatives raised the question of which entities possessed the authority to bring the crisis to an end. Resolution 445, for example, condemned the Rhodesian elections scheduled for April 1979, which were aimed at reaching an "internal settlement," and called on the Committee on Sanctions to strengthen and widen the sanctions.[109] The African states and the Soviet Union feared that the United Kingdom or the United States would send observers to the "internal settlement" elections so as to legitimate them and then use the results to justify terminating their compliance with the sanctions regime.[110]

---

[103] *Id.* at 2–3.   [104] *Id.* at 37.

[105] UN SCOR, 27th Sess., 1640th mtg., at 6, UN Doc. S/PV.1640 (1972).

[106] SC Res. 314, UN SCOR, 27th Sess., Res. & Dec., at 7, UN Doc. S/INF/28 (1972). In abstaining from voting on the African proposal, the United States stated that "we cannot accept those parts of the draft resolution which directly or indirectly affect laws which have been adopted and are now in force and which under our Constitution must be implemented." UN SCOR, 27th Sess., 1645th mtg., at 4, UN Doc. S/PV.1645 (1972).

[107] Letter from the representative of the United Kingdom of Great Britain and Northern Ireland to the President of the Security Council (May 23, 1972), UN SCOR, 27th Sess., Supp. for Apr.–June 1972, at 66 (containing text of speech given in House of Commons by Sir Alec Douglas-Home on May 23, 1972).

[108] *Id.*

[109] SC Res. 445, UN SCOR, 34th Sess., Res. & Dec., at 13, UN Doc. S/INF/35 (1979).

[110] The representative of Ethiopia stated that "Africa is of course fully aware that the moves currently taking place in Washington and London to send observer missions to Rhodesia are primarily intended to lend legitimacy to the process and its results, thus creating a pretext for the lifting of economic sanctions." UN SCOR, 34th Sess., 2119th mtg., at 2, UN Doc. S/PV.2119 (1979). The Soviet delegate continued along the same line; the United Kingdom and the United States were using the internal solution "as a pretext to refuse to enforce or to observe the sanctions established by the Security Council against Southern Rhodesia." *Id.*, 2120th mtg., at 4, UN Doc. S/PV.2120. The representative of Ghana sounded the strongest warning, stating that "measures should be taken . . . against the danger of unilateral action to lift sanctions against Ian Smith." If this were to occur, it would be a "flagrant and appalling breach of Charter obligations." He asked, "What would be left of

Anticipating what was soon to follow, the President of the Security Council's Committee on Sanctions sent a letter to the Council stating:

> The Committee had learned with distress that the United Kingdom Government contemplated the non-renewal of some sanctions . . . and the lifting of the rest, "as soon as Rhodesia returns to legality with the appointment of a British Governor and his arrival in Salisbury". . . . The Committee emphasized that only the Security Council, which had instituted the sanctions in the first place, had a right to lift them.[111]

The next month, the bilateral political settlement known as the Lancaster House accord accentuated the question of authority. On December 12, 1979, the United Kingdom informed the Council that as a result of the Smith regime's acceptance of the resumption of full legislative and executive authority over Southern Rhodesia by a British governor,

> the state of rebellion in the Territory has been brought to an end.
>
> . . . .
>
> . . . In these circumstances, the obligations of Member States under Article 25 of the Charter in relation to [the sanctions] are, in the view of the Government of the United Kingdom, to be regarded as having been discharged. This being so, the United Kingdom is terminating the measures which were taken by it pursuant to the decisions adopted by the Council in regard to the then situation of illegality.[112]

The African Group in the United Nations promptly characterized the unilateral action by the United Kingdom as unacceptable and illegal. "The African Group declares that resolution 253 (1968) can be revoked only by a decision of the Security Council and that any unilateral action taken in this context is a violation of the responsibilities assumed by Member States under Article 25 . . . ."[113] Despite these statements, the United States lifted its sanctions on December 16. Days later, the USSR declared that "these unilateral acts by the countries concerned represent a flagrant violation of the United Nations Charter, since only the Council can terminate the effect of decisions which it has taken."[114] On December 18, 1979, the United Kingdom asked the Security Council to consider the matter of Southern Rhodesia.[115] In light of the seemingly fundamental disagreement over the procedure for termination of sanctions, it is somewhat

---

[the United Nations'] effectiveness if the Security Council, the one organ that can make binding decisions, could be disregarded as lightly as the General Assembly, alas, so often is?" *Id.* at 13.

[111] Letter to the President of the Security Council from the Chairman of the Security Council Committee established in pursuance of resolution 253 (1968) concerning the question of Southern Rhodesia (Nov. 9, 1979), *id.*, Supp. for Oct.–Dec. 1979, at 61, 62 (quoting a statement by the UK Secretary of State for Foreign and Commonwealth Affairs in Parliament on Nov. 7, 1979).

[112] Letter from the representative of the United Kingdom of Great Britain and Northern Ireland to the President of the Security Council (Dec. 12, 1979), UN SCOR, 34th Sess., Supp. for Oct.–Dec. 1979, at 119, 120.

[113] Letter from the representative of Madagascar to the President of the Security Council (Dec. 14, 1979), *id.* at 131.

[114] Letter from the representative of the Union of Soviet Socialist Republics to the President of the Security Council (Dec. 21, 1979), *id.* at 138, 138.

[115] Letter from the representative of the United Kingdom of Great Britain and Northern Ireland to the President of the Security Council (Dec. 18, 1979), *id.* at 137.

surprising that there was no debate at the Council's meeting of December 21, 1979, which terminated the sanctions.[116]

After the vote, the United Kingdom stated: "Our view remains that the obligation to impose those sanctions fell away automatically with the return to legality of the colony. But we have been very conscious that many countries have attached great importance to the adoption by the Council of a resolution on this subject."[117] The United States merely expressed its pleasure that "the Council is calling upon Member States to terminate the measures taken against Southern Rhodesia under Chapter VII of the Charter because the objective of those measures has been achieved. It was in recognition of that fact that the United States made its recent announcement regarding sanctions."[118] Tanzania, however, recognizing the import of what had just occurred, stated that the Council could not "accept individual interpretations concerning [sanctions], because if such a state of affairs is tolerated then the very fabric of international intercourse and international law will be placed in serious jeopardy."[119]

Thus, although not as tidy as the simple references made by the United States and the United Kingdom during the gulf war would have it, the Rhodesian case does stand for the proposition that Council actions must be terminated by subsequent Council action. If there was ambiguity in the view of the two nations at the time of the Rhodesian sanctions, that ambiguity was resolved by their statements toward the end of the gulf war.[120]

The Political Implications of the Reverse Veto

The reverse veto can affect the politics of the Council in two ways. First, if its net effect is to increase the dominance of the permanent members in Council deliberations that revisit an action already taken, then the reverse veto makes the initial decision all the more important. As Marquis wrote:

> i do not think the prudent one
> hastes to initiate
> a sequence of events which he
> lacks power to terminate[121]

In the Council at moments of urgency, not all the details of resolutions can be worked out to everyone's satisfaction. But integral to the perception of dominance is the assertion that *most* members of the Council do not have a say about

---

[116] Resolution 460 passed by a vote of 13-0-2 (Czechoslovakia and the USSR abstaining). The resolution decided, "having regard to the agreement reached at the Lancaster House conference, to call upon Member States to terminate the measures taken against Southern Rhodesia under Chapter VII of the Charter." SC Res. 460, UN SCOR, 34th Sess., Res. & Dec., at 15, UN Doc. S/INF/35 (1979).

[117] *Id.*, 2181st mtg., at 2, UN Doc. S/PV.2181.

[118] *Id.* at 8.   [119] *Id.* at 19.

[120] *See, e.g.*, Statement of Mr. Pickering, representative of the United States, UN Doc. S/PV.2977, at 301 (part II) (closed) (Feb. 23, 1991) ("it is only here in the Security Council that we could agree to lift sanctions against Iraq"); Statement of Sir David Hannay, representative of the United Kingdom, *id.* at 313 ("only the Security Council itself can make that judgement").

As to the views of others, see, e.g., Statement of Mr. Munteanu, representative of Romania, *id.* at 332 ("the sanctions against Iraq can be lifted only by the Council itself").

[121] DON MARQUIS, *Archy and Mehitabel*, poem 42, "Prudence." I wish to thank my colleague, Stefan A. Riesenfeld, for bringing this passage to my attention. He employed it in *The French System of Administrative Justice: A Model for American Law? Part III*, 18 BOSTON U. L. REV. 715, 748 (1938).

the details of resolutions. This situation requires that trust be placed in those who dominate. But if that trust is weak, those who are dominated will be suspicious about the details they cannot influence. Writing on the future of the type of U.S. leadership shown in the Council during the gulf war, three scholars cautioned: "For in order to give leadership concrete meaning, a leader must have followers, those willing to buy into a broad vision of collective goals articulated by a leader in whom both legitimacy and trust are placed."[122] The reverse veto accentuates this dependency because it suggests that the initial action the followers "buy into" will not be reversible. The review process of the institution does not allow much space for trusting a leader, or suffering a mistake.

Second, the reverse veto increases the importance of the initial decision because it curtails the already limited ability of actors both within and without the Council to end a crisis by negotiation. The mere possibility of a reverse veto fundamentally alters the proceedings that follow. For example, in the gulf war, each permanent member's ability to veto any resolution aimed at stopping or altering the authorization to use force meant that the United States or Britain could insist that Iraq accept and implement unconditionally all of the Security Council's resolutions.[123] For those seeking a way to end the fighting, there seemed to be very little ground for discussion and perhaps even less likelihood that any initiative would survive a veto.[124] Indeed, there is a parallel to the Rhodesian situation in the Soviet peace initiative's assertion that ending the factual basis for the resolutions would cause the resolutions to lapse. (However, the UK statement regarding the Rhodesian sanctions was not as far-reaching; it declared that the obligations in the resolutions would lapse, while the Soviet initiative would have had the resolutions themselves lapse.) Specifically, under the Soviet initiative then evolving, the Iraqi troops were to withdraw from Kuwait over a twenty-one-day period and "[i]mmediately after the completion of the withdrawal of troops from Kuwait, the reasons for the adoption of other Security Council resolutions would have lapsed, and those resolutions would thus cease to be in force."[125] The United States observed in response that

> [i]t is difficult for us to see how an unconditional proposal [i.e., that Iraq comply with the Council's resolutions] can be so conditioned, particularly in respect of the idea of declaring that Security Council resolutions somehow cease to exist, are null and void or without effect . . . . We must not dismantle at the stroke of a pen what the Council has built since August 2 until we have reached agreement on how to restore peace and security to the area.[126]

This exchange is not recounted to suggest that the United States and others were not justified in seeking full Iraqi compliance with the resolutions or in opposing any grant of a cease-fire that might have allowed Iraq to consolidate whatever

---

[122] Cooper, Higgott & Nossal, *supra* note 40, at 408.

[123] Paul Lewis, *U.S. and Britain Insist on Deadline: Tell Soviets Iraq Must Agree to Kuwait Pullout in Days*, N.Y. TIMES, Feb. 21, 1991, at A1.

[124] *New Peace Plan at U.N.*, N.Y. TIMES, Feb. 15, 1991, at A6 ("The latest peace proposal calls for a halt to the allied bombing and the appointment of a Security Council commission to examine [by Feb. 25] ways of ending the fighting. . . . Diplomats said the proposal had no chance of being adopted because the United States would certainly veto it.").

[125] Statement of Mr. Vorontsov, representative of the Soviet Union, UN Doc. S/PV.2977, *supra* note 120, at 296.

[126] Statement of Mr. Pickering, *id.* at 303–06.

defenses it retained.[127] Rather, it illustrates how the presence of resolutions and their relative irreversibility due to the veto altered the argumentation employed and the political options possible.

A similar effect on settlement possibilities can be seen in the early stages of the Rhodesian situation. Although Ian Smith might have been able to reach some agreement with the United Kingdom and possibly the United States, the discussions before the Council should have indicated to him that such bilateral settlements would not necessarily result in the lifting of UN sanctions. Consequently, one can see the logic of the British position regarding the Rhodesian sanctions. To pursue a settlement with Rhodesia, the United Kingdom needed to be able to free itself of its obligations under the resolutions, and, even better, to lay the foundation for the argument that the obligations generally had ceased to have force.

These examples point to the importance of distinguishing between the authority to initiate an act and the authority to terminate or modify an action already initiated, and to the recognition that the difference between the two justifies different voting formulas. In a manner analogous to the way the standard of review used by an appellate court determines the distribution of power between the appellate and trial court levels, so does the voting procedure to terminate or modify an action influence the content, and even likelihood, of the actions taken.

Dealing with the Reverse Veto

Although dealing with the veto, and the double standard that may be perpetuated by it, would require amending the Charter, dealing with the threat of a veto on action already taken or authorized need not require such an amendment. The approach would be to incorporate in any resolution taking a decision a modified voting procedure for future use in terminating the action taken. The idea appears both possible and desirable.

The legality of a modified voting clause. When I mentioned the idea of a modified voting clause to a lawyer serving with the mission of one of the permanent members of the United Nations, his reaction was quick and dismissive. He stated that such a bootstrap approach was not possible; a permanent member may not agree to waive its veto.

I can discern no support for the argument as a matter of treaty law. First, if it so desired, the Council could simply designate a termination date or terminating event for any authorization. This approach waives not only the veto, but the vote altogether. In this regard, it is interesting to revisit the positions of the United States and the United Kingdom on the Rhodesian sanctions. In essence, they claimed that the sanctions terminated automatically when the rationale for imposing them ceased to exist. An example of a time-dependent termination, a "sunset provision," is the Council's practice of authorizing peacekeeping forces for only a certain period of time.[128]

---

[127] The discussions that took place in the Security Council at the time of the Soviet initiative make clear that a veto would not have been necessary, since many members demanded that Iraq comply with the resolutions and stated that it was for the Council to authorize any change in the actions taken against it.

[128] *See, e.g.,* SC Res. 426, UN SCOR, 33d Sess., Res. & Dec., at 5, UN Doc. S/INF/34 (1978) (establishing the United Nations Interim Force in Lebanon (UNIFIL) for an initial period of six months). UNIFIL's mandate has been extended continuously every six months since the adoption of

Second and more importantly, the Security Council on at least one occasion has already essentially altered its voting procedures via a resolution. In Resolution 687, the Council created a Compensation Commission to address claims against Iraq arising out of the gulf war and requested that the Secretary-General make recommendations for the Commission's operation.[129] On May 2, 1991, the Secretary-General suggested that the Commission "function under the authority of the Security Council and be a subsidiary organ thereof." He recommended that the "principal organ" and policy-making body of the Commission be a "15-member Governing Council composed of the representatives of the current members of the Security Council at any given time."[130] As for the decision-making process of this Governing Council, he recommended that,

> [e]xcept with regard to the method of ensuring that payments are made to the [Compensation] Fund, which should be decided upon by consensus, the decisions of the Governing Council should be taken by a majority of at least nine of its members. *No veto will apply in the Governing Council.* If consensus is not achieved on any matter for which it is required, the question will be referred to the Security Council on the request of any member of the Governing Council.[131]

The Security Council adopted the recommendations of the Secretary-General in Resolution 692.[132] The overall effect was to delegate a decision—otherwise subject to the veto—to a subsidiary organ (with the same membership as the Council) where the veto does not apply. By analogy, could not the Council delegate all further decisions regarding a sanctions regime to a similar subsidiary body operating without a veto? And if the Council could do so, then why can it not simply alter its own voting procedures for future decisions on a particular action it has taken?[133]

The drafting of modified voting clauses. A modified voting clause requires careful drafting both to avoid a double veto situation and to meet the demands of the situation presented. There should be no need to discuss whether the second resolution modifies the first or whether it creates new obligations, a categorization issue, to which the veto might apply—i.e., a double veto situation. For example, assume that a resolution authorizing sanctions states, "any decisions terminat-

---

Resolution 426. *See, e.g.,* SC Res. 701 (July 31, 1991) (extending mandate of UNIFIL for a further interim period of six months until Jan. 31, 1992).

See also UN Doc. S/5575 (1964) (recommending the stationing of a UN peacekeeping force in Cyprus for a period of three months), most recently extended by SC Res. 759 (June 12, 1992); SC Res. 693 (May 20, 1991) (establishing the UN Observer Mission in El Salvador for an initial period of twelve months).

[129] SC Res. 687 (Apr. 3, 1991), *reprinted in* 30 ILM 852 (1991).

[130] Report of the Secretary-General pursuant to paragraph 19 of Security Council resolution 687 (1991), UN Doc. S/22559, paras. 4, 5 (1991), *reprinted in* 30 ILM at 1706.

[131] *Id.,* para. 10 (emphasis added).

[132] SC Res. 692 (May 20, 1991), *reprinted in* 30 ILM at 864.

[133] Nor would it seem that a permanent member could reassert its veto because of changed circumstances. Article 62 of the Vienna Convention on the Law of Treaties, *opened for signature* May 23, 1969, 1155 UNTS 331, limits the invocation of changed circumstances to situations where the effect of a "fundamental" change "is radically to transform the extent of obligations still to be performed." Putting aside the issue of whether the treaty in question is the Charter or a resolution, it would seem rare indeed that the requirements of Article 62 could be met. *See* Georg Schwarzenberger, *Clausula Rebus Sic Stantibus,* [Installment] 7 ENCYCLOPEDIA OF PUBLIC INTERNATIONAL LAW 22 (1984).

ing or modifying the measures taken in this resolution shall be made by an affirmative vote of [for example] twelve members." If a proposal were made to broaden the economic sanctions ordered in the original resolution to include certain banking transactions, a voting "border question" would arise. Is the proposal a *modification* of the existing regime and therefore subject to the modified voting procedure, or is it a *new* sanction and therefore subject to the voting procedure set forth in the Charter? The border question posed in the hypothetical would seem to be decided by the voting procedures set forth in the Charter, and thus the veto would probably apply to it.

Consequently, the preferred drafting approach would be categorical; for example, "any decision to terminate any or all of the measures taken in [for example] paragraphs 1 through 9 of this resolution shall be made by an affirmative vote of [for example] twelve members." The limitation of the language to an effort to terminate enumerated measures leaves little room for ambiguity and thus steers clear of the border question.

Of course, there could be many variations on the modified voting procedure. The exemplary language above, "an affirmative vote of twelve members," would mean that any effort to terminate a sanction could be blocked by the vote of four states, as opposed to the current possibility that one of the permanent members could block termination. "An affirmative vote of thirteen members" would mean that any effort to terminate a measure could be blocked by the vote of three states. And so on. Note, however, that if the language were "an affirmative vote of all the members of the Council," this would not be equivalent to the current situation because only the permanent members can now exercise the reverse veto, while the quoted language in effect extends the reverse veto to all the members of the Council.[134]

In general, I think the required number of affirmative votes to terminate a resolution should be high so as to prevent political maneuvering by the state at which the resolution is directed. Just as the reverse veto at present means that the target state may have little chance to terminate the authorization or order in a resolution if a permanent member is strongly opposed, so a modified voting procedure—eliminating the reverse veto—might mistakenly encourage the target state to attempt to split the Council. Thus, the required affirmative votes should probably be higher than the nine required as an initial matter, but not so high, say fourteen, as virtually to perpetuate the present situation regarding the reverse veto.[135]

The choice among drafting variations extends not only to the number of votes required, but also to other conditions regarding both the voting and the implementation of the terminating resolution once adopted. For example, if the question involves termination of an authorization to use force, the resolution on modified voting procedure might (1) provide for a particularly high number of states to terminate, for example thirteen; (2) limit efforts at termination to once every six months; (3) provide that if the authorization is terminated, there then be reason-

---

[134] Conversely, if the permanent members did not have a veto at all, the blocking of any effort to terminate a measure already taken, were it not modified in the manner described above, would require negative votes by six states.

[135] In the event, it may not always be desirable for the required number of votes to be higher than nine. Only six votes could be mustered in June 1993 to lift the arms embargo on Bosnia. Richard Bernstein, *Security Council Stops Move to Arm Bosnians*, N.Y. TIMES, June 30, 1993, at A4. The higher number of votes required represents a balance between not encouraging strategic behavior by the target state and trusting in the ability of the Council to modify previous actions when appropriate.

able time for orderly withdrawal; and (4) indicate that any such termination will be without prejudice to the right of the participating states to protect their forces as necessary. Clearly, the drafting choices likely will, and should, be greatly influenced by the particular situation.

Policy and political considerations regarding modified voting clauses. The politics of modified voting clauses raises numerous questions: are such clauses desirable from the perspective of the international community, the United Nations, the nonpermanent members and the permanent members, and, depending on the answers to these questions, how likely is it that such clauses could be adopted?

The nonpermanent members would probably find the modified voting clause desirable in that it would lessen the significance of the initial decision, which because of a sense of urgency is dominated by the permanent members. It is the possibility of the reverse veto that gives an assurance of the continuance of domination. A modified voting clause would empower the nonpermanent members by allowing them to revisit the decision at a later date.

The modified voting clause is not likely to appeal to the permanent members, at least at first glance. On the one hand, if perceptions of illegitimacy are of no particular concern, the increased possibility of revisiting a resolution would seem to be a needless distraction. Moreover, in view of the intensity with which these states defend the prerogative of the veto, the possibility of any modified voting procedure, even if limited, might seem threatening to that prerogative. On the other hand, the permanent members should find such a clause desirable because it would protect them from the abusive veto of any of the other permanent members.

More importantly, the modified voting clause should be attractive to all the members of the Council because it supports the objectives of the Organization. The clause would be desirable from the perspective of collective authority because it would increase the perceived legitimacy of decision making generally by encouraging the maintenance of consensus. It would be desirable in terms of the objectives of sanctions in that it would enable the state targeted by the sanctions to act with a view to ending them. For if the target state and its citizenry conclude that, no matter what they do, the sanctions will remain in place because of the wishes of one or two permanent members, they may simply stiffen their resistance and reject further efforts to satisfy what they see as an unreasonable and unresponsive Council.[136] From the perspective of the design of the United Nations, the clause would be desirable in that the promotion of an ongoing process in the Security Council would tend to lead the General Assembly back to involvement in, rather than opposition to, the Security Council.

Finally, adoption of modified voting clauses is politically feasible even if the permanent members are equivocal as to their value. The votes of the nonpermanent members are necessary for the passage of any Council resolution and, while those members may not be able to offer alternative plans of action in the short term, they may have sufficient power to demand the inclusion of a modified voting procedure for application to future reconsideration of the decision.

---

[136] A related problem is that it is not always clear what is required to end sanctions. "If the Council is so outraged that it imposes coercive sanctions against a State or regime, as in the case of Southern Rhodesia from 1966 to 1980, it might be useful for it to indicate what the offending State or regime must do to be relieved of the sanctions." Bailey, *supra* note 61, at 332. The participatory governance that would accompany the maintenance of consensus on sanctions and the like would result in the elaboration of what is sought from the offending state.

Perhaps the ability to debate, the opportunity to participate, can resolve the concerns about illegitimacy. Thus, reform should encourage the maintenance of consensus. Nevertheless, we must recognize that the opportunity to participate and to seek consensus may only make a lack of consensus more apparent, and that dealing with the reverse veto does not address directly the double standard in governance made possible by the veto power. Rather, dealing with the reverse veto serves to place concerns about legitimacy on the table, leaving it to the member states to find a consensus that addresses those concerns.

CONCLUSION

We will all long consider the implications of the end of the Cold War for the international legal system. The Cold War divided the international community *and* gave rise to communities among the states on each side of the divide. Even as the ending of that bipolar world brought the international community back together, it loosened the "communities of division" and allowed countries to rediscover their own selves, or lack of selves, free of either pole.

The renewed sense of global community means, at least for now, that it is possible in more areas to judge whether the conduct of a state is acceptable. There are trends both toward the tolerance of difference—as states, and parts of states, explore and debate what makes them unique—and toward judgment of the conduct of oppressive states posing foreseeable risks to international peace and security. In the face of both unaccustomed community and diversity, the world must learn to judge and tolerate, and to know whether what is called for is judgment or tolerance. In some instances it will be the Security Council that serves as judge, making, applying and enforcing the law. Therefore, it is critical to determine which parts of the international community accept, and which parts question, the legitimacy of the Security Council's authority regarding threats to international peace and security, and why they do so.

To be effective, international governance must be concentrated in some body other than the whole. The question is how to design this body so that the governed as a whole, both in fact and in perception, are served rather than oppressed. Considering the very different positions of the members of the international community and their citizenries, this article concludes that the problem of legitimacy will be an ongoing one for any effort at international governance, and that effective governance, among other things, therefore requires a process involving ongoing participation, in most cases through representatives. Indeed, the differences may be so great that we must recognize that the search for consensus regarding principled substantive bases for intervention will be difficult and, even if "successful" to some, certainly not adequate to resolve the much harder problem of applying such general principles to any particular case. Similarly, challenges to power framed in terms of the illegitimacy of that power cannot be dealt with merely on the level of general principles. Rather, the means of confronting the challenges to legitimacy must be institutionalized. This conclusion places a heavy emphasis on process, not because I believe justice is merely procedural, but because I believe our diverse global community is more likely to find its vision of substantive justice through a process involving debate.[137] To the degree that the organization and its members can learn from the resulting debates, the challenges expressed in terms of legitimacy may be met.

---

[137] *See* HAAS, *supra* note 19, at 190–94.

[6]

DOES THE UNITED NATIONS SECURITY COUNCIL HAVE THE COMPETENCE TO ACT AS COURT AND LEGISLATURE?

KEITH HARPER*

INTRODUCTION

The demise of the Cold War heralded welcomed change around the globe. Eastern Europe and the former Soviet republics are no longer bound by the "dictatorship of the proletariat."[1] A wave of democratization moves swiftly across Africa and the Americas as super-power patrons will no longer guarantee the positions of privilege held by yesterday's dictators. In addition, the retreat of the daunting political glacier has precipitated a prudent optimism that the world has taken a small step away from nuclear holocaust. However, this optimism and the accompanying euphoria are tempered by the spread of global tragedies—tribal warfare in the former Yugoslavia, famine created and perpetuated by clan warfare in Somalia, and the widespread development of other threats to international peace and security. It seems that the so-called "new world order" has, at least initially, generated more old world disorder evincing an unfortunate truism—positive change does not come easily.

Nevertheless, the world has great reason to celebrate. Static ideological and political bilateralism paralyzed the United Nations during the Cold War years, specifically the U.N. mechanism to ensure international peace and security—

---

* Law Clerk to The Honorable Lawrence W. Pierce, U.S. Court of Appeals, Second Circuit. B.A. 1990, University of California, Berkeley; J.D. 1994, New York University School of Law; Member, Cherokee Nation of Oklahoma. I gratefully acknowledge the helpful comments made on previous drafts by Professors Thomas M. Franck, Paul C. Szasz, and Gregory H. Fox. I would also like to thank the editors of the *Journal of International Law and Politics*, in particular, Heather Shamsai for her endless hours devoted to this piece. This Note is dedicated to my mother, Doreen T. McKissack, and my grandmother, Elsa M. DaLuz. It was made possible and meaningful because of the inspiration of Suzette and our daughter, Nailah.

1. Thomas M. Franck, *The Emerging Right to Democratic Governance*, 86 AM. J. INT'L. L. 46, 48 (1992).

the Security Council.[2] The fall of the Iron Curtain sets the stage for the Security Council to play the role that the drafters of the U.N. Charter envisionsed for it. The new world order has cultivated a homogenization of the super-powers' values and interests. With the growing Security Council collegiality comes a concomitant political momentum to subdue aggressive elements within the international community. The collective action against Iraq[3] highlighted this force. Subsequent Council action against Libya[4] and interventions in Somalia[5] and Bosnia[6] suggest that the Gulf War was not an aberration, but an antecedent to the Council's consistent and continual presence in world affairs.

An increasingly proactive and self-empowering Security Council promises to have a positive effect on the international landscape. Nevertheless, questions that remained dormant

---

2. *See generally* Symposium, *The Prospective Role of the United Nations in Dealing With the International Use of Force in the Post- Cold War Period*, 22 GA. J. INT'L & COMP. L. 9 (1992) [hereinafter Symposium].

3. *See infra* notes 21-73 and accompanying text.

4. *See infra* notes 74-87 and accompanying text.

5. On December 3, 1992, the Security Council unanimously passed a resolution "*Recognizing* . . . the present situation in Somalia . . . constitutes a threat to international peace and security" and allowing for "such measures as may be necessary" to restore peace. S.C. Res. 794, U.N. SCOR, 47th Sess., Res. & Dec., at 63, U.N. Doc. S/INF/48 (1992). The situation in Somalia had deteriorated to the point where the Council found it necessary to send an armed force just to keep the population from starving. *Id.* paras. 6-7. The campaign called for a U.S.-led force to enter Somalia and open up the distribution lines that lead to food centers throughout the country. *Id.* para. 19. In addition, the resolution intimates that the solution goes beyond food lines to a "political settlement" of the conflict "aimed at national reconciliation in Somalia." *Id.* pmbl. The exact goals of this ongoing campaign are unclear. Paul Lewis, *Mission to Somalia*, N.Y. TIMES, Dec. 13, 1992, at A14. The Somalia intervention is unprecedented because of its singular humanitarian purpose in the midst of an entirely domestic situation without a clear international dimension.

6. The Council has taken extensive action in the former Yugoslavia in an attempt to ameliorate the political ills and to put a stop to the arguably genocidal activities. S.C. Res. 743, U.N. SCOR, 47th Sess., Res. & Dec., at 8, U.N. Doc. S/INF/48 (1992); S.C. Res. 740, U.N. SCOR, 47th Sess., Res. & Dec., at 7, U.N. Doc. S/INF/48 (1992); S.C. Res. 727, U.N. SCOR, 47th Sess., Res. & Dec., at 7, U.N. Doc. S/INF/48 (1992); S.C. Res. 724, U.N. SCOR, 46th Sess., Res. & Dec., at 45, U.N. Doc. S/INF/47 (1991); S.C. Res. 721, U.N. SCOR, 46th Sess., Res. & Dec., at 44, U.N. Doc. S/INF/47 (1991); S.C. Res. 713, U.N. SCOR, 46th Sess., Res. & Dec., at 42, U.N. Doc. S/INF/47 (1991).

during the sustained absence of Council activity over the last forty years are now being raised.[7] The exercise of great power by an institutional body appropriately raises fundamental issues concerning the boundaries of that power.

Although Chapter VII confers broad autointerpretative capabilities on the Security Council, the Council is not without legal restrictions on its power.[8] Perhaps more importantly, the Council must protect its institutional legitimacy by acting in ways which most states deem appropriate and within its competence.[9] Without the states' cooperation in its operations, the Council would be paralyzed and ineffective.[10] Therefore, it is not only prudent but it is necessary for the Council to guard its legitimacy by abstaining from action where it may be perceived as acting *ultra vires* and, thus, inappropriately. Put another way, as the source, and indeed, the touchstone of the Council's institutional legitimacy is the support its decisions maintain among the community of states. It must not act in ways the international community will perceive as illegitimate.

Though some recent Security Council decisions were unquestionably legal and have garnered wide international support, other Council actions were based on dubious legal grounds and have been criticized as inappropriate by both states and scholars. I will argue that one source of the debata-

---

7. *See generally* LELAND M. GOODRICH ET AL., CHARTER OF THE UNITED NATIONS—COMMENTARY AND DOCUMENTS (1969). Considerations that the international community currently faces include: What are the limitations of Security Council power? What kind of a role should the General Assembly play in decisional matters concerning peace and security? These questions are the same points of contention central to the debates at the San Francisco conference where the U.N. Charter was drafted. *Id.*

8. *See infra* notes 146-58 and accompanying text.

9. This political check on Council powers has been designated the "CNN factor." Paul Szasz, Remarks at the Conference on the Future of U.N. Collective Security at the New York University School of Law (Jan. 22-24, 1993). Indeed, this factor may be as powerful as the Article 24 procedural check on Security Council action. Council action would be severely constrained if most people of most states politically opposed a particular Security Council action, or did not recognize the competence of the Council in general. The price of losing its institutional legitimacy by acting against the political will of the world community is a powerful check on the Council's powers.

10. As most actions under Chapter VII—sanctions and/or military force—require the cooperation of all states, the Council would be unable to enforce its decisions without state support.

ble illegality and impropriety is the Council's increasing inclination to assume the role of both court and legislature. In its recent actions against Iraq, Libya, and Israel, the Council has demonstrated a willingness to answer juridical questions and impose legal obligations on states through its Chapter VII powers.[11] This Note discusses the legality and appropriateness of the Council as an institutional chameleon. The effect of the Council's assumption of these new roles on its institutional legitimacy will be discussed in two parts.

Part I explains how the Council functions as both court and legislature, and describes the broadening of the historical scope of Council power that this behavior represents. In its attempts to "restore or maintain" international peace, the Council has been willing to make juridical determinations traditionally answered by judicial bodies. In addition, other Council determinations, which could be classified as legislative, essentially create legal obligations for states.

Part II explores whether it is both legal and appropriate for the Security Council to act as a court and a legislature. First, I will argue that the Council should avoid answering questions that are purely juridical in nature; if it undertakes to answer such questions, the Council should establish and observe procedural rules similar to those universally observed by courts, to protect both the rights of state "litigants" and the Council's own legitimacy. Second, I will argue that Article 39 of the Charter generally confers on the Council the authority to create legal obligations for states. However, limitations on that authority exist. The primary limitation is that the Council must avoid creating legal obligations that are in contravention of established international normative standards that reflect the political interest of Security Council members instead of the interest of all states, or that exceed the will and desires of most states. I will also suggest that the Council should seek and follow the advice of the General Assembly, the only representative body of the U.N. system, to ensure that it is acting appropriately.

In conclusion, I will point to areas where the Council may act legislatively and judicially in the future, and suggest that

---

11. Chapter VII of the U.N. Charter authorizes the use of force, both economic and military, to enforce Security Council decisions. U.N. CHARTER ch. VII.

classifying Council determinations as either executive, judicial or legislative would be helpful in ascertaining whether or not an action by the Council is appropriate. Moreover, I will suggest that to prevent an incapacitation of the Council, it is crucial to codify certain political checks to prevent Security Council member states from sacrificing the present institutional legitimacy of the United Nations on the altar of its member states' political interests.

I. RECENT SECURITY COUNCIL DETERMINATIONS—ACTING AS COURT AND LEGISLATURE

The main purpose of the U.N. Security Council is clearly defined in Article 24 of the United Nations Charter (hereinafter "Charter")—"[to have] primary responsibility for the maintenance of international peace and security."[12] To fulfill that responsibility, Article 39, in more ambiguous terms, confers broad power on the Council when acting under Chapter VII.[13] Article 39 requires the Council to make two separate determinations. First, it must answer a threshold jurisdictional question—whether there exists "any threat to the peace, breach of the peace, or act of aggression." Second, once the Council has made this initial determination, it must then "decide what measures shall be taken in accordance with Articles 41 and 42, to maintain or restore international peace and security."[14] In essence, the Charter, and specifically Chapter VII, delineates the Security Council as an executive branch bestowed with policing power and the capacity to use coercive force in the form of military and economic sanctions. Nevertheless, the Council, in recent resolutions involving situations in Iraq, Libya, and Israel, has made decisions more akin to those made by legislatures and judiciaries than by a purely executive organ. Specifically, in answering the threshold jurisdictional question—determining whether a state's action constitutes a

---

12. U.N. CHARTER art. 24.
13. Article 39, the jurisdictional clause of Chapter VII, provides in full:
    The Security Council shall determine the existence of any threat to the peace, breach of the peace, or act of aggression and shall make recommendations, or decide what measures shall be taken in accordance with Articles 41 and 42, to maintain or restore international peace and security.
U.N. CHARTER art. 39.
14. Id.

"threat to the peace"[15] and therefore subjects that state to Council action under Chapter VII—the Council has shed its historical reluctance to create legal obligations for states: it has acted as a lawmaker. Moreover, the Council has been willing to answer purely juridical questions to determine both the existence of threats and the appropriate "measures" necessary to "restore and maintain international peace."

A.   *The Security Council in a Judicial Capacity—Eliminating Threats to the Peace*

This section emphasizes a distinction between political and juridical questions. Primarily, the difference lies in whether the question presented is cognizable under law and whether the system intends to have the question answered by a political or judicial institution. Juridical questions are limited to inquiries where a breach of legally defined norms or an issue of law can be judicially determined and the resolution requires normative application of rules. Political questions, on the other hand, address the policy implications of decisions and the effect of those policies on the polity and constituency—in the international sphere, the relationship among states.

Critical to the distinction within any particular system is the assignment of powers by the institution's constitution. In the case of the U.N. system, the Statute of the International Court of Justice textually commits certain issues to the "primary" judicial organ—the International Court of Justice (hereinafter, I.C.J.).[16] Specifically, Article 36(2) of the Statute defines "legal disputes" as including:

 a. the interpretation of a treaty;

 b. any question of international law;

---

15. If the Council determines that a "breach of the peace" or an "act of aggression" exists they may also act under Chapter VII. *See supra* note 13 and accompanying text. I use "threat to the peace" here and elsewhere as a shorthand, as it is a lesser included event of either a breach of the peace or an act of aggression. A potential occurrence (i.e., "a threat") will always precede an actual "act" or "breach."

16. STATUTE OF THE INTERNATIONAL COURT OF JUSTICE art. 36 [hereinafter I.C.J. STATUTE].

c. the existence of any fact which, if established, would constitute a breach of an international obligation; and

d. the nature or extent of the reparation to be made for the breach of an international obligation.[17]

Article 36(2) is not intended to be a talisman—defining what is a juridical question. Rather, it expresses what the framers of the U.N. Charter intended as the jurisdiction of the I.C.J. as a judicial institution.[18] In this paper, I use the term "juridical question" as a categorization of issues that I believe a judicial, rather than a political, institution has the competence to answer. If a non-judicial institution were to answer such "juridical questions," it must, at a minimum, develop processes to ensure fairness and due process.[19]

Interestingly, the Security Council has answered "juridical questions" on three recent occasions—as part of the cease-fire resolution ending the Gulf conflict, in imposing sanctions against Libya, and in determining that Israel had violated Article 49 of the Fourth Geneva Convention.

The ability of the Council to take action in these and other situations is a direct result of the abandonment of the ideological polarization that accompanied the profound changes in the former Soviet Union, thereby harmonizing the political exigencies of the permanent members of the Coun-

---

17. *Id.* art. 36, para. 2.

18. I mention Article 36, paragraph 2 here only as an illustration of the types of questions normally thought of as "juridical" and thus appropriately decided by judicial institutions. Juridical questions require in-depth analysis of fact and intricate legal reasoning. As I will discuss in part II, the Security Council simply has neither the competence nor the procedural tools required to answer properly these questions I have termed juridical.

19. Part II of this paper will further explore why it is critical that an institution, at a minimum, wear the procedural garb of a judiciary before resolving juridical questions.

My intention in classifying certain questions as "juridical" is not to argue that the historical dichotomy between "political" and "legal" is clear and reliable. I acknowledge this particular distinction to be specious. My claim is simply that recent decisions by the Council resemble questions that a court—that is, an organ instructed to apply norms judiciously—would address, rather than those that a political institution—that is, an organ free to decide issues based on its members' national interests—would answer.

cil.[20] The Iraqi invasion in particular offered an opportunity for the Council to demonstrate its emerging political hegemony by vigorously suppressing a naked act of aggression.

1. Iraq

a. The Invasion of Kuwait and the Unprecedented Response by a Post-Cold War Security Council

On August 2, 1990, Iraq invaded, wholly occupied, and attempted to annex neighboring Kuwait.[21] The Council responded with singular purpose and unprecedented efficiency, condemning the overt act of Iraqi aggression and ordering the immediate withdrawal of Iraqi troops from Kuwait.[22] When Iraq failed to respond, the Council enacted seven successive sanctions in an attempt to coerce Iraq to abandon its claims to Kuwaiti territory.[23] The Security Council's use of coercive

---

20. Such harmony of interest is made necessary because of Article 27 of the U.N. Charter, which requires the "concurring votes of the permanent members" in order to pass a Security Council resolution on any "substantive" issue. U.N. CHARTER art. 27, para. 3. The permanent members are China, France, the Russian Republic (formerly the Soviet Union), the United Kingdom, and the United States [hereinafter permanent five or permanent members]. U.N. CHARTER art. 23, para. 1.

Given the difficulties Boris Yeltsin is currently facing in the Russian Republic, this trend toward political harmonization among the premanent members cannot necessarily be presumed to continue. Nevertheless, recent Council actions—in Iraq, Israel, and Libya, discussed in this part—demonstrate new possibilities that give a unique promise of a functioning international organization. Therefore, the trend, as uncertain as it may be, merits discussion.

21. S.C. Res. 660, U.N. SCOR, 45th Sess., Res. & Dec., at 19, U.N. Doc. S/INF/46 (1990); Oscar Schachter, *United Nations in the Gulf Conflict*, 85 AM. J. INT'L L. 452, 452-53 (1991); Michael R. Gordon, *Iraq Army Invades Capital of Kuwait in Fierce Fighting*, N.Y. TIMES, Aug. 2, 1990, at A1.

22. S.C. Res. 660, *supra* note 21, para. 2. Resolution 660 referred to the invasion of Kuwait as a "breach of international peace and security" although it clearly was an "act of aggression."

23. S.C. Res. 674, U.N. SCOR, 45th Sess., Res. & Dec., at 25, U.N. Doc. S/INF/46 (1990); S.C. Res. 670, U.N. SCOR, 45th Sess., Res. & Dec., at 24, U.N. Doc. S/INF/46 (1990); S.C. Res. 667, U.N. SCOR, 45th Sess., Res. & Dec., at 23, U.N. Doc. S/INF/46 (1990); S.C. Res. 665, U.N. SCOR, 45th Sess., Res. & Dec., at 21, U.N. Doc. S/INF/46 (1990); S.C. Res. 664, U.N. SCOR, 45th Sess., Res. & Dec., at 21, U.N. Doc. S/INF/46 (1990); S.C. Res. 662, U.N. SCOR, 45th Sess., Res. & Dec., at 20, U.N. Doc. S/INF/46 (1990); S.C. Res. 661, U.N. SCOR, 45th Sess., Res. & Dec., at 19, U.N. Doc. S/INF/46 (1990).

measures culminated in historic Resolution 678, which authorized the use of military force[24] if Iraq did not withdraw from Kuwait by January 15, 1991.[25] This eventually led to the overwhelming Allied victory in the Gulf War.[26]

The military campaign was a clear demonstration of the homogenization of superpower interest and the vast capabilities of a unified Security Council. As such, the war redefined the Council's role in the restoration of international peace and security. This was not the first occasion the Council had authorized military force to restore international peace under Chapter VII; the only other instance, however, was the collective action against North Korea after its invasion of South Korea.[27] The Korean situation, however, proved to be an aberration, occurring under unique circumstances that gave rise to Security Council authority.[28] In contrast, the response to Iraq is a reflection of an inchoate but persistent political re-orientation towards the convergence of the political interests of the five permanent members of the Security Council. As a reflection of a transformed political order, the Council's actions will undoubtedly pave the way to increased Security Council utilization of Chapter VII, and may perhaps prove to be the triumph of the principles and purposes of the Charter.[29]

---

24. S.C. Res. 678, U.N. SCOR, 45th Sess., Res. & Dec., at 27, para. 2, U.N. Doc. S/INF/46 (1990). The resolution authorized the use of "all necessary means to uphold and implement Resolution 660" which asked for the withdrawal of Iraqi troops from Kuwait. *Id.*

25. *Id.*

26. *See generally* Schachter, *supra* note 21.

27. S.C. Res. 84, U.N. SCOR, 5th Sess., Res. & Dec., at 5, U.N. Doc. S/INF/5 (1950); S.C. Res. 83, U.N. SCOR, 5th Sess., Res. & Dec., at 5, U.N. Doc. S/INF/5 (1950); S.C. Res. 82, U.N. SCOR, 5th Sess., Res. & Dec., at 4, U.N. Doc. S/INF/5 (1950).

28. Stephen M. De Luca, *The Gulf Crisis and Collective Security Under the United Nations Charter*, 3 PACE Y.B. INT'L L. 267, 267 (1991). The Soviet Delegation was protesting the non-recognition and denial of a seat to the People's Republic of China and, consequently, was not present for the vote on this resolution. Since North Korea was a communist state, the Soviets would certainly have vetoed the resolution if present. *See generally* L. H. Woolsey, *The "Uniting for Peace" Resolution of the United Nations*, 45 AM. J. INT'L L. 129 (1951) (discussing the historic importance of the General Assembly's "Uniting For Peace" Resolution).

29. *See generally* Thomas M. Franck & Faiza Patel, *Agora: The Gulf Crisis In International and Foreign Relations Law, U.N. Police Action in Lieu of War: "The Old Order Changeth,"* 85 AM. J. INT'L L. 63 (1991).

b. *Imposing Peace and Preempting Future Aggression Through Security Council Resolution 687*

It is unquestionable that the Council possessed the institutional competence and legal power to respond to Iraqi aggression.[30] However, the resolution of the conflict, with the imposition of cease-fire conditions on Iraq, was not clearly legal nor prudentially infallible. Recent wars have generally concluded with the signing of peace agreements between warring parties.[31] Such agreements require mutual consent of the parties.[32] Although it may be necessary that the end of conflict be achieved through the use of some duress or force, international law has long held that this reason by itself does not render a treaty invalid.[33]

---

30. Although there is little dispute that the Security Council had the authority to act against Iraq in this situation, a vigorous debate has arisen nonetheless concerning which specific article of the U.N. Charter authorized the Council's actions during the Gulf War. Should Resolution 678 be characterized as an "enforcement action" under Article 42? *See, e.g.*, Franck & Patel, *supra* note 29, at 63; Anthony Clark Arend, *International Law and the Recourse to Force: A Shift in Paradigms*, 27 STAN. J. INT'L L. 1, 4 (1991). Or was Resolution 678 simply affirming the "inherent right" of collective "self-defense" under Article 51? *See, e.g.*, Eugene V. Rostow, *Agora: The Gulf Crisis In International and Foreign Relations Law, Continued*, 85 AM. J. INT'L L. 506, 506 (1991); Nicholas Rostow, *The International Use of Force after the Cold War*, 32 HARV. INT'L L.J. 411, 411 (1991); *see also* Oscar Schachter, *Self Defense and the Rule of Law*, 83 AM. J. INT'L L. 259, 260 (1989). Under a collective self-defense rubric, "no action by the Security Council" is necessary before the right can be "exercise[d]." N. Rostow, *supra*, at 416. This conceives of Security Council action as a mere legitimatizing ritual, offering Allied forces a welcomed, but unnecessary, benediction for their military operation. N. Rostow, *supra*, at 416-17. On the other hand, the Article 42, or what may more correctly be described as a "quasi-Article 42," framework, requires Security Council initiative. Franck & Patel, *supra* note 29, at 63. This view posits that the competence of the military action emanates from the Security Council, not from inherent rights of sovereign states. This debate, however, does not concern judicial or legislative action by the Council and is therefore beyond the scope of this Note.

31. Quincy Wright, *How Hostilities Have Ended: Peace Treaties and Alternatives*, 392 ANNALS AM. ACAD. POL. & SOC. SCI. 51, 52 (1970) (stating that modern wars generally end without formal peace treaties, but that agreements are common).

32. *Id.* at 56.

33. *Id.* For international law to find that "duress" voids treaty obligations—as it voids contracts under domestic law—would effectively eliminate the possibility of creating a peace treaty, because such a treaty, by its very nature, is coercive.

The Gulf War, however, was not terminated by treaty, but by the most comprehensive and complex Security Council resolution in U.N. history.[34] Resolution 687, like all Chapter VII actions, was not based on consensual agreement,[35] but on the powers of the Security Council, upon determining the existence of a "threat to the peace, breach of the peace or act of aggression," to restore international peace and security.[36] The source of Security Council authority for the imposition of peace did not emanate from Iraqi capitulation, but rather from the inherent competency of the Security Council to "*restor[e] international peace and security*."[37] Indeed, such was the stated purpose of the measures imposed on Iraq, similar in many respects to the Versailles treaty.[38]

Implicitly, the measures were an attempt by the Security Council to preempt future regional aggression; it did so in two ways. First, Resolution 687 attempted to eliminate Iraqi capability to wage aggressive war.[39] The measures exceeded merely restoring Iraq to *status quo ante bellum*;[40] they included the

---

34. Schachter, *supra* note 21, at 456.

35. This is not to say that as a pragmatic and political matter, the consent of Iraq was not useful or even necessary. Rather, I am simply noting that as a *legal* matter, the source of Resolution 687's power is not through consensual agreement but, rather, through the inherent powers of the Council to act under Chapter VII. This Resolution was unprecedented and has implications for the precedential value of the cease-fire not found in traditional "peace treaties."

36. *See* U.N. CHARTER art. 39.

37. S.C. Res. 687, U.N. SCOR, 46th Sess., Res. & Dec., at 11, pmbl., U.N. Doc. S/INF/47 (1991) (emphasis added). Implicit in this rationale is that Iraq, even after it forfeited its claim to Kuwait, remained a threat to international peace; this has to be so, because prior measures already worked to ameliorate the initial breach of the peace. The initial breach of the peace, defined in S.C. Resolution 660 as the invasion of Kuwait, was neutralized by this point. S.C. Res. 660, *supra* note 21.

38. *See* Schachter, *supra* note 21, at 456.

39. Lawrence D. Roberts, *United Nations Security Council Resolution 687 and Its Aftermath: The Implications for Domestic Authority and the Need for Legitimacy*, 25 N.Y.U. J. INT'L L. & POL. 593, 595 (1993).

40. Some commentators have argued persuasively that the Council acted appropriately in doing so. One commentator has posited that the restoration of peace means removing the conditions that led to the aggression. Michael Walzer, *Justice and Injustice in the Gulf War, in* BUT WAS IT JUST: REFLECTIONS ON THE MORALITY OF THE GULF WAR 8-11 (David Decosse & Jean Elstain eds., 1992) (suggesting that the disarming of Iraq was just and required to prevent future instability in the region). The Security Council

elimination of all Iraqi chemical and biological agents and components, as well as the research, development, support, and manufacturing facilities for that weaponry.[41] All ballistic missiles with range capabilities of over 150 kilometers were to be destroyed.[42] In addition, Iraq was to divulge the location of all chemical, biological, and nuclear weapon facilities.[43] Among the imposed conditions, Iraq was required to disclose to the International Atomic Energy Agency (hereinafter IAEA) all information about its nuclear capabilities.[44] Finally, Iraq was to refrain from the development of biological, chemical, and nuclear weaponry and would be required to allow for regular inspection.[45]

Secondly, and more importantly for our purposes here, Resolution 687 attempted to eliminate the dispute that precipitated the initial conflict and that may lead to future conflict between Iraq and Kuwait. The Resolution purportedly settled the long-standing border dispute that led, in part, to the initial invasion. In addition, Resolution 687 reiterated earlier Council resolutions that called for Iraq to assume financial liability for all losses as a result of its aggression. In the case of these final measures, the Security Council made legal determinations and assumed the role of a judicial body.

---

cites Iraq's violations of its obligations under four multilateral agreements as a partial explanation for the stringent measures. The treaties are: (1) *International Convention Against the Taking of Hostages, opened for signature* Dec. 18, 1979, U.N. GAOR, 34th Sess., Supp. No. 46, at 245, U.N. Doc. A/34/146 (1979); (2) Protocol for the Prohibition of the Development, Production and Stockpiling of Bacteriological (Biological) and Toxin Weapons and on their Destruction, *opened for signature* Apr. 10, 1972, 26 U.S.T. 583, T.I.A.S. No. 8062; (3) Treaty on the Non-Proliferation of Nuclear Weapons, *opened for signature* July 1, 1968, 21 U.S.T. 483, 729 U.N.T.S. 161; and (4) Protocol for the Prohibition of the Use in War of Asphyxiating, Poisonous and Other Gases, and the Bacteriological Methods of Warfare, June 17, 1925, 26 U.S.T. 571, 94 L.N.T.S. 65 (1929). At least one commentator has argued convincingly that the measures far exceed Iraq's obligations under these treaties. Roberts, *supra* note 39, at 598.

41. S.C. Res. 687, *supra* note 37, para. 8.

42. *Id.*

43. *Id.* paras. 9-10.

44. *Id.*

45. *Id.*

c. *By Calling Upon the Secretary-General to Determine the Boundary Utilizing Specific "Appropriate Materials," the Council Acted Judicially*

Resolution 687 called for Iraq and Kuwait to "recognize the inviolability of the [pre-war] international boundary [as] . . . set out in the 'Agreed Minutes Between the State of Kuwait and Republic of Iraq Regarding the Restoration of Friendly Relations, Recognition and Related Matters.' "[46] Further, the resolution called upon "the Secretary-General to . . . [draw upon] appropriate material," including one particular map, in order to "demarcate the boundary between Iraq and Kuwait."[47] That map, British in origin, was rejected by the Iraqis as not accurately reflecting the actual borderline.[48] Nevertheless, the Secretary-General implemented the Council's request by forming the Iraq-Kuwait Boundary Demarcation Commission (Border Commission) to draw the necessary boundary lines using the Council's specified map.[49] According to the Border Commission's report to the Secretary-General, Iraq participated fully through voting, attendance at meetings, and drafting of the reports. However, Iraq has continually rejected all conclusions of the Border Commission[50] and has criticized the Council for demarcating a boundary line absent agreement between the disputing states.[51] Iraq has, in addition,

---

46. S.C. Res. 687, *supra* note 37, para. 2; Agreed Minutes Regarding the Restoration of Friendly Relations, Recognition and Related Matters, Oct. 4, 1963, Kuwait-Iraq, 485 U.N.T.S 321 (1964) [hereinafter Agreed Minutes].

47. S.C. Res. 687, *supra* note 37, para. 3.

48. Herman F. Eilts, *The Gulf Crisis Through an Historical Looking Glass*, 14 SUFFOLK TRANSNAT'L L.J. 2, 15-16 (1990).

49. S.C. Res. 687, *supra* note 37, para. 3.

50. REPORT OF THE SECRETARY-GENERAL ON THE STATUS OF COMPLIANCE BY IRAQ WITH THE OBLIGATIONS PLACED UPON IT UNDER CERTAIN OF THE SECURITY COUNCIL RESOLUTIONS RELATING TO THE SITUATION BETWEEN IRAQ AND KUWAIT, Annex A, U.N. Doc. S/23514 (1992); FURTHER REPORT OF THE SECRETARY-GENERAL ON THE STATUS OF COMPLIANCE BY IRAQ WITH THE OBLIGATIONS PLACED UPON IT UNDER CERTAIN OF THE SECURITY COUNCIL RESOLUTIONS, at 6, U.N. Doc. S/23687 (1992).

51. IDENTICAL LETTER DATED 6 APRIL 1991 FROM THE PERMANENT REPRESENTATIVE OF IRAQ TO THE UNITED NATIONS ADDRESSED RESPECTIVELY TO THE SECRETARY-GENERAL AND THE PRESIDENT OF THE SECURITY COUNCIL, at 2, U.N. Doc. S/22456 (1991) [hereinafter LETTER FROM THE PERMANENT REPRESENTATIVE]; *see also* LETTER DATED 16 AUGUST 1991 FROM THE PERMANENT REPRESENTATIVE OF IRAQ TO THE UNITED NATIONS ADDRESSED TO THE PRESIDENT OF THE SECURITY COUNCIL, at 5, U.N. Doc S/22957 (1991).

disputed the validity and applicability of the Agreed Minutes.[52]

The determination, by the Council, that the settling of the boundary dispute was necessary to "restore" regional peace and security is clearly within the Council's Chapter VII powers and intuitively seems a prudent decision. Indeed, the war was vivid evidence that the disputed borderline was a "threat to international peace." However, the Council also took what it perceived as "appropriate measures" to "restore" stability by having the Secretary-General use a particular map, not accepted by all parties, to determine the border. In doing so, the Council answered an implicit legal question as to whether the map reflected the actual boundary line. In other words, the Council determined that Iraq's version of the facts to be without merit and therefore drew a legal conclusion that the British-drawn map reflected the actual boundary line. In rejecting Iraq's claim, the Council assumed the role of a court by answering what is ineluctably a purely juridical question.[53]

d. *Iraq's Claims Were Justiciable and Actual Issues of Fact and Law Existed That Required Adjudication*

Iraq's claims are by no means facially spurious; there are legitimate issues of both fact and law that require adjudication. The Council, by presuming particular answers to those juridical questions, is essentially assuming the role of a court. First, Iraq claims that the Agreed Minutes are not dispositive on the border issue because that agreement has "not yet been subjected to the constitutional procedures required for ratification . . . by the legislative branch and President of Iraq."[54] Moreover, Iraq claims that since 1969 it has publicly disputed the boundary evidenced in the Agreed Minutes.[55] Therefore, there is a question as to whether, under the law of treaty construction, Iraq is bound by that agreement.

---

52. LETTER FROM THE PERMANENT REPRESENTATIVE, *supra* note 51, at 2.

53. For a discussion of the appropriateness of the Council acting judicially, see *infra* notes 130-77 and accompanying text. Note that demarcation of a borderline would fit the definition of "legal disputes" under I.C.J. Statute article 36(2). Moreover, it is a question that is traditionally answered by judicial institutions.

54. *See* LETTER FROM THE PERMANENT REPRESENTATIVE, *supra* note 51, at 2.

55. *Id.*

Article 18 of the Vienna Convention of the Law of Treaties is on point in this regard.[56] States do have certain obligations as a result of signing a treaty absent ratification. Specifically, the Vienna Convention provides that the parties are "obliged to refrain from acts which would defeat the object and purpose of a treaty."[57] It does not, however, require that the party accept or approve the treaty provisions. Indeed, Article 18(a) specifies that even the minimum obligation to refrain from acts that "defeat the object" of a treaty cease when the signatory makes "its intention clear not to become a party to the treaty."[58] Iraq claims it has consistently repudiated the Agreed Minutes. The claim of repudiation should be properly adjudicated in a judicial forum, particularly considering that the drawing of boundaries necessarily involves a dispute over title to land affected by that dispute. Disputes over title to land are the prototypical juridical question.[59]

Any international normative system that makes land disputes a political question is inviting aggression. Historically, desires for territorial expansion have been the primary motiva-

---

56. Vienna Convention on the Law of Treaties, May 23, 1969, 1155 U.N.T.S. 331 [hereinafter Vienna Convention]. Although the Vienna Convention is not binding on this treaty because the Convention was not yet in force when the Agreed Minutes were signed and Article 4 of the Convention explicitly proscribes retroactive application of its terms, it has been widely accepted as a restatement of the customary law on treaty construction and interpretation and is therefore appropriate here. *See generally* BARRY E. CARTER & PHILLIP R. TRIMBLE, INTERNATIONAL LAW (1991). Moreover, to the extent that the Vienna Convention is not applicable on this issue, it is only an added argument for my central contention that legally justiciable issues exist and they should be adjudicated.

57. Vienna Convention, *supra* note 56, art. 18.

58. *Id.*

59. It is not at all surprising that the I.C.J. and other judicial tribunals have consistently been the institutions that have adjudicated border disputes. *See, e.g.,* Concerning Territorial Dispute (Libyan Jamahiriha v. Chad), 1991 I.C.J. 44 (Aug. 26); Guatemala v. Honduras, Wash. Survey No. 393, Jan. 1, 1933, *cited in* ALEXANDER M. STUYT, GENERAL PRINCIPLES OF LAW 22 (1946); *see also* Florida v. Georgia, 58 U.S. 478 (1854) (holding that the U.S. Supreme Court is the proper forum for settlement of border dispute between two states of the United States). Settling border disputes tends to involve detailed facts, which are most appropriately analyzed by a judicial institution that has adequate procedural safeguards and that would be less willing than a non-judicial body to sacrifice a just result solely to expedite the decision-making process.

tion to wage aggressive war.[60] Deciding land disputes other than through the normative application of rules would be courting anarchy.

In addition, Iraq claimed that the map identified by Resolution 687 as the "appropriate material" to settle this dispute was reflective of neither the border according to the Agreed Minutes nor the actual line of demarcation.[61] Iraq's objections were not considered by the Border Commission in its settling of this dispute.[62] Whether the British map, submitted by the Council, is the appropriate map is an issue that should not be decided in an arbitrary or capricious manner.

Clearly then, prior to the establishment of the border by the combined efforts of the Security Council and the Secretary-General, fundamental issues of both law and fact existed which required juridical analysis. In deciding the line of demarcation, and assuming that the Council was not acting arbitrarily, the Council must have answered these implicit juridical questions. As such, the Council assumed the role of a judicial organ.

e. *The Determination of Iraq's Financial Liability Raises Issues That Necessitate Adjudication in a Judicial Forum*

Resolution 687 *"reaffirms"* Iraq's financial liability "under international law for any . . . loss, damage, including environmental damage and the depletion of natural resources, or injury to foreign [g]overnments, nationals and corporations, as a result of Iraq's unlawful invasion and occupation of Kuwait."[63] The Council exercised great leverage to force Iraq's compli-

---

60. To allow a political institution to decide which land belongs to a particular state is tantamount to conferring on members of that polity a license to allow or disallow an aggressor state to conquer the land of its neighbors. For example, if it were in the interest of members of the Security Council to allow a particular state to occupy land of another state, then they might be willing to do so. Indeed, political institutions, whose members, by definition, act in the their own interests, would be expected to permit the aggression.

61. LETTER FROM THE PERMANENT REPRESENTATIVE, *supra* note 51, at 3.

62. *See* S.C. Res. 687, *supra* note 37, para. 2 (demanding that Iraq and Kuwait "respect the inviolability of the international boundary . . . set out in the [Agreed Minutes]").

63. S.C. Res. 687, *supra* note 37, para. 16. The term "reaffirms" is used because the Council had already informed Iraq of this liability in Resolution 674, though in more general terms. *See* S.C. Res. 674, *supra* note 23, para. 8.

ance with these provisions—all of Iraq's foreign assets were frozen under a previous resolution,[64] and economic sanctions remained.[65] However, the sanctions also made it impossible for Iraq to pay any type of compensation, as it could not sell its oil and did not possess any monetary assets. Resolution 687, therefore, had to lay out a mechanism for Iraq to fulfill its financial obligations. It did so by "*directing*" the Secretary-General to make recommendations within thirty days for establishing a fund that would give Iraq the ability to pay for both "essentials" for the Iraqi population and compensation for wartime damage.[66] Resolution 706 was later adopted, providing for Iraq to sell petroleum in order to generate funds subject to the approval of a Security Council Committee.[67]

The monies generated from Iraqi petroleum sales were to be placed in a U.N. Compensation Fund that would pay the cost of destroying Iraq's military arsenal, half the cost of demarcating the border, for humanitarian relief for Iraqi citizenry, and for all compensation claims against Iraq, including compensation to Kuwaiti citizens for property seized during the war.[68] After Iraq rejected the provisions of Resolution 706,

---

64. S.C. Res. 661, *supra* note 23, para. 4.

65. *Id.* para. 3.

66. In addition, the Council passed Resolution 692 that set up the Compensation Commission. S.C. Res. 687, *supra* note 37, para. 19. The Commission is comprised of three organs: (1) a Governing Council, comprised of the Security Council members; (2) an Executive Secretary, appointed by the Secretary-General; and (3) various "Commissioner," providing "advice" and appointed by the Governing Council. The Commission is responsible for dispensing compensatory funds to all claimants suffering loss during the Iraqi invasion and occupation of Kuwait. S.C. Res. 692, U.N. SCOR, 46th Sess., Res. & Dec., at 18, para. 3, U.N. Doc. S/INF/47 (1991). States may file claims with the Commission for their citizens who suffered "loss." There is a $100,000 limit on the amount a state can claim for any particular individual. LETTER DATED 2 AUGUST 1991 FROM THE PRESIDENT OF THE GOVERNING COUNCIL OF THE UNITED NATIONS COMPENSATION COMMISSION TO THE PRESIDENT OF THE SECURITY COUNCIL, at 7, U.N. Doc. S/22885 (1991). In addition, a state can claim $2,500 for any individual without any documentation of loss. *Id.* at 6. For an in-depth discussion of how the compensation fund is implemented, see Elyse J. Garmise, *The Iraq Claims Process and the Ghost of Versailles*, 67 N.Y.U. L. REV. 840 (1992); Marian Nash, *Claims Against Iraq: United Nations Compensation Commission*, 86 AM. J. INT'L L. 113 (1992).

67. S.C. Res. 706, U.N. SCOR, 46th Sess., Res. & Dec., at 21, para. 1, U.N. Doc. S/INF/47 (1991).

68. *Id.* at 3; S.C. Res. 692, *supra* note 66, pmbl.

the Council seized $800 million in Iraqi assets that had been frozen.[69]

Compensation for claims against an aggressor seems rationally related to the restoration of peace after a financially devastating war. This Council action, therefore, does not necessarily implicate a judicially-oriented Council. However, the payment of compensation predictably raises questions about the extent of the liability and the validity of claims that require judicial consideration.[70] Deciding that Iraq is responsible for all claims against it, with only minimal levels of judicial scrutiny, implicitly presumes the Security Council made certain legal conclusions.[71] Assuming again that the Council did not act capriciously in structuring compensation relief, the Council must have decided that the vast majority of claims against Iraq were *bona fide*.[72] Moreover, the Council implicitly decided that Iraq was responsible for *all* loss emerging from the war, regardless of the specific origin and whether any other parties were negligent. By drawing such legal conclusions, the Council again assumed the role of a court.[73]

---

69. Paul Lewis, *U.N. Council Votes To Use Iraqi Assets Frozen Abroad*, N.Y. TIMES, Oct. 3, 1992, at A2.

70. The Foreign Minister of Iraq identified this problem in his response letter to Resolution 687. He stated that Resolution 687 "holds Iraq liable for environmental damage and the depletion of natural resources, although this liability has not been established." LETTER FROM THE PERMANENT REPRESENTATIVE, *supra* note 51, at 5.

71. *See* Nash, *supra* note 66.

72. The Committee assembled to hear the claims against Iraq for liability stemming from the Gulf War has, in its proceedings, only minimal procedural safeguards. Most claims are administered without serious judicial scrutiny and payments are made on claims without regard to whether the evidence is substantial or only minimal. Nash, *supra* note 66. As an alternative, the Council could have acted under a theory analogous to "judicial notice," in which a court stipulates that it is common knowledge that a particular fact is true. The Council failed even to stipulate that the facts were as assumed in the resolutions.

73. Determination of financial liability is inherently a legal determination, as it requires application of normative standards and it is a determination almost exclusively made by judicial bodies. For further discussion, see *infra*, text accompanying notes 130-66.

2. *Libya*

a. *The Security Council Set Sanctions Against Libya for Failing to Respond to Requests for Extradition of Libyan Nationals Allegedly Responsible for a Terrorist Bombing*

The Security Council has not limited its operations to a response to the Iraqi invasion of Kuwait. Indeed, over the last two years, the Security Council has explored the uncharted penumbra of its powers and competence with increased zeal. If any skepticism about the Security Council's willingness to expand its enforcement agenda remained, surely the resolutions concerning Libya abated that skepticism. In some respects, the actions taken against Libya were more extraordinary than those taken to end the Gulf War.

The Security Council sanctions against Libya responded to the December 21, 1988, bombing of Pan Am flight 103 over Lockerbie, Scotland, and the bombing of Union de Transports Aerens flight 772 over the Sahara.[74] Two Libyan officials were allegedly involved in the Lockerbie bombing, which killed 270 people.[75] They were indicted in both the United Kingdom[76] and the United States[77] on criminal charges related to the incident. Soon after this indictment, the United States made an extradition request to Libya for custody of the two men, as did the United Kingdom shortly thereafter.[78] After Libya failed to respond to the extradition requests of the United Kingdom and the United States, the Security Council passed Resolution 731 which "*urge[d]* the Libyan [g]overnment immediately to provide a full and effective response to those requests."[79] "Those requests" included not only the extradition of the two Libyans, but also referred to demands delineated in previous

---

74. S.C. Res. 731, U.N. SCOR, 47th Sess., Res. & Dec., at 51, para. 1, U.N. Doc. S/INF/48 (1992).

75. George J. Church, *Wanted: A New Hideout*, TIME, Apr. 6, 1992, at 29.

76. S.C. Res. 731, *supra* note 74, pmbl.

77. Questions of Interpretation and Application of the 1971 Montreal Convention Arising from the Aerial Incident at Lockerbie (Libya v. U.S.), 1992 I.C.J. General List No. 89, para. 2 (Order of Apr. 14) [hereinafter Libya v. U.S.].

78. S.C. Res. 731, *supra* note 74, pmbl.

79. S.C. Res. 731, *supra* note 74, para. 3.

U.N. documents,[80] including the payment of compensation to the victims of the Lockerbie bombing by the Libyan government.[81] Instead of surrendering the accused, the Libyan government filed a claim against the United States and the United Kingdom with the I.C.J.[82] Libya alleged that by seeking redress through the Security Council, the United States and United Kingdom were acting in contravention of the Montreal Convention for the Suppression of Unlawful and Acts Against Safety of Civil Aviation.[83]

Soon thereafter, the United States and the United Kingdom sought and obtained a second resolution, in which the Council, "*[a]cting* under Chapter VII of the Charter, . . . *[d]ecide[d]* that the Libyan Government must now comply without any further delay with paragraph 3 of resolution 731 (1992)" to provide a full and effective response to its requests,[84] and "to cease all forms of terrorist action and all assistance to terrorist groups."[85] The resolution continued by imposing sanctions, including an embargo of arms and aircraft equipment on Libya, which "all States [were required to] adopt, . . . until the Security Council decide[d] that the Libyan government ha[d] complied with" the above request.[86]

---

80. *See generally Letter Dated 20 December 1991 from the Permanent Representatives of France, the United Kingdom of Great Britian and Northern Ireland and the United States of America to the United Nations Addressed to the Secretary-General,* U.N. GAOR, 46th Sess., Agenda Item 125, U.N. Doc. A/46/828, S/23309 (1991); *Letter Dated 20 December 1991 from the Permanent Representative of the United States of America to the United Nations Addressed to the Secretary-General,* U.N. GAOR, 46th Sess., Agenda Item 125, U.N. Doc. A/46/827, S/23308 (1991). *See also* FURTHER REPORT BY THE SECRETARY-GENERAL PURSUANT TO PARAGRAPH 4 OF SECURITY COUNCIL RESOLUTION 731, U.N. Doc. S/23672 (1992).

81. The U.N. documents refer to the compensation requests made by the United States and the United Kingdom in a joint statement of November 27, 1991. This request was adopted by reference in Resolution 731. *See* S.C. Res. 748, U.N. SCOR, 47th Sess., Res. & Dec., at 52, para. 1, U.N. Doc. S/INF/48 (1992) (citing S.C. Res. 731 as a reference in this context).

82. Libya v. U.S., *supra* note 77.

83. Montreal Convention for the Suppression of Unlawful and Acts Against Safety of Civil Aviation, Sept. 23, 1971, 24 U.S.T. 564, T.I.A.S. No. 7470 [hereinafter Montreal Convention]. The Montreal Convention is a multilateral agreement which prohibits state support of international terrorism. *See also Get Quaddafi,* ECONOMIST, Apr. 11, 1992, at 17.

84. S.C. Res. 748, *supra* note 81, para. 1, pmbl. (emphasis in original).

85. S.C. Res. 748, *supra* note 81, para. 2.

86. S.C. Res. 748, *supra* note 81, paras. 3-7.

b. *The Council Implicitly Drew Legal Conclusions in Determining
    That Libya Was Financially Liable to the Victims of
    the Lockerbie Bombing*

In addition to all other requests to comply fully with Resolution 748, Libya would have to pay full compensation to all victims of the bombing.[87] This request was unusual and seemingly premature, given that there had not yet been a trial of the alleged terrorists nor any adjudication of the Libyan government's involvement in the bombing. The Council, in requiring compensation be paid, must have made one of two findings—either that (i) Libya *is* in fact responsible for the Lockerbie incident, or that (ii) the two Libyan nationals *are* responsible, and Libya is liable for the loss through a theory of *respondeat superior*. In either case, legal determinations *were* made. These legal conclusions necessitated review of issues of law and fact that were neither expressly addressed nor fully "litigated" by the Council in any resolution. Assuming the Council did not act arbitrarily, the Council must have acted as a court in determining Libya's financial liability, given the conclusions in Resolution 731 and Resolution 748.

3. *Israel*

a. *Israel Expelled Palestinians From the "Occupied Territories" for
    What It Considered Sufficient Security Reasons*

On December 18, 1992, the Israeli government expelled over 400 Palestinians from the West Bank and Gaza Strip without a full trial.[88] The Palestinians were sent to a "security zone" that Israel had declared in southern Lebanon, but the Lebanese refused them entry.[89] Israel contended that this mass deportation was necessary for security reasons because these individuals, reportedly all members of Islamic fundamentalist groups, including one called "Hamas," were respon-

---

87. This is in reference to a U.S. State Department release, to which the Council refers in the text of Resolution 748. U.S. Dep't of State, *Gist: International Terrorism*, STATE DEP'T DISPATCH, May 18, 1992, *available in* LEXIS, Genfed Library, Dstate File.

88. Clyde Haberman, *Israel Expels 400 From Occupied Lands*, N.Y. TIMES, Dec. 18, 1992, at A1.

89. *Id.* Israel initially intended to deport the Palestinians to Lebanon. However, unlike previous occasions, Lebanon refused to accept the deportees this time. *Id.*

sible for recent uprisings and killings in the Occupied Territory.[90]

The international community responded swiftly, with almost universal condemnation of the Israeli action as illegal.[91] International human rights organizations and foreign governments, as well as the United States, usually an ardent supporter of Israel, strongly condemned the deportation. The United Kingdom, speaking on behalf of the European Community, stressed that such deportations were in violation of the Fourth Geneva Convention.[92]

In addition, the Palestinian delegation to the peace talks reacted by boycotting the final meetings of the first round of negotiations.[93] Representatives of the Palestinian delegation and other Palestinian leaders called for immediate Security Council involvement.[94]

Israel has consistently argued that the Geneva Convention is inapplicable to the occupied territories.[95] The Israeli High

---

90. *Id.*

91. *Id.*

92. *Id.*; Sarah Helm, *Israeli Court Refuses to Oppose Expulsions*, INDEPENDENT, Dec. 23, 1992, at 9, *available in* LEXIS, News Library, Indpnt File. Article 49 of the Geneva Convention provides in pertinent part: "deportations of protected persons from occupied territory to the territory of the Occupying Power or to that of any other country, occupied or not, are prohibited, regardless of their motive." 1949 Geneva Convention IV Relative to the Protection of Civilian Persons in Time of War, Aug. 12, 1949, art. 49, 75 U.N.T.S. 287-417, [hereinafter Geneva Convention]. "Protected persons," as defined in article 4, include "those who, at a given moment and in any manner whatsoever, find themselves , . . . in the hands of a[n] . . . Occupying Power of which they are not nationals." *Id.* art. 4; *see also U.N. Security Council Votes on the Situation in the Occupied Territories*, U.S. DEP'T STATE DISPATCH, Jan. 20, 1992, at 54 (stating that the U.S. government posits that the deportation is in violation of the Geneva Convention).

93. Haberman, *supra* note 88; David Ridge, *Palestinians Tell U.S.: No More Talks Until Deportees are Returned*, JERUSALEM POST, Jan. 14, 1993 *available in* LEXIS, News Library, Jpost File. In addition, the deportation set off widespread strikes in the Occupied Territory. Haberman, *supra* note 88.

94. Clyde Haberman, *Israel's Deportation; Rabin Kicks the Mideast Table*, N.Y. TIMES, Dec. 20, 1992, sec. 4, at 4; *see also* Paul Lewis, *Security Council Votes To Condemn Israeli Expulsion*, N.Y. TIMES, Dec. 19, 1992, at A1.

95. Hugh Carnegy, *A Lull in the Battle for Peace: Middle East Talks Hang in the Balance After the Deportation of Alleged Islamic Militants from Israel*, FIN. TIMES, Dec. 19, 1992, at 6; Sarah Helm, *Middle East: Rabin Finds Backing for "Iron Fist" in Court*, INDEPENDENT, Dec. 18, 1992, at 9, *available in* LEXIS, News Library, Indpnt File. Israel has consistently alleged that the Geneva Conven-

Court, in agreement with Yitzhak Rabin, held, in a December 1992 decision, that such deportations were legally permissible since they were only temporary.[96]

b. *Security Council Declares That the Israeli Deportation of the Palestinians Was a Violation of the Fourth Geneva Convention*

The Security Council disagreed with the Israeli position and enacted Resolution 799 which "*[s]trongly [c]ondemn[ed]* the action taken by Israel, the occupying Power, to deport hundreds of Palestinian civilians."[97] The resolution refers twice to Israel's "contravention of . . . obligations" under the Fourth Geneva Convention and purposely uses the language of Article 49 by consistently referring to Israel as the "occupying Power."[98] In other words, the Council emphasized that the Palestinians are "protected persons," the Gaza Strip and West Bank are "occupied territories," and that Israel is an "occupying Power." Therefore, Article 49 is applicable in this instance. Finally, Resolution 799 "*demands* that Israel, the occupying Power, ensure the safe and immediate return to the occupied territories of all those deported."[99]

---

tion "is designated to prohibit mass deportations" and does not apply to temporary deportations of a few individuals. David Makovsky & Allison Kaplan, *Israel Deports over 400 Inciters Move Complicates Search For Peace*, JERUSALEM POST, Dec. 18, 1992 *available in* LEXIS, News Library, Jpost File. Israeli apologists have also argued that Israel is not an "occupying power" as defined by the Geneva Convention. Samuel Katz, *Rabin's "Great Achievement"*, JERUSALEM POST, Feb. 19, 1993 *available in* LEXIS, News Library, Jpost File. For a compelling discussion on whether the Geneva Convention is applicable to Israel, see *Roundtable on the Expulsion and the Peace Process: Divisions Within the Israeli Peace Movement*, TIKKUM, March 1993, at 33 (interviews with Daphne Golan, Avram Poraz, Aaron Back, Avigdor Feldman, Galia Golan, Yoran Lass).

96. Ethan Bronner, *Israel Expels 400 Palestinians to Lebanon*, BOSTON GLOBE, Dec. 18, 1992, at 1; *see also* David Makovsky, *Israel and U.N. Deadlocked Over Return of Deportees*, JERUSALEM POST, Jan. 11, 1993 *available in* LEXIS, News Library, Jpost File (stating Rabin's assertion that, as they were for only two years, the deportations did not violate the Geneva Convention).

97. S.C. Res. 799, U.N. SCOR, 47th Sess., Res. & Dec., at 6, para. 1, U.N. Doc. S/INF/48 (1992); *see also*, Paul Lewis, *Israeli Expulsions Condemned by U.N.*, N.Y. TIMES, Dec. 20, 1992, at A14.

98. S.C. Res. 799, *supra* note 97, pmbl., paras. 1, 4.

99. S.C. Res. 799, *supra* note 97, para. 4.

c. *The Security Council, by Clarifying the Israeli Obligations Under the Geneva Convention, Is Essentially Acting in a Judicial Capacity*

Resolution 799 clarifies Israeli obligations under international law. In enacting the resolution, the Council answered very specific questions that were clearly juridical. In doing so, it applied international norms codified in a multilateral treaty to a specific situation, despite article 36(2) of the I.C.J. Statute, which specifically places interpretations of treaties under the jurisdiction of that U.N. organ.[100]

As in a court opinion, Resolution 799 explains specific provisions of Article 49 of the Geneva Convention and how the actions taken by Israel fit within those provisions. Moreover, the judicial analysis was integral to the resolution; without the determinations, Israel could have shielded itself with its own interpretation of the convention. Resolution 799 effectively closed the debate and made Israeli obligations explicit and enforceable. In this way, the Council acted as both the judiciary and the executive—applying legal standards in its findings, and establishing a regime to enforce the judicial decisions.

B. *Security Council as Legislature—Creating Legal Obligations for States*

Under Chapter VII, the Security Council is given the authority to determine what constitutes a "threat to the peace." However, if the Council determines that a particular state action, though not a violation of international law, is nonetheless a threat to international peace, is it not in effect creating legal obligations for that state, in light of the Charter's requirements that member states obey Security Council determinations?[101] In certain Council actions against Iraq and Libya, it explicitly created specific legal obligations for those states and

---

100. I.C.J. STATUTE art. 36(2)(a).

101. Article 25 of the U.N. Charter provides that "the Members of the United Nations agree to accept and carry out the decisions of the Security Council in accordance with the Charter." U.N. CHARTER art. 25. If, for instance, the Council determines that a particular state action (e.g., cutting down certain rain forests) is a *per se* "threat to the peace," then that state action would be legally proscribed. In this way, the Council can act as a legislature.

implicitly for all states.[102] The following part explores this un-precedented Council action.

1. *Iraq—Resolution 687 Creates New Legal Obligations for Iraq*

As previously discussed, one of the foremost objectives of Resolution 687 is the disarming of Iraq.[103] That the Council has the legal authority under Chapter VII to find the disarming of Iraq necessary to restore international peace is indisputable.[104] Moreover, because Iraq has demonstrated a proclivity for expansionist aggression and brutality[105] and its *status post bellum* was such that it could still wage aggressive war on its neighbors, the destruction of Iraqi warmaking capabilities was both politically astute and pragmatically necessary.

The resolution did create, however, new obligations for Iraq that did not exist prior to the enactment of Resolution 687. Resolution 687 purported to be based, in part, on Iraqi violation of treaty obligations. Before reciting the extensive measures imposed on Iraq in the operative paragraphs,[106] the Security Council, in the preamble, laid out evidence supporting its finding that Iraq continues to be a threat to international peace. Specifically, Resolution 687 cites Iraq's breach of four multilateral agreements,[107] Iraq's proclivity toward aggression evidenced by its "threats" to use outlawed weaponry, and past instances of aggression as the grounds for applying sanctions and the imposition of arms inspection.[108]

---

102. *See, e.g.*, S.C. Res. 799, *supra* note 97.

103. *See supra* text accompanying notes 41-47.

104. However, we must assume that the Council found that Iraq remained a threat to international peace, even after having forfeited its claim to Kuwait because the initial "breach of the peace," defined in Resolution 661 as the invasion of Kuwait, had been neutralized by this point. *See supra* note 22 and accompanying text.

105. The Gulf War and Iraq's eight-year war with Iran, as well as Iraq's brutal suppression of its civilian Kurdish population, serve as ample evidence of this proclivity.

106. *See supra* text accompanying notes 39-45 (discussing specific measures taken).

107. S.C. Res. 687, *supra* note 37, at 2-3; *see also supra* note 39 and accompanying text. Iraq did not violate most of the treaty obligations cited. Moreover, Iraq was only a signatory, not a party, to two of the agreements. *See, e.g.*, Roberts, *supra* note 39, at 600.

108. S.C. Res. 687, *supra* note 37, pmbl. The preamble specifically notes Iraq's threats to use chemical weapons as a rationale for the measures taken.

Significantly, Resolution 687 did not limit its provisions to Iraq's treaty obligations. For instance, although the Geneva Protocol for the Prohibition of the Use in War of Asphyxiating, Poisonous and Other Gases calls for refrain from "*use*" of chemical weaponry, the Council found it necessary to mandate the "*destruction*" of those weapons and prohibit Iraq from merely possessing the chemicals.[109]

By determining that Iraq's mere possession of such chemicals is a threat to the peace, the Council created new legal obligations for Iraq. The obligations arise out of Article 25, which requires all states to comply with Security Council determinations.[110] The Council has acted legislatively to the extent that Resolution 687 goes beyond Iraq's obligations under international law.

2. *Libya—The Security Council Imposes Obligations on Libya in Direct Contravention of a Multilateral Agreement to Which Libya and a Majority of the Council's Members Are Parties*

In Resolution 748, under its Chapter VII authority, the Council observed that Libya's failure to comply with an extradition request regarding two of its nationals constituted a threat to the peace.[111] This is perhaps the clearest illustration of legislative activity by the Council to date. As Libya has claimed,[112] the Security Council's request exceeds Libya's obligations under the Montreal Convention. The Convention, to which the United Kingdom, the United States, and Libya are parties, requires states *either* to assume jurisdiction *or* to extradite individuals to a state willing to exercise jurisdiction over any individual who has allegedly committed terrorist acts against civil aircraft.[113] At the time the Security Council enacted Resolutions 731 and 748, the Libyan government main-

---

One main purpose for owning such weaponry is for its deterrent effect, which, by definition, is a threat. To suggest that a verbalization of an implicit threat is evidence of such a propensity is slightly disingenuous. More likely, the resolution was based on the use of such weaponry on the Kurds a few years prior to the war and its use during the eight-year war with Iran.

109. S.C. Res. 687, *supra* note 37, para. 8 (emphasis added).

110. U.N. CHARTER art. 25.

111. *See supra* notes 84-86 and accompanying text.

112. Libya v. U.S., *supra* note 77, paras. 38-39.

113. Montreal Convention, *supra* note 83, arts. 5, 7.

tained that it had already asserted jurisdiction over this matter and had, therefore, fulfilled its obligations under the Convention.[114] This was not enough for the Council, which mandated that Libya extradite the two individuals *allegedly* responsible for the Lockerbie bombing to the United States or to the United Kingdom. In this instance, not only is the Council creating new obligations for a state, but it is doing so in contravention of a binding multilateral treaty which directly addresses this issue,[115] and to which a majority of the Council members and Libya are parties.[116] In this way, Resolution 748 is the most far-reaching legislative action taken by the Council.

II. THE PROPRIETY OF THE SECURITY COUNCIL ACTING AS A COURT AND A LEGISLATURE

A fundamental critique of international law is that it lacks adequate enforcement mechanisms and is, therefore, inherently defective.[117] Indeed, some postulate, most notably the Hobbes-Bentham-Austin positivist school,[118] that because of its inability to coerce compliance through force, the international normative system is not "law" at all.[119] Other commentators acknowledge this lack of enforcement as a distinguishing characteristic of international law, but find the distinction unimportant in a "teleological" examination of a normative system that finds general compliance without a "sovereign's command."[120] While I find the assertion that the international

---

114. Libya v. U.S., *supra* note 77, para. 7.

115. It is, of course, true that legally the Council is not bound by other treaty obligations. *See* U.N. CHARTER art. 103. However, creating new obligations in an area already covered by a comprehensive and almost universally accepted multilateral agreement is unprecedented and well worth scrutiny.

116. The I.C.J. has found Article 103—which states that obligations under the Charter trump obligations under any other agreement—dispositive on this issue at least on a preliminary hearing where the Court denied Libya's motion for an injunction. Libya v. U.S., *supra* note 77, para. 42.

117. *See generally* THOMAS M. FRANCK, THE POWER OF LEGITIMACY AMONG NATIONS 27-40 (1990) (repudiating this critique) [hereinafter FRANCK, LEGITIMACY].

118. Eric Stein, *The United Nations and the Enforcement of Peace*, 10 MICH. J. INT'L L. 304, 304 (1989).

119. *See, e.g.*, JOHN AUSTIN, THE PROVINCE OF JURISPRUDENCE DETERMINED 12, 42, 201 (1954).

120. *See generally* FRANCK, LEGITIMACY, *supra* note 117, at 27-40. Franck argues forcefully that most states, most of the time, obey the unenforceable

130   INTERNATIONAL LAW AND POLITICS   [Vol. 27:103

normative system finds compliance much of the time without transparent coercive force indisputable, it is clear that the system is in a constant search to find such authoritative leverage. There is an undeniable benefit to the use of force to compel compliance—to varying degrees, it usually works.[121]

The Security Council was intended to meet the demand for a forceful mechanism to ensure compliance with international law—specifically when non-compliance would or could cause instability in the international system.[122] The Chapter VII powers of the Security Council are the emulsifying element, introduced to solidify the "soft law" of the international system, making it more akin to domestic "hard law."[123] The ultimate purpose of the Security Council is to be the "commanding sovereign" in matters that endanger international peace and security. Therefore, the recent move toward self-empowerment by the Council may be seen as the belated assumption of its institutionally defined and mandated role as enforcer.[124] This should be a welcome development, as it is the realization of an international legal system that more closely fulfills the Austinian requirements of "law."[125]

---

rules of international law. He asserts that they do so because, to the degree these rules have "legitimacy," these rules will have a "compliance pull" even without coercive force.

121. While some commentators have persuasively urged that international law much of the time finds state obedience, *see* FRANCK, LEGITIMACY, *supra* note 117, at 8, most would agree that the system would be enhanced by the ability to use coercive force. Indeed, it is often difficult for many to accept a legal system as legitimate if it cannot use force to coerce compliance. *See, e.g.,* AUSTIN, *supra* note 119, at 12, 42, 201.

122. *See, e.g.,* GOODRICH ET AL., *supra* note 7, at 34.

123. The term "hard law" is generally used to describe rules which are enforced by utilizing coercive pressures, such as criminal or civil penalties (e.g., being placed in prison) in domestic law. "Soft law" describes those rules where compliance is obtained through pressures short of using physical force. FRANCK, LEGITIMACY, *supra* note 117, at 29.

124. U.N. CHARTER arts. 24-25.

125. As noted earlier, Austin believed that "law" required coercive force wielded by a "sovereign." AUSTIN, *supra* note 119, at 211-93. It is immaterial whether one believes or disbelieves that the coercive power to force compliance is necessary for a rule to be "law." I posit here only the proposition that coercive force will inevitably lead to more compliance than would its absence.

The rule Thucydides memorialized—"the strong do what they can and the weak suffer what they must"[126]—has historically guided the international system. The challenge has always been, at least from the international lawyer's perspective, to create relations between nations that are not propelled by force, but rather by law and its objectives of stability and justice. The founders of the United Nations intended the Security Council to guard a new world order based on the rule of law.[127] In the international system, the legitimate enforcement of legal rules compels all nations to consider the consequences of their actions. An enforcement system, such as the Council's Chapter VII powers, enhances efforts to conform the behavior of nations to legal rules that benefit all states.

The establishment of such an enforcement system, however, requires endowing the enforcing instrumentality with substantial power. Endowing the Security Council with broad power raises realistic concerns about the abuse of such power by nations that are members of the Council and that thus control the institution. It is not difficult to recall past abuses and to envision future scenarios where a system entrusted with such overwhelming powers produced illegitimate or unjust results—when the sovereign commanded, and she should not have.[128] Therefore, it is relevant to ask whether the Security

---

126. THUCYDIDES, THE HISTORY OF THE PELEPONNESIAN WAR 403 (Richard Crawley trans., 1950).

127. *See generally* Franck & Patel, *supra* note 29 (discussing the "new order" and the Security Council's powers under the U.N. Charter).

128. Consider, for example, some of the tactics used by the United States to convince other Security Council members to vote in alliance with the United States. In forming the coalition that passed the resolutions against Iraq during the Gulf crisis, the United States reportedly extended favors in exchange for the affirmative votes of several states. Burns Weston, *Security Council Resolution 678 and Persian Gulf Decision Making: Precarious Legitimacy*, 85 AM. J. INT'L. L. 516, 523-26 (1991). These favors included promises to ignore domestic human rights violations and promises of foreign aid and debt forgiveness. *Id.* at 523-25. Specifically, compelling evidence persuasively suggests that to acquire China's alliance with the U.S. position in the Gulf War, the United States effectively bought off China with promises to support World Bank loans and to ignore China's repression of its domestic pro-democracy movement. *Id.* at 523-24. The United States allegedly made similar concessions to insure the support of the Soviet Union and Yemen. *Id.*; Ian Williams, *U.S. Takeover at the U.N.; Leveraging the World*, 255 NATION 392 (1992). One Council diplomat characterized the post-Cold War pressures of the United States as a "reign of terror." *Id.* at 392. Such buying of

Council's propensity to act judicially and legislatively is appropriate and, furthermore, whether such propensity has a deleterious effect on the Council's institutional legitimacy.

This discussion will focus on these two questions. First, I will outline the concerns regarding the Council's assumption of roles not expressly within its competence. I will explore the concerns arising from the Council's increased willingness to answer juridical questions normally in the domain of the I.C.J. In addition, I will discuss issues pertaining to the creation of norms by a small group of states, and the imposition of such norms on all other states. Specifically, I will examine the effect the creation and imposition of that norm will have on the United Nations and on the development of international law.

A discussion of the Council's appropriate behavior is important, as it is what protects the legitimacy of the institution. Without a clear determination of what constitutes legitimate action, the community of states may perceive the Council as rogue. Subsequently, the Council may lose international support, which is vital for the successful execution of the Council's mandate.

A.   The Security Council as a Court

In discussing the appropriateness of the Council's judicial acts, it is first necessary to address the implicit dangers of systems that permit and legitimate decisions of states acting in their own national interests.[129] The Security Council is for all

---

votes and overt and substantial political pressure to change votes emphasizes the central concern—the danger of allowing a political institution to answer legal questions. The acquiescence of Council members to the U.S. enticements is inappropriate behavior by members of a *judicial* instrumentality. It violates fundamental concepts concerning conflicts of interest and is analogous to the acceptance of bribes by judges in the domestic context. Professor Brilmayer punctuates the violation, observing that "the concessions often involve acquiescence to violations of international law." R. Lea Brilmayer, *The Odd Advantage of Reliable Enemies*, 32 Harv. Int'l L.J. 331, 332 (1991).

129. This is not to suggest that the Security Council regularly, or even often, acts contrary to the interests of most states or against the interests of most peoples. There are, however, times when the political interests of the five permanent and other Security Council members are at odds with that of most states. This political motivation creates some concerns when the Council intends to act as a court.

Scholars have charged, for instance, that the permanent members of the Security Council—who are also the only nuclear powers—have sought

intents and purposes a political creature: "political expediency based on the concept of national interest" guides its members.[130] This raises the central query of whether the Council acts appropriately when acting as a court: Can a political institution legitimately make judicial decisions? If it is never appropriate for a political institution to answer juridical questions, it logically follows that a juridical decision by the Security Council is *per se* inappropriate. This would render further discussion moot.

1. *Considerations of Judicial Propriety*

a. *The Propriety of Decisions Influenced by National Self-Interest*

The foremost concern of this analysis regards systemic legitimacy. When national self-interest generally prejudices an institution, it cannot be expected to apply the law judicially. A dichotomy exists between the rule of law and the interests of states, which influences a political institution's adjudication of questions.[131] The dissonance between juridical decisions and

---

to prevent defining threats to use nuclear arms as a violation of international law. Mark Schapiro, *Mutiny on the Nuclear Bounty*, 257 NATION 798 (1993) (stating that the Non-Aligned Movement's efforts to enact such a resolution were terminated by super-power armtwisting); NICHOLAS GRIEF, THE WORLD COURT PROJECT ON NUCLEAR WEAPONS AND INTERNATIONAL LAW 13-16 (1993) (containing a compelling brief arguing that international law and the U.N. Charter proscribe the mere threat of the use of nuclear weapons and seeking an I.C.J. declaration to that effect).

Another example of the permanent five acting in their own self-interest is discernable in the juxtaposition between the environmental perspective of developed nations, led by Security Council members, and that of developing nations. *See, e.g.*, Ranee K.L. Panjabi, *Idealism and Self-Interest in International Environmental Law: The Rio Dilemma*, 23 CAL. W. INT'L L.J. 177, 179-80 (1992) (explaining the developing world's desire for self-interested development as a product of historical oppression); Edith Brown Weiss, *International Environmental Law: Contemporary Issues and the Emergence of a New World Order*, 81 GEO. L.J. 675, 675-76 (1993) (noting differences in interests between the developed and the developing world).

It is important to ask, therefore, how the homogenized interest of the permanent five will affect the decision-making processes when the Council makes legal determinations for a heterogeneous international community. This raises questions involving the appropriateness of a court violating the principle of *nemo judex debet esse in properia sua causa*. *See infra* note 141 and accompanying text.

130. TAE JIN KAHNG, LAW, POLITICS AND THE SECURITY COUNCIL 1 (1969).

131. *Id.*; *see generally* Ebere Osieke, *The Legal Validity of Ultra Vires Decisions of International Organizations*, 77 AM. J. INT'L L. 239 (1983) (examining

political decisions in the international system emanates from the differing functions of law and politics—the former "regulat[es] . . . conduct," while the latter "strive[s] to maximize the power of [a] nation-state[ ] through whatever means are available . . . including the violation of rules of conduct, the validity of which the former purportedly claims."[132] Therefore, to empower the Security Council, which is composed of states primarily guided by political forces, is to invite a non-judicial application of the law.[133] The Council's actions are unjust and, therefore, inappropriate to the extent that a dissonance exists between a legal conclusion and the Security Council's political conclusion.[134]

The dangers of such a situation are manifest. Although the rule of law may provide one answer, the Security Council may provide quite another, if the Council members' political interests guide their decision-making. If, indeed, an institution legitimized such an unjust result, it would force one to

---

emerging principles concerning the legal validity of legislative and judicial acts that international organizations have adopted in excess of their express constitutional powers).

132. KAHNG, *supra* note 130, at 1; *see also* HANS J. MORGENTHAU, POLITICS AMONG NATIONS 251 (2d ed. 1954) (describing the nature of international law as "primitive"). *See generally* HANS KELSEN, THE LAW OF THE UNITED NATIONS: A CRITICAL ANALYSIS OF ITS FUNDAMENTAL PROBLEMS (2d ed. 1964).

133. The Security Council members vote pursuant to orders from the political leaders of their states, based solely on the interests of those states. This is clearly different from the decision-making of judicial bodies, which must act and make decisions according to normative standards and "fairness." For example, Article 20 of the I.C.J. Statute requires every member of the I.C.J. to "exercise his powers impartially and conscientiously," I.C.J. STATUTE art. 20, and "to decide in accordance with international law such disputes." *Id.* art. 38(1); *see also infra* text accompanying notes 157-58 (discussing the principle of *nemo judex debet esse in properia sua causa*).

134. This is not a new concern of the U.N. system; indeed, it was a primary issue at San Francisco when the Charter was drafted. GOODRICH ET AL., *supra* note 7, at 23, 260. Belgium, for instance, had suggested that to curb the possibility of unjust actions, the I.C.J. should have judicial review powers over Security Council action. GOODRICH ET AL., *supra* note 7, at 23.

With the elimination of the Cold War check, however, this long dormant question has been and must continue to be re-examined. *See, e.g.*, W. Michael Reisman, *The Constitutional Crisis in the United Nations*, 87 AM. J. INT'L L. 83 (1992) (providing a legal analysis of the expansion of Security Council powers); Mark W. Janis, *International Law?*, 32 HARV. INT'L L.J. 363, 363-64 (1991) (advocating the rearticulation of international law during a time of changing politics and actors).

conclude that the institution was systemically flawed. Should such a political institution, conferred with executive powers, answer purely juridical questions requiring in-depth legal analysis when there are appropriate fora for the adjudication of such issues?

To allow a biased decision-maker—as this analysis has asserted the members of any political organ clearly are—to answer juridical questions arguably violates a general principle of international law.[135] As Professor Franck writes, "[j]udicial impartiality . . . is the essential ingredient of the legal system of most nations."[136] Indeed, one intuitively expects such a rule: a biased decision-maker is repugnant to any notion of fairness or justice. Procedural rules and structure can ensure that courts will not make biased decisions.[137]

b. *Juridical Questions are Unlike Other Chapter VII Determinations, Which Require Political Considerations*

One may respond that the Council's juridical determinations are similar to other Council determinations under Chapter VII, such as determining the existence of a threat to the peace.[138] However, one fundamental difference exists: the determination of a threat to the peace requires more than mere normative considerations, it also necessitates an analysis of political realities.[139] It is, thus, a political question that a political institution such as the Council should consider.

---

135. International organizations consistently view general principles of law as a source of international law, and, therefore, as constituting binding legal obligations. *See, e.g.*, I.C.J. STATUTE art. 38(1) (ordering the I.C.J. to apply "general principles of law recognized by civilized nations" in deciding cases).

136. 3 THOMAS FRANCK, HUMAN RIGHTS IN THIRD WORLD PERSPECTIVE 1 (1982) [hereinafter FRANCK, THIRD WORLD]. Professor Franck cites numerous cases from many domestic jurisdictions to evidence this point. *See, e.g.*, United States v. Civella, 416 F. Supp. 676 (W. Dist. Mo. 1975), *reprinted in* FRANCK, THIRD WORLD, *supra*, at 31-37; State v. M.A. Oyenubi, 3 U. I.F.E. L.R. 156, (Nigeria High Ct. 1971), *reprinted in* FRANCK, THIRD WORLD, *supra*, at 1-7; *see also infra* text accompanying notes 157-58 (discussing the principle of *nemo judex debet esse in properia sua causa*).

137. FRANCK, THIRD WORLD, *supra* note 136, at 57. *See* 1 GEORG SCHARZENBERGER, INTERNATIONAL LAW 390 (1st ed. 1945).

138. *See, e.g.*, U.N. CHARTER art. 39.

139. For example, see the situations referenced in GOODRICH ET AL., *supra* note 7, at 128.

Collective Security Law

The failure of the League of Nations taught that when answering such political questions, ignoring the existing power realities in the international community can be fatal.[140] The League experience demonstrated the necessity for an organ, composed of state representatives, that could employ devastating coercive power to enforce the law and to answer aggression without undue constraints; the Security Council is that organ.[141] The alternative, an international organ making purely legal decisions, could not deploy adequate force to elicit compliance with its decisions.[142]

The creation of the Security Council acknowledges that, in the international arena, political questions cannot be divorced from political realities.[143] This premise led the framers of the U.N. Charter to give the Security Council broad powers of autointerpretation,[144] enabling the organ to effect its "pri-

---

140. *See infra* note 144.

141. Unfortunately, to empower this organ, the permanent five were exempted from enforcement measures through their veto power. U.N. CHARTER art. 27. This is unfortunate because those states are, in certain cases, the foremost transgressors of international legal standards. For example, the U.S. invasions of Panama and Grenada, and the Russian invasion of Afghanistan, violated Article 2, paragraph 4 of the U.N. Charter.

142. In no way should this be construed as rejecting judicial review of Security Council actions, which I believe would be a positive development. The point is that only an executive organ of an international organization will have the support of states and ultimately states are the only ones capable of "enforcing" its will.

143. The Security Council's seemingly paradoxical existence noted earlier reflects the requirements of the forum in which it operates. The international forum is both political and judicial because it must consider the political viability of a particular action and the effect of that action on the normative system.

144. GOODRICH ET AL., *supra* note 7, at 266. The failures of the Kellogg-Briand Pact and the League of Nations greatly influenced the formation of the U.N. Charter. GOODRICH ET AL., *supra* note 7, at 23; *see generally* 1 EVAN LUARD, A HISTORY OF THE UNITED NATIONS 44 (1982) (discussing the lessons of the League of Nations, the planning of the U.N. Charter, and the San Francisco Conference). The United Nations emerged from the rubble of World War II—a war many of the Charter's framers perceived was the result of the League of Nation's inadequacies. LUARD, *supra*, at 1-16. The League represented the world's initial attempt to "promote international cooperation and to achieve international peace and security." LEAGUE OF NATIONS COVENANT pmbl. However, the League's framers failed by institutionalizing their aspirations instead of their realism. The League's ineffectiveness in preventing World War II was primarily due to fundamental structural incompetencies. Stein, *supra* note 118, at 305. These structural difficulties in-

mary responsibility for the maintenance of international peace and security" unfettered.[145]

This rationale is inapplicable, however, when the Council makes determinations that do not require the analysis of political considerations. When the Council makes legal determinations, it need not and, in fact, *should not,* incorporate political considerations into its decision-making. Considering political factors is inappropriate because law, unlike politics, is primarily based on considerations of fairness and normative application of rules. Unlike the determination of whether something is a threat to the peace, no countervailing political concern exists in answering juridical questions.

c.   *The Security Council's Lack of Procedural Safeguards to Ensure Due Process Underscores Concerns That the Members' National Political Interests Solely Guide the Council*

Courts generally have procedural rules that safeguard the rights of litigants before the tribunal. The I.C.J. Statute, for example, devotes twenty-six articles to delineating procedures of the Court.[146] In addition, the I.C.J. has adopted Rules of the Court that outline further procedural safeguards.[147]

A court is generally presumed to have procedural mechanisms to weigh evidence properly, make findings of fact and law, make determinations in an unbiased fashion, ensure unbiased access to information, permit all parties in a dispute to be heard and to be represented by counsel, and essentially to pro-

---

cluded a failure to establish a determinative norm concerning aggression and a politically realistic instrument to take effective political, economic, and collective military measures to suppress aggression and breaches of the peace. *Id.*; *see* GOODRICH ET AL., *supra* note 7, at 24-27. The Security Council and its seemingly limitless powers in the sphere of "international peace and security," GOODRICH ET AL., *supra* note 7, at 26, coupled with a determinative definition of aggression in Article 2, paragraph 4 of the Charter, were designed to address the primary deficiencies of its institutional predecessor. Symposium, *supra* note 2, at 23-24 (comments by Professor Sohn).

145. U.N. CHARTER art. 24, para. 1.

146. Chapter III of the Statute of the International Court of Justice provides procedural rules that ensure the due process guarantees to a greater extent than in many domestic courts. I.C.J. STATUTE arts. 39-64. The Security Council does not yet have such a comprehensive set of procedural rules.

147. Rules of the Court, 1946 I.C.J. Acts & Docs. 545-83 [hereinafter Rules of the Court].

tect all other due process rights of the persons before it.[148] There is a compelling argument that due process rights and procedural safeguards are general principles of law or customary international law.[149] In any case, it would seem inappropriate for an international tribunal to lack such safeguards.[150]

No such rules, however, guide the adjudication of claims before the Security Council.[151] This is especially pertinent for

---

148. In the domestic arena, we assume that courts have such institutional competency. In the International Covenant on Civil and Political Rights such due process rights are guaranteed in Article 9. International Covenant on Civil and Political Rights, Dec. 16, 1966, art. 9, 991 U.N.T.S. 171 [hereinafter Political Covenant]. Moreover, many commentators have argued that certain "judicial procedures" are general principles of international law. *See, e.g.*, Bin Cheng, General Principles of International Law as Applied by International Courts and Tribunals 258 (1987); Georg Schwarzenberger, A Manual of International Law 237-54 (5th ed. 1967).

149. Cheng, *supra* note 148, at 258-326. Most international treaties regarding rights of individuals guarantee the right to due process of law. *See, e.g.* Political Convenant, *supra* note 148, art. 2, para. 3. (mandating that individuals "have an effective remedy" if the rights in the Political Covenant are violated and that the state provide a competent tribunal to hear claims); art. 6, para. 1; art. 12, para. 4; art. 17; art. 26 (forbidding arbitrary application of the law); and art. 9 (guaranteeing the right to liberty and security of person, proscribing arbitrary arrest and detention, and requiring the State to act "in accordance with such procedures as are established by law"); Universal Declaration of Human Rights, G.A. Res. 217, U.N. Doc. A/810, arts. 9, 10, 17 (1948) (providing, respectively, for no arbitrary arrest, the right to fair hearing by an impartial tribunal, and no arbitrary deprivation of property). In addition, most of the world's legal systems provide due process guarantees. *See, e.g.*, U.S. Const. amend. XIV, sec. 1; *see also* Franck, Third World, *supra* note 136, at 1-172 (citing cases from around the world which expound the right to an unbiased court by ensuring the impartiality of the judge and factfinder, and ensuring a right to counsel); Salvador Commercial Co. Case, 1902 U.S.F.R. 838, 871-72, *quoted in* Cheng, *supra* note 148, at 280.

150. To be free from arbitrary deprivation of rights is a *sine qua non* of freedom and equality. Article 2, paragraph 1 of the U.N. Charter recognizes the "sovereign equality" of all member states. U.N. Charter art. 2, para. 1. It seems that a right to fair litigation of the "sovereign's rights" naturally emanates from any genuine concept of "equality." If the United Nations has the capacity to eviscerate the rights of some states without due process of law, then the alleged "equality" among sovereigns is purely illusory. *See also* Cheng, *supra* note 148, at 290 ("[T]here are two cardinal characteristics of a judicial process, the impartiality of the tribunal and its corollary, *the juridical equality between the part[ies.]*") (emphasis added).

151. Concededly, the Charter requires the Council to give states an opportunity to be heard when the Council discusses matters concerning that state. U.N. Charter art. 31. This, however, is a dramatically insufficient safeguard.

questions before the Council requiring intricate legal analysis.[152] It is self-evident that any tribunal faced with the adjudication of issues of law and fact is far more likely to decide the issues in an arbitrary and capricious manner if it lacks rules of procedure.[153]

In addition, unlike the I.C.J., the Security Council is not required to explain any of its holdings in a published opinion.[154] A published opinion analyzing the pertinent legal and factual issues and explicating the rationale for the court's decision has two effects. First, it requires that the decision be based on normative standards, because a failure to state the law and its relation to the facts would be deemed inappropriate. Second, any judicial impropriety or misinterpretation of the law would be manifest, and thus subject to harsh criticism, while opinions with an appropriate application of international normative standards would be beyond reproach.[155]

Currently, the deliberative process used by the Security Council to arrive at a decision is merely speculative. A failure to outline specifically the decisional process is concededly not problematic when an institution examines political issues.[156] However, questions of law should be resolved through the nor-

---

The Council need not closely scrutinize all documents that may be relevant to an adjudication and need not base its decisions on the application of clear normative standards.

152. *See, e.g.,* the discussion of the demarcation of the border between Iraq and Kuwait, *supra* notes 48-62 and accompanying text.

153. The purpose of procedural rules is to facilitate and ensure the normative application of law.

154. Rules of the Court, *supra* note 147, art. 95 (requiring that when the court announces a judgment, the judgment "shall include," among other items, "a statement of the facts" and "the reasons in point of law" for the decision).

155. This has the added effect of legitimizing rulings by a court that are clearly based on the rule of law while delegitimizing capricious decisions that fail to apply legal rules judiciously.

156. It is appropriate for a member of a political institution to "vote" as he or she wishes considering the many interests of various interested parties. Indeed, it is the purpose of the political institution to fuse all interests to come up with the best possible solution. Of course, the political entity cannot consider voting a particular way because of improper factors (e.g., bribery, or a violation of the overall purpose of the institution), but it is not required to apply normative standards to its decisions. Therefore, it would serve little purpose to have such an institution publish its deliberations when answering political questions.

mative application of rules. Failure to provide a record that supports the Council's conclusions of fact and law precludes any critical analysis of the determinations. Without such analysis, commentators and, more importantly, states would be prevented from effectively criticizing the Council's decisions as unfair or in contravention of law. If the Council is to persist in acting as a court, it must at a minimum establish and follow procedural rules and publish opinions.

Furthermore, if the Council is to act in a judicial capacity, it must not allow its members to adjudicate matters in which its members are interested parties. To do so is inconsistent with the long-standing principle of *nemo debet esse judex in sua propria causa.*[157] This doctrine has been accepted by many international tribunals as a general principle of international law.[158] The Council, when answering juridical questions that affect its members' own national interests, is essentially transgressing this principle.

d.   *The Language of the Charter Does Not Envision the Council Acting as a Court*

The Security Council is given not only the power to determine the existence of threats to the peace but also the authority to take appropriate measures to neutralize those threats.[159] However, the Council is limited to taking measures "in accordance with Articles 41 and 42."[160] The legal determinations made by the Council, such as the demarcation of a border, are clearly "not [decisions] involving the use of armed force," and therefore Article 42, which concerns only the use of force, would be inapplicable. Article 41, on the other hand, concerns the imposition of economic and other sanctions on a state "to give effect to [Council] decisions."[161] Although Article 41 is phrased in permissive terms and does not limit the Council's action to a particular set of measures, it certainly does not envision the Council making legal determinations.[162]

---

157. Cheng, *supra* note 148, at 279-89.
158. *See, e.g.,* Virginius Incident, 65 B.F.S.P. 98, 102-03 (1873); *see also* Cheng, *supra* note 148, at 280-87 (citing numerous cases by international tribunals).
159. U.N. Charter art. 39.
160. *Id.*
161. *Id.* art. 41.
162. Article 41 of the U.N. Charter provides in full:

The question remains—where does the Council find the authority under Chapter VII to assume the role of a court?[163] Indeed, any reasonable, hermeneutic analysis must conclude that this authority is not explicitly conferred upon the Security Council under Chapter VII.[164] There is, therefore, a question of whether the Council can legally assume the role of judiciary.

Furthermore, even if the Council can "legally" make judicial determinations, it is questionable whether the assumption of such power is prudent for an institution so reliant on maintaining legitimacy. The Charter confers different powers upon U.N. organs consistent with the composition of those organs.[165] The Security Council is composed of the most powerful states and, consequently, maintains the inherent capacity to coerce compliance with its decisions. For the Security Council to resolve issues of law in a dispositive manner is inconsistent with its role as executive enforcer. This sentiment is made manifest in the Charter through the conspicuous absence of any bestowal of judicial powers on the Council. That the Charter fails to supply adequate authority for the Council

---

The Security Council may decide what measures not involving the use of armed force are to be employed to give effect to its decisions, and it may call upon the Members of the United Nations to apply such measures. These may include complete or partial interruption of economic relations and of rail, air, postal, telegraphic, radio, and other means of communication, and the severance of diplomatic relations.

U.N. CHARTER art. 41.

163. Again, I am not questioning whether the Council has the authority to decide, for instance, that an indeterminate border is a "threat to the peace." Rather, the question is whether the Council is conferred the power under the Charter to determine, for example, what a disputed boundary line should be.

164. Some commentators argue that the Council has very broad authority under Chapter VII and in no way should be limited by the particular denotation of the Articles. Chapter VII, as they would have it, is a mere description or perhaps litany of examples of these boundless Security Council powers. It should be noted, however, that the U.N. Charter is a treaty and should be interpreted under the rules of treaty interpretation, such as those found in the Vienna Convention, *supra* note 56, arts. 31-32. Clearly, it seems unreasonable to suggest that the Security Council has the authority to assume the role of court under Chapter VII, given that such power is not even intimated through the "ordinary meaning" of the Charter terms or the "preparatory work of the treaty." Vienna Convention, *supra* note 56, arts. 31-32.

165. *See infra* notes 166-71 and accompanying text.

to act as a judicial body will heavily influence any state's conclusions as to the appropriateness of any Council action in this regard.

e.   *The Existence of Other Organs and the Mechanisms to Create Additional Bodies for Proper Adjudication of Juridical Questions Raise Concerns of Comity*

If the United Nations did not have a judicial organ, then it would be sensible for the Council to assume a judicial role. This is, of course, not the case. The Security Council is responsible for ensuring international peace and security, while the I.C.J., in Article 92 of the Charter, is described as the "principle judicial organ of the United Nations."[166] The logical conclusion is that the Council should refer issues of law and corresponding issues of fact, absent political questions, to the I.C.J.

In determining whether a particular Council action is appropriate, a functional analysis of the institutional system as a whole is critical. These considerations automatically raise issues of comity between the organs of the institution. By failing to refer questions of law—which would normally be addressed by a court—to the I.C.J., the Council dramatically diminishes the I.C.J.'s legitimacy as a coordinate organ of the United Nations. In a system that is intended to operate in a unified manner to fulfill the purposes outlined in the Charter, and act "in conformity with justice and international law,"[167] the Council's actions seem counterproductive. By ignoring the clear separation of function and power set forth in the Charter, the Security Council diminishes the legitimacy of the entire U.N. system.[168]

f.   *Alternatively, the Council Can Form a Tribunal Under Article 29 of the Charter to Adjudicate Legal Issues*

The Council, some might respond, is given the power not to respect the integrity of the I.C.J. and should not be limited

---

166. U.N. CHARTER art. 92.

167. *Id.* art. 1, para. 1.

168. In addition, the I.C.J. has more experience in deciding juridical questions such as the demarcation of a boundary line. *See, e.g.,* Concerning Territorial Dispute (Libyan Jamahiriha-Chad), 1991 I.C.J. 44 (Aug. 26).

by that organ.[169] However, the Council has the option of forming a subsidiary tribunal under Article 29 to adjudicate legal issues.[170] Under Article 29, the Council can "establish such subsidiary organs as it deems necessary for the performance of its functions."[171] Thus, instead of deciding questions of law and fact for itself, which raises concerns about institutional competence, the Council can establish a tribunal that properly adjudicates the issues. Much of the disquiet about an institution making legal determinations based on national interest will be ameliorated if the Council establishes a judicial tribunal with the express purpose of answering certain juridical questions. An Article 29 tribunal would provide both a distance from the Council necessary to preserve institutional legitimacy, and only limited autonomy if the Council desires to have more control than it would have over the I.C.J.[172] That the Charter provides yet another avenue where the Council can adjudicate the justiciable issues of a case is further evidence that the Council is not given any implied power to act as a court.

2. *Analysis of Council Actions as a Court*

Recently, the Council has attempted to answer juridical questions at least twice. The issues surrounding the demarcation of the boundary in Resolution 687 and the Security Council interpretation of the Geneva Convention in Resolution 799 provide instructive examples of the difficulties created by Council adjudication.

---

169. I believe that the Council should be limited by the legal determinations made by the U.N. coordinate branch assigned the task of answering legal questions. The Council's failure to respect the I.C.J. may be a reflection of the Council's unwillingness to consider fully the principles of international law as is required under U.N. Charter Article 1, paragraph 1, applicable to the Council through Article 24, paragraph 2. U.N. CHARTER art. 1, para. 1, art. 24, para. 2.

170. U.N. CHARTER art. 29.

171. *Id.*

172. The Security Council would have more control over an Article 29 tribunal than it has over the I.C.J. because it determines the composition of the organ and the procedural rules of the tribunal. Nevertheless, the Council must ensure that it gives the tribunal adequate independence to analyze the issues and decide the questions without undue influence. A failure to distance itself sufficiently from the deliberative process would be tantamount to answering the questions itself.

a.   *The Demarcation of the Iraq-Kuwait Boundary Line Is an
     Example of Why the Council Should Generally Not Act
     as a Court*

The Security Council, as already discussed, answered juridical questions in determining the proper boundary between
Iraq and Kuwait.[173] Resolution 687, in this regard, is an example of why the Council should avoid acting as a court.

The Iraqi government's reaction to the demarcation was
predictably negative. The strength of the Iraqi critique was
nourished by the Council's willingness to answer juridical
questions in a political manner.[174] Iraq had certain legal
claims to the disputed territory which were summarily decided
without any adjudication. The absence of judicial discussion
of those claims and the Council's inability to demonstrate the
utilization of procedural mechanisms to ensure a fair adjudication render its determinations suspect. In essence, it seems
that the Council acted punitively towards Iraq in not considering its claims for title to certain disputed territory. As Professor Eilts points out, the "imposition" of this determination will
not settle the problem in the eyes of the Iraqis. On a pragmatic level, this will allow the political viability of "future successor [Iraqi] government[s] to re-assert the previously
claimed territory" and the United Nations will not be able to
"indefinitely guarantee Kuwait's security."[175] If Iraq had been
allowed to adjudicate its claims in a proper forum with protective procedural guarantees, its legal, and *ipso facto* political,
ability to challenge any determination would have been severely weakened.

---

173. *See supra* text accompanying notes 46-52.

174. It is not my contention that the Security Council could not, or even
should not, act punitively towards Iraq. Indeed, I believe the elimination of
the Iraqi war arsenal, for example, was a prudent measure to ensure future
regional peace and security. Nevertheless, I believe it is inappropriate for
the Council to dispossess Iraq of territory as a punitive measure under Chapter VII; dispossession of land leads down a slippery slope that could end with
neo-colonialism. I believe it is a small step from saying it is appropriate to
dispossess a nation of *some* of its land to saying that it is appropriate to dispossess it of *all* its land.

175. Eilts, *supra* note 48, at 16. In addition, Eilts reminds us that the
boundary line reflected in the "appropriate materials" referred to in Resolution 687 would give title to Kuwait to part of the Rumaila oil fields that were
initially discovered by Iraqi-sponsored oil companies. Such manifest injustice will not die by the passage of a capricious Security Council decision.

On the normative level, the Council's willingness to ignore the legal claims of a party to a dispute will undoubtedly have significant ramifications in garnering international support of its determinations. States may be reluctant to support a Security Council that is willing to adjudicate their claims to land, knowing that the Council may be guided by political expediency. Land issues are especially sacrosanct to states. An institution that is willing to sacrifice arbitrarily a state's claims to that fundamental element of statehood on the altar of "peace and security" may find itself severely rebuked.[176] It is both unwise and unnecessary for the Council to set such a precedent that will cultivate continued regional instability and diminish the Council's legitimacy.

The Council had options other than deciding the border controversy. First, some concerns would have been lessened had the Council assumed the procedural attributes of a court. If, for instance, the Council had discussed its "legal" determinations in a published opinion, the Council could have demonstrated that its determinations were neither arbitrary nor political, but based on a careful analysis of fact and law.[177] Moreover, the opinion would dilute fears and neutralize criticism that the Council acted pursuant to the selfish goals of its members.[178] Second, the Council could have mandated that the two parties respect a particular boundary line while the dispute was being adjudicated in a proper forum.

b. *Alternatively, the Security Council Should Have Mandated That Iraq and Kuwait Submit to the Jurisdiction of the I.C.J. or to an Article 29 Tribunal*

Criticizing the Council's approach would be inappropriate if there were not viable alternative methods of settling the dispute. However, alternatives, which do not share the preca-

---

176. It is no wonder that the Security Council voted unanimously until Resolution 687, when three states—Yemen, Ecuador, and Cuba—dissented. Provisional Verbatim Record, U.N. SCOR, 46th Sess., 2981st mtg. at 82, U.N. Doc. S/PV.2981 (1991).

177. It would have been proper for the Council to show that the evidence of Iraqi claims was considered in its decisions and consequently found to be without merit. The failure to do even this minimal task raises concerns that the Council did not consider Iraqi claims at all.

178. This would in turn violate the principle of *nemo debet esse judex in properia causa.*

rious legitimacy of the Council acting judicially, do exist. One alternative would be for the Council to decide that Kuwait and Iraq must submit their claims to the I.C.J. Although this approach would bypass any criticism and fear that member states may have toward the Council's acting as a court, it has its legal difficulties. For instance, the I.C.J. has jurisdiction over contentious cases only where states voluntarily submit to its jurisdiction.[179] For the Security Council to mandate that the states accept the I.C.J.'s jurisdiction may violate the consensual nature of the court's jurisdiction over contentious cases.

Another option is for the Security Council to request an advisory opinion from the I.C.J. concerning the border demarcation. A request for an advisory opinion, however, raises its own difficulties. Advisory opinions can only be requested by particular organs of the United Nations, in order to seek advice "on any legal question."[180] Although the demarcation of the border is such a legal question, the request may be rejected by the I.C.J. because the legal question is arguably a "contentious case" disguised in advisory opinion garb. Nevertheless, the I.C.J. is not without precedent for rendering an advisory opinion on boundary disputes.[181] Moreover, the I.C.J. has generally been willing to expand the scope of its jurisdiction.[182]

Alternatively, if the I.C.J. is unable to find sound jurisdictional grounds to hear this case or if the Council is wary of requesting I.C.J. advice, the Council may establish an Article 29 tribunal for the express purpose of analyzing the issues of fact and law that are central to this dispute. The Security Council could have mandated that Kuwait and Iraq submit themselves to this *ad hoc* judicial organ in its resolutions. The

---

179. Article 36(1) of the I.C.J. Statutes only permits states to "refer" contentious cases to the I.C.J. I.C.J. STATUTE art. 36(1).

180. U.N. CHARTER art. 96.

181. *See, e.g.*, Concerning Territorial Dispute (Libyan Jamahiriha-Chad), 1991 I.C.J. 44 (Aug. 26); Delimitation of the Maritime Boundary in the Gulf of Maine Area (Can. v. U.S.), 1984 I.C.J. 246 (Oct. 12).

182. *See, e.g.*, Military and Paramilitary Activities (Nicar. v. U.S.), 1986 I.C.J. 169 (May 10) (rejecting the U.S. claim that the Vandenberg Reservation prohibited the Court from assuming jurisdiction, dramatically expanding the scope of I.C.J. jurisdiction); Corfu Channel Case (U.K.-Alb.), 1948 I.C.J. 15 (Preliminary Objections of Mar. 25) (rejecting Albania's objection to I.C.J. jurisdiction).

tribunal could then have made legal determinations based on all the claims of both parties and the Council could have then legitimately enforced the result.

c. *Therefore, the Settlement of the Boundary Dispute Was a Patently Inappropriate Action by the Security Council*

As it stands, the Council's actions concerning the border demarcation simply imbued Iraqi claims of injustice with credibility and added force and may have raised concerns among other states about the Council's overzealous behavior.[183] The Council acted with complete disregard for common notions of fairness in determining the border, without any procedural mechanisms to ensure that Iraq received due process of law. Adjudication is not within the institutional competence of the Council under Chapter VII.[184] More importantly, it reflects a propensity of the Council to be imprudent and inattentive in protecting its fragile legitimacy. States will of course be aware that the Council's willingness to alienate land may, in the future, affect their own territories. Such natural inferences will deflate the wide support the Security Council enjoyed during the Gulf War and create political obstacles for future actions under Chapter VII. At a minimum, the decision to demarcate the borderline was an unnecessary[185] *tour de force* which demonstrated that the Security Council was willing to act as it pleased, without considering the implications that its actions would have on interstate relations.

---

183. *See* U.N. Doc S/PV.2981, *supra* note 176 (statements by Cuba and Yemen). *See also* David D. Caron, *The Legitimacy of the Collective Security of the Security Council,* 87 AM. J. INT'L L. 552, 556-62 (1993).

184. *See supra* text accompanying note 142. Virtually since its inception, the United Nations has been perceived by the world community as a puppet, if not the alter-ego, of the United States. *See generally* Inis L. Claude, Jr., *Collective Legitimization as a Political Function of the United Nations,* 20 INT'L ORG. 367 (1966); Youssef Ibrahim, *Many Arabs See "Double Standard",* N.Y. TIMES, Jan. 15, 1993, at A8. This notion, whether well-founded or not, militates against the moral force of the Security Council and its decisions. Caron, *supra* note 183, at 556-60. When the Council acts lawfully and within its authority, the strength of the criticism that the U.N. is merely a U.S. pawn is severely diminished. *Id.*

185. I use the term "unnecessary" not to insinuate that the United Nations should not have demarcated the border, but rather that there are more appropriate organs of the United Nations than the Security Council for the task—namely the I.C.J. or an Article 29 tribunal.

148   *INTERNATIONAL LAW AND POLITICS*   [Vol. 27:103

B. *Security Council as a Legislature*

The creation of normative rules is perhaps the most significant power any institution can have. To confer on a body the competence to make law is tantamount to permitting that body to become the sovereign. Recent Council measures taken under Chapter VII have manifested themselves in ways that can only be characterized as legislative—that is, they created legal obligations for states.[186]

Although the Council arguably has the power to legislate as a matter of law, this power, if used without constraint, could effectively delegitimate the U.N. system. This is not to say that the Council should refrain from creating legal obligations; on the contrary, the creation of obligations for states by the Council is quite appropriate if it considers the political ramifications of those obligations for all U.N. member states.[187] To protect its institutional legitimacy, the Council must avoid the appearance of acting inappropriately—that is, of acting in the interest of Security Council member states and to the detriment of some or all other states. The following is a discussion of what I believe could be perceived by the international community as inappropriate and why.

---

186. See, for example, the actions taken against Libya, where the Security Council acted in clear contravention of treaty law. This action can only be characterized as legal if the Council had the power to make law. *See supra* note 78 and accompanying text. Kelsen asserts that "the Security Council is not bound strictly to comply with existing law." HANS KELSEN, THE LAW OF THE UNITED NATIONS: A CRITICAL ANALYSIS OF ITS FUNDAMENTAL POWERS 275 (1st ed. 1950). An institution which is unrestrained by existing law and which can compel compliance to its decision by force, is, *ipso facto*, a lawmaker.

187. Moreover, the Council may be the only U.N. organ that can effectively coerce compliance to the norms it creates. The General Assembly is conferred only the authority to encourage "the progressive development of international law," U.N. CHARTER art. 13, para. 1(a), and thus has no authority to enforce the law. Therefore, it is important that the Council have the capacity to create new norms but, as I will argue, not without regard for the interests of the states not represented on Security Council. *See generally* Caron, *supra* note 183 (arguing that the Council's legitimacy is affected by the Council's faithfulness to the concerns of other U.N. member states).

1. *Factors to Consider in Adjudging Legislative Appropriateness*

a. *The Security Council's Authority to Determine Threats to the Peace, by Implication, Confers the Authority to Act Legislatively*

The determination that certain action constitutes a "threat to the peace" is limited by neither the text of Article 39 nor by the record of the preparatory work for the Charter.[188] Indeed, this broad discretion of the Council was the intent of framers of the Charter. During the drafting of the Charter, some of the framers suggested elucidating the terms of Article 39 with greater specificity.[189] Ultimately, however, it was decided that such definitional particularity would serve to limit unnecessarily the Security Council's ability to effectively act against threats to international peace. This is not to say that the Council can act without constraints; the Security Council is required to "act in accordance with the Purposes and Principles of the United Nations."[190] Article 1(1) further requires that the Council act in "conformity with the principles of justice and international law."[191] This limitation does not make legislative action inappropriate for the Council, but does limit *how* the Council legislates. Hence, no legal limitation exists which forbids the Council to use Chapter VII in a legislative capacity. The language of Article 39 is interpreted to stand for the proposition that the Council can create law: when the Council determines that a particular action is a *per se* threat to international peace, states are obligated to avoid such action.[192] Nonetheless, in deciding if it is appropriate for the

---

188. Vienna Convention, *supra* note 56, arts. 31-32. Under Article 31 of the Vienna Convention, the "ordinary meaning" of the terms of the treaty are dispositive in the interpretation of the treaty. *Id.* art. 31. Article 32 permits consideration of "preparatory work" if the text is "ambiguous or obscure." *Id.* art 32. Considering both the plain meaning of the text and the preparatory work of the Charter, it is clear that the Security Council is given broad discretion in exercising its Chapter VII powers. GOODRICH ET AL., *supra* note 7, at 295-97.

189. *See* GOODRICH ET AL., *supra* note 7, at 295-97.

190. U.N. CHARTER art. 24, para. 2.

191. *Id.* art. 1, para. 1.

192. For example, if the Council passed a resolution saying that terrorist acts by state officials of any nation is a threat to the peace, then states would be obliged to prevent their officials from participating in terrorist actions. *See, e.g.,* S.C. Res. 748, *supra* note 81, para. 4.

Council to legislate, we must determine not only whether such action is legal, but also whether it is prudent.

b.   *Concerns of a Non-Representative Institution Creating Legal Obligations for the International Community*

The pentarchy called the Security Council is a patently undemocratic body.[193] At a time when "democracy is beginning to be seen as the *sine qua non* for validating governance" and is becoming an international legal entitlement,[194] the suggestion that an undemocratic, oligarchic body should make law that is imposed on the community of states is anomalous. A small group of states with similar national interests making determinations of "what the law should be" based on those interests is a situation that invites injustice and impropriety.[195]

Furthermore, such a situation is in contravention of basic principles of the international normative system. Some generally accepted, albeit limited, sources of rules regulate state behavior—convention law, customary law, and general principles of law.[196] These sources of law have a common denominator: they require the consent of states.[197] State consent, evidenced

---

193. The Council actually has 17 members. However, it is a "pentarchy" because the permanent five members have extreme influence on the decision-making, given that they have the veto power. *See Open the Club*, Econo-mist, Aug. 29, 1992, at 14 (asserting that many feel the Security Council is becoming "a flag of convenience for old-time neo-imperialists" and asserting that the permanent seats should be expanded).

In response, one may posit that since the Council has over half the world's population represented among its permanent members, it is actually more representative than the General Assembly. Although this argument is compelling, international law is now and has always been perceived as the law between *nations*. Considering that our discussion here concerns international law, the small group of states comprising the Security Council cannot be considered representative of the world, regardless of the population actually represented.

194. Franck, *supra* note 1, at 46.

195. *See* Peter J. Fromuth, *The Making of a Security Community: The United Nations After the Cold War*, 46 J. Int'l Aff. 341, 363 (1993).

196. I.C.J. Statute art. 38(1).

197. Carter & Trimble, *supra* note 56, at 140. The "persistent objector" doctrine is the exception that proves the rule—only states that have continually and persistently objected to the development of a customary rule during its development period are exempt from that rule once it is in force. There would be no need for this doctrine unless consent was of the utmost importance.

both implicitly through practice, and explicitly through agreements to normative regulation, is a logical requirement in a system that respects the "sovereign equality" of nations.[198] Lawmaking does and should require consideration of self-determination; the recognition of the sovereign equality of states represents, albeit inadequately, self-determination in the context of interstate relations. By acting as a legislature, the Council may ignore the sovereign equality of states and play the role of oligarch. While an imperfect world may accept this as perhaps necessary, in our current system, the lawmaker has the obligation to seek constituent acceptance of its enacted norms.[199]

Making law without a comprehensive assessment of state interests has significant implications for the international legal system. The Council's legislative actions may have a chilling effect on the progressive development of international law; this is a risky consequence. Such actions force states to take defensive postures, guarding their sovereign right to be bound only by laws to which they consent.[200] International law traditionally develops through state practice and agreement. If the Council begins to hasten the codification of emerging norms by directly enforcing norms which are not yet law as traditionally defined, member states will be hesitant to demonstrate any indication that they support such emerging norms.[201] The Council may be able to enforce present *lex feranda*, but it risks crippling the system for future progressive development.

---

198. U.N. CHARTER art. 2, para. 1. Arguably, the Council acts illegally when enacting legislation while ignoring the "sovereign equality" of states. Article 2, paragraph 1, stresses that the United Nations is based on "the principle of the sovereign equality of all its Members." A fundamental element of sovereignty is the right to be bound only by the law to which a state consents to be bound. If the Council requires that states abide by new Chapter VII legislation, disregarding the states' protests, it may contravene the traditional interpretation of this provision.

199. A number of commentators have suggested that this, at most, requires the Security Council to seek advice from the General Assembly. *See, e.g.*, Caron, *supra* note 183, at 575; Fromuth, *supra* note 195, at 363; Reisman, *supra* note 134, at 98.

200. *See* Thomas M. Franck, *United Nations Based Prospects for a New Global Order*, 22 N.Y.U. J. INT'L L. & POL. 601, 640 (1990).

201. For example, if states felt that, were they to become parties to an environmental treaty, the Council would eventually extend its terms, through legislative measures, beyond those with which the states desired to comply, the states would be hesitant to sign the treaty at all.

152   *INTERNATIONAL LAW AND POLITICS*   [Vol. 27:103]

Moreover, the creation of norms without broad international support will be viewed as illegitimate, and the Council's legislated rules will not have the same compliance pull as rules viewed as legitimately developed.[202]

c. *The Security Council Must Not Create Legal Obligations That Place the Interest of a Particular Group of States Above Those of Another*

The Security Council is dominated by developed states, which, in certain circumstances, have interests allied against the interests of states in the developing world.[203] It is not difficult to imagine the establishment of laws that will benefit the developed North while hurting the developing South. The Security Council, which essentially represents the interest of nations of the developed world, has a natural political inclination to establish such inequitable norms. Of course, such legislative infirmity will breed contempt by the developing world.

Consider a hypothetical to illustrate this point: The developed nations contend that Brazil's continual destruction of the Amazon should cease because of the serious environmental consequences. Brazil responds that the preservation of the Amazon would not be of such import if the developed world had not destroyed all its natural resources to fuel its development; that being the case, the Brazilians insist that their control of environmental issues must be reciprocated in the form of debt forgiveness. The Security Council, fed up with the protracted negotiations, passes a resolution forbidding Brazil to continue clear cutting the Amazon, because the accompanying environmental degradation is a threat to international peace and security.

The Council, in such a case, effectively eliminates Brazil's valid bargaining position. Such action negatively alters the power dynamic concerning lawmaking, so that only the self-

202. For a discussion of the legitimacy of international rules and how it effects the compliance pull of those rules, see generally FRANCK, LEGITIMACY, *supra* note 117. *See also* Caron, *supra* note 183, at 575.

203. For example, in the area of environmental protection, it is well-known that in negotiating conventions, the developing, southern world tends to stress the need for continued development, while the industrialized, northern countries emphasize conservation. *See generally* Ranee K.L. Panjabi, *From Stockholm to Rio: A Comparison of the Declaratory Principles of International Environmental Law*, 21 DENV. J. INT'L L. & POL'Y 215 (1993).

interests of Council members are represented. Exacerbation of fundamental power and economic inequalities through abuse of Security Council powers is the surest way to delegitimize the Council and to eliminate support for future Council action.

d. *The Charter Confers a Primitive, Quasi-Legislative Capacity on the General Assembly That Gives Rise to Issues of Comity*

The only U.N. organ given any legislative authority in the Charter is the General Assembly. As the Assembly is the most "democratic" institution within the U.N. system, this makes sense.[204] Article 13(1)(a) confers upon the General Assembly the power to make recommendations for the purpose of "promoting international cooperation in the political field and encouraging the progressive development of international law and its codification."[205] This article has been interpreted by some commentators to allot to the General Assembly the primary legislative authority of the institution.[206] At the outside, it bestows on the Assembly a presumption of legislative authority, as no other organ is given any express legislative capacity. The fact that the framers gave the General Assembly these powers indicates that the framers did not intend the Council to use Chapter VII in a legislative sense,[207] or perhaps intended for it to do so only after consultation with the General Assembly. Therefore, the Council should be careful when creating obligations. States that ground their dissatisfaction with Council enactments—that is, the Council's decisions of what

---

204. The General Assembly has representatives from all member states. U.N. CHARTER art. 9.

205. *Id.* art. 13, para. 1. The International Law Commission has been delegated the responsibility by the General Assembly to promote the "progressive development of international law." *See id.* art. 13, para. 1(a).

206. *See* GOODRICH ET AL., *supra* note 7, at 135. For a discussion of whether General Assembly Resolutions are "binding," see R. KIRGIS, PRIOR CONSULTATION IN INTERNATIONAL LAW: A STUDY OF STATE PRACTICE 7-9 (1983). *See also* Oscar Schachter, *International Law in Theory and Practice*, 178 REC. DES COURS. 111 (1982-V) (stating that "few would deny that the General Assembly resolutions have had a formative influence on the development of international law in matters of considerable importance to national States"). *See generally* ROSALYN HIGGINS, THE DEVELOPMENT OF INTERNATIONAL LAW THROUGH THE POLITICAL ORGANS OF THE UNITED NATIONS (1963).

207. If not, the Charter would grant similar authority to the Council.

"the law is"—on the Council's failure to follow the clearly delineated a separation of powers in the Charter wield a compelling argument. This could eventually act to delegitimize the United Nations.

Ultimately, I believe, it is appropriate for the Security Council to create obligations for states; nothing strongly militates for or against the Council assuming a legislative role *per se.* However, the Council must legislate only in a limited manner. The Council should limit its legislative activity to accelerating the progression of *lex feranda* into binding norms. It should avoid creating obligations for states that do not reflect clear emerging normative standards. The alternative is a Council willing to compel compliance with norms which exceed the will or expectation of most states and may severely diminish the Council's legitimacy. Additionally, the Council must not create legal obligations in contravention of established international normative standards. A Council enactment that supersedes or preempts the application of customary law or multilateral treaty provisions would be *prima facie* evidence of the Council's failure to act "in conformity with . . . international law."[208] To ensure that it is not acting illegitimately, the Council should first determine if the obligation it places on states is an acceptable normative standard for most states. As a practical matter, perhaps seeking the *ad hoc* advice of the General Assembly prior to any legislation is the best way to maintain legitimacy.

2. *Analysis of Recent Legislative Council Action*

Part I of this paper described certain recent Council actions that were indicative of the Council assuming a legislative role. The following discussion of two of those legislative activities serves to illustrate the above analysis through actual application.

a. *The Council Has the Legal Authority to Act as a Legislature, But Some of Its Recent Actions Beg for More Political Discretion*

In passing Resolution 687, bringing an end to the Gulf War, the Security Council created certain obligations for

---

208. U.N. CHARTER art. 1, para. 1.

Iraq.[209] These obligations, however, were reasonable extensions of treaties to which Iraq was admittedly a party. For instance, although the Geneva Protocol merely prohibits the use of certain chemical weaponry, Iraq was prohibited from possessing and was ordered to destroy all such chemicals. These increased obligations were logical and reasonable extensions of the Geneva Protocol, especially given the Iraqi propensity to use and threaten to use these weapons.[210]

However, the Council has not always acted so reasonably in legislating new burdens for states. The Security Council's decision to compel Libya to extradite two alleged terrorist rings with impropriety. Resolution 748 characterized Libya's alleged involvement in terrorism as a threat to international peace. Libya was ordered by the Council to extradite two of its citizens; in essence, the Council created additional obligations for Libya.

Unlike the action against Iraq, this legislative act was not prudent. The Council acted in direct contravention of the Montreal Convention to which most of the Security Council members and Libya were parties.[211] This action is inappropriate because a treaty which has been almost universally accepted reflects a consensus that greatly legitimizes the agreed upon norms. To act in defiance of such highly authoritative norms, without compelling justification, is highly questionable.[212] The Montreal Convention offers states reliable evidence of existing law. By changing the bedrock normative understandings of certain international legal standards, the Council, with one swift move, creates unnecessary instability in an already fragile legal system. Therefore, I believe it was improper for the Council to ignore the clear and applicable provisions of the Montreal Convention as they did by adopting Resolution 748.

CONCLUSION

While the Cold War years were characterized by realistic fears of nuclear annihilation, there was a certain predictability

---

209. *See supra* notes 26-41 and accompanying text.

210. *See supra* notes 38-44 and accompanying text.

211. Libya v. U.S., *supra* note 77.

212. *See* Ibrahim, *supra* note 184 (suggesting that the United Nations acts capriciously and vindictively against Arab states).

in that bilateral world. Today, that predictability has been replaced by an uneasy tension. The future has not seemed so indeterminate since the creation of the United Nations following World War II. Nevertheless, with the end of the Cold War, the potential for lasting international peace and security has never seemed so plausible. If the international community realizes a sustained era of peace, it will surely be with significant contribution from the United Nations. It is therefore of the utmost importance to guard zealously the legitimacy of the organization.

In this paper, I have analyzed recent Security Council actions and have suggested that they signify the broadening of Security Council powers under Chapter VII. Further, I have suggested that this expanding role for the Council is ultimately a positive development. It does raise concerns, however, about the propriety of such action and, more importantly, how that action may affect the legitimacy of the United Nations. The delineation of parameters around appropriate Council action is essential to ensure that the Security Council will not be perceived as illegitimate by the community of states and hence, cripple the U.N. system in its mission to instill stability and ensure peace.

I have asserted in the preceding pages that a determination of whether the Security Council is acting in an executive, legislative, or judicial capacity is important in deciding whether the Council is acting properly. By creating a hermeneutic framework based on the type of decision the Council is making, we can better predict the effect which an action will have on the organ's legitimacy. If the Council has acted legislatively, then the correct inquiry is whether the Council has acted appropriately as a legislature. If the Council has acted judicially, then our query should focus on whether it has acted appropriately as a court. The frameworks for analyzing the Council's actions are substantively distinctive.

By acting within broad parameters consistent with the role which the Council is presently playing, the Security Council would be able to fulfill its constitutional mandate while complementing the institutional legitimacy of the U.N. system. Codification of procedures consistent with the functions of the Council would aid in bolstering institutional legitimacy.

When making law, the Council should seek the General Assembly's guidance. I believe that it would be prudent, in this regard, to codify procedures wherein the General Assembly is consulted on all legislative matters. Such codification would reduce the possibility of myopic decision-making by the Council that would negatively impact its legitimacy.

When analyzing issues of law or fact, the Council should adopt procedural rules to ensure due process, including regulating the admissibility and authentication of evidence, providing an opportunity for litigants to be heard, preventing interested parties from adjudicating their own claims, ensuring the equality of all litigants' rights, and mandating the Council to make public its rationale for reaching its decisions in a manner similar to a published opinion of law. Alternatively, the Council should refer juridical questions to a judicial institution with such processes already in place.

The power of the Security Council to effect positive change in international relations and international law is at a critical juncture. To ensure that the Council finds the necessary support for its actions, it must always act within its competence and authority. Garnering wide support will enable the Council to enact normative standards that will add stability to international relations. Moreover, support by the international community will be necessary for the Council to fulfill its constitutional mandate and perhaps to permit the United Nations to realize the principles and purposes memorialized in its Charter.

[7]

The Police in the Temple
Order, Justice and the UN: A Dialectical View

Martti Koskenniemi *

I

Controversy reigns over the Security Council. Was the Council entitled to authorize a United States-led coalition to make war on its behalf to oust Iraq from Kuwait, or to re-establish the Aristide Government in Haiti?[1] Could it impose a peace arrangement, including a liability regime, on Iraq and to strengthen it by an economic blockade, originally set up for another purpose?[2] Was the Council acting within its competence as it prevented Bosnia-Herzegovina from exercising its 'inherent right of self-defence' by an arms embargo directed at the aggressor and the object of aggression alike, or when it short-circuited the International Court of Justice by demanding the extradition of two Libyan citizens over rights accorded to Libya by an international treaty?[3]

Such questions have aroused the anxiety of international lawyers. But there are other questions, too. Is the Council entitled to intervene in the government or misgovernment of States as soon as political agreement has been attained between its principal members that the matter raises a 'threat to international peace and security' under Article 39 of the Charter? This seems suggested by its enforcement action to counter Southern Rhodesia's illegal declaration of independence in 1965 and its reaction to South Africa's policy of *apartheid* since 1977.[4] Yet, white oppression of a black majority remained a special case – until the Council

* University of Helsinki.

1   SC Res. 678 of 29 November 1990; SC Res. 940 of 31 July 1994.
2   SC Res. 687 of 3 April 1991.
3   For the arms embargo, cf. SC Res. 713 of 25 September 1991 and the analysis e.g. in Petrovic, Condorelli, 'L'ONU et la crise Yugoslave', XXXVIII *AFDI* (1992) 35-6 and on the Libyan situation cf. SC Res. 748 of 31 March 1992 and *Lockerbie* (*Libya v. USA*) case, ICJ Reports (1992) 114-127.
4   SC Res. 232 of 16 December 1966 (Southern Rhodesia); SC Res. 418 of 4 November 1977 (South Africa).

6 EJIL (1995) 325-348

Martti Koskenniemi

intervened in the civil wars devastating Liberia, Somalia, Angola and Rwanda[5]and to remove Haiti's military leadership.[6] Clearly, internal crises may create a danger of escalation and thereby implicate international security. But was the Council not stretching it a bit when it declared, at a euphoric moment, that problems of an ecological, social or economic kind may also concern the maintenance of international peace and security?[7] Was it in fact making a *carte blanche* declaration of the limitlessness of its powers?

That the Council frequently makes declarations about the lawfulness of State action may seem a relatively innocent incursion into a judicial function (in spite of the absence of a due process clause from the Council's [provisional] rules of procedure).[8] The setting up of two *ad hoc* war crimes tribunals to issue binding judgments seems already precariously close to international legislation.[9] Is the Council both a Court and a Parliament? What about its propensity to look away from flagrant breaches of the peace, or officially induced massacres, when its key members fail to agree on an appropriate reaction?[10] What is the Council's responsibility? Is it in the position of the Hobbesian sovereign, for whom 'there can happen no breach of Covenant' between himself and his subjects because there is no such Covenant at all. Is it true of the Security Council, that:

> ... because the End of this Institution is the Peace and Defence of ... all; and whosoever has the Right to the End, has the Right to the Means, it belongeth of Right [to him] to be Judge both of the meanes [sic] of Peace and Defence; and also of the hindrances, and disturbances of the same; and to do whatsoever he shall think necessary to be done, both before hand, for the preserving of Peace and Security, by prevention of Discord at home and Hostility from abroad ; and, when Peace and Security are lost, for the recovery of the same.[11]

---

5   E.g. SC Res. 788 of 19 November 1992 (Liberia); SC Res. 794 of 3 December 1992 (Somalia); SC Res. 864 of 15 September 1993 (Angola) and SC Res. 929 of 22 June 1994 (Rwanda).

6   Cf. SC Res. 841 of 16 June 1993, SC Res. 875 of 16 October 1993; SC Res. 940 of 31 July 1994, SC Res. 944 of 29 September 1994 and SC Res. 948 of 15 October 1994.

7   The full text of the relevant part of the statement issued from the Security Council 'Summit Meeting' reads: 'The absence of war and military conflicts amongst States does not in itself ensure international peace and security. The non-military sources of instability in the economic, social, humanitarian and ecological fields have become threats to international peace and security'. UN Doc. S/23500 (31 January 1992).

8   Cf. generally Higgins, 'The Place of International Law in the Settlement of Disputes by the Security Council', 64 *AJIL* (1970) 1-18. But see also the criticism by Graefrath of the Council's 'summary court procedure' in relation to the Libyan sanctions in 'Leave to the Court what Belongs to the Court', 4 *EJIL* (1993) 192 et seq. Also Higgins has later taken a more critical view, labelling the Council's decisions on the Iraqi liability regime as 'extremely unusual' and 'very, very different from anything we have expected of the Security Council before', in *Problems & Process. International Law and How We Use It* (1994) 183, 184. On this same point, cf. also Zedalis, 'Gulf War Compensation Standard: Concerns under the Charter', XXVI *RBDI* (1994) 333-350.

9   SC Res. 827 of 25 May 1993; SC Res. 955 of 8 November 1994.

10   For a discussion of the Iran-Iraq war (1980-1988) from this perspective, cf. O. Russbach, *ONU contre ONU. Le droit international confisqué* (1994) 141-166.

11   Thomas Hobbes, *Leviathan* (1651) Part II, Ch. 18.6 (Penguin 1982, ed. & Intr. by C.B. Macpherson) at 232-3.

The Police in the Temple. Order, Justice and the UN: A Dialectical View

The controversy relates to the Security Council's place in the UN and in the world. Given the Council's composition and working methods, its monopolization of UN resources and the public attention focused on the Council is problematic. The dominant role of the permanent five, the secrecy of the Council's procedures, the lack of a clearly delimited competence and the absence of what might be called a legal culture within the Council hardly justify enthusiasm about its increased role in world affairs.

International lawyers have responded by seeking out normative limits to Council authority from an interpretation of Articles 1, 2, 24(1) and 39 of the Charter, laying down the purposes and principles of the Organization and the formal competence of the Council plus creating a link between them.[12] But the principles and purposes of the Charter are many, ambiguous and conflicting. The relationship between domestic jurisdiction in Article 2(7) and human rights under Articles 1(2), 1(3) and 55-56, for example, can only be determined by successive acts of application by UN political organs in accordance with the political logic of the moment.[13] The purposes and principles are no less indeterminate than the concept of a threat to peace. Textual constraint is practically non-existent. Inasmuch as each organ is the judge of its own competence, procedural constraint seems scarcely more significant.

For this reason, many have taken the 'realist' position that the relevant issue is conclusively settled through an analysis of the politically possible: if the Council – or the permanent five – can agree, then there is little more to say. The lawfulness of their agreement under some – always contested – standard is even at best of only academic interest. As such a standard cannot be successfully invoked against the Council, relying on it in practical politics (in contradistinction to learned articles) would encapsulate a discredited idealism. For better or for worse, what the Council says *is* the law.[14]

From the lawyer's perspective the realist response clearly misses the point. Authority is a normative and not a factual category. Power is distinct from authority: a gunman's orders do not turn into law merely because there happens to be no police around.[15] A nagging doubt remains, however. If the lawyers themselves are divided (and this 'internal' objection is intended to respond to their *Erkenntnisinteresse*) and the permanent members of the Council are always able to

---

12 Cf. Bedjaoui, diss. op., *Lockerbie* case, ICJ Reports (1992) 155-156 (paras. 25-26); Weeramantry, diss. op. ibid. at 170-175 and of the large commentary on the *Lockerbie* case e.g. Chappez, 'Questions d'interprétation et d'application de la Convention de Montréal du 1971 resultant de l'incident aérien de Lockerbie', XXXVIII *AFDI* (1992) 477-479 and Greafrath, *supra* note 8, at 186-187. See also generally O. Schacter, *International Law in Theory and Practice* (1991) 399-400 plus the various essays in *Recueil des Cours*, Colloque: Le développement du rôle du Conseil de sécurité (1992).

13 M. Koskenniemi, *From Apology to Utopia. The Structure of International Legal Argument* (1989) 212-220. For a recent discussion, cf. Bailey, 'Intervention. Article 2.7 versus articles 55-56', XII *International Relations* (1994) 1-10.

14 Pellet, 'Conclusions', in B. Stern (ed.), *Les aspects juridiques de la crise et de la guerre du Golfe* (1991) 490.

15 H.L.A. Hart, *The Concept of Law* (1962) 19-20, 54-60.

Martti Koskenniemi

marshal prestigious names to buttress their reading of the relevant principles, how long is it useful – or possible – to resist?

The impasse of the 'realist' and the lawyer follows from their perspectives inevitably remaining within the controversy they seek to resolve. The competence of the UN relates to questions of order (power) and of justice (authority) but cannot be reduced to either one. The Organization is neither simply a policeman nor a Temple of Justice – though in its individual actions it tends to show itself as one or the other. In this paper I shall propose a 'dialectical' view on its competences that seeks to accommodate concerns of power and of authority and to provide a foothold for reformed institutional policy.

II

The two great problems for international thought have related, in their most abstract formulation, to the conditions of order and the possibility of justice among States.[16] The *problem of order* is about how to establish and maintain effective authority among States that recognize no secular superior or common values – in conditions of 'anarchy' as political theorists like to put it.[17] This seems, at first glance, to be a purely causal-technical problem and has been so treated by much 'realist' political theory from Machiavelli and Hobbes onwards: power and its derivatives – fear and force – become the conditions *sine qua non* for its resolution.

The *problem of justice* has to do with the relationship of order with normative standards. Such standards are sometimes classified as political, sometimes legal, and people disagree about such (and other) classifications.[18] But the point is that they are external to the fact of power and claim to provide a measure for its acceptability and, at least implicitly, a programme for transformation. So described, justice is a purely normative phenomenon, by definition independent from the factual world for which it provides an evaluation.

The contrast (or indeed tension) between solutions to the two problems structures international thought and is present in the controversy about the Security Council. Hard approaches stressing the primacy of the order-problem (the Council's capacity to police its commands) conflict with soft approaches emphasizing the foundational character of justice (the need to assess the sanctity of its commands in the Temple of Justice). Though labels such as 'realism' and 'idealism' seem both tendentious and old-fashioned, the fact remains that as a matter of psychological

---

16   These are problems that take the existence of a states-society for granted and seek reform within it. For cosmopolitan movements that hope to replace States with other political subjects (such as 'mankind'), the problems look different.

17   Cf. e.g. S. Hoffmann, 'Is there an International Order?', in *Janus and Minerva. Essays in the Theory and Practice of International Politics* (1987) 85.

18   One classification is by T.M. Franck for whom justice, legitimacy and legality provide three related but separate standards from which to appreciate the functioning of international institutions. Cf. his *The Power of Legitimacy Among States* (1990).

The Police in the Temple. Order, Justice and the UN: A Dialectical View

orientation or literary genre, 'policing' approaches conflict with 'Temple' ones in any discussion of international issues – including the competence of UN bodies.

This persistence of the dichotomy may seem surprising inasmuch as it has long been clear that the two problems cannot be treated in abstraction from each other. Machiavelli conceded it to be an indispensable condition of an effective order that it enjoy what sociologists (shunning directly normative statements) nowadays call legitimacy. An illegitimate order is an unstable order. This argument is *internal*. It pays no regard to the pedigree of legitimacy: a 'feeling' of legitimacy induced by ignorance or manipulation is as good in supporting existing order as legitimacy based on critical reflection. In a corresponding manner, the complete absence of social institutions makes it impossible to realize standards of justice. Among people and States – unlike among angels – institutions are needed to undertake the distributive and retributive tasks that justice calls for. This argument, too, is internal: it looks at social institutions from the perspective of an anterior conception of justice.

Sophisticated contemporary legal and political theory concedes the interdependence of the problems of order and justice. The modern policy-maker or lawyer is neither a (pure) Hobbesian realist nor a (pure) Rousseauian utopian.[19] Today, everybody is a suave (Grotian) eclectic.[20] We readily recognize that a single-minded pursuit of order will create self-destructive politics. The Nazi order may have been optimally effective; but this could only be so at the cost of the tremendous injustice of its institutions which finally accounted for its breakdown. A single-minded pursuit of justice in secular conditions, failing to pay regard to the effectiveness of (existing or proposed) institutions degenerates into utopian politics that will sooner or later lead to anarchy or dictatorship.

However, such eclecticism works from within the dichotomy between 'police' and 'Temple'. The relationship between order and justice is conceptualized as *internal* to the chosen approach, or instrumental: justice as a means to uphold order, order as a means to realize justice. It fails to pay regard to the *external* relationship between the two, the extent to which both are constitutive of each other.

The very need for and definition of order are normative statements in their own right: conceptualizing 'order' in terms of stability, peace, or the 'securing of the elementary needs of the relevant group'[21] creates an axiological system with a normative premise. So does the definition of the basic units (States, say) or the basic concepts describing their relations (sovereignty, say). The causal-technical world of

19 As Martin Wight famously argued, the correct division is into three: those who stress the predominance of the facts of State power (realists), those who reject the state-centred model and emphasize the foundational character of a human community (revolutionaries) and the 'rationalists' or 'Grotians' trying to work out diplomatic and economic structures to bind States into a coordinative society. Cf. M. Wight, *International Theory: The Three Traditions* (1991). Cf. also Yost, 'Political Philosophy and the Theory of International Relations', 70 *International Affairs* (1994) 263-290.

20 Cf. also the discussion in Koskenniemi, *supra* note 13, at 2-8, 131-191.

21 H. Bull, *The Anarchical Society: A Study of Order in World Politics* (1977).

Martti Koskenniemi

power emerges from a normative description.[22] But conversely, in the absence of natural justice (or at least of our capacity to know it), social norms emerge from the activity of social institutions. Customs, kings and parliaments make laws. Though these laws are sometimes unjust, and we recognize them as such, as Max Weber well knew, in a general sense our ideas about right and wrong emerge from the factual *a priori* that is constituted by our existing social (economic, cultural, religious, etc.) institutions.

The failure of modern internationalism to grasp the external dependence between order and justice means that its proposed reforms have normally been tilted in favour of solving one or the other problem[23] – while of course stressing the need to take account of its counterpart. Such thought, already initially out of balance, is constantly in danger of sliding into supporting what could be called cynic or utopian tyranny.

Cynic tyranny emerges when the system is tilted in favour of the problem of order and encapsulates justice only through an *internal,* instrumental relationship, i.e. by seeing justice as a (perhaps necessary) means towards order. It is a strategy of paying lip service to normative standards while constantly adjusting them in response to the daily requirements of the order's maximal effectiveness. Under such conditions, the distinction between normative beliefs created through manipulation and false consciousness on the one hand, and uncoerced consent on the other, disappears or cannot find institutional expression. Cynic tyranny emerges not only when no attention is paid to the· acceptability of power but also (and more dangerously) when the Temple becomes a vehicle for buttressing the police.

The danger of *utopian tyranny* again, emerges when a society's institutions and its management problems are seen from the perspective of one normative belief. It is premised on the authentic character of an underlying normative world. Its political programme seeks to reformulate social institutions ('superstructure') – including the State and the states-system – to correspond to that foundation. In conditions of agnosticism (in today's diplomatic discourse) utopian tyranny realizes itself through a general degeneration of the Temple into preaching extremism, fundamentalism, nationalism, xenophobia, etc.[24]

In practice, it may be difficult to distinguish between cynic and utopian tyranny. We have seen sufficiently often that what starts out as a demand for authentic (utopian) justice may transform into cynic tyranny. And though perhaps empirically

---

22   On these arguments, cf. generally C. Brown, *International Relations Theory. New Normative Approaches* (1992) and for an incisive recent summary Frost, 'The Role of Normative Theory in International Relations', 23 *Millennium* (1994) 109-119. For a delightful general argument to this effect, cf. MacIntyre, 'The Indispensability of Political Theory', in D. Miller, L. Seidentorp (eds), *The Nature of Political Theory* (1983) 17-33.

23   But there is no equivalence: 'the quest for order in international affairs comes before that of justice', Hoffmann, *supra* note 17, at 118.

24   On this theme, cf. also my 'National Self-Determination Today: Problems of Legal Theory and Practice', 43 *ICLQ* (1994) 241-269 and 'The Wonderful Artificiality of States', *ASIL Proceedings 1994* (1995) 22-29.

The Police in the Temple. Order, Justice and the UN: A Dialectical View

more difficult to ascertain, the psychological process whereby a cynic tyrant at some point starts authentically to believe in his own manipulations is not impossible to envisage.

The point here is that if we conceive of the relation between social order and social justice only from the internal perspective, we fail to create (indeed, even to conceive) institutions that merit political support. Having the system tilt one way or the other may be even more unacceptable than merely staying within the (pre-modern) antagonism of hard and soft, realism and utopia. For unlike the tyrant *sans peur et sans reproche*, the cynic tyrant is able to buttress the edifice of his rule with a string of marvellous temples while the utopian tyrant has all the sophistication of the modern security police to carry out his work of ideological (and sometimes physical) purification – dangers catastrophically realized in the unholy alliance of modernity and the holocaust.[25]

III

Let me sketch the strategy through which 20th century diplomacy within international institutions has sought to deal with the problems of order and justice.

The collapse of the 19th century world in the trenches of the Somme was a shock for the contemporaries and constituted in many fields – but particularly in politics and culture – the defining moment for modernity, and with it, the ideological environment for 20th century internationalism.[26] Despite its far greater quantitative significance, the Second World War and the establishment of the United Nations do not match up to the Great War and the experiment of the League of Nations in the shaping of our understanding of the problems of international policy.

The origins of the Great War – a great mystery to contemporaries – have been explained then and subsequently as stemming from various defects in the political system of the 19th century.[27] For many, the 'system' of Great Power predominance, occasional Congresses and the frantic search for intermittent alliances to deter one's adversary was simply too technically ineffective, European-centred and random to accommodate 'the displacement of an older structure of power by a new one between the leading States'.[28] From this perspective, the primary concern of the peace-makers in 1918-1919 had to be with strengthened, permanent institutions that

---

25   Cf. Z. Bauman, *Modernity and the Holocaust* (1991).
26   For an elaborate discussion of the significance of the First World War and the creation of the League of Nations for the 'discipline of international institutions' (through the themes of 'break, movement and repetition'), cf. David Kennedy, 'The Move to Institutions', 8 *Cardozo Law Review* (1987) 841-988.
27   Cf. also Koskenniemi, *supra* note 13, at 131-3.
28   F.H. Hinsley, *Power and the Pursuit of Peace: Theory and Practice in the History of Relations Between States* (1963) 301, 302.

Martti Koskenniemi

would include every State in a common bond against the potential aggressor (Germany).

Others interpreted the system's collapse by focusing on its unjust character: the Great Power primacy of the first half-century developed into a formal Imperialism in the second, manifested in the secrecy and limited character of Great Power consultations and the opening up of large parts of the globe for an official territorial scramble. It could not accommodate claims for national self-determination nor for the pursuit of internal democracy – indeed, some of it seemed to be actively directed at keeping nationalism, liberalism and socialism under control.

These contrasting interpretations of the failure of the premodern diplomatic structures are famously illustrated by the Versailles peace conference, torn between its desire for effective provisions to curtail German influence and for a just system of political boundaries in Europe. The approach behind the Treaty's exorbitant reparation and other war guilt provisions, imposed on Germany without her presence in the negotiations, collided head-on with Wilsonian ideas about the realization of the self-determination of the peoples formerly under Ottoman and Habsburg rule and about the institution of liberal democracy in as many European countries as possible.[29] At a very general level, this conflict reveals an ambiguity about the League's character: was it a collective military arrangement or a peace organization, committed to renouncing force? It tried to be both – with the result of never being fully convincing as either.

The Covenant encapsulated this tension in various ways. For example, the guarantee for Europe's post-war boundaries in Article 10 was intended to form the basis of Europe's new territorial order.[30] If these were violated, all members would take concerted action. But the guarantee was only reluctantly agreed upon by the States with the principal responsibility to enforce it – and not least because of a doubt about the justness of the agreed boundaries.[31] The much-belaboured principle of 'peaceful change' in Article 19 sought to temper the injustice of the reparations

---

29   The tension between these two aims of the Versailles settlement has been much commented upon. One of the most readable comments being Harold Nicolson's autobiographical account of the loss of high idealism of a young British diplomat: 'We arrived determined that a peace of justice and wisdom should be negotiated: we left it, conscious that the Treaties imposed upon our enemies were neither just nor wise', *Peace-making 1919* (1936) 187. But for the contrary view that 'there has surely never existed a peace of so idealistic a character', cf. G.M. Gathorne-Hardy, *A Short History of International Affairs 1920-1939* (4th ed., 1960) 18.

30   Text of Article 10: 'The Members of the League undertake to respect and preserve, as against external aggression, the territorial integrity and existing political independence of all Members of the League...'

31   On the British attitude, cf. Sir A. Zimmern, *The League of Nations and the Rule of Law* (1945) 199-200, 218-221, 243-247; F.S. Northedge, *The League of Nations: Its Life and Times* (1986) 30-31, 91-95. On the (divided) American view, cf. the account by Wilson's Secretary of State, R. Lansing, *The Peace Negotiations. A Personal Narrative* (1921) 34-35, 53-54, 106-108 and 121-125. The guarantee was the crucial difference between him and Wilson (leading to Lansing's resignation) and one reason for the Senate's non-ratification of the Covenant.

The Police in the Temple. Order, Justice and the UN: A Dialectical View

and territorial provisions agreed at Versailles.[32] But the apparent balance between Articles 10 and 19 was too unstable: the former was the League's hard core, the latter merely a disposable ingredient in fact never resorted to after 1929.

That the Covenant became a part of a controversial peace treaty may have been necessary for there to be a Covenant at all. Wilson's idealism may never have squared with Clemenceau's concern with French security. In this sense, the contradictory character of the settlement was decidedly not a result of the confused ideas of the peace-makers, or their ill will ('it just happened' writes Nicolson),[33] but followed logically from the contradicting understandings of the Congress system's failure and thus opposite theories about what was needed to avoid its recurrence. That the diplomats may not have treated the problem in an optimal fashion is less interesting.

The League system incorporated a number of technically sophisticated solutions to problems of European order and justice. Many of these relied on legal regimes (provision for peaceful settlement, sanctions against non-complying States, internationalized zones, system of plebiscites, etc.).[34] Among the consequences of their collapse later on was the birth of an international 'realism' that concluded that legal regimes are by their very nature useless or perhaps even counterproductive in the search for international order: *de maximis non curat praetor*. They rely for their operation on the existence of the kind of community that they seek to bring about.[35] Though 'realism' may now be on the way out, this is the argument and the experience that today's lawyer needs to confront when arguing for a determined limit on the authority of the Security Council.

But the problems of the League were not exhaustively related to tensions inside the Covenant. At critical moments, Great Powers were not (or no longer) members. But even members showed lack of faith in the collective response system by looking elsewhere during the Vilnius and Memel crises in 1920 and 1923 and the Manchurian occupation in 1931.[36] Though sanctions were adopted against Italy in October 1935, the collective system never recovered from the League's inaction during the German occupation of the Rhineland the following March – with the

---

32 Text of Article 19: 'The Assembly may from time to time advise the reconsideration by Members of the League of Treaties which have become inapplicable, and the consideration of internal conditions whose continuance might endanger the peace of the world'.

33 Nicolson, *supra* note 29, at 188.

34 For a theorization of these legal techniques as part of an international law 'modernism', cf. Berman, '"But the Alternative is Despair": Nationalism and the Modernist Revival of International Law', 106 *Harvard Law Review* (1993) 1806, 1859-1903.

35 Cf. E.H. Carr, *The Twenty-Years Crisis 1919-1939* (1981).

36 These doubts could hardly have been illustrated in a more striking manner than by the conclusion of the Locarno agreements in 1925 which (re-)guaranteed Germany's western frontier – with the direct implication of putting into question the eastern frontier – an arrangement which was 'totally at variance with the League system and went far to destroy it', Northedge, *supra* note 31, at 96-7.

Martti Koskenniemi

Covenant finally abandoned in the summer of 1936 as the sanctions against Italy were lifted.[37]

That the League collapsed because member States did not believe in it is merely a tautology: as an order system it seemed far too compromised by the wish to treat all members on an equal footing and to rely on their good faith in fulfilling their obligations.[38] As a justice system it was too formal and inflexible to provide effective relief to the various grievances concerning the *status quo* of 1919. Neither French obstinacy (indeed obsession) nor German indignation could find an outlet within it. And nothing in the Covenant took account of tyrants, acting *mala fide*, and using the weaknesses of the order system to play the divergent interests of League members against each other (e.g. Japan's policy *vis-à-vis* the western allies during the Manchukuo crisis 1931-32) and the weaknesses of the justice system to buttress their domestic position (e.g. Italy's colonial grievances). That the tyrants now appear utopian and cynic simultaneously – like Marinetti's futurism or Le Corbusier's architecture – is a striking reminder of the limits of politics in modern conditions and a nice counterbalance to the discrediting of law by post-war 'realism'.

IV

The origins of the Second World War have been far less the object of historians' controversy than those of its predecessor – though differences in philosophical or political outlook have led them to stress sometimes structural causes, sometimes personal responsibilities. That Hitler (or Germany, or Versailles) is to 'blame' but that the confused Western policy bears its share of responsibility, too, there is no doubt, at least not since Professor Taylor's defence of the latter thesis.[39] But to understand the peace of 1945 we need less to grasp the 'real' origins of the war than the lessons that contemporaries drew from the twenty-years' crisis as they tried to construct a new peace. Among the most striking of those lessons was the assumption that the League *could* have managed international affairs if only the Covenant had been more adequately drafted. No politician was prepared to argue – as some political scientists did – that peace could *a priori* not be attained through institutions. The continuity between official inter-war and post-war diplomacy was based on the assumption that what was needed was not something new but more of

---

37 A good review of the League's action agaist Italy is e.g. C.L. Brown-John, *Multilateral Sanctions in International Law. A Comparative Perspective* (1975) 59-159.

38 As illustrated by the unanimity rule which 'stultified all action by the League by ensuring that always, on every issue, there were some members who could block action against their interests', Hinsley, *supra* note 28, at 310, 314-315.

39 A.J.P. Taylor, *The Origins of the Second World War* (1961).

The Police in the Temple. Order, Justice and the UN: A Dialectical View

the same: a more effective League with 'clear-cut obligations', 'teeth' and better 'procedures'.[40]

On the other hand, it is striking to what extent our present image of the United Nations differs from the image it had to its midwives. The Charter took shape during three moments: the initial conception had been discussed between London and Washington since 1940; a Great Power conception culminated in the Dumbarton Oaks proposals of 1944, and the final product was refined by the lesser powers' handmark in San Francisco the following year. The discussions took place as the war was still raging and that environmental fact could not but have an impact. Hinsley summarizes:

> The Charter was less interested in legal and just settlement; the great danger was war and any settlement was better than war.[41]

Reading the political documents of the first two moments – the 1941 Atlantic Charter, the 1942 Declaration of the United Nations, the 1943 Moscow Declaration[42] – one finds nothing of the substance of the organization as we have come to know it. There is no mention of the social, economic and humanitarian tasks that have been such a visible part of the UN from the early 1960s onwards. The institutions of the new organization were simply taken over from the model provided by the League. This is not because Great Powers would have ignored these tasks. Apart from the Soviet Union, they accepted that the League's activities in the economic and social fields had been beneficial and should be expanded.[43] They even thought that a proposal to give the UN competence to promote 'the observance of basic human rights' was significant enough to disagree on it.[44] Yet, practically all preparatory discussion focused on the role that the Great Powers would have in policing the coming peace, a question culminating in the form of decision-making in the Security Council.

For the Great Powers, the United Nations was a structure devoted to maintaining order. International justice was simply not dealt with – possibly as the overwhelming problem in this field was still to attain victory from 'Hitlerism',[45] in comparison to which every other grievance must have seemed secondary.[46] Perhaps surprisingly, the San Francisco Conference accepted the main principles of the

---

40 E. Luard, *A History of the United Nations. Volume 1: The Years of Western Domination, 1945-1955* (1982) 4-10.
41 Hinsley, *supra* note 28, at 338.
42 Conveniently reproduced e.g. in L.M. Goodrich, E. Hambro, *Charter of the United Nations. Commentary and Documents* (1946) 305-308.
43 Cf. e.g. Luard, *supra* note 40, at 12, 26.
44 This proposal, originally made by the United States and opposed by the United Kingdom and the Soviet Union, was the source of present Article 1(3).
45 Declaration by United Nations, 1 January 1942.
46 The Western allies – at least Churchill – must also have felt it difficult to agree on entering in a discussion about international justice with Stalin.

proposed order system practically without dissent.[47] Small powers expended their energy to buttress the Assembly's position in the security field. But despite some amendments, the principle that the Assembly could not challenge the Council's absolute primacy, was maintained. The Conference also focused on the Assembly's functions in the economic and social fields and succeeded in upgrading the ECOSOC to a 'principal organ'. As the ECOSOC was to coordinate the activities of specialized agencies, but was also positioned as a subsidiary organ of the General Assembly, the Conference in effect achieved an all-encompassing dichotomy between the organization's 'political' activities and its activities in the economic, social and humanitarian fields, each being headed by a principal organ: the Council and the Assembly.

This dichotomy between *hard UN* (political activities for which the Security Council is mainly responsible) and *soft UN* (activities for which the General Assembly – through the ECOSOC – is mainly responsible) is functionally and ideologically the most significant structuring feature of the organization. It governs everything from the career options of UN staff members and the specialization of diplomats at permanent missions, via the structure of the organization's budget and the permanent tension between Geneva ('soft') and New York ('hard'), to the organization's image in the selective eyes of the mass media. It has been both a source of constant tension in the orientation of the UN's activities as well as an invaluable asset in overcoming difficult periods – most conspicuously by allowing soft activities to compensate for the problems which the Cold War occasioned for carrying out hard ones.[48]

Unlike the Covenant, the Charter does not appear to take on the dual task of maintaining order as well as guaranteeing justice. The contrast between Articles 10 and 19 (territorial guarantee and peaceful change) seems non-existent in the Charter; there is no mention of either concept anywhere. Still, the effect of the principle of non-use of force (Article 2(4)), together with Articles 24 and 25 and Chapter VII is to constitute a guarantee of the *status quo* which is, at least on the surface, procedurally much stronger than the Covenant. And though 'peaceful change' had acquired a bad name under the League, the reasons for providing some way to cope with an unjust *status quo* were no less urgent in 1945 than they had been in 1919. It would be wrong to think that the rather haphazard mention of the organization's 'purpose' to 'achieve international cooperation in solving international problems of an economic, social, cultural or humanitarian character, and in promoting and encouraging respect for human rights and fundamental freedoms' in Article 1(3) was meant to attain that purpose. It was probably put in simply to cover the general

---

47   The two issues in the Dumbarton Oaks proposals that raised most controversy among the smaller powers were the application of the right of veto by a Great Power in a dispute concerning itself, and regional arrangements. Cf. Luard, *supra* note 40, at 45-49, 51-54.

48   For one early periodization of the relative shifts between Assembly and Council, cf. Goodrich, 'The Security Council', in J. Barros (ed.), *The United Nations. Past, Present and Future* (1972) 29-30.

functionalist belief that cooperation in these fields was useful for attaining peace and to provide a justification for the UN's economic and social activities under Chapter IX. Nevertheless, over the decades it has been precisely these activities that have sought to alleviate the patterns of internal and transnational injustice buttressed by the states-system.

Nor were the Charter provisions on trusteeship and non-self-governing territories designed to attain the massive redistribution of sovereignty that decolonization meant in practice. That the relevant provisions were flexible enough (despite colonial powers' constant legal objections to the interpretation of Chapter XI of the Charter so as to internationalize what was supposed to be a national trusteeship) to provide a basis for a programme of pushing into independence a much larger number of territories than were originally listed within the trusteeship system (11 territories) reformed these parts of the Charter into a veritable *de facto* peaceful change mechanism.[49]

The Charter combines in a much more subtle way than the League did, the maintenance of international order with the purpose of providing for (minimal) conditions of international justice. True, its text is tilted in favour of political activities. Therefore it may have been fortunate that the Cold War set in before the Great Powers were able to stabilize their control on the world. This occasioned an immediate transformation of the Organization's core activity from the Council to the General Assembly. Though this *de facto* shift was originally manoeuvred for political purposes, it provided the basis for tackling problems of international injustice, particularly colonialism and underdevelopment – the kinds of injustice that the Assembly's majority felt most acutely. The Charter's *textual* imbalance was compensated by the *practice* that raised social, economic and humanitarian activities to the core. The 'tyranny' of the Great Powers was overruled by the 'tyranny' of the majority.

V

'The Charter was meant to be based on a separation of functions. Therefore, usually, the Council and the Assembly operate independently of one another'.[50] The Charter deals with the relationship between order and justice through a procedural mechanism that uses the two main organs so as to allow the treatment of both types of problem simultaneously and to ensure that neither is fully overtaken by or collapsed into the other. The competence, composition and procedures of each organ is justifiable only as a separation of powers arrangement which seeks to provide optimal efficiency in policing the world as well as a forum for seeking

---

49   For the original (though contested) understanding of the distinction between trust territories and non-self-governing territories, cf. e.g. Hall, 'The Trusteeship System', XXIV *BYIL* (1947) 70-71.

50   Vallat, 'The General Assembly and the Security Council of the United Nations', XXIX *BYIL* (1952) 78.

Martti Koskenniemi

agreement on various economic, social and humanitarian policies, while trying to keep both in check so as to avoid the dangers inherent in establishing a full precedence of one over the other.

As regards *competence*, the Security Council has 'primary responsibility for the maintenance of international peace and security' (Article 24 (1)). This is the Charter resolution to the problem of order; in exercising this competence, the Council should not be seriously obstructed by the other organs, particularly the General Assembly.[51] On the other hand, under Articles 10 and 14, the Assembly may deal with every conceivable international problem and 'recommend measures for the peaceful settlement of any situation, regardless of origin, which it deems likely to impair the general welfare or friendly relations among nations'.[52] The problem of justice is dealt with by establishing a general competence for the Assembly to make it come true.

The *composition and procedures* of the Council are determined by the single-minded purpose to establish a causally effective centre of international power. That the five Great Powers have permanent membership and the right of veto in the Council and that the Council has the authority to *bind* members would be indefensible under any conception of institutional justice worthy of that name. But it is clearly defensible in view of what were held to be the main reasons for the League's ineffectiveness. The UN's collective security-system (unlike the League's) is based on the co-option of overwhelming power. It follows tautologically that if such power is overwhelming it allows co-option only on its own terms.

The Assembly's composition and procedures reflect an equally single-minded purpose to create a global scope for the organization's activities – another conclusion drawn from the League's failure. To co-opt all States, however, requires that all States have a say in the directing of the organization's economic, social and humanitarian activities. As any observer of the annual Assembly sessions may testify, its activity is not geared towards maximal effectiveness; quite the contrary.[53] Its composition and working methods would be nonsensical were it for the Assembly to create or maintain the international order – as illustrated by the controversy in the early sixties about the financing of peace-keeping operations 'demonstrating the limitations of what could be done through the General Assembly majority voting'.[54] But what other way can justice be defensibly discussed or set up than by a voting procedure? That the Assembly may not pass binding resolutions may be ineffective – in a secular world where values differ, however, it is the only

---

51   Article 12(1) of the Charter.
52   Article 14. Cf. also Articles 2(2) and (3).
53   H.G. Nicholas describes the Assembly as a 'talking shop with all the potentialities and disabilities that that implies' – summarizing these implications in a wonderful chain of attributes, namely 'irresponsible, vain, chaotic, extreme', its debates sometimes 'reaching a higher level of hypocrisy, unctuousness, and flatulence than is healthy for any organization', *The United Nations as a Political Institution* (4th ed., 1971) 100, 98, 113.
54   Goodrich, in Barros, *supra* note 48, at 44.

The Police in the Temple. Order, Justice and the UN: A Dialectical View

acceptable solution; justice – unlike order – cannot be created out of the barrel of a gun.

A policeman and a Temple of Justice: neither has been a tremendous success. For decades, the Council was no guarantee of anyone's security: inasmuch as there was security, it depended on external facts, particularly a State's position with respect to the balance of terror. The Organization's soft activities continue to pay the price of the fact that its members are States whose representativeness cannot be taken for granted and whose ulterior motives often make the argument about the Assembly's democratic character seem a tenuous hypocrisy.

The principle of the division of competences, however, remains sound. The Security Council should establish/maintain order: for this purpose, its composition and procedures are justifiable. The Assembly should deal with the acceptability of that order: its composition and powers are understandable from this perspective. Both bodies provide a check on each other. The Council's functional effectiveness is a guarantee against the Assembly's inability to agree creating chaos; the Assembly's competence to discuss the benefits of any policy – including the policy of the Council – provides, in principle, a public check on the Great Powers' capacity to turn the organization into an instrument of imperialism.

VI

Yet, this nice balance has not ensured absence of conflict. The Charter extends the Assembly's power of discussion to matters of international peace and security.[55] The limits to the Assembly's power come from a duty to refer matters to the Council when 'action is necessary'[56] and from the prohibition to make recommendations in situations or disputes pending before the Council, unless the Council so requests.[57] In practice, however, the Assembly has passed resolutions in all conceivable situations, whether they were on the Council's agenda or not.[58] These resolutions have sometimes complemented simultaneous Council action, sometimes contradicted it, the only limit having been set by its inability to pass mandatory decisions or to take formal 'enforcement action'.[59] It has established

---

55 Articles 10, 11(2) and 14 of the Charter.
56 Article 11(2) *in fine*.
57 Article 12(1).
58 A policy defensible by the Council's curious practice never to move an item from its list after it has been received there – with the result that the list now covers nearly all conceivable international (regional) conflicts with some seriousness.
59 This was, of course, the bottom-line rule regarding the delimitation of the competences of the two organs outlined by the ICJ in the *Expenses* case, Reports (1962) 164-166. For a useful overview of cases where Assembly action has sometimes complemented, sometimes pre-empted Council action cf. N.D. White, *Keeping the Peace. United Nations and the Maintenance of International Peace and Security* (1993) 140-157, 161-177.

Martti Koskenniemi

peace-keeping forces,[60] made appeals to States for the establishment of voluntary embargoes[61] – and sometimes bluntly accepted by an overwhelming majority resolutions earlier vetoed in the Council by a Great Power.[62]

The first serious constitutional controversy within the organization concerning the powers of its two main bodies related, of course, to the passing of the Uniting for Peace Resolution in connection with the Council having been blocked by the Soviet veto in the Korean crisis in 1950. A Western manoeuvre resulted in a palace revolution whereby the Assembly took it upon itself to:

> consider the matter immediately with a view to making the appropriate recommendations to members for collective measures, including in the case of a breach of the peace or act of aggression the use of armed force when necessary, to maintain or restore international peace and security.[63]

The controversy over the lawfulness of the Uniting for Peace resolution has long been over. It did not occasion a revolutionary transformation of the organization's activities. The nine Special Emergency Sessions held under the new procedure have scarcely differed from the Assembly's other special sessions. Apart from the setting-up of UNEF I in 1956, they did not initiate operational action. They resulted in condemnatory resolutions whose effect on the political world has been no different from that of its normal resolutions. Even peace-keeping operations have been, since the 1960s, firmly in the Security Council's hands. Nor have the Assembly's efforts to reform the Charter's order-system been impressive. The Assembly's Special Committee on the Review of the Charter ('Charter Committee') has routinely discussed Chapter VII matters at its annual sessions but has so far failed to achieve concrete results. In the 1980s and 1990s the Assembly did pass a number of declarations, drafted by the Charter Committee, on matters relative to international security – but always with the proviso that they would not imply

---

60   Most famously, UNGA Res. 1000 (ES-I) 5 November 1956.
61   For the Assembly's early recommendation on arms embargoes on Portugal and Congo, cf. UNGA Res. 1807 (XVII) 14 December 1962 and Res. 1474 (ES-4) 20 September 1960, 1600 (XV) 15 April 1961. On South Africa, the Assembly still recommended an embargo in 1990, 45/176 B and F (19 December 1990).
62   One recent example having been the United States intervention in Panama in December 1989. A non-aligned draft resolution in the Council (S/21048) would have deplored the intervention but was vetoed on 23 December by the US, France and United Kingdom (the vote having been 10-4-1). A resolution closely following the text of the earlier non-aligned draft was passed by the General Assembly on 29 December, UNGA Res. 44/240 (75-20-40). A comparable method was used by the Assembly in 1980 to condemn the Soviet invasion in Afghanistan – where a resolution essentially similar to that passed in the Assembly had been subject of the Soviet veto; and the US invasion of Grenada – where the Assembly passed a resolution essentially similar to an earlier draft vetoed in the Council by the US. For the former, cf. S/13729 and UNGA Res. ES-6/2 (14 January 1980) and the latter cf. UNGA Res. 38/7 (2 November 1983). Today, the Assembly disagrees with the Council in respect of the maintenance of the Bosnian arms embargo, cf. UNGA Res. 48/88 (20 December 1993), paras. 17-18 and with the United States in respect of the continued Cuban embargo, cf. Res. 48/18 (15 November 1993).
63   UNGA Res. 377 A (V) 3 November 1950 para. A (1).

The Police in the Temple. Order, Justice and the UN: A Dialectical View

changes in the Charter itself.[64] The significance of these declarations has remained small. An *ad hoc* Committee was set up in 1993 to examine the composition of the Security Council.[65] It has, however, so far failed to reach agreement on any proposals.

The new activities of the Security Council have occasioned the first major constitutional crisis in the United Nations since the passing of the Uniting for Peace Resolution.[66] This time, the crisis is in the opposite direction. It is not the Assembly that is trying to deal with the problem of order; the Security Council is attempting to deal with the problem of international justice.

The depth of the crisis is not so much related to the Council's enlarged jurisdiction *ratione materiae*: had it merely started to deal with a larger number of situations, including the internal conflicts and problems of social, economic, or humanitarian character to which it referred in its summit declaration of January 1992, few would have been concerned. The affair's seriousness is occasioned by the Council's willingness to use its exceptionally 'hard' powers of enforcement, binding resolutions, economic sanctions and military force for 'soft' purposes of international justice. This is what is new and problematic. 'It was to keep the peace, not to change the world order, that the Security Council was set up'.[67]

As is well-known, the Council's formal competence to take enforcement action is based on the criteria in Article 39: the presence of an act of aggression, breach of the peace, or a threat to the peace. The enlargement of the Council's powers has been undertaken through a new interpretation of what counts as a 'threat to the peace'. The sense of 'peace' has been widened from the (hard) absence of the use of armed force by a State to change the territorial *status quo* to the (soft) conditions within which – it is assumed – peace in its 'hard' sense depends;[68] a change from a formal to a substantive meaning.[69]

It is generally accepted that UN organs have the authority to determine, at least *prima facie*, the limits of their own jurisdiction.[70] The ICJ, for instance, enjoys no

---

64   Cf. Manila Declaration on the Peaceful Settlement of Disputes, UNGA Res. 37/10 (15 November 1982); Declaration on the Enhancement of the Effectiveness of the Principle of Refraining from the Threat or Use of Force in International Relations, 42/22 (18 November 1987); Declaration on the Prevention and Removal of and Disputes and Situations which May Threaten International Peace and Security and on the Role of the United Nations in this Field, 43/51 (5 December 1988); Declaration on Fact-Finding by the United Nations in the Field of Maintenance of International Peace and Security, 46/59 (9 December 1991); and Declaration on the Enhancement of Cooperation between the United Nations and Regional Arrangements and Agencies in the Maintenance of International Peace and Security, 49/57 (14 December 1994).
65   UNGA Res. 48/26 (3 December 1993).
66   For the volume of the increase in the Council's activity between 1988-1994, cf. the Reports by the Secretary-General, A/49/1 (2 September 1994) 4-6 (paras. 29-33).
67   Sir Gerald Fitzmaurice, diss. op., *Namibia* case, ICJ Reports (1971) 294 (para. 115).
68   Cf. also P.-M. Dupuy, 'Sécurité collective et organisation de la paix', 97 *RGDIP* (1993) 624.
69   This is one of the key themes in the Secretary-General's *Agenda for Peace*; to extend the organization's coercive powers from reactive (peace-keeping, peace-making) to preventive action (peace-building), S/2411, A/47/277 (17 June 1992) e.g. para. 21.
70   *Expenses* Case, ICJ Reports (1962) 168.

Martti Koskenniemi

general authority of constitutional review – however much its advisory or
contentious procedure may be used to decide incidental jurisdictional issues.[71] The
right 'of last resort' of member States to decide, for themselves, on whether an act
has been *ultra vires* is difficult to reject[72] – despite the evident problems it causes to
the credibility of the collective system.

Now the chase for a Somali clan leader, the Libyan sanctions or the Iraqi
liability regime, among a host of other controversial Chapter VII decisions, are
difficult to justify under a coherent theory of 'threat to peace'. Some lawyers have
suggested remedying the situation by a revision of the Council's composition.[73] I
would suggest that the Council simply has no business venturing into such theory-
building, or that even if it does so, there is no compelling argument as to why the
General Assembly could not simply overrule the Council. The kinds of
considerations that make for a wide, substantive definition of peace are of no
concern for the police but must be decided in the Temple.

Before invoking the objections to the wide reading of 'threat to international
peace and security' by the Council, it is first necessary to see that the appeal of such
a reading follows from a real difficulty to separate form from substance, or order
from justice. Indeed, it may appear that such a separation cannot be undertaken, that
social order is always dependent on its perceived 'legitimacy'. Studies of
international security (order) have focused on a wide or a 'comprehensive',
integrated notion of security, pointing out that even if the subjects of security are
'States' (a by no means self-evident moral choice), there are many ways in which
State security may be threatened. A 'State' is not only a territorial unit but also a set
of institutions (e.g. form of government, a secular/religious base) and ideas (e.g.
national, historical or ideological justification).[74] These institutions or ideas may be
subject to a wide variety of partly internal, partly external, political, ideological or
economic threats that are no less dangerous to the State's identity or viability than
clear-cut military threats against its territory. Mass exodus, for example, into a State
may effectively change its linguistic, religious or ethnic base – and thereby also its
identity.

These arguments – originally voiced within peace studies – convince many
politicians who have started to speak about a 'comprehensive' security policy that

---

71   *Namibia* Case, ICJ Reports (1971) 45 (para. 89). But see also ibid., at 53 (para. 115) and e.g.
     Graefrath, *supra* note 8, at 200-205; Bowett, 'The Impact of Security Council Decisions on
     Dispute Settlement Procedures', 5 *EJIL* (1994) 93-99; Gaja, 'Reflexions sur le rôle du Conseil de
     sécurité dans le nouvel ordre mondial', 97 *RGDIP* (1993) 315-317 and Franck, 'The 'Powers of
     Appreciation': Who is the Ultimate Guardian of UN Legality?', 86 *AJIL* (1992) 519-522.
72   Cf. D. Ciobanu, *Preliminary Objections. Related to the Jurisdiction of the United Nations
     Political Organs* (1975) 173-179; Sur, 'Securité collective et retablissement de la paix: la
     résolution 687 (3 avril 1991) dans l'affaire du Golfe', *RdC*, Colloque 1992, at 19-20.
73   Caron, 'The Legitimacy of the Collective Authority of the Security Council', 87 *AJIL* (1993) 552-
     588; Franck, 'Fairness in the International Legal and Institutional System. General Course on
     Public International Law', 240 *RdC* (1993-III) 196-218.
74   Cf. B. Buzan, *People, States & Fear* (2nd ed., 1991) 57-107.

The Police in the Temple. Order, Justice and the UN: A Dialectical View

would take account of various kinds of non-military threats to their countries.[75] Likewise, statements by the Security Council, the Secretary-General and influential scholars have used the vocabulary of security to justify the need for a more effective international governance through the Security Council.[76] In accordance with the arguments made above in section II, however, there are serious theoretical, systemic and practical objections to these proposals.

The *theoretical objections* to the comprehensive concept of security relate to the extent that it seems to assume both that we know (or can reliably ascertain) those social conditions in which security flourishes and that everybody would, of necessity, have good reason to agree on their enforcement through the Security Council. Now it may be true that democratic societies are not in the habit of going to war against each other. And it may also be true that the substance of international law is moving against totalitarianism.[77] It does not, however, follow that the Council should be empowered to make every State a democratic one. It is not only, as J.S. Mill famously argued, that democracy and liberalism cannot be created by force (though that seems plausible enough) but that we simply do not know what 'democracy' would mean for a Russian, Somali, Chinese, Algerian or other non-Western, non-liberal society. But we do have the experience that attempts to insert the political system of European States into Africa by the first generation of non-colonial leaders, trained in Paris or London in the 1960s, failed to create a viable African political life.[78] Our Kantian ethics invites us to assume that everyone wishes to be treated like we would like. This is rubbish; to think in terms of moral universals creates demands on ourselves (and the UN) that we (or the UN) have absolutely no means to fulfil. Our inevitable guilt will need only a small push to turn into cynicism and brutalization (a push daily attempted by journalistic accounts of UN 'failures') – 'Morality is the last refuge of Eurocentrism'.[79]

But even if the Security Council were, miraculously, in possession of a causally credible recipe for global security, it is still not true that it should enforce it. In the first place, the extent to which a given policy or situation, national or international, might contribute to 'security' is merely one, and not self-evidently the most important, criterion whereby it may be evaluated. Nothing in political history has undermined the fact that social transformation for the better might sometimes

---

[75] For example, the special summit of the European Council held in Brussels on 29 October 1993 defined the general objectives of European security by reference to its territorial integrity and political independence of the European Union but also in terms of its democratic character, its economic stability and the stability of neighbouring regions. Cf. Fink-Hooijer, 'The Common Foreign and Security Policy of the European Union', 5 *EJIL* (1994) 195.

[76] Cf. *Agenda for Peace, supra* note 69, paras. 12-16 and e.g. Urquhart, 'International Security after the Cold War', in A. Robert, B. Kingsbury, *United Nations, Divided World. The UN's Roles in International Relations* (2nd ed., 1993) 94-103.

[77] Or, as some say, in 'pro-democratic' directions, cf. Crawford, 'Democracy and International Law', LXIX *BYIL* (1993) 123-133.

[78] Cf. B. Davidson, *The Black Man's Burden. Africa and the Curse of the Nation-State* (1992).

[79] H.-M. Enzensberger, *Civil War* (1994) 59, 56-71.

Martti Koskenniemi

necessitate revolution.[80] In the second place, peoples' views about the peaceful conditions of societies are not technical but political: they do not speak about causality (or not of causality only) but about norms, values and preferred ways of life. There is no necessary harmony between them; they are situational and conflicting. To believe otherwise is to make the classical Utopian mistake – a mistake which translates itself into a politics of tyranny.[81]

These objections do not mean that Article 2(7) of the Charter should be resuscitated. They do not mean that international action should not be taken to relieve absolute suffering and misery merely because national bureaucrats fail to provide UN personnel with a *laissez-passer*. But they do mean that action should be measured in accordance with what is possible; that 'enforcement action' should not be enforced on the people it intends to save; and that the rule must remain the accommodation of local values. Above all, they mean that such action should be exceptional and open to review and revision by a representative body tasked to deal with normative controversy, that is, *faute de mieux*, the General Assembly.

The view that 'security' is comprehensive and depends also on the presence of acceptable conditions of social life is certainly not manifestly implausible. But there is a long way from the truth of that statement to the falsity of the view which says that it is the Security Council's task to bring about those conditions. Dictators always saw everywhere a threat to the *Ordnung*; and no conflict was too small for the intervention of the security force. Theirs, too, was a comprehensive notion.

The *systemic objection* follows from the theoretical one. There is a crucial difference between policies intended to safeguard 'security' and policies intended to bring about the good life – a difference encapsulated in the distinction between the police and the Temple. The former relies on causal-technical assumptions about what type of action most efficiently safeguards communal peace. In a (Hobbesian) world where causal-technical assumptions are opposed to normative ones, and preferred as they are understood to be verifiable in contrast to the latter being of merely 'subjective preference', public policies are always on the move towards setting up a *Leviathan*. This effect is not created simply by liberal agnosticism about norms but through the association of agnosticism with a belief in an overriding, and non-normative, value of 'security'.

Now the position of the Security Council under the UN Charter is, as we have seen, that of the technician of peace, the police. Its composition, procedures and practices are completely indefensible if we assume that its tasks extend to assessing and enforcing the conditions of the good life – including rules of international law – among and within States. These are normative tasks that can be acceptably tackled only through a decision-process that is subject to public criticism and in which every concerned entity can participate. As each organ determines for itself the limits

---

80 As (controversially) declared by the UN General Assembly in respect of decolonial struggle in Res. 2625 (1970). Cf. generally H. Wilson, *International Law and the Use of Force by National Liberation Movements* (1988).

81 On this theme generally, cf. I. Berlin, *The Crooked Timber of Humanity* (1990) especially at 1-48.

The Police in the Temple. Order, Justice and the UN: A Dialectical View

of its own competence, the Assembly can simply assume this role. There is no need for a Council determination to that effect as there is no *general* primacy of Council over the Assembly, the police over the Temple.

The Council's recent activity has brought to light its *practical inappropriateness* as a forum to justice. There is no 'due process' clause in the Council's (provisional) Rules of Procedure. The treatment – or non-treatment – of the Libyan views in connection with the passing of Resolution 731 in January 1992 that effectively determined Libya's guilt in sponsoring terrorism was below all standards of procedural fairness.[82] The moderate proposals by Professor Bowett to reform the Council's procedures would be as necessary as they are unlikely to take place.[83] The Council's internal discussions over the past few years have not brought the prospects of a meaningful reform any closer.

Let me offer just two examples of the Council's lack of concern for procedural 'detail'. First, the Council's economic sanctions are managed by five separate sanctions committees (on Iraq, Yugoslavia, Libya, Somalia and Angola) with completely inadequate secretarial help, each having been established in connection with a particular sanctions resolution and conducting its work in secret and in isolation from the other committees.[84] As a result, the committees routinely make diverging interpretative decisions with significant economic effects not only on the target States but, for instance, on States, organizations and private companies seeking authorizations to make deliveries under the 'humanitarian exceptions' clauses in the relevant resolutions.[85] The committees consist of diplomats of the permanent missions of Council member States who have no access to the economic, humanitarian and other data that would be needed for rational decision on delivery authorizations, and little time or interest to examine the tens of thousands of annual requests and other communications properly.[86] The committees neither publish their decisions nor follow-up on their effects. Reports on the national implementation of sanctions are neither analysed nor commented upon. Unlike the Committee

---

82   Cf. Graefrath, *supra* note 8, at 187-191, 196, 204.
83   Bowett, *supra* note 70, at 100.
84   The principle of secrecy was set up by the Iraqi sanctions Committee in August 1990, more by default than conscious planning. This has then been followed by the other committees. As a result, public analysis and commentary of sanctions management by the Council has remained almost non-existent – the exception being commentary on the work of the Iraqi sanctions committee, its initial protocols having leaked out and been published separately in D. L. Bethlehem (ed.), *The Kuwait Crisis: Sanctions and their Economic Consequences*, Part II, Vol. 2 (1991) 773-985. For comments, cf. Koskenniemi, 'Le comité des sanctions (créé par la résolution 661 (1990) du Conseil de sécurité)', XXXVII *AFDI* (1991) 119-137 and Scharf, Dorosin, 'Interpreting UN Sanctions: The Rulings and Role of the Yugoslavia Sanctions Committee', XIX *Brooklyn Journal of Int'l Law* (1993) 771-827.
85   For Iraq, cf. SC Res. 687 of 3 April 1991 para. 20; For Yugoslavia cf. SC Res. 760 of 18 June 1992; for Libya cf. SC Res. 748 of 30 March 1992 paras. 4(a) and 9. For the provision in respect of Haiti (no longer in force) cf. SC Res. 841 of 16 June 1993, para. 7.
86   The Yugoslavian sanctions committee alone received more than 34,000 communications in 1993 and during the first eight months of 1994 had received already more than 45,000. Cf. Report of the Secretary-General on the Work of the Organization, A/49/1 (2 September 1994) 5 (para. 32).

Martti Koskenniemi

established in 1968 to survey the implementation of the embargo against Southern Rhodesia,[87] they do not even file reports on their activities to the Council itself[88] – a situation casting serious doubt on the meaningfulness of the Council's sanctions policy.

Second, having set up two war crimes tribunals the Council has so far failed to demonstrate its willingness to take these bodies seriously by providing the necessary conditions for their adequate functioning. There has been much publicity on the difficulties of the Yugoslavian war crimes tribunal, and the potential conflict between the 'peace process' and the 'crimes process'. The investigation of the Rwandan war crimes was allocated to a Commission of Experts without adequate funds and technical personnel and unable to conduct the kinds of large-scale investigations outside Kigali that would have been necessary for the setting up of a credible war crimes process.[89] The Chairman of the Expert Committee appealed on 23 August to member States for assistance to provide at least one hundred investigators, 20 doctors and 60 assistants. By the end of November 1994, however, only a handful of investigators had visited the country and the final 36-page report of the Commission falls short of providing an adequate basis for indictments in the Tribunal, established in November.[90]

These are only some examples of the Council's *nonchalance* in regard to the practical implementation of its decisions, made possible by its absence of accountability within the UN system. How else can it be explained that the Council has never required States that have been authorized to 'take necessary measures' under Chapter VII (in respect of Iraq, Haiti, Somalia, Rwanda, or the protection of Bosnia's 'safety zones') to report on those measures to the Council or to members at large – in complete disregard of the implications of the delegation of powers by members to the Council under Article 24(1) of the Charter?

The Council's failure to ensure the implementation of an increasing number of its resolutions in former Yugoslavia, Somalia and Angola may now have demoralized the Council's atmosphere to the extent that serious reform towards some legal culture within it has become impossible. One wishes the situation were otherwise. One thing is certain, however: with the exception of Haiti, all the crises begun after the end of the Cold War are still continuing. The Council will have to face up to the consequences of its inability to make reality of its inflated promises. A test case will be the form through which it will guarantee the partition of Bosnia-Herzegovina having a number of times required respect for its 'territorial integrity' and rejected the aggressor's right to enjoy the fruits of his aggression[91] – indeed

87   SC Res. 253 (1968) 29 May 1968.
88   With the insignificant exception of the Iraqi committee's formal reports on the permanent arms embargo on Iraq, set up in SC Res. 687 (1991).
89   For the setting up of the Commission of Experts, cf. SC Res. 935 of 1 July 1994.
90   SC Res. 955 of 8 November 1994. For the Commission's final report, cf. UN Doc. S/1994/1405 (9 December 1994), especially paras. 22-26.
91   E.g. in SC Res. 757 of 30 May 1992, 3rd preambular paragraph.

The Police in the Temple. Order, Justice and the UN: A Dialectical View

having once put all its eggs in the basket of an International Peace Conference whose Chairmen rejected an earlier partition plan on the grounds that '... such a plan could achieve homogeneity and coherent boundaries only by an enforced population transfer'.[92]

So the question is whether the Assembly might still be able to recover its role as the normative Temple of the Organization, independent of the Great Powers and capable of challenging them. The prospect may appear daunting: the Assembly is clearly a part of Philip Allott's inter-statal 'unsociety' – a fact which alone may seem enough to prevent it from assuming a meaningful normative role.[93] Tragic Utopianism shakes hands with the realist for whom 'international government is, in effect, government by that state which supplies the power necessary for the purpose of government'.[94] For both, the condition of present institutions prevents significant normative transformation.

Despite the paraphernalia, the ineffectiveness, the ulterior motives, the ignorance, the in-fights, it still remains the Assembly that can provide the counterweight to the Council, provided it is determinate enough. Article 14 of the Charter may be only a 'modest approach to the problem of "peaceful change"',[95] but it does provide the Assembly with the formal basis to study and recommend peaceful adjustments of any situation – including unjust *status quo* – and to challenge the Council's authority when that might seem appropriate. The argument that the Assembly is 'less realistic'[96] than the Council and therefore should not be taken too seriously has no effect here (unlike in issues of military security).

Still, the problem is less with formal competence than with *de facto* will and capacity. Recent attempts to reform the Assembly so as to concentrate its work better and to reinforce the coordinating role of the ECOSOC go in the right direction.[97] But they have brought in little by way of strengthening the Assembly in its Charter-based role as a *forum* to decide, by majority votes if necessary, on the economic, social and humanitarian policies that could transform the living conditions of national societies. The *Agenda for Development*, brought in as a timid counterpart to the Secretary-General's *Agenda for Peace*, may have used up its momentum without succeeding in making proposals on the reform of worldwide economic and social decision-patterns. That exercise, as well as, surprisingly, the initial years of the Commission for Sustainable Development, were transformed into

---

92 Report of the Secretary-General on the International Conference on the former Yugoslavia, S/24795 (11 November 1992) 13 (para. 36).

93 P. Allott, *Eunomia. New Order for a New World* (1990) 239-259.

94 Carr, *supra* note 35, at 107.

95 Goodrich, Hambro, *supra* note 42, at 104.

96 Pellet, 'Le Tribunal criminel international pour l'ex-Yugoslavie. Poudre aux yeux au avancée décisive', 98 *RGDIP* (1994) 30.

97 For the recent decision to restructure and revitalize the Assembly's economic, social and related activities, cf. UNGA Res. 48/162 (20 December 1993). For an overview and a moderate analysis of the prospects of serious reform (noting that the taboo against changing the Charter is lifting) cf. Bertrand, 'The Historical Development of Efforts to Reform the UN', in Roberts, Kingsbury, *supra* note 76, especially at 428-436.

Martti Koskenniemi

new forums for North-South controversy. On the other hand, there are some signs of the Assembly seeking seriously to examine the Council's activities. It has, for instance, used its budgetary powers to set limits on Council activity – one (controversial) example having been in connection with the financing of the Yugoslavian war crimes tribunal. It has also called for more transparency in the Council's working methods. In 1994, it requested the Council not only to review its working methods but also to 'provide, in a timely manner clear and informative account of its work, including Security Council resolutions and other decisions, inclusive of measures taken under Chapter VII' and declared its readiness to initiate 'in-depth discussion' of the matters contained therein.[98]

There is, undoubtedly, a new anger feeding the work of the General Assembly and some of its subsidiary bodies. After years of fruitless academic pondering, the Assembly decided in 1994 to request the International Court of Justice for an advisory opinion on the lawfulness of nuclear weapons. There may not be much political wisdom in such a request. But the feeling that lies behind it – that it is perverse to believe that being a Great Power endows one with the right to make a lawful threat of mass destruction – cannot be overlooked. It is a justified feeling of anger, perhaps of frustration. It has three directions in which to grow. It may seek to turn the Assembly into a Temple of Justice; it may conclude that the Assembly can never become such a Temple, and fall back into frustration; or it may be co-opted by the Great Powers handing out again plastic pearls and trinkets for sovereign rights.

VII

The police are ransacking the temple, searching for criminals and those it calls terrorists. The mind of the police – the security police in this case – is a machine, programmed to believe that history ended and we won it; that what remains is a clash of civilizations and we intend to come up first. As it proceeds – helmets, boots, blackjacks and all – towards the altar, the people draw silently away into the small chapels, surrounding the *navis*, each to attend communion before a different god. After the police have gone, the altar hall is empty but for the few that were left to guard it, and their admirers. The frescoes, the bronze statuettes, the stained glass, the marble speak from different ages, through different symbols, and towards a now empty centre. *Quod non fecerunt barbari, fecerunt Barberini*. The peace of the police is not the calm of the temple but the silence of the tomb.

---

98   UNGA Res. 48/264 (29 July 1994).

[8]

THE LEGALITY OF BOMBING IN THE NAME OF HUMANITY

N.D. White*

1 INTRODUCTION

There is no doubt that the situation of extreme violence in Kosovo in the thirteen month period leading up to the NATO bombing between 24 March 1999 and 9 June 1999 was a threat to the peace. Indeed, the Security Council made that determination prior to the bombing.[1] There is little doubt that this determination potentially removed the restriction on *UN* intervention in the internal affairs of a state.[2] UN sanctioned military intervention, though, normally requires the express authority of the Security Council.[3] The issue is whether states can take 'humanitarian' military action 'in support' of resolutions which make determinations of a threat to the peace, breach of the peace or act of aggression,[4] even though there is no express authorization to do so. The interventions in northern Iraq in 1991 and Kosovo in 1999 appear to be context-breaking actions, aimed at creating a new right to take military action in support of Security Council resolutions. In those two cases the justification given by the states using military force was to protect human rights, principally the right to life, the violation of which had been recognized by the Security Council. A further instance of military action being taken to enforce Security Council resolutions is the bombing of Iraq that has occurred since the cease-fire embodied in Resolution 687 of 1991, most recently in December 1998 and regularly thereafter, the purpose being to enforce compliance with the disarmament provisions of that resolution.

This paper will consider, with particular focus on Kosovo, the compatibility of these military actions with the UN collective security system, which since the end of the Cold War has rapidly been developed along decentralized lines. Are the Iraq and Kosovo operations further lawful developments of the system or are they so inconsistent as to be incompatible with the UN Charter? Treaty regimes can be developed quite radically but there are limits to this development (this applies to the NATO treaty as well). Furthermore, for subsequent practice to modify a treaty it must be widely supported by the members. Is the fact that the 19 members of NATO supported the action in Kosovo sufficient by itself, not only to modify the

---

* Professor of International Organizations Law, Law School, The University of Nottingham, UK. This article is based on a paper given at the British International Studies Association Annual Conference, held at Manchester, UK, December 1999.
[1] See eg SC Res. 1199, 23 September 1998.
[2] Art. 2(7) of the UN Charter.
[3] J. Lobel and M. Ratner, 'Bypassing the Security Council: Ambiguous Authorizations to Use Force, Cease-Fires and the Iraqi Inspection Regime', (1999) 93 *AJIL* 124.
[4] Art. 39 of the UN Charter. This is the 'gateway' to chapter VII which contains the Council's economic and military enforcement powers.

JOURNAL OF CONFLICT AND SECURITY LAW (2000), VOL. 5 NO. 1, 27–43

NATO treaty but also the requirements of the UN Charter? This paper will look at the inability of the Security Council to authorize military action as a justification for NATO taking action. The lack of alternatives debated before the UN, apart from the stark choice between bombing or inaction, needs to be considered, as does the possibility of seeking a mandate from the General Assembly. The necessity of UN authorization, both in terms of legality and legitimacy, will be discussed.

2 THE DECENTRALIZED SYSTEM OF COLLECTIVE SECURITY

Collective security can be defined as the combined usage of the coercive capacity of the international community to combat illegal uses of armed force and situations that threaten international peace.[5] It is recognized by collective security experts that there are degrees of collective security, signifying that simply because a system does not match an ideal it does not mean that it is not a collective security system. Indeed, there are considerable disagreements on what constitutes an ideal system.[6] Nevertheless, it is clear that the greater the international consensus behind the operation the greater its legitimacy, although it would be unrealistic to expect un-animity. Certainly, question marks may be raised against the composition of the UN Security Council and its ability to represent the international community, thereby calling into question whether a Council mandate, though having the necessary legal pedigree, gives sufficient legitimacy to the operation. Until there is a major reform of the Council the legitimacy of such military operations will be increased if they also have the support of the General Assembly.[7] Indeed, it is argued here that it is not strictly correct to state that only the *Security Council*, acting on behalf of the UN, can authorize enforcement action,[8] rather it is only the *United Nations*, nor-mally acting through the Security Council, that can authorize such action.

Collective security or collective police actions taken outside the ambit of the UN though are more problematic, for they normally are deficient both in terms of legitimacy and legality. Although the Security Council is in need of reform, it does represent the UN when taking action in the field of peace and security.[9] The

---

[5] K.P. Saksena, *The United Nations and Collective Security* (1974) 4–5.

[6] I.L. Claude, *Power and International Relations* (1962) 110–68. C.A. Kupchan, 'The Case for Collective Security', in G.W. Downs (ed.), *Collective Security Beyond the Cold War* (1994) 42–4.

[7] The Korean action received support from the General Assembly in GA Res. 376, 7 October 1950. Less obvious support was forthcoming in the military response to the invasion of Kuwait – see for example GA Res. 46/135, 17 December 1991. See further GA Res. 49/27, 5 December 1994, on Haiti; GA Res. 49/206, 23 December 1994, on Rwanda; GA Res. 48/146, 20 December 1993, *re* Somalia; GA Res. 50/193, 22 December 1995, on Bosnia. Clearly, most of these endorsements were retrospective. See further T.M. Franck, 'The United Nations as Guarantor of International Peace and Security', in C. Tomuschat (ed.), *The United Nations at Age Fifty: A Legal Perspective* (1995) 25.

[8] D. Sarooshi, *The United Nations and the Development of Collective Security* (1999) 27–9.

[9] Art. 24(1) of the UN Charter.

The Legality of Bombing in the Name of Humanity 29

international community has granted the Security Council this function. Even if states had a collective police power before 1945, at that point they embodied it, for better or worse (though the intention was to improve the ambiguous and selective nature of collective interventions), in the UN Security Council.[10] It seems more precise to state that the parameters, indeed existence, of such a collective power before the advent of the UN Charter was legally highly doubtful. It was by establishing the UN Charter that the vast majority of states decided to establish a body with novel competence. The adoption of the UN Charter in 1945 was a defining moment, not in the sense of defining a legal regime that already existed, but in the sense of creating, for the want of a better phrase, a new world order, with the Charter assuming the foundational significance of the constitution of the international community.[11] Thereafter the UN possessed powers which states did not, arguably never did, possess. Legally speaking only the UN can thereafter delegate its collective security powers of enforcement to a state or states. Two objections may be given to this contention: first that empowerment of the Security Council in article 24(1) of the Charter is 'in order to take prompt and effective action', and second that the Security Council, by the same provision, only has primary, not exclusive, responsibility. Thus it may be contended that if the Security Council is inactive in the face of a threat or breach of the peace then residual responsibility would exceptionally revert to states or other international organizations to take collective action.[12] However, the reference to 'primary responsibility' for peace and security in article 24(1) relates to the division of competence within the UN – it is the General Assembly, and also to a lesser extent, the International Court of Justice, two other principal organs of the UN, that have subsidiary competence in the field of international peace and security,[13] not states acting unilaterally or multilaterally. It will be argued that, in the face of unjustifiable Security Council inaction, it is the General Assembly that has the competence to authorize military enforcement action. Furthermore, the idea of rights reverting back to states in the event of Security Council inaction assumes that they possessed such rights before 1945, and that they could claim them back based on a perception of Security Council inadequacy. Both these claims have little legal pedigree.[14] In particular, they violate the fundamental norm of the international community prohibiting the threat or use of force.[15]

In the Kosovo situation the main NATO contributors did not claim, in the main, to be acting instead of the Security Council, rather that they were furthering or

---

[10] Sarooshi, *op.cit.*, 26–32.

[11] B. Fassbender, 'The United Nations Charter as Constitution of the International Community', (1998) 36 *Columbia Journal of International Law* 529. But see G. Arangio-Ruiz, 'The Federal Analogy and UN Charter Interpretation', (1997) 8 *EJIL* 9.

[12] See the resolution adopted by the North Atlantic Assembly of November 1998 (NATO doc. AR 295 SA), cited in B. Simma, 'NATO, the UN and the Use of Force: Legal Aspects', (1999) 10 *EJIL* 16.

[13] *Certain Expenses of the United Nations*, ICJ Rep.1962, 164–5.

[14] Simma, *loc.cit.*, 17.

[15] Art. 2(4) of the UN Charter.

30   *N.D. White*

supporting Security Council resolutions. However, this goes against the grain of Security Council practice which, in the absence of agreements under article 43 of the Charter, has led to a loose decentralized system of collective security, whereby the Security Council has authorized a state or group of states under chapter VII of the UN Charter to take military action to maintain or restore international peace and security. Command of these operations is vested in those states forming the multinational force. The Security Council's main mechanism for controlling the operations it has sanctioned comes in the form of the enabling resolution and a reporting system, whereby the contributing states provide information to the Security Council, usually via the Secretary General, on the military action taken to fulfil the mandate granted to them by the Security Council. This may be a far cry from the formal provisions of chapter VII of the UN Charter whereby command and control was meant to be centralized under the Military Staff Committee, and ultimately the Security Council.[16]

Strategic control by the Military Staff Committee and overall political control by the Council appear necessary for the achievement of the collective security concept as envisaged by the Charter, in that they embody the centralization of the collective use of force. This argument can be used to criticise the Council's practice in the use of the military option to date, when it has simply delegated authority and control to a state or group of states. However, simply to dismiss a viable alternative system because it does not match the text of the Charter is too formalistic.[17] If the Council simply authorizes a state to use force to achieve an objective within the ambit of the UN's security role, despite the fact that it is being performed by one state, it is still a collective authorization to use force, in that it is being performed to carry out the collective will of the Council on behalf of the UN. This is all the more so when the Council authorizes a group of states to carry out such a function.[18] The question remains whether control by the Council and the Military Staff Committee is essential to properly fulfil the collective security function. It could be argued that the provisions of chapter VII are simply formalities which, if in operation, would facilitate the use of the power contained in article 42. They can be seen as just one method of allowing the Council to fulfil its collective security role. Thus, it would appear to be unnecessary to make these formalities a prerequisite to the use of military enforcement action by the Council.[19]

Nevertheless, whereas an ideal collective security system envisages aggression

---

[16]   Articles 45–47 of the UN Charter.

[17]   But see J. Quigley, 'The United States and the United Nations in the Persian Gulf War: New Order or Disorder?', (1992) 25 *Cornell JIL* 1.

[18]   This seems to be envisaged by art. 48 of the UN Charter which provides in paragraph 1 that 'the action required to carry out the decisions of the Security Council for the maintenance of international peace and security shall be taken by all the Members of the United Nations or by some of them, as the Security Council may determine'. See also paragraph 2 which envisages such action by member states acting in 'appropriate international agencies'.

[19]   T.D. Gill, 'Legal and Some Political Limitations on the Power of the UN Security Council to Exercise its Enforcement Powers under Chapter VII of the Charter', (1995) 26 *NYIL* 61.

and threats to the peace being met whenever they occur, the decentralized system is erratic, its operation often occurring only when the dominant states' interests are at stake, as well as being blocked by the veto when a permanent member sees its interests as being threatened. However, certainly with the end of the Cold War, the collective security system has started to operate in a fashion closer to that envisaged in 1945. What is clear at the moment is that the Council has not yet 'decided' to use military force, it has simply recommended or authorized that states, on a voluntary basis, use force in particular situations and for particular purposes. Inevitably, the voluntary nature of the military option undermines the collective security ideal that every aggression is met with counter-force, since there may be no willing volunteers or, indeed, those initially volunteering may withdraw without any legal hindrance.[20] However, it is difficult to argue against the volunteer system of UN-authorized military action under chapter VII when chapter VIII explicitly accepts it under article 53 as regards regional arrangements.

The thin line between military actions under chapter VII and those under chapter VIII is seen to be even more illusory when considering the legal basis of NATO actions in Bosnia and Kosovo (post NATO bombings) undertaken with UN authority. The resolutions mandating military enforcement actions culminating in the endorsement of IFOR following the Dayton Accords of November 1995,[21] and KFOR following the FRY's withdrawal in June 1999,[22] can either be seen as deriving from chapter VIII, thereby treating NATO as a 'regional arrangement', or as authorizations to each individual member state of NATO, including other contributors to IFOR/KFOR, to form multilateral forces under chapter VII. Both of these are equally plausible, thereby illustrating the overarching decentralized model based on UN authorization.

Although not matching the original Charter scheme, the decentralized military option which has been developed by the Security Council to deal with acts of aggression (Korea and Kuwait), and threats to the peace (Somalia, Rwanda, Haiti, Bosnia, Zaire, Albania and East Timor) is a lawful development of its powers to maintain or restore international peace and security. This does not mean that the system does not have any legal parameters. *De minimis* there must be an authorizing resolution from the Security Council,[23] which, given its import and the fact that it is purporting to delegate potentially devastating powers to states, must be construed narrowly.[24] In the United Nations there is consensus that the phrase 'all necessary measures' or 'all necessary means' in combination with an 'authorization' 'under Chapter VII' signifies that military enforcement action is being sanctioned. Other language will not do. For example US and UK attempts to interpret Security Council resolutions condemning Iraq for non-compliance with weapons inspections during 1998, when 'serious consequences' were indicated by the Security Council,

---

[20] But see Sarooshi, *op.cit.*, 150.
[21] SC Res. 1031, 15 December 1995.
[22] SC Res. 1244, 10 June 1999.
[23] Lobel and Ratner, *loc.cit.*, 125–7.
[24] Sarooshi, *op.cit.*, 44.

failed because there was no support for that position from Russia and China and many other members of the Security Council.[25] Failure to secure the necessary authorizing language in a resolution signifies a lack of consensus over military action, it is disingenuous for certain states to then claim that they can unilaterally interpret resolutions as sanctioning military action. All there is then is an unjustified claim to take military action. The same must be true for the attempt to stretch Security Council authority even further by stating that military action was taken 'in support' of Security Council resolutions. None of the resolutions on which military actions against Iraq and the FRY were, in whole or in part based, provided authority for those actions.[26]

In the case of Kosovo, the subsequent authorization of KFOR by the Security Council[27] cannot be seen as retrospective endorsement of the NATO bombings. First, Russia and China made this particularly clear when the mandating resolution for KFOR was adopted.[28] Second, the Security Council as a political organ concerned with the maintenance or restoration of peace and security will quite often have to 'build upon facts or situations based on, or involving illegalities'.[29] This does not signify an acceptance of their legality. What it does mean is that NATO stepped outside the parameters of the UN Charter when it suited the organization, and then it stepped back in again when it, or rather the G8, had produced a suitable formula for ending the bombing which satisfied Russia and was agreed to by the FRY.

Although binding chapter VII resolutions were breached by Iraq and the FRY, this is not a sufficient justification for what Krisch has labelled the 'unilateral enforcement of the collective will'.[30] The lack of consensus in the Security Council that a simple chapter VII resolution condemning and demanding certain action can give rise to military action by willing states if the resolutions are ignored is telling. Indeed, all that will happen if western states continue to utilize resolutions in this way, is that there will be no agreement on any type of chapter VII resolution in the future in case certain states may take it upon themselves to undertake military action to enforce them.[31] The collective security system has been stretched and pulled by the practice of mainly western states and is quite generous to them, but they still need to seek and gain a Security Council mandate. The desire of western states to base their military actions on Security Council resolutions is significant though, for it seems to undermine the argument that the NATO bombardment of the FRY and the intervention in northern Iraq are strong evidence of a re-emergence of a

---

[25]　See eg SC Res. 1154, 2 March 1998. N.D. White and R.Cryer, 'Unilateral Enforcement of Resolution 687: A Threat Too Far?', (1999) 29 *California Western ILJ* 274.

[26]　SC Res. 688 of 5 April 1991 re Operation Provide Comfort in Northern Iraq; SC Res. 687 of 3 April 1991 *re*, for example, Operation Desert Fox against Iraq; SC Res. 1199 of 23 September 1998 and 1203 of 24 October 1998, *re* Operation Allied Force against the FRY.

[27]　SC Res. 1244, 10 June 1999.

[28]　SC 4011th mtg, 10 June 1999.

[29]　Simma, *loc.cit.*, 11.

[30]　N. Krisch, 'Unilateral Enforcement of the Collective Will: Kosovo, Iraq, and the Security Council', (1999) 3 *Max Plank Yearbook of UN Law* 59.

[31]　*Ibid.*, 94.

unilateral right to humanitarian intervention.[32] After examining the claims of NATO states both before international and national political fora and in pleadings before the International Court in May 1999,[33] Krisch concludes that despite the odd (and inconsistent) statements by the US and the UK which seemed to favour unilateral humanitarian intervention, both those states and the remainder of NATO members tried to justify their action on the basis of the collective authority of the UN rather than on the right of humanitarian intervention. 'Thus, a purely unilateral humanitarian intervention seems even more difficult after the case of Kosovo than before'.[34] It seems that by trying to force the military actions under the UN umbrella, NATO states have probably done more damage to the already precarious and dangerous doctrine of humanitarian intervention, as well as breaching, and therefore undermining the constitutional parameters of the UN collective security system they helped to create. The failure of the Security Council to condemn the NATO action by rejecting a Russian draft on 26 March 1999 by 12 votes to 3,[35] cannot be seen as an authorization of the bombing, nor an endorsement of it, since a major concern for many states voting against the resolution was its lack of balance in that it failed also to condemn the brutality of the repressive measures taken by the FRY.[36] Above all lack of condemnation by the Security Council cannot be seen as an authorization to use force.

3 ACTING ON BEHALF OF THE 'INTERNATIONAL COMMUNITY'

As with the other isolated instances in international practice, it is possible to look at the interventions in Northern Iraq and Kosovo and pick out of the morass of legal justifications certain statements by some states and, assuming acceptance by the international community, present this as evidence of *opinio juris* for a right of humanitarian intervention. However, as with the Indian intervention in Bangladesh in 1971, when the right of humanitarian intervention was seemingly invoked alongside the right of self-defence,[37] recent attempts to resurrect the doctrine have been combined with other justifications which attempt to base the actions on norms acceptable to the international community. India tried, despite the evidence, to

---

[32] But see A. Cassese, 'Ex Inuria ius oritur: Are We Moving towards International Legitimation of Forcible Humanitarian Countermeasures in the World Community', (1999) 10 *EJIL* 23.

[33] See *e.g. Case Concerning Legality of the Use of Force (Yugoslavia v United Kingdom)* Request [by the FRY] for Provisional Measures, 2 June 1999. The Court refused to grant the request, although it did express its concern both at the loss of life in Kosovo, and 'with the use of force in Yugoslavia' which 'under the present circumstances raises very serious issues of international law' – paras.15–16.

[34] Krisch, *loc.cit.*, 93. See his analysis of NATO claims at 81–86.

[35] UN doc. S/1999/328.

[36] See SC 3989th mtg, 26 March 1999. Krisch, *loc.cit.*, 84–5.

[37] SC 1606th mtg, 1971; *Keesing's* (1972), 2503.

34   *N.D. White*

invoke the right of self-defence, a clear and accepted exception to the ban on the use of force.[38] In 1991 the UK, in justifying its part in the intervention in Northern Iraq, at one point invoked the doctrine of humanitarian intervention, while at another it purported to place the action within the context of resolution 688,[39] thereby trying to give the action some sort of UN sanction, knowing that Security Council authorized operations are, alongside self-defence, the universally recognized exceptions to the ban on the use of force.

In 1999, the UK was seen, perhaps above all other NATO states, as trying to rely on humanitarian intervention, but failed overall to invoke it in its pure form. When announcing the launch of airstrikes to the House of Commons on 24 March, 1999, Deputy Prime Minister John Prescott stated that the action was supported by all 19 members of NATO, and was 'intended to support the political aims of the international community' set out in Council resolutions 1199 and 1203, both of which had been breached by the FRY. The action was further 'justified as an exceptional measure to prevent an overwhelming humanitarian catastrophe'.[40] The danger in accepting this sort of layered argument as a justification for unilateral or multilateral humanitarian intervention is that it ignores the reasons why India and the UK did not rely on the doctrine as sole justification. Instead, they tried to invoke recognized exceptions to article 2(4) despite knowing full well that the operations did not fit the requirements of the exceptions – there was no armed attack against India in 1971, and there was no express authority from the Security Council to use force against Iraq or the FRY.

Although the approach taken by the intervening states in Iraq and Kosovo weakens the doctrine of humanitarian intervention, at least in its pure form, probably beyond repair, it still leaves the question of whether military intervention taken in support of or in the spirit of Security Council resolutions is a new and accepted concept in international law. In the absence of a clear mandate from the Security Council, the intervening states have invoked the argument that they are acting on behalf of the 'international community'. The Security Council resolutions represent the will of the international community and the states are enforcing that will. The 'international community' seems to be the concept underpinning the recent actions in Iraq and Kosovo. The increased recognition of this notion, much derided in the past by powerful states,[41] is necessitated when military intervention is taken to uphold fundamental norms of the international community prohibiting crimes against humanity which were undoubtedly being committed in northern Iraq and Kosovo. The UK Foreign Secretary, Robin Cook, seemed to realise that it was pointless trying to find or imply authority from specific resolutions, and instead the argument had to be based on the will of the international community, when he was pushed before the Foreign Affairs Select Committee of the House of Commons in

---

[38]   Art. 51 of the UN Charter.

[39]   See statements by the UK Prime Minister and UK Foreign Secretary in M. Weller (ed.), *Iraq and Kuwait: The Hostilities and their Aftermath* (1993) 149, 723–4.

[40]   H.C. DEB. 24 March 1999, col.484.

[41]   J.M. Grieco, 'Anarchy and the Limits of Cooperation: A Realist Critique of the Newest Liberal Internationalism', (1988) 42 *International Organization* 485.

April 1999 to justify the apparent contravention of the prohibition on the use of force. He stated that 'the legal basis for our action is that the international community [of] states do have the right to use force in the case of overwhelming humanitarian necessity'.[42]

It is easy to invoke the 'international community' to legitimate a military intervention, but who or what is the 'international community'?[43] The dangers of simply basing it on international laws, no matter how fundamental, are clear for there is a huge leap from recognizing that there are laws prohibiting crimes against humanity, and recognizing that states have the right unilaterally or in combination with their allies to enforce those norms. Such a system of law will rapidly descend into self-help, whereby the name of the 'international community' is simply invoked at the discretion of powerful states as a cloak for their military interventions and to further their hegemony. However, in the case of Kosovo and Iraq, some of the discretion has been removed in that there are Security Council resolutions recognizing the gravity of the human rights abuses in those countries. Does this not give a certain objectivity lacking in the old doctrines based on self-help such as humanitarian intervention? Discretion, though, remains, for this new form of intervention is only claimed as a legal right not a duty, though it is often cloaked in the rhetoric of moral obligations.[44] Furthermore it is somewhat disingenuous to claim that the international community's will is embodied in a Security Council resolution, when that organ has the capacity to expressly authorize military action to enforce its will. The determination of a threat to the peace is not the same as a mandate to take military action to combat the threat. Again the argument fails to recognize the gap between statements of the law and their enforcement.

However, in the case of Kosovo, but not in Iraq, there is an authorization from an international organization, NATO. Do 19 democracies acting in concert represent the international community? Can such an organization be in breach of international law? The fact that NATO is composed of liberal democracies does not by itself suggest that it is the fulcrum of the international community, although there has been a significant trend in the international community towards democratic government. In fact in taking decisions to go to war, whether under international authority or not, many of the constitutional checks and balances present in liberal democracies for most other forms of governmental decision making are not applicable. The power to take such decisions rests within the executive, the legislature generally does not approve of such actions except retrospectively. In the case of the UK the decision to go to war is taken by the Cabinet and then is run by a small part

---

[42] Foreign Affairs Committee, Minutes of Evidence, 14 April 1999, para.152.

[43] See generally P. Tsakaloyannis, 'International Society at a Crossroads: The Problem of Conceptualization', in D. Bourantonis and M. Evriviades (eds.), *A United Nations for the Twenty-First Century: Peace, Security and Development* (1996) 19; A. Hurrell, 'International Society and the Study of Regimes: A Reflective Approach', in V. Rittberger (ed.), *Regime Theory and International Relations* (1993) 49; H. Bull, 'The Importance of Grotius in the Study of International Relations', in H. Bull, B. Kingsbury and A. Roberts (eds.), *Hugo Grotius and International Relations* (1992) 71.

[44] See debate in House of Commons. H.C. DEB., 25 March 1999, cols.542–3.

of the Cabinet with military advisers.[45] Parliament debates but decisions have already been taken, and it would cause a constitutional crisis if Parliament were to vote against the actions already taken by the executive. The only real democratic control on such military actions is public opinion, which, to be honest, is often media led. In essence then, NATO has no more claim to represent the international community than would any other organization of a similar size.

The legality and legitimacy of NATO action is also undermined when a consideration of its own Treaty is undertaken. Although it has claimed the right to take 'non Article 5' operations,[46] in other words not simply military action in self-defence, these cannot simply be those determined by NATO alone. NATO can only operate within the framework of international law, in particular the UN Charter which has supremacy over any other international treaty when there are conflicting obligations.[47] Although NATO members, by consensus, can re-interpret their own treaty to allow them to take non-defensive military operations, they cannot somehow contract out of the UN system,[48] to set themselves up, in effect, as a competitor to the UN. It is thus incorrect for the US under Secretary of State, Strobe Talbott, to state that 'we must be careful not to subordinate NATO to any other international body',[49] for the whole international security system is based on a hierarchy with the UN at the apex. To allow smaller groups of states forming alliances or organizations the right of 'self-authorization' to take enforcement action would be to let the genie out of the bottle,[50] and would lead to competing claims to intervention. It is worth noting that the US and UK assert the paramountcy of the UN Charter over other conflicting treaty regimes when it suits. The essence of the two states' arguments in the *Lockerbie* cases is that the obligations imposed on Libya by the Security Council prevail by virtue of the UN Charter over Libya's rights and duties contained in the 1971 Montreal Convention for the Suppression of Unlawful Acts Against the Safety of Civil Aviation.[51] It is inconsistent for these two states to

[45] C. Seymour-Ure, 'War Cabinets in Limited War: Korea, Suez and the Falklands', (1984) 62 *Public Administration* 181. Similar mechanisms were used in the case of Kosovo – see A. McSmith and P. Beaver, 'Commander Blair Goes it Alone', *The Observer*, 18 April 1999, 14.

[46] Resolution on 'Recasting Euro-Atlantic Security', adopted by North Atlantic Assembly, NATO doc. AR 295 SA (1998).

[47] Art.103 of the UN Charter.

[48] In particular articles 42 and 53 of the UN Charter. See H.McCoubrey, 'Kosovo, NATO and International Law', (1999) 14(5) *International Relations* 32–4.

[49] Cited in Simma, *loc.cit.*, 15. See also the position of the UK reflected in the House of Commons Defence Select Committee in its Third Report, 31 March 1999 when it declared that '[i]nsistence on a UN Security Council mandate for such [non Article 5] operations would be unnecessary as well as covertly giving Russia a veto over Alliance action. All 19 Allies act in accordance with the principles of international law and we are secure in our assertion that the necessity of unanimous agreement for any action will ensure its legality' – para.176.

[50] Simma, *loc.cit.*, 20.

[51] *Cases Concerning Questions of Interpretation and Application of the Montreal Convention Arising From the Aerial Incident at Lockerbie (Libya v UK), (Libya v US)* ICJ Rep. 1992, 3 and 114 (Provisional Measures Judgments); (1998) 37 *ILM* 587 (Preliminary Objections Judgments).

argue the supremacy of the UN Charter in the case of Libya, and yet dismiss it in the case of the NATO intervention in Kosovo.

It is because the UN represents the vast majority of the world's states (currently 188) that it has the only legitimate claim to be acting on behalf of the international community. Indeed, practically it is the only organization that can claim to be the international community. When states set it up in 1945 it was imbued with exceptional powers that no state or other organization could possess, unless they received authority from the UN. It was because the UN represented 'the vast majority of the Members of the international community' at the time,[52] and now more so, that it has the powers of the international community. Within the UN, it is the General Assembly that is reflective of the political will of the organization. 'The special value of the General Assembly is its universality, its capacity to be a forum in which the voice of every member state can be heard'.[53]

Certainly after the bombing campaign and the establishment of KFOR under Security Council authority, NATO members seem to recognize, if not the illegality of their bombing campaign, certainly the dangerous precedent that it sets. The perception is that it is being 're-packaged' as a unique situation forced upon NATO by exceptional conditions that somehow set it apart from later catastrophes in East Timor and Chechnya. In the general debate of the General Assembly in October 1999, the representative of Belgium, for instance, hoped that resorting to force without the approval of the Security Council would not constitute a precedent, while expressing concern about a return to the law of the jungle.[54] Germany stated that state sovereignty would remain the guiding principle in international relations.[55] President Clinton portrayed the Kosovo situation not as a triumph for NATO but as a triumph for the United Nations. [56] Even Russia suggested that lessons had been learned from the crisis and would be prepared to develop a legal framework for enforcement actions 'of the international community' in the case of humanitarian emergencies in the future.[57] These statements perhaps show that, without prejudicing the positions of states on the legality of the operation, Kosovo is being labelled as an exceptional action without any legal precedence. Nevertheless, the Netherlands warned the Council that its repeated inaction would push the Organization towards the margins as a custodian of the peace, and it called on the Assembly to demand that the veto power be exercised with maximum restraint.[58]

---

[52] *Reparation for Injuries Suffered in the Service of the United Nations*, ICJ Rep.1949, 185.
[53] Report of the Commission on Global Governance *Our Global Neighbourhood* (1995) 242.
[54] GA 14th plenary mtg, 25 September 1999.
[55] GA 27th plenary mtg, 6 October 1999.
[56] GA 6th plenary mtg, 21 September 1999.
[57] GA Fourth Committee debate, 12th mtg, 20 October 1999. But see China GA 35th plenary mtg, 20 October 1999.
[58] UN Press Release GA/9607 (1999).

4 SECURITY COUNCIL OR UN AUTHORITY?

The statement by the Dutch representative in the General Assembly debates in its 54th session shows the dilemma that NATO states have over whether the Security Council has exclusive competence over military enforcement action, or whether the Assembly has a role. The Dutch suggested that the Assembly act as a mechanism of accountability to ensure that the veto was not misused in similar situations in the future. It did not go so far as to say that the Assembly itself could, if the Security Council was deadlocked, authorize or recommend such action. However, there are strong arguments that the General Assembly has residual enforcement powers in exceptional cases, and indeed it should have been the fall back forum for seeking authority to undertake the bombing of the FRY. The argument by NATO that it had no choice but to undertake the bombing without an authorization from an organ that truly represents the international community is thus revealed to be incorrect. Indeed, if any forum can legitimately claim to represent or indeed embody the international community, then it has to be the General Assembly of the UN. The General Assembly not only has subsidiary competence in the field of collective security, it has primary competence in issues of human rights.[59] Claims to intervene in Kosovo to protect human rights would thus have all the attributes necessary for the Assembly to grant authority, though only if it was convinced by a two-thirds majority of NATO's case.[60]

Debates over the competence of the General Assembly to recommend military measures to be taken when the Security Council has failed to exercise its primary responsibility for collective security, tend to be clouded by question marks over the legality of the Uniting for Peace Resolution adopted by the General Assembly in 1950.[61] The immediate reason for the adoption of the Resolution was the return, in August 1950, of the Soviet Union to the Security Council, leading to the discontinuation of the Council as the body dealing with Korea. In fact the Assembly had adopted an 'enforcement' resolution on Korea after the Soviets had returned to the Security Council but before the Uniting for Peace Resolution was adopted.[62] However, the reasons for Uniting for Peace went beyond Korea, in that the Western influenced majority in the General Assembly at the time was also of the view that the frequent use of the Soviet veto during the period 1946–50 was an abuse of that right, and that the ideal of great power unanimity at San Francisco was no longer attainable. The western states wanted an alternative form of collective security, based not on permanent member agreement in the Security Council, but on the basis of the will of the majority in the Assembly. Such a concept of collective security, whilst opening up the potential for economic and military actions against

---

[59] N.D. White, *Keeping the Peace: The United Nations and the Maintenance of International Peace and Security* (2nd ed., 1997) 169–72.

[60] Abstentions do not count as votes, so the required number of votes in favour of military action may not be as high as perhaps thought – see F.L. Kirgis, *International Organizations in their Legal Setting* (2nd ed., 1993) 213.

[61] GA Res. 377, 3 November 1950.

[62] GA Res. 376, 7 October 1950.

transgressors, also had the potential, in theory, for allowing the General Assembly to recommend military action against one of the permanent members. A more likely scenario would be for the Assembly to recommend military action that would affect the interests of a permanent member. It may be because this system of collective security was potentially dangerous that the resolution restricted the Assembly's power to recommend military measures to the most flagrant violations of international peace, namely breaches of the peace or acts of aggression, and did not expressly permit the Assembly to take such measures as a response to threats to the peace.

The Soviet Union objected strongly to the resolution, in particular it argued that it violated the Charter requirement that coercive power was granted solely to the Security Council.[63] In 1962, the World Court in the *Expenses* case stated that 'action', which is the preserve of the Security Council,[64] refers to coercive action but it failed to state whether this excluded the Assembly from recommending coercive measures. At some points the Court suggested that 'action' is restricted to mandatory, coercive action 'ordered' by the Security Council. In other words the Assembly did not appear to be barred from recommending enforcement action as part of its significant responsibility for the maintenance of peace as recognized by the Court.[65] Furthermore, despite the wording of the Uniting for Peace Resolution, there appears to be no cogent argument against allowing the Assembly to recommend military measures to combat a threat to the peace.[66]

However, when looking at the issue from the perspective of the ban on the use of armed force, a rule of *jus cogens* from which no derogation is allowed, doubts may be cast on the legality of the Uniting for Peace Resolution and the power of the Assembly to recommend military measures. The exceptions to article 2(4) are explicitly stated in the UN Charter to include only action in self-defence under article 51 of the UN Charter and military action authorized by the Security Council under articles 42 or 53. To state that the General Assembly can recommend military action arguably creates a third exception, which would appear to be contrary to the *jus cogens* in article 2(4). However, the Security Council is authorizing military action on behalf of the *United Nations* and so the exceptions to the ban on force are those undertaken in legitimate self-defence and those authorized by the *United Nations*. The question of which organ within the UN authorizes them is an internal issue and does not effect the legitimacy of UN action *vis à vis* a transgressing State.[67] The internal issue can be resolved in favour of both organs having the ability to authorize military action, given that the Assembly effectively has all those recommendatory powers possessed by the Council,[68] albeit at a supplementary level of competence. It is submitted here that the Assembly possessed a power to recommend military action in 1945, though, of course, its conversion from power *in*

---

[63] GA 301st plenary mtg, 1950.
[64] Art.11(2) of the UN Charter.
[65] *Expenses* case, ICJ. Rep. 1962, 162–5.
[66] S.D. Bailey and S. Daws, *The Procedure of the UN Security Council* (3rd ed., 1998) 296.
[67] *Expenses* case, ICJ Rep.1962, 168.
[68] Articles 10 and 14 of the UN Charter.

abstracto, to power in reality, was achieved through the practice of the Assembly. Alternatively, it is possible to derive the power to recommend military action from the practice itself as a valid form of re-interpretation of the Charter. In either case, the end result is a constitutional exercise of competence by the Assembly.

The Uniting for Peace Resolution, whereby the Assembly can be activated in the face of a deadlocked Security Council by a procedural vote in the Council that is not subject to the veto, has been used in the past to gain UN authority for innovative military actions.[69] In the face of a military intervention by two permanent members in the Suez crisis of 1956, and, more relevantly, in the face of a threat to the peace in the Congo in 1960 which was in the state of collapse, the Security Council, unable to take substantive action itself due to the veto, transferred the matter to the Assembly,[70] which duly became the organ of authority in the case of UNEF, a traditional peacekeeping force, and temporarily in the case of ONUC, which acted in a more muscular fashion. Although it may be argued that these two operations were more 'peacekeeping' than 'enforcement', and thus are not direct precedents for seeking an enforcement mandate for an intervention in Kosovo, the Congo operation came very close to enforcement.[71] In addition, the General Assembly had, even before the adoption of the Uniting for Peace Resolution, become involved in the Korean enforcement operation. In fact the Assembly made a substantial contribution to UN action in Korea by passing a resolution which allowed the UN force to continue its operations to establish 'a unified, independent and democratic government of Korea' after the Security Council had been deadlocked by the return of the Soviet representative.[72] This resolution was seen as authorizing General MacArthur's crossing of the 38th parallel and so can be classified as recommending enforcement action. The British Foreign Secretary, Ernest Bevin, who was instrumental in the resolution, saw it as essential to have the authority of the UN for the intervention in North Korea.[73]

The procedure envisaged by the Charter for convoking a special session,[74] does not appear significantly different from that established under the Uniting for Peace Resolution. Both allow for the transference of matters from the Security Council by a procedural vote[75] or by a majority of members of the General Assembly. In addition, the Uniting for Peace Resolution specifically grants the Assembly the power to recommend collective measures and establishes the machinery to enable it to carry out these measures. Article 10 in itself recognizes the power of the Assembly to recommend measures, so that whether in normal, special session, or emergency special session it has the same powers as those purportedly granted by the Uniting

---

[69] For review of practice under Uniting for Peace see White, *op.cit.*, 172–8.

[70] SC Res. 119, 31 October 1956 (UK and France voted against); SC Res.157 17 September 1960 (USSR voted against).

[71] White, *op.cit.*, 254–61. But see *Expenses* case, 177.

[72] GA Res. 376, 7 October 1950.

[73] See A. Farrar-Hockley, *The British Part in the Korean War: Volume 1: A Distant Obligation* (1990), 209.

[74] Art.20 of the UN Charter.

[75] B. Simma (ed.), *The Charter of the United Nations: A Commentary* (1994) 346.

for Peace Resolution. Indeed, its actual powers are wider than Uniting for Peace for it can act to combat threats to the peace as well as breaches of the peace and acts of aggression.[76] What seems to have confused the sponsors of the Uniting for Peace Resolution were doubts over whether the Assembly could recommend enforce-ment measures. They failed to take account of the perfectly valid argument in favour of the Assembly having this power, a power it had already utilized in the Korean situation.

It is somewhat ironic that a procedure advocated by Western states in 1950 was conveniently forgotten in the case of the Kosovo crisis. The cumbersome nature of convening a special session or emergency special session of the Assembly is no real excuse given that NATO first threatened to use force without express authority in October 1998. The matter could have been put forward before the Assembly during its 53rd annual session. Indeed, the Assembly did consider the situation of human rights in Kosovo and adopted a resolution on 9 December 1999 that was very criti-cal of the violations of human rights and international humanitarian law by the FRY, and supportive of the demands made by the Security Council.[77] Although adopted against a background of a reduction in the oppressive actions carried out by the FRY forces in Kosovo, this still represented an opportunity for NATO to seek a mandate for its airstrikes.

5 CONCLUSION

It may be argued that in the Kosovo crisis, as with Iraq previously, the Security Council was failing to take the necessary military action to combat breaches of Security Council resolutions, and in the face of situations that clearly constituted threats to the peace. In these circumstances it was breaching the trust put in it by member states when they established the United Nations. Assuming that the Security Council was being blocked by an illegitimate threat of the veto in a situ-ation that clearly warranted Security Council authorized military action, it is still not legally permissible for states to take it upon themselves, whether in the forum of another organization or not, to enforce those resolutions. Such a contention pre-sumes that states had these powers before they 'collectivized' them in the Security Council, which is very doubtful. It also ignores the fact that legally speaking they must be expressly returned or granted to them by the UN. Furthermore, when the UN Charter speaks of the Security Council having 'primary responsibility' to main-tain or restore international peace and security, it is recognizing that the General Assembly, not states or organizations acting outside the UN, has significant second-ary responsibility in the field of peace and security, which may be invoked when the

---

[76] *Ibid.*, 235.

[77] GA Res. 53/164, 9 December 1998. Adopted by 122–3–34. Russia voted against the resolution and China abstained. The Russian vote against was explained in the GA Third Committee debate on the draft on the basis that the resolution did not sufficiently respect the territorial integrity of the FRY – UN Press Release GA/SHC/3511, 18 November 1998.

Security Council is unable to act. Indeed, when combined with its undoubted competence in matters of human rights and its legitimate claim to represent the international community, the General Assembly was the natural alternative when the Security Council was deemed to have failed to take adequate action in the face of repression by the FRY. The need for the authority of the UN is made graphically clear by Lobel and Ratner:

> Often a real or imagined evil will exert a tremendous centrifugal pull on most of us to support forceful action. Nonetheless, the perils associated with warfare – that great powers can use humanitarian concerns to mask geo-political interest; that major air strikes such as those threatened against Iraq and Serbia in 1998 have serious consequences in lives lost, destruction caused and the resulting destabilization; that warfare is of limited utility as a means of solving complex, long-standing, underlying problems; that a world order that allows individual or coalitions of nations to deploy offensive military might for what they deem are worthy causes amounts to anarchy – these perils require that force be only used as last resort as determined by a world body.[78]

Although Lobel and Ratner see the Security Council as that world body, it is argued above that the world body is the UN, which acts normally via the Security Council, but exceptionally via the General Assembly. If the Security Council were unable to act because of legitimate concerns that the situation does not require it to exercise its primary responsibility to authorize military action, then it would be unconstitutional for the Assembly to have exercised its competence. However, if there is a genuine threat to the peace, breach of the peace or act of aggression so dangerous and overwhelming that it requires a military response then the Assembly is entitled, indeed obliged, to act. Uniting for Peace recognized the latter two situations, but there is no reason why the Assembly does not have this competence as regards threats to the peace. In the Kosovo crisis, the Security Council had determined there to be a threat to the peace, and there was strong evidence of massive repression and crimes against humanity. However, instead of pushing the matter before the Security Council to see if the Russians and Chinese would actually have vetoed a resolution authorizing the bombing, it was simply assumed that it would be the case. This appears to be a correct assumption, although it may be because the Russians in particular wanted to negotiate a less volatile and more humane military intervention than bombing. Furthermore, to have put a resolution before the Council and had it vetoed, would then have freed the NATO states to put forward a procedural resolution before the Council transferring the matter to the General Assembly, where a vote on the proposed NATO action should have been held. Assuming that such a request for authority would have won both a procedural vote in the Security Council and a substantive vote in the General Assembly, NATO then would have had a sound legal basis upon which to launch its air strikes.

[78] Lobel and Ratner, *loc.cit.*, 153.

The Legality of Bombing in the Name of Humanity   43

Why NATO did not follow this course remains a matter of conjecture since, at least on the surface, it does not appear to have been on the agenda. Three reasons may have been pertinent. First of all a fear that the method of military action being put forward – bombing – would not be acceptable to two-thirds of the membership. Bombing in the name of humanity may be a cause for concern for the international community. [79] The main reason why this was the only option on the table for NATO was 'a desire, understandable in itself, to minimize NATO casualties'.[80] Secondly, securing UN authority would have created an expectation, though not a legal obligation, that NATO would launch military action, thereby restricting NATO's freedom of choice.[81] Thirdly, a fear that the use of the General Assembly to sanction military action would set a dangerous precedent and could be used against NATO states in the future. This ignores the fact that the precedents for securing Assembly authority are already there, they have simply been conveniently forgotten, and also the fact that bombing without any UN authority is an even more dangerous precedent.

---

[79] See McCoubrey, *loc.cit.*, 35–6, pp.38–9. Also contains a discussion on whether the bombing breached the requirements of the *jus in bello*.

[80] *Ibid.*, 38.

[81] But see the case of Zaire where the multilateral force under Canadian command decided not to intervene in 1996–7 upon its own assessment of the refugee crisis, despite receiving authorization from the Security Council – SC Res. 1080, 15 November 1996.

[9]

THE 'INHERENT' POWERS OF THE UN SECRETARY-GENERAL IN THE POLITICAL SPHERE: A LEGAL ANALYSIS

by Roberto Lavalle*

1.   INTRODUCTION

The exercise, in the political sphere, of powers traditionally characterized as inherent in his office has become a well-established and particularly important activity of the United Nations Secretary-General.[1]

This activity, which normally brings the Secretary-General into contact with governments,[2] has three essential features: (1) it is undertaken by the Secretary-General on his own authority, i.e., without having received a man-

---

* Former legal officer, United Nations. (The views expressed herein are, however, purely and exclusively personal).

1. In many cases, the initiatives that the UN Secretary-General has taken in the use of his inherent powers have been purely or predominantly of a humanitarian character. A notable example is the efforts he undertook, in 1971 and 1972, for the relief of East Pakistan. For a succinct description of this activity, see *Repertory of Practice of United Nations Organs* Supplement No. 5, Vol. 5 under Art. 98, paras. 48-64. In other cases, the initiatives have been in the human rights area. For an account of the inherent powers activities carried out from the outset to 31 December 1979, see *Repertory of Practice of United Nations Organs*, Vol. 5, under Art. 98, para. 106, and the five supplements thereto, as follows: Supplement No. 1, Vol. 2, under Art. 98, paras. 47-58; Supplement No. 2, Vol. 3, under Art. 98, paras. 253-313; Supplement No. 3, Vol. 4, under Art. 98, paras. 662-709; Supplement No. 4, Vol. 2, under Art. 98, paras. 288-325; and Supplement No. 5, Vol. 5, under Art. 98, paras. 668-762. For information concerning specifically fact-finding activities, see GAOR, Twentieth Session, Annexes, agenda items 90 and 94, A/5694, paras. 313-328. See also E. Gordon, 'Resolution of the Bahrain Dispute', 65 AJIL (1971) p. 560; B.G. Ramcharan, 'The Good Offices of the Secretary-General of the United Nations in the Field of Human Rights', 76 AJIL (1982) p. 130; T.M. Franck, 'The Role and Future Prospects of the Secretary-General', in *The Adaptation of Structures and Methods at the United Nations, Workshop, The Hague 4-6 November 1985* (1986) pp. 81-90; see also, D. Cordovez and N. Elaraby in *The United Nations and the Maintenance of International Peace and Security* (1987) and H. Caminos and R. Lavalle, 'New Departures in the Exercise of Inherent Powers by the UN and OAS Secretaries-General: the Central American Situation', 83 AJIL (1989) p. 395. Needless to say, there can often be room for disagreement as to exactly where the line should be drawn between political initiatives, on the one hand, and initiatives in the humanitarian or human rights areas, on the other.

2. Although he does not appear to have done so yet, there seems to be no reason why, in exercising the powers in question, the Secretary-General could not, in the absence of objections by the government(s) concerned, establish contacts with entities other than governments, as he has often done when acting on his own in the human rights and humanitarian spheres.

0165-070X/90/010022-15
Martinus Nijhoff Publishers/Dordrecht
XXXVII-NILR 1990, 22-36

date, express or implied, from another United Nations organ,[3] (2) it aims to promote or facilitate, directly or indirectly, the prevention, settlement, easing or control of international disputes or tensions, and (3) it is of a discretionary nature.[4]

The principal categories of the activity under consideration, which often involves the appointment of special or 'personal' representatives of the Secretary-General, are appeals, the transmission of communications between governments, good offices, mediation and arbitration,[5] fact-finding, and participation in international conferences and organs of a political nature.[6] But these categories should not be regarded as absolutely discrete or all-inclusive: any particular instance of the activity, which is often extremely fluid, may well merge any two or more of them or be *sui generis*.[7] Appeals differ from the

---

3. There have been cases where, although a certain political action by the Secretary-General is not based on a mandate, express or implied, the General Assembly or the Security Council has taken a prior position on the dispute or situation to which the action relates and that position can be regarded as an incentive to the action. This occurred recently with respect to the situation in Central America. Resolutions adopted by the General Assembly and the Security Council between 1983 and 1986 expressed support for the process to promote peace in the region that was being carried on by a group of Latin American States, but without asking the Secretary-General to take any substantive action. The Secretary-General, acting under his autonomous powers, lent support to that process. (Cf., Caminos and Lavalle, loc. cit. n. 1, pp. 397-398). In such cases one could consider that the Secretary-General has exercised his autonomous powers pursuant to a 'political' mandate, in the absence of which he might have refrained from acting. It may also occur that, before taking action of a political nature in the absence of a formal mandate, he has consulted or sounded out the members of the Security Council regarding the action and ascertained that they do not object to it. This case can perhaps be regarded as another instance of the 'political' mandate (GAOR XV, Supplement 1A, p. 3, right-hand column, and S.D. Bailey, *The Secretariat of the United Nations* (1962) p. 41). The same is true of any situation where the Secretary-General spells out before the Security Council or the General Assembly measures he intends to take in the political sphere without eliciting any reaction, whether from the organ as a whole or any individual member. (For an example of this, see Bailey, *supra* p. 40.)

4. That the Secretary-General is to act pursuant to a mandate does not necessarily mean that he lacks discretion. For one thing, a mandate could, conceivably, provide that the Secretary-General is to give effect to it only if he deems it advisable to do so. Moreover, it often occurs that a political mandate is formulated so generally or vaguely as to leave the Secretary-General with considerable leeway for the exercise of discretion in its fulfilment.

5. In June 1986 the Governments of France and New Zealand asked the Secretary-General to issue a 'ruling' on the dispute that had arisen between them concerning the *Rainbow Warrior* incident, agreeing in advance to abide by the ruling. The Secretary-General, having acceded to the request, handed the two Governments the text of his ruling in July 1986. (See United Nations press releases SG/SM/3883 and SG/SM/3889, of 19 June and 7 July 1986.) Although it would seem clear that the Secretary-General's intervention cast him in the role of an arbitrator, at a press conference held on 30 June 1986, he was less than clear-cut on the matter, referring, in connection with it, to his 'role of mediation or arbitration'. (See press release SG/SM/3886 of 1 July 1986, pp. 3-4.)

6. The Secretary-General broke new ground in 1987, with regard to the Central American situation, by accepting, on his own authority, membership in an international control body. (See Caminos and Lavalle, loc. cit. n. 1, p. 400.)

7. For instance, the action the Secretary-General took, in 1970, with respect to Bahrain involved good offices and fact-finding. See *Repertory of Practice of United Nations Organs,* Supplement No. 5, Vol. 5, under Art. 98, paras. 703 and 712. An example of a *sui generis* autonomous

other types of initiative the Secretary-General takes in the political sphere in that they do not make him a provider of services.[8] They do not, therefore, require any kind of prior consent or co-operation by the conflicting parties. For the Secretary-General to go beyond mere appeals it is necessary that they allow him to intervene, at least on the procedural plane, which is usually that of good offices. But the Secretary-General does not shrink from spontaneously offering his services.[9] He provides them if the interested parties, or at least one of them,[10] ask him to intervene or accept his offer to do so.[11]

This article will discuss the legal basis for the activity in question, a matter that does not appear to have been treated with rigour, whether in the literature or within the United Nations.[12] In so doing the article will have regard to a very important development that took place in 1988, namely, the adoption by the United Nations General Assembly of a declaration on the role of the United Nations in the prevention and removal of international disputes (hereinafter 'the Declaration'),[13] which contains a set of provisions dealing with the activity comprehensively, if without much detail.

As a preliminary step, however, a few *ad hoc* terminological conventions will be adopted to facilitate the treatment of the subject. The activity with which we are dealing will be referred to as 'autonomous activity' (or 'activities'); the term 'autonomous power' (or 'powers') will be used to designate the power (or powers) under which the Secretary-General undertakes

---

activity is provided by the Secretary-General's intervention, in 1983, in a dispute between Guyana and Venezuela. His function in that connection was to provide assistance to the two Governments concerned in the choice of a means of settling the dispute peacefully (see UN press release SG/SM/3461).

8. An appeal may, however, involve the Secretary-General in the substance of the problem addressed by serving as a vehicle for concrete recommendations on how to solve it. An example of this is provided by the Secretary-General's appeals to the Governments of the United States and the Soviet Union regarding the Cuban missile crisis. (*Repertory of Practice of United Nations Organs,* Supplement No. 3, Vol. 4, under Art. 98, para. 672.)

9. The offer may be contained in an appeal. An example of this modality is provided by the appeals to the United States and the Soviet Union referred to in the preceding note.

10. See *Repertory of Practice of United Nations Organs,* Supplement No. 4, Vol. 2, under Art. 98, paras. 298-299. A request to the Secretary-General by a government wishing to send a communication to another one would normally appear to be sufficient to allow him to transmit the communication if he considers it wise to comply with the request.

11. See *Repertory of Practice of United Nations Organs,* Supplement No. 3, Vol. 4, under Art. 98, para. 701; Supplement No. 4, Vol. 2, under Art. 98, paras. 311-312; and Supplement No. 5, Vol. 5, under Art. 98, paras. 693-694.

12. The subject has been dealt with either from a purely political perspective or in a manner that appears legal inasmuch as the Charter or certain of its provisions (particularly Art. 99) are invoked but is without the close reasoning essential to legal analysis.

13. The official title of the Declaration is 'Declaration on the Prevention and Removal of Disputes and Situations which may Threaten International Peace and Security and on the Role of the United Nations in this Field'. It is annexed to res. 43/51, adopted by the General Assembly, on the report of its Sixth Committee and without a vote, on 5 December 1988. The Declaration is based on a draft declaration prepared and adopted unanimously by the Special Committee on the Charter of the United Nations and the Strengthening of the Role of the Organization, the

autonomous activities. The term 'mandated activity' (or 'activities') will designate the activities of a political nature undertaken by the Secretary-General pursuant to a mandate received from another United Nations organ (normally the General Assembly or the Security Council, or, exceptionally, a competent subsidiary organ of one or the other).

2.   THE SITUATION AT THE TIME OF THE ADOPTION OF THE DECLARATION

What was, at the time of the Declaration's adoption, the legal basis for autonomous activities? Were they, as one might well suppose they had to be, the exercise of powers vested in the Secretary-General by the Charter? If so, they were either based on the *travaux préparatoires* of this instrument or implied by it. For the Charter contains no provision explicitly granting any such powers to the Secretary-General.

Since there is nothing in the *travaux préparatoires* of the Charter that could serve as a basis for the autonomous powers, to make a case that they are derived from the Charter it is necessary to demonstrate that they are implied by one or several of its provisions.

But, before seeking to ascertain whether such a demonstration is feasible, one must determine the possible relevance to the problem of certain action that the General Assembly took in 1946. For one might be tempted to view this action as expressing the Assembly's conviction that the Secretary-General derives autonomous powers from the Charter.

In its report, adopted on 23 December 1945, the Preparatory Commission of the United Nations made the following comments on the functions of the Secretary-General:[14]

'The Secretary-General may have an important role to play as a mediator and as an informal advisor of many Governments, and will undoubtedly be called upon from time to time, in the exercise of his administrative duties, to take decisions which may justly be called political. Under Article 99 of the Charter, moreover, he has been given a quite special right which goes beyond any power previously accorded to the head of an international organization, viz: to bring to the attention of the Security Council any matter (not merely any dispute or situation) which, in his opinion, may threaten the maintenance of international peace and security. It is impossible to foresee how this Article will be applied; but the responsibility it confers upon the Secretary-General will require the exercise of the highest qualities of political judgement, tact and integrity.'

---

report of which (UN Doc. A/43/886) was before the Sixth Committee at the Forty-Third Session of the Assembly. The draft declaration was adopted by the Sixth Committee without a vote and without amendments. Nor were any amendments made to it by the plenary.

14. Report of the Preparatory Commission of the United Nations, PC/20, 23 December 1945, Chap. VIII, Section 2, Sub-section B.

These comments are contained in subsection B, entitled 'the Secretary-General, Functions, Terms of Appointment and Procedure of Appointment', of Section 2 of Chapter VIII of the report, a chapter dealing at length with the organization of the Secretariat.

In Section XI of its resolution 13(I), adopted unanimously on 13 February 1946, the General Assembly transmitted Section 2 of Chapter VIII of the report of the Preparatory Commission to the Secretary-General 'for his guidance'.

Can the passage quoted be considered to imply that in the view of the Preparatory Commission the Secretary-General is vested with autonomous powers by the Charter? If so, can one consider that by adopting resolution 13(I) the Assembly endorsed this view?

The first point to be noted is that only the first sentence of the above passage from the report of the Preparatory Commission is relevant to the autonomous powers of the Secretary-General. The reference in the sentence to his functions as 'informal advisor' of governments does not necessarily embrace the performance of autonomous activities. The reference to his role as mediator, a term that most likely has, in the sentence, a wider and less precise meaning than the one normally assigned to it in the context of general international law, appears to imply that in the Commission's opinion the Secretary-General may be entrusted with 'mediation' functions under Article 98 of the Charter. It could also imply that he may assist in the settlement of disputes without having received a mandate to do so under that Article of the Charter. But the reference does not necessarily carry this second implication. It could equally well mean *only* that, in the Commission's opinion, the Secretary-General may play this role if it is entrusted to him under Article 98 of the Charter. As for the observation about some of the decisions taken by the Secretary-General in the exercise of his administrative duties being of a political nature, which is hardly more than a truism, it should be noted that the Secretary-General's autonomous activities are entirely outside the purview of his administrative duties. Finally, looked at as a whole, the first sentence of the passage quoted is too vague and unfocused to serve as a basis for any kind of conclusion as to precisely what, in the opinion of the Commission, the Secretary-General may do in the political arena, whether on his own authority or by virtue of authority conferred on him under Article 98.

Consequently, the fact that the General Assembly, by resolution 13(I), transmitted the passage in question to the Secretary-General 'for his guidance' could be taken as evidence that in its opinion he has the power to perform, on his own, political functions other than the one entrusted to him by Article 99 of the Charter only if the *travaux préparatoires* of the resolution very strongly supported such an interpretation of it. But this is by no means the case, since they contain nothing in any way relevant to the extent of the powers of the Secretary-General.

It is accordingly not surprising that neither the Secretary-General nor any of the writers who have addressed the legal aspects of his autonomous activities has sought to base them squarely on the report of the Preparatory Commission, taken in conjunction with General Assembly resolution 13(I).

Can a rationale for the autonomous activities be based on the mysterious notion that in undertaking them the Secretary-General somehow exercises 'powers inherent in his office'.[15] The notion might have some merit if it could be based either on the *travaux préparatoires* of the Charter or on a demonstration that certain of its objectives can be fulfilled only if the Secretary-General possesses autonomous powers. But, since neither is possible, the notion should be dismissed as no more than an incantation.

Nor can it persuasively be argued that the autonomous powers derive from the provisions of the Charter that have some relevance to them, i.e., Articles 98 and 99 or paragraph 1 of Article 33.

An attempt at deriving the Secretary-General's autonomous powers from Article 99 of the Charter, the provision that is the most frequently invoked as their legal basis, can follow a direct path or a more roundabout one.

The direct path is simply to argue that Article 99, which is the only provision of the Charter that *explicitly* assigns a political function to the Secretary-General,[16] thereby invests his office with a political character, whence his autonomous powers.[17] That this glib line of reasoning is without merit goes almost without saying: from the fact that Article 99 empowers the Secretary-General to perform a specific political function on his own authority, one cannot reasonably conclude that he may perform other political functions under this authority.

Roundabout reliance on Article 99 as the basis for the autonomous powers proceeds from the idea that the Secretary-General's authority under that Article necessarily carries with it the power to investigate disputes or situations that can call the Article into play; for, it is further alleged, he can take action under

---

15. It is under this title that the Supplements to the *Repertory of Practice of United Nations Organs* have dealt with the autonomous activities of the Secretary-General.

16. Since it is clear that nothing precludes the Secretary-General being, under Art. 98 of the Charter, entrusted with political functions, this article implicitly empowers him to perform such functions of this type as may be entrusted to him thereunder. This appears to be borne out by the above-quoted passage from the report of the Preparatory Commission. Since the Security Council is hardly in a position to carry out entirely by itself the investigative activity to which Art. 34 of the Charter refers, it would appear that under this article the Secretary-General may be entrusted with fact-finding functions by the Security Council.

17. According to one author, the power conferred on the Secretary-General by Art. 99 'constitutes, particularly when blended with Article 98, the broad legal base for the Secretary-General's political personality'. (See S.M. Schwebel, *The Secretary-General of the United Nations. His Political Powers and Practice* (1952) p. 24). This is true, but, for the reason given in the text, cannot be relied upon as a basis for his autonomous powers. Although the Covenant of the League of Nations lacked a provision similar to Art. 99 of the Charter, the first Secretary-General of the League took important political initiatives on his own authority (although only behind the scenes and with no subsequent publicity). One can therefore be tempted to argue that if, having, to borrow Schwebel's term, a less pronounced political personality than the United Nations Secretary-General, he was able to take political action on his own authority, then *a fortiori* the United Nations Secretary-General should be able to do likewise. But, whatever its persuasiveness on the political level, this argument is legally worthless. For one does not see why the interpretation of

the Article only if he has available adequate information.[18] But this ingenious argument can justify only autonomous activities that are exclusively of a fact-finding nature. Other autonomous activities cannot reasonably be brought within the scope of the argument. For, far from providing the Secretary-General with the means of applying Article 99, such activities tend to obviate its application. It is doubtful, moreover, that the argument can apply even to autonomous activities that aim exclusively at fact-finding. For one thing, the object of the autonomous activities of this type that have been undertaken has not been to ascertain whether the Secretary-General should, in respect of a dispute or situation, make use of Article 99, but to contribute to the easing or settlement of disputes. Moreover, it appears possible for the Secretary-General to keep abreast of most, if not all, political developments by assiduously tapping the sources of information available to the public.[19]

Shorter shrift can be made of any attempt at relying on Article 33(1) of the Charter:[20] this provision does not refer to the Secretary-General and there is no reason for considering that for its effective application it is necessary that he be one of the entities empowered to provide the dispute settlement services that the Article mentions.

One might also seek a basis for the autonomous activities in the provision in Article 98 of the Charter to the effect that the Secretary-General 'performs ... functions' that are 'entrusted to him' by the General Assembly and the Security Council. At first sight this provision does not appear relevant at all, for, by definition, autonomous activities are carried out in the absence of a mandate. Since, however, a mandate can be conferred retroactively and can also be tacit, could one not argue that if, after either of the two organs has been informed of autonomous activities carried out by the Secretary-General, it has not objected thereto, it has tacitly and retroactively sanctioned them, thus underpinning them, *ex post facto*, by virtue of the Article 98 provision

---

the Covenant and the practice under it should have any bearing on the interpretation of, and the practice under, the United Nations Charter.

18. Cf., the statement made by the Secretary-General before the Security Council on 20 September 1946, at the Council's 70th meeting. (SC, Official Records, First Year, Second Series, p. 405). In public pronouncements the Secretary-General has fairly often cited Art. 99 as the source of his autonomous powers. Cf., for example, the press conference he gave on 20 September 1982, the subject of press release SG/SM/3342 of 20 September 1989, p. 2.

19. A unit of the United Nations Secretariat entitled 'Office for Research and the Collection of Information' provides the Secretary-General with information from public sources capable of facilitating the prevention of conflicts. See, on p. 4 of press release SG/SM/4291, the comments made by the Secretary-General on this unit in the course of an address he delivered in April 1989. See also press release SG/SM/3648, p. 4.

20. Cf., the passage from the Introduction to the Annual Report of the Secretary-General on the Work of the Organization submitted to the General Assembly at its Twenty-Fourth Session quoted in *Repertory of Practice of United Nations Organs,* Supplement No. 4, Vol. 2, under Art. 98, para. 318. In a speech delivered in 1971, the Secretary-General appears to have based his autonomous powers to perform good offices functions, at least partly, on Art. 33 of the Charter. (Cf., Supplement No. 5 to the *Repertory of Practice of United Nations Organs,* Vol. 5, under Art. 98, para. 714.)

just quoted? Thus, whenever the Secretary-General undertakes an autonomous activity he would, according to this theory, act in anticipatory reliance on Article 98, banking, so to speak, on this provision.

It is submitted that this argument is specious. For one thing, many of the autonomous activities of the Secretary-General are not made public. Moreover, even when they are, they are more often made known by communications to the press than by reports to the General Assembly or the Security Council. (The reason for this is, frequently, that the Secretary-General has acted with respect to a dispute or a situation with which neither organ is dealing.) Furthermore, it has never been the practice of either organ to take decisions tacitly.[21]

Since it does not appear feasible to find in the Charter a sound legal basis for the autonomous activities of the Secretary-General, which are nevertheless so firmly anchored in practice that they can hardly be regarded as legally questionable, it is necessary to strike out in a different direction.

The first step in this direction is to note that, although autonomous activities are not in conformity with the Charter, they are not in contradiction with it. They are, in other words, *praeter legem*, but not *contra legem*.

One can then go on to argue that the autonomous activities, rather than being the exercise of powers vested in the Secretary-General by the Charter (or inherent in his office, which comes to the same thing, this office being a creation of the Charter), constitute a practice of the Secretary-General, considered not so much as an organ of the United Nations, but as an actor in his own right in the international arena. Thus, the direct legal basis for the practice would be a permissive rule of customary international law, with the constitutional law of the United Nations operating, so to speak, at a lower level, the office of the Secretary-General being not only created by that order but also endowed by it with the permanence and impartiality that are prerequisites to the effectiveness of the autonomous activities. This practice, although generated, as it were, outside the Charter, is co-ordinated with it, in the sense that it does not empower the Secretary-General to do anything that would violate it, for instance by infringing Article 2(7) of the Charter or running counter to any decision of a United Nations organ to which the Secretary-General is subordinated. The fact that the Secretary-General has, in connection with his autonomous activities, occasionally used the word 'personal' bears out the view that they are marginal to the Charter.[22]

---

21. It goes without saying that the Security Council or the General Assembly, if officially informed of action taken by the Secretary-General under his autonomous powers, may approve the action. For an example of such approval, see GA res. 42/1 of 7 October 1987, in para. 4 of which the General Assembly approved action that the Secretary-General had undertaken under his autonomous powers with regard to the Central American situation. Such an approval retroactively brings action originally undertaken under the autonomous powers within the scope of Art. 98 of the Charter.

22. Some of the representatives whom the Secretary-General has appointed to undertake autonomous activities on his behalf have been styled 'personal representatives'; moreover, he has referred, in the case concerning Thailand to be mentioned later on, to his authority to undertake

The foregoing is a more plausible analysis than the one derived from General Assembly resolution 13(I) or any of those that rest directly and exclusively on the Charter.

As against this, it should be noted that if the autonomous powers of the Secretary-General derive directly from the Charter, no organ may divest him of them,[23] whereas, if they are the product of customary international law the international community, acting through the United Nations General Assembly, could do so. On the other hand, if the autonomous powers do not rest on the Charter, they can, so long as they are not brought into conflict with it, be expanded without any limit, whereas if their source is exclusively the Charter, this may not be possible.[24]

It appears that only one Member of the United Nations, the USSR, has, on legal grounds, challenged the exercise by the Secretary-General of his autonomous powers. It did so, in the 1960s and in 1970, in connection with fact-finding and good offices activities.[25] This notwithstanding, the Declaration on the Strengthening of International Security, which the General Assembly, by its resolution 2734 (XXV), adopted in 1970 with only one vote against and one abstention,[26] refers, in its paragraph 6, to 'good offices', including 'those of the Secretary-General', among the means enumerated in the paragraph for settling disputes and situations likely to endanger the maintenance of international peace and security. Further evidence of how well-established the Secretary-General's autonomous powers were at the time of adoption of the Declaration is the fact that, despite the USSR's objections, which he rebutted,[27] he had never ceased to make extensive use of those powers and to refer to them in numerous reports and public pronouncements.

---

those activities as his 'personal authority'.

23. This would be true only of *complete* divestiture. In respect of any given dispute or situation, the General Assembly or the Security Council may, whatever the legal basis of the autonomous powers may be, deprive the Secretary-General of all or part of them in that respect by either entrusting to him, under Art. 98 of the Charter, functions relating to the dispute or situation or instructing him not to intervene. Moreover, if the Secretary-General takes an initiative in any situation that has been or becomes the object of a decision or a recommendation by either organ he must act in such a way as not to set himself at odds with the decision or recommendation.

24. This presupposes, of course, the possibility of determining, on the basis of the text or the *travaux préparatoires* of the Charter, the precise extent of the autonomous powers, a presupposition that, admittedly, is altogether unrealistic.

25. See *Repertory of Practice of United Nations Organs*, Supplement No. 4, Vol. 2, under Art. 98, paras. 313-319; and Supplement No. 5, Vol. 5, under Art. 98, para. 711.

26. Since the vote was not by roll-call, the identity of the two States that did not go along with the majority is unknown. But the vote in the First Committee on the draft that was to become res. 2734 (XXV) was unanimous except for South Africa, which voted against, and Portugal, which abstained. (GAOR, Twenty-Fifth Session, Annexes, a.i. 32, A/8096, para. 18.) It is therefore very likely that these two States were the odd men out in the plenary. And it is highly improbable that their attitude was dictated by the reference, in the draft resolution, to the good offices function of the Secretary-General.

27. *Repertory of Practice of United Nations Organs*, Supplement No. 5, Vol. 5, under Art. 98, para. 712.

It should be noted, however, that most likely the Secretary-General would never publicly endorse the view that his autonomous powers are not based on the Charter. For, by so doing, he could give the impression of down-grading the Charter or placing himself outside it, which might, politically, smack of apostasy.

What was, at the time of adoption of the Declaration, the extent of the Secretary-General's autonomous powers? Was there any legal impediment to his undertaking thereunder *any* political activity that could promote the objectives of the Charter in a manner not prohibited by it?

Before an answer is sought to this question, it should first be noted, in the interest of realism, that two severe restrictions of a non-legal nature exist on the use of those powers. One is of a practical character: the Secretary-General will exercise them in any particular case only to the extent that in his considered opinion there is a sufficient degree of probability that they will prove useful; above all, he must feel reasonably sure that his initiative will not antagonise or irritate the States directly concerned, other States or the membership at large to such an extent that his initiative would be counter-productive. Moreover the Secretary-General's actions under his autonomous powers will of necessity be subject to financial constraints, since, unlike what will normally occur in the case of mandated activities, the expenses his autonomous activities entail can be met only by the financial resources he has on hand.[28]

It is nevertheless legitimate to seek to determine the purely legal limits of the autonomous powers.

Not unexpectedly, the large body of practice that has been created by the Secretary-General's use of those powers and is known to the public, as well as his numerous public pronouncements on the matter, more often provide evidence of what he may do in the exercise of the powers than of their limits. Two cases, however, the first arising in 1963, the second in 1980, do shed light on those limits.[29]

The first of the two cases resulted from the offer made in 1963 by a number of United Nations Members of 'stand-by' military units to be made available on request to a United Nations peace-keeping force. According to a United Na-

---

28. The Secretary-General may finance autonomous activities by using the power the General Assembly normally grants him every two years, in connection with unforeseen and extraordinary expenses, to enter, up to a certain ceiling, into commitments that he certifies as relating to the maintenance of peace and security. (The latest resolution in this series is General Assembly resolution 44/203 of 21 December 1989, para. 1(a) of which authorises the Secretary-General to make commitments in this manner up to the amount of $ 3 million).

29. In 1964 the Secretary-General, having been requested by three Governments to designate a certain other Government that the former wished to entrust with the function of supervising a cease-fire between them, turned the request down. He based his denial, however, not on legal grounds but on considerations of expeditiousness and practicality. (See *Repertory of Practice of United Nations Organs*, Supplement No. 3, Vol. 4, under Art. 98, para. 700). Given the very *sui generis* character of this case, the manifest unreasonableness of the request and the fact that the Secretary-General did not rely on considerations of a legal nature to deny it, the precedent should not be regarded as marking a limit to the exercise of the Secretary-General's autonomous powers.

tions press release issued in October 1963, the Secretary-General's reaction was to point out that 'generally the peace-keeping operations of the United Nations in which military personnel are employed are undertaken on the basis of specific authorization by one of the competent United Nations Organs . . .'[30]

The second case concerned the relations between Thailand and Kampuchea. By a letter dated 1 July 1980 to the Secretary-General, the Permanent Representative of Thailand to the United Nations, at the same time as he complained about incidents along the Thai/Kampuchean border, requested that the United Nations station an observer team on the Thai side of the border.[31] In his reply, dated 7 July 1980, the Secretary-General stated that he was not in a position to dispatch United Nations observers to Thailand under his 'personal' authority, 'as any such action would normally have to be carried out under the authority of the Security Council.'[32] Since an observer operation of this type is within the realm of peace-keeping and involves military personnel, the Secretary-General's denial of the request should be seen as a corollary of the position he had taken in 1963 that he could not undertake peace-keeping operations under the autonomous powers.

3.   THE IMPACT OF THE DECLARATION

The operative part of the Declaration consists of 25 numbered paragraphs followed by two final unnumbered ones. The numbered paragraphs lay down principles and guidelines that States and the four United Nations organs concerned: the General Assembly, the Security Council, the International Court of Justice and the Secretary-General, are urged to apply in removing or preventing disputes and situations likely to threaten international peace and security. Paragraphs 8 and 9 of the Declaration deal with specific modalities of assistance to be rendered by the Secretary-General to the Security Council. The other provisions of the Declaration that refer to the Secretary-General are contained in paragraphs 20 to 24 inclusive. Paragraph 23 provides that he is to be encouraged to avail himself of Article 99 of the Charter. The remaining four paragraphs referring to the Secretary-General are in the nature of a very rudimentary codification (hereinafter referred to as 'the minicode') of his autonomous activities. They read as follows:[33]

30. *Repertory of Practice of United Nations Organs,* Supplement No. 3, Vol. 4, under Art. 98, para. 703.

31. Security Council, Supplement for July-September 1980, S/14046.

32. Ibid., S/14058.

33. The minicode is blemished by the obscurity of the second sentence of para. 22, with respect to which the *travaux préparatoires* are unhelpful. Fortunately, however, this sentence appears to be redundant. Para. 24 appears to be inspired by the Secretary-General's role in the Central American situation.

' . . .

20.   The Secretary-General, if approached by a State or States directly concerned with a dispute or situation, should respond swiftly by urging the States to seek a solution or adjustment by peaceful means of their own choice under the Charter and by offering his good offices or other means at his disposal, as he deems appropriate;

21.   The Secretary-General should consider approaching the States directly concerned with a dispute or situation in an effort to prevent it from becoming a threat to the maintenance of international peace and security;

22.   The Secretary-General should, where appropriate, consider making full use of fact-finding capabilities, including with the consent of the host State, the sending of a representative or fact-finding missions to areas where a dispute or a situation exists; where necessary, the Secretary-General should also consider making the appropriate arrangements;

. . .

24.   The Secretary-General should, where appropriate, encourage efforts undertaken at the regional level to prevent or remove a dispute or situation in the region concerned;'

What impact, if any, has the minicode had on the legal aspects of the autonomous activities of the Secretary-General?

The precisely calculated dosage of specificity and vagueness that characterises the minicode brings within its compass all the autonomous activities undertaken by the Secretary-General prior to the adoption of the Declaration, but does not inhibit him from future use of his autonomous powers to undertake novel activities. In other words, while it embraces the autonomous powers with which the Secretary-General had (as witness his relevant actions and public pronouncements) considered himself to be vested, it is non-committal with respect to any future widening of those powers.

To dispel all doubts that might conceivably subsist as to this legal neutrality of the minicode, it is necessary to demonstrate that it has not, as a cursory reading of it might make one believe it has, removed the limitations of a legal nature on his autonomous powers that the Secretary-General has had occasion to recognise.

Of these limitations, which are two in number and have been referred to earlier, the first one was fairly broad. It concerned peace-keeping operations in general, which, in the Secretary-General's opinion, he could not undertake in the absence of a specific mandate from one of the competent United Nations organs. It is clearly impossible to read into the minicode anything that could operate to remove this limitation.

The later of the two limits set by the Secretary-General to his autonomous powers arose, it will be recalled, in a more specific context, namely, a request made by Thailand in 1980 that he station an observation team on its side of the Thai/Kampuchean border. As has been noted, the Secretary-General denied this request on the ground that 'any such action would normally have to be carried out under the authority of the Security Council.'

Were the Secretary-General to receive such a request at the present time, the minicode would not preclude him from turning it down on the same ground. For the relevant provision of the minicode, i.e., paragraph 22 of the Declaration, contains the qualifying phrase 'where appropriate', on which the Secretary-General can rely to exclude from the scope of the paragraph cases where, in his opinion, he may not perform fact-finding functions without the authorization of the Security Council. That those cases are likely to be those having a peace-keeping dimension goes without saying.

The minicode has been shown to be neutral with respect to the forms that the autonomous activities may take. It is clear, moreover, that the minicode does not seek to abridge the Secretary-General's discretion in deciding whether or not to approach States concerned in a dispute that do not seek his assistance (cf., paragraph 21 of the Declaration). The same is not true, however, of his position vis-à-vis States in that situation that do request his assistance. For in that case the Secretary-General cannot, without disregarding the minicode, refrain from 'urging the States to seek a solution or adjustment by peaceful means of their choice' *and* 'offering his good offices or other means at his disposal, as he deems appropriate', to them (cf., paragraph 20 of the Declaration). And, if the Secretary-General has offered the States that have approached him some means of assisting them, he can hardly renege on the offer if it is accepted. Thus the minicode abridges, to a certain extent, the freedom of action the Secretary-General enjoyed in the exercise of his autonomous powers prior to the adoption of the Declaration.

Consequently, it is not only of theoretical but also of practical importance to determine whether the minicode might not be in the nature of a blanket mandate conferred by the General Assembly on the Secretary-General to undertake activities of the type characterized here as 'autonomous'. If the minicode constitutes such a mandate, this would mean that the Secretary-General would, in conducting autonomous activities, act not under a practice, but, rather, pursuant to that blanket mandate, contained in the minicode. The minicode would have brought about a situation where any activity undertaken by the Secretary-General that would have qualified as an autonomous one if carried out prior to the adoption of the Declaration would, if carried out subsequently, be a mandated one.[34] In other words, as from the date of adoption of the Declaration the Secretary-General would, strictly speaking, have ceased to possess powers that, although still largely discretionary, could properly be characterised as autonomous within the meaning this adjective has here.

---

34. As pointed out in n. 3 *supra*, the terms of a mandate may well confer discretion on the Secretary-General as to whether or not he should take action under that mandate.

This, however, is not at all the case: far from constituting a grant of power, the minicode does not even qualify as a set of declaratory provisions, but is to be regarded as no more than a series of exhortations.

That the minicode does not amount to a grant of power is implied by its being part of a declaration. Declarations are meant to lay down general principles of a moral or political rather than a legal nature. Moreover, the use, throughout the minicode, of 'should' instead of 'shall' or 'may' in the specification of the actions to be taken by the Secretary-General pursuant to the minicode implies that in adopting the provisions of the minicode the General Assembly's intent was to exhort the Secretary-General to take those actions rather than to empower him to or declare that he may do so.[35]

This basically hortatory nature of the minicode is borne out by the *travaux préparatoires*. It is true that at the meetings of the Sixth Committee of the General Assembly at which the draft that was to become the Declaration was considered, three representatives stated or implied that the minicode amounted to a grant of power to the Secretary-General.[36] But, in introducing, before the Sixth Committee of the General Assembly, the report of the Special Committee on the Charter of the United Nations and on the Strengthening of the Role of the Organization that contained the draft declaration, the Chairman of the latter body stated that 'the aim of paragraphs 20 to 24 [of the draft declaration] was to draw attention to the capabilities of the Secretary-General in taking preventive action', which carries the contrary implication.[37] The same is true of statements made by three other representatives on the Sixth Committee.[38] And five other representatives referred merely to the strengthening of the role of the Secretary-General in the maintenance of international peace and security that the minicode would bring about.[39]

Thus, the minicode has neither widened nor narrowed the autonomous powers of the Secretary-General. Nor has it made any change in their legal basis, which continues to be a practice that has developed on the margin of the Charter but in no way runs counter to it. In other words, the minicode, which is not even, strictly speaking, declaratory in nature, is, from the strictly legal viewpoint, altogether neutral.

The minicode is, however, of considerable importance in that, on the political level, it consolidates and strengthens the practice with which it deals.

35. Cf., the Preliminary Report by K. Skubiszewski on resolutions of the General Assembly of the United Nations, in 61 *Yearbook of the Institute of International Law* (1985) Part 1, pp. 58-59.

36. Statements by the representatives of Czechoslovakia (A/C.6/43/SR.15, para. 16), the Ukranian SSR (ibid., para. 78) and Nepal (A/C. 6/43/SR.19, para. 16).

37. A/C.6/43/SR.14, para. 5.

38. Statements by the representatives of Italy (A/C.6/43/SR.14, para. 18), Morocco (A/C.6/43/SR.19, para. 46) and Iran (ibid., para. 21).

39. Statements by the representatives of Mexico (A/C.6/43/SR.14, para. 81), Egypt (A/C.6/43/SR.16, para. 18), Spain (ibid., para. 64), Senegal (ibid., para. 76) and the United States (A/C.6/43/SR.20, para. 36).

This is no doubt what led the Secretary-General to welcome, in an address delivered to an educational institution in April 1988,[40] the provisions concerning his office contained in the draft that was to become the Declaration. In a similar vein, the representative of the United States on the General Assembly's Sixth Committee at the Assembly's Forty-Third Session aptly characterised those provisions, during the Sixth Committee's discussion of the draft, as 'an important political endorsement of an active role for the Secretary-General.'[41] To promote this role, they lay on the Secretary-General a moral obligation to respond positively to appeals for help from States that are in any way at odds with one another.

40. Press release SG/SM/4124 of 20 April 1988, p. 7. The draft declaration had just been adopted by the Special Committee on the Charter of the United Nations and on the Strengthening of the Role of the Organization.
41. A/C.6/43/SR.20, para. 36.

[10]

JUDGING THE SECURITY COUNCIL

By Jose E. Alvarez*

Should the International Court of Justice (ICJ) "judicially review" Security Council decisions? The question, once fanciful, is now being asked seriously by litigants in and judges on the World Court,[1] nonpermanent members of the Security Council that consider it an "undemocratic" body acting as "a cloak for a new form of imperialism,"[2] and scholars worried about its recent "quasi-legislative" or "quasi-judicial" acts.[3] The recent throng of commentators and advocates[4] includes students of realpoli-

* Professor, University of Michigan Law School. This article is based on a presentation given at the American Society of International Law's Annual Meeting on April 5, 1995. The author thanks Susan Damplo, Gerry J. Simpson, Anne-Marie Slaughter, Eric Stein, Howard Meyer, Richard Pildes, Phillip Trimble, Edward Martin Wise, and anonymous reviewers from the *Journal*'s Board of Editors for their helpful suggestions.

[1] Alleging jurisdiction under the Montreal Convention for the Suppression of Unlawful Acts against the Safety of Civil Aviation, Libya sought interim measures against the United States and the United Kingdom, a request that ultimately would require that the Court consider the legality of Security Council Resolution 748, which imposed economic sanctions to compel Libya to comply with U.S. and UK requests to surrender Libyan nationals accused of the Lockerbie bombing. Questions of Interpretation and Application of the 1971 Montreal Convention arising from the Aerial Incident at Lockerbie (Libya v. UK; Libya v. U.S.), Provisional Measures, 1992 ICJ REP. 3, 114 (Orders of Apr. 14) [hereinafter Lockerbie]. (The Orders are nearly identical.) For its part, Bosnia filed multiple claims against Serbia, principally under the Genocide Convention, which initially included a request for a determination that Security Council decisions imposing an arms embargo be construed as not impairing Bosnia's rights of individual or collective self-defense. Neither Libya nor Bosnia was successful in attaining these requests through the provisional measures stages of these cases. Application of the Convention on the Prevention and Punishment of the Crime of Genocide (Bosnia-Herzegovina v. Yugo. (Serbia and Montenegro)), Provisional Measures, 1993 ICJ REP. 3 (Order of Apr. 8) [hereinafter Order of Apr. 8], *reprinted in* 32 ILM 890 (1993); Application of the Convention on the Prevention and Punishment of the Crime of Genocide (Bosnia-Herzegovina v. Yugo. (Serbia and Montenegro)), Provisional Measures, 1993 ICJ REP. 325 (Order of Sept. 13) [hereinafter Order of Sept. 13]. For one view of the scope of Bosnia's claims before the Court, see Craig Scott, Francis Chang, Abid Qureshi, Paul Michell, Jasminka Kalajdzic & Peter Copeland, *A Memorial for Bosnia: Framework of Legal Arguments Concerning the Lawfulness of the Maintenance of the United Nations Security Council's Arms Embargo on Bosnia and Herzegovina*, 16 MICH. J. INT'L L. 1 (1994) [hereinafter Scott] (although cast as a pleading before the Court and initiated by a Bosnian government request, this document was not filed before the Court). Bosnia's actual pleadings on the merits, not yet public, apparently no longer challenge Security Council action. Conversation with Thomas Franck, counsel for Bosnia (Apr. 5, 1995).

In proceedings before the war crimes Tribunal for the former Yugoslavia, the first defendant has also raised defenses premised on the illegality of the Council's actions in establishing the Tribunal. *See* text at and notes 59–62 *infra*.

[2] ADAM ROBERTS & BENEDICT KINGSBURY, PRESIDING OVER A DIVIDED WORLD: CHANGING UN ROLES, 1945–1993, at 57 (International Peace Academy, Occasional Paper Series, 1994). Developing states' distrust of the post–Cold War Security Council has been especially evident in recent discussions in the Special Committee on the Charter of the United Nations and on the Strengthening of the Role of the Organization. See, e.g., recent annual reports of that committee, UN Docs. A/48/33 (1993) and A/49/33 (1994).

[3] *See, e.g.*, Keith Harper, *Does the United Nations Security Council Have the Competence to Act as Court and Legislature?*, 27 N.Y.U. J. INT'L L. & POL. 103 (1994); Vera Gowlland-Debbas, *Security Council Enforcement Action and Issues of State Responsibility*, 43 INT'L & COMP. L.Q. 55 (1994); Frederic L. Kirgis, Jr., *The Security Council's First Fifty Years*, 89 AJIL 506 (1995).

[4] *See, e.g.*, Scott I. Bortz, *Avoiding a Collision of Competence: The Relationship Between the Security Council and the International Court of Justice in Light of* Libya v. United States, 2 FLA. ST. U. J. INT'L L. & POL. 353 (1993); Thomas M. Franck, *The "Powers of Appreciation": Who Is the Ultimate Guardian of UN Legality?*, 86 AJIL 519 (1992); W. Michael Reisman, *The Constitutional Crisis in the United Nations*, 87 AJIL 83 (1993) [hereinafter Crisis], *also in* DEVELOPMENT OF THE ROLE OF THE SECURITY COUNCIL, COLLOQUE, JULY 21–23, 1992, at 399 (René-Jean Dupuy ed., 1993) [hereinafter COLLOQUE]; Matthias J. Herdegen, *The "Constitutionalization" of the UN Security System*, 27 VAND. J. TRANSNAT'L L. 135 (1994); Robert F. Kennedy, Libya v. United States: *The International Court of Justice and the Power of Judicial Review*, 33 VA. J. INT'L L. 899 (1993); Scott S. Evans, *The Lockerbie Incident Cases: Libyan-Sponsored Terrorism, Judicial Review, and the Political Question Doctrine*, 18 MD. J. INT'L L. & TRADE 21 (1994); MOHAMMED BEDJAOUI, THE NEW WORLD ORDER AND THE SECURITY COUNCIL: TESTING THE LEGALITY OF ITS ACTS (1994); Bernhard Graefrath, *Leave to the Court What Belongs to the Court—The Libyan Case*, 4 EUR. J. INT'L L. 184 (1993); Ken Roberts, *Second-Guessing the Security Council: The International Court of Justice and Its*

2 THE AMERICAN JOURNAL OF INTERNATIONAL LAW [Vol. 90:1

tik warning the Court against any unrealistic attempt to transform the United Nations collective security scheme into a constitutional structure of checks and balances, and legalists grasping hopefully for hints of _Marbury v. Madison_ in recent World Court pronouncements.[5]

For the ostensible realists, the question of World Court review over Council action is about how best to effectuate collective security. For them the UN Charter is not a "constitution" with checks and balances but, rather, a hierarchical collective security scheme with the Council at its apex.[6] The only "check" on its action emerges from realpolitik: the veto and the prospect that the Council will ask for sanctions or force and no one will respond.[7] Realists argue that, in cases like those presented by Libya and Bosnia, the Court's role is limited to ratifying the Council's program or staying out of the Council's way.[8] For the Court to do anything in these types of cases except at the invitation of the Council is to undermine the Charter scheme in a vain attempt to legalize what cannot be legalized.[9] For its opponents, judicial review asks the impossible: the Court cannot "review" the Council, as no rules exist with which to examine the legality of a chapter VII determination.[10] Some realists bluntly characterize the Charter scheme as constituting a "police state" rather than a system based on the "rule of law"; they view the Council as a "law unto itself," with opportunistic flexibility the key to its success.[11]

At the other end of the spectrum, legalists argue that (1) the Court needs to be the "last-resort defender" of the system's legitimacy; (2) the Charter is a constitution of

---

Powers of Judicial Review, 7 PACE INT'L L. REV. 281 (1995); Edward McWhinney, _The International Court as Emerging Constitutional Court and the Co-ordinate UN Institutions (Especially the Security Council): Implications of the_ Aerial Incident at Lockerbie, 1992 CAN. Y.B. INT'L L. 261; Geoffrey R. Watson, _Constitutionalism, Judicial Review, and the World Court,_ 34 HARV. INT'L L.J. 1 (1993); Vera Gowlland-Debbas, _The Relationship between the International Court of Justice and the Security Council in Light of the Lockerbie Case,_ 88 AJIL 643 (1994); Oscar Schachter et al., remarks, _UN Checks and Balances: The Roles of the ICJ and the Security Council, in_ CONTEMPORARY INTERNATIONAL LAW ISSUES: OPPORTUNITIES AT A TIME OF MOMENTOUS CHANGE 280–97 (1993 Joint Conference of the American Society of International Law and Nederlandse Vereniging voor Internationaal Recht, 1994) [hereinafter 1993 JOINT CONFERENCE]; Derek W. Bowett, _The Impact of Security Council Decisions on Dispute Settlement Procedures,_ 5 EUR. J. INT'L L. 89 (1994).

[5] _Compare_ Franck, _supra_ note 4, _and_ Thomas M. Franck, _The Security Council and "Threats to the Peace": Some Remarks on Remarkable Developments, in_ COLLOQUE, _supra_ note 4, at 83 (urging judicial review) _with_ Reisman, _Crisis, supra_ note 4 (counseling against World Court review). The legalist/realist is a categorization adopted here for didactic purposes. Franck, Reisman and the other scholars writing on this issue do not identify themselves as in either camp and this categorization does not do justice to all the nuances of their respective positions.

[6] _See, e.g.,_ Reisman, _Crisis, supra_ note 4, at 83, 84, 95.

[7] _See, e.g.,_ Serge Sur, comments, _in_ COLLOQUE, _supra_ note 4, at 140; Benedetto Conforti, _Le Pouvoir discrétionnaire du Conseil de Sécurité en matière de constatation d'une menace contre la paix, d'une rupture de la paix ou d'un acte d'agression, in_ COLLOQUE, _supra_ note 4, at 51, 60.

[8] _See, e.g.,_ Reisman, comments, _in_ COLLOQUE, _supra_ note 4, at 139–40; Reisman, _Crisis, supra_ note 4, at 83, 92–100; Terry Gill, comments, 1993 JOINT CONFERENCE, _supra_ note 4, at 284.

[9] _See supra_ note 8. _See also_ Sean D. Murphy, _The Security Council, Legitimacy, and the Concept of Collective Security After the Cold War,_ 32 COLUM. J. TRANSNAT'L L. 201, 252–69 (1994); Herdegen, _supra_ note 4, at 150–52; Helmut Freudenshuß, _Article 39 of the UN Charter Revisited: Threats to the Peace and the Recent Practice of the UN Security Council,_ 46 AUS. J. PUB. INT'L L. 1, 36 (1993); Terry Gill, Nico Schrijver, Richard B. Lillich, comments, 1993 JOINT CONFERENCE, _supra_ note 4, at 283–95; Bortz, _supra_ note 4, at 376–78. See also the U.S. arguments in the _Libya_ case summarized in Evans, _supra_ note 4, at 50–54.

[10] _See, e.g.,_ Reisman, _Crisis, supra_ note 4, at 92–93, and Reisman, comments, _in_ COLLOQUE, _supra_ note 4, at 139 (arguing that contemporary jurists' attempts to deconstruct "implied" constraints from the Charter reveal nothing about the intentions of Charter drafters or contemporary expectations, and concluding that judicial review is therefore "quite hollow"); Conforti, _supra_ note 7, at 51–60 (to same effect); Herdegen, _supra_ note 4, at 152 (commenting on the "indeterminacy" of chapter VII).

[11] Serge Sur, Security Council Resolution 687 of 3 April 1991 in the Gulf Affair: Problems of Restoring and Safeguarding Peace (Research Paper No. 12), UN Doc. UNIDIR/92/53, at 8, 61 (1992) [hereinafter Resolution 687]. _See also_ Serge Sur, _Sécurité collective et rétablissement de la paix: La Résolution 687 (3 avril 1991) dans l'affaire du golfe, in_ COLLOQUE, _supra_ note 4, at 18; Reisman, Sur, F. Delon, comments, _in id._ at 139–40, 148, 152; Murphy, _supra_ note 9, at 206, 246–69; Herdegen, _supra_ note 4, at 145–49.

"limited enumerated powers" under the rule of law; (3) the Court is the "one institution in the system" capable of so affirming; and (4) "functional parallelism," not an institutional hierarchy, obtains between Council and Court.[12] To them, Council and Court have complementary but distinct functions, one primarily political, the other legal, and each should operate to permit the other to fulfill its role.[13] They argue that, while the Council has wide discretion, it is not omnipotent and cannot violate fundamental norms of international law such as the principle of inherent self-defense, the laws of war and the Charter itself.[14] To legalists, the Court exists in part to protect institutional legitimacy by preventing the Council from overstepping its limits.

Despite their differing conclusions, many realists and those they would call "judicial romantics"[15] make many of the same assumptions. Both sides suggest that the ICJ now faces a decision like the one the U.S. Supreme Court confronted in 1803 in *Marbury v. Madison*;[16] that is, ICJ judges need to decide whether to "cross the 'Rubicon' "[17] and assume the power, without express constitutional warrant, to render the decision of a coordinate political organ null and void. They tend to ask the question as it seems to be posed in the *Lockerbie* and *Bosnia* cases now before the Court: that is, as either praiseworthy or wrongheaded attempts by states to "judicialize" determinations under chapter VII, especially Article 39. To both sides, the important question is whether or not the Court in these or similar cases will proceed in the fateful direction of *Marbury*.[18] Many, on both sides of the issue, argue that the Court should have staked a clearer position in its Orders on provisional measures in *Lockerbie* since the longer the question of judicial review remains open, the greater the potential for damage to the Court, the Council and the entire UN system.[19] They assume that the Court's answer will be apparent when it comes and that the Court's ability to engage in "review" turns on textual determinacy: that is, legalists posit that there are textually determinate rules judges can

[12] *See, e.g.*, Franck, *supra* note 5, at 110; Thomas M. Franck, *Fairness in the International Legal and Institutional System*, 240 RECUEIL DES COURS 189–221 (1993 III); Franck, comments, 1993 JOINT CONFERENCE, *supra* note 4, at 280–83, 291, 293–96. *See also* Gowlland-Debbas, *supra* note 4, at 658–61; Graefrath, *supra* note 4.

[13] *See* Franck, *supra* note 5, at 110; Franck, *supra* note 12, at 189–221; Franck, comments, *supra* note 12. *See also* Harper, *supra* note 3, at 143–47; Francisco Orrego Vicuña, *The Settlement of Disputes and Conflict Resolution in the Context of a Revitalized Role for the United Nations Security Council, in* COLLOQUE, *supra* note 4, at 41, 47; Gowlland-Debbas, *supra* note 4, at 658–61; Evans, *supra* note 4, at 60–70, 75–76; Kennedy, *supra* note 4, at 910–15; Alain Pellet, *Le Glaive et la balance, in* INTERNATIONAL LAW AT A TIME OF PERPLEXITY 539, 545–50 (Yoram Dinstein ed., 1989); Scott, *supra* note 1, at 91–97.

[14] They argue, for instance, that Charter Article 42 does not authorize the Council to target civilians or deploy disproportionate force. *See, e.g.*, Gowlland-Debbas, *supra* note 3, at 91–93; Order of Sept. 13, 1993 ICJ REP. at 407 (Lauterpacht, J., sep. op.); Michael Bothe, *Les Limites des pouvoirs du Conseil de Sécurité, in* COLLOQUE, *supra* note 4, at 67, 76–80; Watson, *supra* note 4, at 37. Even some of those skeptical of judicial review accept these limits on Council action. *See, e.g.*, Herdegen, *supra* note 4, at 156–57.

[15] Reisman, *Crisis, supra* note 4, at 94 (applying this term to Judge Lachs's opinion in the *Lockerbie* case).

[16] 5 U.S. (1 Cranch) 137 (1803). In this case the U.S. Supreme Court found that it did not have jurisdiction to issue the writ of mandamus sought by Marbury because the act of Congress authorizing the writ extended the Court's original jurisdiction beyond the limits allowed by the Constitution.

[17] Franck, comments, 1993 JOINT CONFERENCE, *supra* note 4, at 282.

[18] The *Marbury* analogy comes up repeatedly, especially among U.S. scholars. *See, e.g.*, Watson, *supra* note 4; Franck, *supra* note 4; Evans, *supra* note 4, at 65–67; Reisman, *Crisis, supra* note 4, at 92; Kennedy, *supra* note 4, at 915; Herdegen, *supra* note 4, at 149; Franck, Lillich, comments, 1993 JOINT CONFERENCE, *supra* note 4, at 280–83, 295; Roberts, *supra* note 4. *See also* Michael J. Glennon, *Protecting the Court's Institutional Interests: Why Not the* Marbury *Approach?*, 81 AJIL 121 (1987). Although none of these writers argue that *Marbury* is directly relevant, neither do they examine the limits of the analogy to *Marbury*.

[19] *See, e.g.*, Reisman, *Crisis, supra* note 4, at 89–96; Paul J. I. M. de Waart, *The UN System at a Crossroads: Peoples' Centre or Big Brothers' Small Club?, in* TOWARDS MORE EFFECTIVE SUPERVISION BY INTERNATIONAL ORGANIZATIONS 49, 61–64 (Niels Blokker & Sam Muller eds., 1994) [hereinafter EFFECTIVE SUPERVISION]. Franck is more cautious, indicating only that the Court should keep the "door open" in the pending *Lockerbie* and *Bosnia* cases and be ready to remedy the Council's "legitimacy deficit" if necessary. *See, e.g.*, Franck, comments, 1993 JOINT CONFERENCE, *supra* note 4, at 293–94.

apply or discover, while realists tend to disagree. Many, on both sides of the issue, also propose that the Court find "the answer" in the text of the Charter and its negotiating history.[20] Finally, both sides tend to see proposals for change in the Council's membership or procedures and proposals for judicial review as rival alternatives, political or juridical, intended to foster institutional legitimacy.[21]

Despite the scholarly attention, the question of "judicial review" over Council action is still seen but "through a glass darkly," its significance obscured by an all-consuming focus on the possibility that the ICJ might find a chapter VII decision by the Council, legally binding under the Charter,[22] void in a case pending before the Court. This article looks skeptically at these prevailing assumptions (part I), critiquing especially the alleged role of textual determinacy in the prospects for Court "legitimation" (part II). Parts III and IV argue that the all-or-nothing alternatives sometimes suggested are deceptive. Part III surveys the many modes of Council action that might generate issues that the Court needs to address, and part IV examines the many ways that the Court could address them. Part V identifies an "expressive" mode of World Court "review" that has not been the focus of attention, while part VI deals with one final objection to judicial review.

My thesis is that neither the proponents nor the opponents of judicial review have adequately come to terms with either the limits of judicial action or its possibilities and that the discussion can be enriched by taking a closer look at the processes for legitimation at issue, as well as constitutional review in comparative contexts. I conclude that the ICJ, neither potential savior nor destroyer of the United Nations, has engaged, and will continue to engage, in variegated forms of "review," but that judicial review will not soon extend to a judicial finding that some particular Council action is "null and void."

I. THE COURT AS ONE OF MANY (DE)LEGITIMATORS

Those considering the question of "judicial review," particularly U.S. scholars, need to reconsider their natural tendency to view the issue through the prism of *Marbury v. Madison*. The *Marbury* analogy misleads in the context of a court that cannot make the Council a party to a binding judgment,[23] that relies on the Council for enforcement of its decisions,[24] and that is operating without clear law on the effects (if any) of a judicial finding of illegality.[25] Unlike the U.S. Supreme Court, which is not empowered to render advisory opinions, the ICJ is likely to have a matter that directly challenges the validity

---

[20] *Compare* Watson, *supra* note 4; Herdegen, *supra* note 4, at 152–54 (finding that the broad terms of the UN Charter, along with the Charter's "*travaux préparatoires*," grant the Security Council broad, but not unlimited, discretion under chapter VII); Scott, *supra* note 1, especially at 75–87, 119–25 (to same effect) *with* Roberts, *supra* note 4, at 289–93 (concluding that the Charter's negotiating history does not favor judicial review).

[21] Reisman, for example, proposes, as an alternative to judicial review, the establishment of an appropriate informational loop with the more representative political body, the General Assembly, when the Council is in a chapter VII mode. Reisman, *Crisis, supra* note 4, at 92–100; Reisman, comments, *in* COLLOQUE, *supra* note 4, at 139–40. *See also* Franck, *supra* note 12, at 41–61, 189–221; Franck, *supra* note 5, at 85–107; Franck, comments, 1993 JOINT CONFERENCE, *supra* note 4, at 280–97; Sur, Resolution 687, *supra* note 11, at 61; Sur, comments, *in* COLLOQUE, *supra*, at 139–40; Roberts, *supra* note 4, at 318–19.

[22] *See* UN CHARTER Arts. 25, 48.

[23] Under Article 34 of the ICJ Statute, only states may be parties to contentious cases. International organizations have the right only to present information to the Court in such cases and, of course, are not parties to any subsequent judgment. Compare Articles 65–68 of the ICJ Statute with Article 96 of the Charter, which permits requests for advisory opinions by certain international organizations.

[24] ICJ STATUTE Art. 59; UN CHARTER Art. 94. *See also* Gowlland-Debbas, *supra* note 4, at 670–73; Scott, *supra* note 1, at 95 n.304.

[25] *See, e.g.*, Elihu Lauterpacht, *The Legal Effect of Illegal Acts of International Organisations, in* CAMBRIDGE ESSAYS IN INTERNATIONAL LAW: ESSAYS IN HONOUR OF LORD McNAIR 88 (1965); Gowlland-Debbas, *supra* note 4, at 670.

of UN action put to it only through an advisory question from a UN organ.[26] Such a request will not result in a binding decision absent a separate treaty obligation that makes it so.[27] Although it might be suggested that, after all, *Marbury* purported to address action by a nonparty—the U.S. Congress was not a party to that suit and the Court nonetheless found an act of Congress unconstitutional—the peculiar limits of the ICJ Statute, which rule out contentious cases against *any* institutional organ as such and vest the Council with responsibility for enforcement, make the judicial leap required to reach the legality of action by the Council all the greater.[28]

At most, we can hypothesize that a decision made in the course of a contentious case by the World Court that a Council decision is *ultra vires* might have an effect on the United Nations *comparable* to the effect on the executive or legislative branch of a finding of unconstitutionality by the U.S. Supreme Court. But such an effect would depend on the international community's respect for the Court as compared to the Council, since it would require that states ignore the dim prospects for Council enforcement of such a decision, as well as Article 59 of the Court's Statute (which makes the Court's judgments binding· only on the parties to them).[29] For an ICJ decision to *effectively* invalidate a Council decision, states would generally have to give the Court's decision more pervasive force than the law requires.[30]

Further, the legal effects of the Court's judgments, even in contentious cases, are not automatic, and are unpredictable and case specific. Even assuming that we ought to be most concerned about the possibility that the ICJ will issue an opinion critical of the Council after the Council has taken action or has begun to operate in a chapter VII mode,[31] existing jurisdictional limits make it unlikely that the Court will find that a Council decision, already taken, is "null and void" or that one being contemplated would be. The most the Court would find is that a particular Council decision as applied to these parties in the circumstances at issue would be illegal.

[26] Except in the unlikely event that all UN members were to join together as parties to a contentious case raising the validity of some UN action, or in the equally unlikely event that all UN members successfully intervened in an ongoing case brought by other litigants under Article 62 or 63 of the Court's Statute; in such an instance, the case would be nearly identical to one involving the United Nations as a party.

[27] For a survey of exceptional treaties that make advisory opinions binding on their parties, see Roberto Ago, *"Binding" Advisory Opinions of the International Court of Justice*, 85 AJIL 439 (1991).

[28] Under the ICJ Statute, it is also impossible to bring a case against a named individual—whether the Secretary-General or the President of the Security Council—and therefore (indirectly) make the Organization a party.

[29] The effect of any ICJ judgment in this regard depends on whether the Court's interpretations of the Charter are generally accepted by the UN membership. *See, e.g.*, Louis Sohn, *Interpreting the Law, in* UNITED NATIONS LEGAL ORDER 169 (Oscar Schachter & Christopher C. Joyner eds., 1995). Acceptance may not emerge. Indeed, to Eugene Rostow, Article 94 renders the duty to comply with any Court decision "precatory, conditional, advisory, and indeed nugatory—entirely nugatory for the permanent members of the Security Council and uncertain, to say the least, for all other members." Eugene V. Rostow, *Disputes Involving the Inherent Right of Self-Defense, in* THE INTERNATIONAL COURT OF JUSTICE AT A CROSSROADS 264, 271 (Lori F. Damrosch ed., 1987).

[30] Arguments that the Council would be bound by "good faith" or "comity" to give effect to determinations made by the Court in the course of a contentious case between states assume that such principles apply to such cases. *See, e.g.*, Scott, *supra* note 1, at 95 & n.304.

[31] *See, e.g.*, Reisman, *Crisis, supra* note 4, at 89 (the Court should be deferential whenever the Council is "factually in a chapter VII mode"). Reisman's concern over the possibility of Court review even when the Council has taken only chapter VI action appears to be all the more justified insofar as it is agreed that the Council is authorized to take legally binding decisions even under chapter VI—pursuant to Article 25 of the Charter. *See, e.g.*, Legal Consequences for States of the Continued Presence of South Africa in Namibia (South West Africa) notwithstanding Security Council resolution 276 (1970), 1971 ICJ REP. 16 (Advisory Opinion of June 21) [hereinafter Namibia]. To the extent that realists worry about Court review because the Court should not be empowered to dispute the legality of any legally binding decision by the Council, that possibility appears to exist under *both* chapter VI and chapter VII. But there appear to be potentially troublesome cases even when parties approach the Court seeking a determination *before* the Council is in a "chapter VII mode."

6   THE AMERICAN JOURNAL OF INTERNATIONAL LAW   [Vol. 90:1

This point is not merely technical. Because the Court is constrained from acting in the classic *Marbury* mode, the question presented by the parties before it becomes crucial from the standpoint of likely effects or practical constraints on Council action. Consider a hypothetical case brought by Syria against another state, in the course of which the ICJ needs to consider whether Syria must abide by UN sanctions against Iraq despite extremely detrimental effects on Syria's economy and citizens. If the Court manages to find, in Article 50 of the Charter or elsewhere, a justification for a humanitarian or other exception to the sanctions that has to date not been authorized by the Council's sanctions committees, neither the Council's legitimacy nor the overall efficacy of its sanctions may suffer a devastating blow.[32] The practical difficulties for the Council will be far different, however, if, as in the *Bosnia* cases, the Court purports to pass on *jus cogens* principles, indicating that these limit all international subjects, including the Council, and concluding that *therefore* the Council's arms embargo violates Bosnia's right to defend itself against genocide.[33]

Moreover, there are even differences between more direct challenges to Council action. The possible delegitimating consequences seem more significant in *Lockerbie* simply because a ruling in Libya's favor could mean that two of the states central to the success of Libyan sanctions would be judicially precluded from enforcing them. Were the United States and the United Kingdom to abide by such a judgment (itself not a foregone conclusion), the entire Council program would probably collapse—quite apart from whether other states voluntarily decided to cease enforcing the sanctions out of deference to the Court. The effects of a hypothetical judgment concluding that the Council's arms embargo violates Bosnia's rights under the Genocide Convention would be more ambiguous, depending on what the Court actually said. Unless the Court were to suggest that the Genocide Convention imposes an affirmative obligation on treaty parties to supply arms to victimized states—an unlikely finding under that Convention—such a ruling need not justify a flow of arms to Bosnia.[34] Further, while an adverse decision would not, in either the *Bosnia* or the *Lockerbie* cases, preclude the Council from taking new measures, the options available to it if Libya wins its case might be more limited than if Bosnia convinces the Court that the arms embargo is illegal.[35]

It is also unlikely that the Court would go so far in either of these instances. As Elihu Lauterpacht argued long ago, international law has scarcely developed the law concerning the consequences of a determination of illegal action by an international organization. We still do not know whether the Court could determine that the Council's

---

These may present graver difficulties for the Court and Council since the intent of such challenges may be to preclude options that the Council ought to retain. *See* Scott, *supra* note 1, at 93 n.300.

[32] This is especially the case if, as has been suggested, the Council itself has turned a blind eye to some violations of the sanctions. *See, e.g.,* FREDERIC L. KIRGIS, JR., INTERNATIONAL ORGANIZATIONS IN THEIR LEGAL SETTING 656 (2d ed. 1993). The hypothetical case in the text is inspired by recent Syrian complaints. *See* Note Verbale Dated 31 January 1991 from the Permanent Representative of the Syrian Arab Republic to the United Nations Addressed to the Secretary-General, UN Doc. S/22193, at 1 (1991).

[33] As argued in Scott, *supra* note 1, but apparently not now being argued in the case as it proceeds to the merits. Conversation with Thomas Franck, *supra* note 1.

[34] *See, e.g.,* Order of Sept. 13, 1993 ICJ REP. at 441, para. 103 (Lauterpacht, J., sep. op.).

[35] This would be the case, for instance, if the Court made the (unlikely) finding that Libyan sanctions impermissibly intrude on Libya's sovereign rights to refuse to extradite its own nationals. Such a broad finding would make it difficult for the Council to take any action to compel Libya to transfer its nationals for trial. This would not be the case, however, if the Court took the view, for instance, that the Council's sanctions were merely intended to impose a duty on Libya to negotiate in good faith and that the Council's limited sanctions do not intrude on Libya's sovereign rights. Of course, if the Court took this view, even this affirmation of the Council's actions would contain an implicit limitation on the future scope of Council sanctions. On the other hand, a judicial finding that the Council's arms embargo violates Bosnia's right to defend itself against genocide need not prevent the Council from taking other measures, such as economic sanctions, that could not be said to violate that right.

act is void with retroactive effect, void from the time of its decision, or merely voidable at the option of the Organization.[36] A cautious Court could easily opt for the third option. Under present circumstances, lacking contentious case jurisdiction over the Organization or the Council as a party, the Court would probably decide that it need not reach this question since it can "never be in a binding jurisdictional relationship that allows its acts to void acts of other organs."[37] For these reasons, the focus on a *generalized* threat of a judicial finding of nullity seems misplaced.

Far from being paradigmatic, the *Marbury*-style challenges to the Council suggested by the initial pleadings in the *Lockerbie* and *Bosnia* cases are aberrational and will likely remain so. If the debate over judicial review necessarily involves instances in which the Council takes such controversial action that a state is emboldened to mount a confrontational case in the World Court *and* manages to find a jurisdictional basis for doing so, one suspects that the issue, however doctrinally interesting to scholars, will have limited real-world consequences.[38] As is argued in part III below, however, the "judicial review" question has a much wider potential ambit—a fact obscured by fixation on *Bosnia-* and *Lockerbie*-type cases.

Similarly, the suppositions that a *Marbury*-style decision will be evident once an opinion is issued and that a fateful decision on the question should emerge during the pending *Lockerbie* cases are belied by disagreements over the meanings of, for example, the *Lockerbie* Orders on interim measures. That people can read those same short orders as an affirmation of Council supremacy,[39] a courageous step toward full-scale *Marbury* review[40] or an erroneous half-step in between[41] suggests that it is wrong to assume that we will know "judicial review" when we see it, that all define "judicial review" the same way or that the "choice" to review is one the Court can quickly make. On the contrary, as part IV below demonstrates, the evolution of constitutional review within national systems suggests a very different course. "Judicial review" often does not arrive fully formed, heralded and portentous; aspects of review are more likely to emerge incrementally, unannounced and, sometimes, unnoticed.[42]

At bottom, the debate on judicial review is less about judicial propriety or the structure of the Charter (real or imagined) than about how proper governance should occur. One side assumes that the ultimate warrantor of legitimacy needs to be a body that is primarily "political," such as the Council or the General Assembly (or, as some would have it, a combination of both),[43] while the other side argues for a body that, at least as a last resort, is primarily judicial, assigning that role to one particular court, the ICJ, and its contentious jurisdiction. The choices presented are too limited.

Once we leave the confines of the *Marbury* analogy, there is little reason to fixate on the World Court's contentious jurisdiction. If the real issue is judicial (de)legitimation,

---

[36] Lauterpacht, *supra* note 25, *passim. See also* Gowlland-Debbas, *supra* note 4, at 670.

[37] As suggested in Scott, *supra* note 1, at 133 n.409. As the Memorial indicates, however, this does not necessarily apply to the effect of an ICJ determination regarding *jus cogens. Id.* at 133–39.

[38] Indeed, the Orders on provisional measures in the *Lockerbie* and *Bosnia* cases reflect the Court's desire to limit the scope of these cases. Bosnia's case has been reduced, on jurisdictional grounds, to issues directly arising from the Genocide Convention. *See* Orders of Apr. 8 and Sept. 13, 1993 ICJ REP. 3, 325. The Court has also limited Libya's cases against the United States and the United Kingdom to action under the Montreal Convention. *See* Lockerbie, 1992 ICJ REP. 3, 114.

[39] *See, e.g.,* de Waart, *supra* note 19, at 62 (criticizing the Orders for "negligen[ce] in protecting the sovereignty of member states").

[40] Franck, *supra* note 5, at 218–19; Franck, *supra* note 4.

[41] *See, e.g.,* Reisman, *Crisis, supra* note 4, at 90–94 (criticizing the Orders for lack of deference to the Council).

[42] Even within the United States, it is well to remember that it was not until its decision in *Dred Scott* in 1857, 54 years after *Marbury* was decided, that the Supreme Court was again to find federal legislation unconstitutional. Scott v. Sandford, 60 U.S. (19 How.) 393 (1857).

[43] Reisman, *Crisis, supra* note 4, at 97–99.

not the threat of a binding finding of nullity, many pronouncements that the World Court might foreseeably make may either help or hurt the Council's image: from an advisory opinion critical of the Council, to a decision dismissing either a request for an advisory opinion or a contentious case incidentally casting doubt on a Council action, or even to a decision affirming the Council's edicts but containing dissenting or concurring opinions that give its actions a particular interpretive gloss.

It cannot be assumed that the Court's advisory jurisdiction poses no threat to the Council.[44] While the Council would not ask for an advisory opinion if the risk of embarrassment were too great or the possibility of an adverse opinion unacceptable, its initial assumptions—about either the course of future events or the ultimate scope of the Court's opinion—might prove wrong. Yet, given the level of compliance with the Court's advisory opinions and the difficulty of enforcing its contentious judgments, the Council's options might be, in practical terms, as constrained by an advisory opinion as they would be by an adverse decision in a case like *Lockerbie*.[45] Ignoring the Court's advisory jurisdiction in this connection seems shortsighted in view of the importance that jurisdiction has had in developing UN institutional law.[46] Indeed, some of the more daring teleological interpretations of the Charter have come in the form of advisory judgments, perhaps because the Court, when asked an abstract question in a technically nonbinding context, is freer to roam.[47]

One should also not ignore the potential for development of that mode of jurisdiction. Although advisory opinions are limited to issues arising directly under the requesting organ's jurisdiction, in the future UN organs or other organizations might be more daring in their interpretation of what lies within their competence. Even so limited, there are plenty of advisory questions another UN organ such as the Assembly or another international organization might pose that overlap with the scope of the Council's opera-

---

[44] Reisman acknowledges the potential for judicial review in the Court's advisory jurisdiction and recognizes that such opinions are not devoid of political and legal force. As he puts it, "[a] statement of the law, rendered according to due process by a court obliged to decide according to law, cannot help but say something authoritative about the law." *Id.* at 92.

[45] *Id. But see* Watson, *supra* note 4, at 27 (asserting that contentious cases have arguably greater "precedential" value).

[46] Much of international institutional law has been influenced by the Court's advisory opinions. Consider, for example, the impact of the *Reparation* case on the doctrines of implied powers, legal personality and treaty-making capacity, and on the interpretive "principle of effectiveness"; the impact of the *Certain Expenses* case on peacekeeping powers, the scope of the General Assembly's powers vis-à-vis the Council's, and the "duty to pay"; the determination of the *Effect of Awards* case of the scope of a UN organ's power to create "independent" subsidiary organs; and the impact of the *Namibia* case on the General Assembly's implied powers, the role of institutional practice in the interpretation of the Charter, and the meanings of such Charter terms as "abstention," "dispute" and "situation." Reparation for injuries suffered in the service of the United Nations, 1949 ICJ REP. 174 (Apr. 11) [hereinafter Reparation]; Certain expenses of the United Nations (Article 17, paragraph 2, of the Charter), 1962 ICJ REP. 151 (July 20) [hereinafter Certain Expenses]; Effect of awards of compensation made by the United Nations Administrative Tribunal, 1954 ICJ REP. 47 (July 13) [hereinafter Effect of Awards]; Namibia, 1971 ICJ REP. 16. Indeed, even once-controversial advisory opinions have proven influential with time. Thus, the *Conditions of Admission* opinion, the subject of a contentious nine-to-six ruling by the Court, expressed the view that "the political character of an organ cannot release it from the observance of the treaty provisions established by the Charter when they constitute limitations on its powers or criteria for its judgment." Admission of a State to the United Nations (Charter, Art. 4), 1948 ICJ REP. 57 (May 28). This acknowledged limitation on the power of UN organs provides the starting point for defenders of judicial review today.

[47] For one example, see the dissenting opinion of Judge Krylov in the *Reparation* case, 1949 ICJ REP. at 219 (pointing out the ways the Court's majority opinion constitutes, in his view, judicial legislation). *See also* Ervin P. Hexner, *Teleological Interpretations of Basic Instruments of Public International Organizations, in* LAW, STATE, AND INTERNATIONAL LEGAL ORDER 119 (Salo Engel ed., 1964). The Court's activism in its advisory capacity would hardly surprise those who have observed similar activism where domestic courts are authorized to render opinions on "abstract" questions. *See, e.g.,* Alec Stone, *Abstract Constitutional Review and Policy Making in Western Europe, in* COMPARATIVE JUDICIAL REVIEW AND PUBLIC POLICY 41, 50–55 (Donald W. Jackson & C. Neal Tate eds., 1992) [hereinafter COMPARATIVE REVIEW].

tions. Even today the Court faces two requests for advisory opinions that could prove embarrassing to permanent members of the Council, if not the Council itself: the requests by the General Assembly and the WHO regarding the legality of the threat or use of nuclear weapons.[48] It is easy to imagine requests for advisory opinions by other organs that might affect the Council's activities or future options.[49]

By the same token, the World Court's right to critique the Council should not be premised on the proposition that the Court is the "only institution" capable of verifying the law. As the drafters of the Charter conceded, the usual test for constitutionality is "general acceptance," and, given the paucity of cases that reach the Court and the need for day-to-day decisions, each UN organ is usually in charge of "verifying legality" and typically does so without incident.[50] As U.S. constitutional scholars have noted, institutional practices have had as much (or more) to do with certain constitutional developments in the United States as the U.S. Supreme Court.[51] Given the huge lacunae in case law and its haphazard nature, it is unwarranted to assume that constitutional development or innovation necessarily relies on a judicial imprimatur or that the legitimation of such developments requires a court's blessing. That notion is particularly problematic in the context of the United Nations and the Security Council—where the Court's involvement, given its jurisdictional limits, is necessarily attenuated when it comes to judging the Council's acts, where some chasms in the law of the Charter are wider than any gaps in U.S. constitutional law, and where many of the constitutional innovations in practice have not involved the Court's participation.[52] Those whose lodestar is *Marbury v. Madison* might also remember that the Supreme Court's opinion in that case merely presumed that the U.S. Constitution's indeterminacy on judicial review should be resolved by having federal courts independently review the Constitution. As Laurence Tribe has noted, no one, including Chief Justice Marshall, has yet demonstrated that the very premise of a written constitution would be disserved or that legislative power "would necessarily be unbounded if Congress itself judged the constitutionality of its enactments"—and, in fact, certain constitutional systems have

---

[48] ICJ Communiqué No. 94/24 (Dec. 23, 1994) (request based on GA Res. 49/75K (Dec. 15, 1994)). For one view of the wide range of issues posed by these cases, see Nicholas Rostow, *The World Health Organization, the International Court of Justice, and Nuclear Weapons*, 20 YALE J. INT'L L. 151 (1995).

[49] Consider, hypothetically, a WHO request for views on the health impact of a particular sanctions regime, or a request by ECOSOC directed at economic effects, or a request by the General Assembly relating to human rights effects. These requests could also someday come in the form of *jus cogens* challenges under Article 53 or 64 of the Vienna Convention on the Law of Treaties between States and International Organizations or between International Organizations, Mar. 21, 1986, UN Doc. A/CONF.129/15 (1986), *reprinted in* 25 ILM 543 (1986). Article 66 of the Convention envisions advisory opinions directed at testing the consistency of existing treaties with *jus cogens* (under either Article 53 or 64 of the Convention) and provides that any such advisory opinions would be "accepted as decisive by all the parties to the dispute concerned."

Note, however, that the potential for *judicial* delegitimation because of the Court's response to such wide-ranging opinions is particularly severe. As James Boyd White has noted in connection with the U.S. Supreme Court, a court's claim to special expertise and singular relevance might be lessened if it opines in the abstract. JAMES BOYD WHITE, WHEN WORDS LOSE THEIR MEANING 264–65 (1984); *see also infra* note 195.

[50] *See, e.g.*, LOUIS B. SOHN, RIGHTS IN CONFLICT: THE UNITED NATIONS AND SOUTH AFRICA 1–7, 39–61 (1994); Sohn, *supra* note 29, *passim.*

[51] *See, e.g.*, Bruce Ackerman & David Golove, *Is NAFTA Constitutional?*, 108 HARV. L. REV. 799 (1995) (discussing the impact of congressional and executive practices on the treaty power); PHILIP BOBBITT, CONSTITUTIONAL FATE 193 (1982) (contending that there are constitutional gaps so vast in U.S. Supreme Court precedent that Congress must have internalized certain limits).

[52] *See infra* note 82 (list of constitutional innovations). Louis Sohn has noted that there is an unfortunate preoccupation with the ICJ and courts generally, to the detriment of close scrutiny of the day-to-day constitutional developments undertaken by other organs. SOHN, *supra* note 50, at 174–75; Sohn, *supra* note 29, at 227.

operated on the premise that the legislature is responsible for resolving conflicts between statutes and the constitution.[53]

If the question is whether an entity exists that can serve as a potential "check" on the Council, the (de)legitimating powers of rival UN bodies need to be considered as well. The General Assembly, for instance, has repeatedly criticized the Council in connection with Bosnia and even for a time challenged the expenditures for the Council's war crimes Tribunal in the former Yugoslavia.[54] The Assembly, considering its authority over the UN budget, its powers to create potentially troublesome subsidiary organs and its ability to refer issues to other UN organs, it not the entirely toothless body that the Court arguably is.[55] The Human Rights Commission, as well as other institutional entities within or outside the UN system, could take an active interest in issues before the Council, for example, with respect to the impact on human rights of Council-imposed sanctions or use of force.[56] Consultations between organs may also help verify legality— as between the Secretary-General and the Council, or the Council and the Assembly.[57]

Prospects for (de)legitimation also exist through bodies created by the Council under its power to establish subsidiary organs (Article 29 of the Charter) or under implied chapter VII authority. These organs, including the Compensation Commission created to adjudicate claims against Iraq, the Iraq-Kuwait Boundary Commission, the Yugoslav and Rwandan war crimes commissions and Tribunals, the special commission created to oversee the destruction of weapons in Iraq, and the sanctions committees charged with overseeing the various regimes in place, are making determinations with possible long-term legal effects.[58] The clearest case of Council legitimation (with potential delegitimating effects) has already occurred within the Yugoslavia war crimes Tribunal. In response to defense arguments in the first case to be tried before that body, both the trial and appellate chambers have attempted to legitimize, in different ways, the Council's decision to establish the Tribunal. Responding to arguments that the Tribunal's establishment was an *ultra vires* action, the trial chamber found that the Council's chapter VII decision was an unreviewable "political question." Nevertheless, that chamber considered in some detail the defense arguments for illegality, refuting these in ways that imply future limits on the Council's powers.[59] By contrast, the appellate chamber, led by Judge Cassese, found

---

[53] LAURENCE H. TRIBE, AMERICAN CONSTITUTIONAL LAW 25 (2d ed. 1988).

[54] *See, e.g.*, GA Res. 48/88 (Dec. 20, 1993), and 47/121 (Dec. 18, 1992); BEDJAOUI, *supra* note 4, at 123–26. *See also* GA Res. 41/31 (Nov. 3, 1986) (calling on the United States to comply with the Court's Judgment in the *Nicaragua* case).

[55] *See* UN CHARTER Arts. 10, 17, 22; BEDJAOUI, *supra* note 4, at 125–26.

[56] For concerns along these grounds, see, e.g., MIDDLE EAST WATCH, HUMAN RIGHTS WATCH, NEEDLESS DEATHS IN THE GULF WAR: CIVILIAN CASUALTIES DURING THE AIR CAMPAIGN AND VIOLATIONS OF THE LAWS OF WAR (1991).

[57] Reisman, *Crisis, supra* note 4, at 98–99; Louis B. Sohn, *The Use of Consultations for Monitoring Compliance with Agreements Concluded under the Auspices of International Organizations, in* EFFECTIVE SUPERVISION, *supra* note 19, at 65.

[58] *See, e.g.*, Murphy, *supra* note 9, at 235–46; John R. Crook, *The United Nations Compensation Commission—A New Structure to Enforce State Responsibility,* 87 AJIL 144 (1993); David J. Bederman, *The United Nations Compensation Commission and the Tradition of International Claims Settlement,* 27 N.Y.U. J. INT'L L. & POL. 1 (1994); THE UNITED NATIONS COMPENSATION COMMISSION (Richard B. Lillich ed., 1995) [hereinafter COMPENSATION COMMISSION].

[59] Prosecutor v. Tadić, Case IT–94–1–T, Decision on Jurisdiction, paras. 16, 40 (Aug. 10, 1995). Thus, the chamber found that the Council had not acted "arbitrarily" in establishing the Yugoslav Tribunal but had acted as a result of a protracted incremental process; that none of the arguable limits on the Council's powers, "whether imposed by the terms of the Charter or general principles of international law and, in particular, *jus cogens,*" were applicable; that the Tribunal was established to prosecute under customary law and not "some eccentric and novel code of conduct or some wholly irrational criterion"; that, while the Council's finding of a threat or breach of the peace was nonjusticiable, establishment of the Tribunal was "a seemingly entirely appropriate reaction to a situation in which international peace is clearly endangered"; that establishment of the Tribunal was an appropriate measure under Charter Article 41 because states believed that it would assist in the restoration of peace and serve a deterrent effect; that the Council, like the General Assembly,

that its inherent "incidental" power to determine the propriety of its own jurisdiction (*compétence de la compétence*) permitted review of the legality of the Council's actions in establishing the Tribunal.[60] It then proceeded to find that the Council's powers, while not "unlimited," encompassed the creation of a judicial tribunal as a measure "not involving the use of force" under Article 41 of chapter VII.[61] Perhaps most interestingly, the appeals chamber found that the Tribunal had been "established by law" because it was created with "full guarantees of fairness, justice and even-handedness, in full conformity with internationally recognized human rights instruments."[62]

While the Council did not establish the Yugoslav Tribunal to buttress its own legitimacy, this and other subsidiary bodies were created as mechanisms for more impartial and apolitical judgments than are possible within the Council.[63] Through these delegations of authority the Council has created potential alternatives to its own politicized processes.[64] As the Tribunal's decisions issued to date suggest, in at least some of these instances the body is "subsidiary" in name only and can render final judgments that even the Council is not authorized to disturb—and that in turn can disturb the Council by suggesting limits on its powers.[65]

Even assuming that international legality needs a more judicialized, "neutral" verifier of legitimacy than a self-judging UN organ or a subsidiary organ that owes its existence and mandate to the Security Council, the Court need not remain the only possibility. Indirect challenges to Council actions might be brought through ad hoc or other arbitra-

---

has the power to create a subsidiary judicial body; and that the principle of *jus de non evocando* (requiring that accused be tried by regular and not specially created courts) is not applicable to action under chapter VII. *Id.*, paras. 16, 17, 19, 23–27, 35, 37.

[60] Prosecutor v. Tadić, Case IT–94–1–AR72, paras. 18–22 (Oct. 2, 1995). In so doing, the appeals chamber rejected the trial chamber's resort to the political question doctrine and affirmed that the first obligation of any court is to ascertain its own competence. *Id.*, para. 18. The appeals chamber rejected as irrelevant the prosecutor's plea that the Tribunal was not established to scrutinize the actions of UN organs. *Id.*, para. 20. Significantly, in deciding that it had jurisdiction to consider this question, the chamber cited the ICJ's Advisory Opinions in *Namibia* and *Effect of Awards*. *Id.*, para. 21.

[61] *Id.*, paras. 28–36. It further found that the Council is empowered to turn to a judicial body as its instrument, citing once again the ICJ's *Effect of Awards* Advisory Opinion. *Id.*, paras. 37–38.

[62] *Id.*, para. 45; *see also* paras. 46–47.

[63] *See, e.g., id.*, paras. 37–38 (arguing that, while the Council is not provided with judicial powers, it can turn to judicial bodies to fulfill its purposes).

[64] These bodies have not escaped criticism. Iraq and others have criticized the one-sided nature of the mandate and structure of the Compensation Commission—which gives Iraq little say in the Commission's work and fails to provide for consideration of any claims by Iraq or Iraqi nationals, including claims stemming from alleged violations of humanitarian law by the allied forces during the Persian Gulf conflict. *See, e.g.,* UN Doc. S/22456 (1991) (letter of Apr. 6, 1991, from Iraqi Minister of Foreign Affairs to UN Secretary-General and President of the Security Council); Murphy, *supra* note 9, at 238–39. *See also* Frederic L. Kirgis, Jr., *Claims Settlement and the United Nations Legal Structure, in* COMPENSATION COMMISSION, *supra* note 58, at 103 (criticizing the Council for, among other things, the lack of procedural safeguards within the Compensation Commission). Similarly, the Boundary Commission's limited mandate assumed the legitimacy and legal status of a treaty, which Iraq contested. UN Doc. S/22456, *supra.* Observers of sanctions committees have criticized the methods and procedures under which these committees operate and have recommended changes to encourage transparency and consistency. Michael P. Scharf & Joshua L. Dorosin, *Interpreting UN Sanctions: The Rulings and Role of the Yugoslavia Sanctions Committee,* 19 BROOK. J. INT'L L. 1 (1993). Some of these problems may be resolved if these "technical" bodies develop processes more akin to those deployed by administrative courts. *Cf.* Mauro Cappelletti, *Fundamental Guarantees of the Parties in Civil Litigation: Comparative Constitutional, International and Social Trends,* 25 STAN. L. REV. 651, 686 (1973) (discussing such transformations within domestic legal systems).

Some have also criticized aspects of the Council's procedures for handling war crimes in the former Yugoslavia. *See, e.g.,* de Waart, *supra* note 19, at 63–64 (criticizing the establishment of the Yugoslav war crimes Tribunal for not taking into account the "vox populi" of the General Assembly); ABA SECTION OF INTERNATIONAL LAW AND PRACTICE, REPORT ON THE INTERNATIONAL TRIBUNAL TO ADJUDICATE WAR CRIMES COMMITTED IN THE FORMER YUGOSLAVIA (1993) (noting some potential problems with protection of defendants' rights).

[65] *See* text *supra* at notes 59–62. Once ad hoc war crimes tribunals are established as "independent," their independence cannot be trammeled. *See generally* Effect of Awards, 1954 ICJ REP. 47.

Collective Security Law

tions[66] or before other institutional fora.[67] From the standpoint of the Council's and the system's legitimacy, we might be as concerned about such challenges as by the possibility of litigation in the World Court. Indeed, given the jurisdictional hurdles to successful pursuit of a contentious case before the Court, the prospect of such challenges—admittedly meager—is worth as much attention as cases before the ICJ. A party to the Chicago Convention, for instance, might bring a challenge, culminating in arbitration, that casts doubt on the legality of a Council sanctions program directed at international aviation.[68] Depending on who participates, the legal or political impact of such arbitral findings might be considerable. Arbitral criticism of Council action could even be seen as having the benefit of greater neutrality than the Court's; unlike ICJ judges, such arbitrators would neither be part of, nor compensated by, the UN system they would be criticizing. National courts may also be the fora for (de)legitimation of the Council's edicts.[69]

Review by the ICJ also needs to be seen on a continuum with nonadjudicative modes of (de)legitimation, including unilateral disobedience by members.[70] The threat to the

---

[66] For a summary of some of these possibilities and their potential significance, see John H. Barton & Barry E. Carter, *International Law and Institutions for a New Age*, 81 GEO. L.J. 535 (1993). One could envision, for example, disputes brought under bilateral investment treaties (BITs) or treaties of friendship, commerce and navigation (FCNs) by parties anxious to test the limits of Council economic sanctions or their interpretation. FCNs typically grant a private right of action, at least in U.S. courts, while BITs give investors the right to take treaty violations to arbitration. A private investor's arbitral claim against a state that invokes a Council resolution as a defense to its BIT obligation to permit the free transfer of profits might be brought, for instance, to test the resolution's purported direct effect on private parties and their contracts. In some cases the Council has anticipated these possibilities and has attempted to terminate private rights of action in domestic courts or under a treaty. *See, e.g.*, SC Res. 687, para. 29 (Apr. 3, 1991). Presumably, those who object to ICJ review are equally willing to deprive private parties of any rights under existing treaties or other laws even when the Council does not explicitly indicate that these actions might undercut the effectiveness of its program. But note that the effect of the termination of such private rights of action goes beyond protecting the Council's supremacy. In practice, if the individual hurt by the sanction has no remedy, each member's interpretation of the scope and domestic effect of Council resolutions has been given primacy. Absent remedial action by the Council, individuals may have no remedy even when a state has applied the sanction too broadly, to the detriment of contractual or other rights.

[67] For instance, a GATT panel proceeding addressing the scope of a UN sanctions regime in response to a GATT party's accusation that certain measures were not required by the Council but are being taken for protectionist reasons.

[68] Convention on International Civil Aviation, Dec. 7, 1944, Art. 84, 61 Stat. 1180, 15 UNTS 295 (Chicago Convention).

[69] *See, e.g.*, Diggs v. Shultz, 470 F.2d 461 (D.C. Cir. 1972) (finding Council sanctions against Rhodesia unenforceable in the face of a later-in-time federal statute); People of Saipan v. United States Dep't of Interior, 502 F.2d 90 (9th Cir. 1974) (finding self-executing a trusteeship agreement supervised by the Council and rejecting as too tenuous the possibility of enforcement by the Security Council); Bosphorus Hava Yollari Turizm Ve Ticaret Anonim Sirketi v. Minister for Transport, [1994] 2 I.L.R.M. 551 (Ir. High Ct.) (addressing the scope of Yugoslav sanctions and the weight to be given to the views of a Council sanctions committee). Indeed, as Council actions implicate a greater number of issues, domestic court challenges to Council action become more likely. *See, e.g.*, Conforti, *supra* note 7, at 144 (noting that municipal courts might be tempted to contest the legitimacy of Council decisions when there is no verification of their legality). Thus, a zealous lawyer, defending the next Duško Tadić prior to the client's transfer to the Yugoslav war crimes Tribunal, would probably attempt to challenge the Tribunal's jurisdiction in domestic court. *Cf. supra* notes 59–62.

[70] Those examining judicial review to date have not considered the possible relevance of other supervisory mechanisms. *Cf.* Ignaz Seidl-Hohenveldern, *Failure of Controls in the Sixth International Tin Agreement*, in EFFECTIVE SUPERVISION, *supra* note 19, at 255, 270–71 (proposing that organizational immunity be lifted in certain cases to give domestic courts a larger role in legitimizing the activities of organizations); Eric Suy, *The Development of Supervisory Mechanisms within the CSCE Framework*, in *id.* at 83, 91–92 (discussing the legitimating role of public access to CSCE meetings); Nicolas Valticos, *Once More about the ILO System of Supervision: In What Respect Is It Still a Model?*, in *id.* at 99 (discussing whether the International Labour Organization's various distinctive methods of supervision remain a model for other international organizations). For an overview of supervisory forms, including "internal" supervision (as by administrative tribunals), and their possible impact, see Niels Blokker & Sam Muller, *Some Concluding Observations*, in *id.* at 275. The (de)legitimating impact of "Legal Opinions of the Secretariat," published annually in the *UN Juridical Yearbook*, is also worth considering. For a survey of alternative ways to make the international system more accountable and expand participation, without judicial review as such, see Note, *Discretion and Legitimacy in International Regulation*, 107 HARV. L. REV. 1099 (1994).

Council's legitimacy is not necessarily greater when it is posed by an adjudicative body. Threats might be more serious when members take the law into their own hands and fail to abide by the Council's edicts because they perceive these to be illegal and/ or unjust—as is suggested by the questionable compliance with many recent Council resolutions by recalcitrant targeted states or third states unwilling to bear the pain of sanctions. Moreover, lack of compliance is not necessarily limited to nonpermanent members. At this writing, the U.S. Congress is mounting an assault on the Executive's power to engage in UN peacekeeping, especially the President's power to commit troops or finances.[71] While realists may be correct that the prospective withholding of financial or other support for Council initiatives, not some possible ICJ decision, is the most serious ongoing threat to the future efficacy and legitimacy of the Council, they do not adequately explain why judicial review is the worse of the two delegitimating evils.

Finally, greater attention must be paid to the connections between complaints about an "unrepresentative" Security Council and proposals for judicial review. "Democratizing" Council reforms and judicial review may not be linked merely by cause and effect. It is not clear that procedural reforms of the Council's operations can serve as a substitute for judicial review.[72] Nor is it clear that judicial review will necessarily ameliorate complaints about the Council's lawmaking.[73] Judicial review and "democratizing" reforms may not be rival formulas to solve a common problem—the flagging legitimacy of the Council—but symbiotic phenomena. As Joseph Weiler's accounts of the history of judicial activism within the European Union might suggest, the effects of more assertive judicial review of Council action may be "bidirectional and even circular."[74]

While in some instances ICJ review culminating in an affirmation of the legality of Council action may, as legalists suggest, legitimize the Council, the long-term effects are less clear. Judicial review by the ICJ, far from being an "answer" to those seeking to buttress the Council's sagging legitimacy, may promote more strident cries for an increase in the number and diversity of permanent members holding the veto power, or at least demands for active participation by more UN members anxious to assert their political voice (as through greater General Assembly involvement in issues relating to peace and security or through reforms in the membership of the Court and the Council). Faced with the prospect of "constitutionalization" of the UN system, nonpermanent

---

[71] *See, e.g.*, International Peacekeeping Policy Act of 1995, S. 420, 104th Cong., 1st Sess. (1995); National Security Revitalization Act, H.R. 7, 104th Cong., 1st Sess.; and Peace Powers Act of 1995, S. 5, 104th Cong., 1st Sess. For background, see WASH. WKLY. REP., Nov. 1994–May 1995.

[72] *Compare* Reisman, *Crisis, supra* note 4, at 98–99 (proposing an "informational loop" between the Council and the Assembly) *with* Bowett, *supra* note 4, at 97 (advocating judicial review since there is no guarantee that legal rights will be protected by the "political" Assembly).

[73] *Cf.* Franck, *supra* note 4.

[74] Generalizing from the EU experience and inspired by Hirschman's work on "exit and voice" in other disciplines, Joseph Weiler has suggested that lawmaking by international bodies may follow a peculiar dynamic: successful international organizations evolve into effective lawmaking institutions when members forgo their sovereign option to "exit" (either totally or selectively) and opt instead to correct organizational inadequacies by exercising a greater "voice" in the organizations' decision-making processes. J. H. H. Weiler, *The Transformation of Europe,* 100 YALE L.J. 2403 (1991) (drawing from ALBERT O. HIRSCHMAN, EXIT, VOICE AND LOYALTY: RESPONSES TO DECLINE IN FIRMS, ORGANIZATIONS, AND STATES (1970)). Weiler argues that the more an international organization successfully "legislates" (in the sense of promulgating rules that are binding both on and within states), the more members consciously involve themselves in the organization's ways of making law. *Id.* at 2466–67. He argues that at times the relationship between legal and political developments in the European Union was "bidirectional and even circular," with the "integrating legal developments at least indirectly influenc[ing] the disintegrating political ones." *Id.* at 2426. *See also* David J. Gerber, *The Transformation of European Community Competition Law?,* 35 HARV. INT'L L.J. 97 (1994) (applying Weiler's insights and finding similar bidirectional effects among Court, Commission and national institutions). Weiler's ideas may also find some resonance in the work of those who have examined the evolution of judicial review in domestic legal systems, especially the constitutionalization of formerly socialist states. *See, e.g.*, William Kitchin, *Establishing and Exercising Judicial Review in the Soviet Union: The Beginnings, in* COMPARATIVE REVIEW, *supra* note 47, at 59.

14   THE AMERICAN JOURNAL OF INTERNATIONAL LAW   [Vol. 90:1

members might, over time, seek a greater voice in the formulation of Council decisions.[75] Faced with judicial review, even permanent members might seek changes in the structure of the Court. Without some attention to this need for a greater "voice," the ultimate legitimacy of the Charter scheme may suffer.

On the other hand, in the short run ICJ judgments that critique Council action could undermine institutional legitimacy, as the realists argue. But the long-term effects are less clear. As judicial review has done within the European Union, ICJ review, particularly if combined with restructuring proposals to give more members a greater voice in the Council (or even perhaps the Court), could legitimize the constitutional order, help avoid unilateral resort to self-help measures in defiance of the collective security system, and strengthen, not weaken, international law.[76] Without knowing whether one is addressing the short or long term, and whether or not one is anticipating restructuring *combined* with more robust forms of judicial review, it is hard to tell whether "judicial review" will be detrimental or helpful to the Charter order.

II. TEXTUAL DETERMINACY AND JUDICIAL LEGITIMATION

Those considering the issue of judicial review rely on the Charter's text and history for two purposes. First, they rely on these texts, and their alleged (in)determinacy, to come to distinct conclusions about whether it would be permissible for ICJ judges to engage in "judicial review." Second, they rely on these texts, and their alleged (in)determinacy, to come to differing conclusions about whether ICJ judges have anything to contribute to the question of the legality of Council acts; that is, to determine whether ICJ judges could engage in "review" even if that were permissible.

As the differing conclusions suggest, one can scarcely rely on the Charter's text or emanations from the Charter's negotiating history to come to any practical conclusions about the Court's options.[77] Such textual or formalist approaches focus either on the lack of explicit license in the UN Charter for judicial review or on the presumed intent behind the founders' rejection of Belgium's proposals during the negotiation of the Charter,[78] or, alternatively, on proposed hidden "core" meanings in such Charter terms

---

[75] For suggestions to this effect, see, e.g., Ruth Gordon, *United Nations Intervention in Internal Conflicts: Iraq, Somalia, and Beyond*, 15 MICH. J. INT'L L. 519, 527 (1994); Mohammed Bedjaoui, *Introduction: On the Efficacy of International Organizations: Some Variations on an Inexhaustible Theme* . . ., in EFFECTIVE SUPERVISION, *supra* note 19, at 7, 18; BEDJAOUI, *supra* note 4, at 37. Moreover, to the extent other groups within states become more aware of the impact on their interests of decisions taken by executive branch officials, we might also expect increased concern with the lack of direct democratic accountability. The "democratic deficit" in UN lawmaking is being increasingly addressed by a restive U.S. Congress, which at this writing seems intent on asserting a greater role with respect to UN peace operations. *See supra* note 71.

[76] *Cf.* de Waart, *supra* note 19, at 61–64 (advocating judicial review by the ICJ *and* that members' representatives to the Assembly act under the democratic supervision of their national parliaments).

[77] *See, e.g.*, Watson, *supra* note 4; Herdegen, *supra* note 4, at 152–54; Scott, *supra* note 1, esp. at 75–87, 119–25; Roberts, *supra* note 4, at 289–93.

[78] During the negotiation of the Charter in 1945, Belgium had sought, first, an amendment providing as follows:

> Any State, party to a dispute brought before the Security Council, shall have the right to ask the Permanent Court of International Justice whether a recommendation or a decision made by the Council or proposed in it infringes on its essential rights. If the Court considers that such rights have been disregarded or are threatened, it is for the Council either to reconsider the question or to refer the dispute to the Assembly for decision.

Doc. 2, G/7(k)(1), 3 U.N.C.I.O. Docs. 335, 336 (1945). When this proposal failed to win support, Belgium attempted to secure an amendment providing that the Committee on Legal Problems "should determine the proper interpretative organ for the several parts of the Charter." Doc. 664, IV/2/33, 13 *id.* at 633, 633. This, too, failed to win support, and one commentator, reviewing this history, concludes that "the framers did not wish the Charter to authorize judicial review 'as an established procedure.'" Watson, *supra* note 4, at 12.

as "threat to the international peace" or on a presumed license for review inherent in Article 25 (making Council decisions binding when "in accordance with the present Charter"). All these approaches are question begging, attractive only to the already converted on the advisability of judicial review. The Charter's negotiating history, even if relevant,[79] is sufficiently ambiguous to permit many avenues of redress in the ICJ, with the possible exception of an "established procedure" under which all legal questions are routinely passed upon by the Court.[80]

The importance of the supposed lack of constitutional warrant for judicial review lies in the eyes of the beholder. Many domestic courts and even some international tribunals have assumed, without formal constitutional warrant, a license to engage in constitutional review or have considerably expanded a constitutional license explicitly conferred.[81] The ICJ itself and the United Nations as a whole have often engaged in creative interpretations of the Charter, creating doctrines and powers out of whole cloth, without Charter amendment or explicit Charter license.[82] The real question is whether and when to engage in

---

[79] Cf. Certain Expenses, 1962 ICJ REP. at 184–97 (Spender, J., sep. op.) (giving reasons why reliance on the presumed original intent of the Charter drafters is "beset with evident difficulties").

[80] See, e.g., Watson, supra note 4; Scott, supra note 1, at 82–87. Reacting to the original Belgian appeal for regularized Court review of Council action (see supra note 78), the U.S. delegate indicated that:

> He did not interpret the Proposals as preventing any state from appealing to the International Court of Justice at any time on any matter which might properly go before the Court. On the whole, he did not consider the acceptance of the Belgian Amendment advisable, particularly since he believed that the Security Council was bound to act in accordance with the principles of justice and international law.

Doc. 433, III/2/15, 12 U.N.C.I.O. Docs. 47, 49 (1945); see also Doc. 873, IV/2/37, 13 id. at 653 (1945). The subcommittee examining the issue at the time rejected the Belgian proposal but decided to approve the report

> on the interpretation of the Charter which suggested that if two member states are at variance concerning the interpretation of the Charter, they are free to submit the dispute to the Court, and that if two organs are at variance concerning the correct interpretation of the Charter they may either ask the Court for an advisory opinion, establish an ad hoc committee of jurists to examine the question and report its views, or have recourse to a joint conference.

Id. at 654. This record implies that those involved in the drafting most probably did not intend to vest the Court with "exclusive power to provide an authoritative interpretation of the Charter." Sohn, supra note 29, at 203.

[81] For constitutional developments within the European Union, see Weiler, supra note 74; Joseph H. H. Weiler, Eurocracy and Distrust: Some Questions concerning the Role of the European Court of Justice in the Protection of Fundamental Human Rights within the Legal Order of the European Communities, 61 WASH. L. REV. 1103 (1986); Paul R. Dubinsky, The Essential Function of Federal Courts: The European Union and the United States Compared, 42 AM. J. COMP. L. 295, esp. 340–46 (1994). Indeed, Dubinsky argues that the European Court of Justice's judicial activism is in part due to the open-ended principles contained in the treaties it has been expounding. Id. at 346. For other examples of the assumption of judicial review powers without explicit constitutional warrant, see ALLAN R. BREWER-CARIAS, JUDICIAL REVIEW IN COMPARATIVE LAW (1989); JUDICIAL ACTIVISM IN COMPARATIVE PERSPECTIVE (Kenneth M. Holland ed., 1991); COMPARATIVE REVIEW, supra note 47.

[82] Today, when we have de facto amended the Charter provisions on deployment of UN forces pursuant to Article 43 agreements and at the direction of a Military Staff Committee; when the Council has delegated important functions to judicial and quasi-judicial bodies such as an international criminal court, a compensation commission and sanctions committees; when the Council has taken purportedly binding action under chapter VI; when the Organization has resorted to budget making by consensus instead of the two-thirds vote envisioned in Article 18; when it has created peacekeeping out of an imagined "chapter VI and one-half" and insisted on forceful implementation of sanctions pursuant to a nonexistent "Article 41 and one-half"; when the Organization has managed to seat Russia instead of the USSR as a permanent member despite the wording of Article 27; and when it has resorted to "peacekeeping with teeth" in situations probably never contemplated by the framers—as in assistance in humanitarian crises (UNISOM II in Somalia, UNPROFOR in Croatia) or in response to prior aggression (UNIKOM in Iraq)—the burden appears to be on those who insist that we need a Charter amendment to permit the Court to interpret the Charter. For other examples, see Sohn, supra note 29, at 226–29 (contending that the UN Charter, in its 50 years, has seen more interpretive changes than the U.S. Constitution in 200); Helmut Freudenschuß, Between Unilateralism and Collective Security: Authorization of the Use of Force by the UN Security Council, 5 EUR. J. INT'L L. 492 (1994) (surveying the Council's innovations in the deployment of force since Aug. 5, 1990). See also Kirgis, supra note 3. Such constitutional creativity absent formal amendment also undermines one conceivable rationale for denigrating judicial review,

16   THE AMERICAN JOURNAL OF INTERNATIONAL LAW   [Vol. 90:1

such creative interpretations. It is time to begin addressing exactly why formal Charter amendment is needed for "judicial review" to occur.[83]

Similarly unsatisfactory is the attempt to rely on textual determinacy to decide whether ICJ judges have the tools to review Council acts. Realists contend that Article 39 and chapter VII generally are so "elastic" that there is nothing to review and no rules to apply. For them, to give ICJ judges the power to fill the Charter's vast normative gaps would contravene the Charter scheme since, for good or ill, the Charter accords power and primacy to a politically accountable body, the Council, and not to unrepresentative, unaccountable judges. Realists question both the existence of rules and the ability of judges to function without them.

The argument fails to consider how domestic judges in constitutional and other settings have dealt with similar challenges or why such comparisons are necessarily inapplicable to the UN setting.[84] It fails, for instance, to consider how noninternational scholars have confronted similar challenges—as when the role of national judges has had to be defended from the claim that theirs is an inherently value-laden enterprise, not a mechanistic one producing right answers under fixed and settled rules.[85] Further, even assuming that rule skeptics are right about the "elastic" content of chapter VII of the Charter, not all potentially relevant rights of sovereigns are similarly elastic or content free. Merely because some Charter rules are void because of vagueness does not indicate that all sovereign rights are.[86] Realists' arguments would be more satisfying if they explained precisely which institutional or other flaws prevent ICJ judges from doing what national judges do when interstices in the law must be filled. Are they claiming that ICJ judges have no new or distinct perspectives to bear on an issue such as the legality of Council-approved sanctions against Libya?[87] Or that ICJ judges inhabit a system incapable of generating legal determinations perceived as "objective" and therefore worthy of being obeyed?[88]

That some of the rules in the Charter may be textually "indeterminate" does not foreclose the propriety of judicial review. The ICJ, other international tribunals and

---

namely, that an ICJ decision interpreting the Charter would be nearly impossible to "reverse" given the difficulty of amending the Charter under its Article 108.

[83] *Cf.* Dubinsky, *supra* note 81, at 342–44 (suggesting, in the context of the European Union and the United States, that explicit constitutional amendment facilitates acceptance of judicial activism). This assumes that there is an "antimajoritarian" difficulty to be addressed as regards the European Union. *But see* Weiler, *supra* note 81, at 1115–19 (explaining why the antimajoritarian difficulty did not seem applicable to the European Court, at least in 1986).

[84] *See, e.g.*, David M. Beatty, *Human Rights and the Rules of Law*, in HUMAN RIGHTS AND JUDICIAL REVIEW: A COMPARATIVE PERSPECTIVE 1 (David M. Beatty ed., 1994); Weiler, *supra* note 81; Watson, *supra* note 4, at 28–33; Alec Stone, *Judging Socialist Reform: The Politics of Coordinate Construction in France and Germany*, 26 COMP. POL. STUD. 443 (1994). For a summary of arguments addressing the "countermajoritarian" difficulty posed by the U.S. federal judiciary, see Steven P. Croley, *The Majoritarian Difficulty: Elective Judiciaries and the Rule of Law*, 62 U. CHI. L. REV. 689, 700–13, 748–53 (1995).

[85] *See, e.g.*, Heidi Feldman, *Objectivity in Legal Judgment*, 92 MICH. L. REV. 1187 (1994).

[86] *Cf.* Oscar Schachter, *United Nations Law in the Gulf Conflict*, 85 AJIL 452, 468–69 (1991) (suggesting that even aggressors retain some inalienable rights).

[87] *Cf.* text at and notes 187–96 *infra* (discussion of J. B. White model of review). For an examination of how adjudicative models contribute to perceptions of procedural justice, see E. ALLAN LIND & TOM R. TYLER, THE SOCIAL PSYCHOLOGY OF PROCEDURAL JUSTICE (1988).

[88] If so, critics of the Court need to address why its 15 members, sitting in a setting far less politicized than the Security Council and enjoying a mandate to take a more long-term perspective, will invariably produce opinions that fail to generate perceptions of "objectivity" whenever Council actions are at issue. Compare Feldman, enumerating factors tending to produce such perceptions, *supra* note 85, at 1230–47 with, e.g., those who have sought to explain how the ICJ has "mediated positivism" by producing "a degree of certainty," invoking principles familiar to lawyers, or adopting a "magisterial" style, *see, e.g.*, Oscar Schachter, *The Nature and Process of Legal Development in International Society*, in THE STRUCTURE AND PROCESS OF INTERNATIONAL LAW 767 (Ronald St. J. Macdonald & Douglas M. Johnston eds., 1983).

many arbitral bodies have all handed down decisions rendered no less effective because the rules they were asked to apply were "indeterminate."[89]

Rule skepticism proves too much. If indeterminacy alone requires judicial abstention, then the Court should probably not have entertained any of the numerous maritime boundary disputes it has resolved over the years. Although the Court has arguably not carved out clear rules regarding the role of "equity" in such demarcations,[90] its success at settling these disputes has not been damaged thereby and their resolution remains, for most observers, the Court's most singular contribution. As these cases suggest, courts, including the World Court, are not just rule clarifiers: they are dispute settlers and their achievement and prospects may be evaluated on a basis other than whether their opinions produce determinate rules with predictable application. Moreover, if the rule skeptics were right, the Court would have no business adjudicating even those disputes which the Council invites it to consider. If questions presented under Article 39 or chapter VII are nonjusticiable, the Council's permission would not make the underlying norms any more determinate.[91] Worse, indeterminacy would also bedevil Council efforts to submit "legal" disputes likely to endanger the international peace to the Court under chapter VI. The challenge is to examine the legitimating powers international courts do have— despite indeterminacy—and explain why those powers fail before the Council. Without isolating those criteria that make only certain types of its judgments "legitimate" and legitimating, it is impossible to say that the World Court should not hear cases merely because the Council is involved.

Even opponents of judicial review implicitly acknowledge that rule indeterminacy is not the problem it appears to be. Realist proponents of Council supremacy note, for example, that the Council cannot impose an absolute embargo denying a targeted population access to medicine or food, in violation of peremptory norms of the laws of war and/or human rights, and that its actions must generally be proportionate to the aims sought. They also contend that the Council must respect some essential core of sovereignty so that targeted states are not deprived of their right to statehood, including their right to self-preservation and to manage and govern their territory.[92] These argu-

---

[89] This assumes, of course, that some international legal norms are not "indeterminate." For an examination of the alleged "indeterminacy" of virtually every rule applied by the World Court, see MARTTI KOSKENNIEMI, FROM APOLOGY TO UTOPIA: THE STRUCTURE OF INTERNATIONAL LEGAL ARGUMENT (1989). For a look at the "indeterminacy" of many human rights norms, see Bruno Simma, *International Human Rights and General International Law: A Comparative Analysis, in* 4 COLLECTED COURSES OF THE ACADEMY OF EUROPEAN LAW, bk. 2, at 153 (1995). As both Koskenniemi and Simma would concede, that both ICJ and human rights judges have given content to "indeterminate" norms has not prevented the successful resolution of the underlying disputes.

[90] *See, e.g.,* L. D. M. Nelson, *The Roles of Equity in the Delimitation of Maritime Boundaries,* 84 AJIL 837 (1990); Jan Schneider, *The Gulf of Maine Case: The Nature of an Equitable Result,* 79 AJIL 539 (1985).

[91] *Cf.* Reisman, *Crisis, supra* note 4, at 88–89 (suggesting that in *Lockerbie*-type cases the proper course for the Court is to divine the Council's intent). This course requires that the Court make initial judgments on whether and what the Council wants reviewed. These determinations may themselves undermine the program of the Council since it may fail to anticipate the scope of the Court's subsequent judgment and might be as embarrassed by the result as by an "uninvited" judgment. This result is made more likely by the difficulties of any judicial attempt to divine the Council's "intent." To do so, the Court probably must determine, for example, the significance and status of interpretive statements by the Council's President—itself a controversial issue. *See, e.g.,* Anthony Aust, *The Procedure and Practice of the Security Council Today, in* COLLOQUE, *supra* note 4, at 365, 370–71. Certainly, its secretive consultations, the usual absence of legal advisers, and the lack of agreed records of nonpublic deliberations make study of the workings of the Council exceptionally difficult. *See, e.g., id.* at 366–68. Further, to the extent the Council's decisions, such as the imposition of complex sanctions against Iraq in 1991, need to be interpreted in light of underlying reports by the Secretariat, intriguing difficulties would arise for the Court if those reports were alleged to have been drafted with subsequent interpretation in mind.

[92] *See, e.g.,* Herdegen, *supra* note 4, at 154–59. Sur defends the legality of the Council's comprehensive measures against Iraq after the gulf war on the grounds, among others, that Resolution 687 required Iraq's "acceptance" of its provisions, that the Council did not itself "establish" Iraq's boundary with Kuwait, that

ments accord with legalists' views that the Council is not omnipotent and that some legal limits to its powers and competence exist. Where realists disagree is on the legitimacy of Council self-judgment.

On the other hand, merely affirming that rules exist for judges to apply—as some legalists do—does not indicate that the UN Charter creates an "état de droit" with built-in separation of powers. That the Council might be limited to action permitted by the Charter or international law or that the Council's institutional practice might plausibly be said to rest on principled and articulable standards does not address the ICJ's proper role.[93] Textual determinacy is not the key here, either.[94] If, as legalists argue, the ICJ legitimizes the rule of law, a more important question is that posed by some domestic scholars in the context of national courts: by what *process* does it do so? If, as some suggest for domestic courts, the role of the ICJ should be to promote perceptions that help ensure that the subjects of law need not be coerced into obeying it, how does the Court best accomplish this purpose?[95]

More generally, the legalists' view of the Court's legitimizing role is less persuasive than it might be for failure to articulate more precisely what "legitimation" means in this context. As Joseph Weiler has noted with respect to the European Union, there are various possibilities: "democratic legitimacy" generated by perceptions of real participation in governance; "formal legitimacy" generated by results produced from institutions or systems created through democratic processes; and "social legitimacy" connoting empirically determined social acceptance, which occurs when relevant actors display a commitment to and actively guarantee values that are part of the general political culture (such as justice, freedom and the general welfare).[96] The first two are troublesome at the UN level since the Security Council (and, arguably, the Organization generally) is not designed to be a democracy in the sense of equal participation by all sovereign states. Moreover, even if the Article 2 principle of "sovereign equality" were taken as the normative goal of the Charter, to be given effect by the Court despite the Council's membership and voting structure, it is not clear why the equal participation of states' executive branch officials should be assumed to be the exclusive or best touchstone for

---

the restrictions on weaponry did not amount to a complete "disarmament" of Iraq but rather were focused on weapons that were threatened or actually used during the war, and that the Council did not purport to find violations of treaties concluded outside the framework of the United Nations to which the United Nations was not a party. Sur, Resolution 687, *supra* note 11, at 17, 19, 25, 31. *See also* IAN JOHNSTONE, AFTERMATH OF THE GULF WAR: AN ASSESSMENT OF UN ACTION 19–23 (International Peace Academy, Occasional Paper Series, 1994).

[93] *Compare* Franck, *supra* note 12, at 192–218 (attempting to answer whether the Council "treat[s] like cases alike," and finding evidence of "principled standards") *with* Peter H. Kooijmans, *The Enlargement of the Concept of "Threat to the Peace," in* COLLOQUE, *supra* note 4, at 111 (concluding that it is difficult to find a "straight line" in the Council's threat-to-the-peace determinations, as "political considerations seem to be the determining factor"). Even Franck admits that what becomes clearest in examining the Council's practice is the evidence of changing views of certain basic Charter norms, such as a decrease in the impact of Article 2(7) (noninterference in domestic jurisdiction) as a limit on UN action. Franck, *supra*, at 211.

[94] As Professor Macdonald has noted, it is a mistake to attempt to distinguish law from politics by reference to "some quality of the legal rules and norms themselves. The distinctiveness of law lies instead in the particular style of reasoning and the way in which rules are used." Ronald St. J. Macdonald, *Changing Relations between the International Court of Justice and the Security Council of the United Nations,* 1993 ANNUAIRE CANADIEN DE DROIT INTERNATIONAL 3, 7.

[95] *Cf.* Feldman, *supra* note 85, at 1253.

[96] Weiler, *supra* note 74, at 2468–69. For one attempt at empirical measurement of the public legitimacy of the European Court of Justice, see Gregory A. Caldeira & James L. Gibson, *The Legitimacy of the Court of Justice in the European Union: Models of Institutional Support,* 89 AM. POL. SCI. REV. 356 (1995). For discussions of alternative formulations and possible components of "legitimacy," compare THOMAS M. FRANCK, THE POWER OF LEGITIMACY AMONG NATIONS 80, 81, 85, 86–88, 171–72 (1990) with Jose E. Alvarez, *The Quest for Legitimacy,* 24 N.Y.U. J. INT'L L. & POL. 199, 228–35 (1991) (reviewing FRANCK).

legitimacy. In an age of human rights and relativistic conceptions of "sovereignty,"[97] why should state-centric notions of "democratic" governance be central to the Court's determination? If the Council, with the full concurrence of a majority of the General Assembly, were to consent to genocide, should the Court affirm the legality of that act? Yet, to the extent the Court considers other values, aside from "democratic" participation by a sufficiently diverse body of states, which values should these be? Is there agreement on the touchstones for "social legitimacy" that the Court would confer?

Without a clearer description of the Court's mission and how it is supposed to accomplish it, one is hard put to discern which of several theoretical justifications for judicial review legalists have in mind (or, for that matter, which model of judicial review realists are intending to refute). The possibilities include (1) a consent-based model, grounded in the proposition that whatever the Court does is ultimately subject to correction via amendment of the Charter;[98] (2) a minority protection model, under which the Court's role is to protect a particular state or minority group of states whenever the majoritarian or hegemonic processes of the Council threaten their rights;[99] (3) a participation-based model, under which the Charter scheme is premised, more narrowly, on sovereign equality as to participation in UN governance, so that the Court is authorized to step in only when a state's participation rights are denied (but is not authorized to alter the substantive outcomes produced by those processes);[100] (4) a teleological model, grounded in achieving international peace and security at all costs;[101] and, most broadly of all, (5) a rights-based model, according to which the Charter is ultimately grounded in protecting the human rights of people, not states, and which authorizes the Court to review all legislative outcomes, including those produced by the Council, for consistency with these norms.[102] Each of these presents a very different conception of the Court's (de)legitimation role.

Moreover, even if one of these models seems most appropriate, legalists need to demonstrate why, of all possible adjudicative (de)legitimation fora, the ICJ is the best or most capable of being the last-resort defender of the chosen model. The ICJ seems an awfully slender reed on which to place such reliance. If the rule of law depends ultimately on the ICJ and its meager caseload as "last-resort defender," it is in trouble. Surely the realists are right to be skeptical about the ability of the Court to adopt at least some of these legitimation models. While the Council's "quasi-judicial" determinations—such as its findings on Iraq's financial liabilities[103]—might bear legal scrutiny under each of the legitimation models noted above, its more politicized (not to say ad hoc) judgments—such as the decision that there is sufficient political will to authorize

---

[97] *Compare* Louis Henkin, *An Agenda for the Next Century: The Myth and Mantra of State Sovereignty*, 35 VA. J. INT'L L. 115 (1994) (endorsing current trends) *with* Ernest S. Easterly, *The Rule of Law and the New World Order*, 22 S.U. L. REV. 161 (1995) (bemoaning the threatened loss of sovereignty).

[98] Compare, for example, the view of U.S. constitutional scholars who have stressed that judicial review can only be understood in the shadow of constitutional amendment processes. Akhil Reed Amar, *Philadelphia Revisited: Amending the Constitution Outside Article V*, 55 U. CHI. L. REV. 1043, 1044 (1988); *see also* Croley, *supra* note 84, at 750 n.179.

[99] *Cf.* Croley, *supra* note 84, at 750. *See, e.g.*, de Waart, *supra* note 19, at 49 (proposing a similar democratic governance model for the United Nations).

[100] *Cf.* Croley, *supra* note 84, at 751 & n.181. One concrete example might be South Africa's pleas in the *Namibia* case alleging denial of its participation rights in the Security Council. Namibia, 1971 ICJ REP. 16, paras. 23–25.

[101] *See, e.g.*, Sohn, *supra* note 29, at 186–87.

[102] *Cf.* Croley, *supra* note 84, at 704–05, 751. *See also* Bedjaoui, *supra* note 75, at 26 (suggesting a need to verify the legality of the Council's acts not only to reassure members but also "to assure 'the peoples,' when it is sought to mobilize them through world opinion, that there is nothing pernicious about the action contemplated by the Security Council").

[103] *See, e.g.*, SC Res. 687 (Apr. 3, 1991), *reprinted in* 30 ILM 847 (1991).

20   THE AMERICAN JOURNAL OF INTERNATIONAL LAW   [Vol. 90:1

sanctions against Libya but not against, say, Israel for its alleged international law violations—are difficult to scrutinize from a judicial perspective. Indeed, disentangling the difference between a quasi-judicial and a political judgment is itself problematic, and problems with the distinction do not necessarily lead to finding most disputes justiciable[104]—especially given the absence of a clear "equal protection" type of principle in the Charter (except the Article 2 reference to "sovereign equality").[105] A frontal attack on the Council's alleged "double standards" is an unlikely place for Council/Court interaction.[106] Few litigants are likely to go to the World Court to insist that the Council is legally obligated either to make an Article 39 determination or to undertake specific Article 41 or 42 action, and fewer still will be able to find a jurisdictional basis for doing so.[107]

III. THE MANY MODES OF COUNCIL-GENERATED "LAW"

ICJ judges may find it increasingly difficult to avoid "reviewing" Council action not because of a likelihood of relatively direct challenges like those brought initially by Libya and Bosnia, but because the law they may be asked to review relates to or relies on Council determinations. "Judicial review" in this broad sense, rather than in the narrow sense of *Marbury* in which a court finds action unconstitutional and void, is probably not an option that the Court can choose to forgo. As the Council generates more law, ICJ judges, elected to decide the law, will find it difficult to avoid reexamining some of that Council-generated law.

Particularly since its reactivation after the Cold War, but even before, the Council, more than other UN organs, has been generating abundant institutional law and significant precedents.[108] The instances are so numerous that they require but short summary here. Although the Council is not required to find a breach of international law to act, in several cases it has found such breaches (e.g., in connection with Southern Rhodesia,

---

[104] *See, e.g.*, Harper, *supra* note 3; André Beirlaen, *La Distinction entre les différends juridiques et les différends politiques dans la pratique des organisations internationales*, 11 REVUE BELGE DE DROIT INTERNATIONAL 405 (1975); Gowlland-Debbas, *supra* note 4, at 648–53.

[105] While equal protection-type arguments, perhaps inherent in the Charter's highly elastic reference to "sovereign equality," surfaced in certain Iraqi complaints about post–Persian Gulf war sanctions, *see* UN Doc. S/22456, *supra* note 64, these arguments have scarcely emerged to date in either the *Bosnia* or the *Lockerbie* cases. *But see* Order of Sept. 13, 1993 ICJ REP. at 438, para. 95 (Lauterpacht, J., sep. op.) (noting the unequal effects of the Council's arms embargo on Bosnians as opposed to Serbs). *Compare* Sur, Resolution 687, *supra* note 11, at 7 (arguing that no such principle applies since the Council has total discretion) *with* Watson, *supra* note 4, at 35 (contending that Articles 1(2) and 55 contain "equal protection" principles that may be applied by the Court).

[106] *But see* Franck, *supra* note 12, at 192–218 (asking whether the Council in such instances treats "like cases alike").

[107] Not even Judge Lauterpacht, the judge most favorable to Bosnia's request for interim relief, would go that far. Order of Sept. 13, 1993 ICJ REP. at 441, para. 103 (Lauterpacht, J., sep. op.) (indicating that "it would be difficult to say" that members are "positively obliged [under the Genocide Convention] to provide the Applicant with weapons and military equipment"). "Operational triage," however distasteful, also seems inherent in both the Council's and the Clinton administration's criteria for authorization of "peace operations." Security Council Sets Out Factors to be considered in Establishing United Nations Peacekeeping Operations, UN Press Release SC/5837 (May 3, 1994); The Clinton Administration's Policy on Reforming Multilateral Peace Operations (White House, May 5, 1994).

[108] As Kirgis has noted, some of the Council's actions have the three essential characteristics of "legislative" acts within international organizations: "they are unilateral in form, they create or modify some element of a legal norm, and the legal norm in question is general in nature, that is, directed to indeterminate addressees and capable of repeated application in time." Kirgis, *supra* note 3, at 520 (quoting EDWARD YEMIN, LEGISLATIVE POWERS IN THE UNITED NATIONS AND SPECIALIZED AGENCIES 6 (1969)). The Council has also undertaken "findings of fact" and drawn "conclusions of law." *Id.* at 527–32. *See also* BEDJAOUI, *supra* note 4, at 42–53. Of course, not everything the Council does either is premised on legal considerations or leads to legally relevant precedents. Indeed, for some, it is this fact that justifies judicial review. *See, e.g.*, Macdonald, *supra* note 94, at 18–19.

South Africa, Iraq, the former Yugoslavia, Libya and Somalia), raising obvious questions about whether the activities that prompted Council actions should generally be regarded as violations of international law and interpretive issues about the nature of those "breaches" in each case.[109] The Council has usually accompanied a finding of breach with a finding of attribution, raising (and perhaps settling) questions that are still the subject of debate in the International Law Commission.[110] In other cases, the Council has gone beyond attributing responsibility to states and has found or suggested that individuals may be accountable for internationally wrongful acts (as with the accused before the Yugoslav war crimes Tribunal, Iraqi individuals alleged to have committed grave breaches of humanitarian law, and Libyan officials allegedly involved in the Lockerbie bombing).[111] These actions in turn give rise to further questions concerning, for example, the interpretation and possible development of the Nuremberg Principles: such as the status under customary international law, as opposed to treaty law, of individual account-ability for "ethnic cleansing" and "mass rape," even in contexts not involving proven aggression;[112] the scope of humanitarian law (including its potential application to peacekeepers and other nonparties to the relevant conventions);[113] and, in the context of Libya, the status of terrorism as an international "crime" and the limits of extradition vis-à-vis national sovereignty.[114] In general, the Council's actions implicate many issues, among others, the existence and content of *jus cogens;* the effect of Council declarations of nullity and their opposability; the interplay between Article 41 sanctions and customary international law; the legal impact of Council decisions (or indecision) on the termination of sanctions; reparations and their scope; the duty to implement Council measures; the relationship between Council measures and municipal law and domestic contracts; the impact of Council measures on extraterritorial domestic laws and doctrines of extraterrito-riality; and reconciliation of Council measures with implementation by regional or other organizations and other treaty obligations.[115]

---

[109] Gowlland-Debbas, *supra* note 3, at 64–66.

[110] *Id.* at 67–71.

[111] *Id.* at 67–68. *See also* Giorgio Gaja, *Réflexions sur le rôle du Conseil de Sécurité dans le nouvel ordre mondial,* 97 REVUE GÉNÉRALE DE DROIT INTERNATIONAL PUBLIC 297 (1993).

[112] *See, e.g.,* Theodor Meron, *War Crimes in Yugoslavia and the Development of International Law,* 88 AJIL 78 (1994); Jordan J. Paust, *Applicability of International Criminal Law to Events in the Former Yugoslavia,* 9 AM. U. J. INT'L L. & POL'Y 499 (1994); ANNE T. GOLDSTEIN, RECOGNIZING FORCED IMPREGNATION AS A WAR CRIME UNDER INTERNATIONAL LAW (Center for Reproductive Law & Policy, 1993).

[113] *See, e.g.,* Murphy, *supra* note 9, at 229–33; Jarat Chopra & Thomas G. Weiss, *Sovereignty Is No Longer Sacrosanct: Codifying Humanitarian Intervention,* 6 ETHICS & INT'L AFF. 95 (1992); David J. Scheffer, *Toward a Modern Doctrine of Humanitarian Intervention,* 23 U. TOL. L. REV. 253 (1992); Juan Antonio Carrillo Salcedo, *Le Rôle du Conseil de Sécurité dans l'organisation et la règlementation du "droit d'assistance humanitaire,"* in COLLOQUE, *supra* note 4, at 157; Maurice Torrelli, *La Dimension humanitaire de la sécurité internationale,* in *id.* at 169.

[114] See, e.g., the views of individual judges in *Lockerbie,* text and notes 158–67. *See also* Gianluca Burci, *The Maintenance of International Peace and Security by the United Nations: Actions by the Security Council under the Chapter VII of the Charter,* in ITALIAN SOCIETY FOR INTERNATIONAL ORGANIZATION, PROSPECTS FOR REFORM OF THE UNITED NATIONS SYSTEM 123, 144–46 (1993).

[115] Gowlland-Debbas, *supra* note 3, at 74–90; *see also* Harper, *supra* note 3; Kirgis, *supra* note 3. Even realists acknowledge that the Council has been making quasi-judicial determinations with legal effect, *see, e.g.,* Murphy, *supra* note 9, at 210–35, as have the Council's "subsidiary" bodies. Thus, the decisions of the Compensation Commission for Iraq may have at least as great an impact on the law of state responsibility as those of the Iran-U.S. Claims Tribunal. *See, e.g.,* Crook, *supra* note 58, at 148–50. *But see* Bederman, *supra* note 58, at 35–40 (expressing doubts about the status of Commission precedents). Some have noted that Council presidential statements have also been deployed to make quasi-legislative and quasi-judicial determinations. *See, e.g.,* Kirgis, *supra,* at 519–20.

Questions also arise with respect to possible limits on the Council's enforcement powers. Gowlland-Debbas, *supra,* at 90–94; Kirgis, *supra,* at 520–39; Gordon, *supra* note 75, *passim.* To cite but one example: could the Council, to secure funds for the payment of claims against Iraq, go beyond its Resolution 778 (which now authorizes the "borrowing" of certain Iraqi assets on a temporary basis) and demand the permanent expropria-tion of all Iraqi assets wheresoever held, including Iraqi embassy bank accounts? Such action would have

These issues of potential Council/Court overlap also relate to the work of other international, regional and domestic courts. And this overlap is not subject to the simple solution that the Council should merely pursue "executive" or "enforcement" action and eschew more general lawmaking or quasi-judicial determinations.[116] The Council has not necessarily exceeded its authority in raising these issues. Determinations on the scope of sanctions by the Council or by one of its sanctions committees, for example, or a finding that Iraq needs to forgo the use of certain weapons because it has been an aggressor—however "legislative" or "quasi-judicial" these might appear to be—do not constitute *prima facie* violations of the Charter.[117] While some criticize the Council's more recent "quasi-judicial" pronouncements—as with respect to Iraq's financial liabilities after the Persian Gulf war[118]—and while the Council could benefit from a measure of normative restraint,[119] some Council "lawmaking" is inescapable. Making law, both in interpreting the Charter and in developing the doctrine of state responsibility, has always been part of the Council's job.[120] Its finding, for instance, that Iraq's purported annexation of Kuwait was "null and void"[121] would have been implicit in its decision to use force to dislodge Iraq from Kuwait—whatever the Council had actually said. And even when the Council does not purport to make "quasi-judicial" pronouncements, the precedential impact of a resolution like 688 (requiring Iraq to permit the entry of humanitarian organizations to protect the Kurds) can scarcely be ignored by lawyers. That decision, like many others the Council has recently made, bears on the meaning of Article 2(7) and the present status of human rights law.[122]

Whenever the Court is asked to interpret the Charter or principles of international law that have been the subject of Council action—whether or not any specific Council action is indirectly challenged—the Court will be using, interpreting, and extrapolating from, among other things, Council precedents. Moreover, should the Court be asked to apply a Charter or international law principle to a new situation that is not then the subject of chapter VII action by the Council, whatever the Court says about, e.g., the scope and meaning of Article 2(7) or 2(4) will constitute a precedent that the Council will be called upon at least to consider the next time a similar instance arises in its work—even under chapter VII. What each organ does, no matter how solicitous it is of each organ's respective tasks, inevitably forms part of the web of emerging law and practice under the Charter and of international law. Making law through a dialogue between judicial interpreter and lawmaker is the essence of constitutional adjudication and cutting off that dialogue seems as unlikely as avoiding instances of overlap altogether.[123]

Seeing the issue of judicial review through the lens of *Lockerbie* and *Bosnia* emphasizes aberrant cases at the expense of potentially more likely scenarios that may eventually result in Council/Court conflicts over international legal doctrine. As the range of the Council's "lawmaking" surveyed above suggests, Court and Council, no matter how solicitous of each other's sphere of action, may find themselves addressing the same or

---

potential implications in diplomatic law, extraterritorial application of law, and attribution and expropriation rules within the doctrine of state responsibility.

[116] *But see* Harper, *supra* note 3, *passim.*

[117] *See, e.g.,* Schachter, *supra* note 86.

[118] *See, e.g.,* Elihu Lauterpacht, comments, 85 ASIL PROC. 46 (1991); Kirgis, *supra* note 3, at 532.

[119] *See, e.g.,* Harper, *supra* note 3, at 132–55.

[120] *See, e.g.,* Kirgis, *supra* note 3, *passim.*

[121] *See* SC Res. 662 (Aug. 9, 1990), *reprinted in* 29 ILM 1327, 1328 (1990).

[122] *See, e.g.,* Gordon, *supra* note 75, *passim.* Other examples include Council or sanctions committee decisions with respect to humanitarian exceptions, which may establish precedents in humanitarian and human rights law. *See* Scharf & Dorosin, *supra* note 64, *passim.*

[123] *See generally* Stone, *supra* note 84. See also, more generally, text at and notes 187–96 *infra.*

similar legal questions.[124] A case involving the extraterritorial nature of a state's domestic law, or the scope of *jus cogens*, or the scope of reparations may require the Court to revisit questions raised by prior Council sanctions. The Court's determinations may in turn affect the course of future Council activity or its options. Whichever body acts first has the potential to "check" the other—at least in the sense of imposing on the other some need to distinguish or reinterpret what it has done or said in the past. These aspects of a judicial—or, if one prefers, a constitutional—system result from the creation of a Court charged with examining law, including the law of the Charter, and of a Council that necessarily makes it or gives it effect.

The Court has decided that it is not precluded from considering either questions relating to peace and security or issues pending in the Council.[125] An alternative rule instructing ICJ judges to ignore those questions or requiring automatic deference to the Council's wishes seems impracticable and unworkable; it tells judges that they may no longer fully adjudicate a broad range of basic legal issues. What is the Court supposed to do, for instance, the next time a party raises the contentious issue of damages or permissible countermeasures for intentionally caused environmental harm? Is the Court not to pass on the question merely because, in Resolution 687, the Council found Iraq financially liable for such harm? Is the Court instead supposed to affirm, contrary to the views of many, that the issue has been resolved in favor of liability in all such cases merely because the Council found Iraq liable?[126] Is the Court free to find that liability is due only after instances of aggression? or only after a chapter VII finding? or whenever damage was intentionally caused? or whenever particularly grave damage results? Is the Court supposed to consider whether the Council or its members expressed views on the subject when it approved Resolution 687? Is the Court bound by such views no matter how ill-considered or contrary to other evidence of the state of the law? Whatever it does, the Court will find it difficult to avoid conveying a message about the state of the law on this controversial subject and, incidentally if not directly, on the scope (if not the validity) of the precedent set by the Council.

Under the circumstances, the Council also needs to be concerned with the implications of possible "judicial review." In a future case the Council might have to consider, for example, whether to make a finding of liability or to authorize sanctions or use of force in response to a state's having placed a mine in another state's harbor without warning neutral shippers. In such a case, the Council should consider the Court's Judgments in

---

[124] As noted by Gowlland-Debbas, *supra* note 4, at 661 (discussing the possibility of overlap in the context of state responsibility, where the outcome in one forum "could deprive the solution in the other of all meaning"). The point is not restricted to state responsibility. Thus, Court, Council and Assembly have all participated in the changing interpretation of Article 2(7), as in connection with apartheid and South Africa. *See, e.g.,* SOHN, *supra* note 50, *passim;* Sohn, *supra* note 29, *passim.*

[125] *See, e.g.,* Military and Paramilitary Activities in and against Nicaragua (Nicar. v. U.S.), Jurisdiction and Admissibility, 1984 ICJ REP. 392 (Nov. 26); United States Diplomatic and Consular Staff in Tehran (U.S. v. Iran), 1980 ICJ REP. 3 (May 24). For an advocate's view of the significance of these cases, see Scott, *supra* note 1, at 75–87.

[126] Indeed, the extent of financial liability for environmental harm, intentionally or negligently caused and for "direct" or "indirect" harm, has proven to be a controversial subject, as is clear from the International Law Commission's recent debates. *See, e.g.,* Report of the International Law Commission on the work of its forty-fifth session, UN GAOR, 48th Sess., Supp. No. 10, at 43–132, UN Doc. A/48/10 (1993). While, for some, Resolution 687 on Iraq's postwar responsibilities merely "reaffirmed" what Iraq plainly owed under established international law, *see, e.g.,* Jeremy P. Carver, *Dispute Resolution or Administrative Tribunal: A Question of Due Process,* in COMPENSATION COMMISSION, *supra* note 58, at 69; and John R. Crook, *The UNCC and Its Critics: Is Iraq Entitled to Judicial Due Process?, in id.* at 77, 82, others have been more critical of these "quasi-judicial" determinations. *See, e.g.,* Kirgis, *supra* note 64; and Kirgis, *supra* note 3, at 527–32 (noting, e.g., the legal ambiguities in the Council's determinations that Iraq's foreign debt is null and void).

the *Corfu Channel* and *Nicaragua* cases.[127] Also, as the Council already had occasion to do when it approved measures to enforce the Court's decision in the *Case concerning the Territorial Dispute* between Libya and Chad,[128] the Council (or even national courts) may be compelled to decide whether to enforce a judgment of the Court, and it might be tempted to "consider itself a review body of some type" in connection with that decision.[129] Further, if in either of these two types of cases the Council were to take action inconsistent with the Court's prior findings, it could be accused of undermining the Charter scheme by undermining the Court. In some instances, then, the Council has a duty to adopt a "quasi-judicial" stance, at least in the sense that it may need, through its decisions or through a presidential statement or otherwise, to distinguish prior ICJ judgments or to modify its actions in light of the Court's pronouncements.[130] In some cases, the Council ignores the Court at its own and the system's peril. The legitimacy of both Council and Court is implicated by how each deals with issues of overlap.[131]

IV. THE MANY MODES OF "REVIEW"

If the Court has occasion to "review" legal doctrines related to Council actions without ever being asked to challenge those actions, it is likely that ICJ judges may not consciously exercise an obvious option to "judicially review." Judicial review may creep up on the Court and Council unannounced. This would be consistent with the development of judicial or constitutional review within domestic legal systems.

As comparativist constitutional scholars have demonstrated, most countries accepted judicial power over the constitutionality of legislative acts in the relatively recent past— many as late as the mid-twentieth century—and, what is more important, many have approached it gingerly or grudgingly, in a series of half-steps, sometimes even reversing course.[132] Brewer-Carias demonstrates that, in Europe, previously discretionary powers of government gradually gave way to judicial control of legality. Describing the process in connection with European administrative law, Brewer-Carias contends that such control was derived from the principles of "proportionality, rationality, non-discrimination, equity and justice."[133] He and others characterize "judicialization" as usually the product of an ongoing process rather than of a single fateful and irreversible judicial choice— with many countries still wrestling over, for example, how to permit constitutional review

---

[127] Corfu Channel case (UK v. Alb.) (Merits), 1949 ICJ REP. 4 (Apr. 9); Military and Paramilitary Activities in and against Nicaragua (Nicar. v. U.S.), Merits, 1986 ICJ REP. 14 (June 27). *See also* Sohn, *supra* note 29, at 174–87.

[128] 1994 ICJ REP. 6 (Feb. 3).

[129] Mary Ellen O'Connell, comments, 1993 JOINT CONFERENCE, *supra* note 4, at 290–91. *See also* Mary Ellen O'Connell, *The Prospect of Enforcing Monetary Judgments of the International Court of Justice: A Study of Nicaragua's Judgment against the United States*, 30 VA. J. INT'L L. 891 (1990).

[130] As Judge Bedjaoui put it: "The Security Council . . . will not gain in credibility, authority or efficiency unless the conviction takes root that it acts not as an institution above the Charter and international law but as their servant." BEDJAOUI, *supra* note 4, at 7.

[131] Those concerned with the legitimacy of the Council cannot ignore the legitimacy of the Court and vice versa. *But see* David D. Caron, *The Legitimacy of the Collective Authority of the Security Council*, 87 AJIL 552 (1993); Burns H. Weston, *Security Council Resolution 678 and Persian Gulf Decision Making: Precarious Legitimacy*, 85 AJIL 516 (1991).

[132] *See generally* Cappelletti, *supra* note 64. In Europe the first constitutional tribunals were directly influenced by Hans Kelsen, e.g., in Austria and Czechoslovakia in 1920. Other continental countries established such tribunals only in the 1940s. BREWER-CARIAS, *supra* note 81, at 32; Stone, *supra* note 47, at 41. For some states, such as Russia, judicial review came as late as 1989. Kitchin, *supra* note 74, at 59. Others, such as Israel, are still struggling with limited judicial review in the absence of a written constitution. Martin Edelman, *Judicial Review and Israel's Struggle for a Written Constitution*, *in* COMPARATIVE REVIEW, *supra* note 47, at 157.

[133] BREWER-CARIAS, *supra* note 81, at 34.

of "political" acts by an executive once seen as exempt from such review.[134] Similar evolutionary processes have taken place in international adjudicative fora apart from the ICJ.[135]

Comparative study of "judicial review" in domestic systems reveals shades of meaning in the concept[136] and enormous varieties in methods, even within countries that have ostensibly accepted the possibility of a final judicial say over the constitutionality of legislation. Domestic systems also differ widely in the effect attributed to a court determination that legislation violates the constitution.[137] In some systems, "judicial review" or aspects of it have been instigated by legislative action, not by courts.[138] Of course, one finds great differences in approaches to constitutional interpretation among domestic legal systems and the European Union—on a continuum from "activist" and teleological to more "passive" or literal, focusing on text and/or "original intent."[139]

---

[134] *See, e.g., id.* at 32 (discussing the history of Spain, Italy and France with respect to such acts). Cf. the United States and executive decisions dealing with "foreign affairs," as addressed by, e.g., HAROLD H. KOH, THE NATIONAL SECURITY CONSTITUTION (1990).

[135] *See supra* note 74. *See also* John H. Jackson, *The Legal Meaning of a GATT Dispute Settlement Report: Some Reflections, in* EFFECTIVE SUPERVISION, *supra* note 19, at 149 (discussing the evolution of rule-based GATT dispute settlement).

[136] In some cases, one supreme body has the power to overturn legislation for violation of constitutional norms, while other systems give such power to all courts. BREWER-CARIAS, *supra* note 81, at 91; C. Neal Tate, *Comparative Judicial Review and Public Policy: Concepts and Overview, in* COMPARATIVE REVIEW, *supra* note 47, at 3, 7. Some permit review prior to enactment of a law, and some only after the law has come into effect, while others permit both. BREWER-CARIAS, *supra*, at 92; Tate, *supra*, at 6; Stone, *supra* note 47, at 41. In some states a constitutional question may be raised only as an independent action, while others permit such consideration if incidental to another litigable case or question. BREWER-CARIAS, *supra*, at 92; Carl Baar, *Social Action Litigation in India: The Operation and Limits of the World's Most Active Judiciary, in* COMPARATIVE REVIEW, *supra* note 47, at 77. Some courts are permitted to raise the constitutional question *sua sponte.* BREWER-CARIAS, *supra*, at 133 (discussing Venezuela and Greece). Other states permit organs of the state to raise such questions, while yet others grant this privilege to individuals in all or in some instances (such as for violation of fundamental rights). *Id.* at 92.

[137] Some decisions purport to be effective *erga omnes,* some only for the parties to the action. *See, e.g.,* Tate, *supra* note 136, at 7–8. Constitutional decisions may or may not have *stare decisis* effect. BREWER-CARIAS, *supra* note 81, at 129 (discussing Mexican amparo and its effects). Some such decisions have only prospective effect, others retroactive, and many states, including the United States, have adopted positions somewhere in between. *Id.* at 93, 151–54. The German Federal Constitutional Court, for instance, has developed an elaborate, nuanced set of rules on the effect of such judgments. While in Germany a finding of unconstitutionality normally results in the annulment of the law, in certain cases, the court decision leaves the legislature with other options. Where the alleged defect is the unequal application of the law, the Court may choose not to annul the law as such but to leave it to the legislature to decide whether to extend the law to cover the neglected group of persons or to abolish the benefit entirely. Where the Court deems the harm caused by immediate invalidation to be too great, it may allow the legislature some time to fix the problem or the Court may decide whether to permit the law to apply in the interim. In some cases, the Court may itself "enact" some alternative transitory rule. Dieter Grimm, *Human Rights and Judicial Review in Germany, in* HUMAN RIGHTS AND JUDICIAL REVIEW, *supra* note 84, at 267, 291–92.

[138] Venezuela, for instance, established judicial control over administrative action through legislation; others have done so through case law development. BREWER-CARIAS, *supra* note 81, at 36. Note as well developments in the United Kingdom where parliamentary supremacy has seemingly given way to the European Union, with local UK courts giving effect to its supremacy. *See, e.g.,* Maurice Sunkin, *The Incidence and Effect of Judicial Review Procedures against Central Government in the United Kingdom, in* COMPARATIVE REVIEW, *supra* note 47, at 143.

[139] Some domestic courts apply extremely literalist approaches, while judges on the Swiss Federal Tribunal, for instance, see their task in human rights cases as "perfecting" unwritten norms of "democratic" society. BREWER-CARIAS, *supra* note 81, at 107. Differences in approaches to judicial interpretation, combined with other aspects of domestic legal culture, lead to dramatically different results—even between systems with similar judicial structures. At one extreme may be the Supreme Court of Japan, which, from 1947 to the present, has managed to find legislation unconstitutional in only a handful of instances—despite a U.S.-inspired constitution that explicitly sanctions judicial review. Itsuo Sonobe, *Human Rights and Constitutional Review in Japan, in* HUMAN RIGHTS AND JUDICIAL REVIEW, *supra* note 84, at 135, 172. The German Federal Constitutional Court, by contrast, has been extremely activist in developing constitutional norms and especially in elaborating human rights in ways that exceed the jurisprudence of most countries with judicial review. Grimm, *supra* note 137, at 294. *See also* Baar, *supra* note 136, at 77 (describing India's as the "world's most active judiciary").

26   THE AMERICAN JOURNAL OF INTERNATIONAL LAW   [Vol. 90:1

The differences in national styles, methods and effects of judicial review undoubtedly affect the views of judges on the World Court who, no matter how "international" in outlook, are influenced by their respective domestic legal systems. If the Court's Orders on provisional measures and the individual opinions in the *Libya* cases do not achieve a fully coherent conception of "judicial review" or even its desirability, is that any surprise? How can one expect these judges to have a readily formed opinion on a relatively stark challenge to the Council's supremacy such as that presented by Libya, when the Court has had relatively few occasions to pass on even more oblique constitutional questions and when many of the judges come from judicial systems that have only recently subscribed to more robust forms of judicial review? If the scope, nature and effects of judicial review are a lengthy, evolutionary process, still changing even in the United States after two hundred years of practice,[140] it is no surprise that the World Court will not be able to resolve the question once and for all in the course of the *Lockerbie* cases.[141]

Even assuming that the Court's jurisdictional Statute were amended to permit the United Nations to be a party to contentious cases or that the Court were bold enough to attempt to ignore the jurisdictional difficulties in a particular case, it would not follow that *Marbury*-style review would emerge fully developed and in a form that U.S. constitutional lawyers would recognize.[142] Yet some modes of review, both inevitable and discretionary, will occur even without amending the Court's Statute. Depending on which models for review the judges use by way of analogy, the results need not be as disastrous for the Charter order as some fear.

Extremely deferential review, as deployed by the Japanese Supreme Court[143]—establishing the Court's ultimate power and its potential for legitimacy but recoiling from its effects—might be attractive, at least for the near term. The judges could confine judicial scrutiny to whether there is a nexus between the impugned Council decision and its intended purposes, applying a test of "manifest irregularity" or abuse of power/discretion, for instance.[144] Alternatively, the Court could further develop an informally bifurcated process whereby extremely deferential review would prevail in contentious cases or for purposes of requests for provisional measures while more wide-ranging, even

---

Of course, even within one legal system, changes along the continuum may occur over time or with respect to particular issues. *See, e.g.*, Gerber, *supra* note 74, esp. at 126–30. The choice of interpretive options may vary with the goals of the court and the needs of the particular legal system. Dubinsky argues, for example, that the European Court's resort to interpretive methods responds to the Community's particular goals: namely, (1) assuring that the rule of law is observed; (2) maintaining a stable balance of power among Community institutions; and (3) providing for uniform application of Community law. Dubinsky, *supra* note 81, at 323.

[140] Philip Bobbitt begins his book, *Constitutional Fate,* with these words: "The central issue in the constitutional debate of the past twenty-five years has been the legitimacy of judicial review of constitutional questions by the United States Supreme Court." BOBBITT, *supra* note 51, at 3.

[141] *Contra* de Waart, *supra* note 19; and Reisman, *Crisis, supra* note 4.

[142] Compare the history of Japanese judicial review despite U.S. attempts to replicate *Marbury*-style review. *See supra* note 139.

[143] *See supra* note 139.

[144] *See, e.g.*, Gowlland-Debbas, *supra* note 4, at 670–73. See also the approach of the Indian Supreme Court described by B. P. Reddy & Rajeev Dhavan, *The Jurisprudence of Human Rights, in* HUMAN RIGHTS AND JUDICIAL REVIEW, *supra* note 84, at 175, 184.

From a U.S. lawyer's perspective, the ICJ might more readily choose this approach if Council decisions (or aspects of them) were seen less as "quasi-legislative" actions and more as agency decisions owed deference by virtue of agency expertise. Then the relevant comparison might not be with *Marbury v. Madison* as much as with Chevron, Inc. v. Natural Resources Defense Council, Inc., 467 U.S. 837 (1984) (federal court, when applying an ambiguous statute, must defer to any reasonable interpretation adopted by an agency administering the statute).

teleological, concerns would be vented in appropriate advisory opinions.[145] Or it could demarcate in both its advisory opinions and contentious cases areas of "political discretion" that are not reviewable, as many domestic systems have done, spelling out, for instance, that it will not review, or review only with the utmost deference, whether a matter is a "threat to the international peace,"[146] but that it will review other consequences of that initial determination (such as whether any sanctions imposed are consistent with humanitarian law, including requirements of proportionality). Or it could decide only to scrutinize Council decisions when "fundamental" norms of the international system (such as the right of a state to defend itself against genocide) are implicated, along the lines of some domestic courts with respect to fundamental human rights. It could distinguish different standards of review for different issues, just as U.S. courts have established distinct levels of scrutiny. Even if the Court were to decide to review all Council action on the same terms as all other legal questions, it would probably still leave it to the Council to decide what, if any, effect—prospective, retroactive, *erga omnes/ inter partes*—such decisions would have.[147]

Evolutionary possibilities can also be envisaged for the Court's advisory jurisdiction. If the organs now able to request advisory opinions have the necessary political will, that mode of jurisdiction can develop to the extent that UN organs will more routinely ask for the Court's opinion either shortly before or shortly after controversial action is taken. Used wisely, such recourse to the ICJ could assist the Council in undertaking action that would otherwise be seen as controversial, such as authorizing sanctions against Libya. Members that might be inclined to question the legality of Council action might be convinced by a judicial determination of legality and be more willing to comply with Council action in the wake of such an opinion.[148] Certain national systems, like those of France and Germany, permit "abstract review"; constitutional courts are authorized to pass on the constitutionality of parliamentary legislation immediately on its adoption and before its implementation. Although abstract review in France and Germany is premised on binding decisions, the nonbinding nature of the World Court's advisory

---

[145] But in that case the Court may need to articulate why such distinctions are permissible and desirable. *Cf.* text at and notes 44–47 *supra* (suggesting that both advisory opinions and contentious cases may raise similar concerns). Moreover, whatever interpretive options the Court chooses to pursue need to be connected to instrumental goals appropriate to the UN system. Among possible instrumental goals, ensuring that the rule of law is observed will probably remain as important for the Court as maintaining a stable complementarity of functions among all UN organs, including the Council.

[146] See the trial chamber decision in the *Tadić* case, *supra* note 59, para. 23. Deference need not mean abdication. *See, e.g.*, THOMAS M. FRANCK, POLITICAL QUESTIONS/JUDICIAL ANSWERS 107–25 (1992) (comparing U.S.-style abdication under the political question doctrine with German courts' very different approach to foreign relations issues).

[147] *See supra* text at and notes 36–37. *Cf.* Watson, *supra* note 4, at 39–40 (proposing "Jeffersonian" review whereby the Court's determination would not be dispositive except with respect to the parties to the case). This approach is also suggested by Judge Lauterpacht in the *Bosnia* case, where he writes that it is not necessary for the Court to determine whether the arms embargo as applied to Bosnia violates *jus cogens:*

> Instead, it would seem sufficient that the relevance here of *jus cogens* should be drawn to the attention of the Security Council, as it will be by the required communication to it of the Court's Order, so that the Security Council may give due weight to it in future reconsideration of the embargo.

Order of Sept. 13, 1993 ICJ REP. at 441, para. 104 (Lauterpacht, J., sep. op.) (Lauterpacht here seems to be anticipating the "cueing" function discussed in text at and notes 169–73 *infra*). Significantly, Lauterpacht is anticipating such limited effects even in the context of *jus cogens*, the substantive area in which, arguably, the Court has the widest license to disagree with the Council.

[148] As occurred with respect to the *Certain Expenses* Advisory Opinion. After the ICJ approved the legality of the contested peacekeeping expenses in its Advisory Opinion, certain members reluctantly paid their share of these expenses out of respect for the Court. *See* 13 Whiteman, U.S. DIGEST §16, at 320–25. Of course, more routine referral to the Court would probably follow if the Secretary-General were granted, as has been proposed, the right to ask for an advisory opinion.

28   THE AMERICAN JOURNAL OF INTERNATIONAL LAW   [Vol. 90:1

jurisdiction might facilitate experimentation and reduce the likelihood of antimajoritarian criticisms of the Court.[149] While abstract review is controversial in France and Germany, it has also had beneficial effects. The specter of court intervention has resulted in legislative compromises (sometimes called "auto-limitation") intended to avoid constitutional controversies, a process of self-restraint especially evident where French and German constitutional courts have approved legislative acts but conditioned them on strict guidelines of interpretation.[150]

The potential development of the Court's advisory jurisdiction suggests one more reason why the *Marbury v. Madison* analogy misleads: the possibilities presented by abstract advisory review in practice are even greater than those under the U.S. legal system, premised on review of only live "cases" and "controversies."[151]

V. REVIEW IN AN EXPRESSIVE MODE

Over the near term, the Court will likely attempt to avoid decisions that directly question the Council's actions or their effects.[152] At the end of the *Lockerbie* and *Bosnia* cases, the Court, simply on jurisdictional grounds, may leave questions concerning Council prerogatives unresolved. Nonetheless, unless these cases are rendered moot or settled, the Court will issue further decisions and those will likely be accompanied by the opinions of individual judges. Even such decisions, denying jurisdiction or upholding the Council's actions, engage the Council in an ongoing dialogue, an "expressive" mode of review.

The provisional Orders issued to date in the *Lockerbie* cases are instructive. In its Orders of April 14, 1991, the Court, by a vote of eleven to five, rejected Libya's pleas for interim relief, finding that Libya, along with the United States and the United Kingdom, has a Charter-based duty "to accept and carry out" Council Resolution 748.[153] The Court limited itself to determining that Libya's rights under the 1971 Montreal Convention could not prevail, at least for purposes of a request for interim relief, and it cited in justification Articles 25 and 103 of the Charter.[154] On their face these majority opinions may be read to endorse the supremacy of Council decisions under the Charter and to determine that a chapter VII decision by the Council extinguishes whatever customary and/or conventional rights Libya might have previously enjoyed.[155] Others read these cases differently: as softly affirming that the Court is authorized in an appropriate case to engage in *Marbury*-style review over the Council.[156] Both interpretations are plausible.[157] But the significance of the *Lockerbie* opinions does not rest merely on what they say about the possibility that someday the Court will find a Council decision *ultra vires*.

---

[149] *See generally* Alec Stone, *In the Shadow of the Constitutional Council: The "Juridicisation" of the Legislative Process in France*, W. EUR. POL., Apr. 1989, at 12. The controversy surrounding "abstract review" in France and Germany is hardly surprising, given the consequential effects on both the legislatures and the courts in those countries. As Stone has noted elsewhere, such review has both "judicialized" the legislators, who increasingly pursue political goals through the medium of legal discourse—citing prior constitutional decisions, constitutional text and history, and legal scholars—and "politicized" the judiciary, now more closely "meshed" in the policy-making legislative process. Stone, *supra* note 84. *Cf.* Weiler, *supra* note 81 (noting the absence of such fears, at least through the late 1980s, within the European Union).

[150] Stone, *supra* note 84, at 447–48. Stone concludes that the process has made the French and German constitutional courts "powerful policymakers whose impact on legislative process and outcome is extensive and multidimensional." *Id.* at 466.

[151] *See, e.g.*, TRIBE, *supra* note 53, at 67–69.

[152] As it arguably has done with respect to the Libyan and Bosnian requests for interim relief.

[153] Lockerbie, 1992 ICJ REP. at 15, para. 39, and 126, para. 42.

[154] *Id.* at 15, para. 39, and 126, para. 42.

[155] Reisman, *in* COLLOQUE, *supra* note 4, at 407.

[156] Franck, *supra* note 5, at 108; Franck, *supra* note 4.

[157] Hardly a surprise, since the 11-5 decision was evidently a compromise and did not prevent 8 of the 11 judges in the majority from separately explaining their respective rationales. *See* text at and notes 158–64 *infra*.

In the course of these cases, individual ICJ judges have issued separate opinions criticizing the Council's actions. These opinions constitute warnings to the Council, quite apart from any threat to render Council action "void."

Criticism appears even in the opinions of judges who joined in the majority vote against Libya's claim for provisional measures. In his individual opinion, Judge Oda argued that Libya's problem was jurisdictional. He read the case as a mismatch between the rights Libya sought to protect and the jurisdictional basis for its claims. He contended that Libya's claim against being "coerced" into extraditing its own national was grounded in "sovereign rights under general international law," and not in the Montreal Convention, and hence was not cognizable in a case brought under the latter treaty.[158] Judge Oda seemed to be suggesting that the Council might have violated customary international law, and, significantly, he did not add that Article 103 of the Charter licenses the Council to do so with impunity. Judge Ni affirmed, strongly, the right of simultaneous consideration of a dispute by Council and Court but found that Libya had failed to abide by the six-month waiting period provided for in the Montreal Convention as a precondition to ICJ review. He invited Libya to return at the end of those six months.[159] A terse joint statement by four other concurring judges noted that the circumstances of the case did not merit provisional measures.[160] Judge Lachs, like Judge Ni, affirmed that the Charter anticipates "fruitful interaction" between Council and Court and that the Court is the "guardian of legality for the international community as a whole."[161] He noted that it is important that the two organs act "in harmony—though not, of course, in concert—" and found that the Court was faced with a "new situation which allowed no room for further analysis nor the indication of effective interim measures."[162]

Judge Shahabuddeen argued that "at this stage" the Court must "presume" the validity of the Council's sanctions resolution, not because of the Council's "superior authority—there is none—" but because of Article 103 of the Charter. For Judge Shahabuddeen, Libya's rights arose under the Montreal Convention and the Charter provides that such treaty rights cannot prevail over a decision of the Council. Nonetheless, Judge Shahabuddeen questioned whether an impartial trial for the Libyan defendants is even possible in the United States, given the U.S. demand for compensation from Libya—a demand premised on the defendants' guilt.[163] In a now oft-quoted passage, Judge Shahabuddeen also speculated about the limits to the Council's "powers of appreciation" and whether a body exists to determine those limits.[164]

The dissenters, Judges Bedjaoui, Weeramantry, Ajibola and El-Kosheri, would have given Libya some of its requested provisional relief and all of them criticized the Council, sometimes trenchantly. Judge Bedjaoui found that the Montreal Convention's right to extradite or prosecute is a right recognized by international law, suggested that the Council turned to chapter VII as a pretext, cast doubt on whether the failure to extradite nationals accused of committing a bombing three years earlier was "today" an "urgent" threat to the international peace, affirmed that the Council must respect the Charter and international law and that the Court has competence to tell it to do so, and even speculated that the Council's Resolution 748 (issued while the Court's decision on provisional measures was pending) may have been "manifestly incompatible with the

---

[158] 1992 ICJ REP. at 131 (Oda, J., declaration).
[159] 1992 ICJ REP. at 132–35 (Ni, J., declaration).
[160] 1992 ICJ REP. at 136–37 (Evensen, Tarassov, Guillaume, & Aguilar Mawdsley, JJ., joint declaration).
[161] 1992 ICJ REP. at 138 (Lachs, J., sep. op.).
[162] *Id.* at 139.
[163] 1992 ICJ REP. at 140–41 (Shahabuddeen, J., sep. op.).
[164] *Id.* at 142.

Charter" if intended to prevent the exercise of the Court's judicial function.[165] Dissenting Judge Weeramantry indicated that the Council is required to act in accordance with the principles and purposes of the Charter (Article 24) and in conformity with international law. To this end, he, together with dissenting Judge Ajibola, would have granted provisional relief to conserve Libya's rights to the extent such measures were not inconsistent with Council Resolution 748.[166] Dissenter El-Kosheri focused on the United States' and the United Kingdom's failure to abstain in connection with Council Resolution 731, openly questioned whether UN members are obligated to carry out all decisions of the Council, argued that Resolution 748 (which impeded the Court's jurisdiction in this case) was an exercise of *excès de pouvoir,* and affirmed that the sovereign right to refuse to extradite one's nationals belongs to all states equally.[167]

Apart from whether the Court or individual judges were threatening to issue a decision that finds the Council's action illegal, the Court's Orders in *Lockerbie* warned the Council to exercise care in undertaking similar action in the future, particularly any action contrary to international legal obligations that it may take in the face of the Court's consideration of a pending case.[168] Many of the judges were deploying their prerogative[169] to "cue" a coordinate constitutional actor—while, at least in the context of interim relief, refusing to find that a Council edict was *ultra vires.* As constitutional scholars have noted in connection with the U.S. Supreme Court, this phenomenon is not rare. Sometimes a court indicates possible limits to constitutional action through dicta even while affirming the legality of challenged action in its holding.[170] This may also occur when a court does not have the power to annul or override a legislative act but engages in what some have called "indirect" review. In such a case, for instance, a constitutional court may affirm a challenged action but indicate that the parliament "could not have intended" one particular interpretation.[171]

Like domestic judges, ICJ judges probably hope that the Council will heed their "cues." Indeed, some of the individual opinions in the *Lockerbie* Orders constitute nearly plaintive pleas for the Council to exercise some normative restraint to avoid Judge Shahabuddeen's difficult questions about its margin of appreciation.[172] They are cueing the Council to internalize the limits suggested and impose restraints on itself that would prevent violations of the law—and the threat of further litigation.[173]

---

[165] 1992 ICJ REP. at 143–59 (Bedjaoui, J., dissenting).

[166] 1992 ICJ REP. at 160–81 and 183–98 (Weeramantry & Ajibola, JJ., respectively, dissenting).

[167] 1992 ICJ REP. at 199–217 (El-Kosheri, J., dissenting).

[168] The dissenting and concurring judges seem to have gone beyond disagreeing with the "manner" in which the Council took its decisions. *Cf.* Reisman, *in* COLLOQUE, *supra* note 4, at 416–17. These judges had substantive qualms about Council Resolution 748.

[169] The Court's prerogative to consider the substance of Council Resolution 748 (*see* note 168 *supra*) seems inherent in its competence to decide the scope of its jurisdiction under Article 36(6) of its Statute. *See also supra* note 60.

[170] *See* BOBBITT, *supra* note 51, at 191–95; Watson, *supra* note 4, at 30, 43. The speed with which the Court disposed of these requests for interim relief may lessen fears that judicial review will invariably preclude prompt Council action. *Cf.* Doc. 498, III/2/19, 12 U.N.C.I.O. Docs. 65 (1945) (UK fears to this effect).

[171] *See* Scott, *supra* note 1, especially at 138–39. This course may be taken under the rubric of avoiding constitutional difficulties where any other construction is possible. *See, e.g.,* Tate, *supra* note 136, at 5–6. Even the trial chamber in the *Tadić* case, while affirming the Council's action in establishing the Yugoslav war crimes Tribunal, arguably sent abundant "cues" to the Council as to the limits of future action. *See supra* text at note 59.

[172] *See* text at note 164 *supra.*

[173] *See, e.g.,* Stone, *supra* note 84. McWhinney, *supra* note 4, at 270–71, argues that some of the individual opinions in the *Libya* case stand as a "form of legal vindication of the plaintiff's claim" and he sees these opinions as all contributing to an "unfolding of the legal dialectic and to the making of new constitutional law." *Cf.* Franck, *supra* note 5, at 108–09 (focusing on another type of "cue": a warning to the Council that the Court is keeping the door open on judicial review).

Whether or not the Court's "cues" in the *Lockerbie* cases will prove effective remains uncertain.[174] The potential use of the "cueing" function is greater at the international than at the national level, given the relative dearth of alternative enforcement possibilities. In the end, the international system relies almost exclusively on "cues" for enforcement. The successful implementation of the Court's advisory opinions, as well as any institutional innovations by UN organs, relies, after all, on "general acceptance."[175] Cues like those issued by the Court and judges in *Lockerbie* are one of the few "enforcement" tools generally available against the Council.

The Court performs a related, but distinct, role even when it upholds Council action. In some cases, as constitutional scholars have noted, a constitutional court undertakes to express *community* goals. Some constitutional opinions not only seek to cue a coordinate constitutional body but also aspire to "shape people's vision of their Constitution and of themselves."[176] The World Court speaks through its "expressive function" to the international community as a whole. Much of the effectiveness of the UN collective security system is due not to the realistic threat of UN force but to the successful espousal of ideas and principles—peace, decolonization, human rights—and, most importantly, to the idea that when international subjects act, they do so under the rule of law. The United Nations and its component parts are essentially a "theatre for standard-setting and myth-making."[177] The Court and Council both are organs through which the community expresses these ideas.

The *Bosnia* cases reveal an attempt to deploy the Court's expressive function in this second sense. Despite the Court's and most of the judges' refusal to deal with the broader reaches of Bosnia's claims, the two Orders on provisional measures and the individual opinions of some of the judges, particularly those portions of the latter that have given rise to the most controversy, evince an attempt to express community sentiments in opposition to "ethnic cleansing." To this end, portions of both Orders imply that genocide had occurred in the former Yugoslavia and that one of the states, Serbia and Montenegro, bore a greater degree of responsibility for it.[178] By the time of the second Order, the Court's abrupt refusal to consider Serbia and Montenegro's request for provisional relief[179] spoke volumes about the Court's view of Serbian actions. Judge Shahabuddeen served notice of these concerns in his separate opinion, which, among other things, cast doubt on Serbian denials of involvement in the military actions of Bosnian Serbs, implied that the Serbian Government knew of genocidal acts inside Bosnia, and suggested that the Serbian Government was not in a position to ask for relief when it had failed to implement the Court's prior provisional measures.[180]

The adjudication of Bosnia's claims, and the individual opinions of some of the judges, also expressed another important community goal: to document the historical record of atrocities. As Judge Lauterpacht noted in his separate opinion to the second Order, Bosnia was seeking, in its second request for provisional measures, judicial cognizance

---

[174] Some see "auto-limitation" operating with respect to the humanitarian exceptions now more routinely incorporated into the Council's sanction programs. Gowlland-Debbas, *supra* note 4, at 667.

[175] *See* text at and note 50 *supra*.

[176] BOBBITT, *supra* note 51, at 219 (quoting Hans A. Linde, *Judges, Critics, and the Realist Tradition*, 82 YALE L.J. 227, 238 (1972)).

[177] Adam Roberts & Benedict Kingsbury, *Introduction: The UN's Roles in International Society since 1945, in* UNITED NATIONS, DIVIDED WORLD 1, 21 (Adam Roberts & Benedict Kingsbury eds., 2d ed. 1993). As another observer of the Council put it, the Council serves a "global community function": galvanizing political and moral support. Murphy, *supra* note 9, at 208–09.

[178] *See, e.g.,* Order of Sept. 13, 1993 ICJ REP. at 346–47, 348–49, paras. 46, 52–53, 57, 59; Order of Apr. 8, 1993 ICJ REP. at 24, para. 52.

[179] Order of Sept. 13, 1993 ICJ REP. at 346–47, para. 46.

[180] *Id.* at 362–63, 368 (Shahabuddeen, J., sep. op.).

of facts that "shock the conscience" of humanity.[181] To this end, Judge Lauterpacht believed that it was necessary, even in the context of a request for mere interim relief, to summarize the abundant evidence of genocidal practices and Serbian acquiescence and/or participation presented by the applicant, including media reports.[182] As Judge Lauterpacht put it:

> To refrain from confronting the facts simply because the proceedings are ones for provisional measures would suggest a degree of formalism inconsistent with one of the tasks of the international judicial process in circumstances so unusual as those involved here. . . .
>
>   . . . There is also a reason of policy for looking at the facts—a policy which the principal judicial organ of the United Nations can properly take into account. As is well known, the justification for the war crimes trials following the Second World War was seen to lie not solely in the requirement that the perpetrators of heinous crimes should be brought to justice. It lay also in the belief in the necessity of placing on historical record the character and extent of those crimes so that they should never be forgotten and that the recollection of the sacrifice of the victims should not be dimmed by time. . . . It may, of course, be said that such a record will appear in the Court's treatment of the case at the merits stage. However, . . . there is a distinct possibility that the merits stage of these proceedings will not be reached. What will those in later years who are not well instructed in our contemporary history understand of the real thrust and significance of the Court's Order if they cannot read therein some narrative of the circumstances which have led to it?[183]

At least one paragraph in the second Order itself reflects the entire Court's sensitivity to these concerns.[184]

The Orders on provisional measures in the *Bosnia* cases may ultimately gain fame not for what they said (or failed to say) about Bosnia's claim that the Council's arms embargo was *ultra vires* but for having given voice to community sentiments. The judges who elected to reject Serbian requests for interim relief, or who thought it necessary to express certain views of the facts even though such fact-finding is exceptional at the provisional measures stage, were saying that Serbian actions constituted such an affront to international norms that the usual rules for more "balanced" or "even-handed" treatment of applicants to the Court did not apply.[185] The Court and its judges proclaimed to the international community as a whole and to the Council that territorial acquisition through genocidal practices lies outside the bounds of the post-Holocaust international order.

The judges' individual opinions in the *Lockerbie* and *Bosnia* cases suggest a Court that is ready to engage in this expressive mode of judicial review, even if in advance or defiance of the expectations of some UN members.[186] At first glance, this mode of review seems consistent with a model of judicial review articulated by James Boyd White in the context of U.S. courts. According to this view, judicial review is premised on the unique

---

[181] Order of Sept. 13, 1993 ICJ REP. at 422, para. 38 (Lauterpacht, J., sep. op.).

[182] *Id.* at 425–31, paras. 50–67.

[183] *Id.* at 424–25, paras. 47–48.

[184] Order of Sept. 13, 1993 ICJ REP. at 348, para. 52.

[185] This might be analogous to the U.S. Supreme Court's finding a constitutional violation because of the "expressive harms" of certain public action. *See, e.g.,* Richard H. Pildes & Richard G. Niemi, *Expressive Harms, "Bizarre Districts," and Voting Rights: Evaluating Election-District Appearances after Shaw v. Reno,* 92 MICH. L. REV. 483 (1993).

[186] Of course, this route has been taken by other constitutional courts as well. *See, e.g.,* BOBBITT, *supra* note 51, at 185, 211–12 (noting, among other things, how the Supreme Court's standards have helped change the United States as a nation).

way courts, in contrast to legislatures and executive actors, make decisions.[187] White sees judicial decision making as a vehicle for a collective and intertemporal conversation about the political community's values, a vehicle that is justified because it is not otherwise replicated in other institutional actors.[188] From this perspective, the UN Charter, like the U.S. Constitution, creates a "rhetorical community," by establishing a "set of speakers, defining the occasions for and topics of their speech," and serving itself as a "text that may be referred to as authoritative."[189] Having constituted a community and a culture, the Charter creates, in the ICJ, an organ with the potential to reconcile the irreconcilable, find peace and order in conflict, and produce a self-reflective, self-corrective body of identifiably legal discourse that will bind its audience together by engaging it in a common language and a common set of practices.[190] Under White's view, the ICJ would be seen as uniquely situated to expound the Charter in the "pure and disinterested way it requires"[191] since it alone can convincingly propound the language and "culture of law" on which the Charter relies.

Premised on a fluid view of "law" and language,[192] White's model would probably seem quite alien to some legal cultures.[193] It is also a conception of law that at least its expounder sees as requiring live cases between active parties, not advisory opinions, since only in the former instance does a court possess an analytically distinct type of competence not available to the legislature.[194] For this and other reasons,[195] notwithstanding the appeal of White's model, one hesitates to associate the ICJ too closely with it. What can be said with greater confidence, however, is that the ICJ judges have engaged the Council and the international community in a conversation as to possibilities—as to the variegated forms of possible "review"—and that they will most probably continue to do so.[196]

While a definitive appraisal of the Court's actions in the *Lockerbie* case remains premature, the substantive decision reached by the Court as a whole in response to Libya's claims is defensible. The *Lockerbie* majority and individual opinions respect the Council's

---

[187] WHITE, *supra* note 49, at 231–74.
[188] *See also* Croley, *supra* note 84, at 751 n.181.
[189] WHITE, *supra* note 49, at 246, 245.
[190] *Cf. id.* at 251.
[191] *Id.* at 262.
[192] White's elegant conception of "law" is perhaps clearest when he writes:

> To conceive of the law as a rhetorical and social system, a way in which we use an inherited language to talk to each other and to maintain a community, suggests in a new way that the heart of law is what we always knew it was: the open hearing in which one point of view, one construction of language and reality, is tested against another. The multiplicity of readings that the law permits is not its weakness but its strength, for it is this that makes room for different voices and gives a purchase by which culture may be modified in response to the demands of circumstance. It is a method at once for recognizing others, for acknowledging ignorance, and for achieving cultural change.

Id. at 273.
[193] Compare, e.g., the positivistic resistance to judges as law "creators" as well as law "interpreters." *See, e.g.,* GENNADY M. DANILENKO, LAW-MAKING IN THE INTERNATIONAL COMMUNITY 253–60 (1993).
[194] WHITE, *supra* note 49, at 264–65.
[195] The "uniqueness" of the ICJ with respect to these issues is, as discussed *supra* in part II, in question. Note, too, that White's model addresses the U.S. federal judiciary. It assumes that judges have something distinct to offer in part because, owing to life tenure, they are more removed from the political dictates of the day than other actors. These assumptions cannot be wholly applied with respect to ICJ judges who are elected for renewable nine-year terms. *Cf.* Croley, *supra* note 84, at 748–90 (noting the difficulties in finding a principled justification for elected judiciaries within the U.S. states).
[196] For examples of the Court's contribution to international institutional law, see *supra* note 46. For recognition of common aspects of "transjudicial communication," see Anne-Marie Slaughter, *A Typology of Transnational Communication*, 29 U. RICH. L. REV. 99 (1994).

discharge of its functions and are solicitous of the Court's own complementary role.[197] For the Court to have gone further in the context of Libya's request for provisional measures and opined, as some have recommended, that it could not review Council decisions under chapter VI or VII unless that is so intended by the Council would have been to reach for and prematurely decide a constitutional issue not yet presented to it.[198] When the Court rendered its decision, Council Resolution 748, a decision under chapter VII, had overtaken the Council's prior Resolution 731, premised on chapter VI. That, combined with the limited nature of the facts presented and the relief sought, was sufficient to dispose of the immediate issue on the narrowest basis possible.[199] In doing so, the Court in *Lockerbie* left open other possibilities—including the possible courses of action surveyed above—while individual judges began, in the time-honored fashion of many constitutional courts, a conversation as to possible legitimation models.[200]

The more interesting question is not why the individual judges in *Lockerbie* and the *Bosnia* cases stopped where they did but why they went so far in the direction of criticizing the Council in *Lockerbie* and articulating community norms in the *Bosnia* cases. Why engage in the "expressive mode of review"? Reisman has suggested that "[l]egal language carries, virtually *in ossibus*, the idea of legal restraints,"[201] noting that the "juridical mind inclines to assume that, as [the creature of a treaty], the Council simply could not be discharged, when fulfilling its mandate, from the application of some principles of international law or compliance with some of the terms of the United Nations Charter."[202] Reisman disparages both notions, suggesting that the ICJ is a mere "college of people" not "enfranchised" to undertake judicial review by the political process that resulted in the Charter.[203]

Whether or not Chief Justice Marshall was in any sense "enfranchised" by the U.S. political process to do what he did in *Marbury* would seem to be a matter of some dispute. Certainly, the accounts by U.S. commentators of Marshall's achievement in *Marbury* or later in *McCulloch v. Maryland*[204] would lead one to wonder what the fuss was all about if Marshall was merely following the political dictates of the electorate.[205] Other constitutional lawyers—dealing with either domestic courts or international tribunals—might take umbrage at any suggestion that constitutional review needs to be "enfranchised" by a political process. If "enfranchisement" means that judges must be charged with constitutional review by a document formally approved by the electorate such as a constitution or legislation, this view does not take into account that judges are political actors with their own agendas, biases and potential for politically risky action. It is entirely too dismissive of the evolutionary potential inherent in the creation of an interpretive body in a constitutive charter.

---

[197] *Cf.* Reisman, *Crisis, supra* note 4, at 94.

[198] *Cf. supra* note 171 (noting canon of constitutional interpretation of avoiding constitutional issues).

[199] It might be said that the *Lockerbie* judges wisely "tempered the mechanical arrogance of abstractions with the life blood of the concrete problem," and that, by refusing to yield to the charm of "generalizing abstraction," they sought to reassure observers that the Court was not being "excessively creative." *Cf.* Schachter, *supra* note 88, at 769 (discussing international judges in general). It is also true that, given the evident splits within the Court, if there was to be a majority opinion, such an opinion would necessarily take the narrowest possible ground.

[200] Its focus on Resolution 748 does not foreclose the possibility that the Court would have come to the same conclusion based on a chapter VI action by the Council. That issue did not need to be decided in this case.

[201] Reisman, *Crisis, supra* note 4, at 92.

[202] *Id.*

[203] *Id.* at 94.

[204] 17 U.S. (4 Wheat.) 316 (1819).

[205] *Cf.* WHITE, *supra* note 49, at 247–68.

One cannot explain the role, both actual and potential, of the ICJ (or any tribunal) without some account of the people that constitute it. Judicial review, in whatever form, is also about judges—their backgrounds, education, and institutional or other expectations.[206] Just what the "career expectations" of the judges on the ICJ are—with their nine-year terms and possibilities for reelection—may be speculative, but their common legal expertise is not. Whatever their nationality and differences in judicial temperament, the judges on the ICJ, by virtue of education, career background and selection through politicized UN processes, are likely to be eminent subscribers to what David Kennedy has called the "internationalist sensibility," that is, they are likely to be strong believers in and advocates of international law as "law."[207] They are most likely to be part of Kennedy's "informal priesthood of believers" in international law and institutions.[208] They are likely to manifest what Kennedy describes as "utopian preacherliness" or "holier-than-thou realism" in pursuit of at least one common agenda: establishing for all to see that international law is no less "law" than national law.[209] Whether we describe them as part of the "invisible college" of international lawyers[210] or as prominent members of an "epistemic community,"[211] ICJ judges as a whole are not likely to accept total deference to the Council, even if that were possible despite the cases of overlap discussed above.[212] For ICJ judges, as for most lawyers, unchecked power in the hands of any single organ is "law" in name only.[213]

Even if it were possible for ICJ judges to take the extreme realist position—that unless invited by the Council, they may express no view with respect to Council action—such a stance by a majority on the Court demands that these internationalists deploy the Court's expressive powers on the side of the rule of the powerful instead of the rule of law. For most, this would come uncomfortably close to denying the very reason they became judges on the Court.[214] It is nearly as unrealistic to expect such fettered judicial

---

[206] Certainly, Stone's account of the role of French judges and Ramseyer's account of the role of Japanese judges place considerable emphasis on the political backgrounds of French judges and the career expectations of Japanese judges, respectively. *See, e.g.,* ALEC STONE, THE BIRTH OF JUDICIAL POLITICS IN FRANCE 8 (1992) (noting the political backgrounds of the majority of judges on the French Constitutional Council, as well as the political nature of their appointment); J. Mark Ramseyer, *The Puzzling (In)Dependence of Courts: A Comparative Approach,* 23 J. LEGAL STUD. 721 (1994) (arguing that until recently one-party rule in Japan "controlled" judges through job assignments).

[207] David W. Kennedy, *A New World Order: Yesterday, Today, and Tomorrow,* 4 TRANSNAT'L L. & CONTEMP. PROBS. 329, 332–36 (1994).

[208] *Id.* at 335.

[209] *Id. See also* Shirley V. Scott, *International Law as Ideology: Theorizing the Relationship between International Law and International Politics,* 5 EUR. J. INT'L L. 313 (1994).

[210] Oscar Schachter, *The Invisible College of International Lawyers,* 72 NW. U. L. REV. 217 (1977).

[211] *See* 46 INT'L ORG. 1, *passim* (1992) (issue devoted to studies of various international "epistemic communities," usually defined as groups of people sharing technical or other expertise and a particular value orientation).

[212] As Judge Lauterpacht asked in the *Bosnia* case, does anyone really believe that the Court would or should affirm the legality of a Council decision that, for example, would compel states to be accomplices to genocide? Order of Sept. 13, 1993 ICJ REP. at 440, para. 100 (Lauterpacht, J., sep. op.).

[213] *See, e.g.,* Admission of a State to the United Nations (Charter, Art. 4), 1948 ICJ REP. 57, 64 (Advisory Opinion of May 28) (asserting that UN political organs must still adhere to the Charter). *See also* Bedjaoui, *supra* note 75, at 19 (noting that it is not acceptable that "sovereign states should have created an international organization equipped with broad powers of control" but that is itself exempted "from the duty to respect both the Charter which gave it birth and international law"); BEDJAOUI, *supra* note 4, at 32–36 (to same effect); BREWER-CARIAS, *supra* note 81, at 81 (arguing that two fundamental objectives of judicial review under the "état de droit" are "to ensure that all those acts of the state are adopted or issued in accordance with the law" and "to ensure that state acts respect the fundamental rights and liberties of citizens"); and Beatty, *supra* note 84, at 89 (arguing the importance of structural checks and balances over a bill of rights).

[214] Moreover, to the extent absolute deference to the Council demands that ICJ judges cease deploying what Anne-Marie Slaughter has identified as a "common judicial identity and methodology"—including common methods of legal reasoning and belief in the solemnity of precedent—such deference would demand that ICJ judges cease being judges. *See generally* Slaughter, *supra* note 196, at 125–26.

license as to expect Council decision making to ignore a permanent member's national
security.

VI. THE LIBERAL CHALLENGE TO JUDICIAL REVIEW

The most formidable argument in the realists' arsenal is that they are the true heirs
of realpolitik: states, and particularly the permanent members of the Council, have not
decided to turn the Charter into a quasi-governmental system where the Court is licensed
to perform the tasks routinely accorded to domestic courts.[215] From this perspective, the
Court should resist its natural inclination to acquire a nonexistent review power. For
these propositions realists might be able to draw considerable support from "liberal"
theorists as well.

Liberals might contend that comparisons with the evolution of constitutional review
at either the domestic or the European Union level are fundamentally mistaken because
those systems draw upon a common liberal culture and institutions, and especially a
common acceptance of the possibility of law as "*law*, as a body of rules interpreted and
applied by a nonpolitical entity."[216] They might rally to the realist cause by arguing that
neither the United States nor most of the military powers capable of making a collective
security system effective are yet ready to accept internationally what liberal regimes have
accepted internally: a "well-functioning judicial system insulated from direct political
influence."[217]

Judicial review has come so late to so many parts of the world because its acceptance
is premised on a decision by elites to share power. After all, judges able to render a
legislative or executive action void because of constitutional infirmities are policy makers
in all but name, and, at least from the perspective of political scientists who study the
phenomenon, another lawmaking branch.[218] Comparative constitutional scholars have
demonstrated how "closely connected judicial review is with the development and, indeed, the manufacture of democratic government."[219] Judicial review has been seen
virtually everywhere as a bulwark against authoritarianism, as a mechanism to protect
human rights, and as a reaction to fascism. Judicial review *is* governance, and if the ICJ
judges at the merits stage in *Lockerbie* or elsewhere were to declare a Council decision
ultra vires, there is no question that such a decision would fundamentally change the
Court and the UN system of governance.

Furthermore, such a change would entail serious risks. As the observers of the "judicialization" of the legislative process in European states would remind us, enmeshing
the courts in the Council's "legislative" process may result in the longed-for état de
droit only by creating a system antithetical to creative innovation and necessary change.[220]

---

[215] *See, e.g.*, Reisman, *Crisis*, *supra* note 4. *See also* Edward Gordon, *Legal Disputes under Article 36(2) of the
Statute, in* THE INTERNATIONAL COURT OF JUSTICE AT A CROSSROADS, *supra* note 29, at 183, 202 (arguing that
while in principle the World Court is as free as the Supreme Court to undertake certain creative solutions
not expressed in the Charter, "it lacks the justification for doing so that derives from the checks and balances
written into the structure of government that the Constitution—but not the Charter or Statute—creates");
Gill, comments, 1993 JOINT CONFERENCE, *supra* note 4, at 283–86 (denying that the Charter creates a "federal
structure").

[216] *See* Anne-Marie Slaughter Burley, *International Law and International Relations Theory: A Dual Agenda*, 87
AJIL 205, 234 (1993); Anne-Marie Slaughter, *International Law in a World of Liberal States*, 6 EUR. J. INT'L L.
(forthcoming) (copy on file with author) [hereinafter *Liberal States*]. As Mohammed Bedjaoui has put it:
"essentially built upon liberal concepts, the Charter of the United Nations was from the outset unable to
blend the underlying philosophies of different world perceptions into a synthesis or leave any place for other
philosophies alongside that of liberalism." Bedjaoui, *supra* note 75, at 13.

[217] Murphy, *supra* note 9, at 284. *See also* Slaughter, *Liberal States*, *supra* note 216.

[218] *See, e.g.*, Stone, *supra* note 149, at 29–30; STONE, *supra* note 206, at 225–53.

[219] Tate, *supra* note 136, at 8.

[220] *See, e.g.*, Stone, *supra* note 149, at 29.

Involving the Court in judging the legality of the Council's actions may even have costs beyond those that the realists have so far enunciated. Judicial review may not just hamper the Council's program. To the extent the World Court becomes more systematically involved in the partisan struggles of the Council, it may be "politicized," as happened in France with respect to its Constitutional Council.[221] As Stone asserts has occurred at least in France and Germany, increased judicial review may blur the present distinctions between the proper roles for Court and Council, politics and law.[222] While the blurring of these distinctions may not pose so serious a legitimacy problem for domestic legal rules, which are backed by effective institutionalized sanctions, the consequences for the legitimacy of international law may be much graver. Given the tenuous legitimacy of ICJ judges,[223] turning them into umpires of the Council's political games is too risky.

However, the Court and Council have so many options that such fears need not be realized. UN processes remain a long way from "judicialization" as in France or Germany or the European Union. An antimajoritarian critique of the World Court at this early stage in its development does not seem plausible.[224] Nor, in view of the Court's real limitations (jurisdictional and doctrinal), are all-or-nothing confrontations with the Council very likely.[225] Further, even in those countries where "abstract" constitutional review has been institutionalized, the process has been neither permanent nor uniformly applicable across all lawmaking issues.[226] In addition, as is suggested in part III, some "judicialization" of UN lawmaking processes, including the Council's, is an inevitable concomitant of the creation of a supreme judicial organ charged with review over international law. The Court, no matter how deferential to the Council, may, in either contentious cases or through advisory opinions, pass on legal questions related to Council activity—that is, in cases where politics and law are already inextricably enmeshed. Also, nothing that the Court might do can prevent the Council's legitimacy from being called into question by other UN organs, other bodies or even members themselves, and, if so, the question is not whether the Council will be second-guessed but by whom.[227]

The liberal challenge to judicial review is not merely overstated. Its basic presuppositions are open to question. Opponents of judicial review should not be given the benefit of the doubt on the supposed limitations faced by the "illiberal" UN order. History does not demonstrate that illiberal systems or systems characterized by heterogeneity cannot have a functioning judiciary capable of some constitutional review, or that even if this were so for domestic systems, the same holds true for the United Nations.[228] Historical support for the latter supposed truism is clouded by the ICJ's successful

---

[221] Cf. id. at 13. If both Council and Court become engaged in the same tasks, it may become increasingly difficult to maintain that the World Court is "primarily legal," while the Council is "primarily political." Cf. Harper, supra note 3.

[222] See, e.g., Stone, supra note 84, at 460–61.

[223] See, e.g., Gordon, supra note 215, at 185–87 (analyzing the Court's "political" nature).

[224] See, e.g., Watson, supra note 4, at 30–33; Roberts, supra note 4, at 314.

[225] Nor would the Council be helpless before a prospective Court challenge. Council members, should they anticipate an adverse opinion relating to the Council's decisions, can distance themselves from an ongoing case by, for example, not filing memorials before the Court or otherwise participating in the proceedings, the better to contend that the arguments on behalf of the Council's actions were simply not presented to the Court.

[226] See, e.g., Stone, supra note 84, at 447 (noting particular substantive areas of the law in both France and Germany in which "judicialization" has had more profound effects than in others).

[227] Some members that might otherwise be encouraged to oppose or defy Council decisions may turn to judicialization of the process instead. See generally Stone, supra note 84, at 447 ("[o]ppositions judicialize legislative processes to win what they would otherwise lose in normal political processes.").

[228] For attempts by one court to exercise judicial review even under martial law, see C. Neal Tate, Temerity and Timidity in the Exercise of Judicial Review in the Philippine Supreme Court, in COMPARATIVE REVIEW, supra note 47, at 107.

38 THE AMERICAN JOURNAL OF INTERNATIONAL LAW [Vol. 90:1

assertions of constitutional review in various advisory opinions.[229] Given the many modes for Council action and Court review, it is unwarranted to assume that "judicial review" by the ICJ is inconceivable absent direct penetration or "direct effect" of international law in domestic legal orders. If this feature is what liberals contend is required for effective judicial review, at least some ostensibly "liberal" states lack "judicial review" so narrowly conceived.[230]

Nor has it been demonstrated that the UN order, "illiberal" as it may now be, cannot change or "learn."[231] Consider Mary Volcansek's description of Italy in 1946 on the eve of its attempt to replicate the U.S. constitutional order:

> Italy was unified as a nation only in the late nineteenth century, and that unification was the result of diplomatic agreements and military conquests. Its resulting governing structure could not meet even the minimal requirements of a democracy and it was easily converted into a totalitarian state, with the acquiescence of the monarch and Parliament, under the leadership of Mussolini. Italy had no democratic tradition, nor did those who wrote the new constitution share the same assumptions about or visions of government and governing. Marxists, Leninists, liberals, conservatives, Catholics, and neofascists gathered to find a compromise scheme of government.[232]

Replace "Italy" with "the international community," and the comparison becomes apt. As Volcansek demonstrates, the system of judicial review that has evolved in Italy since 1946 bears scant resemblance to the one it attempted to transplant, because judicial review has a way of adapting to each cultural setting. As this and other tales of transitions to more liberal orders suggest, regimes change and judicial review has sometimes taken root under extremely unfavorable, illiberal conditions.[233]

Nor should the "romantics" cede "realism" too readily. What seems politically unreal today, when the United States sees itself as holding most of the economic cards and nearly all of the military ones, can change; indeed, the United States may soon find itself in a world where its increasingly illusionary veto power is less important than the protection of consistently applied rules.[234] Over the long term, the U.S. national interest may in fact be served by judicial review. If so, as "P1," the United States is in a position to lead other permanent members to the same conclusion.

CONCLUSION

The question of judicial review should not remain a sterile debate between "legalists" and "hard-headed realists." Both sides need to recognize that they are engaged, with the Court and the Council, in the pursuit of an effective, *but legitimate*, collective security scheme. Both the Council and the Court are engaged in supervising rule compliance by members. Both must maintain a "delicate" balance "between securing continued

---

[229] *Cf., e.g.,* Goler T. Butcher, *The Consonance of U.S. Positions with the International Court's Advisory Opinions, in* THE INTERNATIONAL COURT OF JUSTICE AT A CROSSROADS, *supra* note 29, at 423.

[230] *See* part IV *supra.*

[231] For a general approach to organizational "learning," see ERNST HAAS, WHEN KNOWLEDGE IS POWER: THREE MODELS OF CHANGE IN INTERNATIONAL ORGANIZATIONS (1990).

[232] Mary L. Volcansek, *Judicial Review and Public Policy in Italy: American Roots and the Italian Hybrid, in* COMPARATIVE REVIEW, *supra* note 47, at 89, 99.

[233] In some cases, judicial review has arisen or been strengthened because of perceived abuses by state authorities. *See, e.g.,* Cappelletti, *supra* note 64, at 681. For arguments premised on the need for an evolving United Nations, see Scott, *supra* note 1, at 97–98.

[234] As Richard Falk has noted, it is a "mistake to assume an inherent conflict between geopolitics and respect for international law." Richard A. Falk, *The United Nations and the Rule of Law,* 4 TRANSNAT'L L. & CONTEMP. PROBS. 611, 619 (1994). For a more general critique of realist assumptions, see Slaughter, *Liberal States, supra* note 216.

co-operation from the members on the one hand, and obtaining and maintaining the integrity" of their roles as supervisors on the other.[235] If the simultaneous pursuit of these goals is required for "institutional legitimacy," both Council and Court have roles to play and need to coexist in a state of inevitable and sometimes desirable tension.

No one model of judicial review for Council/Court interaction has yet been articulated by the Court and perhaps no *one* model is appropriate. In the meantime, reality cannot be denied. Aspects of "review" by the Court are already here and, especially through the Court's advisory jurisdiction, have been here for some time.[236] They are as real— and probably as inevitable—as the Security Council's need to represent the interests of the effective police powers and to respond flexibly to crises.

The World Court exists today as one of many possible (de)legitimating agencies. Through its advisory and contentious case capacities, it has "cued" other actors as to lawful possibilities and expressed important community aspirations—while also sending a message that affirms its view of itself.[237] The Court, as well as other national and international adjudicative bodies, will be required, sooner or later, to pass on legal issues emerging from the Security Council's proliferating legal determinations and precedents. The ICJ's judges will almost certainly "expound" on at least some issues of Council/ Court overlap and will continue to operate in an "expressive mode," if for no other reason than that they are members of a "court" charged with the interpretation of "law" who also tend to share an "internationalist sensibility."

The prospects for Court/Council interaction will almost certainly not be conclusively determined in the course of the pending *Lockerbie* or *Bosnia* cases. Nor are the possible future modes of ICJ review either limited to those suggested by the *Marbury* analogy or necessarily constrained by realpolitik to those dictated by the Council. The Council and the Court face a continuum of options and interpretive modes for which both domestic systems and other international tribunals serve as sources of inspiration. Judicial review is an evolutionary process, emerging from a dialogue among all international actors. Fortunately, the Court has a ready body of comparativist expertise to draw upon to evolve its own powers.

Given the many modes of Council action with potential legal effect and the many possible modes of World Court "review," the issue need not be seen as a choice between hegemonic (or systemic) needs and the "rule of law." Even more activist forms of judicial review than have appeared to date may prove to be neither utopian nor calamitous— especially if the permanent members of the Security Council come to appreciate that they have long-term interests in pursuing peace through law.

---

[235] Blokker & Muller, *supra* note 70, at 280–81.

[236] For recent surveys of the Court's attempts at "review," see, e.g., BEDJAOUI, *supra* note 4, at 15–29; Roberts, *supra* note 4, at 293–312.

[237] *Cf.* BOBBITT, *supra* note 51, at 217–19 (discussing the U.S. Supreme Court's expressive function in the *Nixon Tapes* case).

[11]

THE ROLE OF THE INTERNATIONAL COURT OF JUSTICE IN THE MAINTENANCE OF INTERNATIONAL PEACE

DAPO AKANDE*

I. INTRODUCTION

The coincidence of the fiftieth anniversary of the International Court of Justice (the Court) and the imminent close of the twentieth century sets the stage for an assessment of the activities of the Court over the last half century and for speculation as to the role that the Court is likely to be called on to play in the coming century. It is no doubt true to say that one of the issues that has most troubled the world this century is the task of finding appropriate international institutions that can guarantee peace and security among nations. The purpose of this paper is to consider the role and contribution of the International Court of Justice in maintaining international peace. The paper first attempts to address the general question of whether an international court can play any significant part in the settlement of important disputes between nations. It argues that the dichotomy between legal and political disputes is one that does not stand up to scrutiny. It then examines the record of the Court to see how far and in what ways it has in fact been involved in peacemaking among nations.

The International Court of Justice, as the principal judicial organ of the United Nations,[1] is in many respects the leading international judicial tribunal. Its Statute charges it with the function of settling disputes in accordance with international law.[2] Though the members of the United Nations have, through the Charter, conferred on the Security Council the primary responsibility for the maintenance of international peace and security,[3] the Court has itself explained in a number of cases that that "primary" responsibility does not mean "exclusive" responsibility.[4] In these cases the Court refused to accept that the Security Council alone has the mandate to maintain international peace and the Court did not exclude the possibility that it shouldered some responsibility itself for this task. Several

---

* LLB (Ife), LLM (London), PhD Candidate at Magdalene College, Cambridge and Part-time Lecturer at the London School of Economics and Political Science. Special thanks to Judge Rosalyn Higgins, Amazu Asouzu, Dino Kritsiotis, Lai Oshisanya and Roger O'Keefe for reading earlier drafts of this article and for making helpful suggestions. Responsibility for any errors or omissions is of course mine alone.

1 See Art. 92 of the Charter of the United Nations.
2 Art. 38(1) of the Statute of the International Court of Justice.
3 Art. 24(1), Charter of the United Nations.
4 *Certain Expenses of the United Nations* (Advisory Opinion), 1962 ICJ Reports 151 at 163; 34 ILR 281 at 292; *Military and Paramilitary Activities in and against Nicaragua*, 1984 ICJ Reports 392 at 434 at para. 95; 76 ILR 145.

8 RADIC (1996)

members of the Court have endorsed the view that one of the purposes, if not the primary purpose, of the Court is the securing of international peace. Judge Sir Hersch Lauterpacht in the very first sentence of his seminal work, *The Development of International Law by the International Court,* stated that "it would appear that the primary purpose of the International Court ... lies in its function as one of the instruments for securing peace in so far as this aim can be achieved through law".[5] President Basdevant in his opening remarks at the oral hearings of the *Reparations for Injuries Advisory Opinion* said, in relation to the role of the Court, that "it is asked of the Court that it should contribute to peace by deciding the disputes submitted to it".[6] Again, President Nagendra Singh in his Separate Opinion at the Merits Phase of the *Nicaragua Case* stated that "the Court as the principal judicial organ of the United Nations has to promote peace, and cannot refrain from moving in that direction".[7] The Court itself noted in the *Border and Transborder Actions Case* between Nicaragua and Honduras that "the purpose of recourse to the Court is the peaceful settlement of disputes".[8]

This last quoted statement of the Court only restates what is obvious, but is often overlooked: the purpose of judicial settlement is the peaceful settlement of disputes. Yet the proposition that an International Court might have any significant role in the maintenance of international peace is one which for several generations was rejected by many international lawyers. From the time of Vattel to at least the early part of the 20th century the prevailing view among both international lawyers and statesmen was that there were certain inherent limitations in the judicial function and that obligatory judicial settlement of some, if not most, disputes was inappropriate.[9] This doctrine of the inherent limitations of the judicial function in international law classified disputes into those that were justiciable and those that were non-justiciable, disputes as to rights as opposed to disputes arising out of conflicts of interests, and legal in contradistinction to political disputes (all these terms being different ways of saying the same thing).

II. THE SCOPE OF THE JUDICIAL FUNCTION IN THE SETTLEMENT OF INTERNATIONAL DISPUTES: THE DICHOTOMY BETWEEN LEGAL AND POLITICAL DISPUTES

The alleged dichotomy between legal and political disputes was the defining intellectual framework in the conception of the international judicial function. Both governments and international lawyers consistently put forward the view

---

5 Lauterpacht, *The Development of International Law by the International Court* (1958), p.3.
6 Pleadings, Oral Arguments, Documents – *Reparation for Injuries in the Service of the United Nations,* p.46.
7 *Military and Para-Military Activities in and against Nicaragua* (Merits) 1986 ICJ Reports, p.153; 76 ILR 487
8 1988 ICJ Reports 91; 84 ILR 246; para 52 of the judgment.
9 For a review of the development of "the doctrine of the limitations of the judicial process in international law", see the seminal work of Hersch Lauterpacht, *The Function of Law in the International Community* (1933).

594   *Dapo Akande*

that international arbitration or judicial settlement were of limited value in settling certain classes of disputes. A memorandum prepared by the Russian delegation for use in the First Hague Conference shortly before the turn of the century is
illustrative of the then prevailing view. The memorandum included a note concerning a proposed article on mediation. This note insisted that although arbitration was in general more effective than mediation, the application of arbitration
"is essentially and even exclusively restricted to cases where there is a conflict of
international rights, while mediation, although of a political character, is equally
applicable to the conflicts of interests which most often threaten peace among
nations".[10] The preferred solution for "conflicts of interests which most often
threaten peace among nations" was therefore mediation. Baron Descamps, who
participated in the two Hague Conferences and went on to become President of
the Committee of Jurists that drafted the Statute of the Permanent Court of
International Justice, stated that "apart from important disputes, which require the
machinery of mediation, there are legal disputes".[11] The general report of one
committee at the first Hague Conference explained the limitation of the scope of
disputes suitable for arbitration or judicial settlement on the ground that the
arbitrator is a judge and as he is bound to act according to law, arbitration is not
applicable to disputes involving "conflicting interests" and "differences of a
political nature".[12] The purpose and effect of limiting the types of disputes
thought suitable for arbitration was therefore to exclude those disputes "which
most often threaten peace among nations" from the purview of judicial settlement.

Though this distinction between justiciable and non-justiciable, legal and
political disputes was well accepted by the prevailing doctrine, there were considerable problems in defining which disputes were political and thus excluded from
the application of the judicial function. One approach was to enumerate the
classes of disputes that could properly be regarded as legal disputes.[13] A more
popular view, however, was that such disputes as could be settled by the application of the principles and rules of international law were legal, and such disputes
as could not be formulated in juridical terms were political and unsuitable for
judicial settlement. However, the test which seemed to prevail in terms of its
influence in the practice of States was one which regarded all important disputes
as political and therefore unsuitable for judicial settlement. As Hersch
Lauterpacht pointed out

> the test of the limitation of the judicial function based on the appli-
> cability of legal rules is not the most important in practice. This attribute
> must be reserved for the distinction between legal and political

---

10   *Reports to the Hague Conferences of 1899 and 1907*, ed. by J.B. Scott (1917), p.95. (Hereinafter
      referred to as *Hague Reports*.)
11   Quoted by Hersch Lauterpacht in his book *The Function of Law in the International Community*
      (1933), p.142. (Hereinafter referred to as *The Function of Law*.)
12   *Hague Reports*, note 10 above, p.56.
13   See Lauterpacht, *The Function of Law*, p.16.

disputes based on the relative importance of the subject matter of the controversy. According to this test those disputes are political, and therefore non-justiciable, which affect the important, or – to use the current expression – the vital interests of States.[14]

Any important dispute or any dispute affecting the vital interests of States was therefore thought unsuitable for judicial settlement. One reason for this position was that it was thought that governments would not be willing to have important matters determined judicially.[15]

It is this view that important disputes are political and therefore non-justiciable that assigns to the judicial function a very small role in the maintenance of international peace. This view found expression in several arbitration treaties concluded after the Hague Peace Conferences. Many of those treaties limited the obligation to arbitrate to disputes of a legal nature provided that such disputes do not "affect the vital interests, the independence, or the honour of the two contracting States or do not affect the interests of third States".[16] The argument was that nations cannot surrender questions of national honour or questions of independence to the decision of foreign judges and that they are the sole judges of their own dignity and of the rights which guarantee that dignity.[17] This argument reveals what Hersch Lauterpacht regarded as the principal function which the doctrine of the inherent limitation of the judicial function has been called to fulfil since its inception: the doctrine has supplied "a legal cloak for the traditional claim of the sovereign State to remain the ultimate judge of disputed legal rights in its controversies with others".[18]

A. Is there a Dichotomy between Legal and Political Disputes under the Charter?

In order to assess the role of the International Court of Justice in the maintenance of international peace, it is important to determine whether the distinction between legal and political disputes is one which is maintained under the Charter of the United Nations. There is some scope for the argument that this distinction is one which still exists under the Charter. Firstly, Article 36(3) of the Charter provides that in making recommendations for the settlement of disputes, the Security Council should take into consideration that *legal disputes* should as a

14 *The Function of Law*, p.139.
15 See, for example, Vattel who asserted that "when one should seek to rob [a nation] of an essential right, of a right without which it cannot hope to maintain its existence", the duty of the nation is for it not ever to attempt pacific settlement but to "exhaust its resources, and nobly shed the last drop of its blood": *Le Droit des Gens, ou Principes de la Loi Naturelle, appliqué a la Conduite et aux Affaires des Nations et des Souverains* (1758), Book II. chapter xviii. Quoted by Hersch Lauterpacht in *The Function of Law*, p.9.
16 See, for example, Art. 1 of the arbitration treaty between Great Britain and France of 14 October 1903, Hertslet, *Treaties*, vol xxiii, p.402.
17 See Calvo, *Le droit international théorique et practique*, (6th ed., 1888), vol. iii, p.472. Quoted by Hersch Lauterpacht in *The Function of Law*, p.12.
18 *The Function of Law*, p.6-7.

general rule be referred to the ICJ. Secondly, Article 36(2) of the Statute of the Court provides that States Parties to the Statute may declare that they recognise as compulsory *ipso facto* the jurisdiction of the Court in all *legal disputes*. It then goes on to enumerate four classes of disputes. The argument may therefore be made that the Charter and the Statute intended to carry on the division between legal and political disputes and that they exclude political (meaning "important") disputes from settlement by the Court, with the effect that the Court is assigned a small or insignificant role in the maintenance of international peace.

However, a more thorough reading of Article 36 of the Statute does not support this conclusion. In the first place Article 36 (1) provides that "the jurisdiction of the Court comprises all cases which the parties may refer to it and all matters specially provided for in the Charter of the United Nations or in treaties or conventions in force". This provision in no way limits the function of the Court to the settlement of small disputes or disputes other than those affecting the vital interests of States. The Court, under this provision, has the jurisdiction to decide all cases submitted to it and its function under Article 38 of the Statute is to decide such disputes in accordance with international law.[19]

It is however with respect to compulsory adjudication that the doctrine of the inherent limitation of the judicial function was most frequently deployed. As a matter of fact, it was paradoxically felt that the doctrine would serve to promote obligatory arbitration or judicial settlement as it would limit the scope of the advance obligation to resort to judicial settlement therefore making the undertaking of such an obligation easier for States.[20] It is therefore with regard to Article 36 paragraph 2 of the Statute that one needs to examine whether the distinction between legal and political disputes survives in the Charter. As earlier noted, Article 36(2) allows the parties to recognise the compulsory jurisdiction of the Court in all *legal disputes*. It then lists four classes of disputes, namely – (a) the interpretation of a treaty, (b) any question of international law, (c) the existence of any fact which, if established, would constitute a breach of an international obligation and (d) the nature or extent of the reparation to be made for the breach of an international obligation. In spite of the use of the phrase "legal disputes" and in spite of the enumeration of the disputes considered as falling in that category, it is submitted that the Statute in no way intended to exclude from the competence of the Court important disputes or "conflicts of interests which most threaten the peace of nations".[21] Hersch Lauterpacht has demonstrated that the term "legal disputes" is used descriptively in Article 36(2) and was in no way intended to qualify the classes enumerated in Article 36(2).[22] He also points out that category (b) "any question of international law" is wide enough to cover the three remaining classes, and indeed any conceivable dispute in which the parties

---

19   This rule applies except the parties agree that the Court decide the dispute *ex aequo et bono*. Art 38(2) of the Statute of the Court.
20   See Lauterpacht, *The Function of Law*, p.4-6.
21   See note 10 above.
22   *The Function of Law*, p.35-6.

ask for their rights. It may be added that in so far as international law covers important questions and in so far as international law covers questions relating to peace among nations, as it clearly does,[23] the Court has jurisdiction over such matters.

B. The Dichotomy between Legal and Political Disputes in the Decisions of the Court

The Court itself has on several occasions had to consider the assertion that its competence was excluded in particular cases owing to the fact the dispute was political and not legal. The Court has clearly indicated that the fact that a dispute has political aspects or that its decision will have political implications does not debar the Court from exercising its jurisdiction once it is properly seised of a dispute. As the Court stated in the Jurisdictional Phase of the *Nicaragua Case*[24] (a case involving questions relating to the use of force), "the Court has never shied away from a case brought before it merely because it had political implications or because it involved serious elements of the use of force".

The Court has also taken the view that once a dispute is susceptible to the application of legal rules it is generally within the scope of its judicial function. In fact the Court has noted that very often political and legal aspects are intertwined in cases brought before it. In the jurisdictional phase of the *Case Concerning Border and Transborder Armed Actions* between Nicaragua and Honduras (another case involving the use of force), the Court stated that it was

> aware that political aspects may be present in any legal dispute brought before it. The Court, as a judicial organ, is however only concerned to establish, first, that the dispute before it is a legal dispute in the sense of a dispute capable of being settled by the application of principles and rules of international law and secondly, that the court has jurisdiction to deal with it, and that jurisdiction is not fettered by any circumstances rendering the application inadmissible.[25]

The point therefore is that it is artificial to attempt to separate legal disputes from political disputes. As Judge Lachs pointed out in his Separate Opinion in the *Nicaragua Case* (Merits Phase) "almost all disputes arising between States have both political and legal aspects; politics and law meet at almost every point of the

---

23   See the statement of Hersch Lauterpacht written as far back as 1933 where he said "Can it, with any degree of accuracy be said that international law is concerned only with minor issues between States? Such an assertion is on the face of it contrary to the actual content of international law as at present constituted", *The Function of Law*, p.169-170. How much more true is this statement in the face of the enormous expansion of international law since the end of the Second World War?

24   *Military and Paramilitary Activities in and against Nicaragua, (Nicaragua v. The United States of America)* 1984 ICJ Reports, p.435, para 96; 76 ILR 146.

25   1988 ICJ Reports 91 para. 52; 84 ILR 246.

598   *Dapo Akande*

road".[26] Hersch Lauterpacht expressed the same opinion when he said that "the State is a political institution, and all questions which affect it as a whole, in particular in its relations with other States, are therefore political".[27] The terms "legal" and "political" are by no means opposites. They are concepts that do not have the same frame of reference and in fact refer to totally different things. To say that a dispute is political is often to refer to the way in which the dispute has arisen and developed and to the emotion and feeling that it has aroused. Even the smallest of disputes in terms of subject matter may arouse the greatest of feeling and may lead to its classification as political. To say that a dispute is legal, however, is to say it calls into play the application of rules and principles of law. Clearly these statements are not contradictory. Disputes arousing feeling and emotion very often call into play legal rules. For example, Judge Bedjaoui noted in his dissenting opinion in the *Lockerbie Case*[28] that that case comprises a political dispute relating to State terrorism and a legal dispute concerning extradition. What is important for the Court in any case that comes before it is whether the questions before the Court can be settled by reference to international law. If they can, the Court is competent to answer those questions regardless of the "political" circumstances surrounding the case.

Some writers are of the opinion that to attempt to distinguish between "legal disputes" and "political disputes" is not only to undertake an artificial inquiry but to undertake the wrong inquiry. Thomas Franck, for example, has said that

> the right question ... is not whether the dispute is essentially legal or political but whether it is more likely to be settled by recourse to a political or legal forum.[29]

In this view, there is no inherent distinction between legal and political disputes and the distinction between a legal and a political question lies in the method through which settlement of the dispute is being pursued or is best pursued.[30]

The Court has also stated both in its advisory function and in relation to contentious cases that it would not concern itself with the fact that there is some political motivation behind the bringing of a case to the Court. In two Advisory Opinions relating to admissions to the United Nations,[31] the Court stated that it could not attribute a political character to a request which invited it to perform the essentially judicial task of interpreting the Charter – a multilateral treaty. Again in

26   1986 ICJ Reports, p.168; 76 ILR 502.
27   Lauterpacht, *The Function of Law*, p.153.
28   *Questions of Interpretation and Application of the 1971 Montreal Convention Arising from the Aerial Incident at Lockerbie (Libya v. UK;Libya v. US)*. 1992 ICJ Reports at 34, 144.
29   See Thomas Franck, *Judging the World Court*, (1986), p.41.
30   See Hans Kelsen, *Principles of International Law*, 526 (R.W. Tucker ed., 2d rev. ed. 1966) quoted by Vera Gowlland-Debbas in "The Relationship between the International Court of Justice and the Security Council in the light of the *Lockerbie Case*", 88 (1994) AJIL 643.
31   *Admission of a State to the United Nations* (Advisory Opinion) 1948 ICJ Reports 57; *Competence of the General Assembly For the Admission of A State to the United Nations*, (Advisory Opinion) 1950 ICJ Reports 4.

the *Certain Expenses Case,* it had been argued that the question put to the Court was intertwined with political questions and that the Court should therefore refuse to give an opinion. The court however noted that "it is true that most interpretations of the Charter of the United Nations will have political significance, great or small. In the nature of things it could not be otherwise."[32] The Court then went on to repeat its earlier pronouncements that it could not attribute a political character to a request inviting it to undertake the judicial task of treaty interpretation. In the *Border and Transborder Case* Honduras had argued that Nicaragua's application to the Court had been politically inspired. The Court said that "it cannot concern itself with the political motivation which may lead a State at a particular time, or in particular circumstances, to choose judicial settlement."[33]

Despite these pronouncements by the Court, some States have continued to make the argument, at least in the context of a request for an advisory opinion, that certain issues are political and therefore beyond the remit of the Court. This argument, with nuances and variations, was made by certain States in their pleadings in the proceedings relating to the *Legality of the Use by a State of Nuclear Weapons* (Request for an Advisory Opinion).[34] These proceedings related to two similar requests, from the World Health Organisation (WHO) and the General Assembly, for an advisory opinion on the legality of the use of nuclear weapons.[35] At a general level one may say the Court was here being called to make its most direct foray into peace and security issues. The Court was not being asked to settle a bilateral issue affecting peace among nations but was being asked to pronounce on the legality of the use of what some might consider the greatest threat to the existence of mankind – nuclear weapons.

In their written statements and oral arguments before the Court, certain States (including four of the five declared nuclear weapons States) argued that the Court should not render the advisory opinion requested of it. They argued that the Court has a discretion whether or not to render advisory opinions and that in the case at hand the Court should exercise its discretion by refusing to render an opinion. Various arguments were put before the Court in support of this position. These included the contention that the WHO lacked the competence to request the

---

32   1962 ICJ Reports at p.155.
33   1988 ICJ Reports at p.91 at para. 52; 84 ILR 246.
34   See *Legality of Use by a State of Nuclear Weapons in Armed Conflict,* (Advisory Opinion of 8 July 1996 – request by the WHO), and *Legality of the Threat or Use of Nuclear Weapons* (Advisory Opinion of 8 July 1996 – request by the General Assembly).
35   Though the questions put to the Court by the WHO and the General Assembly were similar they were by no means the same. The question asked by the World Health Assembly, the governing body of the WHO, in May 1993, was – "In view of the health and environmental effects, would the use of nuclear weapons by a State in war or other armed conflict be a breach of its obligations under international law including the WHO Constitution?". (Res. WHA 46/40). The question put to the Court by the General Assembly, in December 1994, was – "Is the threat or use of nuclear weapons in any circumstance permitted under international law?" (GA Res. 49/75k). Though the Court joined the oral proceedings relating to these two requests, the cases themselves were not joined and it remains to be seen whether the Court will deliver a single opinion.

600   *Dapo Akande*

opinion[36] and that though the General Assembly had the competence to request the opinion, the question was abstract and an answer would serve no useful purpose. Also, it was argued that the question before the Court was essentially political and therefore the Court lacked the competence to give an answer. In the light of the previous jurisprudence of the Court, this argument was rarely put in the blunt form that it had been put in previous cases. For example, the United Kingdom argued with respect to the request by the WHO, that where the motivation behind the request is essentially political and is extraneous to the proper aim of seeking guidance as to the legitimate functions of the organ or organisation requesting the opinion, the Court should not answer the question put to it. The UK further stated that the true basis of this exclusion is not simply that political motives lies behind the request, but that where the Court is being tempted to get involved in an essentially political debated (in this case nuclear disarmament), the issue of propriety arises and it would be improper for the Court to get involved.[37] Also, France, at the oral hearings, argued that (i) the questions were of a purely political nature (ii) in order to reply to them, the Court would have to act as an international legislator and take into consideration political and moral factors and that (iii) the Court would be interfering in an essentially diplomatic and political process.[38] This argument was echoed by the Counsel for Germany who, at the oral hearings, said that "in the view of my Government the question before the Court is basically of a political nature."[39]

Although these arguments did go some way towards taking into account the concerns that have been expressed about this alleged dichotomy between legal and political disputes, they were rejected by the Court. States like the UK based their arguments not so much on the incompetence of the Court as on the impropriety

36   This contention was upheld by the Court which held that international organisations do not possess a general competence but are governed by the "principle of speciality" and that the question put to the Court by the WHO did "not arise 'within the scope of [the] activities' of that Organization as defined by its Constitution." *Legality of the Use by a State of Nuclear Weapons in Armed Conflict* (Advisory Opinion), paras. 25-26.

37   Written Statement of the United Kingdom – *Legality of the Use by a State of Nuclear Weapons in Armed Conflict* (Request for an Advisory Opinion by the World Health Organisation), pp.53-58. It is interesting to note that this argument relating to the political nature of the question put to the Court was not repeated by the UK in relation to the request by the General Assembly. Also this argument was not put before the Court by the UK at the oral hearings phase of the proceedings.

38   Oral Pleadings, *Legality of the Use by a State of Nuclear Weapons* (Request for an Advisory Opinion), CR95/23 (translation), p.5 *et. seq.* (Professor Pellet). Of course, many other States took a different view. See for example the statement of Counsel for Qatar (Dr. Al-Nauimi) that "while the question may have a political background, or political implications, the nature of the question before the Court today is not a political one." CR95/29 p.29, para. 14.

39   Oral Pleadings, *Legality of the Use by a State of Nuclear Weapons* (Request for an Advisory Opinion), CR95/24, p.35 *et. seq.*, para. 12 (Mr. Hillgenberg). Earlier Mr. Hillgenberg had said "Mr. President, we are aware that many highly respected experts believe that progress to date in the field of nuclear arms control and disarmament is still not sufficient, and that a judicial ruling on the legality or illegality of the use of nuclear weapons may help expedite the process. This Court, however, according to the Charter of the United Nations and its own Statute, is called upon to give advisory opinions on legal questions. It should be not enter the political field of promoting disarmament through opinions on political matters pending in various international political fora." CR95/24, p.35, para. 7.

of using the Court in a political debate wholly unrelated to constitutional questions affecting the organ in question.[40] However, the Court relied on its prior jurisprudence and held that the questions asked of it were framed in terms of law and thus legal questions and also that it could not consider the political aspects or political motives surrounding the requests.[41]

Some of the arguments put forward related to the inability of the Court with respect to political *questions* as opposed to political *disputes*. In this regard the argument was not so much that the context of the issue at hand was political (though this was also argued) but that international law as it presently stood had nothing to say about whether the use of nuclear weapons was *per se* legal or illegal and that therefore the question was not one fit for a judicial body. It was therefore argued that the Court would have to play the role of legislator as there was no existing law in this regard.[42] However, the Court was of the view that the question put to it was legal and it examined, in relation to the opinion requested by the General Assembly, various areas of international law that bear on the legality or otherwise of the use of nuclear weapons. It held that:

> the threat or use of nuclear weapons would generally be contrary to the rules of international law applicable in armed conflict, and in particular the principles and rules of humanitarian law

but that:

> However, in view of the current state of international law, and of the elements of fact at its disposal, the Court cannot conclude definitively whether the threat or use of nuclear weapons would be lawful or unlawful in an extreme circumstance of self-defence, in which the very survival of a State would be at stake.[43]

---

40 It should be noted that though the Court had on several occasions stated that it could not concern itself with the political motivation behind a request for an advisory opinion, those advisory opinions had related to the workings of the organ that had requested the opinion. See *Admission of a State to the United Nations* (Advisory Opinion) 1948 ICJ Reports 57; *Competence of the General Assembly For the Admission of a State to the United Nations* (Advisory Opinion) 1950 ICJ Reports 4; *Certain Expenses of the United Nations* (Advisory Opinion) 1962 ICJ Reports 155. However, it should also be noted that Article 96 of the Charter of the United Nations empowers the General Assembly and the Security Council to request advisory opinions on any legal questions and does not limit the questions that these organs may ask to questions relating to the work of the organ or organisation as is the case with other bodies that may request advisory opinions.

41 *Legality of the Use by a State of Nuclear Weapons in Armed Conflict* (Advisory Opinion of 8 July 1996), paras. 15-16. *Legality of the Threat or Use of Nuclear Weapons* (Advisory Opinion of 8 July 1996), para. 13.

42 See, for example, the statement of the German Counsel (made when arguing that the matter before the Court was political) that, "I submit that ... up to this present moment, there is no convention, international custom, or general principle of law which would support that nuclear weapons, as part of a defensive strategy, are illegal under any circumstances." CR95/24, p.35, para. 7. See also the French argument, CR95/23 (translation), p.53 *et. seq.*

43 Paragraph 2E of the *dispositif* of the Opinion, *Legality of the Threat or Use of Nuclear Weapons* (Advisory Opinion). This sub-paragraph was approved by the casting vote of President Bedjaoui, the Court having been deadlocked with seven votes in favour and seven against.

602   *Dapo Akande*

This distiction between political *questions* and political *disputes* is implicitly approved by the second part of this paragraph in the *dispositif*. As is argued in this paper politicisation of a dispute in terms of its importance to the interests (vital or otherwise) of the States concerned or in terms of the emotion it generates does not exclude the dispute from the purview of the Court. So far the Court has not concerned itself with the fact that a given case has political undertones. This cannot but be so. Every case brought before the Court has political undertones as it involves political entities. It may even be argued that the very fact that the case has come before the Court is indicative of political disagreement. Every case which comes before the Court relates to a dispute that the parties have failed to settle by negotiation and this fact itself gives some political colour to the case. Therefore to admit as part of positive law the doctrine relating to the exclusion of political disputes would be to undermine the very nature of judicial settlement of disputes. As Hersch Lauterpacht put it, to accept the suggestion that the Court should refrain from dealing with political questions "would mean a speedy and radical liquidation of the activities of the Court".[44]

However, it is another thing to say that a particular question before the Court, either in advisory or contentious proceedings, is a political question because it cannot be answered by reference to law or there are no legal guidelines for its resolution. If it is in fact the case that international law has nothing to say on the legality or otherwise of a particular matter, then it does follow that the question is not one that the Court is able to answer as the Court's function is to apply international law and not to make it.[45] For example it may be argued that the question whether a particular act is a threat to or breach of the peace under Article 39 of the United Nations Charter is a political question because international law contains no rules for determining the matter and the Charter entrusts that determination to a political body – the Security Council – which is entitled to act in accordance with political and not legal considerations.[46] The essential question is therefore whether a particular question is capable of a legal answer. If it is, the Court is competent in that regard. Again the fact that a particular *question* is political does not debar from the Court being competent with respect to the dispute in which the question arises. For example, it may be argued that though the determination of a threat to the peace or breach of the peace is political and thus within the sole competence of the Security Council, there are nevertheless

44   Lauterpacht, *Function of Law*, p.155.
45   Article 38(1) of the Statute of the Court. See also the statement of the Court in the *Fisheries Jurisdiction Case (United Kingdom v. Iceland)* (Merits), 1974 ICJ Reports 3 at pp.24-5, para. 53, that "the Court, as a court of law, cannot render judgment *sub specie legis ferendae*, or anticipate the law before the legislator has laid it down." See also the *Fisheries Jurisdiction Case (Federal Republic of Germany v. Iceland)* (Merits), 1974 ICJ Reports 175 at p.192, para. 45.
46   See generally, Gill, "Legal and Some Political Limitations on the Power of the UN Security Council to Exercise its Enforcement Powers Under Chapter VII of the Charter", 1995 Netherlands Yearbook of International Law 33; Alvarez, "Judging the Security Council" 90 AJIL 1 (1996); Bedjaoui, *The New World Order and the Security Council: Testing the Legality of its Acts* (1994); Gowlland Debbas, "The Relationship Between the International Court of Justice and the Security Council in the Light of the *Llockerbie Case*", 88 AJIL 643 (1993).

legal restraints imposed on the Security Council in deciding how to respond to that threat to or breach of the peace.[47]

Ongoing Armed Conflicts

Aside from the general argument that there is a class of political disputes that is not appropriate for judicial settlement, a more specific argument has been made that the Court is not competent to deal with cases involving *ongoing* armed conflicts. Cases like the *Corfu Channel Case*[48] and the two cases examined in Part II below demonstrate that the Court is capable of deciding cases involving *limited* uses of armed force and cases involving armed incidents where that is not the substance of the case.

However, in the *Nicaragua Case*[49] the United States argued that the case was inadmissible because it involved an ongoing armed conflict. It asserted that ongoing armed conflicts were never intended by the drafter of the Charter to be encompassed by Article 36(2) of the Statute. The US also argued that

> resort to force during ongoing armed conflict lacks the attributes necessary for the application of the judicial process, namely a pattern of legally relevant facts discernible by the means available to the adjudicating tribunal, establishable in conformity with applicable norms of evidence and proof, and not subject to further material evolution during the course of, or subsequent to, judicial proceedings.[50]

The argument therefore was not that the dispute was political and not legal but that (i) there had been no intention to subject such disputes to judicial settlement; and (ii) it would be difficult for the Court to make findings of fact in such a situation. The Court unanimously dismissed these submissions of the United States. With respect to fact finding, the Court held that it is the litigant seeking to establish a fact that has the burden of proving it and that in cases where evidence may not be forthcoming, a submission may be rejected as unproved. It also noted that it is not only in cases of ongoing armed conflict that fact finding may be difficult.[51]

Judge Schwebel (who voted with the rest of the Court on this point at the

---

47 This issue has arisen before the Court in both the *Lockerbie Case* (*Libya v. United States and theUnited Kingdom*) (Provisional Measures), 1992 ICJ Reports 3 and the *Bosnian Genocide Convention Case* (*Bosnia and Herzegovina v. Yugoslavia (Serbia and Montenegro)*) (Further Requests for the Indication of Provisional Measures) 1993 ICJ Reports 324.

48 1949 ICJ Reports 35.

49 *Military and Paramilitary Activities in and against Nicaragua* (Jurisdiction and Admissibility), 1984 ICJ Reports 439; 76 ILR 147.

50 1984 ICJ Reports 439, para. 99; 76 ILR 147.

51 On the problems of fact finding by the Court, see Schwebel, "Three Cases of Fact-Finding by the International Court of Justice" reprinted in Schwebel, *Justice in International Law* (1994), p.125. See also Highet, "Evidence and Proof of Facts", in Damrosch (ed.) *The International Court of Justice at a Crossroads* (1987), p.355; Lillich (ed.), *Fact-Finding Before International Tribunals* (1992).

604   *Dapo Akande*

Jurisdiction and Admissibility phase) returned to this question in his dissent on the merits of the case. Whilst agreeing that the Court is competent to deal with ongoing use of force,[52] he argued that the case at hand was non-justiciable because of its circumstances. He took the view that the Court would be required to pass judgment on the motives and policies of the States involved, as a prerequsite to deciding the necessity of continued US recourse to measures of self defence. This, he stated, the Court would find difficult as it was not

> in a position to subpoena the files of the Central Intelligence Agency and the White House - or the files of the Nicaraguan Government, not to speak of the files of the Government of Cuba and of the supporters of the subversion of El Salvador.[53]

Therefore the main concern was one of fact finding. It has already been pointed out that this is not a problem that is singularly restricted to cases of ongoing armed conflicts but may occur in other contexts also. The approach of the Court was to remind the parties that the burden of proof lay on the party seeking to prove a fact. Surely this must be correct. However, it underscores the essential question which is whether the State or States concerned wish to litigate such a dispute before the Court. In the *Nicaragua Case*, neither the US nor the Central American States that were being assisted by the US wanted to litigate such issues before the Court. The US later stated that

> much of the evidence that would establish Nicaragua's aggression against its neighbours is of a highly sensitive intelligence character. We will not risk US national security by presenting such sensitive material in public or before a Court that includes two judges from Warsaw Pact nations. This problem only confirms the reality that such issues are not suited for the International Court of Justice.[54]

The problem is thus not one of the competence of the Court but of the desire of the parties to settle such disputes by judicial means. It will be suggested below that the Court's role in the settlement of disputes can only be exercised to its full potential when the States involved want to settle their disputes. This is particularly true in cases involving the use of force. However, it cannot be excluded that in certain circumstances States will find political advantage in submitting a case involving ongoing armed conflict to the Court. In such a case the Court has a

---

52   Responding to the US argument that it was not the intention of the drafters to include ongoing armed conflicts in the scope of the Court's competence, Judge Schwebel stated that "while that argument is perfectly plausible, it is, in my view, insufficient. It is insufficient because nowhere in the text of the Statute of the Court is there any indication that disputes involving continuing use of armed force are excluded from its jurisdiction." He then examined Article 36(1) and (2) of the Statute and referring to the terminology used in those texts stated that "these capacious terms do not exclude disputes over the continuing use of force from the Court's jurisdiction." 1986 ICJ Reports 289; 76 ILR 623.
53   1986 ICJ Reports 294-5, para. 71; 76 ILR 628-9.
54   "Statement Concerning US Withdrawal from the *Nicaragua Case*", January 18, 1985; See Damrosch (ed.), *The International Court of Justice at a Crossroads* (1987), p.472 at 474.

number of means by which it may seek to determine the relevant facts. For example, under Article 50 of the Statute, the Court may "entrust any individual, body, bureau, commission or other organisation that it may select, with the task of carrying out an enquiry or giving expert opinion." The Court utilised this provision in the *Corfu Channel Case* when it appointed naval experts to inquire into whether Albania could have had knowledge of the laying of the mines in its territorial waters. The Court may also use materials in the public domain, testimony of witnesses, inferences and admisssions against interest in its task of finding the relevant facts.

Indeed one of Judge Schwebel's criticisms of the decision in the *Nicaragua Case* was that the Court did not use its fact-finding capabilities to the full.[55] He argues that the "Court might have manifested a greater willingness than it did in that case to use its power to obtain evidence, to call for additional evidence, and to seek expert inquiry".[56] He states that the Court's findings of fact with respect to the US activities in issue were largely sound and easy enough but that its findings of fact with respect to the activities of Nicaragua, whilst far from easy, were unsound. According to him, the Court decided many questions relating to Nicaraguan activities in other Central American States against the weight of evidence. In so arguing, Judge Schwebel appears to concede that the problem was not that the case was non-justiciable, as he had stated in his dissenting opinion, but that the Court, in his view, carried out its tasks (which might have been difficult but were possible) unsatisfactorily.[57]

Having regard to these considerations, one may therefore agree with Schachter who states that "one cannot conclude as an *a priori* matter that the limits on the fact-finding capabilities of the Court preclude adjudication in cases involving the use of force".[58] It is not the case that the Court lacks the competence to settle disputes involving the ongoing use of force but that such attempts at adjudication might be unproductive because of the unwillingness of one side to submit to such a mode of dispute settlement.[59] As Schachter points out, "the problems of justiciability and juridiction in regard to disputes involving force are largely the same as those raised in other cases in which a respondent state (or a potential respondent) has strong reasons to resist adjudication."[60]

The Court is therefore not debarred from acting in the promotion of peace and

---

55   See Schwebel, "Three Cases of Fact-Finding by the International Court of Justice", in Schwebel, *Justice in International Law* (1994), p.125 at 139.

56   See previous note, at p.135.

57   See Schwebel, "Indirect Aggression in the International Court", in Schwebel, *Justice in International Law* (1994), p.140.

58   Schachter, "Disputes Involving the Use of Force", in Damrosch (ed.), *The International Court of Justice at a Crossroads* (1987), p.223 at 236.

59   Note that the *Bosnian Genocide Convention Case* relates to an armed conflict which at the time when it was filed was ongoing. At no time has the respondent – Yugoslavia (Serbia and Montenegro) – raised this as a bar to the jurisdiction of the Court. See *Case Concerning the Application of the Convention on the Prevention and Punishment of the Crime of Genocide* (Jurisdiction and Admissibility), Judgment of 11 July 1996.

60   See previous note, at p.240.

606   *Dapo Akande*

security by any doctrine limiting its competence to disputes concerning small matters or matters other than the vital interests of states. As Gowlland-Debbas has said:

> the practice of the International Court, beginning with the *Corfu Channel Case* has involved cases with widespread political implications that concerned vital state interests and at times, explosive issues, if not outright hostilities.[61]

The function of the Court is to settle disputes according to international law. If a case involves a disagreement as to the legal rights of the States involved, the Court has the power to hear the case.

C. Dispute Settlement and the Maintenance of Peace

It is submitted that the fact that the function of the Court is the peaceful settlement of disputes according to law shows that it was intended to have a role to play in the maintenance of peace. Many of the disputes that have come before the Court involve not only the vital interests of States but constitute a real source of tension between the parties. Territorial and maritime questions, for example, involve not just the mere determination of a boundary line but also relate to the allocation of resources and of competence and jurisdiction. These disputes are often a source of tension between neighbouring states and are the sorts of disputes that are likely to lead to a breach of the peace. The Court has come to play a significant role in the settlement of some of these disputes and such judicial settlement has prevented the escalation of disputes which might threaten the stability of nations.[62] Judge Shahabuddeen in the opening sentence of his dissenting opinion in the jurisdictional phase of the *Case relating to the territorial dispute between Qatar and Bahrain*,[63] stated that "the judgement of the Court [in these sorts of cases] opens the way to the peaceful settlement of a long-standing dispute between two neighbouring States".

Unsettled disputes between States are often a cause of tension in the relations between those States. International law does not impose an obligation on States to settle disputes, it only obliges them to settle such disputes peacefully, if they decide to settle. International law is not a panacea for the settlement of all disputes but in so far as a dispute contains legal aspects, the authoritative pronouncement on such legal aspects, be it the interpretation of a treaty or the judicial ascertainment of a fact establishing the breach of an international obligation, may play an important part in the final settlement and disposition of the dispute. The Court itself noted in the *Tehran Hostages Case* that

---

61   See Gowlland-Debbas, note 30 at p.652.
62   See, for example, the two cases discussed below.
63   *Case Concerning Maritime Delimitation and Territorial Questions Between Qatar and Bahrain,* Jurisdiction and Admissibility, Judgment of 15 Feb. 1995, 1995 ICJ Reports p.51.

it is for the Court, the principal judicial organ of the United Nations, to resolve any legal question that may be in issue between parties to a dispute; and the resolution of such legal questions by the Court may be an important and sometimes decisive factor in promoting the settlement of the dispute.[64]

III. RECORD OF THE INTERNATIONAL COURT IN CASES INVOLVING DISPUTES LIKELY TO LEAD TO A BREACH OF THE PEACE

Let us now turn to an examination of some cases in which the judicial function of the Court has led to a settlement or an amelioration of a dispute directly threatening international peace. The two I intend to look at involve territorial questions between African States.

(i) Frontier Dispute between Burkina Faso and Mali Case[65]

This case concerned a dispute between the two countries over the ownership of a 100 mile stretch of land known as the Agacher Strip reputedly rich in mineral resources. The demarcation of the frontier between the two countries had been disputed since both countries attained independence and the two States had engaged in negotiations to settle the dispute. In 1974 armed hostilities broke out and a Mediation Commission under the auspices of the OAU was established to seek a solution. This Commission was, however, unable to fulfil its mandate and both parties agreed in 1983 to submit the dispute to a Chamber of the International Court of Justice.

Whilst the Chamber was seised of the case further hostilities broke out and Christmas Day of 1985 saw the start of a few days of armed conflict between the parties. A cease-fire was organised on the 29th of December but both parties also applied to the Chamber of the Court for the indication of provisional measures of protection. The Chamber acceded to this request speedily and on the 10th of January 1986,[66] it ordered both parties to ensure that no action of any kind be taken which might aggravate or extend the dispute. The Chamber also ordered that both parties continue to observe the cease-fire and that they should withdraw their forces to such positions, or behind such lines, as may be determined by an agreement between them to be reached within 20 days of the Order of the Chamber. The terms of the troop withdrawal were to be contained in the said

---

64 *United States Diplomatic and Consular Staff in Tehran (United States v. Iran)*, 1980 ICJ Reports p.22, para. 40.

65 *Frontier Dispute Case (Burkina Faso/Mali)* 1986 ICJ Reports 554. For an analysis of the judgment in this case see Gino Naldi *"Case concerning the Frontier Dispute (Burkina Faso/ Republic of Mali)*: Uti Possidetis in an African Perspective", 36 ICLQ (1987) 893.

66 *Frontier Dispute Case (Burkina Faso/Mali)* Provisional Measures, Order of 10th January 1986, 1986 ICJ Reports p.3. For an analysis of this order and the events leading up to it see Gino Naldi, *"Case concerning the Frontier Dispute between Burkina Faso and Mali*: Provisional Measures of Protection", 35 ICLQ (1986) 970.

608 *Dapo Akande*

agreement and if the parties failed to reach an agreement the Chamber itself would indicate those terms by means of an Order. The Chamber also ordered that with regard to the administration of the disputed area, the situation which prevailed before the armed conflict that gave rise to the request for provisional measures should not be modified.

The parties complied with the terms of this Order and they reached agreement on the terms of the troop withdrawal within 8 days of the Order of the Chamber. The case then proceeded to the merits phase and the Chamber gave judgment on the merits in December 1986 in which it upheld the principle of *uti possidetis* relied on by Burkina Faso. The Chamber then indicated the course of the boundary in the disputed region.

This case illustrates the positive and influential role the International Court can play in the settlement of disputes directly threatening the peace. In the first place, the indication of provisional measures by the Chamber appears to have been instrumental in ameliorating the situation of armed hostilities that erupted in the Christmas period of 1985. Though the parties had agreed to a ceasefire, both of them still felt a need to approach the Chamber for provisional measures in order to reinforce the cessation of hostilities. The Order of the Chamber indicating provisional measures required the parties to reach an almost immediate agreement on the withdrawal of troops failing which the Chamber itself would indicate the terms of the troop withdrawal. It may be argued that this Order in fact facilitated the troop withdrawal and strengthened the ceasefire. Secondly, the judgment of the Chamber on the merits has settled finally the question between the parties. Acceptance of the judgment by both parties and compliance with it has removed this source of tension between the parties.[67] The Court, by deciding the legal issues between the parties, settled decisively a dispute that had twice resulted in armed conflict between the parties.

(ii) *Libya v. Chad* (Territorial Dispute)[68]

This case involved the longstanding dispute between the two countries over the ownership of a huge amount of territory. The area in dispute comprised some 530,000 square kilometres of land and included the Aouzou strip which is reportedly rich in uranium. This strip of land had been occupied by Libya since 1973 and had been the source of often intense armed conflict between the two countries at various points in time. The importance of the dispute is also signified by the fact that the disputed area relates to the whole frontier between the two countries

---

67 See the respective letters of the Presidents of Burkina Faso and Mali addressed to the President of the Chamber that decided the dispute and annexes to ICJ Press Communique No. 87/1. In those letters both Heads of State stated their intention to comply with the judgment of the Chamber and they expressed their appreciation to the Chamber for helping in the reconciliation of the two peoples.

68 *Case concerning the Territorial Dispute between Libya and Chad*, 1994 ICJ Reports, p.6. For an analysis see Gino Naldi, "*Case concerning the Territorial Dispute (Libyan Arab Jamahiriya/Chad)*, 44 ICLQ (1995) 683.

The Role of the ICJ in the Maintenance of International Peace   609

– this frontier being at least 500 miles.

After some prodding by the OAU,[69] both parties agreed to submit the dispute to the International Court of Justice and they signed a special agreement to this effect in August 1989. The case was heard in 1993 and the Court gave judgment in February 1994. The Court upheld the Chadian contention that the boundary between the two countries was conclusively determined by a 1955 treaty between France and Libya. The Court thus held that the whole of the area in dispute, including the Aouzou strip, belonged to Chad.

After some initial anxiety as to whether Libya would comply with the judgment and surrender control of the Aouzou strip, the parties reached agreement on the implementation of the judgment including Libyan troop withdrawal from the Aouzou strip. This agreement was implemented and on the 31st of May 1994, less than four months after the delivery of the judgment of the Court, Libya formally returned the Aouzou strip to Chad after more than 20 years of Libyan occupation.[70] This withdrawal of Libya from the area was overseen by the U.N. in accordance with Security Council Resolution 915.[71]

This case presents another example of role the Court may be called to play in the peaceful resolution of disputes. The case involved a matter of no mean importance and demonstrates that the judicial function may involve the settlement of disputes affecting the vital interests of States.

These cases demonstrate the fact that the Court does have a role to play in the maintenance of peace.[72] The role of the Court is not political in the sense that Court does not utilise political methods of settlement but is confined to settling disputes by applying legal considerations and methods. As Judge Weeramantry stated, in relation to the Court, in his dissenting opinion in the *Lockerbie Case*

> the concept it uses are juridical concepts, its criteria are standards of legality, its methods is that of legal proof. Its tests of validity and the bases of its decision are naturally not the same as they would be before a political or executive organ of the United Nations.[73]

---

69 See resolution of the Assembly of Heads of States and Governments of the OAU – AHG/RES.6 (XXV).

70 See the agreement of 4 April 1994 between Libya and Chad on the practical modalities for the implementation of the Judgment of the Court. Reproduced in 33 ILM 619. See also the report of the Secretary General (S/1994/512) on the implementation of the judgment – reproduced in 33 ILM 785.

71 See also Security Council resolution 910 (1994) by which the Security Council exempted from the application of the flight embargo imposed on Libya, flights by the UN reconnaissance team that preceeded the UN observers that monitored the Libyan withdrawal.

72 See also the *Case Concerning the Land and Maritime Boundary Between Cameroon and Nigeria (Cameroon v. Nigeria)* (Provisional Measures), 1996 ICJ Reports 13. This case also relates to longstanding boundary dispute between the two countries in an area presumed to contain oil. The dispute was submitted to the Court after an armed incident early in 1994 and a request for provisional measures was made by Cameroon after another armed incident in February 1996. Through the mediation of the President of Togo, a ceasefire had been agreed to after the latter incident but Cameroon nevertheless saw benefit in obtaining an order for provisional measures from the Court which granted Cameroon's request.

73 1992 ICJ Reports 56, 166.

610   *Dapo Akande*

This however does not debar the Court from playing a role, perhaps a decisive role, in maintaining peace amongst nations. The Court is often able to clarify authoritatively legal or factual points at issue between the parties and this in turn may have the effect of providing the basis of settlement of the dispute between the parties.

IV. THE COURT AND INTERNATIONAL DISPUTE SETTLEMENT

However, the fact that the Court itself is not able to enforce its judgment means that the Court can only play a useful role if the parties themselves are seeking a settlement of the dispute. A cynical observer may regard this as a fact that prevents the Court from playing any meaningful role in the maintenance of peace. However, the fact is that there are several factors that may inhibit the settlement of disputes between States even when the respective governments desire a settlement. Unsettled disputes are inevitably a source of tension between the States concerned. History shows that if disputes, territorial disputes in particular, are not settled they are likely to lead to frequent and persistent breaches of the peace with the possibility of escalation of such disputes leading to further hostilities.[74] The territorial dispute between Ecuador and Peru,[75] the dispute over the Spratly islands in the South China Sea[76] and the dispute between Turkey and Greece over certain islands in the Aegean[77] are recent examples of how such disputes can threaten or lead to a breach of the peace.

Submission of a dispute to the Court gives the parties an opportunity to settle a dispute they may otherwise be unable to settle. A negotiated settlement of a dispute may be precluded by various factors. Negotiation is only usually successful when there is some compromise on both sides. It may therefore be difficult to achieve a negotiated settlement of a problem that can only be solved by one side or the other getting the disputed territory. Furthermore previous intransigence by the parties may prevent them from withdrawing from already stated and widely publicised positions. Recourse to the Court allows for an authoritative and more palatable vindication of the position of one side over the other.

Settlement of disputes by negotiation and agreement may also be prevented by domestic considerations. A State may be unwilling to reach agreement on a particular matter because it is anxious about how such an agreement may be perceived domestically. Submission of the dispute to the Court provides a State with an instrument that can be played before the domestic constituency in support of an unfavourable outcome to the dispute. As Thomas Franck has so aptly put it

the prestige of the World Court also can conduce to settlement. Even

---

74   See, for example, the cases discussed above.
75   For reports of the fighting between the two countries in early 1995 and a brief history of the dispute, see Keesings's Record of World Events, 1995, at pp.40356, 40404, 40458, 40609.
76   For reports of recent events, see Keesing's Record of World Events, 1994, at pp.40234 and 40383 and 1995, at p.40412.
77   For reports of events in early 1996, see Keesing's Record of World Events, 1996, at p.40923.

where a negotiated settlement has been precluded by domestic politics, a government that cannot openly "bargain away" claims may be
able to retreat before "the majesty of law".[78]

However, the role of the Court is not confined to settling disputes that cannot
be solved by negotiation. The Court can often play a role *within* the negotiation
process either to support negotiations or to inspire the parties to negotiate. In the
North Sea Continental Shelf Cases,[79] the parties had unsuccessfully attempted to
negotiate full delimitation of the continental shelf adjoining their respective
coasts and decided to ask the Court to declare the principles upon which the
continental shelf was to be delimited (as opposed to asking the Court itself to
delimit the continental shelf). The Court did so in its 1969 Judgment after which
the parties negotiated a delimitation on the basis of the legal principles identified
by the Court. This is an example of the role the court can play in supporting
negotiations between States where those negotiations have stalled owing to a lack
of agreement on fundamental legal issues. As the Court remarked in a different
case, "[i]n the fresh negotiations which are to take place on the basis of the
present Judgment, the Parties will have the benefit of the above appraisal of their
respective rights, and of certain guidelines defining their scope."[80]

The Court in the *North Sea Continental Shelf Cases* was in some senses being
asked to play an advisory role in a contentious case as it was only asked to declare
the applicable principles and not to apply those principles. This however should
not be seen as inconsistent with the function of the Court in contentious cases as
the Court is being asked to give what is actually a declaratory judgment binding
on the parties with the effect that if one party fails to apply the declared principles, it is possible for the other party to apply to the Court for the interpretation or
application of its judgment.[81]

The Court may play an important role in getting the parties to a dispute to the
negotiating table and in encouraging a negotiated settlement of the dispute between the parties. The finding by the Court that it has jurisdiction over a dispute
sometimes has this effect. In the *Phosphates Lands in Nauru Case*[82] Nauru, after
failing to get Australia to negotiate the dispute, brought action against Australia
in respect of damage done to the island nation by Australia at the time when
Australia (together with New Zealand and the United Kingdom) was the Administering Authority of Nauru under the UN Trusteeship system. Australia contended that the Court was not competent to hear the case because the Court lacked
jurisdiction and also argued that the case was inadmissible under the *Monetary*

---

78 Thomas Franck, *Judging the World Court* (1986), p.55.
79 *North Sea Continental Shelf Cases (Denmark v. Germany; Netherlands v. Germany)*, 1969 ICJ
    Reports 4; 41 ILR 29.
80 *Fisheries Jurisdiction Case (United Kingdom v. Iceland)* (Merits), 1974 ICJ Reports 3 at p.33,
    para. 78. See also the *Fisheries Jurisdiction Case (Federal Republic of Germany v. Iceland)*
    (Merits), 1974 ICJ Reports 175 at p.202, para. 69.
81 See Art 60 of the Statute of the Court.
82 *Phosphates Lands in Nauru (Nauru v. Australia)*, Jurisdiction and Admissibility, 1992 ICJ
    Reports 241; 97 ILR 1.

612 *Dapo Akande*

Gold principle[83] as the UK and New Zealand were not parties to the case. The Court rejected these arguments and held that it was competent to hear the case. This judgment had the effect of persuading Australia to seek a negotiated settlement of the dispute with the result that it agreed to pay about Aust.$107,000,000 to Nauru, *ex gratia*.[84]

Another case in which the Court played an important role in the achievement of a negotiated settlement of an international dispute is the *Great Belt Case*.[85] This case concerned a Danish project to build a bridge over the main navigable channel of the Great Belt strait. The Great Belt is one of the three Danish straits which form the natural entrances between the North Sea and the Baltic Sea. Finland, alarmed that the bridge would affect the passage of oil rigs and drill ships to and from its ports and yards, brought proceedings in the ICJ in which it asked the Court to declare (i) that there is a right of free passage through the Great belt (being a strait used for international navigation); (ii) that this right extends to drill ships, oil rigs, other special ships and reasonably foreseeable ships; (iii) that the construction of a fixed link over the Great Belt as planned by Denmark would be incompatible with the right of passage mentioned above; and (iv) *that the two parties should start negotiations in good faith, on how the right of free passage shall be guaranteed*. Finland also made an application for provisional measures under Article 41 of the Statute of the Court in which it asked the Court to order a cessation of construction work. However, the Court took the view that the circumstances were not such as to require provisional measures and it dismissed the application for such measures. Nevertheless the Court stated in its Order that:

> pending a decision of the Court on the merits, any negotiation between the parties with a view to achieving a direct and friendly settlement is to be welcomed.[86]

The parties did start negotiations with a view to settling the dispute after the Court's judgment on provisional measures, whilst at the same time proceeding with their preparation of the case through the submission of the Memorial and Counter Memorial and the fixing of the date for the oral hearing. The negotiations stalled at various stages but on 3 September 1992, only 11 days before the date fixed for the opening of the oral hearings, the Prime Ministers of Denmark and Finland agreed, on the telephone, to settle the case. Denmark agreed to pay 90 million Danish kroner and Finland withdrew the case.[87] As there are no public

---

83 *Case Concerning Monetary Gold Removed from Rome in 1943*, (Preliminary Questions), 1954 ICJ Reports p.22 at 32. The principle in question states that, as the Court's jurisdiction is based on consent, the Court will not hear a case where the very subject matter of that case concerns the international responsibility of a third state not before the Court.
84 For the agreement recording the settlement of the dispute, see 97 ILR 110.
85 *Case Concerning Passage through the Great Belt (Finland v. Denmark)*, Provisional Measures, Order of 29 July 1991, 1991 ICJ Reports 12; 94 ILR 446.
86 See paragraph 35 of the Order, 1991 ICJ Reports a p.20; 94 ILR at p.458.
87 For a brief statement of the issues in the case and the settlement, see the note by Martii Koskenniemi (Co-Agent for Finland in the case), 32 ILM 101 (1993).

documents on the settlement, it is not certain what the precise influence of the Court proceedings was, but it is thought that the Court's nudge towards negotiation and the fact that the case was before the Court did have some influence in promoting the negotiated settlement.[88]

Though this role of the Court in the negotiation process has not been particularly well received by all,[89] it can hardly be doubted that in so far as the Court is in this way contributing to dispute settlement it is acting in the promotion of peaceful settlement of disputes and contributing to the maintenance of international peace. It is difficult to understand the criticism of the role of the Court in these cases. The role of the Court is to achieve a peaceful settlement of disputes according to law. When the fact that a dispute is before the Court leads the parties to a negotiated settlement of the dispute, the Court is in fact advancing the object which both adjudication and negotiation serve: the settlement of disputes by peaceful means. Again it is difficult to agree with the implicit suggestion of Judge Bedjaoui[90] that the use of the Court to pressure the other side to negotiate or settle

88   In February 1996, the United States and Iran reached a settlement of the *Case concerning the Aerial Incident of 3 July 1988*, 1996 ICJ Reports 9. This case was brought by Iran against the US in relation to the downing of Iran Air 655 by a US Navy Cruiser in 1988. The oral hearings phase of the case had been scheduled for September 1994 but was postponed *sine die* by agreement of the parties. The parties subsequently reached an agreement under which the US will pay $61.8 million to the heirs of the Iranian victims. See Mealey's International Arbitration Report, Vol. 11, Iss. 2 (2/96) at p.3, Section G, for a copy of the Settlement Agreement. Also in 1995, Senegal and Guinea Bissau discontinued the proceedings before the Court relating to their maritime boundary after reaching agreement as to the joint exploitation of the maritime zone in issue. See 1995 ICJ Reports p.423.

89   See the remarks of Judge Oda in the *Great Belt Case* where he said, at pp.26 -27 ICJ Reports and 464-465 ILR, "Moreover, if what the Court wishes to encourage is that the parties should negotiate as to their respective attitudes or conduct pending judgment of the merits, it should be obvious that neither side will be willing to risk prejudicing its case by making concessions. Until the Court has resolved some central legal issues, the chances of stalemate is therefore so great that for the Court to point the Parties in that direction may be of little avail. I therefore have difficulty in endorsing the sentiment expressed by the Court... The only fruitful direction in which the Court can bend its efforts is towards ensuring 'that the decision on the merits be reached with all possible expedition.'" See also the remarks of Judge Bedjaoui in his book *The New World Order and the Security Council: Testing the Legality of its Acts* (1994). He says, at pp.100-101 that "there are also cases where the Court, though seised, has been unable to proceed to the full accomplishment of its functions but has willy nilly played the part of a deterrent brandished by the applicant State to bring a respondent to a composition. Hardly a glorious role for the Court, or one enabling it to shine. But it has no power to prevent itself from being so used and can only lend itself to such tactics ... The case referred to it thus disappears more often than not after the pronouncement of its decision on a request for provisional measures, the goal having been achieved by the parties reaching a compromise solution." See again the disquiet of Judge Oda in relation to the Court's judgment in the *Case Concerning Maritime Delimitation and Territorial Questions Between Qatar and Bahrain*, 1994 ICJ Reports 112 at 133 *et seq.* (especially paragraphs 5 and 36) which afforded the parties time to present the whole of the dispute to the Court. In the second judgment in the case on jurisdiction and admissibility (February 1995, 1995 ICJ Reports 6), Judge Oda refused to call the 1994 decision a judgment and referred to it "as a record of the Courts attempt at conciliation" (at p.40, para. 2).

90   See the previous footnote. However, both Judge Oda and Judge Bedjaoui are not entirely opposed to this development. In the *Great Belt Case*, Judge Oda went on to say that (in the very next sentence after the passage quoted in the previous footnote), "Indeed, it is the very readiness of the Parties to negotiate on a basis of law that makes it imperative to finish the case as speedily

614 *Dapo Akande*

is an unwelcome development which perhaps ought not to be encouraged. Most writs issued in domestic courts have this very purpose and most cases initiated in domestic courts never go through to full trial and hearing of the case. The purpose of legal rules is not always to impose norms but to create a framework which the parties know is there and will be applied if they fail to agree on norms of conduct amongst themselves. Therefore when the "threat" of legal proceedings leads parties to a dispute to agree on a settlement which is satisfactory to them, the law has not failed nor has there been an abuse of the judicial process. The presence of that process has simply facilitated one of the objects of law which is the peaceful and just settlement of disputes.

The Court also exercises a role in maintaining peace through its role in the development of and clarification of principles of international law.[91] As Sir Hersch Lauterpacht pointed out in an earlier quoted statement,[92] the Court is an instrument for securing peace only in so far as this aim can be achieved through law. Authoritative clarification of legal principles by a body with legitimacy serves the cause of peace in at least two ways. Firstly, it promotes certainty in the law and this not only reduces disputes arising from the uncertainty of the legal position of the parties, but also enables States to form expectations as to the conduct of other States. Secondly, clarification of the law by the Court, if consistent, strengthens and promotes respect for the rule of law.[93]

However, the potentialities of the Court in the maintenance of peace should

---

as possible." Also Judge Bedjaoui, in the passage quoted in the previous footnote, and after stating that the Court has no power to prevent itself from being used in the manner being described, remarked that, "Afterall, the main thing is to see a conflict replaced by a peaceful settlement, even one to whose birth the Court only contributed by its passive existence."

91 See B.S. Chimni, "The International Court of Justice and the Maintenance of Peace and Security: The Nicaragua Decision and the United States Response", 35 ICLQ (1986) 960 at 969.

92 See note 5 above and text thereat.

93 Many of the States that argued that the Court should render the opinion requested of it in *The Legality of the Use by a State of Nuclear Weapons* advisory proceedings based their arguments on the proposition that such an opinion would not only clarify the legal position for States but would contribute to what they saw as the ultimate goal of nuclear disarmament. For example, Counsel for Egypt (Professor George Abi-Saab) argued at the oral hearings that "[I]t would be too presumptuous to assume that an advisory opinion would settle once and for all the problem of nuclear weapons for the international community. But it can clarify all or part of the legalities of this problem." CR95/23 p.32. He went on to refer to the *Status of South West Africa Opinion* saying that that Opinion was a building block in the reestablishment of the rule of law in South Africa and "an advisory opinion on the legalities of the threat or use of nuclear weapons [would] be a building block in the legal regime of a future nuclear safe and reconciled world." CR95/23, p.34. Also, the Australian Foreign Minister (Senator Gareth Evans) argued before the Court that if the members of the Court were "minded to address the substantive issues raised in the questions before [them, their] advice can and will materially effect the achievement of that nuclear disarmament." CR95/ 22, p.73, para. 73. See also the statement of the Australian Solicitor General (Mr. Gavan Griffith) that "an opinion from the Court that the use of nuclear weapons was not illegal in some circumstances could have very negative implications for global nuclear non-proliferation norms." CR95/22, p.37, para. 15. See also the statement of the Counsel for Iran (Mr. Javad Zarif) that a ruling on the question asked of the Court "will be of immense help to the United Nations, as well as to the cause of peace and security of the international community." CR95/26, p.19, para. 11.

not be exaggerated.[94] Writing in 1954, Sir Hersch Lauterpacht noted that the Court had been "debarred from directly acting as an important instrument of peace." Earlier on in the same page he had pointed out that

> governments have not availed themselves of [the] potentialities of international justice. This is the main reason why the Court has not been in the position to make that contribution to peace which would stem from a general conviction of the members of the international community that no State should deny to other States the elementary benefit of a contested legal right being adjudicated by a tribunal administering international law.[95]

One main obstacle to the Court playing a wider role in the maintenance of peace is the fact that resort to the Court is based on consent[96] and that most States seem to want it that way. States appear to be very reluctant to engage in litigation between one other except where they have consented to litigating with the other State with respect to that particular dispute.[97] It is interesting to note that in all but three cases between 1960 and 1995 where the means of seising Court was other than by special agreement, the respondent State entered a challenge or prelimi-

---

94 For an analysis of the advantages and disadvantages of international adjudication, see Richard Bilder, "International Dispute Settlement and the Role of the International Adjudication", in Lori Damrosch, *The International Court of Justice at a Crossroads* (1985) p.155 especially at p.162 *et. seq.* See also Thomas Franck, *Judging the World Court*, p.53.

95 *The Development of International Law by the International Court* (1958), p.5.

96 See Article 36 of the Statute of the Court.

97 The record of litigation between States in other international tribunals that provide for the possibility of inter-state adjudication is much worse than that of the ICJ. Though Article 170 of the Treaty of Rome, setting up the European Economic Community, provides for the possibility of inter-state cases before the European Court of Justice, to date only three such cases have been referred to the Court with two being settled without a judgment from the Court. See *France v. UK*, Case 141/78 [1979] ECR 2923, *Ireland v. France*, Case 58/77 (settled) and *Spain v. United Kingdom*, Case 349/92 (discontinued). Most actions against member States of the EU for breach of Community Law are brought by the European Commission. Articles 24 and 48 of the European Convention of Human Rights also provide for the possibility of States Parties submitting complaints to the Convention institutions against other States Parties for violation of the Convention. However, to date there has only been one inter-state case decided by the European Court of Human Rights – *Ireland v. United Kingdom* (1978) 2 EHRR 25. There have also been seventeen inter-state complaints to the European Commission of Human Rights which deal with only six fact situations. See *Austria v. Italy* 788/60, 4 Yearbook of the European Convention of Human Rights 139; *Greece v. United Kingdom* (two complaints) 176/56 & 299/57, 1 Yearbook 139, 2 Yearbook 177; *Denmark, Norway, Sweden & Netherlands v. Greece* 3321-23/67, 3344/67, 11 Yearbook 699 and 4448/70 13 Yearbook 108; *France, Norway, Denmark, Sweden & Netherlands v. Turkey* 9940/82 – 9944/82; *Cyprus v. Turkey* (three applications), (1993) 15 EHRR 509. It appears that there have been no communications to the United Nations Human Rights Committee by a State Party to the International Covenant on Civil and Political Rights against another State Party as permitted by Article 41 of the Covenant. The one exception to this general trend is the dispute settlement mechanism of the General Agreement on Tariffs and Trade (GATT)/ World Trade Organisation (WTO). Since the inception of the GATT in 1948 over 200 disputes have been referred to it with about 100 of them settled by quasi-adjudicatory panels or working parties. See Jackson, *The World Trading System: Law and Politics of International Economic Relations* (1989), p.95; Hudec, *Enforcing International Trade Law: The Evolution of the Modern GATT System* (1993) p.273.

616 *Dapo Akande*

nary objection either to the jurisdiction of the Court or to the admissibility of the case.[98] This reluctance of States to engage in international litigation of this kind reflects an attitude among States that resort to judicial procedures only has a limited role in the settlement of international disputes.

V. CONCLUSION

In this period after the end of the Cold War, we have seen changes in the level of confidence that States now have in relation to the Court. The Court is in its most productive years in its history, it has what is for it a full case load[99] and as someone writing in *The Times of London* in 1995 put it, "the health of the [International] Court furnishes a more reliable indication of respect for the rule of law and of legal process than most other tests."[100] The limitations of the Court must however be recognised. What it can achieve is necessarily limited by the nature of international relations and the state of the international society at any point in time. The Court's contribution to peace is only fully attainable when respect for international law and for the rule of law is high. However, the Court performs a valuable function in relation to the maintenance of peace by settling disputes according to law and by thus removing these disputes from the list of international disputes. Though this process is invariably dependent on the willingness of States to settle their differences and despite the fact that the Court cannot force States to settle their disputes the Court can and does often play a crucial role in the settlement of disputes that negotiation and armed force have failed to put to rest. This is the contribution of the Court to the maintenance of international peace.

---

98 The three exceptions, which are all recent, are – (i) *Case Concerning the Arbitral Award of 31 July 1989 (Guinea Bissau v. Senegal)*, 1991 ICJ Reports 53; (ii) *Case Concerning Passage through the Great Belt Case (Finland v. Denmark)*, 1991 ICJ Reports 12; and (iii) *Maritime Delimitation in the Area between Greenland and Jan Mayen (Norway v. Denmark)*, 1993 ICJ Reports 38.
99 See the address to the 48th Session of the General Assembly (1993) by Sir Robert Jennings, then President of the Court, recorded in the ICJ Yearbook No. 48 (1993-94), p.219-223.
100 *The Times of London*, 13 July 1995, p.19.

Part III
UN Collective Security Measures

[12]

Boom and Bust?
The Changing Nature of UN Peacekeeping

DAVID M. MALONE and KARIN WERMESTER

The emergence of peacekeeping as one of the most important instruments of the United Nations Security Council was a product of necessity rather than design. Although Article 42 of the UN Charter left open the possibility of taking 'action by air, sea, or land forces as may be necessary to maintain or restore international peace and security', the Founding Members' notion of creating a permanent standing UN army to serve as the tool of collective security never materialized. Instead, peacekeeping emerged as an instrument for the UN to manage inter-state conflict.

With the end of the Cold War, peacekeeping has undergone something of a revolution. In the decade of the 1990s, the Council rose to the challenge of intra-state conflict, often in a strikingly intrusive manner and with mixed success. The changing nature of peacekeeping derived from a permissive political context in which, crucially, the five permanent members of the UN Security Council (P-5) more often than not cooperated in the maintenance of international peace and security. P-5 cooperation in the Security Council unfolded in three phases: the first, at the beginning of the decade, was marked by enthusiasm for far-reaching peacekeeping operations (PKOs); the second, mid-decade, saw a retrenchment in peacekeeping after the failure of UN missions in Rwanda, Somalia and Bosnia, even though working relations among the P-5 remained good; the third, at the end of the decade, saw the deployment (and in the case of Sierra Leone, expansion) of four significant PKOs in Kosovo, East Timor, Sierra Leone and the Democratic Republic of Congo *despite* serious disunity between members of the Council, and especially the P-5, on key issues.[1] With the Security Council now adrift on how to approach several major threats to peace and security across the globe, the ambitious peacekeeping mandates of 1999 appear to be improvisations of last resort.[2]

This contribution seeks to outline the two major shifts, spearheaded by the Security Council, that have occurred in peacekeeping in the past decade: first, in the goals pursued by PKOs, and second, in the level of enforcement they have brought to bear. After a brief survey of peacekeeping during the Cold War, this inquiry aims to address the new structure, components and tasks of PKOs. And the final section will examine the increasing resort to peace enforcement over the past ten years.

The Evolution of Peacekeeping

The first ever peacekeeping operation was christened the United Nations Truce Supervision Organization (UNTSO) and was deployed to Jerusalem in 1948, just three years after the signing of the UN Charter. Although more of a monitoring mission, it became the model on which subsequent peacekeeping operations were created.

Until the end of the 1980s, PKOs were developed and deployed in order to bolster peace processes, observe the peace, and keep the peace – with the exception of the UN intervention in the former Belgian Congo between 1960 and 1964, which involved peace enforcement[3] (see Adebajo and Landsberg in this volume). The 'blue helmets' were defenders of the status quo, and operated with light arms under the strict instruction to use force only in self-defence. Such operations were baptized 'Chapter VI and a half' PKOs and required, in principle, an invitation or consent on the part of the recipient state. They operated under UN command, and were primarily mandated with the implementation of activities agreed upon by belligerents, such as the cantonment and separation of warring parties, the monitoring of borders, the withdrawal of foreign troops, and the verification of the cessation of aid to irregular or insurrectionist movements. These missions have come to be known as 'classic' or 'traditional' PKOs.

Although the P-5 were often instrumental in the provision of superior logistical support, they rarely provided troops for UN peacekeeping missions. Instead, middle and small powers such as the Scandinavian countries, Poland, Canada, Bangladesh, Fiji, Ghana and Nepal became regular 'troop contributing nations', and served to uphold the impartiality of the operations. The initial PKOs largely served as deterrents to the renewal of conflict.[4] Between 1948 and 1987, the Security Council launched 13 peacekeeping and military observer operations of this nature. The majority of these operations (seven of the 13) were deployed in the Middle East, a region of clear geostrategic importance to key permanent members of the Security Council.

The UN Transition Assistance Group (UNTAG) operation in Namibia, 1989–90, marked a transition from 'traditional' to 'complex' PKOs.[5] UNTAG was formally established in 1978 with the mandate of assisting the Special Representative of the Secretary-General to ensure the independence of Namibia through free and fair elections under the supervision and control of the UN.[6] However, UNTAG remained effectively dormant until 1989 when, in the improved post-Cold War international climate, implementation of the peace plan began.[7] Between 1978 and 1988, 'Chapter VI and a half' operations had been 'on hold': no new operations were launched during this period despite a rash of regional conflicts around the globe. This *de facto* suspension of PKOs was largely due to a lack of political will within the Security Council to address threats to international peace and security. The reticence of Member States resulted from several factors including continuing tension between East and West, a global economic downturn and perceptions in Washington that the UN had become the bastion of Third World agitation, as demonstrated by demands for a New International Economic Order (NIEO) and the 1975 General Assembly resolution equating Zionism with racism.[8]

In spite of various violations of the agreements underpinning the UN's presence in Namibia, elections there were ultimately successful and Namibia joined the UN on 23 April 1990. This achievement proved to be a watershed. It helped anchor confidence within the Council that its decisions, even ambitious ones involving significant nation-building components within states, could be implemented. Although Namibia in some ways constituted a late case of decolonization (which the UN had also asserted elsewhere in modest ways), it also encouraged the Council to experiment further with concepts such as the resolution of intra-state conflicts through elections and the promotion of democracy.

With the thaw in the Cold War, the Security Council, between 1989 and 1993, was able to draw on an unprecedented level of political will on the part of most of its 15 members, most significantly the P-5, to address a broad range of internal conflicts erupting throughout the world. Many of these conflicts were legacies of Cold War rivalries often conducted through local proxies. Five UN PKOs were launched in 1988 and 1989. By 1993, an additional 12 PKOs had been launched. Most of these addressed situations of *internal* conflict and generally represented a serious departure from past peacekeeping models.

Multifunctional Peacekeeping Mandates in the 1990s

The transformation of PKOs in the past decade reflects more than mere hybridization. The goals of PKOS have in fact changed significantly: from assisting in the maintenance of ceasefires during the Cold War, peacekeeping operations, during the 1990s, increasingly became peacebuilding missions, launched with the goal of implementing the foundations of a truly self-enforcing peace – no small undertaking.[9] Indicative of the change in strategy was an April 1999 report by the UN Department of Peacekeeping Operations (DPKO) titled *Multidisciplinary Peacekeeping: Lessons from Recent Experience*. The report stated that 'mandates should be conceptualized flexibly and could include elements of peace-building and emergency reconstruction of war-torn economies.'[10] The

40   MANAGING ARMED CONFLICTS IN THE 21st CENTURY

changing goals of peacekeeping have seen concomitant changes in the
structure of PKOs, the creation of new components, and the assignment of
additional tasks. These changes will be addressed in the following sections.

Emerging Structure of PKOS

PKOs, traditionally, were mostly military operations with limited political
goals and tasks. Consequently, they were generally placed under the
supervision of a Force Commander, with any political functions directed from
UN Headquarters. However, given the nature of the 'new generation' of
multidisciplinary PKOs and the need for rapid decision-making in the field in
areas of considerable political sensitivity, these new missions were normally
placed under the overall supervision of a Special Representative of the
Secretary-General (SRSG) to whom both military and civilian components
reported. A number of these diplomats achieved widely recognized distinction
in difficult circumstances. Particularly notable were Alvaro de Soto (ONUCA,
Central America, September 1989–February 1992); Iqbal Riza (ONUSAL, El
Salvador, July 1991–March 1993); Aldo Ajello (ONUMOZ, Mozambique,
October 1992–December 1994); and Lakhdar Brahimi (several missions but
perhaps most notably UNMIH, Haiti September 1994–March 1996).[11] The
increasing use of SRSGs endowed PKOs with a greater political mediation
capacity in the field. In addition, SRSGs were able to communicate country-
specific requirements to UN headquarters, allowing for context-specific
adaptation of mandates. In this way, Special Representatives were able to
spearhead, in many instances, the consolidation of peace at the local level.
Indeed, the function of the SRSG is now understood to be critical, and is
examined incisively in *Command from the Saddle: Managing United Nations
Peace-building Missions*,[12] a report arising from discussions with and among a
large group of mostly successful SRSGs in 1998.

Adapting Components and Tasks

The past decade has also witnessed the proliferation within PKOs of civilian
components, corresponding to the fundamentally altered objectives of these
missions. These include civilian police functions (CIVPOL), electoral
monitoring and democratization, humanitarian relief, economic
reconstruction and longer-term development work, civil engineering,
human rights monitoring and, increasingly, protection, de-mining, and
occasionally other tasks. The following section will address four
components of multifunctional peacekeeping mandates that have either
emerged or undergone significant transformation in the past decade:
elections, humanitarian assistance, human rights and civilian police.

Electoral Components

In the early 1990s, in missions like UNTAG in Namibia, the UN Transitional Authority in Cambodia (UNTAC), the UN Operation in El Salvador (ONUSAL) and the UN Operation in Mozambique (ONUMOZ), the Security Council relied primarily on elections as a means of fostering stability and creating legitimacy for new governments. The success of this approach has been mixed. In Cambodia, 1993 saw the promulgation of a new Constitution for the Kingdom of Cambodia, elections on 23–28 May 1993, and the creation of a new government. However, UNTAC's success at establishing self-enforcing peace was undermined by the palace coup of Cambodian Second Prime Minister Hun Sen against his co-Prime Minister Norodom Ranariddh in July 1997. Hun Sen subsequently won a majority in parliament in highly questionable elections in 1998. Similarly, although the UN was not directly involved in the implementation of elections in Bosnia, the experience of the international community did little to usher in a genuine democracy or self-sustaining economic growth in any part of the country. There, the international community focused heavily on promoting 'multi-ethnicity,' almost as if the mere co-existence of different groups would create a modern, liberal democracy.[13] But experience was to demonstrate that the elections in Bosnia were held too early after the Dayton Peace Agreement of December 1995. Elections were to prove only one feature of democratization, a lesson the UN seemed to learn only in the latter part of the decade, and an experience pregnant with implications for future PKOs. It is a lesson that seems to have been borne in mind in the design of more recent PKOs in Kosovo and East Timor, where elections will be held only after conditions are seen as favourable and, in the case of Kosovo, with a multi-tiered approach, starting with local elections.

In an effort to improve upon this mixed track record, the electoral mandate of PKOs was broadened in the 1990s, adopting a more multifaceted approach to elections and democratization. For instance, the UNMIK mandate in Kosovo included a subsection of the 'institution-building component' described as 'democratization and institution-building', as well as one on 'elections'.[14] Similarly in East Timor, the mission includes a 'governance and public administration' component, in addition to an 'electoral operations' component.[15] In both cases, UN staff have been tasked under this rubric with multiple short and medium-term electoral duties – from voter registration and creating electoral law to supporting capacity building for self-government – in an effort to build institutions that can serve as local conflict management mechanisms.

Humanitarian Assistance Components

At the start of the decade, the Security Council responded to humanitarian crises by expressing concern and by prodding states and UN agencies to

42   MANAGING ARMED CONFLICTS IN THE 21st CENTURY

take more robust action. For instance, Security Council Resolution 688 on Iraq in 1991 made clear the Council members' concern over humanitarian conditions in the northern regions of Kurdistan and mandated some humanitarian activities there.[16]

The international community's initial involvement in Somalia intensified the Security Council's focus on humanitarian affairs, hitherto a domain perceived as resting mainly within the purview of UN agencies like the UN High Commissioner for Refugees (UNHCR). Early in the decade, UN peacekeeping missions like the Somalia operation (UNOSOM I)[17] and the UN Mission in Rwanda (UNOMUR)[18] were given a coordinating role and in certain instances were tasked with escorting humanitarian convoys. However, successful efforts to coordinate the operational tasks of humanitarian agencies require serious attention to the political and security dimensions of crises on the ground.[19] The Council, recognizing that its efforts were being consistently thwarted in Somalia and, as a result, its credibility undermined, sought a new approach. Basking in the afterglow of Operation *Desert Storm* against Iraq in early 1991, the Council authorized the use of force in order to ensure the delivery of humanitarian assistance. Resolution 794 of 3 December 1992 called for the 'use of all necessary means', under a Chapter VII mandate, to establish a US-led Unified Task Force to create a safe and secure environment for the delivery of humanitarian assistance. Earlier that year, the Council had expanded the UN Protection Force's (UNPROFOR) mandate in Bosnia, calling on states to 'take nationally or through regional agencies or arrangements all measures necessary' to facilitate, in coordination with the UN, the delivery of humanitarian assistance in Bosnia and Herzegovina.[20]

By the end of the decade, it became clear that the use of force to protect the delivery of humanitarian assistance was of limited effectiveness, and at worst detrimental, unless it was combined with, or preceded by, serious strategic coordination and planning.[21] Inattention to strategic coordination led to continued overlaps and significant gaps in the mandates of UN agencies, even when combined with the mandates of the multiplicity of NGO humanitarian actors in the field, and posed the single greatest challenge to the successful delivery of humanitarian assistance in conflict-torn societies. Moreover, the provision of humanitarian relief did little to promote medium and long-term stability and development. Bridging the gap between relief and development was no small task. On the ground, humanitarian assistance lent itself to manipulation by spoilers. In Somalia, for instance, peacekeepers were accused of upsetting, even destroying, the local economy.[22] In other contexts of prolonged armed conflict perpetuated by complex and highly organized 'shadow' economies, humanitarian assistance was denounced for contributing to the continuation of war, as in the Great Lakes region for instance.[23]

With renewed authorization of large-scale peacekeeping late in the 1990s, the Council took serious steps to tackle obstacles to the successful delivery of humanitarian assistance by incorporating, for the first time, humanitarian tasks under the rubric of a 'humanitarian component' in the PKO mandates for Kosovo and East Timor. Instead of coordinating the actions of others and providing protection, humanitarian tasks were, for the first time, delegated to peacekeepers themselves. These tasks included the delivery of humanitarian assistance, protection of returning displaced persons and provision of adequate needs upon their return, rehabilitation of key infrastructure, and the promotion of social well-being and restoration of civil society: all markedly new developments[24] (see Griffin and Jones in this volume). In the Democratic Republic of Congo, when MONUC was expanded in early 2000, its mandate included enhanced responsibilities in the field of humanitarian assistance (although it remained woefully understaffed to fulfil the tasks).[25] The development of humanitarian assistance components within UN PKOs and the far-reaching tasks entrusted to them constituted significant developments in peacekeeping practice.

Human Rights Components

A by-product of the effort to bring peace to countries wracked by internal strife was a growing understanding among member states that the transition from self-enforcing ceasefires to self-enforcing peace is next to impossible in the face of continued gross violations of human rights. The increasingly widespread, although selective, media coverage of humanitarian devastation and massive human rights breaches (the so-called CNN effect) resulting *inter alia* from intense pressure exerted by NGOs, served to highlight, in the deliberations of the Security Council, the challenges faced by civilians in countries engaged in civil war and in post-conflict societies. As a result, in the past decade, the Security Council started to link the security and human rights agendas of peacekeeping operations. On the ground, the UN often integrated human rights components into PKOs and, where this was not the case, as in Haiti and Rwanda, provided encouragement for the General Assembly to authorize separate human rights missions operating alongside PKOs.

At the beginning of the decade, the promotion and monitoring of human rights became an important component of the peacekeeping strategy in countries like El Salvador, Guatemala, Cambodia, Haiti and Rwanda. In these cases, peacekeepers or related UN personnel provided observation and reporting on human rights issues. The success of the first of these, with ONUSAL in El Salvador, which was tasked with the verification of the implementation of the Human Rights Agreement, was critical to the subsequent wider success of the peace agreement in spite of many other obstacles along the way.

44   MANAGING ARMED CONFLICTS IN THE 21st CENTURY

At the peak of the Security Council's human rights fervour, involving widespread human rights abuses and, in Rwanda, genocide, it established two International Criminal Tribunals under Chapter VII of the UN Charter with mandates to prosecute individuals responsible for the perpetration of gross human rights abuses in the former Yugoslavia (1993)[26] and in Rwanda (1994).[27] The creation of these tribunals, in turn, intensified pressure for an International Criminal Court (ICC) with universal jurisdiction. Within a few years, the Statute of an ICC was agreed in Rome in 1998. Sufficient ratifications for the Court to become operational should be registered within the next five to seven years.

By the mid 1990s, significant failures and manifest inaction – not least in Africa's Great Lakes region and the Balkans – called into question bold peacekeeping endeavours to protect human rights. Moreover, many states, in particular members of the G-77, were reluctant to accept the emergence of a universal human rights norm. As a result, there emerged, in some instances, a tacit and only implicit agreement on incorporating human rights objectives as a baseline for new PKO mandates. For instance, while the UN Transitional Authority in East Timor (UNTAET) and the UN mission in Sierra Leone (UNAMSIL) do not in themselves have a 'human rights component,' many if not all tasks mandated speak to the protection and promotion of human rights, and not least, in Sierra Leone, to the protection of civilians.[28]

Indeed, the protection of civilians in war became the major theme at the end of the decade through which the Council addressed the issue of human rights. In September 1999, the Council passed Resolution 1265 which called for a broad range of measures to protect civilians in armed conflict, including a measure for PKOs to provide special protection and assistance for women and children in war.[29] In a significant development in early 2000, UNAMSIL in Sierra Leone was authorized, under Chapter VII of the Charter, to use force to protect civilians where resources and circumstances allowed.[30] This represented not only a major shift in focus from states to individuals within states on the part of the Council, but an increasing willingness to use force to protect the human rights of individuals.

Civilian Police Components

The role of local civilian police has become understood as both one of the most important peacebuilding mechanisms in war-torn societies and one of the most significant challenges facing the Security Council today.[31] In the past decade, the role of UNCIVPOL has expanded dramatically in countries where local police have been unable – or unwilling – to fulfil their proper functions. Although police units were deployed in previous missions such as ONUC in the Congo and the UN Temporary Authority (UNTEA) in West New Guinea (now Irian Jaya), the units were attached *ad hoc*, with insufficient attention paid to the provision of resources and strategic planning. The first formal UN civilian police component was deployed in 1964 as part of the UN peacekeeping force in Cyprus (UNFICYP). Under the broad mandate of restoring peace and security to the island, its specific tasks included liaising with the local Cypriot police, accompanying local police patrols and monitoring checkpoints.

Despite their uncertain beginnings, these fledgling civilian police components served as a model for UNCIVPOL during the 1990s. In March 1990, the Council sent a contingent of 1,500 police officers from 25 countries to Namibia with the mandate of monitoring local police forces and assisting in the creation of the necessary conditions for the holding of elections. Subsequent missions encompassing large civilian police components were deployed as part of UNTAC in Cambodia, UNPROFOR and successor missions in Bosnia, the UN Mission in Haiti (UNMIH) and its successor missions, and the UN Mission in Kosovo (UNMIK) and UNTAET in East Timor.

During the Cold War, CIVPOL contingents fulfilled two main functions: monitoring and supervising local law enforcement units; and training and mentoring local police forces.[32] In the 1990s, a third role, with far reaching goals and significant implications for peacekeeping emerged: the performance of law enforcement functions.

The problems encountered by CIVPOL, particularly in the domain of law enforcement, have been significant. The 'blue berets', as they became known, faced the same dilemma as the 'blue helmets': unarmed, they were unable to enforce the law, and armed, they potentially became part of the problem rather than the solution, and constituted targets for spoilers. In practice, the perception of increased security created by their presence was often unmatched by capacity and the illusion of their effectiveness in some instances rapidly collapsed. In addition, although there is a clear underlying logic in separating the military component (authorized to provide macro-level security over the short term in the immediate aftermath of the cessation of hostilities) from the policing component (entrusted with ensuring micro-level public security and begin to reconstitute trust and confidence over the long-term), problems have abounded. At best, the trade-off on the ground has been the division of legitimacy, and thus accountability, of public security writ large. At worst, this has led to not insignificant security 'gaps'. The lack of a pre-existing judicial structure with legal, institutional and logistical capacity to sustain policing functions encountered in 'failed states' has only exacerbated these difficulties.[33]

Significant differences in policing 'culture' among countries providing personnel to the UN have also plagued CIVPOL in the field. For example in Haiti, the values and methods of the French contingent of *gendarmes* clashed

46   MANAGING ARMED CONFLICTS IN THE 21st CENTURY

with the 'community based' policing culture of the Royal Canadian Mounted Police (RCMP) contingent, leading to raw hostility between the two groups at times.[34] In addition, some UN police officers, notably in ONUSAL (El Salvador), proved corrupt and brutal. In Kosovo, bitter criticism of the CIVPOL contingents by ethnic Albanians sparked finger-pointing by UN police against the military command of the local NATO-led security force (KFOR) in northern Kosovo.[35] Such divisions among international personnel in Kosovo contributed little to the image of a united effort that has often been depicted in the media and by UNMIK's leader, Bernard Kouchner, as failing on several fronts.

At the end of the 1990s, the Security Council bowed to realities on the ground. For the first time, as part of the UNMIK and UNTAET mandates, UN police officers were authorized to be on 'active patrol', and in Kosovo, they were armed and given 'executive law enforcement authority'.[36] In these transitional authorities, CIVPOL in fact acts *in lieu* of local police forces, an unprecedented occupation of political and administrative space at the local level.[37] However, the roster of such dangerous law-enforcement assignments adds up to many more police officers than the organization can assemble, and will need to be addressed urgently if the Council is to avoid another – potentially calamitous – failure.

The changing goals of peacekeeping in the past decade have seen peacekeepers become, in a sense, peacebuilders. With mixed success, PKOs have become involved in the creation of an operational and political space in which international actors – from grass-roots NGOs to the UN and its family of agencies – have come to take on a host of peacebuilding activities that seek at once to consolidate peace in the short term and increase the likelihood that future conflicts can be managed withouta resort to violence.[38]

Enforcement Action

The Security Council's willingness to involve itself in a broad range of *internal conflicts* – encompassing inter-communal strife, crises of democracy, fighting marked by a fierce struggle for control of national resources and wealth, and several other precipitating causes or incentives for continuation of war – forced it to confront hostilities of a much more complex nature than the inter-state disputes with which it had greater experience.[39] In so doing, it brought to bear an unprecedented level of enforcement under Chapter VII of the UN Charter. Despite this, the Council's ambitious objectives proved significantly more difficult to attain in many circumstances than it seemed to have anticipated. Even Security Council-mandated military activities encountered significant resistance by frequently shadowy belligerents, leading to incidents involving heavy loss of life among peacekeepers and civilians (in Rwanda, Somalia and the former Yugoslavia). The Council's inability to induce compliance with its decisions fuelled two apparently contradictory but all too frequently complementary responses: on the one hand, the Council moved to enforce decisions which had failed to generate consent in the field, notably in the former Yugoslavia,[40] Somalia[41] and Haiti;[42] on the other, in the face of significant casualties, the Council cut and ran, as in Somalia and at the outset of genocide in Rwanda.[43]

The Use of Force

Resort to the provisions of Chapter VII of the UN Charter and to the enforcement of Security Council decisions was not new: Council decisions were enforced in Korea in the 1950s and to a much lesser extent in the Congo in the 1960s. Nevertheless, the extent to which the Council adopted decisions under Chapter VII during the 1990s was totally unprecedented. At first, it was hoped that the UN would prove capable of launching and managing enforcement operations. In the face of disappointing, occasionally catastrophic results in the former Yugoslavia and Somalia, it became clear to Member States – as many within the UN Secretariat, notably Under-Secretary General for Political Affairs, Marrack Goulding, had argued all along – that the transition from peacekeeping to peace enforcement represented more than 'mission creep' (see Berdal in this volume). The two types of operations were, in fact, fundamentally different – one requiring consent and impartiality, the other requiring international personnel to confront one or several belligerent groups, even if in defence of a Council mandate conceived as neutral relative to the parties to the conflict. Decision-making for enforcement operations also proved more difficult than for most 'classic' UN PKOs, given the attendant risks for UN personnel.[44] Powerful Security Council members like the US and UN Secretary-General Boutros Boutros-Ghali, concluded by 1994 that the UN should not itself seek to conduct large-scale enforcement activities. Consequently, for enforcement of its decisions the Security Council increasingly resorted to 'coalitions of the willing', such as Operation *Uphold Democracy* (in Haiti, 1994–95); the NATO-led implementation force (IFOR) and subsequent stabilization force (SFOR) in Bosnia since 1995; the Inter-African Mission to Monitor the Implementation of the Bangui Agreements (MISAB) in the Central African Republic, 1997; and the International force in East Timor (INTERFET) in 1999.[45] The Council also alternately both worried about and supported in qualified terms enforcement activities by regional bodies, notably ECOMOG, the Ceasefire Monitoring Group of the Economic Community of West African States (ECOWAS), in Liberia and Sierra Leone.[46] One enforcement technique, employed only once previously by the Council, against Rhodesia, was the resort to naval blockades to control access of prohibited goods to regions of conflict. Such blockades were mandated with varying success during the 1990s: against Iraq in the Persian Gulf and the Gulf of Aqaba, against various parties in the former Yugoslavia on the Danube and the Adriatic Sea, and against Haiti.[47]

One problem relating to both the use of force and persuasion by international actors is the now widely understood notion that third parties cannot, in most circumstances, impose peace if there is no political will among the protagonists to solve the problem.[48] The withdrawal of much of the UN Angola Verification Mission (UNAVEM I) from Angola in 1993 in the wake of failure of the rebel group, the National Union for the Total Liberation of Angola (UNITA) to respect the outcome of UN-monitored elections, is a case in point. In establishing UNAVEM II in early 1995, the Council requested that the Secretary-General condition UN deployment on the behaviour of parties on the ground.[49] Even this failed, over time, as signalled by the withdrawal of the UN Mission of Observers in Angola (MONUA, the successor observer mission to UNAVEM III) in February 1999, in the face of considerable hostility by both protagonists.[50]

An exceptional and controversial case was NATO's bombing of Serbia, Montenegro and Kosovo in the spring of 1999 in a bid to halt 'ethnic cleansing' by Serb forces in Kosovo. NATO's action followed the failure of negotiations at Rambouillet, which involved Belgrade and a 'contact group' of countries (including the USA, France, the UK and the Russian Federation) seeking the implementation of earlier Security Council resolutions on Kosovo.[51] NATO countries proceeded to attack Serb targets from the air, as of 24 March 1999, without Security Council authorization, pointing to threatened vetoes by Moscow (and possibly Beijing) in justifying their decision to forego such authorization.[52] Russian efforts to rally Security Council condemnation of, and an end to, NATO's action failed, on 26 March 1999, with 12 countries opposed to Moscow's text and only three in favour.[53] A settlement of sorts was negotiated within the veto-free Group of Eight (G8) forum in May 1999 and estimated in Security Council Resolution 1244 of 10 June 1999. NATO countries retained the lead role in the military force (KFOR, a coalition operation rather than a UN PKO, authorized under Chapter VII of the UN Charter), providing security in Kosovo, alongside a UN police force, which as of 1 March 2000 remained woefully under-staffed and inadequate to the task. But the UN was placed in charge of the civil administration of the province, working with the European Union and the Organization for Security and Cooperation in Europe (OSCE).[54] Strong differences remain over the legality of NATO's action (although perhaps less so its legitimacy). NATO, undergoing something of an existential and, to a lesser degree, operational crisis in the wake of its successful Kosovo operation – a campaign marked by a great deal of luck – did not seem particularly keen to engage in any further such interventions.[55] Nevertheless,

NATO will continue to play an important role alongside the UN in promoting stability in the Balkans (and possibly elsewhere in Europe). This insight is hardly new: as early as 1993, Kofi Annan, at the time UN Under-Secretary-General of Peacekeeping, suggested that NATO could play a key role in 'peacekeeping with teeth'.[56]

Humanitarian Intervention

At the end of the 1990s, a wide-ranging and unusually sharp debate arose over humanitarian intervention as a result, in part, of NATO's air campaign against Serb forces in the Balkans, which had not been explicitly authorized by the UN Security Council. This debate coincided with greater resort by the Council to the provisions of Chapter VII of the Charter and an increasing focus by its members on the plight of civilians in war. However, many states were reluctant to accept that an 'international norm in favour of intervention' had developed, as claimed by Kofi Annan in a landmark speech to the General Assembly on 20 September 1999.[57] In response to Annan's speech, Algerian President Abdelaziz Bouteflika stated that at least three questions would need to be resolved before the debate on intervention, or indeed 'interference' as he called it, could be closed: 'First, where does aid stop and interference begin? Second, where are the lines to be drawn between the humanitarian, the political, and the economic? Third, is interference valid only in weak or weakened states or for all states without distinction?'[58] Annan was widely seen as being on strong moral and political ground in advocating humanitarian intervention without Security Council authorization in extreme cases, but, by the end of 1999, there seemed little hope of developing a legal framework of principles to govern such intervention.[59] Thus, humanitarian intervention was likely to continue to be practised only in exceptional circumstances and authorized only on a case-by-case basis by the Security Council. Harsh Russian military tactics employed against civilians in Chechnya in late 1999 and early 2000 demonstrated that humanitarian action would remain subject to double standards, as has been the record of the UN and of the Security Council since 1945. Nonetheless, Annan was widely admired for championing a meaningful debate over humanitarian action and for promoting human rights at every opportunity. By the turn of the millennium he had contributed to a significant development of norms favouring the citizen over the state, and civilians over militaries.

Sanctions

More common than military enforcement decisions by the Council was the resort to mandatory economic (and, increasingly, diplomatic) sanctions under Chapter VII of the UN Charter.[60] While arms embargoes remained in vogue, the imposition of comprehensive trade and other economic sanctions, once

50   MANAGING ARMED CONFLICTS IN THE 21st CENTURY

seen as more benign than the resort to force, faded noticeably once the humanitarian costs of sanctions regimes against Haiti and Iraq became widely known by the end of the 1990s. The capacity of government elites in countries struck by sanctions to enrich themselves greatly by controlling black markets in prohibited products also took some time to sink in. Indeed, the criminalization of the economies of Iraq, the former Yugoslavia and Haiti while under sanctions was striking. By the mid-1990s, more targeted sanctions such as the ban on air flights to and from Libya aimed at inducing Tripoli's cooperation with Council efforts to address several terrorist aircraft bombings, gained favour. Diplomatic sanctions, such as the reduction in the level of diplomatic representation mandated by the Council against Sudan following an assassination attempt in Addis Ababa against Egyptian President Hosni Mubarak, also gained favour.[61] Targeted sanctions (addressing financial transactions and air links) also went into effect on 14 November 1999 against the Taleban in Afghanistan in response to the protection the regime has provided to the alleged terrorist Osama Bin Laden.[62]

Several research projects have recently illuminated the difficulty of designing and implementing effective sanctions, including the 'Interlaken process' (dealing with financial sanctions) sponsored by the Swiss, and a German-sponsored project on arms embargoes and other forms of targeted sanctions.[63] The Canadian government has also recently brought to the attention of the Security Council the need for more effective, less counter-productive sanctions regimes in general,[64] and has emphasized the need for more rigorous application of the Council's sanctions mandate in Angola to suffocate UNITA's ability to fund its war effort through the sale of diamonds.[65] This has resulted, *inter alia*, in the decision of the De Beers corporation to close down its operations in Angola.[66] The Security Council has recently undertaken to curb the sale of 'conflict' diamonds in Angola and Sierra Leone.[67]

The distinction between 'classic' peacekeeping operations of interposition adopted under Chapter VI of the UN Charter and those involving an element of enforcement adopted under Chapter VII had, by the end of the 1990s, become fairly moot. Indeed, the new operations launched in 1999 by the Security Council in Kosovo, East Timor, Sierra Leone and the Democratic Republic of the Congo, were all Chapter VII operations. The only non-Chapter VII operation on the planning boards in early 2000 was a hypothetical deployment between Eritrea and Ethiopia.

Conclusion

The UN Security Council's willingness to tackle complex civil wars during the 1990s owed much to a favourable conjunction of events involving a new-found

THE CHANGING NATURE OF UN PEACEKEEPING 51

political will, particularly among the P-5, that led to the Council expending considerable resources and running some real risks to promote global peace. However, in spite of the significant efforts by the UN system and many of its member states, results have been mixed at best. Complex PKOs involving a multiplicity of civilian components, such as ONUMOZ in Mozambique, UNMIH in Haiti, ONUSAL in El Salvador, MIGUA in Guatemala, UNTAC in Cambodia and UNTAG in Namibia, proved successful to varying degrees. Several others, such as UNOSOM I and II in Somalia, UNPROFOR in Bosnia, UNAMIR in Rwanda and the successive incarnations of UNAVEM in Angola failed, sometimes spectacularly. 'Coalitions of the willing', sometimes able to command greater resources and enjoying much greater administrative and decision-making flexibility, were generally more adaptable. A great number of case studies have generated useful 'lessons learned' material. However, the Council's woolly decision in early 2000 to authorize conditionally a woefully understaffed and unclearly-tasked peacekeeping operation for the Democratic Republic of Congo and the appalling shortcomings of UNAMSIL in Sierra Leone as of early 2000 suggest that while individuals may absorb lessons and benefit from experience, collective bodies like the Security Council have limited memories and are prepared to seize upon any benefit of doubt to indulge political expediency.[69]

Depressing as these conclusions may be, there is little doubt that the Council's decisions in the 1990s, often of a strikingly intrusive nature, fundamentally altered conceptions of state sovereignty and promoted further international intervention (with or without the consent of belligerent parties, across borders and within states).[70] Whether the trends of the 1990s will survive the newly heightened tensions among the Permanent Five following NATO's war in Kosovo remains to be seen. Nevertheless, as pointed out elsewhere in this volume (see Griffin and Jones), the expansion of peacekeeping in the post-Cold War era to embrace ambitious programmes of civil administration often underpinned by the threat or actual use of force appeared only to intensify in 1999 with sizeable operations in both Kosovo and East Timor. The next two years should instruct us as to whether these missions represent a 'bridge too far' for the UN, although here again results may well be mixed and clear lessons with universal application hard to extract.

ACKNOWLEDGEMENTS

We are grateful to friends and colleagues for their extremely helpful comments and suggestions, in particular Bruce D. Jones, Leila Kazemi and Katia Papagianni.

NOTES

1. On 24 Feb. 2000, paradoxically under heavy US pressure, in Security Council Resolution 1291, the Security Council agreed conditionally to expand its monitoring operation, the UN

52 MANAGING ARMED CONFLICTS IN THE 21st CENTURY

Mission in the Democratic Republic of the Congo (MONUC) into a medium-scale, although no doubt ill-fated (5,537 strong) PKO in a bid to build momentum towards a cessation of hostilities.

2. See the 'Report of the Panel on United Nations Peace Operations – A far-reaching report by an independent panel', 23 Aug. 2000, which notably argues that 'the United Nations has repeatedly failed to meet the challenge, and it can do no better today'. The report is available on the UN's website at: www.un.org/peace/reports/peace_operations/.

3. Thomas G. Weiss, David P. Forsythe and Roger A. Coate, *The United Nations and Changing World Politics*, 2nd Ed., Boulder, CO: Westview Press, 1997, p.53.

4. See Chantal de Jonge Oudraat, 'The United Nations and Internal Conflict', in Michael E. Brown (ed.), *The International Dimensions of Internal Conflict*, Cambridge Mass: Center for Science and International Affairs, John F. Kennedy School of Government, Harvard University, 1996.

5. Note that this does not imply that there is a linear evolution from traditional to other forms of peacekeeping operations, as the possibility of new PKOs of interposition remains. The point is simply that the 1990s have witnessed a proliferation of substantively new peacekeeping activities.

6. UN Security Council resolution 435, 29 Sept. 1978.

7. UN Security Council resolution 632, 16 Feb. 1989.

8. UN General Assembly resolution 3379, 10 Nov. 1975.

9. In 1992, Boutros Boutros-Ghali defined post-conflict peacebuilding as 'the creation of a new environment to forestall the recurrence of conflict' in *An Agenda for Peace*, A/47/277-S/24111, 17 June 1992. For an excellent articulation of the evolution and current state of the art of peacebuilding, see Elizabeth M. Cousens' Introduction, in Elizabeth M. Cousens and Chetan Kumar (eds.) with Karin Wermester, *Peacebuilding as Politics: Cultivating Peace in Fragile Societies*, Boulder, CO: Lynne Rienner, forthcoming 2000.

10. 'Multidisciplinary Peacekeeping: Lessons from Recent Experience', United Nations DPKO, Apr. 1999.

11. Kofi Annan also briefly served as SRSG in Bosnia (UNPROFOR, 1 Nov.–20 Dec. 1995); see *The Blue Helmets: A Review of UN Peacekeeping*, New York, NY: UN Department of Public Information, 1996.

12. Rick Hooper and Mark Taylor, 'Recommendations Report of the Forum on the Special-Representative of the Secretary-General: Shaping the UN's role in Peace Implementation', Fafo report No.26, Oslo, Norway: *Peace Implementation Network, Programme for International Cooperation and Conflict Resolution*, 1999.

13. Alexander T. Knapp, 'Vision and Craft – Elections in Kosovo', presentation to UNA-USA, 30 Nov. 1999, New York.

14. UN Security Council resolution 779, 12 July 1999.

15. UN Security Council resolution 1024, 4 Oct. 1999.

16. UN Security Council resolution 688, 5 Apr. 1991.

17. UN Security Council resolution 751, 24 Apr. 1992.

18. UN Security Council resolution 872, 5 Oct. 1992.

19. See Sue Lautze, Bruce D. Jones and Mark Duffield, 'Strategic Humanitarian Coordination in the Great Lakes Region, 1996–1997: An Independent Study for the Inter-Agency Standing Committee', New York: Office for the Coordination of Humanitarian Affairs (OCHA), UN (Mar. 1998).

20. UN Security Council resolution 770, 13 Aug. 1992.

21. Ibid. According to Lautze, Jones and Duffield, strategic coordination refers to two sets of tasks in particular: (1) 'negotiating access to affected populations, advocating respect for humanitarian principles and law, and liaising with international political and military actors' and (2) 'setting the overall direction and goals of the UN humanitarian programme, allocating tasks and responsibilities within that programme, ensuring correspondence between resource mobilization and established priorities, and monitoring and evaluating system-wide implementation of the programme' (see n. 19 above), p.2.

22. See in particular, Ameen Jan, 'Somalia: Building Sovereignty or Restoring Peace?', in Cousens and Kumar (eds.) with Wermester, *Peacebuilding as Politics*.

THE CHANGING NATURE OF UN PEACEKEEPING   53

23. See Alex de Waal, 'En toute impunité humanitaire,' *Le Monde Diplomatique*, Apr. 1998, p.32.
24. See, on Kosovo, S/1999/779, 12 July 1999, and on East Timor, S/1999/1024, 4 Oct. 1999.
25. See UN Security Council Resolution 1291, 24 Feb. 2000, and S/2000/30, 17 Jan. 2000.
26. UN Security Council resolution 808, 22 Feb. 1993.
27. UN Security Council resolution 955, 8 Nov. 1994.
28. UN Security Council resolution 1024, 4 Oct. 1999.
29. UN Security Council resolution 1265, 17 Sept. 1999. Olara Otunnu, President of the International Peace Academy, 1990–98, had undertaken a vigorous campaign as UN Under-Secretary-General to highlight the plight of children in war. The Security Council's decision underscores his remarkable success in this endeavour.
30. UN Security Council resolution 1270, 22 Feb. 2000.
31. See Tor Tanke Holm and Espen Barth Eide (eds.), *Peacebuilding and Police Reform*, London and Portland, OR: Frank Cass,1999.
32. Robert B. Oakley, Michael J. Dziedzic and Eliot M. Goldberg, *Policing the New World Disorder: Peace Operations and Public Security*, Washington DC: National Defense University, 1998, p.23.
33. See Gareth Evans, *Cooperation for Peace: The Global Agenda for the 1990s and Beyond*, Sydney: Allen & Unwin, 1993.
34. See David M. Malone, *Decision-Making in the UN Security Council: The Case of Haiti*, 1990–1997, Oxford: Clarendon Press, 1998.
35. R. Jeffrey Smith, 'French Troops in Kosovo Accused of Retreat; UN Police Cite lack of Support in Mitrovica Uprising, Inadequate Aid to Civilians', *The Washington Post*, 9 Feb. 2000, p.A14.
36. See Barbara Crossette, 'The UN's Unhappy Lot: Perilous Police Duties Multiplying', *The New York Times*, 22 Feb. 2000, and for quote see UN Security Council resolution 779, 12 July 1999.
37. See Michèle Griffin and Bruce D. Jones in this volume for an elaboration of this point.
38. See Cousens (n.9 above).
39. For a discussion of the importance of economic factors in many civil wars of the 1990s, see Mats Berdal and David M. Malone (eds.), *Greed and Grievance: Economic Agendas in Civil Wars*, Boulder, CO: Lynne Rienner, 2000.
40. There is a plethora of literature regarding the former Yugoslavia and constraints and obstacles encountered in the field, including: Adam Roberts, 'Communal Conflict as a Challenge to International Organization: The Case of Former Yugoslavia,' *Review of International Studies*, Vol.21 (1995), pp.389–410; International Crisis Group, 'Kosovo: Let's Learn from Bosnia – Models and Methods of International Administration,' Sarajevo, Bosnia, 17 May 1999.
41. See John L. Hirsch and Robert Oakley, *Somalia and Operation Restore Hope: Reflections on Peacemaking and Peacekeeping*, Washington DC: United States Institute for Peace Press, 1995 and more recently Mark Bowden, *Black Hawk Down: A Story of Modern War*, Atlantic Monthly Press, 1999.
42. Malone (n. 35 above); also James F. Dobbins, 'Haiti: A Case Study in Post-Cold War Peacekeeping', *ISD Reports* II.I, Washington DC: Institute for the Study of Diplomacy, Georgetown University, Oct. 1995; and on Haiti and Somalia see David Bentley and Robert Oakley, 'Peace Operations: A Comparison of Somalia and Haiti,' *Strategic Forum* 30, Washington DC: Institute for National Strategic Studies, National Defense University, May 1995.
43. See in particular Gérard Prunier, *The Rwanda Crisis : History of a Genocide*, New York: Columbia University Press, 1995; Michael Barnett, 'The UN Security Council, Indifference and Genocide in Rwanda,' *Cultural Anthropology*, Vol.12, No.4 (1997), p.551; and J. Matthew Vaccaro, 'The Politics of Genocide: Peacekeeping and Disaster Relief in Rwanda,' in William J. Durch (ed.), *The UN, Peacekeeping, American Policy and the Uncivil Wars of the 1990s*, New York: St. Martin's Press, 1996. See also Adebajo and Landsberg in this volume.
44. The UN Secretary-General's report on UNPROFOR's catastrophic failure to deter attack at Srebrenica in 1995 details a case in point. See A/54/549 of 15 Nov. 1999.

54   MANAGING ARMED CONFLICTS IN THE 21st CENTURY

45. For an excellent reference work covering UN peacekeeping operations from 1947 to the present, see Oliver Ramsbotham and Tom Woodhouse, *Encyclopedia of International Peacekeeping Operations*, Santa Barbara, CA: ABC-CLIO, 1999.
46. For an excellent analysis of regional peacekeeping, see Hilaire McCoubrey and Justin Morris, *Regional Peacekeeping in the Post-Cold War Era*, The Hague, The Netherlands: Kluwer Law International, 2000.
47. UN Department of Political Affairs, 'A Brief Overview of Security Council Applied Sanctions', *Interlaken 2*, 1998.
48. For a statement on this by the Secretary-General Boutros Boutros-Ghali, see SG/SM/5589, 21 Mar. 1995.
49. UN Security Council resolution 976, 8 Feb. 1995.
50. UN Security Council resolution 1229, 26 Feb. 1999.
51. UN Security Council resolution 1199, 23 Sept. 1998 and UN Security Council resolution 1203, 24 Oct. 1998.
52. See S/PV.3988, 24 Mar. 1999 and S/PV.3989, 26 Mar. 1999, and, for a justification of the NATO air strike, see the Press Statement by NATO Secretary-General Javier Solana No.041, 24 Mar. 1999.
53. UN Security Council draft resolution 328, 1998, failed to be adopted on 26 Mar. 1999.
54. See Crossette, 'The UN's Unhappy Lot: Perilous Police Duties Multiplying,' and Smith, 'French Troops in Kosovo Accused of Retreat; UN Police Cite Lack of Support in Mitrovica Uprising, Inadequate Aid to Civilians'.
55. Lieven, 'Kosovo: Implications for the International System', Ditchley Conference Report 00/01 reporting on a conference at Ditchley Park, 14–16 Jan. 2000.
56. Kofi A. Annan, 'UN Peacekeeping Operations and Cooperation with NATO,' *NATO Review* 41, no.5 (Oct. 1993).
57. UN document A/54/PV.4, 20 Sept. 1999, p.4.
58. UN document A/54/PV.4, 20 Sept. 1999, p.14.
59. For a sophisticated discussion of these issues, see Anatol Lieven (n.59 above).
60. For an in-depth discussion of the Council's experience with sanctions regimes since 1990, see David Cortright and George Lopez, *The Sanctions Decade: Assessing UN Strategy in the 1990s*, Boulder, CO: Lynne Rienner, 2000.
61. For another recent discussion of sanctions and the increasing use of targeted sanctions, see Daniel W. Drezner, *The Sanctions Paradox: Economic Statecraft and International Relations*, Cambridge: Cambridge University Press, 1999.
62. See Security Council resolution 1267 of 15 Oct. 1999.
63. See the German Permanent Mission to the UN website for details on this: http://www.undp.org/missions/germany/state.htm
64. See Canada on the UN Security Council 1999-2000: http://www.un.int/canada/english.html
65. For a recent articulation of the Canadian initiative on Angola, see Ambassador Robert R. Fowler, 'Notes for an Intervention by H.E. Robert R. Fowler, Ambassador and Permanent Representative of Canada, to the United Nations Security Council on the Humanitarian Situation in Angola,' Canada on the UN Security Council 1999–2000, 23 Aug. 1999.
66. 'Le négociant De Beers arrête tout achat de diamants d'Angola', *AFP*, 6 Oct. 1999.
67. The Sanctions Committee on Angola was established by UN Security Council resolution 864 in 1993. For a report regarding recent developments in the committee, see UN document S/1999/147.
68. The Report of the Panel (Brahmin Report) of August 2001 highlighted one growing problem: the unwillingness of industrialized countries to expose their troops to physical risks in far-off countries where they have no national interests at stake. On this practically and ethically reprehensible head, see Ramesh Thakur and David Malone, 'Rich and Afraid of Peacekeeping', *International Herald Tribune*, 25 October 2000.
69. MONUC, UN Security Council resolution 1291, 24 Feb. 2000.
70. See David M. Malone, 'The UN Security Council in the 1990s: Boom and Bust?,' Proceedings of the 28th Annual Conference of the Canadian Council on International Law, Keynote Address, in *From Territorial Sovereignty to Human Security*, Cambridge, MA: Kluwer Law International, forthcoming 2000.

[13]

The Applicability of International Law Standards to United Nations Economic Sanctions Programmes

W. Michael Reisman* and Douglas L. Stevick**

Abstract

In the first half-decade after the fall of the Berlin Wall, the UN Security Council repeatedly decreed mandatory economic sanctions programmes under Chapter VII of the UN Charter. Some of the programmes were severely criticized for their allegedly disproportionate effects on the populations of target states. The authors identify economic sanctions as a coercive instrument and assess the applicability of international law standards, including the traditional criteria of necessity, proportionality and discrimination, to mandatory UN economic sanctions programmes. After an overview of the theory of economic sanctions and their place among strategic instruments of enforcement, the authors review the instances of mandatory UN economic sanctions programmes, assessing their effects on the populations of the target states and the extent of the Council's consideration of international legal norms in designing and carrying out sanctions. Concluding that the Council has given inadequate consideration to international law standards in implementing these programmes, the authors propose five legal principles for mandatory economic sanctions programmes: that highly coercive sanctions follow prescribed contingencies; that they be necessary and proportionate; that the sanctioners reasonably maximize discrimination between combatants and non-combatants; that sanctions programmes be periodically assessed; and that relief be provided to injured third parties.

* Hohfeld Professor of Jurisprudence, Yale Law School, P.O. Box 208215, New Haven, Connecticut 06520–8215, USA.

** J.D. Yale 1996. The comments and suggestions of Carlos Viana, J.D. Yale 1997 are gratefully acknowledged. Early versions of the theoretical sections of this article were read to the American Society of International Law (*Proceedings ASIL* (1996) 351) and the American branch of the International Law Association. In the light of comments received, significant changes were made in the theoretical approach.

1 Introduction

Economic sanctions have become a preferred policy instrument of foreign policy-makers in recent years. With the end of the Cold War, multilateral sanctions regimes in particular have proliferated, especially at the United Nations: nine times since the fall of the Berlin Wall, the Security Council has acted under Chapter VII of the UN Charter to create mandatory economic sanctions programmes.

The effectiveness of economic sanctions has long been a subject of debate among policy-makers and jurists. Largely missing from this debate, however, has been any sustained analysis of the international law standards that should govern decisions about the use of economic sanctions. Only recently, as concerns have mounted in a number of circles over the manifest deprivations endured by the people of Iraq and Haiti as a result of the application of mandatory UN sanctions, has this issue drawn the attention of international legal scholars, policy-makers, and ethicists.[1] In this article, we analyse the question of the mandatory applicability of critical international law standards to the design and implementation of economic sanctions programmes, focusing in particular on the inadequacies of UN practice in clarifying a legal framework under which policy-makers can effectively and properly assemble and enforce economic sanctions regimes.

2 Preliminary Considerations

'Economic sanctions' may take many forms and may be applied unilaterally or multilaterally. They involve the purposive threat or actual granting or withholding of economic indulgences, opportunities and benefits by one actor or group of actors in order to induce another actor or group of actors to change a policy. Targeted policies may be external, such as the withdrawal of the target state from territory it has seized or illegally occupied (e.g., South Africa's long occupation of Namibia in defiance of the United Nations' termination of the Mandate), or internal, such as ending patterns of human rights violations (as in present-day China). Economic sanctions may even seek the replacement of the elite in the target state (e.g., Peron in Argentina after the Second World War or Saddam Hussein in Iraq at the moment).

A *Prevalence*

Economic sanctions are often used as a unilateral technique in international politics, though not necessarily explicitly — indeed, sometimes demurrers or denials are declared by the sanction-feasor, who may insist that the consequences, which are, of course, regrettable, are the ineluctable result of some other lawful action.[2] An

---

[1]   See, e.g., United Nations Sanctions as a Tool of Peaceful Settlement of Disputes: Non-Paper Submitted by Australia and the Netherlands, UN Doc. A/50/332 (1995); Damrosch, 'The Civilian Impact of Economic Sanctions', in L.F. Damrosch (ed.), *Enforcing Restraint: Collective Intervention in Internal Conflicts* (1993), 274, 305; Pierce, 'Just War Principles and Economic Sanctions', 10 *Eth. & Int'l Aff.* (1996) 99.
       In this respect, we would depart from the approach taken by G.C. Hufbauer et al., *Economic Sanctions Reconsidered* (2nd. ed., 1990), which is the indispensable work in this field and must be consulted for any

agriculture-exporting state's perishable products aboard a ship in harbour may slowly compost, as the importing state's customs inspectors, with unprecedented care, examine each hold 'by the book', all this occurring at a moment when the two states are engaged in a critical negotiation. Denials or not, the target state always gets the message.

Uses of power by one actor against another are, by definition, based on a general or momentary power-superiority, whose fluidity can be obscured by stereotyping terms, in common parlance, such as the 'strong' and the 'weak'. Economic sanctions are not quite 'equal opportunity' instruments, but their use is certainly not limited to the greatest states against the smallest states. Any disparity in power — in general or as a result even of a transitory situation — can provide the basis for the design and application of an economic sanctions programme. For example, during the stormy election of the Secretary-General of the Organization of American States (OAS) some three years ago, some Caribbean states angrily accused Costa Rica of using banana diplomacy to persuade certain states to support the candidate it had put forward.[3] Costa Rica is hardly a superpower.

Conversely, immunity from economic sanctions is a matter of degree. Even large and powerful states such as the United States may be targeted effectively. The People's Republic of China has mounted an extraordinarily effective economic sanctions programme against the United States, through which it has secured virtually all the adjustments it seeks in America's China policy. One of the most fascinating aspects of this particular economic sanctions programme is that the target, the United States, seems possessed of the idea that *it* is the economic sanctioner, while China is the target! The seemingly interminable national debate about the utility and wisdom of economic sanctions proceeds on this flawed assumption. The point of emphasis is that opportunities to use economic sanctions unilaterally are rather widely distributed.

B *Effectiveness of Economic Sanctions*

Are economic sanctions effective? If that question means: 'When used without the military strategy, can and do economic sanctions induce desired adjustments in the external or internal policies of the target?', the answer is, under certain conditions, yes, decisively and demonstrably so. In 1919, Woodrow Wilson, one of the great enthusiasts of economic sanctions, said:

---

inquiry. The authors only examine explicit cases of economic sanctions. We believe that the 'implicit' use of economic sanctions is much more common than they allow and that it is particularly important to consider, *inter alia*, covert uses of the economic instrument, such as shifts of hard currency reserves to strengthen or weaken the currency of the target state before an election. See generally W.M. Reisman and J. Baker, *Regulating Covert Action* (1992).

[3] On this issue, see Collymore, 'Banana Squabble Helps Gaviria Gain OAS Presidency', *Inter Pr. Serv.*, 28 March 1994, available in Westlaw.

> A nation that is boycotted is a nation that is in sight of surrender. Apply this economic, peaceful, silent, deadly remedy and there will be no need for force. It is a terrible remedy. It does not cost a life outside the nation boycotted, but it brings a pressure upon the nation which, in my judgment, no modern nation could resist.[4]

Wilson was speaking as a propagandist for the League of Nations and did not need, in that role, to specify the conditions for the success of the instrument. But his basic point still holds: economic sanctions can be highly effective.

Part of Wilson's subtext — that economic sanctions are, in his words, silent, deadly and terrible — also holds. Another part of his subtext, however — that the instruments are 'peaceful' — certainly does not apply to the targets of the sanctions. It is that comfortable astigmatism that prompts the present inquiry. Precisely because economic sanctions are now used more frequently by the international community, a re-examination of what they are, how they stake and how they miss, and how they should be normatively organized is timely.

Economic sanctions are a potentially powerful instrument in the right circumstances. They are also of great potential destructiveness. If nothing else, the case of Haiti,[5] which we consider in detail below, where sanctions were used with tremendous and indiscriminate force, should prompt a fundamental reconsideration — in terms of social science, international law and natural law — of the mechanisms, politics, and law of the use of non-lethal sanctions in the international arsenal and of the contingencies and policies that should be applied to their role in international enforcement action.

C *Strategic Instruments of Enforcement*

To understand the way economic sanctions are used, it is necessary to locate them in the context of all strategic instruments and to understand the sequences in which these instruments are deployed. Analytically, policies can be implemented by combinations of four strategic instruments: the military instrument, involving the application of varying degrees of coercion by specialists in violence against a target; the economic instrument, involving the granting or withholding of indulgences or deprivations from a target; the diplomatic instrument, involving communications ranging from persuasion to coercion, directed against the elite of a target; and the ideologic or propagandic[6] instrument, involving the modulation of carefully selected signs and symbols to politically relevant parts of the rank and file as a means of influencing the elite that governs it.

All strategic instruments are directed toward reducing the ambit of choice of the target by constraining it to adopt policies or positions it would otherwise eschew.

---

[4]　S.K. Padover (ed.), *Wilson's Ideals* (1942), 108, cited in G.C. Hufbauer *et al.*, *Economic Sanctions in Support of Foreign Policy Goals* (1983), at 9.

[5]　See *infra* part 3.E.

[6]　We apologize for the rather ugly term 'propagandic', but this inquiry needs a clear designation for what Lasswell called the 'ideological' instrument.

90 *EJIL* 9 (1998), 86–141

Indulgent techniques seek to secure this compliance by promising rewards or giving bribes. The consequence of an indulgent strategy is still to attenuate the freedom of choice of the target, which must forego advantages or opportunities it expected to gain, but neither the target nor the people nor things on its peripheries suffer manifest damage. Deprivatory techniques, in contrast, try to secure compliance by seques- tering or destroying certain power bases or instruments of influence of the target elite.

D *Sanctions and Threat Theory*

Threats are an actor's credible communication of interest, capacity, and contingent intention; they are designed to warn another actor that if it does not desist from or adjust certain behaviour, more destructive instruments will be applied. Although the term 'threat' suffers a generally pejorative connotation in ordinary language usage, threats are a critical, indeed indispensable, part of politics. Like anything else, they can be abused, but they can be beneficial to certain public order configurations, precisely because they facilitate adjustments without requiring overt conflict.

Sanctions are, in part, an application of the theory of threats. Like threats, all instruments of strategy are designed to change the attitudes and behaviour of the target. They do this in two stages. The first stage involves the credible communication of capacity and intention to carry out a particular programme: 'do such and such *or else*'.[7] Let us refer to this stage as the 'communication' stage. The second stage involves the effective application of the sanctions, the actual delivery of the 'or else'. We shall call this the 'application' stage. Sanctions accomplished by the communi- cation stage alone certainly have transaction costs,[8] but they involve fewer costs to the sanctioner and the target than do sanctions that require the second, applicative phase.

Generally, insofar as the actors involved are rational, the communication stage should ensure the desired change in behaviour if two cumulative conditions are met: (i) the content of the programme is clearly sufficient to accomplish its manifest objectives; and (ii) the communication of capacity and intention ('political will') is credible. The target will obviously not comply when the content of the threatened programme is manifestly inadequate, for instance, where the target perceives the programme as essentially symbolic, staged for certain internal or external audiences. Nor will the target comply when the content of the programme is manifestly adequate, but the target has reason to believe that the sanctioner will not follow through. For example, the target, monitoring the sanctioner's internal political processes, may detect at the elite level a most fragile unity of purpose. Or the target may conclude from prior cases that the sanctioner's political will often collapses when sanctions are resisted by a target. Under both conditions, the target will have cause to believe that the sanctioner will be unable to initiate or to sustain the application stage of the

---

[7] The 'or else' may also be an 'and': a promise of a reward as well as the threat of a deprivation.
[8] For the sanctioner, the direct costs are incurred in mobilizing and pre-positioning the various assets to be used in the sanctions programme. Opportunity costs, which are lost once those assets have been diverted to the sanctions, are also incurred.

programme. Whether the target's perceptions are correct or not, the communication phase alone will not suffice to ensure compliance, and the enforcement programme will have to proceed to application.

The relevance of threat theory varies depending on the strategic instrument being used. The communications stage of a credible military sanctions programme is more likely to be a successful application of threat theory than is the communications stage of a credible economic sanctions programme and, *a fortiori*, a credible propaganda programme. Excluding for the moment military actions such as quarantines, which are actually economic deprivations accomplished by carefully defined and limited military means, the effect of the military instrument is generally rapid and, if effective, irreversible. When the economic instrument is used, in contrast, the effects are slow and cumulative, especially if they are being 'cranked up' in measured increments. Faced with a credible threat of overt military sanctions, a 'wait-and-see' attitude is not a rational option for the target. But 'wait-and-see' could be rational if the programme about to be mounted against the target is an economic or propagandic one, for the target can still haggle over terms of compliance or, indeed, turn off the programme directed against it at any time, simply by saying 'yes'. That is not to say that 'wait-and-see' has no costs for the target. The infrastructural costs of sanctions and the sunk costs of reactive attempts to transform the economy may prove as durable and politically costly as those following limited use of the military instrument, even if the target subsequently responds affirmatively. Indeed, in some ways it may prove more politically costly, for damage from the military instrument is easily and plausibly blamed on outsiders; damage from internal preventive, anticipatory action is not.

'Wait-and-see' is not always the strategy that a target will or should follow. In at least two instances, economic sanctions have obtained the desired policy goals at the communication stage: the League of Nations' sanctions against Yugoslavia in 1921 and the American and Canadian sanctions against South Korea to stop nuclear reprocessing in 1975.[9] Whether the target should follow such a passive strategy depends on the credibility of the threat, based on the target's observation of the sanctioner's previous behaviour and other contextual indications of authority and control intent, and on the ability of the target's elites to hedge the impact of the threatened economic shocks.

The target's elites may adopt a defensive strategy at the communication stage. But, as suggested above, such a strategy is not costless and its adoption will depend on a balancing of expected costs and rewards. These strategies may include, but are not limited to, transforming the economy's structure toward import substitution or seeking temporary alternative markets in which to purchase and sell goods and services. The expected benefit from these strategies, in turn, will depend on the costs of redirecting production, on the size of the internal market, and on the elasticity of world supply and demand for those goods in which the target trades.

---

[9]   Van Bergeijk, 'Success and Failure of Economic Sanctions', 42 *Kyklos* (1989) 385, at 388.

92 *EJIL* 9 (1998), 86–141

In most cases, the costs of adopting these reactive strategies at the communication stage may be prohibitively high. As a result, economic sanctions would tend to be less effective at the communication stage than uses of the military instrument, unless the sanctioner has a well-known record of threatening sanctions and carrying them out if necessary. Mere assertions of power or authority are unlikely to make the target change its policies at this stage for they convey little information about the sanctioner's credibility. The differential effect of threat theory on enforcement instruments means that the quantum and nature of damage flowing from a sanctions programme will vary depending on which instrument is selected as the primary sanction tool.

E *Collateral Damage*

The destruction of people and objects on the periphery of a target is called, euphemistically, 'collateral damage'. Some collateral damage is a virtually inescapable feature of destructive strategies, for no weapon regularly delivers its punch with the 'surgical precision' claimed by its manufacturers and operators. Customary international law, now codified, has long tried to define lawful primary targets and to establish boundaries of tolerance for collateral damage. Weapons are not *per se* lawful or unlawful, but must be selected for particular contexts and missions, taking account of their properties and, in particular, their capacities to discriminate between the combatants and non-combatants in the actual circumstances of the case.

The critical notions of damage and collateral damage have been conceived for and applied primarily to uses of the military instrument. Some scholars and politicians believe that the other strategic instruments are essentially, or at least comparatively, non-damage-causing. But if one examines facts contextually and systematically, it is readily apparent that none of the four instruments of policy is inherently non-destructive. Each may be used in ways that produce significant destruction, often on the peripheries rather than on the target itself.

This is obviously the case with military weapons in many contexts. Consider a recent example: the destruction, by 'smart' missiles, of Iraqi intelligence headquarters in Baghdad, which President Clinton ordered in reaction to the Iraqi plot to assassinate former President Bush, produced some collateral damage in the suburb of Baghdad in which the intelligence headquarters was situated.[10]

The inevitability of collateral damage is less obvious for some of the other instruments. The propagandic instrument — the purposive modulation of signs and symbols by one side to a conflict against the rank and file of the adversary — was used prior to, during and after Desert Storm, to encourage the Shi'a in the south of Iraq and the Kurds in the north of Iraq to rise against the Ba'ath regime. In both cases, it could be anticipated that the propaganda, if it were successful, would ignite a chain of events ultimately causing substantial collateral damage in the insurrection and the brutal

[10] See Reisman. 'The Raid on Baghdad: Some Reflections on its Lawfulness and Implications'. 5 *EJIL* (1994) 120.

suppression that would follow it, especially if the coalition that had encouraged the insurrection did not come to its assistance.

Two points must be emphasized. First, damage — in an empirically referential sense — is not caused exclusively by uses of the *military* instrument. The other instruments are often used in highly destructive ways. In fact, though often counter-intuitive, the military instrument, as we have seen, in its communicative or threat stage, can be and usually is used in non-destructive and essentially communicative ways. The sequence is quite simple. Threats and coordinate demonstrations of power are perceived by the intended target; they concentrate its mind in a way that words alone do not; and they stimulate careful assessments of relative power positions correlated with the degree of importance of the issues at stake. Where the assessments indicate probabilities of net losses, they lead to appropriate non-belligerent adjustments. The military instrument is more likely than the other instruments to be effective in this stage, precisely because 'wait-and-see' is an inappropriate response.

Second, damage is not caused exclusively by the application of *material* assets, the 'sticks and stones' of the arsenal. Words can cause direct and collateral damage as well. One of the common methods of propaganda — 'psychwar' — seeks to exacerbate latent conflicts between different ethnic groups within the adversary in order to undermine elite control or to require the elite to divert resources to suppress internal resistance. Propaganda of this sort is hardly without potentially severe collateral damage: tensions between ethnic groups may produce violent incidents or even widespread pogroms. Even if they do not, long after the particular conflict has ended, the residue of hatred that has been endorsed and made more acute will lurk in people's consciousness, like a time bomb or a quiescent virus to be transmitted from one generation to the next until it bursts forth or is detonated. Propaganda, unlike lawful land mines, cannot be set to self-destruct.

In sum, then, considered in terms of threat theory, the collateral damage caused by non-military instruments — the economic and propagandic — may be greater than that of the military instrument, precisely because the elite, presented with a credible threat of the application of one of these non-military instruments, will often adopt, quite rationally, a 'wait-and-see' posture. During the time that this posture is followed, collateral damage can accumulate. Precisely because 'wait-and-see' is always irrational in the face of a credible threat to use the military instrument, its effective employment may actually cause less collateral damage than the use of non-military instruments.

F *The 'Appeal' of Economic Sanctions*

Economic sanctions are unquestionably the flavour of the year nationally and internationally for enforcement action. They are preferred in advanced industrial democracies because they engage comparatively less *internal* political resistance than other candidate strategies. Comparatively speaking, economic sanctions are politically cheap. To be sure, they do have retro-costs, which may be considerable, that are borne by particular sectors of the national economy of the sanctioning state. But

94 *EJIL* 9 (1998), 86–141

economic sanctions do not generate sombre processions of body bags bringing home the mortal remains of the sons and daughters of the constituents. Even when it is glaringly obvious that economic sanctions are not going to be effective, as for example with the US grain embargo mounted against the Soviet Union in response to its invasion of Afghanistan in 1979, or when it is clear in advance that economic sanctions will actually prove more costly to the party imposing them than to the target, the sanctions are not without important political consequences: they still reinforce public commitment to the norm that has been violated and generate a sense of civic virtue, without incurring unacceptable domestic political costs. Whatever their economic costs, they are often likely to be the cheapest feasible political option. When, as often happens in democratic polities, political forces cannot agree on the appropriateness of response to some perceived international delict, economic sanctions become an easy point for compromise: not necessarily the most rational of options, but certainly the lowest common denominator.

Yet international tolerance for unilaterally applied economic sanctions may be declining. Economic interdependence is a long-standing fact. The *perception* of just how integrated the international economy has become, however, and how inclusively disruptive some heretofore tolerated unilateral actions can be to that interdependence has increased. One manifestation of this perception is the growing criticism of the unilateral application of economic sanctions. But the concern about the use of these sanctions has been motivated entirely by self-interest rather than by a concern for the essential lawfulness and morality of the general or particular use of economic sanctions. Indeed, those who press for general or particular economic sanctions programmes feel that it is they who control the moral high ground.

It is the militant sense of virtue and moral superiority that attaches to the application of economic sanctions that is so fascinating. Economic sanctions have enjoyed great popularity among people of pacifistic bent because they seem to offer wholly non-violent and non-destructive ways of implementing international policy. 'At least', one hears again and again, 'we're not killing anyone'. 'At least, we're giving non-lethal sanctions a chance.' In this line of thinking, economic sanctions are always to be preferred to the application of military strategy and, in any case, are always to be exhausted before military action is initiated. As we have seen, however, such assumptions are unfounded.

G *The Relevance of the Law of Armed Conflict*

The basic postulates of the law of armed conflict are the sharp distinction between combatants and non-combatants and the imperative that any use of force be demonstrably necessary, proportional to the necessity, and capable of discriminating between combatants and non-combatants.[11] It is a cardinal principle of the

---

[11] See generally W.M. Reisman and C. Antoniou, *The Laws of War: Basic Documents on the Law of International Armed Conflict* (1994); M.S. McDougal and F.P. Feliciano, *Law and Minimum World Public Order: The Legal Regulation of International Coercion* (1961), reprinted with new introduction as *The International Law of War: Transnational Coercion and World Public Order* (1994).

international law of armed conflict that military strategies are to be planned and appraised taking due account of these criteria. Prospectively, rules of engagement must be designed to accommodate these principles in the anticipated context. Major military campaigns are subjected to critical post-mortems to determine the extent to which those principles were met and whether the application of coercion in that case was internationally lawful.

The same type of examination is not transposed, *mutatis mutandis*, for prospective assessment of applications of the other three instruments. The apparent reason for this persistent blind spot in international legal analysis has been the incorrect assumption that only the military instrument is destructive. The assumption that non-military strategies are inherently non-destructive or non-lethal has also insulated their prospective and retrospective appraisal in terms of basic human rights instruments. The consequences of this blind spot can be very grave. State-sponsored propaganda, for example, is often used to exacerbate hatred between different groups. Surely this is a violation of the Convention on the Elimination of Racial Discrimination.[12]

Non-military instruments should be tested rigorously against the criteria of the international law of armed conflict and other relevant norms of contemporary international law *before* a decision is made to initiate or to continue to apply them. If the non-military instruments were so tested, it is quite probable that, in some cases, they would be found to fail and to require adjustment or abandonment. The economic and propagandic instruments are problematic, mainly because of their relative incapacity to discriminate between licit targets and because of their durable resultant collateral injuries, which persist long after the conclusion of the campaign in which they were deployed.

These considerations should apply, *a fortiori*, to international organizations when they elect to use the economic instrument.[13] Since GATT and WTO prescriptions are placing an increasing number of limitations on the unilateral uses of economic sanctions, their most common and intensive lawful use in the future is likely to be through international organizations. Our thesis is that in these applications, compliance with international law, and particularly the criteria of lawfulness of the law of armed conflict, is mandatory. A preliminary, factual question is whether and to what extent the international organizations that have mounted economic sanctions programmes have complied with this requirement. Thereafter, we will turn our attention to the question of under what circumstances and through which procedures economic sanctions programmes should be planned and applied in the future.

---

[12] Convention on the Elimination of All Forms of Racial Discrimination, opened for signature 7 March 1965, 660 UNTS 195 (entered into force 4 January 1969; adopted by the United States 20 November 1994).

[13] Convention on the Safety of United Nations and Associated Personnel, 9 December 1994, 34 *ILM* (1995) 482.

96 *EJIL* 9 (1998), 86–141

3 The Application of Economic Sanctions by the United Nations

Although the UN General Assembly has periodically passed non-binding resolutions calling on all Member States to apply economic sanctions,[14] it is the UN Security Council that has decided upon and applied the regimes of UN-enforced economic sanctions.[15] In the first 50 years of existence of the United Nations, the Security Council, acting pursuant to Chapter VII, has on ten different occasions mandated that Member States implement economic sanctions of varying degrees of stringency against offending states. Our question here is not whether these sanctions programmes succeeded in achieving their objectives, a subject that is keenly disputed among scholars and policy-makers.[16] We are concerned, rather, with the question whether UN bodies and decision-makers have considered the requisite legal issues of proportionality and discrimination when using any coercive instrument and, if so, the procedures and criteria by which key UN actors have reached their judgments. As the following case studies reveal, UN practice has generally been to either ignore the legal issues raised by the effects of economic sanctions on the population of target states or to address these issues only on an ad hoc basis. It is only as a result of the persistent complaints of Iraq regarding the allegedly unjust impact of post-Gulf War sanctions on its populace and the perception among many in the international community that UN economic measures against Haiti primarily harmed the impoverished people of the country rather than the Haitian military and its supporters that the legal questions raised by sanctions have become a subject of sustained international concern.

A *Southern Rhodesia, 1965–1979*

The Security Council first acted under Chapter VII to define and enforce a mandatory programme of economic sanctions in 1968 in response to the crisis in Southern Rhodesia.[17] The genesis of the Security Council's actions lay in the illegal unilateral declaration of Rhodesian independence (UDI) from the United Kingdom made by the

---

[14] For example, the UN General Assembly, together with the Organization of African Unity (OAU), passed resolutions throughout the 1960s and early 1970s calling on all Member States to impose economic sanctions on Portugal for its failure to permit self-determination by the peoples of its colonial holdings in southern Africa. See M.P. Doxey, *International Sanctions in Contemporary Perspective* (1987), 34–35.

[15] Chapter VII of the UN Charter empowers the Security Council to 'determine the existence of any threat to the peace, breach of the peace, or act of aggression' (UN Charter, Art. 39). When the Security Council determines that such a situation exists, it may decide on measures short of armed force that the United Nations and its Member States must implement to restore international peace and security (Art. 41). Of course, the Security Council may also decide to resort to the use of force (Art. 42). Security Council decisions made under Chapter VII are binding on UN members (Art. 25).

[16] For a sampling of the debate, see Doxey, *supra* note 14; G.C. Hufbauer *et al.*, *Economic Sanctions Reconsidered: History and Current Policy* (2nd ed., 1990); G.C Hufbauer *et al.*, *Economic Sanctions Reconsidered: Supplemental Case Histories* (2nd ed., 1990). This last volume contains case histories of virtually all instances of unilateral and multilateral economic sanctions from the First World War to 1990 and, using a variety of criteria, assesses the effectiveness of the sanctions regimes.

[17] The literature on UN dealings with Southern Rhodesia, including sanctions, is enormous. See, e.g., M.P. Doxey, *Economic Sanctions and International Enforcement* (2nd ed., 1980), at 65–79; Doxey, *supra* note 14,

white minority government of Prime Minister Ian Smith on 11 November 1965. Acting on behalf of the British Commonwealth, the United Kingdom immediately imposed a series of economic sanctions against Southern Rhodesia to pressure the Smith government into renouncing the UDI and guaranteeing political participation by the disenfranchised black African majority. By early 1966, the UK sanctions included a complete ban on imports from and exports to Southern Rhodesia as well as a series of drastic financial measures ranging from the removal of Rhodesia from the sterling area and a prohibition on capital exports to Rhodesia to the freezing of Rhodesian assets in the United Kingdom.[18] Other nations, including France and the United States, also implemented selective sanctions programmes, and the OAU declared a total economic boycott. In November 1965 the Security Council also acted, passing Resolution 217, which recommended that all states 'break off all economic relations' with Southern Rhodesia.[19]

When the sanctions failed to achieve the quick reversal of the UDI that had been hoped for, the Security Council turned to a programme of mandatory sanctions under Chapter VII. In December 1966, the Security Council decided that Member States should implement selective mandatory sanctions against the Smith government, including a prohibition on exports to Rhodesia of petroleum, armaments, vehicles and aircraft, and a ban on imports of Rhodesian agricultural products and minerals.[20] These selective sanctions also failed to bring about an end to the Rhodesian 'rebellion' or to persuade the Smith regime to terminate its racist policies.

Accordingly, in May 1968 the Security Council passed Resolution 253, which imposed a ban on all exports to and imports from Rhodesia, prohibited the transfer of funds to Rhodesia for investment, denounced the purported Rhodesian passport, and severed air links with the country.[21] A limited humanitarian exception existed for exports to Rhodesia of foodstuffs and medical, educational and informational materials.[22] Because this resolution was expressly passed under Chapter VII, it was binding on all Member States. Resolution 253 also established a special Sanctions

---

at 35–46, 110–123; V. Gowlland-Debbas, *Collective Responses to Illegal Acts in International Law: United Nations Action in the Question of Southern Rhodesia* (1990); L.T. Kapungu, *The United Nations and Economic Sanctions against Rhodesia* (1973); D.L. Losman, *International Economic Sanctions: The Case of Cuba, Israel, and Rhodesia* (1978) 80–123; J. Nkala, *The United Nations, International Law, and the Rhodesian Independence Crisis* (1985); R. Renwick, *Economic Sanctions* (1981), at 25–58; H.R. Strack, *Sanctions: The Case of Rhodesia* (1978); Anglin, 'United Nations Economic Sanctions against South Africa and Rhodesia', in D. Leyton-Brown (ed.), *The Utility of International Economic Sanctions* (1987), 23. Unless otherwise noted, the narrative that follows is based on commonly-known events as detailed in these sources.

[18] The UK economic sanctions are detailed in Doxey, *supra* note 14, at 37.

[19] SC Res. 217 (1965).

[20] SC Res. 232 (1966).

[21] SC Res. 253 (1968).

[22] *Ibid*, para. 3(d).

98 *EJIL* 9 (1998), 86–141

Committee of the Security Council to monitor compliance of Member States with the mandatory sanctions.[23]

The compulsory UN sanctions regime endured for 11 years, expanding to prohibit, *inter alia*, transportation to or from Southern Rhodesia;[24] insuring exports to and imports from the territory; licensing trade names, trademarks and franchises there; and transferring Southern Rhodesian funds to or from, or using such funds in, Member States.[25] By the time the Security Council terminated the economic sanctions in late 1979, after the signing of the British-mediated Lancaster House agreement that provided for a constitutional transition to African-majority rule and an independent Zimbabwe,[26] the programme of mandatory economic sanctions was, at least on paper, quite comprehensive.

In framing this sanctions regime, UN bodies did periodically discuss the effects that sanctions might have or were having on the Rhodesian economy. Prior to the passing of Resolution 253, for example, the UN Secretary-General commissioned a report on the effects on Southern Rhodesia of an embargo on petroleum products.[27] In debates in the Security Council leading up to the enactment of comprehensive economic sanctions by Resolution 253, the representatives of many countries noted the ambiguous effects on the Rhodesian economy of the selective sanctions mandated by Resolution 232.[28] The only formal measure that the Security Council expressly took to ascertain the impact of the sanctions on Rhodesia, however, was extending the mandate of the Sanctions Committee to study ways to increase the sanctions' effectiveness. As a minor part of its activities, the Sanctions Committee did analyse the Rhodesian economy in recommending measures to expand the sanctions.[29] Yet despite the comprehensive nature of the sanctions, for the 13 years in which they were in force against Southern Rhodesia, there was virtually no formal consideration within the United Nations of the extent to which these sanctions were having a disproportionately injurious impact on the Rhodesian populace and economy.

---

[23] *Ibid*, para. 20.

[24] SC Res. 277 (1970).

[25] SC Res. 409 (1977).

[26] SC Res. 460 (1979).

[27] Renwick, *supra* note 17, at 28, 110 note 6 (citing W.J. Levy, Inc., *The Economics and Logistics of an Embargo on Oil and Petroleum Products* (1966)). Before implementing its unilateral sanctions measures, the United Kingdom had considered the prospects of a Rhodesian economy subject to sanctions. For example, on 12 November 1965, Prime Minister Harold Wilson stated before the House of Commons that the 'whole financial and banking structure of Rhodesia revolves around tobacco farming in such a way that the decision [to impose sanctions] will have a pretty serious and speedy effect'. *Ibid*, at 26.

[28] See, e.g., UN Doc. SPV1399 (1968) (statement of Ethiopian representative); UN Doc. SPV 1408 (1968) (statement of Pakistani representative); UN Doc. SPV 1428 (1968) (statement of Soviet representative). For an overview of the issues discussed in these debates, see Kapungu, *supra* note 17, at 59–69.

[29] For example, the Sanctions Committee rejected a proposal to cut off all communication links with Southern Rhodesia after debating the consequences of the measure for Rhodesia. See Gowlland-Debbas, *supra* note 17, at 438–439. The committee, however, was primarily concerned with investigating cases of sanctions evasion. See *ibid*, at 605–625.

Three features of the sanctions programme account for this omission. First, the United Nations was primarily concerned with sanctions evasion by both Member States *and* non-members, which was widespread throughout the life of the sanctions. Western multinationals continued to engage furtively in commerce with Southern Rhodesia, many African regimes closed their eyes to trade links between their nationals and Rhodesia, and the US Congress disregarded the mandatory Security Council resolutions by enacting the Byrd Amendment in 1971, which permitted the import of chrome, a strategic mineral, from Southern Rhodesia. Portugal, which still ruled Southern Rhodesia's eastern neighbour, Mozambique, and South Africa, the regional power directly to Rhodesia's south, condemned and openly flouted the UN sanctions regime: for the first decade of the sanctions' operation, the governments of both nations sympathized with Smith's white minority regime and actively sought to help Southern Rhodesia mitigate the effects of the sanctions.

Thus, it was the issue of non-compliance with the sanctions regime which virtually monopolized the Security Council's consideration of Southern Rhodesia. This was the near-exclusive concern of the 13 reports filed by the special sanctions committee of the Security Council established by Resolution 253.[10] Moreover, rather than considering the moral issues raised by the impact of the sanctions on the target populace, the General Assembly repeatedly called on the Security Council to widen the scope of the sanctions to include all measures permissible under Charter Article 41, condemned Member States (particularly the United States) for failing to comply with Security Council resolutions imposing sanctions, and demanded that the Security Council extend the sanctions to Portugal and South Africa.[11] This crisis in sanctions enforcement left little space for considering whether the sanctions were disproportionate.

The second reason that neither the United Nations nor its Member States considered the effects of the sanctions programme on the Rhodesian populace was the manifestly limited impact that the sanctions were having on Southern Rhodesia's economy.[12] In short, at least for the first decade or so of their imposition, the sanctions were ineffective. Anticipating such a response to UDI, the Smith government had taken preparatory measures, such as encouraging the formation of long-term contracts, in order to minimize the impact of the sanctions. Furthermore, after

---

[10]   The Sanctions Committee held its meetings in secret, Kapungu, *supra* note 17, at 134, so it is impossible to say that the Committee never addressed the issue of proportionality — although the absence of any evidence to that effect on the record strongly suggests that it is unlikely that the Committee did so in any depth. This pattern of secrecy in the administration of sanctions by the bodies established for that purpose by the Security Council has persisted to the present.

[11]   A representative General Assembly resolution to this effect is GA Res. 2652 (XXV) 1970.

[12]   The discussion that follows of the effects of the economic sanctions on the Rhodesian economy is based on G. Arnold and A. Baldwin, *Rhodesia: Token Sanctions or Total Economic Warfare?* (1972); Doxey, *supra* note 14, at 41–46; Hufbauer, *Supplemental Case Histories*, *supra* note 16, at 288–290; Losman, *supra* note 17, at 84–92, 97–121; Renwick, *supra* note 17, at 31–34, 37–38, 45–50; R.T. McKinnell, 'Sanctions and the Economy of Rhodesia', unpublished paper presented before the African Studies Association, 19 October 1968.

sanctions were imposed, Southern Rhodesia did a remarkable job at thwarting them by internalizing its economy, successfully promoting rapid import-substitution and economic diversification, and minimizing harm to the white settlers who constituted its political base. Indeed, morale remained high in the white community as it rallied around the common purpose of defying the UN. Although traditional export sectors, such as tobacco and mining, were initially hard hit, and other sectors, including petroleum imports, never fully adjusted to economic isolation, after the first year of sanctions the Rhodesian economy — much to the exasperation of the international community — resumed its rapid growth. Not until the mid-1970s did the economic distortions caused by the sanctions, factored, at this point, by the withdrawal of Portuguese and South African support, the external shock of the 1973 OPEC oil embargo, and intensifying guerrilla warfare, truly begin to bite. In such a situation of ambiguous effects, questions about a disproportionate or discriminatory impact of the sanctions on the population of the target state and its economic bases of support simply did not arise.

A third possible reason for the world community's obliviousness to the plight of the bulk of the African population caused by the sanctions may have been a self-serving stereotypical view of a 'Third World' dual economy. In this stereotype, all the Europeans in Rhodesia were exclusively engaged in the modern sector and were most likely to be affected by international sanctions, while Africans were exclusively engaged in the traditional sector, which was not incorporated into the global economy and, hence, not susceptible to injury by the sanctions. This, however, was not a realistic appraisal of the Rhodesian economy.

The Security Council and other UN bodies had ample opportunity to consider such questions. For example, evidence indicated that the sanctions disproportionately harmed Rhodesia's black population, which was particularly concentrated in the sanctions-sensitive sector of tobacco cultivation.[33] Moreover, the Security Council did authorize relief measures for Zambia, Rhodesia's neighbour to the north, to alleviate the considerable economic harm and dislocation that this nation suffered as result of the sanctions.[34] The predominant attitude towards the Africans' plight, however, was symbolized by the chairman of Zimbabwe's African National Council, who declared in a statement before the Security Council that sanctions should not be weakened solely because they were hurting Africans; pain was a price for freedom, and the white minority was suffering as well.[35] The ease with which these self-authorized affirmations and waivers of others' human rights were accepted by a United Nations

---

[33] Contemporary studies noted these disproportionate effects on Africans. See, e.g., M.P. Doxey, *Economic Sanctions and International Enforcement* (1st ed., 1971), 76–77, 79; Losman, *supra* note 17, at 114–116; McKinnell, *supra* note 32, at 19–20.

[34] Zambia's economy had been heavily dependent on trade with and employment of its nationals in Southern Rhodesia. In 1973 the Security Council passed a series of resolutions that authorized aid to Zambia to ameliorate the effects of the Rhodesian sanctions. See, e.g., SC Res. 329 (1973).

[35] See (1972) *UNYB* 113, UN Sales No. E.74.I.1. The UK-sponsored Pearce Commission that was sent to Rhodesia to gauge the reaction of black Africans to the sanctions reached an identical conclusion. See Renwick, *supra* note 17, at 44.

ostensibly bent on protecting human rights manifested a troubling disregard for the welfare of 'non-combatants'. The presumed consent of African Rhodesians to the hardships engendered by the sanctions was, thus, a fourth feature that contributed to the failure of the United Nations systematically to address questions of proportionality.

In brief, the persistent problem of sanctions evasion and the extraordinary ability Rhodesia demonstrated to minimize the impact of the sanctions did not create the conditions for considering the legal implications of the disproportionate impact of an economic sanctions programme on the population of a target state. The Sanctions Committee set up by the Security Council to monitor the sanctions regime addressed itself exclusively to technical problems of enforcement and effectiveness.

B *Iraq: 1991–Present*

The United Nations adopted its most comprehensive programme of mandatory sanctions under Chapter VII against Iraq in response to that country's invasion of Kuwait on 1 August 1990. On 6 August, the Security Council adopted Resolution 661, which forbade all imports from and exports to Iraq, froze the assets of the Iraqi government and nationals abroad,[36] and suspended pre-existing commercial contracts with Iraqis and Iraqi entities.[37] The trade embargo did not apply to 'supplies intended strictly for medical purposes, and, in humanitarian circumstances, foodstuffs',[38] or to the financial transactions necessary to effect such supplies.[39] Resolution 661 also established a Sanctions Committee, whose membership consisted of the members of the Security Council, to monitor implementation of the sanctions.[40] The original intent of the sanctions was to peacefully compel Iraq to withdraw from Kuwait.

The sanctions programme was quickly modified and expanded. In Resolution 666, the Security Council delegated to the Sanctions Committee the task of determining what constituted 'humanitarian circumstances' under Resolution 661.[41] To minimize sanctions evasion, the Council also reiterated that humanitarian shipments of foodstuffs and medical supplies should be provided under the auspices of international humanitarian agencies, not the Iraqi government.[42] The extent of the 'humanitarian circumstances' exemption became a point of concern in the Sanctions Committee, particularly among those states with nationals working as expatriates or guest workers in Iraq and Kuwait.[43]

---

[36] SC Res. 661 (1990).
[37] *Ibid*, para. 5.
[38] *Ibid*, para. 3(c).
[39] *Ibid*, para. 4.
[40] *Ibid*, para. 6.
[41] See SC Res. 666 (1990).
[42] *Ibid*, paras. 6, 8.
[43] For these debates, see the summaries of 'Sanctions Committee Meetings in the Late Summer and Fall of 1990', D.L. Bethlehem (ed.), *The Kuwait Crisis: Sanctions and Their Economic Consequences*, vol. 2 (1991) 773–985. The work of the Sanctions Committee is described by its former deputy secretary in Conlon,

To enforce the trade embargo, the Security Council authorized Member States to halt Iraq's inward and outward maritime shipping in order to inspect the cargoes of ships suspected of trading with Iraq or Kuwait.[44] The Council also banned air traffic to and from Iraq and required Member States to deny overflight rights to Iraqi aircraft.[45] When the Council judged that the sanctions regime had failed peacefully to dislodge Iraqi forces from Kuwait, it passed Resolution 678, which authorized Member States to 'use all necessary means' to ensure Iraq's withdrawal.[46]

Pursuant to this authorization, Member States whose forces had been deployed in the Persian Gulf region launched air and land operations against the Iraqi armed forces in January and February of 1991, and decisively expelled Iraq's army from Kuwait. As part of the ceasefire that ended the Gulf War, the Security Council decided in Resolution 687 to maintain the programme of sanctions against Iraq.[47] Medical and health supplies were completely exempted from the trade embargo, and proposed shipments of foodstuffs were also exempted so long as they were notified to the Sanctions Committee.[48] The Council also authorized the Sanctions Committee to approve 'materials and supplies for essential civilian needs' under an accelerated no-objection procedure.[49] The trade and financial embargo would terminate when Iraq complied with the provisions of Resolution 687 requiring it to destroy its weapons of mass destruction and to permit international monitoring to ensure that it did not resume its nuclear, chemical and biological weapons programmes.[50] Because Iraq refused fully to comply with Resolution 687, particularly its provisions regarding the destruction of weapons of mass destruction, the Chapter VII sanctions regime remained in effect without significant modification from August 1990 to December 1996.

The continued maintenance of mandatory UN sanctions against Baghdad has been controversial, in part due to the harm that the sanctions have inflicted on the Iraqi people. The Security Council and the Sanctions Committee have been aware of the

---

'Lessons from Iraq: The Functions of the Iraq Sanctions Committee as a Source of Sanctions Implementation Authority and Practice', 35 *Va. J. Int'l L.* (1995) 633.

[44] SC Res. 665 (1990).

[45] SC Res. 670 (1990).

[46] SC Res. 678 (1990).

[47] See SC Res. 687 (1991).

[48] *Ibid*, para. 20. This resolution represented a change in policy towards shipment of foodstuffs: the Sanctions Committee no longer had to determine that the supply of food was justified by humanitarian circumstances. See Conlon, *supra* note 43, at 640–641.

[49] See SC Res. 687 (1991), para. 22.

[50] In October 1992, the United States persuaded the Security Council to pass Resolution 778, which froze the remaining foreign assets of the Iraqi government. See SC Res. 778 (1992). Iraq had previously used these assets to purchase humanitarian goods. Rouleau, 'The View from France: America's Unyielding Policy Toward Iraq', *Foreign Affairs* (January/February 1995) 59, at 64–65.

injuries suffered by Iraqis and have sought to minimize the impact of the sanctions on innocent Iraqi civilians by creating a liberal regime of humanitarian exceptions to the sanctions programme. Indeed, in 1994 the Sanctions Committee received $6 billion in requests for humanitarian shipments to Iraq, leading the Committee's former deputy secretary to charge that 'the magnitudes eventually came to resemble normal commercial deliveries of no particular humanitarian merit'.[51] In 1991, the Security Council approved arrangements whereby Iraq could export oil to earn funds to purchase food and other humanitarian goods.[52] However, Iraq initially refused to participate in the oil-for-food scheme, claiming that the arrangement would violate Iraqi sovereignty.[53]

The sanctions have caused a significant deterioration in the economic and social welfare of the Iraqi populace. The Iraqi economy virtually collapsed. Prior to the embargo, oil accounted for 95 per cent of Iraq's foreign exchange earnings, and medical and other advanced services were largely operated by (since-departed) foreign expatriates.[54] The dinar deteriorated from $ .60 to the dollar in 1990 to 1,200 dinars to the dollar in April 1995.[55] By mid-1994, inflation since 1990 had reached 6,000 per cent.[56] In 1993, industry was operating at only 10 to 15 per cent of capacity, and industrial unemployment was estimated to exceed 70 per cent.[57] The sanctions-induced economic collapse hit the poor particularly hard: the prices of staples such as bread, infant formula and flour have increased by several thousand per cent,[58] and the World Food Programme estimated that the cost of the average basket of goods had increased 50 times by 1993.[59] The middle and professional classes have also seen their incomes dramatically erode and have been reduced to selling durable goods and

---

[51]   Conlon, *supra* note 43, at 647.

[52]   See SC Res. 712 (1991); SC Res. 706 (1991).

[53]   See Iraqi Compliance with UN Sanctions: Hearing Before the Near Eastern and South Asian Affairs Subcomm. of the Senate Foreign Relations Comm., 104th Cong., 1st Session (3 August 1995) (testimony of Patrick Clawson, Senior Fellow, Institute for National Strategic Studies, National Defense University), available in LEXIS, Congress Library, Testimony File. Particularly objectionable to Iraq were the provisions requiring it to use a percentage of the revenues generated in the oil-for-food scheme to pay the expenses of UN monitoring of Iraq and to compensate victims of Iraqi aggression.

[54]   Reuther, 'UN Sanctions Against Iraq', in D. Cortright and G.A. Lopez (eds.), *Economic Sanctions: Panacea or Peacebuilding in a Post-Cold War World?* (1995) 121, at 127.

[55]   'Down but Not Out', *Economist*, 8 April 1995, at 21; 'Iraqis Count the Cost of Sanctions', *Economist*, 19 February 1994, at 46.

[56]   Joffe, 'Iraq — The Sanctions Continue', 6 *Jane's Intelligence Rev.* (1 July 1994) 314, available in LEXIS, News Library, Mags File.

[57]   Kocher, 'The Sanctions Against Iraq', *Swiss Rev. World Aff.*, August 1993, available in LEXIS, World Library, Swswld File.

[58]   See Al-Samarrai, 'Economic Sanctions against Iraq: Do They Contribute to a Just Settlement?', in Cortright and Lopez, *supra* note 54, 133, at 137.

[59]   Kocher, *supra* note 57. For a comprehensive evaluation of the effects of the sanctions on the Iraqi people, see Food and Agricultural Organization of the United Nations, Evaluation of Food and Nutrition Situation in Iraq (1995) (visited 17 March 1997). <http://leb.net/IAC/FAO1–10t.html>.

104 *EJIL* 9 (1998), 86–141

family heirlooms to survive.[60] By 1993, living standards had been reduced by one-third,[61] and the situation has since worsened considerably. The deterioration of the economy has led to skyrocketing levels of crime, particularly in urban areas.[62]

Iraq's economic collapse has precipitated a crisis in health, nutrition and education. An oft-cited 1992 study published in *The New England Journal of Medicine* reported that the Gulf War, civil strife and UN economic sanctions caused a threefold increase in infant mortality in Iraq between January and August 1991.[63] International organizations warned in 1993 that only 50 per cent of water purification and sewage treatment plants were functioning; UNICEF, for example, found in January 1993 that only 25 of Basra's 135 waste-water pumps worked.[64] In November 1993, Food and Agriculture Organization (FAO) nutritionists reported 'pre-famine' conditions characterized by 'very high food prices, collapse of private incomes, depletion of personal assets and rapidly increasing numbers of the destitute'.[65] The food ration that had previously provided most of the daily calorie intake of most Iraqis was cut by up to half by the government in October 1994.[66] In December 1994, UNICEF issued a report estimating that 3.5 million Iraqi civilians were at a significant health risk of malnutrition and death due to the sanctions, including 1.58 million children under the age of fifteen and 230,000 pregnant or nursing women.[67] A 1995 World Health Organization report noted shortages of medicine, medical supplies, foodstuffs, and water purification and sanitation parts and equipment.[68] At one point, Iraq had less than one-tenth of the medicines needed,[69] and minor surgeries were performed without anaesthesia.[70] The UN reported in May 1995 that 23 per cent of children under the age of five suffered from malnutrition and that water treatment systems had

[60] See Al-Radi, 'Iraqi Sanctions — A Postwar Crime', 260 *Nation* (27 March 1995) 416; see also Al-Samarrai, *supra* note 58, at 173 (reporting that doctor's average income deteriorated from $1,400 in 1990 to $270 in 1992).

[61] Clawson, 'Sanctions as Punishment, Enforcement, and Prelude to Further Action', 7 *Ethics & Int'l Aff.* (1993) 20, at 27–29.

[62] Joffe, *supra* note 56.

[63] Ascherio *et al.*, 'Effect of the Gulf War on Infant and Child Mortality in Iraq', 327 *New Eng. J. Med.* (24 September 1992) 931. The study did not establish the share that sanctions had in causing the increase in infant mortality.

[64] Kocher, *supra* note 48.

[65] 'Iraqis Count the Cost', *supra* note 55, at 46.

[66] 'Down but Not Out', *supra* note 55, at 21.

[67] Figures from the UNICEF study are cited by Clark, 'Sanctions on Iraq Take Toll on Children', *NY Times*, 21 January 1995, at 22 (letter to editor); Gibbs, 'A Show of Strength: Clinton's Charge Sends Saddam into Retreat, but Taming Him Is Another Matter', *Time*, 24 October 1994, at 34; Rouleau, *supra* note 50, at 64. The National Council of Churches confirmed this finding. See 'Easing of Iraq Sanctions Urged', 112 *Christian Century* (1 March 1995) 231, at 231.

[68] Iraqi Compliance with UN Sanctions, *supra* note 53 (testimony of Rend Francke, Director, Iraq Foundation). This report confirmed similar findings of the British Red Cross in December 1994. See Clark, *supra* note 67, at 22.

[69] 'Down but Not Out', *supra* note 55, at 21.

[70] Rouleau, *supra* note 50, at 64.

fallen apart, leading to water-borne diseases such as malaria and tuberculosis.[71] Alarms about the crisis in the health of the Iraqi people have also been sounded by British medical groups,[72] a German medical study group,[73] and the Red Cross.[74] Furthermore, the UN estimates that one in five students has dropped out of school because of shortages in educational materials and financial hardship.[75]

While many have excoriated the Security Council for maintaining economic sanctions in the face of the economic, health and educational crisis endured by innocent Iraqi civilians,[76] others have charged that Iraqi policy has aggravated the harmful impact of the sanctions on the populace and that Iraq has overstated the effects of the sanctions to garner support for their lifting.[77] In October 1991, Saddam Hussein's regime pulled all government workers and services out of Kurdish Iraq in the north, forcing the United Nations to provide humanitarian aid.[78] The Iraqi government pursued the same policies towards the Shiite provinces in the south, which had rebelled after the termination of the Gulf War.[79] Most of the nation's transportation and energy infrastructure has been rebuilt, particularly around Baghdad,[80] and a 1993 US Congressional investigation found that Iraq had rebuilt most of its conventional weapons arsenal.[81] The government also initiated a massive self-sufficiency campaign in agriculture that was successful for the first few years of the sanctions;[82] even in December 1996, when the oil-for-food deal was implemented,

---

[71]   Iraqi Compliance with UN Sanctions, *supra* note 53 (testimony of Omar Duwaik, President, Reema International).

[72]   See 'Starvation in Iraq', 338 *Lancet* (9 November 1991) 1179.

[73]   In 1995 a German medical study group found that death rates for children under the age of five from January to November 1994 were 6.5 times higher than in 1989; death rates were 3.5 times higher during that period for all other age groups. Clark, *supra* note 67, at 22.

[74]   International Federation of Red Cross and Red Crescent Societies, *World Disasters Report 1995* (1995), at 26.

[75]   Rouleau, *supra* note 50, at 66.

[76]   See, e.g., Al-Samarrai, *supra* note 58; Clark, *supra* note 67; Davidson, 'Ten Myths about the Sanctions against Iraq', *Gulf States Newsl.*, 15 July 1994; 'Easing of Iraqi Sanctions Urged', *supra* note 67, at 231. For essays bitterly attacking UN sanctions, see R. Clark *et al.*, *War Crimes: A Report on United States War Crimes against Iraq* (1992) 99–101, 164–169.

The Iraqi Action Coalition (IAC) has established an Internet site devoted to documenting the deleterious effects of UN sanctions on the Iraqi people. The site has extensive hyperlinks to related Web sites. See <http://leb.net/IAC/>. The IAC describes itself as 'a broad-based, independent, grassroots coalition dedicated to providing information on the devastating consequences of the blockade on Iraq and to providing assistance to the people of Iraq ... IAC supports an unconditional lifting of the illegitimate blockade on the people of Iraq.' *Ibid.*

[77]   See, e.g., Reifenberg, 'How Iraq, Defying the West, Keeps Its Economy Going', *Wall St. J.*, 3 October 1996, at A11.

[78]   Waterbury, 'Strangling the Kurds: Saddam Hussein's Economic War against Northern Iraq', *Middle East Insight*, July/August 1993, at 31–38.

[79]   Reuther, *supra* note 54, at 127.

[80]   Dowty, 'Sanctioning Iraq: The Limits of the New World Order', 17 *Washington. Q.*, (Summer 1994), at 179.

[81]   Gibbs, *supra* note 67, at 34.

[82]   *Ibid*; Joyner, 'Sanctions, Compliance and International Law: Reflections on the United Nations' Experience against Iraq', 32 *Va. J. Int'l L.* (1991) 1, at 39–40.

there was food on the shelves — poor Iraqis just lack the resources to buy much of it.[83] Poor management of the Iraqi economy over the past four years, which resulted from Saddam Hussein's decision to become personally involved in economic policy, has aggravated the deteriorating humanitarian situation provoked by the sanctions.[84] Saddam Hussein has also insulated his family, the military command, and his supporters in the ruling Ba'ath party from the impact of the sanctions.[85] The Iraqi regime's deliberate policy of using the sanctions for domestic political purposes has resulted in a situation in which, in the words of a Catholic Relief Services official, '[t]he rich and the strong survive, the poor and the weak starve'.[86]

Pressure that had been building for the Security Council to modify or terminate economic sanctions against Iraq initially diminished following revelations in the autumn of 1995 that Iraq had consistently deceived international monitors about the extent of its programme to develop weapons of mass destruction.[87] Some of that pressure, at least in the Security Council, arose more from the desire of European countries to do business with Iraq than from concern over the impact of the sanctions on innocent Iraqi civilians. Nevertheless, many developing countries continued to urge the Security Council to repeal or lighten the sanctions,[88] and the humanitarian situation for the majority of Iraqis steadily worsened.[89] Accordingly, in 1995 the Security Council passed a resolution that would permit Iraq to export $1 billion in oil every three months to generate the funds to import food and medicine.[90] In January 1996, the UN and Iraq began a series of negotiations to finalize the oil-for-food agreement, with areas of disagreement centring on, *inter alia*, monitoring Iraqi imports and the 'equitable distribution' of food and medicines to the Kurds in the north and the Shiites in the south.[91] Indeed, the mere announcement of negotiations in

[83]   See Al-Radi, *supra* note 60, at 416.

[84]   See Iraqi Compliance with UN Sanctions, *supra* note 53 (testimony of Patrick Clawson).

[85]   See *ibid* (testimony of Rend Francke). Then-US Ambassador to the United Nations Madeline Albright has charged that the Hussein regime has built 50 new palaces for regime supporters since the end of the Gulf War at a cost of $1.5 billion. Iraqi Compliance with UN Sanctions, *supra* note 53 (testimony of Madeline Albright, US Ambassador to the United Nations).

[86]   Al-Samarrai, *supra* note 58, at 137. The Iraqi regime even used the introduction by the United States of a new $100 bill to swindle ordinary Iraqis out of their hard currency reserves by falsely claiming that the US government had cancelled the old $100 notes. See 'Scare over US Bills Fills Baghdad Coffers', *Chi. Trib.*, 3 April 1996, at 7.

[87]   On the massive extent of Iraqi deception in this regard, see Tenth Report of the Executive Chairman of the Special Commission, UN Doc. S/1995/1038 (1995); Bruce, 'Playing Hide and Seek with Saddam', *Jane's Defence Wkly.*, 3 January 1996, at 15.

[88]   See 'UN, Iraq Expect to Reach Deal on Oil-for-Food Plan', *Xinhua News Agency*, 16 April 1996, available in LEXIS, News Library, Curnws File.

[89]   Jehl, 'Government Dexterity Eases Misery for Iraqis', *NY Times*, 15 April 1996, at A9.

[90]   See SC Res. 986 (1995).

[91]   See 'Oil-for-Food Plan', *supra* note 88; Crossette, 'UN and Iraq Report Progress in Talks to Allow Limited Oil Sales', *NY Times*, 14 February 1996, at A1; Goshko, 'Negotiators Near Agreement on Deal to Ease Impact of Sanctions on Iraq', *Washington Post*, 13 April 1996, at A27; Jehl, *supra* note 89, at A9.

January 1996 caused food prices in Iraq to fall from 30 to 50 per cent overnight and the Iraqi dinar to stabilize.[92]

The oil-for-food arrangement was not finalized, however, until early December 1996, after six months of negotiations between the Iraqi government, the Security Council and the Secretary-General. The final plan permitted Iraq to sell $2 billion worth of oil over six months to raise funds to buy food, medicines and other humanitarian goods. Funds earned from the oil sales were to be placed in an escrow account in New York administered by the United Nations. About $260 million was to be reserved for the Kurdish population of northern Iraq, and $600,000 placed in a special fund established to compensate victims of the Iraqi 1990 invasion. The UN Special Commission charged with monitoring Iraq's destruction of its weapons of mass destruction was to receive $20 million to cover operating expenses, with the remainder of the money to be distributed in Iraq. The Security Council could renew the oil-for-food plan after six months if Iraq complied with conditions; finding no major violations, the Council extended the plan for a second six-month term in June 1997.[93] Diplomats were confident that Iraq could not easily evade the restrictions: in the words of the US Deputy Representative to the United Nations, 'We designed a resolution for a cheater. . . . We know [Saddam Hussein] well.'[94] Since its implementation, the oil-for-food scheme has been criticized for chronic administrative delays.[95]

The plight of innocent Iraqi civilians raises one of the thorniest legal dilemmas of any comprehensive, effective sanctions programme: the proper response of the UN to the government of a target state that deliberately adopts policies which aggravate the sanctions' impact on the most vulnerable, who are then exploited in public relations as a way of eroding the legitimacy of the sanctions programme. As one international aid worker characterized the dilemma, 'If [Saddam Hussein's] last weapon is the sacrifice of millions of Iraqis to the horrors of starvation and disease until the Western alliance is shocked into saying, "Enough!" and relaxing sanctions, then Mr. Hussein will not hesitate to reach for this weapon.'[96]

C *Libya, 1992–Present*

In the spring of 1992 the UN Security Council imposed mandatory sanctions against the Qadhafi regime in Libya. The primary rationale for the sanctions was Libya's failure to extradite to the United Kingdom or the United States two Libyan nationals allegedly responsible for the bombing of Pan Am Flight 103 over Lockerbie, Scotland, in 1988.

---

[92] 'Iraqis Celebrate Fall in Food Prices', *Agence Fr. Press*, 25 January 1996, available in LEXIS, News Library, Curnws File; Jehl, *supra* note 89, at A9.

[93] Crossette, 'UN Extends Plan for Iraq to Sell Oil to Buy Food', *NY Times*, 5 June 1997, at A1.

[94] Crossette, 'Iraq Gets Approval to Sell Oil to Meet Civilian Needs', *NY Times*, 10 December 1996, at A1. The account in the text of the oil-for-food plan is drawn from this article.

[95] See, e.g., 'Iraqi Health System near Collapse, WHO Says'; *Reuters*, 27 February 1997, available at <http:leb.net/IAC/> (visited 16 March 1997).

[96] Tyler, 'Iraq: A Clear and Continuing Danger', *NY Times*, 1 December 1991, § 4.

108 *EJIL* 9 (1998), 86–141

The Security Council had previously passed a non-binding resolution urging the Libyan government, in effect, to extradite the two individuals.[97] Libya promptly filed suit in the International Court of Justice (ICJ) against the United States and the United Kingdom, invoking its rights under the Montreal Convention[98] not to extradite the accused Libyans. After oral argument in the provisional measures phase of the case, the Security Council, acting under Chapter VII, passed Resolution 748,[99] which imposed sanctions on Libya. The ICJ refused to disturb the UN sanctions regime and denied the provisional measures requested by Libya, holding, by virtue of Charter Articles 25 and 103, that the Security Council's decision pursuant to Chapter VII trumped Libya's rights under the Montreal Convention.[100]

Resolution 748 banned air travel to and from Libya; prohibited supplying, servicing and insuring Libyan aircraft; imposed an embargo on arms shipments and military training and assistance to Libya; and directed all states to prevent the operation of Libyan Arab Airlines offices.[101] The Council established a Sanctions Committee to monitor implementation of the sanctions, report on violations, consider special economic problems that implementing the sanctions might cause for any state, and approve special flights to or from Libya on grounds of significant humanitarian need.[102] The sanctions programme went into effect on 15 April 1992,[103] and the Council was to review the sanctions measures every 120 days (or sooner if necessary) in light of the compliance by the Libyan government with the requests that Libya extradite the two accused Libyan nationals and that it cease supporting terrorism.[104]

Despite regular reviews of the sanctions measures, the Security Council elected not to modify the sanctions. Indeed, mounting frustration with Libya's perceived non-cooperation led the Council in November 1993 to pass a resolution significantly tightening the sanctions regime.[105] The new Resolution 883, also enacted under Chapter VII, directed all states to freeze the assets of the government or public authorities of Libya and of any Libyan undertaking, and to ensure that none of the frozen assets be made available to any of those Libyan entities.[106] The resolution

---

[97] See SC Res. 731 (1992).

[98] Convention for the Suppression of Unlawful Acts against the Safety of Civil Aviation (Sabotage), opened for signature 23 September 1971, 24 UST 564, 31 *ILM* 718 (entered into force 26 January 1973).

[99] SC Res. 748 (1992).

[100] See *Case Concerning Questions of Interpretation and Application of the 1971 Montreal Convention Arising from the Aerial Incident at Lockerbie (Libya v. UK; Libya v. US)*, ICJ Reports (1992) 3, at 114 (Provisional Measures of 14 April 14). For comment, see Franck, 'The "Powers of Appreciation": Who is the Ultimate Guardian of UN Legality?', 86 *AJIL* (1992) 519; Reisman, 'The Constitutional Crisis in the United Nations', 87 *AJIL* (1993) 83.

[101] SC Res. 748 (1992), paras. 4, 5(a)–(b), 6(b).

[102] *Ibid*, para. 9(b)–(f). The principal rationale for permitting humanitarian flights was to facilitate pilgrimages to Mecca.

[103] *Ibid*, para. 2.

[104] *Ibid*, para. 13.

[105] See SC Res. 883 (1993).

[106] *Ibid*, para. 3. A 'Libyan undertaking' was defined as 'any commercial, industrial, or public utility undertaking' owned or controlled, directly or indirectly, by (1) the Libyan government or public

forbade the sale, supply or maintenance of specified equipment used in oil refining and the petrochemicals production process.[107] Finally, the Council tightened the measures relating to servicing and supplying Libyan aircraft and to Libyan Arab Airlines.[108] But in a significant concession to Western European states, many of which are heavily dependent on Libyan oil and have major oil-related investments in Libya, the resolution did not freeze assets derived from the sale or supply of Libyan petroleum, natural gas and agricultural products after 1 December 1993.[109] The sanctions took effect on that date.[110]

The Security Council insisted that it had considered the possible effects of the sanctions on the Libyan people in designing and imposing the initial sanctions regime of Resolution 748 in March 1992. Representatives from Iraq and Zimbabwe, for example, called the Council's attention to the impact that sanctions would have on innocent civilians.[111] In response, the US Ambassador to the UN argued that '[t]he means chosen in this resolution are appropriate; these sanctions are measured, precise and limited. ... They are tailored to fit the offence — Libya's wanton and criminal destruction of civilian aviation — and are designed to penalize the Government of Libya, not its neighbors or any other State.'[112] The UK and French representatives similarly argued that the sanctions, which were targeted to aviation and diplomatic privileges, fitted the crime, with the French Ambassador stating that the sanctions were 'not aimed at the Libyan people, who are not responsible for the acts of their leaders'.[113]

Similar exchanges occurred when the Security Council expanded the sanctions in November 1993. The Libyan representative reported that the air embargo had had deleterious effects on the populace because of the government's inability to arrange medical evacuations.[114] Egypt warned that intensifying the sanctions would increase the harm to the Libyan people and called on the Council to monitor the humanitarian situation.[115] In response, US Ambassador Albright flatly asserted that the sanctions were 'balanced and precisely targeted'.[116]

---

authorities, (2) any entity owned or controlled by the Libyan government or public authorities, or (3) any person acting on behalf of the entities identified in (1) and (2). *Ibid*

[107] *Ibid*, para. 5. The list of proscribed equipment appears in the appendix to the resolution.

[108] *Ibid*, para. 6.

[109] *Ibid*, para. 4.

[110] *Ibid*, para. 2.

[111] UN Doc. S/PV.3063 (1992) (statement of Iraqi representative); *ibid*, at 52 (statement of Zimbabwe's representative).

[112] *Ibid*, at 67 (statement of US representative).

[113] *Ibid*, at 74 (statement of French representative). For the British statement, see *ibid*, at 69.

[114] UN Doc. S/PV.3312 (1993) (statement of Libyan representative).

[115] *Ibid*, at 29–30 (statement of Egyptian representative).

[116] *Ibid*, at 40 (statement of US representative).

110   *EJIL* 9 (1998), 86–141

Since the tightening of the sanctions in December 1993, however, the Security Council has not investigated, or even formally considered, the possibility that the sanctions might be having a disproportionate or discriminatory impact on the Libyan populace. Indeed, there has been sentiment in the Council, particularly on the part of the United States, for widening the sanctions to prohibit the sale of Libyan oil abroad as well as foreign investment in oil-related projects in Libya.[117] Such a move, opposed by Western European states dependent on Libyan oil, would have a devastating effect generally on the Libyan economy.[118] The Sanctions Committee established by Resolution 748 has issued only one report on its activities; that report did not address the issue of the effects of the sanctions on the Libyan people.[119] Of the Council's permanent members, only China has questioned the sanctions on the humanitarian grounds that they aggravate the suffering of the Libyan people, without, however, supplying confirming data.[120]

In fact, the impact of the sanctions on the Libyan people has been relatively mild, at least until recently. The prolonged internal debates in the Security Council prior to the adoption of Resolution 883, which tightened the sanctions programme, permitted Libya to anticipate and minimize the impact of the sanctions by concealing its overseas assets.[121] Furthermore, financial manoeuvring by Libya and half-hearted enforcement of the sanctions by some Middle Eastern and Western European governments have led to widespread sanctions evasion.[122]

Despite the difficulties in gathering data on the Libyan economy, it appears that the sanctions have recently become more effective. The oil-refining, petrochemicals and tourism sectors have experienced sanctions-induced setbacks.[123] In 1994, it was reported that Libyan factories were running at about 50 per cent of capacity due to a shortage of raw materials.[124] Inflation in mid-1995 was estimated at around 300 per cent.[125] The value of dinar-denominated salaries has plummeted, while the prices of imports and unsubsidized agricultural products (such as fruits) have risen dramatically.[126] The economy experienced a 7 per cent contraction in 1993 and 1994, and

---

[117] See 'The Wrong Pressure on Libya', *NY Times*, 30 March 1995, at A22 (Editorial).

[118] 'Libya Will Face Tougher Situation from 1996, with Embargo Squeeze Getting Painful', *APS Diplomatic News Service*, 5 June 1996, in LEXIS, Mdeafr Library, Zme1 File.

[119] See Report of the Security Council Committee Established Pursuant to Resolution 748 (1992) concerning the Libyan Arab Jamahiriya, UN Doc. S/1996/2 (1996).

[120] UN Doc. S/PV.3312 (1993) (statement of Chinese representative). China abstained from the votes on Resolutions 748 and 883.

[121] Lewis, 'UN Tightens Sanctions against Libya', *NY Times*, 12 November 1993, at A10.

[122] See Pound and El-Tahri, 'Sanctions: The Pluses and Minuses', *US News & World Rpt.*, 31 October 1994, at 58.

[123] On oil and petrochemicals, see 'Libya's Domestic Oil Refining and Petrochemical Sectors', *APS Rev. Downstream Trends*, 12 June 1995, available in LEXIS, Mdeafr Library, Zme1 File. On tourism, see Hedges, 'Sanctions Keep West Off the Road to Libya', *NY Times*, 28 June 1992, § 1, at 8.

[124] Barrouhi, 'Libya: With Gaddafi at Bank Helm, Libyan Economy Slips', *Reuters*, 23 September 1994, available in LEXIS, World Library, Txtmde File.

[125] 'Libya Will Face Tougher Situation', *supra* note 118.

[126] 'Sanctions Bite', *APS Diplomat Recorder*, 10 February 1996, available in LEXIS, Mdeafr Library, Zme1 File.

unemployment, which has been growing, hovers at about 30 per cent.[127] High and rising unemployment led Libya to seek permission from the Security Council to expel over a million African and Palestinian immigrant workers in the autumn of 1995.[128] Col. Qadhafi has also put down at least one coup attempt since the sanctions were imposed.[129]

Libya has aggressively sought to portray the sanctions as having a devastating impact on its people, particularly in the area of health.[130] In August 1994, the Qadhafi government submitted a report to the Security Council that detailed the allegedly 'extremely harmful' effects of the sanctions on the Libyan health care system and on the agricultural, stock-raising, transportation, communications, industrial, financial and commercial sectors of the economy.[131]

The Libyan initiative was not without effect. Support for UN sanctions against Libya among developing and Arab states, which had initially implemented the measures, has weakened. In 1994, the League of Arab States[132] and the Non-Aligned Movement[133] expressed 'concern' over the negative impact that the sanctions were having on the Libyan populace. The OAU, '[g]reatly concerned about the human and material damage that the Libyan Arab people and those of the neighbouring States are suffering as a result of the unjust sanctions imposed on Libya,' has called on the Security Council to lift the sanctions.[134]

Some outside observers, however, regard the primary impact of the sanctions as 'psychological'[135] — 'It is generally recognized that irritating though the current sanctions might be, they come nowhere near exerting sufficient economic pressure on the Libyan regime to make it think seriously about complying with the UN demands.'[136]

---

[127] See 'Libya Politics', *International Country Risk Guide: Middle East & North Africa*, 1 October 1995, available in LEXIS, Mdeafr Library, Zme1 File.

[128] See Elthaway, 'Egypt: Bad Economy behind Libyan Expulsions-Diplomats', *Reuters*, 19 October 1995, available in LEXIS, World Library, Txtmde File.

[129] Hedges, 'Qaddafi Reported to Quash Army Revolt', *NY Times*, 23 October 1994, at 5.

[130] See 'Libya Politics', *supra* note 127.

[131] Consequences of the implementation of Resolutions 748 (1992) and 883 (1993) during the period from 15 April 1992 to 15 April 1994, UN Doc. S/1994/921 (1994).

[132] See e.g., Resolution Adopted by the Council of the League of Arab States on 27 March 1994: Coercive Measures and Threats by the United States of America, the United Kingdom of Great Britain and Northern Ireland, and France against the Socialist People's Libyan Arab Jamahiriya, UN Doc. S/1994/373 (1994).

[133] Paragraph 117 of the Final Document of the Eleventh Conference of the Foreign Ministers of the Non-Aligned Countries, held at Cairo from 29 May to 4 June 1994, UN Doc. S/1994/681 (1994).

[134] Resolution on the crisis between the Great Libyan Arab Jamahiriya and the United States of America, the United Kingdom and France, UN Doc. S/1995/596 (1995). The OAU's request that the Council reconsider and terminate the sanctions appears in paras. 7 and 8 of the resolution.

[135] 'Libya-Internal Strategic Perspective', *APS Diplomat Strategic Balance in the Middle East*, 5 February 1996, available in LEXIS, Mdeafr Library, Zme1 File.

[136] 'Libya Politics', *supra* note 127.

D Yugoslavia (Serbia and Montenegro), 1992–1995

The Security Council imposed mandatory sanctions against the Federal Republic of Yugoslavia (Serbia and Montenegro) (FRY) in 1992 as part of an international effort to contain and end the violent strife associated with the disintegration of the former Socialist Federal Republic of Yugoslavia. War in the Balkans broke out in the summer of 1991 between the Serb-dominated federal government and army and the republics of Slovenia and Croatia after the latter declared their independence from the federal state. In an effort to contain the conflict, the Security Council on 25 September 1991, imposed a Chapter VII arms embargo on the former Yugoslavia,[137] and in December of 1991 the Council created a special committee of the Council to monitor its implementation.[138]

The arms embargo failed to bring an end to the Balkan conflict. Moreover, many in the international community concluded that primary responsibility for prolonging the war rested with the FRY, led by Serbia, and the Bosnian Serbs. Accordingly, on 30 May 1992, the Security Council, acting under Chapter VII, passed Resolution 757, which imposed an expansive, mandatory trade embargo against the FRY.[139] Resolution 757 prohibited exports to and imports from the FRY; banned foreign financial assistance to enterprises in the FRY; cut off the FRY's air links to the rest of the world; and severed scientific, technical and cultural cooperation and sporting exchanges with the FRY.[140] Foodstuffs and medical supplies were exempted from the trade embargo.[141] The Security Council also expanded the mandate of the special committee, established by Resolution 713, to monitor the arms embargo, to overseeing the implementation of the economic sanctions.[142] Two weeks later, another Security Council resolution permitted the sanctions committee to approve, via its accelerated, no-objection procedure, requests to export to the FRY any non-food, non-medical 'commodities and products for essential humanitarian needs'.[143]

Over the next three-and-a-half years, the UN modulated the economic sanctions programme against the FRY in repeated attempts to compel the government of Serbian President Slobodan Milosevic to bring about an end to the war in neighbouring Bosnia and Herzegovina. When the economic sanctions and arms embargo proved porous, the Security Council sought to prevent shipments of strategic goods, such as fuel and industrial inputs, through the FRY.[144] At the same time, NATO and Western European Union forces began to monitor the FRY's borders and ply the

---

[137] SC Res. 713 (1991). The arms embargo against all states of the former Yugoslavia remained in effect even after economic sanctions were imposed against the FRY alone. See, e.g., SC Res. 762 (1992).

[138] SC Res. 724 (1991).

[139] SC Res. 757 (1992).

[140] *Ibid*, paras. 4–5, 7, 8(b)–(c). The most important item of trade that the sanctions affected was oil. The sanctions regime did not apply to overland transportation to the FRY.

[141] *Ibid*, para. 4(c).

[142] See *ibid*, para. 13.

[143] See SC Res. 760 (1992).

[144] See SC Res. 787 (1992).

Adriatic Sea to minimize sanctions evasion.[145] In April 1993, the Security Council tightened the sanctions by freezing the FRY's financial assets and overseas property and by extending the economic sanctions regime against the FRY to areas of Bosnia and Herzegovina controlled by the Bosnian Serbs.[146] Sanctions against Bosnian Serb territory were eventually widened to include a ban on all 'commercial, financial, and industrial activities and transactions' with Bosnian Serb persons and entities and a freeze of Bosnian Serb assets held abroad.[147]

In deciding whether to remove sanctions against the FRY, the UN pursued a carrot-and-stick approach that focused on influencing the behaviour of President Milosevic, with scant concern for the possible disproportionate or discriminatory impact that the sanctions might have had on the FRY populace. In September 1994, the Council partially suspended the sanctions programme pending certification that the FRY had closed its border with Serb-controlled Bosnia and Herzegovina and had ceased to provide military and financial support to the Bosnian Serbs.[148] International passenger air traffic with Serbia and Montenegro, passenger ferry service to Bari, Italy, and FRY participation in international sporting and cultural exchanges were permitted[149] — measures which benefited primarily the people of the FRY, not their rulers. Similar partial suspensions of the sanctions programme occurred in 1995 to reward the Milosevic regime for continuing to deny support to the Bosnian Serbs.[150] Only when FRY President Milosevic agreed to the Dayton Peace Accords on 21 November 1995, did the Security Council completely lift the economic sanctions against the FRY and provide for the gradual lifting of the arms embargo against all republics of the former Yugoslavia.[151] Moreover, continued relief from the sanctions depends on Serbia and Montenegro's fulfilment of the Dayton Agreement; sanctions can be reimposed without a Security Council vote if there is evidence that the FRY is violating the peace accords.[152]

The empirical evidence indicates that UN sanctions contributed to a significant decline in the Serbian economy, but socialist mismanagement of the economy and the dislocations produced by the war were also important factors in the FRY's economic

---

[145] Woodward, 'The Use of Sanctions in Former Yugoslavia: Misunderstanding Political Realities', in Cortright and Lopez, *supra* note 54, at 141, 143.

[146] SC Res. 820 (1993). The resolution permitted exports to and imports from territory controlled by the Bosnian Serbs only when authorized by the governments of Croatia and of Bosnia and Herzegovina. *Ibid,* para. 12.

[147] SC Res. 942 (1994).

[148] SC Res. 943 (1994).

[149] *Ibid,* para. 1.

[150] See, e.g., SC Res. 970 (1995); SC Res. 988 (1995); SC Res. 1003 (1995); SC Res. 1015 (1995); SC Res. 1021 (1995); SC Res. 1021 (1995); SC Res. 1022 (1995). Sanctions were terminated in October 1996. SC Res. 1074 (1996).

[151] See Goshko and Harris, 'UN Votes to Withdraw Sanctions on the Balkans', *Wash. Post,* 23 November 1995, at A1.

[152] *Ibid.* The resolution provided that the sanctions imposed by Resolution 942 could be lifted against the Bosnian Serbs only when they signed the Dayton Agreement and removed their forces into designated areas. *See ibid.*

114 *EJIL* 9 (1998), 86–141

collapse.[153] When UN sanctions were first imposed, it appeared that the FRY might be able to withstand them. The Belgrade government had stockpiled goods and fuel;[154] the Serbian economy had a relatively low dependence on foreign trade;[155] domestic oil production was constant and geared towards industry, rather than (dramatically reduced) consumer demand;[156] and analysts believed that the FRY could be agriculturally self-sufficient for some time.[157]

In fact, however, the Serbian economy quickly began to deteriorate.[158] By early 1994, industrial production was estimated to be at about 20 to 30 per cent of its pre-war capacity.[159] Shortages of petroleum for industrial use and of heating oil for homes threatened the country's economy and health.[160] Food self-sufficiency was jeopardized when farmers began to hoard their harvests instead of selling them to the government for nearly worthless Yugoslav dinars.[161] Analysts estimate that the Serbian economy shrank anywhere from 35 to 65 per cent between 1989 and 1995.[162]

---

[153] Woodward characterizes the situation as follows: 'Under these conditions of political and economic collapse, it is extremely difficult to evaluate the separate effectiveness of sanctions [from the effects of the transition to a market economy during the 1980s]. It is, for example, impossible to determine what percentage of the decline in production has been due to the sanctions, to the collapse of the state and its economy, to the end of the communist system, or to the collapse of trade with the Eastern bloc and the Middle East.' Woodward, *supra* note 145, at 146. Similar conclusions are reached in *World Disasters Report 1995*, *supra* note 74, at 22–23; Mojzes, 'Sanctions Observed: To Belgarde and Back', 110 *Christian Century* (27 October 1993) 1051 'Serbia's Difficult Return to Europe', *Swiss Rev. World Aff.*, 1 February 1996, available in LEXIS, World Library, Swswld File.

[154] Church, 'A Chronic Case of Impotence', *Time*, 8 June 1992, at 39.

[155] Hoeltschi, 'Belgrade under the Blockade', *Swiss Rev. World Aff.*, August 1993, available in LEXIS, World Library, Swswld File.

[156] *Ibid*; 'The Sanctions Alternative', *Economist*, 12 February 1994, at 44. The government also attempted to substitute away from oil to other sources of energy. Hoeltschi, *supra* note 155.

[157] Hoeltschi, *supra* note 155.

[158] For an account of the effects of the economic sanctions on the FRY's economy written by Serbian government officials, see Filipovic *et al.*, 'Production and Services in 1994', *Yugo. Surv.* (1995) no. 1, at 59. Recent issues of this journal contain a number of articles from the perspective of the FRY government that directly and indirectly discuss the impact of sanctions on Serbia and Montenegro.

[159] 'The Sanctions Alternative', *supra* note 156, at 44.

[160] 'Serbs Step Up Anti-sanctions Campaign', *UPI*, 12 September 1993, available in LEXIS, News Library, Arcnws File.

[161] Branson, 'Paying the price', *MacLean's*, 1 November 1993, at 39.

[162] For estimates, see Pomfret, 'Balkans Must Confront a History of Hatred', *Washington Post*, 17 December 1995, at A1 (claiming that Serbian economy shrank 65 per cent from 1990 to December 1995); 'The Sanctions Alternative', *supra* note 156, at 44 (stating that GNP fell 50 per cent from 1989 to February 1994); 'All Things Considered: Bosnia Peace Talks Continue in Dayton', Ohio (NPR radio broadcast, 3 November 1995) (transcript No. 2020–13) (reporting EC official's estimate that economy had shrunk 35–45 per cent by November 1995), available in LEXIS, News Library, Curnws File. A FRY minister reported that GNP per capita fell from $2,230 before the sanctions to $1,194 after sanctions were terminated. 'Anti-Yugoslav Sanctions Devastate Economy', *Xinhua News Agency*, 4 April 1996, available in LEXIS, News Library, Curnws File.

With the economic collapse came massive unemployment, which reached levels of 60 to 70 per cent.[163] Aggravating the effects of such high levels of unemployment on family income was a hyperinflation that rivalled that of Germany after World War I; the Belgrade government had taken to printing money to subsidize the economy and household consumption,[164] and annual inflation in January 1994 reached the incredible level of 313 million per cent before being halted.[165] At the same time, real wages were declining: a Red Cross study found that real household income had fallen to one-tenth of its 1990 level by 1994.[166] The same study showed that 2.2 million of the FRY's 10.5 million people lived in poverty, and half a million of those individuals lived in extreme poverty.[167] Competing for scarce domestic and international resources were 850,000 refugees from other parts of the former Yugoslavia.[168] Such dire circumstances provoked the emigration of professionals and the middle class — those most likely to oppose the Milosevic policies that had led to UN sanctions.[169]

The sanctions also took a toll on the health of the populace. The government in Belgrade and international health officials claimed that the FRY had exhausted its foreign currency reserves and was thus unable to buy medical supplies, medical equipment and pharmaceuticals, which had been exempted from the trade embargo.[170] Raw materials for manufacturing drugs domestically, however, were not exempted.[171] FRY doctors who headed three Belgrade hospitals warned that UN sanctions had caused a sharp rise in suicides and heart attacks in Serbia and Montenegro.[172] Mental health services also deteriorated; international observers

---

[163] Branson, *supra* note 161, at 39 (70 per cent by November 1993); Post, 'A Price No One Can Justify', *Newsweek*, 6 December 1993, at 30, (66 per cent in December 1993); 'The Sanctions Alternative', *supra* note 156, at 44 (60 per cent in February 1994).

[164] Hoeltschi, *supra* note 155.

[165] MacKay, Comment, 'Economic Sanctions: Are They Actually Enforcing International Law in Serbia-Montenegro?', 3 *Tul. J. Int'l & Comp. L.* (1995) 203, at 225. Inflation in December 1993 alone was 25,000 per cent. Post, *supra* note 163. The annualized rate of inflation for January to September of 1993 was 1.7 billion per cent. Branson *supra* note 161. The government managed to halt the hyperinflation in January 1994 by pegging the dinar to the Deutschmark. *World Disasters Report 1995*, *supra* note 74, at 23.

[166] *World Disasters Report 1995*, *supra* note 74, at 23. UNICEF reported similar data. See 'All Things Considered', *supra* note 162. One international visitor noted that 'some retirement pensions are barely sufficient to buy two rolls of toilet paper'. Mojzes, *supra* note 153.

[167] *World Disasters Report 1995*, *supra* note 74, at 23. A FRY minister put the poverty figure at 3.5 million people. 'Anti-Yugoslav Sanctions Devastate Economy', *supra* note 162.

[168] See 'All Things Considered', *supra* note 162 (statement of FRY Ambassador to UN).

[169] Woodward, *supra* note 145, at 148.

[170] For the observations of international health officials, see Black, 'Collapsing Health Care in Serbia and Montenegro', 307 *Brit. Med. J.* (20 October 1993) 1135. For the claims of the FRY, see Effects of the Security Council Sanctions on the Health Situation of the Population of the Federal Republic of Yugoslavia, UN Doc. S/1994/506 (1994); 'The Impact of International Community's Sanctions on the Health of the Population of FR Yugoslavia', *Yugo. Surv.* (1994) no. 1, at 97; 'Serbs Step Up Anti-sanctions Campaign', *supra* note 160.

[171] Black, *supra* note 170.

[172] 'Yugoslav Doctors Say UN Sanctions "Genocide"', *Reuters*, 18 February 1994, available in LEXIS, News Library, Arcnws File.

reported a tripling of mortality in mental institutions in less than one year, and mental health budgets were cut drastically.[173]

Accordingly, preventive health care suffered; the government claimed that it declined by 50 per cent between mid-1992 and late 1993.[174] A report issued by the Milosevic government also claimed that because the sanctions regime prohibited the import of chemicals used to purify water, the incidence of preventible contagious diseases rose substantially: in the first six months of 1993, 108 people died of contagious diseases, a figure that was 5.4 times higher than the same period in 1992.[175] The Red Cross found that a decrease in vaccinations also contributed to the increase in disease.[176] FRY officials noted, both during and after the sanctions programme, that malnutrition and infant mortality had increased significantly,[177] assertions confirmed by the Red Cross.[178] This situation was aggravated by growing food shortages, which led the FRY to begin rationing food in September 1994 for the first time since 1948.[179]

However, throughout the life of the sanctions, despite the economic downturn and declining health situation, stores in the FRY were filled with goods, restaurants remained open, and gas was freely available on the black market.[180] Indeed, it was estimated that 40 per cent of all economic activity occurred in the black market,[181] a phenomenon that the Belgrade government encouraged in order to meet the large needs left unfulfilled by its relatively unsuccessful reassumption of socialist-like control of the economy.[182] On the other hand, profits from black marketeering went primarily to the criminal gangs that controlled it.[183]

Four factors must be taken into account in evaluating the legality of UN sanctions against the FRY. First, it is difficult to measure how much of Serbia and Montenegro's post-1991 economic crisis is attributable to the sanctions and how much to other factors, such as economic mismanagement. Second, it is not clear that the Yugoslav people suffered disproportionately from the sanctions: while some claim that the average family struggled just to meet its basic needs,[184] others argue that the

---

[173] Black, *supra* note 170.

[174] 'Serbs Step Up Anti-sanctions Campaign', *supra* note 160.

[175] Effects of Sanctions on the Yugoslav Economy and the Humanitarian Situation, Agenda Item: Strengthening of the Coordination of the Humanitarian Emergency Assistance of the United Nations (1993), cited in Licht, 'The Use of Sanctions in Former Yugoslavia: Can They Assist in Conflict Resolution?', in Cortright and Lopez, *supra* note 54, at 160. See also 'Effects of the Security Council Sanctions', *supra* note 170, at 3 (providing additional statistics on incidence of contagious disease).

[176] *World Disasters Report 1995*, *supra* note 74, at 23–24.

[177] 'Effects of the Security Council Sanctions', *supra* note 170, at 3–4; 'Anti-Yugoslav Sanctions Devastate Economy', *supra* note 162; 'Serbs Step Up Anti-sanctions Campaign', *supra* note 160.

[178] *World Disasters Report 1995*, *supra* note 74, at 23, 24.

[179] MacKay, *supra* note 165, at 225.

[180] Hoeltschi, *supra* note 155.

[181] 'The Sanctions Alternative', *supra* note 156, at 44.

[182] See Woodward, *supra* note 145, at 149.

[183] See Hoeltschi, *supra* note 155.

[184] See, e.g., *ibid.*

sanctions did not unduly burden the populace and that they brought about long-needed changes in the FRY's previously state-dominated and inefficient economy.[185] Third, at least some evidence supports the conclusion that the Serbian and Montenegran people were not innocent victims of UN sanctions; in December 1992, voters in the FRY chose Slobodan Milosevic, and his vision of a Greater Serbia, over Milan Panic, who had 'promised a change of policies that could have led to a lifting of the sanctions'.[186] The question that must be faced in such a situation of apparent consent by citizens in the target state to the governmental policies that brought on international economic sanctions is what role such consent should play in assessing the legality of the impact of sanctions on innocent parties, such as children. Finally, the sanctions did appear to have influenced policy-makers in the FRY: Western diplomats attribute Milosevic's willingness to cease supporting the Bosnian Serbs and to negotiate the Dayton Peace Agreement in part to the effects that sanctions had on his country.[187]

E *Haiti, 1993–1994*

The UN Security Council imposed economic sanctions under Chapter VII most recently against Haiti. On 30 September 1991, the Haitian military, under the command of General Raoul Cedras and supported by the country's small and wealthy elite, overthrew the left-wing populist government of President Jean-Bertrande Aristide. The Haitian electorate had voted for Aristide by a large majority in December 1990 in an election that international monitors, including the UN and the OAS, had judged to be free and fair. Following the coup, President Aristide went into exile in the United States.

While both the UN General Assembly[188] and the OAS condemned the coup, the locus of the first phase of sanctions against Haiti was the OAS. Within ten days of the coup, the Ministers of Foreign Affairs of OAS Member States had passed two resolutions recommending diplomatic, economic and financial sanctions against the Haitian government, requesting the suspension of non-humanitarian aid, and urging OAS Member States to freeze the assets of the Haitian government and to impose a trade embargo on all but humanitarian goods.[189] By mid-1992, the OAS was calling upon Member States to reinforce the embargo, to freeze the private assets of the Haitian military and those who supported the coup, and to deny port access to ships

---

[185] See Bonner, 'Balkan Accord: In Belgrade, The Serbs Hopes Rise as the Sanctions Fall', *NY Times*, 28 November 1995, at A15.

[186] Damrosch, *supra* note 1, at 305.

[187] Goshko, *supra* note 91 Kempster and Meisler, 'UN Suspends Serbia Sanctions', *LA Times*, 23 November 1995, at A1; Tran *et al.*, 'UN Suspends Sanctions', *Guardian*, 23 November 1995, at 13.

[188] See GA Res. 46/7 (1991).

[189] See OAS Res. 1/91, OEA/Ser.F/V.1, MRE/RES.1/91 (2 October 1991); OAS Res. 2/91, OEA/Ser.F/V.1, MRE/RES.2/91 (8 October 1991).

118   *EJIL* 9 (1998), 86–141

trading with Haiti.[190] Consistent with the OAS resolutions, the Bush Administration froze Haitian government assets in the United States and imposed an embargo on imports from and exports to Haiti.[191]

Implementation of the OAS sanctions programme by OAS Member States was haphazard. Sanctions evasion was particularly egregious along Haiti's porous eastern border with the Dominican Republic. The Haitian military and its supporters further minimized the impact of the sanctions by continuing to trade with countries from other regions, such as Western Europe, that were not subject to the OAS regime. In sum, the sanctions failed to dislodge the Haitian military, which had begun a savage campaign of repression to eliminate domestic supporters of President Aristide.

When the ineffectiveness of the OAS sanctions became manifest, the focus of activities shifted to the UN Security Council. In June 1993, acting under Chapter VII of the Charter, it passed Resolution 841, which imposed an embargo on the sale and supply of oil and arms to Haiti, froze the funds of the Haitian government and its officials, and established a Sanctions Committee to monitor compliance with the sanctions regime as well as to approve requests, on a no-objection basis, to ship petroleum to Haiti 'for essential humanitarian needs'.[192] The sanctions were suspended when UN and US negotiators brokered an agreement between General Cedras and Haiti's government-in-exile at Governors Island, New York in July 1994 for the gradual return of President Aristide to power by 30 October 1993.[193] The Security Council reimposed the sanctions when the Haitian military violated the Governors Island Agreement by refusing to allow US military personnel to land in Haiti in mid-October as part of a UN mission.[194]

In view of the failure of renewed efforts to mediate an end to military rule, the ongoing human rights violations and the deteriorating economic situation in Haiti, the Security Council in May 1994 passed Resolution 917.[195] This resolution required UN Member States to deny landing and overfly permission to all but regularly scheduled commercial passenger flights flying to or from Haiti;[196] to deny entry into their territories of members of the Haitian military, its agents, and Haitian government officials;[197] to ban imports to or exports from Haiti;[198] and to observe a trade embargo with Haiti.[199] The resolution also strongly urged, but did not require,

---

[190] See OAS Res. 3/92, OEA/Ser.F/V.1, MRE/RES.3.92 (17 May 1992). For a summary of early OAS actions taken against the military regime in Haiti, see The Situation of Democracy and Human Rights in Haiti: Report of the Secretary-General, UN Doc. A/47/599 and Corr.1 (1992).

[191] An overview of the programme of economic sanctions implemented against Haiti by the United States appears in Matthews, 'Economic Sanctions and Economic Strategies: Toward Haiti's Integration into the World Economy', 6 *St. Thomas L. Rev.* (1994) 281, at 286–289.

[192] SC Res. 841 (1993).

[193] See SC Res. 861 (1993).

[194] See SC Res. 873 (1993).

[195] SC Res. 917 (1994).

[196] *Ibid*, para. 2.

[197] *Ibid*, para. 3.

[198] *Ibid*, paras. 6–7.

[199] *Ibid*, para. 9.

Member States to freeze the funds of members of the Haitian military, its agents, and Haitian government officials.[200] The Sanctions Committee that had been established by Resolution 841 was authorized to use the no-objection procedure to grant individual exemptions to the ban on the export to Haiti of food and fuel for humanitarian purposes.[201]

With international frustration mounting at the failure of the sanctions to dislodge the Haitian military or to persuade it to agree to a negotiated solution, the Security Council approved Resolution 940, under Chapter VII, in July 1994.[202] This resolution authorized Member States 'to form a multinational force ... to use all necessary means to facilitate the departure from Haiti of the military leadership'.[203] Economic sanctions were to be lifted only upon the return of President Aristide to power.[204] Acting under the authority of this resolution, President Clinton gave the Haitian military an ultimatum: surrender power by 19 September 1994, or face invasion by a multinational force under the leadership of the United States. Following a frenzied weekend of negotiations between General Cedras and President Clinton's special emissaries, former President Jimmy Carter, former Chairman of the Joint Chiefs of Staff Colin Powell, and Senator Sam Nunn, the Haitian military agreed to relinquish power and permit President Aristide to return and resume power. On 19 September 1994, a multinational force led by the United States was deployed in Haiti pursuant to the Cedras-Carter agreement. President Aristide returned to a tumultuous welcome in Haiti on 15 October 1994, and economic sanctions against the country were lifted the next day pursuant to Security Council resolutions.[205]

Because of their devastating effects on the Haitian economy and their impact on the health and social well-being of the mass of impoverished Haitians, the OAS and UN sanctions programmes against Haiti were particularly controversial.[206] Within four months of the imposition of OAS sanctions, Representative Robert Torricelli of New Jersey was urging President Bush to terminate the embargo and intervene militarily to oust the Haitian military regime because the economic situation in Haiti had reached the point where military intervention was 'the most humane solution'.[207] In October

---

[200] *Ibid*, para. 4.

[201] *Ibid*, para. 7.

[202] SC Res. 940 (1994).

[203] *Ibid*, para. 4.

[204] *Ibid*, para. 17.

[205] See SC Res. 948 (1994); SC Res. 944 (1994).

[206] For a sample of both the effects of OAS and UN sanctions on the Haitian economy and people and the debate over the advisability of the sanctions, see Constable, 'Dateline Haiti: Caribbean Stalemate', *Foreign Policy*, 22 December 1992, at 175; Matthews, *supra* note 191, at 285–294; Booth, 'Still Punishing the Victims', *Time*, 11 April 1994, at 55; Cleaver, 'Notes from the Hell That Is Haiti: On the Verge of Collapse', *New Leader*, 17 January 1994, at 5; Farah, 'Fuel Aid Sharpens Debate over Haiti', *Washington Post*, 15 January 1994, at A13; 'Voodoo Politics', *Economist*, 21 May 1994, at 47; Werleigh, 'The Use of Sanctions in Haiti: Assessing the Economic Realities', in Cortright and Lopez, *supra* note 54, at 161.

[207] Letter from Rep. Robert Torricelli to President George Bush (30 January 1992), quoted in 'United States to Fine-Tune Embargo against Haiti, State Department Says', *Int'l Trade Rep.* (BNA) (12 February 1992) 264.

120 *EJIL* 9 (1998), 86–141

1992, one year after the coup, an inter-agency committee under the direction of the UN Secretariat's Department of Humanitarian Affairs issued a report detailing the desperate economic and humanitarian situation in Haiti. As a result of the OAS sanctions, tens of thousands of jobs in the industrial and service sectors had been lost and unemployment had risen. Farm income and production had dropped off and deforestation had accelerated due to the embargo on petroleum imports.

The resulting decline in family purchasing power had led to increased levels of malnutrition, particularly among children. Other indicators of social welfare, such as the delivery of health services and education, had also reached a state of crisis.[208] An influential study by the Harvard Center for Population and Development Studies found that the embargo and cessation of foreign aid may have caused up to 1,000 extra child deaths per month.[209]

The impoverished majority of Haitians continued to suffer the brunt of OAS and UN sanctions.[210] Particularly galling to many in the international community was the ease with which Haiti's economic elite and military avoided their impact; indeed, many military officers amassed huge fortunes by controlling the black market in food and fuel spawned by the sanctions.[211]

The international community, and in particular the United Nations, was slow to consider formally the disproportionate and discriminatory impact of the sanctions on Haiti's poor and negligent in tailoring sanctions so as to maximize their impact on the Haitian military and its supporters. In addition to reports from humanitarian agencies in Haiti and accounts in the popular press, UN decision-makers were apprised through official channels of the disproportionate effects of the sanctions on Haiti's poor. In November 1992, the Secretary-General bluntly informed the General Assembly that Haiti's economy was 'in a state of free fall' and detailed the effects of the OAS sanctions regime on different sectors of the Haitian economy and on the social welfare of the impoverished masses.[212] The Secretary-General repeated these characterizations to the Security Council after it imposed mandatory UN sanctions in 1993, noting, for example, that Haiti was 'economically paralysed'[213] and that

> [t]he Haitian economy is on the verge of collapse. Since last month, the national currency has lost 40 per cent of its value. There is galloping inflation, and shortages are becoming more

---

[208] The findings of this report are summarized in 'November 1992 Secretary-General's Report', *supra* note 190, at 14–15.

[209] Harvard Center for Population and Development Studies, *Sanctions in Haiti: Crisis in Humanitarian Action* (1993). The methodology of this study has been criticized. See *World Disasters Report 1995, supra* note 74, at 24.

[210] As late as August 1994 the Secretary-General was warning the Security Council of continued economic deterioration in Haiti. See Report of the Secretary-General on the Question Concerning Haiti, UN Doc. S/1994/1012 (1994).

[211] On the minimal impact of the sanctions on the Haitian economic elite and the military's profiteering from sanctions evasion, see Cleaver, *supra* note 206; Farah, *supra* note 206; French, 'Explosion of Black-Market Fuel Exposes Leaks in Haiti Embargo', *NY Times,* 14 February 1994, at A1.

[212] 'November 1992 Secretary-General's Report', *supra* note 190, at 14–15.

[213] 'August 1994 Secretary-General's Report', *supra* note 210, at 1.

> severe. The prices of staple food products have more than doubled. According to
> international economists, almost four fifths of the population are unemployed.[214]

Despite the early evidence that the sanctions were crippling Haiti's poor, the world community was generally slow to react. In February 1992, the Bush Administration lifted US implementation of the OAS embargo on a case-by-case basis for US-owned maquiladora plants in Haiti.[215] The State Department characterized this measure as 'fine-tuning' and 'retarget[ing]' the sanctions so as not to 'hurt innocent people' — in this case, the 40,000 Haitians who had been employed in the US-owned maquiladoras prior to the coup.[216] Critics charged that the measure was ill-conceived[217] and that the Bush Administration had merely caved in to pressure from corporate lobbyists.[218]

There was no mention of the possibly disproportionate or discriminatory impact of economic sanctions on the poor in the Security Council meeting in which UN sanctions were first imposed.[219] The Council, however, did gradually refine the sanctions regime in the face of the public outcry over the ravages the sanctions inflicted on the Haitian economy. During the interregnum in the summer and autumn of 1993 during which the sanctions were suspended pending implementation of the Governors Island accord, the Council repeatedly issued Presidential Statements warning the Haitian military that non-compliance with the agreement would result in the reinstatement of sanctions 'appropriate to the situation, with particular emphasis on those measures aimed at those deemed responsible for the non-compliance with the Agreement'.[220] When the Haitian military disregarded the Governors Island Agreement and the Security Council reimposed the sanctions regime set up under Resolution 841, the Council's president stated that it was 'deeply concerned by the suffering of the Haitian people'.[221] The Council attributed responsibility for that suffering 'directly' to 'the refusal of the military authorities to comply with the Governors Island Process'.[222] Two weeks later in another Presidential Statement, however, the Council did express 'its determination to minimize the impact of the present situation on the most vulnerable groups and call[ed] upon Member States to continue, and to intensify, their humanitarian assistance to the people of Haiti'.[223]

Such expressions of concern for the plight of the Haitian people surfaced with more frequency in centres of power in the United Nations over the following few months.

---

[214] *Ibid*, at 2.

[215] 'United States to Fine-Tune Embargo', *supra* note 207, at 264.

[216] *Ibid*, at 264, 265.

[217] *Ibid*, at 265.

[218] See Constable, *supra* note 206, at 175.

[219] See UN Doc. S/PV.3238 (1992). The representatives from Canada and Venezuela did express concern over the ineffectiveness of the OAS sanctions in returning Aristide to power.

[220] UN Doc. S/26480 (1993); see also UN Doc. S/26567 (1993) (repeating this language).

[221] UN Doc. S/26668 (1993).

[222] *Ibid*.

[223] UN Doc. S/26747 (1993).

For example, when the 'Friends of the Secretary-General on Haiti' — France, Canada, Venezuela and the United States — called for 'new comprehensive trade sanctions' against Haiti in February 1994, they were careful to note that the sanctions should be 'aimed at the military authorities in Haiti and their supporters'.[224] Nevertheless, not until May 1994 did the Security Council specifically target its sanctions at the wrongdoers, when the Council required that Member States deny entry visas to the Haitian military and its supporters.[225] In the same resolution, however, the Council merely 'strongly urge[d]', rather than required, Member States to freeze the financial resources of those persons.[226] Furthermore, the sanctions imposed by Resolution 917 supplemented UN sanctions already in place;[227] none of the previous sanctions that had placed such an onerous burden on the destitute Haitian economy were lifted or adjusted.

Statements by representatives of Member States in the Security Council in the meeting in which Resolution 917 was approved show the Council's awareness of the desperate situation of the Haitian people. The representatives of Canada, Venezuela, Argentina, Spain, the United States, France and Brazil all expressly referred to the suffering that sanctions had inflicted on Haiti's poor.[228] US Ambassador to the UN Madeline Albright acknowledged that sanctions are 'a blunt instrument'.[229] Many Security Council members attempted to shift blame for the economic and human crisis to the Haitian military: in the words of Canada's representative, '[i]t is the failure of the military authorities to fulfil their commitments which is solely responsible for the plight of the Haitian population'.[230] Other Security Council members, in what can charitably be regarded as an expression of pious hope rather than a hard-headed assessment of the probable real-world effects of policy, echoed France's declaration that

> [t]he Council has seen to it that that objective [of returning Aristide to power] will not be achieved at the cost of the infliction of intolerable suffering on the Haitian people, which has suffered too much already. The Council intends to censure a minority, including through the use of measures that are exceptional in that they are aimed at individuals. In so doing, the Council has also made sure that the poorest people will not be crushed even more.[211]

---

[224] Letter dated 2 February 1994 from the Representatives of Canada, France, the United States and Venezuela to the President of the Security Council, UN Doc. S/1994/116 (1994). At this time the Security Council also trumpeted the arrival of fuel approved by the Sanctions Committee for humanitarian purposes. See UN Doc. S/PRST/1994/2. The fuel shipment was greeted with cynicism in Haiti, however, in light of the ineffectiveness of the embargo and military profiteering on black-market oil sales. See Farah, *supra* note 206, at A13.

[225] See SC Res. 917 (1994), para. 3.

[226] *Ibid*, para. 4.

[227] See *Ibid*, pmbl., para. 1 (reaffirming Resolutions 841 and 873).

[228] See UN Doc. S/PV.3376 (1994).

[229] *Ibid*, at 7.

[230] *Ibid*, at 4.

[211] *Ibid*, at 8 (statement of French representative). Similar sentiments and prognoses were offered by the Spanish representative. *Ibid*, at 6.

Although the Brazilian representative expressed some trepidation about the additional suffering that the expanded sanctions might engender in Haiti, only the Chinese representative addressed the Security Council's responsibility to craft proportionate and discriminatory sanctions:

> Ironically, this suffering [of the Haitian people] is at least partially attributable to the sanctions already applied to Haiti by the Security Council and by other bodies. The question is then whether the newly introduced sanctions regime, if applied, could possibly increase the suffering of the ordinary people in Haiti; and we cannot but express concern about this.[212]

While some Council members undertook to continue to review the humanitarian situation in Haiti,[233] the economic plight of the Haitian people caused by the sanctions subsequently received virtually no formal attention from the Security Council and played no explicit role in its decision to authorize a multinational force to remove the Haitian military and restore President Aristide to his post.[234]

Two reasons account for the world community's delay in recognizing the disproportionately harmful impact the sanctions were having on the Haitian people and the inadequate tailoring of sanctions to affect primarily the Haitian armed forces and their supporters. First, Jean-Bertrande Aristide, Haiti's elected president, strongly supported wide-ranging economic sanctions against his country from the time of the coup up to the day the multinational force was deployed in Haiti.[235] President Aristide's unwavering support for imposing, maintaining and expanding economic sanctions would have made it politically difficult for the OAS or the Security Council to loosen the sanctions programme, even had it been inclined to do so.

A more important factor in the poorly-designed sanctions regime was Haiti's strategic insignificance to the great powers on the Security Council. On the one hand, the human rights violations committed by the Haitian military and the desperate economic plight of the Haitian people aroused international and popular outrage. The Haitian coup also bucked the post-Cold War trend toward democratization in the Western Hemisphere, a matter of particular concern to the OAS. On the other hand,

---

[212] *Ibid*, at 10.

[233] *Ibid*, at 8 (statement of French delegation).

[234] The Secretary-General included a brief reference to Haiti's woeful economy in an August 1994 report to the Security Council. See 'August 1994 Secretary-General's Report', *supra* note 210, at 2. Moreover, in approving Resolution 940, which authorized the use of force to dislodge the Haitian military, the Nigerian and the Spanish representatives mentioned the unintended suffering of the Haitian people brought about by the sanctions. See UN Doc. S/PV.3413 (1994). While the Sanctions Committee continued to make exceptions to the sanctions regime and approve shipments of food and fuel for humanitarian reasons, on no other occasion did the Security Council formally address — or even informally refer to — the economic crisis in Haiti and the issues of proportionality and discrimination in applying its sanctions regime.

[235] For example, in late October 1993 President Aristide in an address before the General Assembly called for a total blockade against Haiti, (1993) *UNYB* 335. He also requested tougher sanctions through his representatives in meetings of the Security Council, see UN Doc. S/PV.3376 (1994), and in correspondence for the Security Council routed through the Secretary-General, see, e.g., Letter dated 15 October 1993 from the President of the Republic of Haiti addressed to the Secretary-General, UN Doc. S/26587 (1993).

124 *EJIL* 9 (1998), 86–141

no state — and, in particular, not the United States — had a strategic interest in intervening militarily in Haiti. Caught on the horns of this dilemma, the international community took the path of least resistance: It demonstrated its moral outrage by imposing 'tough' sanctions, but took the politically safe course of not intervening militarily, despite the manifest mistargeting of the impact of the sanctions. Indeed, President Clinton's September 1994 ultimatum to the Cedras regime to relinquish power or face UN-authorized military intervention was arguably motivated more by the Clinton Administration's need to shore up its sagging international credibility than concern for the suffering that the indiscriminately applied sanctions had inflicted on the Haitian people.

F *Mandatory UN Arms Embargoes and Other Measures*

A less-comprehensive instrument applied by the United Nations to influence the behaviour of elites in target states is the mandatory arms embargo. Since 1992, the Security Council, acting pursuant to Chapter VII of the Charter, has imposed mandatory embargoes on supplying weapons and military assistance to Somalia, Liberia, Angola and Rwanda. In these situations, the Security Council has acted in response to ongoing civil strife that has led to internal anarchy and humanitarian crises of international dimensions.

In Somalia, the Security Council imposed an arms embargo in January 1992 in an effort to limit intense factional fighting among the country's clans and to prevent the collapse of civil authority.[236] In November 1992, the Council decreed an arms embargo with respect to Liberia,[237] where the 1989 rebellion of forces led by Charles Taylor and the 1990 assassination of President Samuel Doe plummeted the country into an anarchy from which it has yet to fully emerge. The refusal of Jonas Savimbi's National Union for the Total Independence of Angola (UNITA) to recognize the legitimacy of the results of UN-supervised elections in 1992 and to lay down its arms led the Security Council to impose an embargo on the supply of arms and petroleum to UNITA on 15 September 1993.[238] Finally, the Security Council imposed an arms embargo against Rwanda in May 1994, when the country descended into genocidal carnage after the Rwandan President's plane was shot down over Burundi.[239]

A universal arms embargo is a useful tool that the international community can make use of when it is foreseeable that mandatory economic sanctions will either be

[236] See SC Res. 733 (1992).
[237] See SC Res. 788 (1992). The arms embargo was reaffirmed in 1993, see SC Res. 813 (1993), and a committee was established in 1995 to monitor its porous enforcement, SC Res. 985 (1995).
[238] See SC Res. 864 (1993). Although UNITA claims that the oil embargo is hurting innocent civilians, see 'Angola Hurt by UN Embargo', *AP Online*, 5 April 1994, available in LEXIS, News Library, Arcnws File; there is no evidence that the suffering of Angolans in UNITA-controlled territory is the result of anything other than the civil war in the country.
[239] See SC Res. 918 (1994). When tensions in the Great Lakes region of Central Africa increased, the Council lifted the embargo on armaments as applied to the Rwandan government, subject to some administrative restrictions. See SC Res. 1011 (1995).

ineffective or will unjustly impact the innocent. For example, imposing economic sanctions against Somalia would have served only to deepen the existing humanitarian crisis by harming the starving civilians who were caught in the crossfire of the degradations of contending warlords. Liberia, Somalia and Rwanda have effectively been without national governments for much of the periods during which these countries have been subject to UN arms embargoes. Thus, it would have been difficult in these cases to identify a target elite whose behaviour could have been influenced by the application of sanctions — and the brunt of sanctions would likely have been felt most of all by the already-pressed civilian populace rather than by the fighters responsible for the violence. Finally, an arms embargo against a particular faction in a country can be an appropriate policy tool in some situations. The arms and petroleum embargo against UNITA in Angola, for example, is easier for the Security Council to apply than a programme of economic sanctions, and it avoids the danger that the Angolan government might use an international sanctions regime in a less than humanitarian fashion to advance its domestic political agenda. Furthermore, in Angola UNITA is the primary wrongdoer, and the civilian population already suffers tremendously from the effects of war alone.

Nevertheless, there are situations in which mandatory economic sanctions are preferable to, or should be a complement of, an arms embargo. For example, an arms embargo against Libya in response to the latter's involvement in the bombing of civilian aircraft would not have been adequately tailored to the illegal acts involved. Alternatively, as was the case with Iraq, countering an aggressor's threat to international peace and security can at times require not only cutting off a state's access to armaments, but also undermining its ability to make war by using economic sanctions to weaken its economy.

There are also situations when the imprecise application of an arms embargo can unjustifiably endanger a state to which the embargo applies. Thus, many have argued that the UN's maintenance of the arms embargo against all the republics of the former Yugoslavia prolonged the Balkan wars by indirectly giving an international imprimatur to Serbia and Montenegro's military advantages over the state of Bosnia and Herzegovina. Thus, even arms embargoes must be measured against the criteria of proportionality and discrimination.[240]

The Council has also recently enacted Chapter VII measures that fall short of an arms embargo or a comprehensive programme of economic sanctions. In 1995, the Sudanese government gave refuge to terrorists who had attempted to assassinate Egyptian President Hosni Mubarak in Addis Ababa. In response, the Council passed a series of resolutions designed to increase pressure on Sudan to extradite the terrorists to Ethiopia for trial. After unsuccessfully calling on Sudan to extradite the accused individuals,[241] the Council acted under Chapter VII first by mandating diplomatic

---

[240] For further observations on the legal issues raised by arms embargoes, see Damrosch, *supra* note 1, at 284–291.

[241] SC Res. 1044 (1996).

126 *EJIL* 9 (1998), 86–141

sanctions against Sudan[242] and then by requiring states to deny aircraft substantially owned or controlled by the Sudanese government permission to take off from, land in or overfly their territories.[243] Such measures represent, in appropriate circumstances, viable alternatives to arms embargoes and economic sanctions programmes.

4 Proposed Principles with Respect to Economic Sanctions

As these foregoing case studies demonstrate, a striking feature of the economic sanctions programmes and arms embargoes implemented by the United Nations under Chapter VII of the Charter is the Security Council's almost complete failure to consider international law standards, particularly the criteria of proportionality and discrimination, in defining and enforcing sanctions regimes. In only two cases, those of Iraq and Haiti, has the Council expressly acknowledged that the impact of economic sanctions on the population of the target state has a role to play in policy formation. While the oil-for-food arrangement was adopted in response to the deteriorating humanitarian situation in Iraq, there is no evidence that the Security Council's decision was guided by anything more than a superficial reference to international law standards. Moreover, in the case of Haiti, while the Council did formally recognize the devastating impact that the sanctions were having on the poor, instead of grappling with the legal issues raised by the sanctions programme, Council members in their public statements simplistically attempted to shift responsibility for their effects to the Haitian military.[244]

In response to the acknowledged shortcomings of its sanctions programmes, the five permanent members of the Security Council issued a short policy statement on the humanitarian impact of sanctions.[245] The document states that 'further collective actions in the Security Council within the context of any future sanctions regime should be directed to minimize unintended adverse side-effects of sanctions on the most vulnerable segments of targeted countries' and that the 'structure and implementation of future sanctions regimes may vary according to the resource base of the targeted country'.[246] Among the considerations that the Council deems relevant to designing sanctions regime are 'assess[ing] objectively the short- and long-term humanitarian consequences of sanctions in the context of the overall sanctions regime' and 'giv[ing] due regard to the humanitarian situation'.[247] Such a policy

---

[242] SC Res. 1054 (1996).

[243] SC Res. 1070 (1996).

[244] See *supra* notes 219–234 and accompanying text.

[245] Letter dated 13 April 1995 from the Permanent Representatives of China, France, the Russian Federation, the United Kingdom of Great Britain and President of the Security Council, UN Doc. S/1995/300 (1995) ('Humanitarian impact of sanctions').

[246] *Ibid.*

[247] *Ibid.*

statement from the Security Council is welcome. We believe, however, that the Council's consideration of the humanitarian impact of sanctions can and should be much more searching and systematic than the terms of that brief policy statement. To that end, and drawing on principles of international law and the experiences of the United Nations and individual nations in implementing economic sanctions programmes, we propose the following principles with respect to economic sanctions.

A *Highly Coercive Economic Sanctions Must Follow Prescribed Contingencies*

1 *Lawful Contingencies*

The use of *highly* coercive economic sanctions, like any other strategic instrument of high coercion, must be based on lawful contingencies. International law permits coercion to be used, but only for prescribed contingencies and under prescribed conditions. For the United Nations, the contingencies are set out in Article 39 of the Charter. For individual states, acting unilaterally or in combination with others, the customary law of self-defence and the emerging law of counter-measures will prescribe the contingencies.

Whether sanctions are applied by the United Nations or unilaterally, the analysis of prospective programmes and the criteria for determining their lawfulness, as distinct from the contingencies for their operation, should be the same. While scholars may argue over whether determinations under Article 39 are to be governed by principles of law embedded in the Charter and subjected to judicial review in their light, we take it as unexceptional that when the community of nations applies coercion in defence of public order, it is subject to the same laws of war or humanitarian law that have been prescribed for others.

Economic sanctions are not required to precede the application of military sanctions. Chapter VII of the Charter, which establishes the authority of the Security Council to use intense coercion to support binding decisions and prescribes the procedures to be followed, implicitly acknowledges the potentially destructive capacity of any strategic instrument of coercion. And there is no reason to doubt that the drafters of the UN Charter were not aware of the highly deprivatory consequences and destructive potential of any instrument of policy. The initiation of *any* instrument requires, as a precondition, a finding of one of the contingencies for action under Article 39 — threats to the peace, breaches of the peace or acts of aggression. Nor does the Charter suggest that one instrument is inherently more destructive than another. Although a number of scholars have suggested that there is a necessary sequence of steps leading up to the use of the military instrument, implying that the military is viewed in the Charter as the most destructive instrument and hence the last to be used, this is not correct. While Article 41 of the Charter introduces 'measures not involving the use of armed force' before its discussion of the military instrument, Article 42 states explicitly:

> Should the Security Council consider that measures provided for in Article 41 would be
> inadequate or have proved to be inadequate, it may take such action by air, sea, or land forces
> as may be necessary to maintain or restore international peace and security...[248]

Thus, the Charter authorizes the Council to commence with any strategic instrument, depending on its assessment of which would be optimum in the context of each case.

International law, however, does not prescribe restrictive contingencies for the use of economic sanctions of low coercion. These actions fall into the category of 'retorsions', that is, discretionary punitive actions, whether diplomatic, ideological or economic, to which states may resort to indicate their displeasure with the policies or comportment of another state. If a low level of coercion is exceeded, the state initiating the action is obliged to justify its action by reference to the law of self-defence or countermeasures.

2 Level of Coercion Must be Correlated with Predictable Consequentiality of Economic Effects

For the inquiries we propose, the level of coercion is determined, not by the structure or name of the programme, but by its *predictable consequentiality*. Thus, if state A unilaterally mounts a general embargo against state B, the action, despite its avowed comprehensiveness, may only be retorsive in terms of its consequences because many other states continue to maintain full and significant economic relations with state B. But if state A is in a monopolistic or monopsonistic position *vis-à-vis* state B, a self-described, partial, unilateral embargo may have effects that go beyond the bounds of retorsion. Thus, to take one well-known example, the United States' collapse of Cuba's sugar quota in 1959 was more than retorsive, in terms of the test of predictable consequentiality because it had foreseeable and substantial harmful economic effects.

If this were so, it would have to be substantively justifiable under international law. Within the framework of prospective effectiveness developed in this paper,[249] an economic sanctions programme would be retorsive only if the sanctioner cannot foresee, in formulating its impact assessment, that substantial economic harm is reasonably likely to follow from implementation.

B *Economic Sanctions Must Be Necessary and Proportional*

Comparative examinations of 'more-than' or 'less-than' do not address the fundamental question of quantum: How much, if any, collateral damage is permissible in a particular case? The concept of necessity in the law of war is supposed to deal with this matter, but it is often interpreted to mean whatever is minimally necessary to achieve a given military objective without relating the inquiry to the legal quality of the *political* objective for which the military objective is only an instrument. Necessity, in this sense, would not be a restrictive criterion, but would become extensive and facilitative. Yet the concept of necessity must be elastic enough to allow for substantial collateral damage when the dangers to public order warrant it. Otherwise, the

---

[248] UN Charter, Art. 42.
[249] See *infra* Part 4.C.2.

economic instrument, indeed all instruments, become, definitionally, techniques which must be ineffective in order to be lawful. The question, then, is how to incorporate the necessity factor into calculations of lawfulness of prospective economic sanctions programmes.

In first impression questions like these, the Natural Law criteria of necessity and proportionality are indispensable, for they help us to consider and then fashion and appraise legal instruments in terms of social goals, costs and alternative consequences. The bigger the bullet, the bigger the hole. Assume that the more lethal the sanctions, the more likely the corresponding collateral damage is to be extensive. Would we not all agree that it would be unacceptable, in a period of breakdown of public order, for police to be ordered to shoot looters, with the collateral damage such rules of engagement might entail? And would it not be equally unacceptable for police not to be ordered to shoot armed irregulars with a record of terrorism who were moving to seize an undefended elementary school? In the first instance, whatever damage might ensue to seizure of property by looters could be largely repaired by ordinary police work *after* public order is restored. In the second instance, the damage that might ensue could not be repaired after public order is restored. In other words, the tolerance for lawful violence, with the corresponding level of collateral damage that will ensue, varies, in part, according to the degree of injury that is posed to public order and the degree of irreparability of injuries if they occur.

This type of analysis can, it is submitted, be applied to determine the level of tolerance for quanta of collateral damage in economic sanctions programmes. Contrast the sanctions programmes against the dictatorships of Saddam Hussein and Fidel Castro. The precipitating events for the sanctions against Saddam were past and projected aggressive wars and the development of nuclear, chemical and biological weapons arsenals for illicit adventures. The sanctions are designed to prevent the development and use of such weapons in future aggressive wars. The precipitating events for the sanctions against Castro (which are not, in fact, comprehensive and effective) are internal authoritarianism and systematic denial of human rights. The sanctions are designed to hasten the end of the dictatorship, but not to forestall any aggressive external policy. Both sanctions programmes will cause collateral damage. Surely a higher level of collateral damage should be legally tolerable for Saddam than for Castro.

But consider the complexity of the problem through the lens of a hypothetical case. Assume that chemical weapons are being assembled in state A from materials produced in five different factories, each employing several thousand people. A precise sanctions programme can effectively deny state A access to the raw materials needed in three of the factories. The programme commences, the factories close and the chemical weapons production is suspended. Ten thousand workers in the three factories are furloughed, they and their families suffer nutritional, health, educational and psychological deprivations, the cities in which they live slide into recession, the mortality and epidemiology of economic collapse manifests itself, and so on.

The workers and their families have suffered collateral damage. That does not

130 *EJIL* 9 (1998), 86–141

necessarily render the programme unlawful. Lawfulness will turn, in part, on the degree of precision of the instrument and the consequent limitation of damage. How can that be measured? By comparing the projected effects of this programme with other possible uses of the economic instrument or with the other instruments. For example, imagine a construct in which the chemical weapons production is terminated by a total embargo against state A, with much more widespread deprivation and infrastructural deterioration. In the first hypothetical situation, there would be considerably less collateral damage.

But contrast these examples with an enforcement programme applying a different strategic instrument, e.g., a surgical bombing raid against the factories using visually corrected 'smart bombs', on the model of the Israeli attack on the Osirak reactor in Iraq. Assume that there are five fatalities.

These three hypothetical programmes indicate, we submit, that, when planning an enforcement programme, international law requires, among other things, that an assessment be made of the collateral damage of different strategic options through comparative projections of the costs to non-combatants or non-responsible parties of the application of the military, economic or propagandic instruments, alone or in various combinations. These comparative projections will force the sanctioner to evaluate the consequences of its acts and facilitate internal, and perhaps external, appraisal of the programme's lawfulness.

The value spectrum of the New Haven School may be useful in this regard, for it provides a focus on changes precipitated by specific sanctions programmes in the production and distribution of values, whether prospectively or retrospectively and at whatever level of detail is desired and in every social sector. International law now prescribes for virtually all of these social slices,[250] in some instances with non-derogable human rights norms. Hence, appraisals of projected enforcement programmes must be made not simply in terms of quanta of collateral damage, but in terms of priorities of human rights norms. As in other social scientific research, investigation here should distinguish between structural or infrastructural inquiry and short-term deprivation. It must also develop techniques for assessing cumulative injury.

The principle of necessity in the law of armed conflict requires that, once a valid contingency is identified, alternative strategies be prospectively evaluated. Assuming various sufficient strategies, instruments and programmes should be selected on the basis of which ones accomplish the necessary objectives with the least possible quanta of harm. The cognitive process is necessarily comparative, but, in the end, it should

---

[250] International law has now assumed explicit responsibility for supervising protection of the environment. With regard to uses of the military instrument, environmental concerns are a venerable part of the literature, from prohibitions with regard to the poisoning of wells until the present. It is clear that any inquiry undertaking to assess the prospective lawfulness of a particular sanctions programme must consider the implications for the environment.

yield selection of the least harmful, yet effective at a nation's level, of instrument technology.

The principle of proportionality under international law caps the quanta of damage that the necessity inquiry suggests. Therefore, even if necessary, a sanctions programme cannot exceed the somewhat broadly construed bounds of proportionality. Collateral damage, as part of general damage, must also be proportional. The referential point of evaluation for proportionality under the law of armed conflict is the immediate or prospective consequences of the act that triggered the contingency. This inquiry into proportionality must also necessarily be prospective.

C *Sanctioners Must Reasonably Maximize Discrimination between Combatants and Non-Combatants*

1 *The Need for Discrimination*

Economic sanctions are destructive. Potentially, they could be even more destructive, at least in terms of collateral damage, than uses of the military instrument. This is especially so if one takes into account the military instrument's effectiveness at the early communication stage. To allow unilateral or multilateral actors to use economic sanctions in a manner inconsistent with the minimization of collateral harm would undermine the fundamental goals of international law that are expressed in the prescribed law of armed conflict.

In all cases, the essential character of economic sanctions must be squarely faced. The theory of 'trickle down' economic programmes is that development strategies that primarily benefit wealthy strata rather than the neediest are morally defensible because they will ultimately prove more inclusively beneficial: thanks to a process in which greater amounts of wealth will drizzle down on the wretched poor at the base of the social pyramid, they will be better off than they could expect if they were made direct beneficiaries. 'Trickle up' economic sanctions theories, in contrast, contend that the increased pain of lower social strata will percolate upward, by some remarkable osmosis, to those who have the capacity to influence decision. This percolation would occur because the political elites either prioritize the public interest or are particularly responsive to the claims of interest groups.[251] The leadership will, indeed, 'feel your pain'.

There is no empirical evidence to support either theory. An economic sanctions programme may not be justified on a 'trickle up' theory of deprivation any more than a military strategy, such as carpet bombing of urban concentrations of non-combatants, can be justified on the theory that the pain of death and injury will rise to the higher, politically responsible levels. From a legal standpoint, it is not enough to say that our economic sanctions are permissible because 'we are hurting country X' or even that 'we are hurting the government of country X', any more than it would be persuasive to use this type of reasoning to defend unfocused bombing.

---

[251] See generally Kaempfer and Lowenberg, 'The Theory of International Economic Sanctions: A Public Choice Approach', 78 *Am. Econ. Rev.* (1988) 787.

132 *EJIL* 9 (1998). 86–141

It follows that, at a theoretical level, economic sanctions, as opposed to retorsions, whether applied by the United Nations under Chapter VII of the Charter or unilaterally, must be designed with regard to the techniques selected, with as much attention to context and capacity for discrimination as must a lawful sanctions programme using the military instrument. Economic sanctions may be used when they are capable of discrimination. Sanctions that deprive an adversary of war *matériel* are presumptively lawful, for they are directed against combatants. Sanctions that are designed to change the political programme of an adversary may be lawful when they visit their impacts on the target elite or on rational economic maximizers within the target who have the capacity to influence the political elite.

The political structure of the target may then be an important consideration. More collateral damage may be permitted when the target is democratic, for more adults may be deemed to support and be implicated in the comportment that is the target of international condemnation and sanction. Far less collateral damage may be permissible when the target state is a dictatorship in which the population has no meaningful say in decisions.

More limited and precise economic sanctions are to be preferred over more general and undiscriminating programmes. Given the destructiveness of economic sanctions programmes, it would seem that genuinely effective general embargoes, which, by definition, cannot discriminate between combatant and non-combatant, should be impermissible and that there is now a need for a much more refined use of the economic sanction. In this respect, UN Security Council Resolution 661 was probably exorbitant in its sweeping restriction on foodstuffs for Iraq; it was ameliorated in Resolution 666 of 13 September 1990, which assigned a certain discretionary competence to the Sanctions Committee to determine whether 'humanitarian circumstances' warranted a departure from Resolution 661.[252] But paragraph 5 of Resolution 666 did not make clear that the Security Council would be obliged to take account of the recommendations of the Sanctions Committee.[253] Our review of the ten cases of UN sanctions programmes indicated that there have been few if any prior examinations of the prospective lawfulness of an economic sanctions programme against the target state before a political decision was made to put it into place. We know of no case in which the Security Council or the Council of the League of Nations commissioned a study of projected collateral damage likely to be caused by economic sanctions before ordering the programme. We submit that any economic sanctions programme, to be lawful, must undertake a preliminary 'impact assessment' study, based on contextual inquiry.

2 Realistic and Operable Techniques of Impact Assessment Must be Developed

In the past, economic sanctions have caused large amounts of collateral damage in the form of civilian loss of life and property. Even if other criteria of lawfulness were satisfied (i.e. contingency, necessity and proportionality), the goal of minimizing

---

[252] See *supra* notes 41–43 and accompanying text.
[253] See *supra* note 41.

civilian harm through discrimination requires that prospective sanctioners inform themselves about the nature of the circumstances in which they undertake to change the behaviour of the target. Due to the nature of economic mechanisms, it is virtually impossible to contain harm *a priori* to those elites in the target state from whom policy changes are sought.[254] Myriad macroeconomic multipliers and linkages simply do not allow for such precision. The law of armed conflict does not impose a complete prohibition on the use of weapons that cannot perfectly discriminate; in each case, lawfulness will turn on many factors. But the capacity of an instrument to discriminate relative to other available instruments will always be an important criterion, given the goals of humanitarian law.

With respect to the economic instrument, the principle of discrimination must be assessed through an *ex ante* determination of expected policy-effectiveness of the programme contemplated by the putative sanctioner. A policy-effective sanctions programme is one that accomplishes the objective of changing an external or internal policy while minimizing collateral damage. A policy-effective programme minimizes collateral damage by reducing the duration of economic suffering, concentrating harm on those who have material influence in policy-making, and targeting resources that are not essential for civilian survival or bodily integrity but whose neutralization is likely to lead to desirable adjustments in the target's policies. A policy-effective programme thus maximizes discrimination because it is narrowly tailored to achieve its policy goals subject to the constraint of harming non-combatants as little as possible. By requiring an *ex ante* determination of policy-effectiveness, in the form of an impact assessment, the target sanctioner, third-party states and other relevant international actors, who can impose real political costs on the target sanctioner at an early stage, would be able to invoke international law upon appraisal of the impact assessment. Collateral harm, therefore, would be prevented at an early stage through a process of authoritative communication.

Any estimate of the policy-effectiveness of a projected programme will necessarily be probabilistic, but past experiences and rigorous techniques of contemporary social inquiry may provide important insights into prospective effectiveness. These insights may serve as an initial evaluatory guidepost that, with the accumulation of evidence, may evolve into a technically sophisticated dialogue between sanction-planners and the international decision process that must assess the propriety of the programme under international law. The increasing sophistication of the cognate genre of environmental impact assessments exemplifies the process of communication that is likely to arise once sanctioners are required to conduct the type of assessment that we propose. Precisely this type of authoritative communication, indeed, seems to have commenced since the Security Council implicitly acknowledged the normative requirement to minimize the collateral damage caused by economic sanctions.

---

[254] See Kaempfer and Lowenberg, 'A Model of the Political Economy of International Investment Sanctions: The Case of South Africa', 39 *Kyklos* (1986) 377, at 377.

The criterion of policy-effectiveness, rather than an a-contextual bright line rule, seems to be the most appropriate, and probably the only feasible, rule of decision for achieving, in the idiosyncrasies of each case, the articulated goals of international law. Conclusions about the policy-effectiveness of an economic sanctions programme in any particular case are the outcome of two interrelated stages: first, economic effectiveness that produces the desired 'shock' in the target and, second, and causally, political change. An inquiry into policy-effectiveness, therefore, must disaggregate the concept into its component parts of economic effectiveness and political effectiveness. Economic effectiveness, which is also relevant in determining predictable consequentiality as we postulated earlier, is the capacity of a sanctions programme to cause a substantial economic shock. Political effectiveness is the capacity of such shock to make relevant actors introduce desired changes in the target's policy. Relevant actors may include the political elite, the economic elite, or any other social grouping with the capacity to change, in whatever way and through whatever means, the policy that has been targeted by the sanctioner. The following guidelines derived from past experiences and social-scientific approaches suggest that a reasonably reliable evaluation of policy-effectiveness is both practicable and administrable.

(a) Economic Effectiveness

Economic sanctions may take a wide variety of forms, but frequently they are embodied in trade restrictions (export controls and import barriers), investment restrictions (prohibition or licensing), and embargoes (specific or general). Theoretically, their capacity to create an economic shock in the trade or the capital accounts of the target state depends on contextual variables. In practice, the choice of instrument is usually constrained by other legal regimes such as the General Agreement on Trade and Tariffs, WTO or internal export control law.[255]

Economic effectiveness depends on the sanctioner's ability to increase significantly the prices of inputs and goods that the target country imports and/or to lower significantly the prices of goods and services that the target state exports by collapsing demand. In order for this to occur, the trade linkages between the sanctioners and the target must be substantial, although they do not need to be in a monopolistic-monopsonistic relationship.[256] At either the communication or the implementation stage, the target will likely try to undertake reactive policies to neutralize those price effects. The effectiveness of reactive policies, however, will be limited by the flexibility of domestic means of production in redirecting toward import substitution or different exports, by the existence or development of alternative markets, and by the elasticity

---

[255] See Leidy, 'The Theory of International Economic Sanctions — A Public Choice Approach: Comment', 79 *Am. Econ. Rév.* (1989) 1300.

[256] See van Bergeijk, *supra* note 9, at 395. Even when they are not, the same effect may be achieved by military or political instruments directed against third parties with whom the target does have substantial economic relations. This, however, moves inquiry from primarily economic sanctions programmes to primarily military or political sanctions programmes with economic components.

of the worldwide demand or supply for an affected good or input.[257] The tendency of local capitalists to engage in capital flight upon sudden increases in country risk, in the absence of offsetting inflows from third-party countries, is also likely to hamper, effective reaction by depleting investment.

While it is counter-intuitive, some empirical studies suggest that sanctions programmes of shorter duration tend to be more effective. Economic shock, apparently, should be sudden to prevent conditioning.[258] This finding, however, is only valid when the goods or inputs cannot, by their nature, be stockpiled, or, if possible, if both the communication and implementation come so unexpectedly that the need for developing warehousing sources is unforeseeable or too costly as a reactive strategy.

An impact assessment would require a factor analysis based on these guidelines for each target. Although complex dyadic and multi-country simulations have been available since the introduction of computers,[259] once a legal requirement for impact assessment becomes clarified, the technical configuration of such assessment would, because of the legal requirement, evolve rapidly towards scientific optimality, as resources are devoted to its perfection. More importantly, an impact assessment of economic effectiveness would communicate to the international community what the sanctioner's expectations are. The world community thus could have access to, and perhaps mobilize itself about, otherwise private or unintegrated information. Relevant actors in the international arena would impose political costs on unilateral sanctioners who use inadequate methodologies or unreliable data in making their case.

(b) Political Effectiveness

(i) Yessibility

Economic sanctions are more likely to be effective when the change in policy sought from the target is, in Roger Fisher's terms, an essentially 'yessible proposition', i.e., the party to whom it is addressed can accept it without suffering a critical value loss. There are several corollaries to the theorem of 'yessibility'. First, the degree of yessibility of the policy adjustment sought will, in direct proportion, increase or decrease the quantum of destructive force necessary for the effectiveness of the sanctions programme. Put bluntly, the less yessible the policy adjustment sought from the target state, the more coercion the sanctioner must be prepared to invest in a sanctions programme.

A second corollary holds that yessibility will be increased by an accommodative formulation of the policy adjustment that is sought, i.e., a formulation that takes

---

[257] See Kaempfer and Lowenberg, 'Determinants of the Economic and Political Effects of Trade Sanctions', 56 S. African J. Econ. (1988) 270, at 270–272.

[258] Van Bergeijk, supra note 9, at 394.

[259] See, e.g., Hubner-Dick and Seidelmann, 'Simulating Economic Sanctions and Incentives: Hypothetical Alternatives to United States Policy on South Africa', 2 J. Peace Res. (1978) 153.

account of the needs or circumstances of the target elite. In particular, change that can be accomplished in ways that permit the target to save face are more yessible. In some circumstances, a package deal, in which the sanctioner appears to be making a concession to the target in return for the target's concession to the sanctioner, may also increase yessibility. When this happens, economic sanctions programmes are more likely to be seen as part of a larger negotiation process, in which the economic instrument's role is not prominent and the result is likely to be attributed to negotiation rather than to the application of sanctions.

A third corollary, which is put forward much more tentatively, holds that adjustments in external policies will be more yessible than adjustments in internal policies, insofar as internal policies are likely to undermine the targeted political elite's power.

(ii) Political Regime

Sanctions aimed at securing policy changes are more likely to be effective when the political elite in the target state is itself composed of rational, profit-maximizing economic actors or when the internal political structure of the target is such that the political elite, though not economically oriented, must take account of the interest of other rational economic actors. The effectiveness of sanctions, from a political standpoint, thus depends on the particular coalition of relevant political actors that sustains the target's domestic political regime. Different patterns of political mobilization and legitimacy would yield different degrees of effectiveness, even assuming the same type and amount of economic harm. By examining the patterns of power and authority in a country's political system, a sanctioner can determine, at least in probabilistic terms, the political effectiveness of projected programmes. Such an inquiry would also focus the sanctioner on the *ex ante* maximization of such effectiveness.

A sanctioner will confront a wide variety of domestic political arrangements. Any typology of regimes is necessarily only a set of snapshots of discrete stages within a very broad and infinitesimally divisible spectrum of arrangements. Hence the need for contextuality in each case rather than reliance on standardized models. Economic sanctions that are directed against the rank-and-file will be less effective against totalitarian regimes in which tight and centralized political controls operate. Similarly, they will be less effective when elites and rank-and-file in the target share symbols communicating a common fundamental ideology, religion or nationality, especially if the sanctioner does not share that commonality or is viewed as unassimilably alien in it. Under these latter circumstances, the political elite of the target will easily be able to recharacterize the economic sanctions to the domestic polity as part of a larger military programme of foreign intruders aimed at destroying the nation's or group's physical or symbolic integrity. The domestic elite would thus be able to fend off the population's complaints regarding the sanctions' economic effects, redirecting them outwards.

In post-totalitarian regimes, i.e., those in which theretofore politically powerful symbols have lost their capacity to influence popular support, the regime's repressive mechanisms may still reduce the sanctions' effects on stability and increase the ability to resist policy pressures. Although the political costs of repression are not zero for the domestic elite, the threshold level at which the population, goaded by the economic pain of the sanctions, is likely to challenge the regime's authority is actually quite high. The low political cost of repression that this implies, however, can be offset by sanctions aimed at reducing the repressive capabilities of the sanctioned state. Wholly aside from the human rights windfall, economic sanctions aimed at raising the cost of military goods used in repression, if economically effective, may create a new social equilibrium in which the costs of repression are high enough and the costs of popular mobilization against the elites are low enough for change to become effective.

The effectiveness of economic sanctions is also likely to be low against despotic or sultanistic regimes, or societies in which the effective symbols of power and authority are not objective but personalized. In these regimes, characteristically, the essential vehicles through which political dissent can be effectively channelled are lacking. Low educational levels or socialization into value orders that encourage submission to patriarchal figures pose formidable obstacles to mobilization for change in the direction of the targeted internal or external policy.

As one moves away from domestic political systems in which mobilization depends on reactions to symbols or repression, economic sanctions seem to promise more effectiveness. Authoritarian regimes, which are usually sustained by a coalition between the military as government and the professional or middle classes, are probably more sensitive to economic sanctions than other non-pluralistic polities, but less so than democracies. These regimes tend to prioritize the protection of pre-capitalist economic interests, the 'liberalization' of civil society by incorporating interest groups into decision-making processes through institutionalization or cooptation, and the preservation of domestic public order through involvement of the military as a specially indulged institution. Because of its main bases of support, the stability of these regimes is highly dependent on the continuing expectation of the efficient and efficacious achievement of the middle classes' economic policy goals and the military's goal of public order. Under these conditions, economic sanctions aimed at commercial interests or the military as an institution are likely to be politically effective to the extent that they are economically effective.

Democracies, or regimes approaching it, indeed seem the most vulnerable to economic sanctions. The critical factor determining vulnerability appears to be the degree of the atomization or polarization of political groupings and the relative real influence of interest groups. In countries that have not consolidated their democracies, for example, the installation of authoritarianism or even a resurgence of post-totalitarianism could be triggered by economic shock. This should underline our caveat about reliance on models: real-world political configurations are likely to fall in between the broad categories discussed here. Moreover, economic sanctions will, to

138 *EJIL* 9 (1998), 86–141

some degree, dynamically affect the political configuration of the target, a second-order consequence that the sanctioner must always assess.

The relative vulnerability of pluralistic regimes is intriguing, for, of course, it is the liberal democracies that have, to date, made the most manifest use of economic sanctions and frequently, but not exclusively, used them against non-pluralistic governments. But non-pluralistic governments can also play the game, and this theorem should alert us to the possibility that they might be able to wield economic sanctions more effectively than their democratic counterparts. Consider the interesting situation in US-China relations: The threat and/or application of US sanctions against China in the post-Tianamen period has been ineffective in changing China's human rights policies and practices. In contrast, the threat and/or application of Chinese sanctions against the United States, in terms of reducing economic opportunities in China for US business while increasing them for our economic competitors, has been quite effective. Indeed, the current US administration has largely surrendered our hitherto major economic sanctions technique for securing Chinese compliance with international standards of human rights by decoupling the granting of Most Favored Nation status from human rights performance — exactly as demanded by the Chinese government!

In terms of this theorem, the sanctions target against which an American programme conducted or initiated is likely to be most effective is a state such as apartheid South Africa, in which a distinct commercial elite stands to suffer significant deprivations as a result of the sanctions *and* is in a position to influence the political elite. For the same reasons, the United States is likely to be a prime target for effective economic sanctions programmes mounted by other states with whom we have important economic ties. The least auspicious sanction target is a post-totalitarian regime such as Castro's Cuba, where there is no independent economic elite and the political elite and its security apparatus are not likely to be affected or threatened by wealth deprivations.

The critical factor in this theorem is the degree of political relevance of the internal wealth elite. A corollary to this theorem holds that the sanctions programme will fail, despite the political relevance of a wealth elite that is suffering the brunt of the sanctions, when the sanctions programme itself generates a new politically relevant wealth elite that actually benefits from the sanctions. Thus, in General Cedras' Haiti, the existing wealth elite suffered from the sanctions, but its removal of support for the military dictatorship was more than counter-balanced by a new elite which was enriching itself through trade in contraband and other transactions that had become profitable, thanks to the sanctions programme itself.

Sanctions programmes will be less effective when the target's elite has or can acquire supportive contacts within the sanctioning state. Thus, China can retain law firms, public relations firms, business lobbies and consulting firms composed of former high officials who continue to have great influence on policy in the United States, while the United States is unable to acquire comparable instruments of influence in China.

(iii) Reactive International Mobilization

The more civilians and non-combatants suffer in the target, the more popular indignation in other states (and even in the sanctioning state) will be directed against the sanctions. Hence the target will use the propaganda instrument intensively. Planning for extended sanctions programmes that cause widespread collateral damage will, accordingly, require coordinate propagandic programmes that justify the continuation of sanctions to politically relevant strata whose support is necessary for the sanctions programme.

(iv) Interdependence and Political Feedback

In circumstances in which there is a high degree of interdependence between the sanctioner and the target, such that many of the deprivatory effects of the sanctions programme will be felt by economic factors within the sanctioner state, the sanctions programme is less likely to be effective in proportion to the political relevance of the domestic factors likely to be hurt by the sanctions — for there will be pressure within the sanctioning state to reduce the scope and intensity of the programme to an essentially symbolic level. In these circumstances, one may find, under the rubric of an economic sanctions programme, what is essentially a propagandic programme, one of whose critical targets is that part of the targeting state's constituency that is demanding action and that is, thus, reassured that 'everything' possible is being done, when, in fact, virtually nothing is being done. This does not mean that the resulting symbolic sanctions programme has no political meaning, as we noted earlier. US responses to China may be an example of this theorem.

(v) Power Differentials in the Global Context

In situations of bipolarity, an economic sanction imposed by one superpower against a smaller state is unlikely to be effective because the smaller state has the capacity to turn to the other superpower to supplement what has been deprived. Thus, during the Cold War, Stalin's economic sanctions programme against Tito's Yugoslavia failed because Tito was able to turn to the West, which eagerly and generously embraced him. Conversely, the US sanctions programme against Cuba at the end of the Eisenhower Administration and thereafter was largely ineffective because Cuba could turn to the Soviet Union.

A corollary to this theorem is that in situations of competitive multipolarity, the unilateral imposition of sanctions is less likely to be effective. The operational implication of this corollary is that in situations of multipolarity, unilateral sanctions should be channelled through international organizations so that as many states as possible are obliged to participate in them. The compromises necessary to win organizational support may be more than offset by the effectiveness of the narrower, but mulitlateral, programme.

(vi) Plurilateralism and Multilateralism

Many of the preceding theorems suggest that the effectiveness of a sanctions programme may be enhanced by making it plurilateral or international. A sanctions programme conducted through the UN Charter, under Chapter VII, has the benefit of being obligatory on all other states parties by virtue of Article 25 of the Charter. It also benefits from a monitoring mechanism that is not associated directly with the state primarily interested in having the sanctions programme.

D *There Must be a Periodicity of Assessment*

Everything, Herakleitos teaches, changes. Hence, economic sanctions programmes must continuously update their information as the programme proceeds to ensure that they are consistent, in their effects, with international law. The necessity for the use of explicit contextuality here is very important to ensure compliance no less than to test allegations of abuse. In sanctions programmes, the target state is likely to seek to exaggerate the injuries it is suffering and, in particular, the burden falling on non-combatant strata of the population as a way of challenging the lawfulness and morality of the sanctions programme and undermining the political will to continue it. Fidel Castro, for example, has insisted that the US economic embargo is wreaking havoc among Cuban children by denying them access to medicine. But, of course, virtually all of the other states in the Western hemisphere have economic relations with the Castro government, and in all of them medicines are far, far cheaper than in the United States. Castro is, in fact, conducting a propaganda programme through which he is trying to blame the United States for the woeful state of Cuba's political economy. A contextual examination of the allegation readily exposes it. One is struck by the lack of such a rigorous analysis by the media that report these claims.

E *Provision for Injuries to Third Parties Must be Provided*

Collateral damage for economic sanctions programmes is not always limited to sectors within the targeted state. Third parties may also suffer collateral damage and are entitled to relief. Article 50 of the Charter provides:

> If preventive or enforcement measures against any state are taken by the Security Council, any other state, whether a Member of the United Nations or not, which finds itself confronted with special economic problems arising from the carrying out of those measures shall have the right to consult the Security Council with regard to a solution of those problems.[260]

This form of collateral damage has received the most attention from the sanctions committees of the United Nations. When the committees have been persuaded, they have often waived the trading prohibition for the third state (as was done for Zambia, for instance, with respect to the Rhodesian sanctions).

5 Conclusion

Future non-retorsive uses of the economic strategy, whether by the international community or on a unilateral basis, should be examined prospectively in terms of the requirements of the law of armed conflict: in each case much more refined economic

---

[260] UN Charter, Art. 50.

sanctions programmes should be designed. If this is to be a meaningful and not a cosmetic exercise, the egregious and potentially long-term social, economic and environmental consequences of uses of economic strategies must be acknowledged. Mid-term and long-term as well as the short-term consequences of a prospective economic sanctions programme must be projected and appraised. As we noted, we know of no case in which the political decision, whether at the UN or unilateral level, to undertake an economic sanctions programme was preceded by an inquiry into the lawfulness of the programme based upon considerations of necessity, proportionality and the capacity for discrimination of the technique to be used. All too often, consideration of these issues after a sanctions regime has become entrenched has been disingenuous.[261]

Policy-makers must undertake rigorously contextual and honest assessments of the collateral damage likely to occur and run inter-instrument comparisons of projected collateral damage. They must give more consideration to the use of the military instrument as a technique for conveying credible threats and achieving its objectives with a lower likelihood of collateral damage if that instrument is used first *and* credibly. Sometimes a precise use of the military strategy will more efficiently achieve the international objective and more closely approximate the tests of lawful international coercion than would an undefined economic sanctions programme. Thus, the conventional wisdom that one must advance, through a slow process of escalation, from diplomatic, to propagandic, to economic, to military instruments should be re-examined. The sequence may sometimes have to be reversed. Ideally, a political decision should be taken to compel a target to comply with a particular international decision or policy and then a group of experts should be tasked to determine the best and most lawful instruments to achieve compulsion in the circumstances of that case. Only then should the particular sanctions instrument or programme of instruments be selected. In some cases, the military instrument may have to be used first, initially by threat communication and, if that fails, by actual application.

---

[261] The statements made in the Security Council once it became undeniable that UN sanctions were crushing the Haitian people and enriching the military elite exemplify this. See *supra* notes 219–234.

[14]

The United Nations System: A Place for Criminal Courts?*

*Colin Warbrick***

---

* This is a revised version of a lecture given in a series organised by the Department of Public Law at the University of Edinburgh in celebration of the fiftieth anniversary of the United Nations.

** Professor of Law, University of Durham, United Kingdom. I am most grateful to a wide variety of members and officials of international and national institutions and non-governmental organisations for the provision of information over the years. I hope that they will remain as cooperative when they see what use I have made of it.

I. INTRODUCTION: THE IDEA OF AN INTERNATIONAL LEGAL COMMUNITY

The institutional weaknesses of the international legal system often remarked upon include: no legislature; effectively no executive; and intermittent judicial settlement of disputes. Whether a direct consequence of these deficiencies or not, there is less variety in the kinds of rules in the international legal order than there is in those found in a municipal system. The standard model is a bilateral, delictual rule, carrying an obligation of reparation. The primary right, the new right in the event of a violation of the primary right, and the right to take measures to enforce those rights, typically belong in one State and operate against another State.[1] Most distinctive is the relative paucity of anything which might be called the "public law" of international law: Where is the constitution of the international legal system to distribute power between such institutions as there are in the international system and to set out the fundamental values of the international system? Should not a system of administrative rules exist to regulate and control the use of public power? And why is there no criminal law system to contribute to the maintenance of international order?

It will be objected that this picture of international law is no longer true, if indeed it ever was. Has it not been the case that, despite its original ambition to produce a single and uniform statement of the law on state responsibility, the International Law Commission (ILC) has discovered that a lack of homogeneity in the nature of international legal rules exists? The process began in the Vienna Convention on the Law of the Treaties with the introduction of the idea of *jus cogens*[2]—a concept of a hierarchy of norms where the lower rule yields its legal validity to a conflicting, but higher rule. The identification of such rules is provided for in an inadequate and circular way. However, part of the test—"a norm accepted and recognised by the international community of States as a whole"[3]— envisions the international system as a single, shared interest of the collective, rather than the mere coincidence of similar interests of individual States.[4] For the moment, it is noted only that Article 53

---

1. IAN BROWNLIE, PRINCIPLES OF INTERNATIONAL LAW ch. XX (4th ed. 1990).

2. Vienna Convention on the Law of Treaties, *done on* May 23, 1969, art. 53, 1155 U.N.T.S. 331, 344 [hereinafter Vienna Convention]. *See* IAN SINCLAIR, THE VIENNA CONVENTION ON THE LAW OF TREATIES 203-25 (2d ed. 1984).

3. Vienna Convention, *supra* note 2, art. 53.

4. *See* Gordon Christenson, *Jus Cogens: Guarding Interests Fundamental to International Society*, 28 VA. J. INT'L L. 585 (1988).

refers to the "international community of *States* as a whole" and not to "the international community" *simpliciter.*[5]

The next kind of international legal rule is found in the *obiter dictum* of the *Barcelona Traction* case.[6] Here, the International Court of Justice (ICJ) distinguished ordinary, inter-State obligations from "obligations of a State toward the international community as a whole . . . they are obligations *erga omnes.*"[7] Here, the ICJ did not simply define their nature,[8] but provided some examples of such rules: "the outlawing of acts of aggression, and of genocide, as also . . . the principles and rules concerning the basic rights of the human person, including protection from slavery and racial discrimination."[9]

The device of obligations *erga omnes*, whether included in treaty arrangements or as a feature of some customary law rules, provides a middle ground between the atomistic nature of the individual State and the establishment of institutional structures to identify and protect the interests behind those important rules.[10] For different reasons, the idea has been of some significance in the development of the law of human rights and aspects of international environmental law.

There are two aspects to international criminal law: State conduct and individual conduct. The ILC still gamely struggles with the elaboration of the notion of "crime of State," introduced by Article 19 of its Draft Articles on State Responsibility. The intellectual and practical obstacles to completing this project remain considerable but, if the ILC can succeed, it will, in the words of Article 19, have identified a species of international legal rule which embodies "an international obligation so essential for the protection of the fundamental interests of the international community that its breach is recognised by that community as a whole [as constituting] an international crime."[11]

---

5. Vienna Convention, *supra* note 2, art. 53.

6. Barcelona Traction, Light and Power Co., Ltd. (Belg. v. Spain) (Second Phase), 1970 I.C.J. 3, paras. 33-34 (Feb. 5).

7. *Id.* para. 33.

8. "In the view of the importance of the rights involved, all States can be held to have a legal interest in their protection . . . ." *Id.* para. 33.

9. *Id.* para 34.

10. *See generally* Claudia Annacker, *The Legal Régime of "Erga Omnes" Obligations in International Law*, 46 AUSTRIAN J. PUB. INT'L L. 131 (1994).

11. For the latest consideration, see Gaetano Arangio-Ruiz, *Seventh Report on State Responsibility*, International Law Commission, 47th Sess., U.N. Doc. A/CN.4/469/Adds.1-2 (1995).

Even if the ILC can develop a coherent regime for "crimes of State," reservations remain as to whether it can convince the "community as a whole" that it has accepted or ought to accept international crimes of States. The legal provenance of this first aspect of "international criminal law," if defined as crimes of State, is problematic. The other part of "international criminal law" does not encompass the conduct of States at all, but instead refers to the criminal liability of individuals, a long-established institution of the international system. The difficulty here has been the proper analysis of the obligation, rather than any question of its existence.

In the absence of international criminal courts, the implementation of individual criminal responsibility has been through national tribunals. This has led to two different kinds of confusion. In some cases, conduct deemed criminal by international law will also be criminal by domestic law, *e.g.*, killing prisoners of war will usually also be a violation of national homicide laws. The international criminal element may be of no significance or only as it is mediated through national understandings of its international character.[12] The other confusion arises because of the inevitable need to rely on national prosecutions. This causes States sometimes to forbear criminalising conduct in international law, and to create an obligation on States to criminalise the conduct in their own law. The collection of anti-terrorism treaties generates obligations of this kind.[13] Not only the absence of a criminal tribunal but also the absence of agreement, at least a sufficiently widespread agreement, on the international criminality of the proscribed conduct compels this technique. No institution of the "international community of States" exists to answer this question other than the States themselves, severally. This domestic alternative has taken some of the urgency out of the need for international criminal tribunals, a fortunate contingency given the remote political possibilities of setting up such courts. The insubstantial quality within any agreement of the identification and implementation of international criminal law, even for individuals, is one weakness of the idea of international community permeating this "new" kind of rule.

"International community" may also refer to contexts other than the legal and political. For example, legal notions conjoined the various aspirations to a "new world order," accompanying the

---

12. *See generally* Leila Sadat Wexler, *The Interpretation of the Nuremberg Principles by the French Court of Cassation: From Touvier to Barbie and Back Again*, 32 COLUM. J. TRANSNAT'L L. 289 (1994).

13. These treaties commonly include an *aut punire, aut dedire* obligation.

operations to reverse Iraq's invasion of Kuwait.[14] The community value was the protection of a State against extinction by armed aggression.[15] If the actual instrument to repel the Iraqi forces was not strictly a community force, it was probably the most practical compromise which could be fashioned between a truly international (or U.N.) operation and a reliably effective force against a powerful opponent. The United Nations, specifically the U.N. Security Council, was involved. It used its powers to identify the situation as one falling within Chapter VII of the U.N. Charter and to require compliance by member States with economic measures directed against Iraq. It later authorised the coalition of States to use "all measures necessary" to eject Iraqi forces from Kuwait and continues to expect and require that States will compel Iraq to comply with the terms of the settlement imposed by the U.N. Security Council. The Chapter VII arrangements of the U.N. Charter are the nearest thing to a legal manifestation of an international community.

Professor Hedley Bull's categories in "The Anarchical Society"[16] distinguish between a "system of States": "where states are in regular contact with one another, and where in addition there is sufficient interaction between them to make the behaviour of each a necessary element in the calculations of the other . . . ."[17] A "society of States" is "when a group of states, conscious of certain common interests and common values, form a society in the sense that they conceive themselves to be bound by a common set of rules in their relations with one another . . . ,"[18] and "world order" consists of "those patterns or dispositions of human activity that sustain the elementary or primary goals of social life among mankind as a whole."[19]

There is not, in this sense, a world legal order. Rather, there exists a series of regimes of relationships between States, some of which might merit the title "society" of the States involved. The United Nations is an example; others, such as the European Union, exceptionally involve individuals and might even, in Bull's terms, be

---

14. For consideration from a legal point of view, see Christopher Greenwood, *New World Order or Old? The Invasion of Kuwait and the Rule of Law,* 55 MOD. L. REV. 153 (1992).

15. This is not to deny that individual State rights, most notably Kuwait's, were at stake. For the position that only State rights were involved, see generally Eugene V. Rostow, *Until What? Enforcement Action or Collective Self-Defense?,* 85 AM. J. INT'L L. 506 (1991).

16. HEDLEY BULL, THE ANARCHICAL SOCIETY: A STUDY OF ORDER IN WORLD POLITICS (1977).

17. *Id.* at 10.

18. *Id.* at 13.

19. *Id.* at 20.

"regional orders." Sometimes lawyers bring several of these regimes together and consider them as a single system.[20] Conclusions about the place of international criminal courts depend upon the view of the international context in which they are to operate. Which institutions create the criminal standards to protect what values? Why are individuals punished by international procedures for violations of international criminal law? When considering the proposals for a permanent international criminal court, it may be discovered that it is directed toward ends different from the two Ad Hoc Tribunals set up by the U.N. Security Council for Yugoslavia and Rwanda.

II. THE PROPOSAL FOR A PERMANENT INTERNATIONAL CRIMINAL COURT

When the ILC and the ICJ made their pronouncements on the "new" kinds of rules, the first example they gave was the rule prohibiting aggression. If ever a breach of that rule occurred, Iraq's attack on Kuwait would appear to be an instance. However, the U.N. Security Council did not so characterise the situation. Resolution 660 determined that a breach of international peace and security had occurred and condemned Iraq's "invasion" of Kuwait.[21] Although the most extensive measures taken against Iraq occurred after its forces had been driven out of Kuwait,[22] they did not include any element of a criminal nature, neither for the aggression itself nor for the numerous violations of the international humanitarian law[23] noted by the U.N. Security Council.

Would it have made any difference if there had been an international criminal court with jurisdiction to which the defendants could have been subjected? That it might have remains one item on a list which has prompted present interest in establishing a permanent international criminal court.[24] It is important to appreciate that a variety of forces were at work behind the initiation of the ILC's

---

20. For a recent, elaborate study, see J. Murphy, *International Crimes, in* 2 UNITED NATIONS LEGAL ORDER 993 (Oscar Schachter et al. eds., 1995).

21. S.C. Res. 660, U.N. SCOR, 45th Sess., 2932d mtg. at 19, U.N. Doc. S/INF/46 (1991).

22. S.C. Res. 687, U.N. SCOR, 46th Sess., 2981st mtg. at 11, U.N. Doc. S/INF/47 (1991).

23. *See, e.g.*, S.C. Res. 666, U.N. SCOR, 45th Sess., 2939th mtg. at 22, para. 2, U.N. Doc. S/INF/46 (1990).

24. Robert Rosenstock, *The Forty-fourth Session of the International Law Commission*, 87 AM. J. INT'L L. 138, 138-40 (1993); James Crawford, *The ILC's Draft Statute for an International Criminal Tribunal*, 88 AM. J. INT'L L. 140, 140-42 (1994).

project, which shortly is to go before the U.N. General Assembly. In addition to the events in the Gulf, the ILC was nearing a conclusion about the Draft Code of Crimes against the Peace and Security of Mankind.[25] These were to be unequivocally crimes against international law; should such crimes be identified without an international criminal court? The altercation between the United States and the United Kingdom with Libya about the handing over of suspects in an international terrorism incident suggested that an international criminal court could serve to settle some disputes between States. Another element favouring progress toward an international criminal court was the concern of several small States that an international body, rather than a multiplicity of national ones, could more effectively prosecute major drug-traffickers. These different forces pushing in a similar, if not precisely the same, direction gave political weight to what had previously seemed, in the worst sense of the word, only an academic possibility. The events in Yugoslavia and Rwanda dramatically brought appalling barbarisms, both coordinated and extensive, to public attention and strengthened these forces.

The ILC's original proposal[26] has undergone a number of modifications but has retained certain essential features.[27] Perhaps the most important feature was that the court was envisaged as a "facility" for States—something of which they might avail themselves if they found it useful or expedient to do so. A treaty, which, of course, requires State consent, was to establish the court. The jurisdiction of the court was subject to an optional clause; through this optional clause a State indicates the offences within the court's general jurisdiction for which it specifically acknowledges the court's competence. There is yet an additional stage before bringing a specific case before the court; this stage might involve the consent of a further State. This structure is comprehensible only if the court is intended to serve the several interests, discrete and possibly different, of those States willing to take advantage of the facility created. It is an impression reinforced not only by the affirmation that the

---

25. *Draft Code of Crimes against the Peace and Security of Mankind, Report of the International Law Commission on its Forty-Third Session,* U.N. GAOR, 46th Sess., Supp. No. 10, at 238, U.N. Doc. A/46/10 (1991).

26. *Report of the Working Group on the Question of an International Criminal Jurisdiction, Report of the International Law Commission on the Work of its Forty-Fourth Session,* 47th Sess., Supp. No. 10, Annex, U.N. Doc. A/47/10 (1992).

27. On the intervening stages, see Crawford, *supra* note 24, at 140-42. For the final version of the Draft Statute for an International Criminal Court, see *Report of the International Law Commission on the Work of its Forty-Sixth Session,* 49th Sess., Supp. No. 10, at 43-161, U.N. Doc. A/49/10 (1994); James Crawford, *The ILC Adopts a Statute for an International Criminal Court,* 89 AM. J. INT'L L. 404 (1995).

international criminal court is not intended to supplant national criminal jurisdiction (the idea of "complementarity"[28]) but also by the absence of an independent right of initiative in the prosecutor to investigate cases and bring proceedings.[29] The court will be a creature of a non-coercive, cooperative system. It is not, in Bull's term, a court of the world community.

To have an international criminal court, international crimes must first be identified. The ILC has consistently emphasised the need to respect the principles of non-retroactivity and legality in setting the jurisdiction of the proposed court, and this has resulted in a degree of tentativeness in identifying the crimes. The Ad Hoc Committee on the Establishment of the International Criminal Court,[30] to which consideration of the ILC's proposal was passed by the U.N. General Assembly,[31] failed to resolve this uncertainty. Doubts were expressed about all proposed offences to come within the general jurisdiction of the court.[32] Some doubts related to the desirability of jurisdiction and others to the definitions of the offences themselves. For instance, on aggression, a division exists between those States relying on Article 6(a) of the London Charter of the International Military Tribunal (IMT)[33] and those adhering to G.A. Resolution 3314 on the Definition of Aggression.[34] Not all States believe that violations of the law of internal armed conflict are criminal breaches of international law.[35] Doubts were also expressed about the exact reach of crimes against humanity, in particular whether they were capable of being committed in peace-time.[36] If these doubts about the legal existence and reach of crimes were not enough, a further possible conflict with the principle of legality emerges from the desire to restrict the

---

28. *See Report of the Ad Hoc Committee on the Establishment of an International Criminal Court* [hereinafter *Report of the Ad Hoc Committee*], 50th Sess., Supp. No. 22, at 6-7, U.N. Doc. A/50/22 (1995).

29. The limited independence of the prosecutor is one of the chief criticisms of the ILC's proposal made by Amnesty International. *See* AMNESTY INTERNATIONAL, ESTABLISHING A JUST, FAIR AND EFFECTIVE INTERNATIONAL CRIMINAL COURT 7, 27-31 (1994).

30. *Report of the Ad Hoc Committee, supra* note 28.

31. G.A. Res. 49/57, U.N. GAOR, 49th Sess., Supp. No. 49, at 296, U.N. Doc. A/49/49 (1995).

32. *Report of the Ad Hoc Committee, supra* note 28, at 11-18.

33. Agreement for the Prosecution and Punishment of the Major War Criminals of the European Axis, Aug. 8, 1945, art. 6(a), 59 Stat. 1544, 1547, 82 U.N.T.S. 279, 288.

34. *Report of the Ad Hoc Committee, supra* note 28, para. 63.

35. *Id.* para. 76.

36. *Id.* para. 79.

jurisdiction of the court to "serious" violations.

The ILC has always maintained that the trial process before the courts should be "fair" and has proposed the incorporation of certain human rights standards into the basic instrument for the court.[37] If Nuremberg and Tokyo are considered the only approximate precedents for an international criminal court, a significant change has occurred since then in the development of international human rights law. On most calculations, human rights law (or parts of it, at least) would be a candidate for inclusion into the special regimes of law referred to earlier. Particularly if a human right has the status of *jus cogens*, States would be obliged to condition the jurisdiction of an international criminal court by the same human rights constraints as they accept with respect to their national criminal procedures. This is necessary for an additional reason: Jurisdiction of the international criminal court will in most cases involve a surrender of national jurisdiction. In many States, there are likely to be constitutional obstacles to surrendering an individual to criminal proceedings in a jurisdiction where these fundamental rights were not guaranteed or there was not the possibility of an application to human rights tribunals.

Noteworthy is the document produced by the Ad Hoc Committee of States' representatives which suggests addressing a very wide range of questions indeed, amounting to full codes of criminal responsibility and procedure and international criminal cooperation.[38] This markedly contrasts with the U.N. Security Council Tribunals, where substantial rule-making powers were conferred on the Tribunals themselves and judicial assistance was to be provided in response to mandatory decisions of the U.N. Security Council or decisions of the Tribunals deriving from this authority. Many matters remain unresolved or unconsidered and much ground remains to be covered, now that the U.N. General Assembly has decided to convene a conference to draft a treaty on an international criminal court.

III. THE SECURITY COUNCIL'S AD HOC TRIBUNALS FOR YUGOSLAVIA AND RWANDA

While the proposal for a permanent international criminal court has been under consideration, suggestions have been made that any scheme for implementing the proposal should take into account the experiences of the two existing Ad Hoc Tribunals established by the

---

37. *See* Crawford, *supra* note 24, at 148-50. For further consideration of the procedural guarantees appropriate to an international criminal court, see AMNESTY INTERNATIONAL, *supra* note 29, at 31-51.

38. *Report of the Ad Hoc Committee, supra* note 28, Annexes I-II.

U.N. Security Council for Yugoslavia[39] and Rwanda.[40] Indeed, the practice of the Yugoslav Tribunal was specifically called in aid to identify the criminality of breaches of the law of internal armed conflict.[41] Before investing too much in analogies between the court and the two Tribunals, it would be as well to investigate precisely the nature of the Tribunals set up by the U.N. Security Council in order to see if they are intended to serve the same, or at least, the same kind of international community. It will be suggested that the Tribunals are a different kind of institution as compared to that envisaged for the permanent criminal court.

The two Tribunals were established by binding U.N. Security Council resolutions under Chapter VII of the U.N. Charter. Each is set up by a statute articulating the offences over which each has jurisdiction as well as territorial and temporal competence. The Statutes provide for the election of judges by the U.N. General Assembly on the nomination of the Security Council and for the appointment of an independent prosecutor by the Security Council. The minimum human rights guarantees for defendants are set out in each Statute and, within these limits, the judges are given an extensive role in preparing the Rules of Procedure and Evidence. The Tribunals' jurisdictions are given priority over national jurisdictions. Based on both the Resolutions and the Statutes themselves, all States have binding obligations to cooperate with the Tribunals, for instance, in handing over defendants and in deferring cases initiated by their own authorities. Practically every one of these characteristics, except the specific rights of defendants, contrasts with those proposed for the permanent criminal court. While the analogy between the permanent court and a national criminal court is very similar, it does not appear that the same can be said for the Ad Hoc Tribunals. The explanation is that they are, in the way that the permanent court will not be, courts of the international legal community regulated by Chapter VII of the U.N. Charter. The narrowness of that community must be appreciated. Although not narrow in membership in the sense that all States are members, it is narrow in the substance of its legal rules, which are confined to those connected with the maintenance of international peace and security.

---

39. S.C. Res. 827, U.N. SCOR, 48th Sess., 3217th mtg. at 2, U.N. Doc. S/RES/827 (1993); *see generally* James C. O'Brien, *The International Tribunal for Violations of International Humanitarian Law in the Former Yugoslavia*, 87 AM. J. INT'L L. 639 (1993); Daphna Shraga & Ralph Zacklin, *The International Criminal Tribunal for the Former Yugoslavia*, 5 EUR. J. INT'L L. 360 (1994).

40. S.C. Res. 955, U.N. SCOR, 49th Sess., 3453d mtg., U.N. Doc. S/RES/955 (1994); *see generally* Lyal S. Sunga, *The Commission of Experts on Rwanda and the Creation of the International Criminal Tribunal for Rwanda*, 16 HUM. RTS. L.J. 121 (1995).

41. *Report of the Ad Hoc Committee, supra* note 28, para. 79.

A. *The Interpretation of the Procedure of the Tribunal*

The remainder of the discussion will be largely confined to the Yugoslav Tribunal and two of its decisions, which serve to illustrate the proposition just made. International human rights law on criminal procedure and fair criminal trial is addressed in the first instance to "ordinary" criminal trials, *e.g.,* standard offences, like homicide and theft in circumstances of domestic stability. Even if conceded for the sake of argument that the Yugoslav Tribunal should be subject to the same minimum procedures as a national criminal court, it surely should be recognised that comparison should not be made with a criminal court trying ordinary offences in conditions of tranquillity. International human rights law and practice recognises that the obligations of States with respect to the criminal process may be modified to take into account exceptional circumstances,[42] or, in an extremely dire situation, dispensed with altogether.[43]

Two examples of how basic rights may be altered can be given. The United Kingdom was faced with a serious threat to public order in Northern Ireland as a result of paramilitary and terrorist actions in the Province. The government, which was anxious to portray these activities as criminal, faced the problem of obtaining convictions because of the difficulty in collecting evidence in the disturbed situation in Northern Ireland and because of the intimidation of witnesses and jurors. The government asked Lord Diplock to devise a system of criminal procedure which would address these problems but which simultaneously would be compatible with the U.K.'s obligations to secure a fair criminal trial under Article 6 of the European Convention on Human Rights. Lord Diplock suggested a series of reforms which included the abolition of jury trial for certain offences and changes in the laws of evidence, particularly with respect to confessions.[44] "Diplock Courts" operating under his scheme have sat in Northern Ireland since 1975. They have achieved the government's purpose of convicting those accused of paramilitary and terrorist offences, whilst at the same time withstanding allegations that trials before the Diplock Courts were unfair.[45]

In another respect, the British government was unable to show the

---

42. *See* ANTONIO VERCHER, TERRORISM IN EUROPE: AN INTERNATIONAL COMPARATIVE LEGAL ANALYSIS 341-52 (1992).

43. *S e e generally* JAIME O RAÁ, HUMAN RIGHTS IN STATES OF EMERGENCY IN INTERNATIONAL LAW (1992).

44. REPORT OF THE COMMISSION TO CONSIDER LEGAL PROCEDURES TO DEAL WITH TERRORIST ACTIVITIES IN NORTHERN IRELAND, 1972, Cmnd 5185.

45. For an assessment, see JOHN JACKSON & SEAN DORAN, JUDGE WITHOUT JURY: DIPLOCK TRIALS IN THE ADVERSARY SYSTEM (1995).

compatibility of changes in pre-trial procedure with its duties under the European Convention. Usually a suspect must be brought before a judicial officer within forty-eight hours after arrest. The provision here allowed for post-arrest detention beyond the usual period. A member of the executive, the Northern Ireland minister, could grant an extension up to five days. Extensions which resulted in judicially unauthorised detentions beyond four days were found to be in violation of Article 5(3) of the Convention in *Brogan*.[46] The government reacted by making an emergency declaration under Article 15 of the Convention, which claimed that the campaigns of violence in Northern Ireland "threatened the life of the nation" and that the extended periods of pre-trial detention were "strictly required by the exigencies of the situation."[47] The legitimacy of each of these claims was sustained by the European Court of Human Rights (EHCR) in *Brannigan*.[48] In *Brannigan*, the EHCR rejected an argument which has won favour with the Inter-American Court of Human Rights[49]: Due process guarantees may not be dispensed with, even in an emergency.[50]

The circumstances in which the Yugoslav Tribunal operates are far from normal. As the Trial Chamber in *Tadic* said: "[It] is operating in the midst of a continuing conflict and is without a police force or witness protection program to provide protection for victims and witnesses."[51] While amendments to the Statute which would take into account these circumstances are unlikely, the Tribunal has fashioned

---

46. Brogan v. United Kingdom, 145 Eur. Ct. H.R. (ser. A) (1988).

47. European Convention for the Protection of Human Rights and Fundamental Freedoms, *done on* Nov. 4, 1950, 213 U.N.T.S. 221.

48. Brannigan and McBride v. United Kingdom, 239 Eur. Ct. H.R. (ser. B) (1993); *see also* Susan Marks, *Civil Liberties at the Margin: the UK Derogation and the European Court of Human Rights*, 15 OXFORD J. LEGAL STUD. 69 (1995).

49. Advisory Opinion OC-9/87 on Judicial Guarantees in States of Emergency (Arts. 8, 25, & 27(2) American Convention on Human Rights), Inter-Am. Ct. H.R. (ser. A, No. 9) (1987).

50. *See* Protocol Additional to the Geneva Conventions of 12 August 1949, and Relating to the Protection of Victims of International Armed Conflict (Protocol I), *adopted on* June 8, 1977, 1125 U.N.T.S. 3, art. 85(4)(e) (stating that depriving a protected person of a "fair and regular trial" is a grave breach, even in conditions of international armed conflict).

51. The Prosecutor v. Dusko Tadic a/k/a "Dule," Decision on the Prosecutor's Motion Requesting Protective Measures for Victims and Witnesses, International Tribunal for the Prosecution of Persons Responsible for Serious Violations of International Humanitarian Law Committed in the Territory of Former Yugoslavia Since 1991, In the Trial Chamber, Case No. IT-94-1-T, Aug. 10, 1995, at para. 27 [hereinafter Decision on the Prosecutor's Motion].

and, indeed, re-fashioned its Rules in light of its unique situation.[52] It does not have an Article 15 clause which will allow it to dispense with certain defence rights, however compelling it might find the need to do so. But, as the Tribunal stated, it is not faced with "ordinary criminal adjudications": "By contrast, the International Tribunal is adjudicating crimes which are considered so horrific as to warrant universal jurisdiction. The International Tribunal is, in certain respects, comparable to a military tribunal, which often has limited rights of due process and more lenient rules of evidence."[53] As an example it gave the acceptance of affidavit evidence, a practice endorsed by many national criminal procedure systems when conducting war crimes trials. While the Yugoslav Tribunals may not avoid the provisions of the Statute,

> the Trial Chamber agrees with the Prosecutor that the International Tribunal must interpret its provisions within its own context and determine where the balance lies between the accused's right to a fair and public trial and the protection of victims and witnesses within its unique legal framework. While the jurisprudence of other international judicial bodies is relevant when examining the meaning of concepts such as "fair trial," whether or not the proper balance is met depends on the context of the legal system in which the concepts are being applied.[54]

The particular issues before the Tribunal concerned the confidentiality of witnesses' and victims' identities from public identification, confrontation between witnesses and the accused, and the anonymity with respect to the defence of certain witnesses. While the Chamber agreed that the identity of some witnesses should be withheld from the public and the media, disagreement arose between the majority (Judges McDonald and Verah) and the minority (Judge Stephen) about withholding the identity of witnesses from the defence. The majority was more prepared to balance the interests of the witnesses and, of the Tribunal itself, against those of the accused.[55] Judge Stephen found in the language of the Statute and the Rules, stronger protection for the rights of the defence. In particular, Article

---

52. *International Tribunal for the Prosecution of Persons Responsible for Serious Violations of International Humanitarian Law Committed in the Territory of the Former Yugoslavia Since 1991: Rules of Procedure and Evidence*, U.N. Doc. IT/32 (1994), *amended by* U.N. Doc. IT/32/Rev.6 (1995). An earlier version of the Rules is reproduced in 5 CRIM. L.F. 651 (1994) in a form convenient to see the amendments.

53. Decision on the Prosecutor's Motion, *supra* note 51, para. 28.

54. *Id.* para. 30.

55. *Id.* para. 77.

20(1) required that proceedings be conducted *"with full respect"* for the rights of the defendant, whereas *"due regard"* was required for the protection of victims and witnesses.[56] Judge Stephen required more convincing evidence for a departure from the ordinary right of a defendant to know a witness's identity than did the majority.[57]

It is not easy to anticipate where questions like this will arise again. However, one suspects that matters of the admissibility or exclusion of evidence are likely to be prominent, as well as conditions of pre-trial detention and interrogation, some of which, of course, may have taken place in the custody of State authorities rather than of the Tribunal. The approach of the Chamber appears correct, though it will be interesting to see to what extent the formulation of the Statute and the Rules may preclude the Tribunal from following a course which it deems to be desirable. It may be unnecessary speculation. One gains the impression that the Prosecutor's staff are confident that compliance with even a strict interpretation of the governing documents will not be an insurmountable hurdle to obtaining convictions.[58]

The Trial Chamber's reference to the nature of the Tribunal and the context in which it operates raises two questions: What purpose does the Tribunal serve?[59] Why, given the availability of national jurisdictions for the trial of persons accused of offences within the Tribunal's jurisdiction, was it necessary to have recourse to this international body? Some answers to these questions can be obtained from the decision of the Appeals Chamber when it considered a series of challenges to the jurisdiction of the Tribunal made in the *Tadic* case.[60]

---

56. Statute of the International Tribunal, art. 20(1), *cited in* S.C. Res. 827, *supra* note 39, Annex (emphasis added).

57. Decision on the Prosecutor's Motion, *supra* note 51, separate opinion of Judge Stephen.

58. I base this on the proceedings of a meeting organised by the TMC Asser Instituut in the Hague in January 1995, in which some members of the Prosecutor's office took part.

59. *See generally* Theodor Meron, *The Case for War Crimes Trials in Yugoslavia*, FOREIGN AFF., Summer 1993, at 122; Payam Akhavan, *Punishing War Crimes in the Former Yugoslavia: A Critical Juncture for the New World Order*, 15 HUM. RTS. Q. 262 (1993).

60. The Prosecutor v. Dusko Tadic a/k/a "Dule," Decision on the Defence Motion for Interlocutory Appeal on Jurisdiction, International Tribunal for the Prosecution of Persons Responsible for Serious Violations of International Humanitarian Law Committed in Former Yugoslavia Since 1991, In the Appeals Chamber, Case No. IT-94-1-AR72, Oct. 2, 1995 [hereinafter Appeals Chamber Decision on the Defence Motion]. For the Trial Chamber's Decision see The Prosecutor v. Dusko Tadic a/k/a

B. Substantive Jurisdiction

Dusan Tadic, a Serb, was the first defendant to be brought before the Yugoslav Tribunal. Proceedings began against him in Germany for genocide, murder, and torture in Bosnia. At the request of the Prosecutor, the Tribunal asked Germany to defer to the proceedings in the Hague. After the necessary legislation had been enacted in Germany to allow the authorities to accede to this request and to transfer prisoners to the Tribunal, Tadic was sent from Germany to the Hague in April 1995. The indictment originally laid against the defendant accused him of a number of offences under Article 2 (grave breaches of the Geneva Conventions), Article 3 (violations of the laws and customs of war which, the indictment averred, included Article 3 of the Geneva Conventions), and Article 5 (crimes against humanity) of the·Statute of the Tribunal. The charges under Articles 2 and 3 were put in the alternative in order to accommodate the question of the nature of the conflict in Yugoslavia: Were any of them international armed conflicts such that the Geneva Conventions and Protocol I applied or were they internal armed conflicts governed, *inter alia*, by Article 3 of the Geneva Conventions?

Tadic filed a number of motions in the proceedings, among which was the following three part challenge to the jurisdiction of the Tribunal:

> (a) that the Tribunal had not been legitimately established by the U.N. Security Council;

> (b) that the grant of primacy to the Tribunal over national proceedings was in violation of the sovereignty of States which had jurisdiction; and

> (c) that the Tribunal lacked subject-matter jurisdiction over the offences of which the defendant was charged.

The most radical of Tadic's challenges to the Tribunal's jurisdiction was that it lay beyond the powers of the U.N. Security Council to create it. It is, of course, an intriguing jurisprudential question, for, if Tadic were right, the conclusion appears to be that neither a legitimate Tribunal nor judges existed to decide even this fundamental question of competence. The Appeals Chamber did decide, however, that it had the jurisdiction to determine this basic

---

"Dule," Decision on the Defence Motion for Interlocutory Appeal on Jurisdiction, International Tribunal for the Prosecution of Persons Responsible for Serious Violations of International Humanitarian Law Committed in Former Yugoslavia Since 1991, In the Trial Chamber, Case No. IT-94-1-T, Aug. 10, 1995 [hereinafter Trial Chamber Decision on the Defence Motion].

issue. It concluded that the Tribunal had been established lawfully. Neither the ultimate authority of the Appeals Chamber nor the way in which it decided the question is of present concern.[61] However, one aspect of its answers is relevant, for it shows the Appellate Chamber's understanding of the special nature of the Tribunal. Tadic argued that the Tribunal was not "established by law"; he contended that there was a general principle of law, the evidence for which he gave as the very similar provisions of the International Covenant on Civil and Political Rights, the European Convention on Human Rights, and the American Convention on Human Rights. The Appellate Chamber's response deserves emphasis. It would not accept that a general principle applicable to domestic criminal proceedings was necessarily identically appropriate to an international court. Attention needed to be paid to the institutional differences between the international legal system and a domestic one. The former had no legislature; no doctrine of separation of powers existed in international law. In the international context, the principle that a criminal court should be "established by law" required that "[it] be established according to the rule of law, it must be established in accordance with proper international standards, it must provide all the guarantees of fairness, justice and even-handedness in full conformity with international human rights instruments."[62]

This was not as close as might appear to the defence argument that had just been rejected. What the President envisioned was the creation of "extraordinary" courts by extraordinary means. That is to say, the only means available in the international system. The ad hoc nature of the Tribunal and the contingency of its existence on the political powers of the U.N. Security Council might not, *mutatis mutandis*, be acceptable for a municipal court, but they were indispensible features of an international criminal court. This is quite similar to the Trial Chamber's approach in the Victims and Witnesses decision.[63] This part of the judgment is not as convincing as other sections. Possibly this is because the Appeals Chamber sought to avoid discharging the U.N. Security Council's purposes, which might be put in jeopardy if convictions became too hard to win—whether those purposes were the assembling of an effective deterrent to breaches of international humanitarian law or assisting the process of reconciliation by identifying and subjecting to condign punishment those responsible for terrible crimes. This was an acknowledgement that the Tribunal serves a community of States, the values of which

---

61. Appeals Chamber Decision on the Defence Motion, *supra* note 60, paras. 13-48. Compare the separate opinion of Judge Li.

62. *Id.* para. 45.

63. *See generally* Decision on the Prosecutor's Motion, *supra* note 51.

were expressed and interpreted by binding decisions of the U.N. Security Council. The President confirmed this when he disposed of another of Tadic's claims—that no justification existed for substituting an international jurisdiction for a national one. The U.N. Security Council, he said. acted "on behalf of the community of nations."[64] Individuals could have no complaint because they would be brought before a tribunal "at least equally fair, more distanced from the facts of the case and taking a broader view of the matter"[65] than their national tribunal. As to the comparative advantage in procedural matters, perhaps one had better wait and see.

The Appeals Chamber reiterated its view of its role by making another observation. The President said, confirming that initiating the Tribunal had been a proper exercise of the U.N. Security Council's authority, that "[t]he Security Council has resorted to the establishment of a judicial organ in the form of an international criminal tribunal as an instrument for the exercise of its own principal function of maintenance of peace and security . . . ."[66] Whether it was the appropriate thing to do was for the Security Council, "which enjoys wide discretionary powers in this regard,"[67] to decide.

Why did the U.N. Security Council so decide? In view of the emphasis placed on the need to obtain convictions, it is proper to notice that Resolution 827 says that the Tribunal is for the *"prosecution"* of those responsible for serious violations of international humanitarian law.[68] Also, the preamble discusses bringing such persons to "justice," which certainly implies minimum procedural criteria. The prosecutor has spoken of the need for trials as a precondition for reconciliation,[69] an aim made explicit in the Resolution establishing the Rwanda Tribunal: that the *"prosecution"* of offenders would contribute to national reconciliation.[70] In fact, the debates in the U.N. Security Council on Resolutions 808 and 827 add very little to the text of Resolution 827 in order to explain how U.N. Security Council members related the establishment of the Tribunal to the U.N. Security Council's powers. The statements made by the representative of France in the debate on Resolution 808 were a rare exception. He said:

---

64. Appeals Chamber Decision on the Defence Motion, *supra* note 60, para. 62.

65. *Id.*

66. *Id.* para. 38.

67. *Id.* para. 39.

68. S.C. Res. 827, *supra* note 39, pmbl. & para. 2 (emphasis added).

69. Ed Vulliamy, *The Times of Trial*, THE GUARDIAN, Oct. 31, 1995, at T6.

70. S.C. Res. 955, *supra* note 40, pmbl. (emphasis added).

> Prosecuting the guilty [sic] is necessary if we are to do justice to the victims and to the international community. Prosecuting the guilty will also send a clear message to those who continue to commit these crimes that they will be held responsible for their acts. And finally, prosecuting the guilty is, for the United Nations and particularly for the Security Council, a matter of doing their duty to maintain and restore peace.[71]

Later he stated that "[t]oday the criminals know they will be pursued and punished. This warning is important with regard to those who respected no moral values; it will surely deter those who are afraid only of force."[72] In their more robust formulation, these sentiments seem more calculated to serve the U.N. Security Council's responsibility for the maintenance of peace, however optimistic they may be, than the more carutious language of the Resolutions. It is impossible to see how the aims of restoring and maintaining peace can be fulfilled other than through the real prospect of conviction.[73]

On the question of subject-matter jurisdiction, the defence raised different objections to the legitimacy of the three heads of offences under Articles 2, 3, and 5. It should be remembered that the Report of the U.N. Secretary-General emphasised that the substantive jurisdiction of the Convention was to be confined to rules of international law which were "beyond any doubt part of customary law."[74] The defence's first argument about Article 2, which refers to "grave breaches" of the Geneva Conventions, claimed that no international conflict in Bosnia existed at the time of Tadic's alleged offences, as is required by common Article 2 of the Conventions. Making a similar argument concerning Article 3, the defence contended that the "laws and customs of war" applied only to international conflicts. With respect to crimes against humanity, Article 5 violations, the defence claimed that the violations must have been committed in execution of an international armed conflict, following the Charter of the Nuremberg Tribunal.

The Appeals Chamber confirmed by four votes to one the conclusions of the Trial Chamber, rejecting all defence objections to

---

71. U.N. SCOR, 48th Sess., 3175th mtg. at 8, U.N. Doc. S/PV.3175 (1993).

72. *Id.* at 27.

73. Prior to conviction, custody must, of course, be obtained over defendants. *See generally* Kenneth S. Gallant, *Securing the Presence of Defendants before the International Tribunal for the Former Yugoslavia: Breaking with Extradition*, 5 CRIM. L.F. 557 (1994).

74. *Report of the Secretary-General Pursuant to Paragraph 2 of Security Council Resolution 808* (1993), para. 34, U.N. Doc. S/25704 (1993).

substantive jurisdiction. President Cassese gave the majority judgment; Judge Sidhova dissented. On subject-matter jurisdiction, the Appeals Tribunal faced a new issue: Whether an armed conflict of any description existed in the region where and when the alleged offences were committed. The conclusion, drawn from the texts of the Geneva Convention and Protocol I as a whole was that "[u]ntil [achievement of a peaceful settlement], international humanitarian law continues to apply in the whole territory of the warring States or, in the case of internal conflicts, the whole territory under the control of a party, whether or not actual combat takes place there."[75] The Appeals Chamber had no difficulty finding these conditions satisfied at the time and in the place in which the offences were alleged to have been committed.

Of more consequence was the Appeals Chamber's treatment of the challenges to the subject-matter jurisdiction of the Tribunal. The essence of the defence claims about Articles 2 and 3 was that they delineated offences which could be committed only in international armed conflicts, and the conflict in which the defendant's alleged conduct had taken place was not an international one. The President's judgment said that the question could not be determined by a reading of the Statute alone. While nothing in Articles 2 and 3 necessarily restricted them to international armed conflicts, Article 5 expressly referred to internal and international armed conflict and an *a contrario* reading might, therefore, limit Articles 2 and 3.[76] To resolve the matter, he adopted a "teleological interpretation" of the Statute. The U.N. Security Council's purpose for establishing the Tribunal was to hold accountable those responsible for serious violations of humanitarian law in Yugoslavia, thereby deterring future violations and contributing to the restoration of peace: "The context in which the Security Council acted indicates that it intended to achieve this purpose without reference to whether the conflicts in the former Yugoslavia were internal or international."[77] Having reviewed Security Council resolutions and the statements of representatives of the States, he concluded that the objective of the Security Council was to give the Tribunal jurisdiction over conduct which was criminal regardless of whether committed in an international or internal armed conflict. This response failed to completely answer the defence plea, which sought to illustrate that the nature of the conflict was an aspect of the criminality of conduct. This point was taken obliquely when the judgment conceded that the interpretation of the Statute in line with the Security Council's purpose could be only "[t]o the extent

---

75. Appeals Chamber Decision on the Defence Motion, *supra* note 60, para. 70.

76. *Id.* para. 71.

77. *Id.* para. 72.

possible under existing international law . . . ."[78]

The next question remained, therefore, to what extent international law allowed an interpretation of Articles 2 and 3 of the Statute which would apply them to internal as well as international armed conflicts. President Cassese rejected the prosecutor's claim that Article 2 applied to non-international armed conflicts and, thus, differed from the Trial Chamber. He properly related the concept of "grave breaches" in the Geneva Conventions to the system of mandatory and universal jurisdiction introduced to secure enforcement. It was true, he said, that the conclusion was inconsistent with developments in State practice and human rights law which "tend to blur in many respects the traditional dichotomy between international wars and civil strife."[79] As for a statement in the U.S. *amicus curiae* brief that "grave breaches" in Article 2 of the Statute did apply to internal armed conflicts, the President noted that it was "unsupported by any authority."[80] Nevertheless, he welcomed it as "the first indication of a possible change in the *opinio juris* of States."[81] There existed, he said, a certain amount of practice to suggest that States were, as a matter of customary law, moving toward using the "grave breaches" system for conduct occurring in internal conflicts. However, though change may have been coming, it had not yet arrived.

President Cassese took a different view of what had been transpiring in the customary development of the "laws or customs of war," as referred to in Article 3 of the Statute. The Trial Chamber had concluded on this point "that the character of the conflict, whether international or internal, does not affect the subject-matter jurisdiction of the International Tribunal under Article 3 . . . ."[82] In particular, the Trial Chamber said the provisions of common Article 3 of the Geneva Conventions were part of customary law and violations of them entailed individual criminal responsibility. In this connection, the judges noted, *inter alia,* that the Nuremberg Tribunal had found individual criminal responsibility for breaches of Hague Convention IV and the Geneva Convention on Prisoners of War, 1929, even though neither made express reference to the criminal nature of its prohibitions.[83] The President said that Article 3 set out an illustrative list of conduct which amounted to a violation of the laws or customs of

---

78. *Id.* para. 77.

79. *Id.* para. 83.

80. *Id.*

81. *Id.*

82. Trial Chamber Decision on the Defence Motion, *supra* note 60, para. 58.

83. Appeals Chamber Decision on the Defence Motion, *supra* note 60, para. 128.

war. After an extensive review of a variety of State practice, the Trial Chamber concluded that this conduct was criminal by customary international law regardless of the nature of the conflict in which it took place.[84]

The argument, although carefully made, was ambitious: Article 3 was a residuary provision which gave the Tribunal jurisdiction over all breaches of international humanitarian law not otherwise falling within Articles 2, 4, or 5. "International humanitarian law" was the law applicable in international and internal armed conflicts. The preparatory work of the U.N. Secretary-General and the comments of the members' representatives of the U.N. Security Council indicated that Article 3 of the Statute was intended to apply to international humanitarian law. The only limitation, which reflected the position in customary law, was that the jurisdiction of the Tribunal was limited to *serious* violations.[85]

However, only part of the argument had been made. It remained necessary to show that rules of customary law, which applied to internal conflicts, existed and that violations of them entailed individual criminal responsibility. Some of the customary law established to the satisfaction of the Appeals Chamber had a treaty origin, *e.g.*, common Article 3 of the Geneva Conventions, Article 19 of the Hague Convention on the Protection of Cultural Property, and "the core" of Protocol II to the Geneva Conventions. Some customary prohibitions went beyond treaty provisions, such as the proscription of the use of chemical weapons. The conclusion was that only some of the rules of humanitarian law applicable to international armed conflicts had become applicable to civil wars, and, where there had been such a transformation, it was of "the general essence" of the rules of international armed conflicts and not all their detailed regulation.[86]

The President made an interesting remark about the content of State practice by which these developments had been achieved. It was not possible, he said, to discover what exactly went on in the field. Assessing the formation of customary law necessitated relying primarily on "such elements as official pronouncements of States, military manuals and judicial decisions."[87] This is certainly an important matter. It properly puts the emphasis on *State* practice: What the rebels do or do not do becomes less significant. On the other hand, those who argue for a customary law of human rights often take

---

84. The judgment contains much of the material in Theodor Meron, *International Criminalization of Internal Atrocities*, 89 AM. J. INT'L L. 554 (1995).

85. Appeals Chamber Decision on the Defence Motion, *supra* note 60, para. 127.

86. *Id.* para. 134.

87. *Id.* para. 99.

too lenient a view of the formal position of States as expressed in their legislation and official pronouncements compared with the actual practices of State officials or security personnel. While the actual practice may be difficult to discover, if it can be discovered and shows a clear pattern contrary to the formal proscriptions of State law, then it should not be disregarded. This became a more important matter when the Appeals Chamber faced its final question: Did breaches of the customary humanitarian law of internal conflicts entail individual criminal responsibility?

This judgment naturally began with reference to the judgment of the Nuremberg Tribunal. The IMT did not regard the absence of a specific criminal provision in the various humanitarian treaties, which the defendants were charged with violating, as precluding a finding of individual criminal responsibility. The IMT relied on State practice to demonstrate the nature of the prohibitions and cited a policy justified in support of the practice: Only by such responsibility could the law be enforced. The Appeals Chamber reversed the relationship between law and policy. Strong interests existed in the ascription of criminal responsibility to violations of the humanitarian law of war, regardless of whether the conflict was international or internal. The "international community" had an interest in prohibiting violations. The judgment then recited a large body of practice, including statements from military manuals, some domestic case law, and resolutions of the U.N. Security Council (the latter as evidence of *opinio juris*) and concluded that:

> [a]ll of these factors confirm that customary international law imposes criminal liability for serious violations of common Article 3, as supplemented by other general principles and rules on the protection of victims of internal armed conflict, and for breaching certain fundamental principles and rules regarding means and methods of combat in civil strife.[88]

Finally, the judgment noted that the law of the former Yugoslavia and the law of Bosnia made conduct, of which the accused was charged, criminal under their general law as well as under the laws implementing the Additional Protocols. This was a sufficient answer to any claim of retrospectivity about the U.N. Security Council's decision on the Tribunal's judgment.[89]

The treatment of the objection to subject-matter jurisdiction under Article 5, crimes against humanity, was rather brief. The defence had claimed before the Trial Chamber that the reference in Article 5 to "crimes when in armed conflict, whether international or internal in

---

88. *Id.* para. 134.

89. *Id.* para. 135.

character,"[90] violated the rule against retrospectivity insofar as it referred to internal conflicts. The claim was abandoned before the Appeals Chamber. The Appeals Chamber confirmed that "it is by now a settled rule of customary international law that crimes against humanity do not require a connection to an international armed conflict."[91]

This limitation derived from the Nuremberg Charter and the Resolution reaffirming the Nuremberg Principles. Because the matter was no longer being contested, the Appeals Chamber had no need to delve into this question further, but it would not be surprising if it would need to return to it. The category of crimes against humanity beyond the Nuremberg principles suffers from vagueness, legal uncertainty, and inconsistency in practice. That another aspect of the formulation of Article 5 might fail the test of legitimacy because of a lack of specificity—"imprisonment," "other inhumane acts," "directed against any civilian population"—cannot be ruled out.

The conclusions on Article 3 do not shock, though they may surprise. A more obvious reading of Articles 2 through 5 of the Statute together was that they provided comprehensive coverage of the worst excesses of the Yugoslavian conflicts without serious overlap between them and with the least problems concerning the legal provenance of the various offences: Articles 2 and 3 covering international conflicts; Article 4 covering genocide, regardless of the nature of the conflict; and Article 5 dealing primarily with acts committed in internal conflicts. Only the last raised any difficulties about its legal status, and those problems were relatively insignificant given the U.N. Security Council's inclusion of the Nuremberg limitation in Article 5, although the inclusion of internal conflicts leaves some scope for argument. The Appeals Chamber's approach provides more comprehensive coverage. Indeed, as it recognised, Article 3, as the Appeals Chamber understood it, might have covered most of the conduct upon which it was likely to have to adjudicate. To reach the conclusion that it did, the Tribunal began by attaching great significance to the language of Article 3 and the intention of the U.N. Security Council members. The analytical approach of the judgment allowed extraction of the maximum reach of Article 3, but ultimately everything turned on whether State practice supported the international criminality of serious breaches of the law of internal armed conflict.

The Appeals Chamber treated these questions more thoroughly than the IMT. Referring to breaches of the Hague and Geneva

---

90. Statute of the International Tribunal, art. 5, *cited in* S.C. Res. 827, *supra* note 39, Annex.

91. Appeals Chamber Decision on the Defence Motion, *supra* note 60, para. 141.

Conventions, the IMT simply said "[t]hat violations of these provisions constituted crimes for which the guilty individuals were punishable is too well settled to admit of argument."[92] The obstacle facing the Yugoslav Tribunal was that some provisions of the Geneva Conventions do carry individual criminal responsibility as a consequence of their breach, implying that others do not. However, it has been suggested that the "grave breaches" regime concerns mainly the establishment of a mandatory implementation regime, based on universal jurisdiction and the *aut dedire, aut punire* principle.[93] International criminality is neither assured nor precluded by this kind of obligation. A straightforward adoption of the IMT's statement might then suffice. The Appeals Chamber did provide some evidence of State practice to make the argument about the rules which apply to internal conflicts. It was appropriately done because the parties to internal conflicts commonly do not accept the legal equality of the contesting parties, which also characterises inter-State conflicts. There remains a major hurdle to surmount in order to establish that States have accepted not only obligations to limit governmental use of force when dealing with rebellion and insurrection, but also that State officials who ignore those standards should be internationally criminally liable. The absence of an unqualified resolution of this matter in customary international law reflects the institutional immaturity of the international legal system: In the absence of an international criminal court until now, the proposition could not be authoritatively tested.[94]

IV. CONCLUSION

The U.N. Security Council Resolutions creating the Ad Hoc Tribunals for Yugoslavia and Rwanda indicate that the *one* place for criminal courts in the U.N. system is in support of the U.N. Security Council's function of preserving and maintaining international peace and security. We should recognise that this is the objective and not expect that it will be best filled by creating international tribunals identical with domestic criminal courts. The decisions of the Yugoslav Tribunal have demonstrated an awareness of this through their extensive interpretation of the Articles on substantive jurisdiction— perhaps a matter of progressive development, rather than crystallisation of the law—and their functional approach when

---

92. Judgment of the Nuremberg Tribunal, 22 INTERNATIONAL MILITARY TRIBUNAL, TRIAL OF MAJOR WAR CRIMINALS 411, 471 (1948).

93. Meron, *supra* note 84, at 568-71.

94. *See* Michael Bothe, *War Crimes in Non-International Armed Conflicts,* 24 ISR. Y.B. HUM. RTS. 241 (1995).

assessing the rights of the defence. Of course, presently an experiment exists to see *if* the Tribunals can make an effective contribution to the discharge of the U.N. Security Council's responsibilities.[95]

Whether there is a place for a permanent criminal court is less certain. If the court is given a narrow jurisdiction, it may not command the support of a large number of States because it will not be able to do enough. On the other hand, if it is given a wide jurisdiction, it may not command the support of a large number of States because it may be able to do too much. It remains to be seen if there exists a community based on the cooperation of States which feels the need for the facility that the permanent court will provide, especially if it is required to approximate a national tribunal.[96]

When first considering the various proposals for international criminal courts, the following human rights adage may come to mind: We have to start somewhere. The development of, for instance, the system of the European Convention on Human Rights was hardly conceivable when the institutions were created forty-five years ago. Might not the same thing happen with an international criminal jurisdiction given time and some successes? For the time being, it remains doubtful that such a process will unfold.[97] Establishing a legal and political international community in which the identification of criminal standards and the shared expectation that they will be made effective remains problematic.[98] Unsurprisingly, the ILC is finding its "international community" projects difficult to bring to fruition. The answer is: International criminal courts fit into the U.N. system as instruments for the discharge of the U.N. Security Council's role in maintaining international peace and security and should accordingly be fashioned in a way that makes them effective to do so.

---

95. There is no space here to consider the relationship between the prosecutor's powers and the powers of the U.N. Security Council when reaching a political agreement, including guarantees of immunity from prosecution before the Tribunal incompatible with decisions the prosecutor may already have taken. The U.N. Security Council has made it clear that it expects the investigation of crimes committed in the territory of Yugoslavia to go ahead with the improved cooperation of the authorities in the area as part of the Dayton settlement of the conflict in Bosnia-Hercegovina. *See* S.C. Res. 1034, U.N. SCOR, 50th Sess., 3612th mtg., U.N. Doc. S/RES/1034 (1995).

96. The General Assembly has established a committee to draft a statute for a permanent international criminal court at two sessions in March and August 1996. G.A. Res. 50/46, U.N. GAOR, 50th Sess., U.N. Doc. A/RES/50/46 (1995).

97. Though no principled reason to object to such a development is evident, compare Alfred P. Rubin, *An International Criminal Tribunal for Former Yugoslavia?*, 6 PACE INT'L L. REV. 7 (1994).

98. *See* Gilbert Guillaume, *The Future of International Judicial Institutions*, 44 INT'L & COMP. L.Q. 848, 856-58 (1995).

[15]

UNITED NATIONS LAW IN THE GULF CONFLICT

By Oscar Schachter*

This was written shortly after the gulf war of 1990–1991 came to an end. The collective action taken under the aegis of the United Nations has been hailed as a vindication of international law and of the principle of collective security. At the same time, it has also been perceived by many as still another example of the dominant role of power and national self-interest in international relations. A plausible case can be made for each of these views. An optimist may conclude in the rosy glow of the desired outcome that law and power have happily converged in this case. Even so, the massive devastation of civilian life during the war and the threat of renewed violence are troubling features. The promise of a new world order based on the rule of law still seems far from fulfillment, but there is renewed hope that the UN Charter will be taken seriously as an instrument of collective responsibility.

The response of governments to the Iraqi invasion of Kuwait raised this hope. It was evident that the governments acting through United Nations processes were mindful of the UN Charter and related general principles of law. Indeed, the consensus required for Security Council decisions and common action could not have been achieved unless they had been seen as legitimate measures under the basic compact. But governments and political organs do not act like courts and are not expected to. National interests and power are the important determinants of state action, especially in time of crisis. Hence, the unfolding of the gulf conflict cannot be viewed as if it were solely a legal scenario. Yet it is not unimportant that the governments referred to and applied the UN Charter. They did so not as a set of constraints on action but, rather, as a basis for agreement on aims and means. The Charter, it may be said, was seen as a resource, rather than as a restraint.

This article focuses mainly on the Charter provisions involved expressly or implicitly in the Security Council decisions. My comments are designed to throw some light on the implications of those decisions for future action. True, one should not expect an event as extraordinary as the gulf conflict to be repeated in the future. Yet, it is not unreasonable to expect that the features of the legal landscape revealed in that conflict will be of future significance.

The commentary that follows is presented under the following headings: (1) The Implicit Affirmation of Article 2(4) of the Charter; (2) Nonforcible Sanctions under Article 41 before and after Hostilities; (3) Collective Self-Defense under Article 51; (4) The Applicability of Article 42; (5) The Place of Article 48; (6) Special Agreements under Article 43; (7) The Humanitarian Rules of Armed Conflict; (8) Sovereign Rights and UN Authority in the Aftermath of the War; and (9) Collective Security as Ideal and Reality.

I. THE IMPLICIT AFFIRMATION OF ARTICLE 2(4)

On August 2, 1990, the UN Security Council was faced with the massive Iraqi invasion of Kuwait and the purported annexation. This was the first time since the

* Of the Board of Editors. The author gratefully acknowledges helpful suggestions made by Theodor Meron.

founding of the United Nations that the entire territory of a member state was forcibly annexed. It was not the first time that a state used force to seek recovery of territory it claimed as its own.

The Council acted with unanimity to condemn the invasion. It referred expressly to Articles 39 and 40 of the Charter, thus bringing the matter under chapter VII and the power of the Council to impose mandatory measures. The resolution demanded the immediate and unconditional withdrawal of Iraqi forces.[1] It also called on both countries to begin "intensive negotiations" to resolve their differences. The resolution did not specify what those differences were, but presumably they included the territorial and financial claims. Considering that Iraq was asserting its sovereignty over the entire territory of Kuwait, the Council resolution might have seemed to be calling on Kuwait to "negotiate" a claim to its extinction. This twist was surely not intended, but it is a reminder of the problem faced by the Council in seeking a peaceful solution to a conflict. At that stage the Council would normally wish to avoid legal judgments and leave room for negotiations.

It is surprising, however, that the Council did not condemn the invasion as a violation of Article 2(4) and an act of aggression. Clearly, it was both. Yet Council Resolution 660 determined only that a breach of the peace had occurred, a finding sufficient to apply measures under chapter VII. Why was there not a finding of a violation of Article 2(4) or explicit reference to aggression? Even the second resolution,[2] adopted four days after the first, did not explicitly refer to Article 2(4) or aggression, although it did refer to the right of self-defense as applicable in response to the Iraqi attack and it also imposed sanctions under Article 41. To be sure, the statements made in the Council by governmental representatives and those made by political leaders left no doubt that they considered Iraq's action as aggression and a violation of Article 2(4). I would not therefore attribute any legal significance to the omission of these conclusions from the resolutions. The omission may only have reflected the hope of some members of the Council that Iraq would be more likely to negotiate if it were not expressly condemned for the "supreme crime" of aggression. This omission may also have facilitated the decision-making process in the Security Council.

Iraq's claim to Kuwait as "lost" Iraqi territory was not regarded by any member of the Council as a legal justification for the invasion. This point is significant since other invading states have justified their use of force as legal on the ground that the territory invaded was their own. For example, India said in 1961 that there was "no legal frontier" between it and Goa because the latter territory had been under the "illegal domination" of Portugal for 450 years and consequently that the armed takeover by Indian troops was legal.[3] Similarly, Argentina had long claimed that the Malvinas (Falklands) were its territory despite British control for 150 years and therefore that its use of force in 1982 to "recover" the islands was "self-defense."[4] Although the Argentine position was not accepted by the Security Council, it received support from several states, especially those with active territorial claims.

---

[1] SC Res. 660 (Aug. 2, 1990), *reprinted in* 29 ILM 1325 (1990).

[2] SC Res. 661 (Aug. 6, 1990), *reprinted in* 29 ILM at 1325.

[3] 16 UN SCOR (987th mtg.) at 10–11, UN Doc. S/PV.987 (1961). A majority in the Security Council voted in favor of a draft resolution requesting India's withdrawal from Goa, but the USSR vetoed the draft. *See* Q. Wright, *The Goa Incident*, 56 AJIL 617 (1962).

[4] Statement of Argentina in UN Doc. A/37/PV.51 (Nov. 2, 1982).

In view of the persistence of irredentist claims, the Council's unequivocal rejection of Iraq's claim is likely to be recalled in the future. It affirms that armed force may not be used to change the existing boundary of a state even if that boundary was established unjustly or by conquest. The unanimity on this issue of principle strengthens its force as an interpretation of Article 2(4). The Council underlined its position in this regard by its decision in a later resolution "to guarantee the inviolability" of the international boundary between Iraq and Kuwait, which had been agreed to by the two states in 1963.[5]

II. Nonforcible Sanctions under Article 41

The Security Council acted with unprecedented speed to impose a trade and financial embargo on a defiant Iraq. Only four days after the demand for immediate withdrawal, the Council, noting Iraq's failure to comply, decided to require mandatory sanctions of a comprehensive character.[6] There was never any question of its legal authority to do so. Article 41, though not mentioned in the resolution, clearly empowered the Council to take measures not involving the use of force to give effect to its decisions and to call on all members to apply such measures. The Council decision (not simply a recommendation) was legally binding under Article 25 of the Charter.

Article 41 is open-ended; it does not list all the measures that the Council may take under its authority. It does mention the complete interruption of economic relations and of air, sea and other means of communication. The Council acted accordingly. Resolution 661 required all states (not only member states) to ban imports to, and exports from, Iraq and Kuwait. It barred the transfer of funds to Iraq and Kuwait and, in effect, required a freeze on the bank accounts affected. These sweeping sanctions were required notwithstanding any prior contract or license. Exceptions were made to provide for medical supplies and foodstuffs in strictly humanitarian circumstances.

A committee of the Council was set up to monitor the implementation of the resolution through reports of states on actions taken by them. A few weeks after the embargo resolution, the Council found that Iraqi vessels were still being used to export oil. Alarmed by this, the Council called on the states "co-operating with the Government of Kuwait" that had maritime forces in the area to use such measures as might be necessary "to halt all inward and outward maritime shipping in order to inspect and verify their cargoes and destinations and to ensure strict implementation" of the embargo decision.[7] This resolution was understood to authorize states to use naval force to halt the shipping in question. The only previous example of use of force authorized by the Council in regard to an embargo was a specific authorization to the United Kingdom to use naval force to block a particular vessel from delivering oil to Mozambique that was destined for Southern Rhodesia in violation of the embargo against the regime of that territory.[8]

The Council's embargo of Iraqi trade was later augmented by Resolution 670, which ordered all states to deny permission to any aircraft destined for Iraq or

---

[5] SC Res. 687 (1991), adopted April 3, 1991, after the fighting ceased. It is *reprinted in* 30 ILM 846 (1991).

[6] SC Res. 661, *supra* note 2.

[7] SC Res. 665 (Aug. 25, 1990), *reprinted in* 29 ILM at 1329.

[8] SC Res. 221 (Apr. 9, 1966).

Kuwait to overfly their territory except where the United Nations had given prior approval. The resolution also included provisions to strengthen compliance with the economic sanctions. It authorized the Council's sanctions committee to continue monitoring the air embargo and also to continue gathering information from all members on their measures regarding trade and financial aspects of the embargo.[9]

In connection with the embargo, the Council took account of Article 50 of the Charter.[10] That article provides that any state which finds itself confronted with special economic problems arising from preventive or enforcement measures taken by the Security Council shall have a right to consult the Council regarding a solution of those problems. This "relief" provision was invoked by twenty-one states that had suffered from the trade embargo.[11] They included oil-importing countries dependent on Iraqi oil and countries that made substantial exports to Iraq and Kuwait. It also was invoked by countries that had many migrant workers in Kuwait and were heavily dependent on them for financial remittances. Recommendations of the Council's committee on sanctions urged states to increase financial and development assistance to the countries injured by the embargo. The UN specialized agencies and other international organizations were also asked to increase their aid to those countries. The Council did not arrange for any direct financial reimbursement to the claimant countries, but it declared that Iraq is liable to pay compensation for damage to Kuwait and other countries in connection with the invasion and occupation.[12] As a condition of the cease-fire, Iraq accepted in principle its liability, as required by the Council.[13]

Probably the most controversial issue faced by the Council during the gulf conflict was whether the sanctions under Article 41 would prove to be adequate to achieve the Council's objective. After the first two months, it was evident that the embargo was largely effective, particularly in stopping Iraq's oil exports and in cutting off the supply of significant imports of a technical and military nature. There appeared to be little doubt that the Iraqi economy was substantially damaged. However, it was much less clear whether such damage, even if continued, would bring about the demanded change in policy on the part of the Iraqi leadership and, if so, when. The United States Government concluded by November 1990 that military action would probably be required to compel Iraq to withdraw from Kuwait. It persuaded most of the other Council members to support a resolution authorizing the states cooperating with Kuwait to take the necessary means to uphold and implement the prior resolutions and to restore peace and security in the area.[14] This authorization was to be effective on January 16, 1991, if Iraq did not comply by that date. The two members of the Council opposed to the resolution (Cuba and Yemen) questioned its validity on the ground that the Council had authorized the use of force without determining that the Article 41 sanctions

[9] SC Res. 670 (Sept. 25, 1990), *reprinted in* 29 ILM at 1334.

[10] SC Res. 669 (Sept. 24, 1990), *reprinted in* 29 ILM at 1333.

[11] UN Docs. S/22021 (1990), and S/22193 (1991).

[12] SC Res. 674, paras. 7, 8 (Oct. 29, 1990); SC Res. 686 (Mar. 2, 1991), *reprinted in* 30 ILM 568 (1991).

[13] Iraq notified the Council in April 1991 of its acceptance of liability in principle as demanded by Resolution 686. UN Doc. S/22456 (Apr. 6, 1991). See also the response of the President of the Security Council, UN Doc. S/22485 (Apr. 11, 1991) (calling the Iraqi statement an "irrevocable and unqualified acceptance").

[14] SC Res. 678 (Nov. 29, 1990), *reprinted in* 29 ILM at 1565.

would be inadequate. In their view, that determination was required when force was authorized under the terms of Article 42.[15]

There are two possible answers to this point. One is that Article 42 was not being applied; this issue is examined below. The other answer is that even if Article 42 was applied, the Council discussion showed that members considered that the economic sanctions would not be adequate to achieve the withdrawal of Iraq. Whether this supposition was well-founded can only be a matter of speculation inasmuch as armed force was used on January 16, 1991.

The end of the hostilities and the Iraqi withdrawal did not bring an immediate end to the sanctions under Article 41. The Security Council decided to maintain a selective embargo in order to ensure compliance by Iraq with all the conditions in the resolutions. The resolution adopted by the Council in April 1991 called for the acceptance by Iraq of a great number of conditions imposed by the Council as a basis for a formal cease-fire.[16] The sanctions under Article 41 were modified to a limited extent, in particular to allow the import of food and material for certain essential civilian needs and humanitarian purposes. The export of petroleum and petroleum products would be permitted to the extent necessary to meet claims on Iraq and the cost of imports.

The conditions imposed on Iraq in the resolution fell broadly into three categories. One related to Iraq's military capabilities. It required Iraq to destroy all chemical and biological weapons and all ballistic missiles beyond a limited range. It also demanded that Iraq agree not to acquire or develop nuclear weapons and to place all nuclear-weapons-usable material under the exclusive control of the International Atomic Energy Agency. It further required that Iraq agree to an international commission that would inspect weapon capabilities and supervise the destruction or removal of those prohibited. A second category of conditions related to the liability of Iraq for loss and damage to foreign governments, nationals and corporations as a result of the invasion and occupation of Kuwait. Specific reference was made to environmental damage and the depletion of natural resources. The resolution called for a fund to pay compensation claims and for a mechanism to determine the appropriate share to be contributed by Iraq, based on the value of its petroleum exports and the needs of its economy. A third category of items in the resolution related to the boundary between Iraq and Kuwait (discussed in the previous section) and to the deployment of a UN observer unit to establish conditions for the withdrawal of the coalition forces from Iraq. Other provisions in the resolution related to the repatriation of Kuwaiti and third-country nationals and to a commitment against terrorism. Some of the provisions of this resolution are reminiscent of terms of such treaties of peace as the Versailles Treaty.

The April 1991 resolution is probably the most complex decision ever adopted by the Council. Its implementation requires a number of administrative and institutional measures by the UN Secretary-General, as well as by national governments and international bodies. From the standpoint of the Charter and, in particular, of Article 41, the resolution shows that economic and other nonforcible sanctions may be a means for enforcing UN requirements that extend beyond repelling aggression or ending hostilities. Iraq accepted the conditions while pro-

---

[15] Article 42 of the UN Charter begins: "Should the Security Council consider that measures provided for in Article 41 would be inadequate or have proved to be inadequate, it may take such action by air, sea, or land forces."

[16] SC Res. 687 (1991), *supra* note 5.

testing that the sanctions were illegal and unfair.[17] Neither Iraqi contention is persuasive. Article 41 expressly allows for sanctions to give effect to the Council's decisions taken under chapter VII. Such decisions must of course fall within the terms of Article 39 and therefore within the broad aim of maintaining or restoring peace and security. In this case, the Council's decisions rest in part on the premise that the measures taken serve to maintain the peace by reducing the military capabilities of a state that has been guilty of aggression and may be a continuing threat to international peace and security. Other provisions, particularly those on compensation for loss, are measures reasonably related to the establishment of a just peace in keeping with international law. While those measures go beyond the original demands for Iraqi withdrawal, the Council had ample reason to take such action as part of the restoration of peace and security in the area. It is hard to take seriously the claim of an aggressor that its sovereign rights are violated by restraints on its military capability or by requiring it to pay for damage it caused. A distinction might have been drawn, in respect of reparations, between the heavy responsibility of the Iraqi leaders and the burden of reparations on the people as a whole. One would expect this issue to arise when reparations are actually implemented.

III. Collective Self-Defense under Article 51

The legal concept of collective self-defense was invoked in the gulf conflict almost immediately after the invasion by Iraq. Kuwait requested the aid of other countries and steps were taken by the United States, the United Kingdom and Saudi Arabia to lend assistance. The Security Council in its Resolution 661, which, as we saw, adopted sanctions under Article 41, also included in its preamble a paragraph that affirmed "the inherent right of individual or collective self-defence, in response to the armed attack by Iraq against Kuwait."[18]

This was the first time the Council recognized in a resolution that the right of collective self-defense applied in a particular situation. It is interesting that the Council did so in the same resolution in which it adopted economic sanctions. Presumably, the members did not consider at the time that measures of self-defense were inconsistent with, or terminated by, the Council's nonforcible sanctions. I will return to this issue below.

In affirming the applicability of collective self-defense in the gulf situation, the Council recognized (again by implication) that third states had the right to use force to aid Kuwait, even though those states themselves had not been attacked and had no treaty or other special links with Kuwait. The point has some importance because earlier legal commentary by respected scholars such as Bowett and Kelsen had suggested a contrary position.[19] The Council's affirmation supports the position that any state may come to the aid of a state that has been illegally attacked. However, the Council took no position on whether such aid must have been requested by the victim state, as held by the International Court of Justice in the *Nicaragua* case of 1986.[20] That question was not an issue in the Iraq-Kuwait case since Kuwait had expressed its desire for assistance.

---

[17] Iraq's response to Resolution 687 is in UN Doc. S/22456 (Apr. 11, 1991).

[18] SC Res. 661, *supra* note 2.

[19] D. W. BOWETT, SELF-DEFENCE IN INTERNATIONAL LAW 216–18 (1958); H. KELSEN, THE LAW OF THE UNITED NATIONS 792 (1950).

[20] Military and Paramilitary Activities in and against Nicaragua (Nicar. v. U.S.), 1986 ICJ REP. 14, 105, para. 199 (Judgment of June 27).

While the Council's affirmation of the right of collective self-defense was not legally required, it served to bolster the case for naval action against Iraq to enforce the embargo. It also supported the contention that it would be legitimate for the third states to use force, if necessary, against Iraq to compel its withdrawal. Since there had been an armed attack, the only additional requirements would be the conditions imposed by general international law—namely, that the self-defense measures would be necessary and proportional to the end sought.[21] The determination of those conditions would be left, in the first instance, to the states resorting to self-defense, but the Council could, if it so decided, order termination of the self-defense measures.

The right of collective self-defense, however, came into question a few weeks after the United Nations imposed the sanctions under Article 41. The perception that such sanctions were not likely to bring about an Iraqi withdrawal had led to proposals for military action. The United States, the United Kingdom, and some other governments considered that such action would be permissible collective self-defense, based on the necessity to compel the aggressor to withdraw unconditionally. As against this position, it was argued by other governments and some international lawyers that the right of self-defense no longer applied when the Security Council had adopted measures it considered necessary to repel the armed attack.[22] This argument rested on the language of Article 51, which safeguarded the right of self-defense "until the Council has taken measures necessary to maintain international peace and security." If these words are taken literally, the right of self-defense would be overridden whenever the Security Council adopted measures considered necessary in case of an armed attack on a state. This would be an implausible—indeed, absurd—interpretation. A Council decision that calls on an invader to withdraw and to cease hostilities is certainly a necessary measure, but it could not be intended to deprive the victim state of its right to defend itself when the invader has not complied with the Council's order. A reasonable construction of the provision in Article 51 would recognize that the Council has the authority to adopt a measure that would require armed action to cease even if that action was undertaken in self-defense. However, this would not mean that *any* measure would preempt self-defense. The intent of the Council as expressed in its decision would determine whether the right to use force in self-defense had been suspended by the Council.

In the Iraq-Kuwait case, the principal argument that collective self-defense was superseded by Council action relied on the fact that the Council had adopted mandatory economic sanctions under Article 41. It was obvious that such economic sanctions were adopted in the hope that they would be effective in bringing about the withdrawal of Iraqi forces. While this was the hope, the resolutions contained no indication that self-defense rights were meant to be terminated by the adoption of sanctions. Indeed, the very resolution, No. 661, that first adopted the economic sanctions included the preambular paragraph, referred to above, affirming rights of individual and collective self-defense. The adoption of sanctions and the simultaneous affirmation of self-defense are surely inconsistent with an intention to bring an end to self-defense measures. It is, however, fair to say that the Council discussions showed that the Council members desired economic

---

[21] *Id.* at 103, para. 194.

[22] P. Lewis, *U.S. Preparing Draft on Claims Against Baghdad*, N.Y. Times, Nov. 1, 1990, at A12, col. 1.

sanctions to be used in lieu of military measures. On the other hand, it was made clear by some participating states, notably the United States and the United Kingdom, that the failure of economic sanctions might make it necessary to resort to armed force under Article 51. In their view, no further authorization by the Council was required if collective self-defense proved to be necessary.

Significantly, no government contested the ultimate right of the Council to prohibit all military action by a state, even if defensive. Article 51 is entirely clear that self-defense claims are subject to the Council's authority. The Council may order a claimant to cease military action even if that action was legitimate defense. However, a decision of that character would need the unanimous concurrence of the permanent members; hence, it could not be adopted over the objection of one or more of those members. In the gulf case, the Council would not have been able to adopt a resolution terminating or suspending the right of self-defense as long as a permanent member opposed that proposal.[23]

The controversy over preemption ended when the Security Council adopted Resolution 678 on November 29, 1990, authorizing the states cooperating with Kuwait to use "all necessary means to uphold and implement" the Council's resolutions if Iraq did not unconditionally withdraw on or before January 15, 1991. It was amply clear that necessary means included the use of armed force to bring about Iraq's withdrawal and compliance with other provisions of the twelve resolutions adopted between August 2 and November 29. As of January 16, Resolution 678 was treated as the legal basis of the large-scale military action by the coalition of states that brought about the defeat of Iraq at the end of February 1991 and its withdrawal from Kuwait.

The precise Charter basis of Resolution 678 was somewhat uncertain. The resolution itself declared that the Council was acting under chapter VII, but it did not specify which article of chapter VII. It thus left several possibilities open to conjecture. One was that chapter VII in general provided an adequate legal basis. Another view was that a resolution authorizing armed force necessarily came within Article 42 and had to meet the requirements of that article. Still a third position was that the authorization came properly within the scope of collective self-defense and that the Council was exercising its authority under Article 51 (which is also in chapter VII).

A good case can be made for this latter position. I will comment on it here and leave for later discussion the applicability of Articles 42, 48, and 43. One reason for treating Resolution 678 as falling within Article 51 is that it authorized the group of states identified as cooperating with Kuwait in resisting the invasion to take the necessary means to achieve the objectives previously declared by the Council and, in addition, to restore peace and security in the area. It is significant in this respect that the Council did not decide that the armed forces of the cooperating states were to be placed at the disposal or under the control of the Security Council. No United Nations command was set up; no reference was made to a

---

[23] It has been suggested that if a proposed resolution authorizing force such as 678 had been vetoed, collective self-defense action would have been barred. *See* M. E. O'Connell, *Enforcing the Prohibition on the Use of Force: The UN's Response to Iraq's Invasion of Kuwait,* 15 S. ILL. U.L.J. 453, 478 (1991). This suggestion is clearly wrong. It does not make sense to conclude that failure of the Council to endorse action by a state should bar that action when it is otherwise permitted by the Charter and international law. A veto can obviously prevent a Council decision and therefore block the Council from prohibiting action. But a veto of a resolution that would approve or authorize otherwise permissible action cannot have the legal effect of precluding that action.

United Nations force or to use of the UN flag. These were features of the UN-authorized force in Korea; their omission here is further evidence that the Security Council intended to leave the choice of means, timing, command and control to the participating states.

It may be asked why a new resolution was required when the Council had already affirmed the right of collective self-defense soon after the invasion. Moreover, collective self-defense action did not require Council approval or authorization; member states were free anyway to use force against the aggressor within the limits of self-defense. However, the resolution served the political purpose of underlining the general support of the United Nations for the military measures if Iraq did not withdraw before January 16, 1991.[24] In addition, the resolution, supported by all of the cooperating states committed to collective action, clarified the objectives of the collective defense action.

Considering the action of the United Nations and the coalition as legally within collective self-defense calls for some further comment. To characterize the military action as collective self-defense rather than as a United Nations action does not imply that the use of force was wholly a matter of discretion for the cooperating states; nor does it mean that the Council lacked authority to place limits on the military action. Article 51 expressly recognizes that, in cases of self-defense, the Council retains the authority and responsibility to take such action as it deems necessary to restore international peace and security. This language makes it clear that the Council may decide on the limits and objectives of the military action authorized as collective self-defense.

Resort to collective self-defense (*jus ad bellum*) is also subject to requirements of necessity and proportionality, even though these conditions are not expressly stated in Article 51. Both requirements were discussed in the Security Council and by the governments concerned for several months. Indeed, the length and intensity of the open debates on these issues are without precedent in international bodies. One important issue—already noted—was whether economic sanctions would be effective enough to make military action unnecessary or excessively costly in human lives and material. Though these issues were (and remain) controversial, the conclusions reached by a majority of the Council and reflected in its authorization to use armed force may be regarded from the legal standpoint as an authoritative determination of "necessity" by the competent international organ acting on behalf of the entire United Nations.

It is worth noting that the debate in the Council and elsewhere on whether the use of force was "necessary" self-defense took a direction rather different from the way the issue had previously been discussed by international lawyers. The argument advanced by opponents of the use of force contended, as noted above, that the economic embargo would prove to be effective in due course; hence, in their view, force was not required as a matter of self-defense. The debate then centered on whether that contention was well-founded.

The criterion of necessity thus debated is quite different from the view previously accepted that an illegal armed attack on a large scale is in itself sufficient to meet the requirement of necessity for self-defense. Thus, when the Japa-

---

[24] Many governments supporting action against Iraq regarded it as important for domestic political reasons to have UN authorization. *See* T. Friedman, *Allies Tell Baker Use of Force Needs U.N. Backing,* N.Y. Times, Nov. 8, 1990, at A14, col. 1. The UN resolution authorizing force was probably of decisive importance in obtaining U.S. congressional approval.

nese attacked Pearl Harbor or when the Germans invaded Poland to begin World War II, it was taken for granted that armed self-defense by the victim states met the requirement of necessity. The possibility that an economic blockade might cause the aggressors to turn back was not seriously considered to be a legal reason for denying the right of self-defense. Admittedly, there might be prudential reasons for concluding that peaceful means in lieu of armed force would be sufficient to redress the wrong of an armed attack. But to introduce this possibility as a ground for concluding that armed self-defense against an attack or invasion is not "necessary" until peaceful means are sought and found unavailing would radically change the prevailing view of self-defense.[25] It is unlikely that states will move in that direction under existing international conditions.

IV. THE APPLICABILITY OF ARTICLE 42

It has generally been assumed that the Council's authority to apply armed force under chapter VII can only be found in Article 42. This assumption was also evidenced in statements made by some of the Security Council members. This is not surprising. For one thing, Article 42 is the only provision in the Charter that expressly empowers a UN organ "to take action by air, sea, or land forces" as may be necessary to maintain or restore international peace and security. Moreover, Article 39, the "basic" provision of chapter VII, authorizes the Council to "decide what measures shall be taken in accordance with Articles 41 and 42, to maintain or restore international peace and security." A reasonable inference is that if the Council decides on measures, they should be under either Article 41 (i.e., not involving force) or Article 42 (if military action is taken).[26] Hence, if Resolution 678 is a "measure decided on" by the Council involving armed force, Article 42 would necessarily apply.

The argument is not entirely compelling. Although Article 42 is the only Charter article that expressly empowers a UN organ to take action by armed force, it does not follow that other provisions may not also apply. This point was made by the International Court of Justice in its advisory opinion in the *Expenses* case. The Court then rejected the argument that the armed force authorized by the United Nations in the Middle East and the Congo had to be based on Article 42. It declared, "The Court cannot accept so limited a view of the powers of the Security Council . . . ."[27] The Court's Delphic comment does not point to any alternative article, but it suggests that the Council could act on a liberal construction of its authority derived from its general powers to maintain and restore international peace and security. On that approach,[28] the reference to chapter VII in Resolution 678 would call for no further specification. As in the case of consensual peacekeeping operations, the Council would draw on the broad language of the Charter provisions.

[25] *See* O. Schachter, *The Right of States to Use Armed Force*, 82 MICH. L. REV. 1620, 1635 (1984); Y. DINSTEIN, WAR, AGGRESSION AND SELF-DEFENCE 216 (1988).

[26] *See* H. KELSEN, *supra* note 19, at 744–45. *See also* Russett & Sutterlin, *The U.N. in a New World Order*, FOREIGN AFF., Spring 1991, at 69 (assumes Article 42 applies to Resolution 678).

[27] Certain expenses of the United Nations (Article 17, paragraph 2, of the Charter), 1962 ICJ REP. 151, 167 (Advisory Opinion of July 20).

[28] This position was taken by C.-A. Fleischhauer, Legal Counsel to the Secretary-General of the United Nations, in a panel at the ASIL Annual Meeting on April 19, 1991. In his statement, Mr. Fleischhauer also stated that Resolution 678 was not adopted under Article 42 since it did not provide "for a collective enforcement action by the United Nations, let alone under its command."

There are, of course, advantages to constitutional interpretation of such flexibility in cases where decisions are generally acceptable. On the other hand, invoking UN authority for coercive armed force touches an especially sensitive area, often with far-reaching effects. Confusion or uncertainty about the precise legal basis may well create friction. By avoiding reference in Resolution 678 to any particular article of chapter VII, the Council left the matter in doubt, giving rise to questions of authority that may require specific legal grounds. One hypothesis, suggested earlier, is that Resolution 678 is more compatible with an authorization of collective self-defense than with a conception of the Council as itself taking action by air, sea or land forces. There is no reason to doubt that the Council has authority under Article 51 to express approval of collective defense actions in a particular case. This may not be incompatible with Article 42 since its terms are flexible, allowing for a variety of actions.

To put it in another way, Resolution 678 may be read as consistent with both Article 51 and Article 42. In regard to the latter, the Council's resolution is an example of "action" taken by the Council involving the use of military forces. The word "action" does not have to mean that those armed forces are under the control or command of the Council. That such command and control was contemplated under other articles of chapter VII should not be read into Article 42. Recognizing Article 42 as a relevant source of authority together with Article 51 would not in itself enhance the Council's authority over the armed forces. It should not be forgotten that Article 51 gives the Council full authority and responsibility in cases of self-defense to take measures to maintain and restore international peace and security.

To be sure, the use of the term "action" in Article 42 may mean "enforcement" in a mandatory sense rather than an authorization. But even if Article 42 allows for mandatory "action," this should embrace the lesser power to recommend or authorize action.[29] It does not make sense to require a mandatory decision where a recommendation or authorization would suffice to achieve the desired action.

If we assume that the Council's Resolution 678 is also a form of "action" within the meaning of Article 42, the question arises (as it did in the Council) whether the conditions of that article have been met. One such condition is that the Council shall have made the determination required in Article 39. The Council did so when in Resolution 660 it found that a breach of the peace had occurred. It also took provisional measures under Article 40 when it ordered withdrawal and negotiation.[30]

Article 42 requires that the Council, before acting under that article, "consider that measures provided for in Article 41 would be inadequate or have proved to be inadequate." At least two members of the Council argued that the Council never did decide that the sanctions under Article 41 would be inadequate; consequently, they questioned the legal validity of Resolution 678. While it is true that the Council did not formally declare the inadequacy of the economic sanctions under Article 41, the debates indicate that several members believed that the sanctions would prove to be inadequate to bring about a withdrawal by Iraq. Moreover, it is not unreasonable to infer that the Council decision authorizing the cooperating states to use force ("all necessary means") impliedly recognized that sanctions would not prove adequate to compel Iraqi withdrawal. The defiant position taken by the Iraqi regime even after six months of sanctions added sup-

---

[29] *See* H. KELSEN, *supra* note 19, at 756.   [30] SC Res. 660 (1990), *supra* note 1.

port to the belief that military action was needed to bring about its compliance. Whether a longer period would have been effective remains conjectural, but there is no doubt that the Council had the legal right to decide on the need for military action.

V. The Place of Article 48

Another relevant Charter article in chapter VII is Article 48, which imposes an obligation on members to take action required to carry out the decisions of the Council, "as the Council may determine." Article 48 is a key article in chapter VII. It implements the enforcement measures decided upon by the Council by giving the Council the right to impose a duty to act upon some or all member states. It is more specific than Article 25, which provides generally that members have agreed to carry out decisions of the Council; Article 48 centralizes within the Council the power to determine which members shall take action required by Council decisions under chapter VII. Hence, the mandatory decisions by the Council in the gulf conflict are covered by Article 48, whether or not it is mentioned.[31] For example, the sanctions not involving force imposed by Resolution 661 under Article 41 are given obligatory effect by Article 48. Article 48 is particularly applicable where the Council requires action by a given state or group of states. Presumably, that is why the Council referred expressly to Article 48 (as well as to Article 25) in its Resolution 670, which prescribed action in regard to air transport and freezing of assets by states in a position to take such action.

Article 48 was not applicable, however, to the use of armed force authorized by the Council in Resolution 678. For it was clear under that resolution (as well as under Resolution 665 on the naval blockade) that the military measures were not required action. Hence, by its terms Article 48 did not apply to such permissive action, whereas it did apply to the mandatory economic and transportation embargoes required of all members.

Article 48 is also significant as the basis for the binding character of the Council's decisions that imposed conditions on Iraq to be carried out after the cease-fire, in particular in Resolution 687, discussed earlier. These conditions were accepted by Iraq, obviously under duress, but they are obligatory by virtue of Articles 48 and 25, irrespective of Iraq's "acceptance."

VI. Special Agreements under Article 43

It has been suggested that the resolution authorizing force is incompatible with the requirement of Article 43 that the Security Council conclude special agreements with member states for the provision of armed forces and facilities to be on call for Security Council action. During the early years of the United Nations, and even recently, it was thought that such agreements were a condition precedent to collective military measures by the Security Council. Article 106 clearly suggests that interpretation.[32] This view was held by the governments at the San Francisco

---

[31] Although Article 48 refers generally to "the action required to carry out the decisions of the Security Council," it must mean "the decisions" that are made under chapter VII involving action that is legally required. It would not apply to all decisions made by the Council in the sense of Article 27 (on voting). The important distinction between binding and nonbinding decisions is not erased or blurred by Article 48.

[32] Article 106 of the Charter reads, in part: "Pending the coming into force of such special agreements referred to in Article 43 as in the opinion of the Security Council enable it to begin the exercise of its responsibilities under Article 42."

Conference[33] and was often expressed by commentators on the Charter.[34] On the other hand, no explicit language in Article 42 or in Articles 43, 44, and 45 (which refer to the special agreements) precludes states from voluntarily making armed forces available to carry out the resolutions of the Council adopted under chapter VII.[35] The voluntary response to the resolutions in the Korean action is in point. In that case, sixteen states provided armed forces and military facilities to assist South Korea in repelling the North Korean aggression.[36] They did so in response to a recommendation, and no legal argument was made by any government that a mandatory decision was necessary.

Article 43, though drafted in obligatory language, has never been applied. The Security Council has not taken the initiative to negotiate such special agreements, though Article 43 requires that this be done "as soon as possible." It does not appear that any member state has ever requested such a negotiation. In effect, Article 43 has become a dead letter. Even when a majority of UN members (including the United States) emphasized the need for states to make armed forces available for service under the United Nations aegis, they did not urge recourse to Article 43 agreements. Thus, the General Assembly adopted resolutions during the Korean War that recommended that "each Member maintain within its national armed forces elements so trained, organized and equipped that they could promptly be made available, in accordance with its constitutional processes, for service as a United Nations unit or units, upon recommendation by the Security Council or the General Assembly."[37] It is not surprising, of course, that at that time no consideration was given to agreements negotiated by the Security Council, then hopelessly split by the Korean action and more generally by the Cold War. The Collective Measures Committee, set up by the General Assembly in 1950 to consider means of strengthening collective military action, reported on various proposals but did not suggest any use of Article 43.[38] Whatever measures were considered (including stand-by forces and even a "reserve" of individual volunteers) were not linked to the agreements under Article 43. The underlying premise was that if member states supported use of armed force under the United Nations, they would be expected to provide the means without legal compulsion.

The fact that Article 43 agreements have not been concluded and have not been found necessary for military measures does not mean that the article is devoid of present interest. One implication of the article is important. It makes clear that member states cannot be legally bound to provide armed forces unless they have agreed to do so. It thus affirms a limitation on the authority given to the Council by Article 42 and by Articles 48 and 49. True, this important point rests

[33] See interpretation in Report on Chapter VIII, Section B, Doc. 881, III/3/46, 12 UNCIO Docs. 502, 508 (1945), *quoted in* H. KELSEN, *supra* note 19, at 756.

[34] *See* L. GOODRICH & A. SIMONS, THE UNITED NATIONS AND THE MAINTENANCE OF INTERNATIONAL PEACE AND SECURITY 398–405 (1955); H. KELSEN, *supra* note 19, at 756; K. P. SAKSENA, THE UNITED NATIONS AND COLLECTIVE SECURITY 93 (1975). In 1948 UN Secretary-General Lie also stated that action under Article 42 required the agreements under Article 43. *See* 3 UN GAOR, pt. 2, Annexes, at 10, UN Doc. A/656 (1948).

[35] *See* D. W. BOWETT, UNITED NATIONS FORCES 277 (1964); L. Sohn, *The Authority of the United Nations to Establish and Maintain a Permanent Force*, 52 AJIL 230 (1958).

[36] *See* D. W. BOWETT, *supra* note 35, at 30–39.

[37] GA Res. 377 (V), para. 8 (Nov. 3, 1950); GA Res. 503 (VI), para. 2 (Jan. 12, 1952) (to the same effect).

[38] Report of the Collective Measures Committee, 7 UN GAOR Supp. (No. 17), UN Doc. A/2215 (1952).

on an inference, not express language. However, there is added support in the legislative history of the Charter and in the process of ratification for concluding that the Security Council may not impose an obligation on a member state to make armed forces available unless that state has agreed to do so through a special agreement with the Council.[39]

VII. The Humanitarian Rules of Armed Conflict

An especially tragic aspect of the gulf war was the extensive destruction of civilian lives and property that resulted from the coalition's aerial bombing and long-distance missiles. Critics of the war, and not only critics, have called attention to apparent violations of the prohibitions in the international law of armed conflict against causing disproportionate and unnecessary suffering to noncombatants. International lawyers, faced with cynicism, are not likely to be comfortable in reviewing the events.

It is worth noting that no government in the coalition and no military commander suggested that the aggressor state or its inhabitants should be denied the protections of the law of armed conflict. Such suggestions have not been lacking in the past. For example, the prosecution in the International Military Tribunal in the case against Nazi leaders at Nuremberg argued that the criminal behavior of the defendants meant that their actions could not be regarded as legal warfare and therefore must be considered to be common crimes such as murder, theft, and the like.[40] This argument was not accepted by the Tribunal. But from time to time it has been suggested that armed forces resisting aggressors were not fully bound by the requirements of the *jus in bello*. In 1952, during the Korean War, some doubt was expressed by a committee of the American Society of International Law that the laws of war were "fully applicable" to a United Nations force opposing an aggressor.[41] The committee suggested that the United Nations should not feel bound by all laws of war but should select those rules that "fit its purposes."[42] In contrast, the Institut de Droit International concluded in 1971 after some years of study and debate that UN forces engaged in hostilities, even if against an aggressor, must comply in all circumstances with the humanitarian rules of armed conflict, including the rules for protection of civilian persons and property.[43] While this conclusion concerned UN forces, it would surely apply equally to national forces opposing an aggressor.

The coalition forces in the gulf war expressed no doubt as to the applicability of the rules of armed conflict to their operations. They did charge from time to time that Iraqi actions violated those rules. The Security Council also accused Iraq of grave breaches of the fourth Geneva Convention on protection of civilian persons and property and the Council affirmed the liability of Iraq and of individuals who committed or ordered such grave breaches.[44] However, it was never suggested by

---

[39] *See* UNCIO Report, *supra* note 33. *See also* M. Glennon, *The Constitution and Chapter VII of the United Nations Charter*, 85 AJIL 74 (1991); Note, *Congress, the President and the Power to Commit Forces to Combat*, 81 HARV. L. REV. 1771, 1800 (1968).

[40] *See* B. Meltzer, *A Note on Some Aspects of the Nuremberg Debate*, 14 U. CHI. L. REV. 455, 461 (1946–47).

[41] Report of Committee on Study of Legal Problems of the United Nations, *Should the Law of War Apply to United Nations Enforcement Action?*, 46 ASIL PROC. 216 (1952).

[42] *Id.* at 220.

[43] 54 INSTITUT DE DROIT INTERNATIONAL, ANNUAIRE 465–70 (1971 II).

[44] SC Res. 670 (Sept. 25, 1990), *reprinted in* 29 ILM at 1334; and SC Res. 674, *supra* note 12. On violations by Iraq, see T. Meron, *Prisoners of War, Civilians and Diplomats in the Gulf Crisis*, 85 AJIL 104 (1991).

any responsible authority that violations by Iraq, however serious, would release the coalition forces from their obligations under the law of armed conflict.

Questions were raised in the Council and the media as to whether the bombing by the coalition forces of Iraqi civilian dwellings and facilities violated the law's proscriptions of indiscriminate or excessive (disproportional) attacks. The military leaders of the coalition responded that only sites of military significance were targeted, but they acknowledged that heavy "collateral damage" affecting civilians had occurred. Some of that damage evidently resulted from inadequate information or error and involved the unintended destruction of noncombatant personnel and civilian dwellings. More important was the strategic bombing aimed at the infrastructure that supports military capacity such as power plants, bridges, roads, communications. Such bombing predictably devastated civilian life. A United Nations survey after hostilities ended found that most means of modern life support in Iraq were destroyed or rendered "tenuous," including food supply, water purification and other essentials.[45] The enormous devastation that did result from the massive aerial attacks suggests that the legal standards of distinction and proportionality did not have much practical effect.

The international law issues raised by the aerial bombings of Iraq are too complex to be discussed here in any depth. Nonetheless, some observations can be offered. As we noted earlier, the separation of the *jus ad bellum* and the *jus in bello* has been implicitly affirmed in the specific sense that responsibility under the former was not considered to affect the position of the parties under the latter; all are equally bound, aggressor and defender alike. Second, all parties accepted in principle the customary law rule of "distinction," that is, noncombatant protection.[46] All agreed that armed force may be directed only against military objectives. However, the hostilities revealed how difficult it can be to make a sharp separation between the military targets and civilian objects, especially in an industrial society where their commingling is widespread. The proposed lists of lawful targets, beginning with the 1923 Hague Air Rules and including the more recent enumeration in the authoritative commentary of the International Committee of the Red Cross, mention structures and installations that may serve, in some circumstances, both military and civilian objectives.[47] No matter how "smart" the bombs may be, when they destroy a power plant partly serving military needs, civilian life is also likely to be profoundly damaged. The attempt of Protocol I of

---

[45] *See* UN Doc. S/22366 (Mar. 20, 1991) (Report of Secretary-General's mission to assess humanitarian needs).

[46] Article 48 of Protocol I Additional to the Geneva Conventions of 1949 provides: "In order to ensure respect for and protection of the civilian population and civilian objects, the Parties to the conflict shall at all times distinguish between the civilian population and combatants and between civilian objects and military objectives and accordingly shall direct their operations only against military objectives." Protocol Additional to the Geneva Conventions of 12 August 1949, and relating to the protection of victims of international armed conflicts, *opened for signature* Dec. 12, 1977, 1125 UNTS 3, *reprinted in* 16 ILM 1391, 1412 (1977).

This fundamental principle is generally accepted and regarded as customary law. *See* T. MERON, HUMAN RIGHTS AND HUMANITARIAN NORMS AS CUSTOMARY LAW 62–70 (1989).

[47] Hague Rules of Air Warfare, drafted December 1922–February 1923, in THE LAW OF ARMED CONFLICTS 207 (D. Schindler & J. Toman 3d rev. ed. 1988); COMMENTARY ON THE ADDITIONAL PROTOCOLS OF 8 JUNE 1977 TO THE GENEVA CONVENTIONS OF 12 AUGUST 1949, at 632–33 n.3 (Y. Sandoz, C. Swinarski & B. Zimmermann eds. 1987). For discussion of restrictions on attacks against dams, dikes and nuclear power stations, see G. Aldrich, *Progressive Development of the Laws of War: A Reply to Criticisms of the 1977 Geneva Protocol I*, 26 VA. J. INT'L L. 693, 714–16 (1986).

1977 to prescribe a presumption in favor of considering an object to be "civilian" (Article 52) remains controversial, particularly as the presumption is believed by some to encourage a state to camouflage its military installations.[48]

This possibility also suggests the importance of clarifying the responsibility for violations of the principles of distinction and proportionality in connection with collateral civilian casualties. Here, too, the problem is increased by the commingling of civilian uses and military objectives. In the gulf war, commanders of the coalition forces maintained that they took every reasonable precaution to minimize civilian casualties, but they did not conclude that aerial bombing of legitimate military objectives was prohibited because civilian casualties would result. A relevant provision of Protocol I (Article 57) requires that a commander do everything "feasible" to minimize civilian casualties. What is "feasible" is not defined and it is far from clear that it provides much direction to the commanders in a war situation.[49]

The gulf war also raised an issue, long debated by experts, in regard to the responsibility of a state subjected to the threat or actuality of aerial bombing. It has been maintained that under customary law, the government in control of an area under attack and of its population has a legal obligation to protect the non-combatant civilians from casualties. Protocol I also recognizes that obligation,[50] though critics of the Protocol have charged that it is unduly disposed to place responsibility on those engaged in the aerial attack.[51] In the controversy over the bombing of Iraq, the coalition forces charged that Iraq had placed important military facilities in civilian areas in some cases and had also moved civilians close to places of military importance. To what extent these charges were well-founded has not been evident in public records, but they do point up the complexity of determining responsibility for collateral damage resulting from aerial warfare. Since it is unlikely that new technology will entirely eliminate such collateral damage, the goal of providing protection to civilian populations remains a daunting task for governments and their military branches.

VIII. Sovereign Rights and UN Authority in the Aftermath of the War

The Security Council initially called for the withdrawal of Iraqi forces from Kuwait and the restoration of the legitimate Government of Kuwait. Other objectives expressed in later resolutions included the payment by Iraq of compensation for damage to Kuwait and to third states, the punishment of persons responsible for breaches of the fourth Geneva Convention, and the restitution of assets taken by Iraq or under its authority. A more general objective was included in Resolution 678—namely, to restore international peace and security to the area. This aim appeared to leave room for almost any action by the Security Council that might reasonably be related to ensuring continued peace and security in the gulf region. Even apart from that resolution, the Charter includes several articles that empower the Council to make recommendations or to take binding decisions under chapter VII to maintain and restore international peace and security. It is

---

[48] See W. H. Parks, *Air Law and the Law of War*, 32 Air Force L. Rev. 1, 138–39 (1990).
[49] *Id.* at 156–58.
[50] See, e.g., Arts. 51(7) and (8), and 58 of Protocol I, *supra* note 46.
[51] See Parks, *supra* note 48, at 157–64. *See also* Arts. 51(8), 57, and 58 of Protocol I, *supra* note 46.

relevant that enforcement action taken under chapter VII is not subject to the restriction of Article 2(7) against intervention in matters which are essentially within the domestic jurisdiction of any state.

The discussions within and outside the Security Council during the conflict referred to various proposals to ensure that Iraq would not be a future threat to peace and security in the region. As mentioned above, the Council decided to destroy the installations in Iraq capable of mass destruction and particularly of nuclear, chemical and biological weapons. Limitations on the supply of arms and of high-technology instruments were also mandated in the Council's resolution of April 3, 1991. However, the Council did not call for the ouster of the Iraqi leader, Saddam Hussein, and of his regime. The broad legal issue raised by these decisions and proposals relating to the sovereign rights of Iraq is whether they would be considered compatible with the principles and purposes of the UN Charter, a requirement made explicit in Article 24 of the Charter. Presumably, a regime that has shown itself to have been an aggressor could be subject to some limitations in respect of its capability to use force. On the other hand, the principles of the Charter require respect for "sovereign equality" and the right of states to political independence and territorial integrity. These principles and the related Charter purposes may be considered to limit the authority of the Council to impose a regime on the defeated aggressor, even if the leaders responsible for aggression and war crimes might be subject to prosecution by victim states. The people of the country would still be entitled to self-government and basic political rights.

The Council resolution setting the conditions for a final cease-fire implicitly recognized these rights by refraining from imposing constitutional decisions or changing the Iraqi regime. However, the savage repression of dissident minorities by the Iraqi forces after hostilities ended imposed severe strains on the policy of nonintervention in internal affairs. The humanitarian concerns led to demands for United Nations involvement and proposals for military action by the coalition forces. The reluctance of some members of the Council to intervene with armed force in an "essentially internal" affair has been attributed to their fear that it would be a precedent for coercive intervention into their countries, which faced ethnic or religious opposition. An added element in the Iraq situation was the large-scale exodus of the Kurdish and Shiite opponents into Turkey and Iran, giving rise to tension between those countries and Iraq. Taking account of that factor, a majority of the Council supported a resolution that condemned Iraq's repression of the Kurds and other groups as a threat to international peace and security.[52] The resolution went on to say that the Council "insists" that Iraq allow access by international humanitarian organizations to all who need assistance in all parts of Iraq. It also requested that the Secretary-General use all the means at his disposal to address the critical needs of the displaced population of Iraq. The resolution was understood to provide further ground for continuing economic sanctions, but it did not refer to renewed military action.

Pressure for military protective measures by the coalition forces increased as Iraqi troops continued their attacks on the dissident minority refugees. Safety zones or enclaves were proposed, to be guarded by the armed forces of the coalition. Iraq objected on grounds that the internal conflict was a matter for Iraq alone to handle and that its acceptance of the cease-fire terms of the Council did not extend to the exercise of authority and police powers by foreign forces in

---

[52] SC Res. 688 (Apr. 5, 1991), *reprinted in* 30 ILM at 858.

domestic affairs. Initially, the United States, the United Kingdom and France hesitated to establish such enclaves, mainly because they feared continuing involvement in a civil war that raised difficult issues of a constitutional character. Subsequently, they did take such action over the objections of Iraq and the expressed misgivings of several other governments. But the Security Council was not asked to authorize or endorse the protective measures in the safety zones, presumably because not all of the permanent members were prepared to support them. The absence of explicit Security Council endorsement, together with the basic Charter provision against intervention in matters essentially within domestic jurisdiction, was cited by dissenting UN members as grounds for condemning the use of troops in the safety zones as Charter violations of serious import. All states, it was argued, had reason to fear the effect of that precedent.

The legal case in support of the protective enclaves rests in part on the Council's finding that Iraq's repression of the minorities constituted a threat to international peace and security. This was a credible proposition in light of the transborder consequences and the resulting tension with neighboring states. Added to this consideration was the close relation between the plight of the displaced Iraqis and the war against Iraq. It could not be ignored that the internal strife was in some respects a consequence of the international military action, placing responsibility of a political and humanitarian character on the coalition to prevent massive attacks by Iraqi forces against noncombatants belonging to particular ethnic and religious communities.

A further point of legal significance is that the foreign forces in the enclaves were limited to the necessary protective action for a relatively short period to allow for relief and the eventual return of the refugees. They did not seek to impose an internal regime of autonomy or minority rights. United Nations police forces were expected to replace the coalition forces. Iraq's acceptance of the UN relief operations, however, did not extend to UN armed forces. The Secretary-General concluded that he could not legally send in a UN force unless the Security Council ordered Iraq to accept it or Iraq agreed to it.[53]

The impasse drew attention to proposals that UN peacekeeping troops be deployed where internal strife or disorder gave rise to the need for humanitarian assistance. It is unlikely that most governments would approve a broad right of the United Nations to introduce troops for humanitarian purposes against the wishes of the government. However, one cannot exclude the possibility that the United Nations would invoke chapter VII, and its mandatory authority under Articles 42 and 48, in cases of humanitarian necessity when the territorial government is unwilling or unable to provide relief and protection. In a case of this kind, the Council is almost certain to premise its decision on a finding that the situation constitutes a threat to international peace and security in view of its transborder implications.

---

[53] However, in May 1991, the Secretary-General did dispatch a small contingent of UN "guards" to perform minimal policing in an area where displaced Kurds were located and UN relief operations carried out. While the guards were not equipped to defend Kurds from Iraqi military attacks, their presence alone was expected to deter such attacks. The Secretary-General's action was not expressly authorized by the Security Council or by Iraqi agreement. However, it could reasonably be regarded as implicitly authorized by Council Resolution 688 of April 5, 1991, paragraph 5, which requested that the Secretary-General "use all the resources at his disposal . . . to address urgently the critical needs of the refugees and displaced Iraqi population." No objection was raised in the Security Council to the deployment of the UN guards.

IX. COLLECTIVE SECURITY AS IDEAL AND REALITY

The ideal of collective security dominated much of the debate during the gulf conflict. The political leaders of the coalition and their representatives in the United Nations proclaimed the necessity of common action against the aggressor in terms reminiscent of statements earlier in the century by Woodrow Wilson, Henry Stimson, Maxim Litvinov, Winston Churchill and Franklin Roosevelt. One could have gone back three centuries earlier for similar statements by philosophers and public figures. A legal historian could have observed that collective security was given legal effect in 1648 after the Thirty Years' War since the Treaty of Münster (a part of the Peace of Westphalia) declared it to be the common obligation of the states party "to protect each and all" and to aid the victim of aggression with "advice and arms."[54] The aphorism "an attack on one is an attack on all" was much quoted as the way to deter aggression and to "enforce the peace."[55] The nineteenth-century Concert of Europe had elements of the idea, though it was animated more by the idea of balance of power than by the conception of a common responsibility.[56]

The latter conception, put in global perspective, was given legal form in the Covenant of the League of Nations. All League members accepted the legal obligation to act against an aggressor; they were committed to maintaining an indivisible peace and to defending any state attacked.[57] The analogy to criminal law appealed to lawyers: a potential outlaw state would face community sanctions and therefore would be deterred from aggression. This optimistic prospect, deceptively simple, had a powerful appeal. However, it was not universally applauded. Many feared it would sweep their countries into wars that were of no direct interest to them. Some historians and political scientists viewed the idea as illusory, unworkable in a world dominated by national interests and power.[58] The skeptics found confirmation of their views in the failures of the League of Nations to halt the aggressions of Japan, Italy, Germany and the Soviet Union. In contrast, World War II was perceived as a successful collective mobilization of law-abiding states against the Fascist aggressors. The victors, especially the United States, moved to place the wartime alliance on a permanent institutional basis that would eventually include all states.

The UN Charter did not expressly refer to "collective security," but it did declare that "collective measures" against aggression and to prevent breaches of the peace were a major aim of the Organization. Unlike the Covenant, it did not rely on a self-executing obligation to deter aggression. The responsibility to take collective measures was placed in the Security Council, a political body with wide, almost unlimited, authority to permit, and even compel, action by all member states. The price for that unprecedented grant of authority was the requirement of unanimity of the five permanent members. This ensured that coercive action could not be applied against a major power—or, as it turned out, against any state a permanent member chose to protect. The veto and the Cold War, taken together, operated to bring collective security virtually to the vanishing point.

---

[54] *Quoted in* G. MANGONE, A SHORT HISTORY OF INTERNATIONAL ORGANIZATION 32 (1954).

[55] I. CLAUDE, POWER AND INTERNATIONAL RELATIONS 106–07 (1962).

[56] F. H. HINSLEY, POWER AND THE PURSUIT OF PEACE 225–37 (1963).

[57] *See* W. SCHIFFER, THE LEGAL COMMUNITY OF MANKIND 202–23 (1954). *See also* A. ZIMMERN, THE LEAGUE OF NATIONS AND THE RULE OF LAW 265 (1936).

[58] *See* I. CLAUDE, *supra* note 55, at 153; H. MORGENTHAU, POLITICS AMONG NATIONS 470–71 (1961); R. Stromberg, *The Idea of Collective Security,* 17 J. HIST. IDEAS 250–63 (1956).

Understandably, the gulf conflict and the success of the collective action under UN authority have led to a new perception. That success showed, for one thing, that unanimity of the permanent members is not a will o' the wisp and that a good part of the international community would be prepared to support measures against aggression adopted by the Security Council. It also revealed—though this aspect has not been highlighted—that governments may legitimately give effect to collective security without obtaining the authorization of the Security Council or of any UN body. This is not new. As we saw, the Charter always included collective self-defense as a legal basis for coercion when a state has been attacked and other states are prepared to aid that state by economic sanctions and armed force. Both NATO and the Warsaw Pact, and the earlier Rio Pact, relied on the principle of collective self-defense as the legal ground for commitments to aid the victims of aggression.[59]

Thus, the experience of the gulf conflict underlined two legal grounds for collective security. It showed that the Council was no longer hopelessly thwarted in meeting aggression by the absence of great-power unanimity. The Council could adopt nonforcible sanctions of a binding character and it could authorize military measures. But the gulf episode also indicated that Council action was not required where collective self-defense could provide the legal basis for measures against aggression. On that basis, authorization by the Council would not be required as a matter of Charter law. Of course, as mentioned earlier, the Council could use its authority to prohibit or terminate collective self-defense measures. However, as this would require a decision of the Council, it could not be accomplished without the support of the five permanent members and the nine required votes. Once again, the veto would impose itself as crucial. In a case of this kind, the veto could be employed, not to impede the collective action, but to ensure that such measures would not be barred by the Council's decision. To take the example of the gulf conflict: hypothetically, a majority of the Council might have favored relying solely on the nonmilitary sanctions to compel Iraq to withdraw, whereas (say) at least two of the permanent members might have considered military measures essential. As the majority could not adopt a decision (in view of the veto) to terminate or prevent military action under Article 51, a collective self-defense action would have been legal under the Charter.

Since collective self-defense may well be the legal basis for future collective security actions, it becomes important to remind states that the conditions for self-defense, collective and individual, are imposed by international law. The states claiming the right to use force in collective self-defense cannot be the final arbiters of its legality.[60] It is for the international community acting through the competent organs of the United Nations, or, *faute de mieux*, through the decentralized responses of states, to pass judgment on the legality of the claim to self-defense. Such judgments have in fact been made by the General Assembly (where the veto does not apply), as well as by the Security Council. In its much-discussed Judgment, the International Court in the *Nicaragua* case passed on the collective self-defense claim of the United States. The Court in that case affirmed the requirements of necessity and proportionality, as well as the necessity of a prior armed attack and a request for aid by the attacked state.[61] The discussion in the

---

[59] See Y. Dinstein, *supra* note 25, at 230–53; M. Virally, *Panorama du droit international contemporain*, 183 RECUEIL DES COURS 9, 298 (1983 V).

[60] O. Schachter, *Self-Defense and the Rule of Law*, 83 AJIL 259 (1989).

[61] See *supra* notes 20, 21.

gulf conflict showed sharp differences of opinion over the necessity and proportionality of the military action taken by the coalition. It is likely that such questions will arise whenever collective self-defense measures are taken.

In consequence, UN organs, and especially the Security Council, will have a responsibility under Article 51 to consider issues of legality regarding the collective defense actions. In order to do so effectively, the Council will need adequate reports on the self-defense measures. Such reports should be timely and should give enough information concerning necessity, proportionality and the ends sought to enable the Council to make an informed judgment as to the legality of the actions taken. It is doubtful that the reports submitted to the Security Council on the military actions by the coalition in the gulf conflict were intended to be reviewed by the Council. Of course, postaudits by the Council on compliance with such abstract standards as necessity and proportionality might be unproductive and perhaps even counter to the proper ends of collective self-defense. This suggests the need for further consideration by the Council and other appropriate bodies of the requirements of legitimate collective self-defense and of the role of the Council under Article 51. Up to now, this subject has not received much attention.

An obvious question raised by the Iraq case is whether the precedent of collective measures supported by the near-unanimity of the Security Council will prove to be a deterrent against acts of aggression, at least against such aggression as clear as Iraq's invasion. An expectation that the Council will act similarly in future cases has been viewed hopefully as a factor that will deter governments with territorial claims or designs against their neighbors. It has been suggested that small and weak states may take comfort from the precedent.

But blatant aggressions such as Iraq's annexation of Kuwait are rare. National interests in taking costly action against a law-violating state may not seem as compelling in other cases. The application of collective security is bound to have a selective and uneven character, and extrapolation from the gulf conflict is uncertain. A desirable outcome of the gulf conflict, from an optimistic perspective, would be a sustained effort to strengthen preventive measures through collective action. Among the more obvious steps would be greater use of international peacekeeping forces under United Nations or regional authority to perform monitoring and "trip-wire" functions in threatened regions. The introduction of military confidence-building measures, as suggested for Europe by the Conference on Security and Co-operation in Europe, is also likely to win support as a useful preventive measure. High on an agenda for preventive action in the Middle East and other troubled areas are arms limitation measures. These would be directed not only to countries in the region but to the supplying states. One principal aim would be to eliminate nonconventional weapons and to cut down on buildups of conventional military capabilities. The obstacles to achieving such restraints are generally recognized and easy solutions are not expected. The Security Council's resolution on conditions of a cease-fire is but a first step.[62]

---

[62] In May 1991, President Bush proposed arms control measures for the Middle East region, including (1) limits on the supply of conventional weapons, (2) elimination of production and acquisition of material used for nuclear weapons, (3) a freeze on producing and testing of ballistic missiles and their eventual ban, and (4) prohibition of poison gas and biological weapons. *See* N.Y. Times, May 30, 1991, at A1, col. 6. President Mitterand of France also proposed several arms limitation measures to be adopted by all countries.

The gulf conflict has also increased an awareness of the economic and social deficiencies that contribute to internal tensions and to interstate conflicts. Economic development and enhanced employment opportunities are now seen as linked to the maintenance of peace. Observance of the internationally recognized human rights and of democratic processes is also given more prominence on the agenda for creating a more stable international order. It remains to be seen how seriously these goals will be taken by governments and to what degree a collective responsibility to maintain peace will be given practical effect. The gulf conflict, in some respects a great calamity, did demonstrate that many countries recognize a common responsibility to combat aggression, although they remain somewhat ambivalent about meeting the costs in lives and material resources. It may well be utopian to expect that wars will be prevented by a common obligation to "protect each and all," but it is surely realistic for governments to press for the goal of security through preventive measures and the commitment to uphold—and, if necessary, to enforce—the basic law of the UN Charter.

[16]

BYPASSING THE SECURITY COUNCIL: AMBIGUOUS AUTHORIZATIONS TO USE FORCE, CEASE-FIRES AND THE IRAQI INSPECTION REGIME

*By Jules Lobel and Michael Ratner**

Introduction

In January and February 1998, various United States officials, including the President, asserted that unless Iraq permitted unconditional access to international weapons inspections, it would face a military attack. The attack was not to be, in Secretary of State Madeleine Albright's words, "a pinprick," but a "significant" military campaign.[1] U.S. officials, citing United Nations Security Council resolutions, insisted that the United States had the authority for the contemplated attack. Representatives of other permanent members of the Security Council believed otherwise; that no resolution of the Council authorized U.S. armed action without its approval.[2] In late February, UN Secretary-General Kofi Annan traveled to Baghdad and returned with a memorandum of understanding regarding inspections signed by himself and the Iraqi Deputy Prime Minister. On March 2, 1998, the Security Council, in Resolution 1154, unanimously endorsed this memorandum of understanding.[3]

In the March 2 meeting, no country asserted that Resolution 1154 authorized the unilateral use of force, and a majority stated that additional Council authorization would be necessary before force could be used.[4] Only after that meeting did U.S. officials claim otherwise; Ambassador Bill Richardson said the UN vote was a "green light" to attack Iraq if President Clinton should decide that Iraq was not living up to the agreement.[5] This assertion in the face of the Security Council's pointed refusal to grant such authority views the Council as a source of the authority to use force, but not as an instrument for limiting its use. With at least one notable exception,[6] however, the United States did not claim to be entitled to use force without the Council's authorization to compel Iraqi compliance with the UN inspection obligations. Rather, U.S. and British officials argued that Resolution 678 of 1990, which empowered the United States and other states to use force against Iraq, still governed and continued to provide authority to punish Iraq for cease-fire violations.[7] This position assumed that Resolution 678's authorization to use

---

* Professor of Law, University of Pittsburgh Law School; and Attorney, Center for Constitutional Rights, respectively. The authors would like to thank Lisa Price, Todd Piczak and Neeli Shreiber for their valuable research assistance, and Jane Stromseth for her invaluable comments on earlier drafts of this article.

[1] *See* Jim Wolf, *U.S. Won't Seek Saudi Sites for Iraqi Raids, Albright Says Air Strikes Could Begin Within Weeks*, Boston Globe, Feb. 7, 1998, at A1.

[2] *See* Christopher Wren, *Standoff With Iraq: The Law; UN Resolutions Allow Attack on the Likes of Iraq*, N.Y. Times, Feb. 5, 1998, at A6; John F. Harris & John M. Goshko, *Decision to Strike Iraq Nears; Clinton Advisors Lean Toward Attack to Force Compliance with UN*, Wash. Post, Jan. 24, 1998, at A1.

[3] SC Res. 1154 (Mar. 2, 1998), *reprinted in* 37 ILM 503 (1998).

[4] *See* UN Doc. S/PV.3858, at 14, 17 (1998).

[5] *See U.S. Doesn't Mince Words With Iraq*, AP, Mar. 3, 1998, *available in* LEXIS, News Library, AP File.

[6] U.S. officials were initially cautious about Annan's agreement with Saddam Hussein and Secretary of State Madeleine Albright stated that if "we don't like" Annan's agreement, "we will pursue our national interest." *See* Dan Morgan, *Administration Weighs Steps in Case UN-Iraq Deal Doesn't Satisfy U.S.*, Wash. Post, Feb. 23, 1998, at A15.

[7] SC Res. 678 (Nov. 29, 1990), *reprinted in* 29 ILM 1565 (1990). *See* Undersecretary of State Thomas Pickering, *USIA Foreign Press News Briefing*, Federal News Service, Mar. 3, 1998, *available in* LEXIS, News Library, Fednew File (a "material breach would mean that the prohibition on the use of force, which arose as a result of the cease-fire, was no longer in effect").

Collective Security Law

BYPASSING THE SECURITY COUNCIL

force remained valid, albeit temporarily suspended—a loaded weapon in the hands of any member nation to use whenever it determined Iraq to be in material breach of the cease-fire. The refusal of the United States to accept limitations on its power by the Security Council thus depended on creatively interpreting the Council's resolutions to accord authority, despite the contrary positions of a majority of its members.

The U.S. and British claim highlights an important problem regarding the Security Council's method of authorizing individual member states or regional organizations to use force on behalf of the United Nations. This "contracting out" mode leaves individual states with wide discretion to use ambiguous, open-textured resolutions to exercise control over the initiation, conduct and termination of hostilities. Such states may seek to apply resolutions by the Security Council in conflict with its aims and objectives or the view of many of its members, as occurred in the 1998 Iraqi inspection crisis. This crisis thus raises questions regarding (1) whether the Security Council has authorized the use of force; (2) how the scope and extent of an authorization are determined; and (3) whether the authorization has terminated.

We argue that two fundamental values underpinning the United Nations Charter— that peaceful means be used to resolve disputes and that force be used in the interest and under the control of the international community and not individual countries—require that the Security Council retain strict control over the initiation, duration and objectives of the use of force in international relations. To ensure that UN-authorized uses of force comport with those two intertwined values, this article argues for three rules derived from Article 2(4) of the Charter: (1) explicit and not implicit Security Council authorization is necessary before a nation may use force that does not derive from the right to self-defense under Article 51; (2) authorizations should clearly articulate and limit the objectives for which force may be employed, and ambiguous authorizations should be narrowly construed; and (3) the authorization to use force should cease with the establishment of a permanent cease-fire unless explicitly extended by the Security Council.

The questions raised by the Iraqi inspection crisis of 1998 are likely to arise in the future.[8] The claim of the U.S. Government to an ongoing UN authorization to use force against Iraq to enforce the cease-fire agreement has resurfaced often over the past seven years and is unlikely to be withdrawn. Moreover, the tendency to bypass the requirement for explicit Security Council authorization, in favor of more ambiguous sources of international authority, will probably escalate in coming years. The recent controversy over NATO's threat to intervene militarily in Kosovo raises similar issues as to the requirement for explicit authorization.[9]

---

[8] Unfortunately, our prediction that the United States and the United Kingdom would continue to assert the right to use force against Iraq without Security Council authorization proved to be accurate. In December 1998, as this article was in its final stages of editing for publication, the United States and the United Kingdom launched air strikes against Iraq, claiming that Iraq had not complied with its inspection obligations. The legal arguments made by the two states in support of their use of force, and the counterarguments presented by countries opposing the attacks were identical to those presented by the contending sides in February 1998 and discussed in this article. As of this writing, the United States and Britain have ceased the air bombardment but are suggesting that it may continue early in 1999. The December air strikes will be evaluated in a short postscript; all references to the Iraqi inspection crisis in the article refer to the events of February and March 1998.

[9] U.S. officials have argued that the mere invocation of Charter Chapter VII with regard to the Kosovo situation is sufficient to authorize a resort to force. *See* John M. Goshko, *U.S., Allies Inch Closer to Kosovo Intervention; UN Council to Vote on Key Resolution*, WASH. POST, Sept. 23, 1998, at A21. The *New York Times* reported that on Kosovo, "as on Iraq, there is a recurring disagreement over how much authority individual nations or regional organizations have to take military action without the clear support of the Security Council." Barbara Crossette, *Security Council Tells Serbs to Stop Kosovo Offensive*, N.Y. TIMES, Sept. 24, 1998, at A1.

THE AMERICAN JOURNAL OF INTERNATIONAL LAW   [Vol. 93:124

I. THE GENERAL PRINCIPLES UNDERLYING UN AUTHORIZATIONS OF FORCE

The UN Charter established an international organization in which states, pursuant to Article 43, would make armed forces available to the Security Council to counteract threats to the peace. This has not occurred. In its stead, the Security Council has authorized member states to use force, in essence franchising UN members to act in the Organization's behalf. The Security Council has authorized member states to use force in Korea in 1950, against Iraq in 1990, and in Somalia, Haiti, Rwanda and Bosnia in the early 1990s.

Smaller, nonaligned states, as well as some scholars, have voiced concern over the legitimacy of Security Council authorizations to individual states to use force. They argue that the resulting situation allows the powerful states to control decisions whether to employ force, how to use it, and when to terminate hostilities. These determinations are made without accountability and control by the Security Council.[10] Despite these concerns, the authorization method is likely to dominate UN practice for the foreseeable future. While we believe that the long-term interest of world peace and security supports revitalizing Article 43, the United States, among others, appears unwilling to submit command and control over its forces to anything more than perfunctory UN supervision. In this context, the United Nations becomes only an authorizing body, ceding control of the actual military operations to individual states.

Problems with the authorization method surface in several related areas. First, states might use force on the basis of actions by the Security Council that could impliedly be interpreted to authorize force, but where its intent to do so was unclear. For example, in 1991 the United Kingdom, the United States and France used force to provide humanitarian aid to the Kurds and to establish safe havens and no-fly zones in northern Iraq partly on the basis of ambiguous authority in Resolution 688. That resolution made no mention of military force, nor was it intended to authorize such force. The Economic Community of West African States (ECOWAS) intervened militarily in Liberia in 1990 without any explicit authorization by the Security Council, although the Council later did issue statements and a resolution approving ECOWAS's actions.

Second, states acting under the authorization of the Council might interpret their mandate to be broader than it had intended. The potential for conflict is most pronounced where the Council has delegated wide authority to a coalition of states to address a major problem, such as the Iraqi invasion of Kuwait. For example, Resolution 678, while motivated by the goal of expelling Iraq from Kuwait, also contains broad language authorizing force "to restore international peace and security in the area." That language could mean virtually anything, depending on how one defines "peace and security" and "area."[11] During the Persian Gulf war, a dispute arose as to whether the

---

[10] See John Quigley, *The "Privatization" of Security Council Enforcement Action: A Threat to Multilateralism*, 17 MICH. J. INT'L L. 249 (1996); Burns H. Weston, *Security Council Resolution 678 and Persian Gulf Decision Making: Precarious Legitimacy*, 85 AJIL 516, 525–28 (1991); Richard Falk, *The Haiti Intervention: A Dangerous World Order Precedent for the United Nations*, 36 HARV. INT'L L.J. 341, 341 (1995); Stephen Lewis, *A Promise Betrayed*, 8 WORLD POL'Y J. 539 (1991). See statement of January 25, 1991, by Malaysia indicating that its support for Resolution 678 in the Security Council was premised on a "continuing central role of the United Nations." Malaysia worried that the coalition members were drawing a "blank cheque from the Security Council resolution" and wanted to see "greater accountability of the actions by participating forces." Malaysia claimed that its concerns were being expressed by many UN members. UN Doc. S/22149 (1991), *reprinted in* IRAQ AND KUWAIT: THE HOSTILITIES AND THEIR AFTERMATH 358 (Marc Weller ed., 1993) [hereinafter IRAQ AND KUWAIT].

[11] Professor Henkin has noted the difficulty of defining threats to international peace and security. He has pointed out that the term "threat to international peace and security . . . is not capable of legal definition, but only of political determination by a political body." Such imprecision requires Security Council authorization to use force to combat threats to peace and security. Louis Henkin, *Conceptualizing Violence: Present and Future Developments in International Law*, 60 ALB. L. REV. 571, 575 (1997).

elimination of Iraq's war-making power, a goal asserted by some of the leaders of the coalition states, was authorized by Resolution 678.[12] The dispute over interpretation of Resolution 678 has continued to fester. In the February 1998 crisis, the United States and the United Kingdom interpreted the broad language "to restore international peace and security" as authorizing the use of force to ensure that Iraq destroyed its biological and chemical weapons—a condition not imposed upon Iraq until after the gulf war was over. Similar questions and disputes over Security Council authorizations to use force arose during the Korean War and the Bosnian and Somalian conflicts.

Furthermore, when the authorizations are not temporally limited, questions arise about their termination. As the Iraqi inspection crisis illustrates, the states acting under Security Council authorization might want to continue to employ force after the basic goal of the mission has been achieved. Conflicts often continue to simmer after hostilities have ended. A key question is whether a permanent cease-fire or other definitive end to hostilities terminates Security Council authorizations to use force.

To resolve these issues, two interrelated principles underlying the Charter should be considered. The first is that force be used in the interest of the international community, not individual states. That community interest is furthered by the centrality accorded to the Security Council's control over the offensive use of force. This centrality is compromised by sundering the authorization process from the enforcement mechanism, by which enforcement is delegated to individual states or a coalition of states. Such separation results in a strong potential for powerful states to use UN authorizations to serve their own national interests rather than the interests of the international community as defined by the United Nations. The decentralization and delegation of the actual use of force is likely to predominate for many years, necessitating stricter Security Council control over such authorizations.

To uphold the principles of the Charter, the Security Council must retain clear control over authorizations to use force (with the exception of force pursuant to Article 51), even if political and military considerations require that it delegate military command to individual nations. The difficulties of controlling the scope and extent of the use of force when its employment is delegated to individual states require, at a minimum, strict control by the Council over the initiation and termination of hostilities. Such control is achieved by the application of normative rules stipulating clear Council approval of non–Article 51 uses of force and termination of that authorization when a permanent cease-fire or other definitive end to the hostilities is realized.

Controlling the military tactics and objectives of the contractee nations will obviously be a difficult task for the Security Council as long as the contracting-out model prevails. Authorization to engage in a large-scale, long-term military operation will often be viewed as requiring that contractees be granted broad discretion so that they can effectively operate and cope with unpredictable military situations. Yet even in this situation, which the Security Council obviously cannot micromanage, it ought to limit the mandate to ensure that the contractee states employ force to secure the UN objectives and not their own. Moreover, overly broad and ambiguous authorizations should be interpreted narrowly to ensure that the Council retains appropriate control over the military operation it spawns.[13] As part III below demonstrates, such a rule would not unduly interfere with the military requirements of the contracting-out model.

---

[12] *See* Bruce Russett & James S. Sutterlin, *The UN in a New World Order*, FOREIGN AFF., Spring 1991, at 69, 77.

[13] There are two important questions that can arise when interpreting ambiguous language in an authorizing resolution. The first, dealt with by this article, concerns a basic policy decision: what are the objectives for which the Security Council has authorized the use of force? We argue that the Council must clearly specify its objectives. Language that broadly authorizes a range of unspecified goals ought to be narrowly interpreted to

128   THE AMERICAN JOURNAL OF INTERNATIONAL LAW   [Vol. 93:124

Security Council control over authorization of the use of force is required not merely to ensure that states resort to force for international rather than national ends. It is also required to fulfill a second constitutive principle of the United Nations, stated in the Charter's stirring preamble: "to save succeeding generations from the scourge of war." A preeminent purpose of the Charter, set forth in Article 1, is "to bring about by peaceful means . . . settlement of international disputes . . . which might lead to a breach of the peace." While Article 1 also articulates as a purpose of the United Nations "to take effective collective measures for the prevention and removal of threats to the peace, and for the suppression of acts of aggression," it is nonetheless true "that the United Nations was founded to be attentive first and foremost to peaceful settlement of international disputes and to rely on the military instrument of policy only as an extreme last resort."[14]

The Charter presumption that peaceful means will be used to settle international disputes is a substantive principle that confers responsibility on the Security Council not only to control uses of force, but also to use force solely as a last resort and to minimize its extent. The general Charter principle that strongly promotes the peaceful resolution of disputes entails the following: (1) that implicit authorizations of force be disfavored; (2) that explicit authorizations be interpreted narrowly to prevent contractee states from formulating the objectives so as to exceed the Council's clear intentions; and (3) that authorizations terminate when the goals of the operation are met and a permanent cease-fire established.

The Charter requirement of explicit authorization by the Security Council for the use of force is supported by Articles 33 and 42. The provision in Article 42 that the Council

---

ensure Council control over the pursuit of the stated objectives and to prevent an escalation of fighting to achieve goals not clearly intended.

The second issue is whether an authorizing resolution supports the military tactics employed by the contractee states. For example, while the resolution might clearly articulate the Council's goal, disputes might arise over the extent of violence used by the authorized states. In this context, it could be argued that the Charter's preference for peaceful settlement of disputes requires a narrow reading of the authorizing resolution, not merely as to the ends of the operation, but as to the means to be employed. This article does not address that question.

However, we do offer some tentative comments on that second issue. First, by way of example, issues as to the appropriate ends and means arose in the coalition's bombing of Iraq during the gulf war. Some nations criticized the bombing campaign as directed at destroying Iraq's military and industrial capacity—an objective they claimed was not intended by Resolution 678. Had the United States and the United Kingdom argued that the bombing campaign was justified by the broad language "restoring international peace and security," we would urge that this language should be interpreted narrowly, and only supported the aim clearly intended by the Council, forcing the Iraqi withdrawal from Kuwait.

However, the United States and Britain argued that the bombing was directed at forcing Iraq from Kuwait. That claim could be evaluated from the perspective of two sources of law. The first is not based on the authorizing resolution but, rather, deals with limitations imposed by the general laws of warfare, particularly rules regarding proportionality. Here, the main question is which rules apply? One position would apply the customary laws of war and whatever treaty norms the contractee states happen to have accepted. A competing view would hold that customary law and those multilateral treaties negotiated under UN auspices and ratified by a majority of UN members should apply.

Second, the Resolution 678 authorization of "all necessary means" to force Iraq out of Kuwait could be read narrowly to limit the coalition's military tactics to those directly related to forcing an Iraqi withdrawal. This would not include bombing bridges and buildings far from the theater of military operations. Our reading of the preference for peaceful settlement in the Charter leads us to sympathize with this view. Nonetheless, such a narrow reading is certain to be rejected by many contractee states and scholars on the ground that it unduly interferes with military effectiveness in ensuring that the Security Council's objectives are met. We might like to see such a rule applied, but the practical and theoretical difficulties of implementation in the current situation make it difficult. Consequently, we argue for greater Council control and a narrow interpretation of the strategic objectives for which force can be used, rather than of the military means used to achieve those objectives. Of course, there can be a very hazy line between tactics and objectives—and, therefore, at times it will be difficult to implement the rule we suggest. *See generally* part III *infra.*

[14] Weston, *supra* note 10, at 526 n.60; *see also id.* at 527, 533; Richard A. Falk, *The United Nations and the Rule of Law,* 4 TRANSNAT'L L. & CONTEMP. PROBS. 611, 634 (1994).

Collective Security Law

may authorize force only after determining that nonlethal sanctions under Article 41 would be or are inadequate suggests that open-ended or vague delegations of authority are inappropriate. Certainly, a rule that the Council must determine that nonmilitary measures are inadequate would also mean that it must clearly determine that military measures are necessary. Both rules flow from the principle underlying Article 42: that armed force should be used only as a last resort.[15] Embedded in the substantive principle that force be used only as a last resort is a procedural requirement that the deliberative body authorizing force do so clearly and specifically. The obligation under Article 33 that the parties to any dispute must first seek a resolution by peaceful means further supports the Article 41 principle. Requiring clear Security Council authorization acts as a brake on the use of force by the international community: it is a procedural condition designed to fulfill the Charter's substantive goal of ensuring that force be employed only when absolutely necessary.

The requirement of explicit authorization can be met by language evincing a clear intent on the part of the Security Council. Diplomatic considerations may require that the text of a resolution not use the term "force" explicitly. In 1990 the United States apparently wanted an explicit reference to the use of military force against Iraq, but owing to Soviet objections the Council substituted the language "all necessary means."[16] In that case, however, it was clear that the Council's intent was to authorize the use of force. While the Council's language may occasionally bow to diplomatic necessity, a core requirement of the Charter would be transformed if individual nations were permitted to use force when the Council's language and intent are both ambiguous.

Second, although the Charter clearly empowers the Security Council to employ force to combat threats to or breaches of the peace, Council authorizations of force must be interpreted in light of the Charter's goal of minimizing violence in the international community. It should not be presumed that the Security Council has authorized the greatest amount of violence that might be inferred from a broad authorization. The opposite presumption should apply: while force can be used to carry out the specific objectives in the authorizing resolution, ambiguous or broad language in the resolution that might be read to encompass force for objectives not clearly intended by the Council should be interpreted narrowly. For example, Resolution 678 clearly authorized force to oust Iraq from Kuwait, but the broad provision on restoring international peace and security ought to be read in the context of that purpose. It should not be interpreted to authorize an escalation of the fighting that would remove the Government of Iraq or enforce weapons inspections.

Finally, the Charter's preference for settling disputes by peaceful means and the Article 2(4) prohibition on the use of nondefensive force require that a UN authorization of force terminate when a permanent cease-fire is negotiated. Armed responses to breaches of cease-fire agreements cannot be made by individual states; a new Security Council authorization must be adopted.

These principles ought to be in the interest of the permanent members of the Security Council, as well as the smaller states that constitute a majority of the United Nations. If contractee states refuse to accept clear limitations on the scope and duration of their delegated authority, construe unclear Security Council language to imply authority to use force where no such authority was intended, or stretch the terms of their contracted authority beyond what most Council members support, the result may be increased reluctance to contract out the use of force. The consequence of such a conflict in the

---

[15] *See* Frederic L. Kirgis, *The Security Council's First Fifty Years*, 89 AJIL 506, 522 (1995).

[16] *See* Quigley, *supra* note 10, at 262 (citing Bob Woodward, The Commanders 334 (1991)).

current geopolitical circumstances would be to undermine the Security Council's role in multilateral collective security and probably increase the unilateral uses of force by militarily powerful nations.

II. THE REQUIREMENT OF CLEAR SECURITY COUNCIL AUTHORIZATION OF FORCE

Disputes have arisen over whether a state or group of states claiming to be acting pursuant to implied or ambiguous Security Council authorization are acting lawfully. Both the Iraqi inspection dispute of early 1998 and the looming Kosovo crisis later that year raised questions whether Security Council ambiguity, acquiescence, approving statements or even silence suffices to provide authorization for the use of force. As a textual matter, the Charter requires the Security Council to approve affirmatively of nondefensive uses of force. Acquiescence does not suffice. To infer Council authorization either from silence, or from the obscure interstices of Council resolutions, undermines this Charter mandate.

Nonetheless, governments and scholars have argued with regard to various international incidents involving the use of force that it was lawfully employed pursuant to implied authorization by the Security Council. These claims of implied authorizations have been disputed within the international community. However, such claims may well multiply in the future as interventionist pressures increase and the Council resists acting directly. The post–Cold War environment militates against forceful unilateral intervention, increasing pressure on states to find at least some form of multilateral authority to justify their forceful action.

Claims of Implied Authorizations of Force

The general political pressure to find implied authorization in Security Council acquiescence or ambivalence rests on construing the purpose of the United Nations to maintain international peace and security as requiring forceful action to remove threats to the peace. Rogue states that flout Council resolutions or otherwise threaten the peace, or states that commit gross human rights violations against their citizens, ought to be penalized. Thus, in the absence of effective UN sanctions, world order requires that individual states or regional organizations provide an effective remedy. As one commentator notes, "Article 2(4) was never an independent ethical imperative of pacifism" but can be understood only in the context of an organization premised on the "indispensability of the use of force to maintain community order."[17]

The inability of the Security Council to authorize force when some believe it to be clearly needed propels the search for implied authorizations. Some argue that diplomatic and political reality may preclude the Council from publicly authorizing actions that its members privately desire or at least would accept.[18] When a group of states act to enforce a Security Council resolution that the Council itself is unwilling to enforce—as

[17] W. Michael Reisman, *Coercion and Self-Determination: Construing Charter Article 2(4)*, 78 AJIL 642, 642 (1984).

[18] *See* Anthony D'Amato, *Israel's Air Strike upon the Iraqi Nuclear Reactor*, 77 AJIL 584, 586 (1983) ("There is a subtle interplay of politics and acquiescence that renders any demand for 'unambiguous authorization' unrealistic."); *see also* Jane E. Stromseth, *Iraq's Repression of Its Civilian Population: Collective Responses and Continuing Challenges*, in ENFORCING RESTRAINT: COLLECTIVE INTERVENTION IN INTERNAL CONFLICTS 100 (Lori F. Damrosch ed., 1993) (ambiguity of Resolution 688, which the allies relied on for legal support of their military operation to provide safe havens, was viewed as both necessity and virtue by allowing China and other nations to acquiesce in the action without authorizing it de jure); Barbara Crossette, *UN Rebuffs U.S. on Threat to Iraq if it Breaks Pact*, N.Y. TIMES, Mar. 3, 1998, at A1 (State Department spokesman James Rubin calling final wording of Resolution 1154 "not as relevant as . . . private discussions").

was arguably the case in the recent Iraqi inspection crisis—the argument can be made that those states are not acting unilaterally, but on behalf of a clearly articulated community mandate.

Political necessity finds a home in legal realist theory. That theory eschews or tempers formal textual rules, in favor of the law's operational code, which can be derived only from a contextual and empirical analysis of how elites actually behave. From this perspective, arguments that an implied Security Council authorization exists and is sufficient, reflect the elite's willingness to tolerate certain forceful action by individual states, even if such behavior conflicts with the formal rules embodied in the UN Charter.

An examination of six international incidents[19] in which implied authorization has been suggested cautions against this approach because of the difficulty of determining when an action has been impliedly authorized, the uncertainty in the law and the potential for abuse.

(1) In 1961 India seized Goa from Portugal, arguing, inter alia, that it was enforcing UN resolutions against colonialism. Professor Quincy Wright rejected this reasoning, which he considered to be a claim based upon an implied authorization.[20] While a majority of the Security Council opposed India's claim,[21] many newly independent states in Africa, as well as the Soviet Union, believed that colonization was such an evil that the use of force against it should be tolerated. This political view led to the United Nations' de facto acquiescence in India's takeover of Goa, which might be perceived as an implicit, after-the-fact authorization. Such an implied authorization loosens the restraints on the use of force; it encourages states to use force when they believe their actions will be tolerated for political reasons by a majority of states.

(2) In 1962 the United States, admitting that it was not explicit, argued that it had implied Security Council authorization to interdict Soviet ships en route to Cuba.[22] The key factors supporting this alleged implied authorization were that the Council, by general consent, had not voted on the Soviet resolution disapproving the U.S. action and had encouraged a negotiated settlement.[23]

The U.S. case for implied authorization seems strained. In fact, the Council had also refrained from acting on a U.S. draft resolution that would have expressed approval of the U.S. action.[24] Moreover, if failure to adopt a resolution condemning the use of force is dispositive, what if the Council votes to condemn by a wide margin, but the resolution is vetoed by a permanent member? At a minimum, the analysis calls for a deeper

---

[19] For the argument that the study of key actors' responses to a critical event or incident is an important methodology for understanding whether formal laws have genuine significance, see INTERNATIONAL INCIDENTS, THE LAW THAT COUNTS IN WORLD POLITICS (W. Michael Reisman & Andrew R. Willard eds., 1988).

[20] Quincy Wright, *The Goa Incident*, 56 AJIL 617, 629 (1962).

[21] A draft resolution by the three permanent Western members and Turkey on behalf of Portugal's complaint of Indian aggression called for a cease-fire and Indian withdrawal. Seven Council members supported the resolution, which was vetoed by the Soviet Union. The Council also failed to adopt a resolution supported by four members to reject the Portuguese complaint. In these circumstances, Council silence suggests implied disapproval and not authorization. *Id.* at 628.

[22] *See* Abram Chayes, *Law and the Quarantine of Cuba*, 41 FOREIGN AFF. 550, 556 (1963):

> [T]he debates in the Security Council in the case of the Dominican Republic revealed a widespread readiness to conclude that the requirement of "authorization" does not impart prior approval, but would be satisfied by subsequent action of the Council, or even by a mere "taking note" of the acts of the regional organization.

See also Leonard Meeker, *Defensive Quarantine and the Law*, 57 AJIL 515, 522 (1963) (paralysis of the Council and UN constitutional evolution undermine requirement of explicit authorization).

[23] *See* Chayes, *supra* note 22, at 556; Meeker, *supra* note 22, at 522.

[24] *See* Michael Akehurst, *Enforcement Action by Regional Agencies, With Special Reference to the Organization of American States*, 42 BRIT. Y.B. INT'L L. 175, 217 (1967).

understanding of why the resolution was not enacted. But such an analysis will often be impossible, since we can never know dispositively what motivated each Security Council member.[25]

(3) Professor Anthony D'Amato's claim that the Israeli 1981 air strike against the Osiraq nuclear reactor was an example of implicit Security Council approval of an armed action takes the 1962 U.S. argument to its extreme.[26] In this case, the Security Council was not silent but "[s]*trongly condemn[ed]*" the air strike.[27] Yet for D'Amato the condemnation was pro forma because it contained no sanctions against Israel. D'Amato relies on this failure to claim that "it is often politically expedient for the community to condemn a forceful initiative in explicit terms, yet to approve of it in fact by stopping short of reprisals against the initiator."[28]

D'Amato's argument that symbolic condemnation illustrates that the international community politically tolerates the act may express a certain reality in international affairs.[29] But to take the additional step and argue that explicit disapproval constitutes implied consent renders the concept of authorization indeterminate and highly speculative. Are human rights resolutions that denounce abuses but impose no sanctions merely expressions of implied approval of those abuses? Who determines whether a particular Security Council action or series of actions is strong enough to constitute genuine disapproval?

(4) The one time that the Security Council may very well have implicitly authorized a use of force was in Liberia in 1990, although it was after the fact. In August 1990, armed forces from five member states of ECOWAS intervened in Liberia to attempt to stop a civil war. ECOWAS had no explicit Security Council authorization to do so, although subsequent Council actions tacitly accepted and expressed praise for the intervention.[30] This appears to be the only case in which the Security Council's implicit approval was uncontested. The Liberian example, however, still presents the danger that it will encourage regional organizations to use force first in the hope of inducing later Security Council approval.

(5) The 1991 effort by the United States, the United Kingdom and France to provide safe havens to the Kurdish refugees in northern Iraq and to enforce no-fly zones in both northern and southern Iraq has been justified on the ground that these actions were implicitly authorized by UN resolutions.[31] Those legal claims were disputed by Secretary-General Javier Pérez de Cuéllar, who concluded that a foreign military presence on Iraqi territory required either the express authorization of the Security Council or Iraqi consent. While many UN members acquiesced in the safe-haven operation, some raised concerns about the absence of explicit Council endorsement; furthermore, both Soviet

---

[25] Professor Akehurst claims that the U.S. attempt to equate authorization with acquiescence contradicted U.S. policy prior to 1960 and that the United States apparently abandoned its creative definition of authorization in the 1965 Dominican dispute, although his evidence for the latter position seems inconclusive. *See id.* at 219. Apparently, most states rejected the U.S. position on implied authorization. *See* David Wippman, *Enforcing the Peace: ECOWAS and the Liberian Civil War, in* ENFORCING RESTRAINT, *supra* note 18, at 157, 187.

[26] D'Amato, *supra* note 18; Anthony D'Amato, *Israel's Air Strike Against the Osiraq Reactor: A Retrospective,* 10 TEMP. INT'L & COMP. L.J. 259, 262–63 (1996).

[27] SC Res. 487, UN SCOR, 36th Sess., Res. & Dec., at 10, UN Doc. S/INF/37 (1981).

[28] D'Amato, *supra* note 18, at 586; *see also* D'Amato, *supra* note 26, at 262 (resolution can only be seen as covert support for Israel's air strike).

[29] *See also* W. MICHAEL REISMAN & JAMES E. BAKER, REGULATING COVERT ACTION: PRACTICES, CONTEXT AND POLICIES OF COVERT COERCION ABROAD IN INTERNATIONAL AND AMERICAN LAW 101–13 (1992).

[30] *See* Wippman, *supra* note 25, at 165, 185–86; Lori F. Damrosch, *Concluding Reflections, in* ENFORCING RESTRAINT, *supra* note 18, at 348, 357 ("authorization" could arguably have been inferred within the meaning of Charter Article 53 from acquiescence or from a previous cautiously worded statement on the Council's behalf).

[31] *See* Stromseth, *supra* note 18, at 77.

and Chinese officials opposed deploying either UN forces or foreign states' military forces to protect Iraqi civilians without their government's consent.[32] Baghdad ultimately agreed to the deployment of five hundred armed UN guards on Iraqi territory to protect UN humanitarian workers.

The establishment of the no-fly zones in northern and southern Iraq was based on similar theories of implied authorization and acquiescence. In August 1992, the proposed southern no-fly zone was "widely criticized" in the United Nations as going beyond any legal mandate and the Non-Aligned Group said that any move to attack Iraqi planes would not receive Security Council backing.[33] After the last of the January 1993 raids on Baghdad, the UN Legal Department endorsed a chorus of criticism of the raids, stating that "the Security Council made no provision for enforcing the bans on Iraqi warplanes."[34] When, in September 1996, the United States conducted military strikes to enforce an extended southern no-fly zone, it earned only lukewarm support from its allies and criticism from Russia and most of the members of the Security Council.[35]

(6) Finally, the present U.S. claim to the forcible enforcement of the inspection regime also relies on implied authorization. Undersecretary of State and former UN Ambassador Thomas Pickering adopted the U.S. position taken in 1962 regarding Cuba by arguing that Resolution 1154 does not preclude the unilateral use of force. Pickering argues that a key factor in interpreting that resolution is that the United States was able to persuade other Security Council members not to include language explicitly requiring it to return to the Council to obtain authorization for force.[36] But the failure to adopt a resolution opposing U.S. action cannot be deemed dispositive when any such resolution would have been fruitless in the face of the U.S. and UK veto power. Still, the Council did the next best thing: it adopted a resolution that did not provide the United States with the authority it sought and the members stated their understanding that the resolution was intended to preclude any such authority.

In sum, this admittedly brief survey of state and Security Council practice on implied authorization arguments suggests three propositions: (1) that while there have been occasional attempts to justify uses of force under the theory of implied authorizations, those incidents do not amount to a "systematic, unbroken practice"—to use Justice Frankfurter's phrase from the *Youngstown Sheet and Tube* case[37]—that warrants a "gloss" on the Charter's requirement of explicit Security Council approval; (2) that most of these claims of implied authorization have been strongly contested; and, most important, (3) that the difficulty of determining whether an authorization has been implied and the resulting uncertainty for world order counsel caution in adopting any such reading of Security Council actions. There are others who might view the incidents we have discussed through a different prism. However, the difficulty of divining and attributing motivations to state actors and of interpreting unrecorded or informal Security Council discussions suggests that a world order that permits implied Council authorizations to

---

[32] *See id.* at 90.

[33] Alan Philps, *Allies deny plan to dismember Iraq,* DAILY TELEGRAPH (London), Aug. 22, 1992, at 9.

[34] *See France Says U.S. Raid Exceeded UN Resolutions,* SAN DIEGO UNION-TRIB., Jan. 21, 1993, at A1.

[35] *See* Alain E. Boileau, *To the Suburbs of Baghdad: Clinton's Extension of the Southern Iraqi No-Fly Zone,* 3 ILSA J. INT'L & COMP. L. 875, 890 (1997).

[36] *See* Pickering, *supra* note 7, at 5.

[37] Youngstown Sheet & Tube Co. v. Sawyer, 343 U.S. 599, 610–11 (1952) (Frankfurter, J., concurring).

use force would depend not on the clearly held expectations of states but, rather, on the nuanced interpretation of ambiguous state actions. That seems to be a dubious way to implement a basic international norm.

Explicit Security Council Authorization and Peace and World Order

The UN Charter requirement that nondefensive uses of force be explicitly authorized by the Security Council comports with both the purposes of the Charter and the needs of a peaceful and stable world public order. The maintenance of collective security was and remains an important goal of the Charter. However, another key purpose, perhaps even the overriding one, was to develop an international system that, while not pacifist, strongly favors resolution of disputes by peaceful means. That presumption of peaceful means requires that ambiguity be interpreted against warfare, a mandate that supports a rule that Security Council authorizations to use force must be clear and unambiguous. Article 42 reflects the presumption of peaceful means by specifying that the Council may decide to authorize the use of force only after determining that other measures are insufficient.

Implied Security Council authorization to use force is often inferred from the Council's condemnation of a nation's action as a threat to the peace.[38] But making that inference is unwarranted; it contradicts the Charter's requirement that the Security Council must determine both that a threat to the peace exists and that peaceful means cannot resolve the situation. In many cases, as in the Iraqi and Kosovo crises of 1998, the Council will have declared a threat to the peace but will not have affirmed the need for military action. In those situations, the requirement of explicit Security Council approval of uses of force reflects the substantive value that force not be used too hastily to resolve international disputes. The more nations understand that the authority to use force can be difficult to obtain, the greater their efforts will be to find peaceful, creative negotiated solutions to problems.

A world order that would allow nations to use force unilaterally under the guise of creative or disputed interpretations of vague language in Security Council resolutions or by the Council's failure to act would undermine Article 2(4). Powerful member states could use that theory to justify the use of force in their own national interest. The potential havoc wreaked by such a legal regime counsels restraint—restraint to be found in the legal requirement that Security Council delegations of authority to use force be both clear and narrowly construed.

If the Security Council is dysfunctional or paralyzed by the exercise of the veto, as arguably occurred during the Cold War, the case for implied authorization might be stronger. However, Council practice since the Cold War simply does not support any great need for a flexible reinterpretation of the Charter to support the actual behavior of states. Five times in the past eight years the Security Council has clearly authorized the use of force to address threats to world peace.[39]

---

[38] For example, in both the Iraqi and the Kosovo crises, the Council's determinations that the respective Iraqi and Serb actions posed Chapter VII threats to the peace were claimed by the United States to permit the use of force without the need for explicit Council authorization.

[39] *See, e.g.*, SC Res. 678, *supra* note 7 (authorizing use of "all necessary means" to liberate Kuwait); SC Res. 794, UN SCOR, 47th Sess., Res. & Dec., at 63, UN Doc. S/INF/48 (1992) (authorizing "all necessary means to establish as soon as possible a secure environment for humanitarian relief operations in Somalia"); SC Res. 940, UN SCOR, 49th Sess., Res. & Dec., at 51, UN Doc. S/INF/50 (1994) (authorizing member states "to form a multinational force . . . and . . . to use all necessary means to facilitate the departure from Haiti of the military leadership"); SC Res. 929, *id* at 10 (authorizing France to use "all necessary means" to protect civilians in Rwanda); and SC Res. 770, UN SCOR, 47th Sess., Res. & Dec., *supra*, at 24, and 816, *id.*, 48th Sess., Res. & Dec., at 4, UN Doc. S/INF/49 (1993) (authorizing states to take "all measures necessary" to facilitate delivery of

Collective Security Law

At times, such an authorization is hard to obtain, but that is the way things ought to work. That China, India, Russia and occasionally France balk at what they consider an inappropriate use of force is not cause for concern; rather, it should lead observers to conclude that the Council retains some vitality as a restraint on war making. It was established to be not merely a forceful initiator of collective enforcement measures, but also a restraining influence on the unwarranted or hasty rush to forcible solutions. While the situation may have changed from that prevailing in the early 1990s and authorization may be harder to obtain, that fact does not warrant bypassing the Security Council. Indeed, the recent controversies regarding Iraq afford hope that the Council will play its contemplated role of authorizing force only as a last resort. World order requires a Security Council that can find the proper balance between authorizing the collective use of force when there is both a compelling need and no peaceful alternative, and not succumbing to economic and political pressure by powerful nations[40] seeking a multi-lateral cover for what is in essence the unilateral use of force.

In the long-term interest of world order, it is imperative that the Security Council be actively engaged in determining whether force ought to be employed by the international community.[41] A rule that allows acquiescence to constitute authorization and that substitutes ambiguity for clear intent would encourage the Security Council to avoid deciding when the use of force is necessary and appropriate. Acquiescence begets more acquiescence, and once a custom of allowing nations to take forceful action under claims based on ambiguous authority is established, it will develop a momentum of its own. For example, the failure to provide explicit legal authority for the ECOWAS intervention suggests that the Security Council, which seemed unanimously to approve of the action, nevertheless chose to avoid its responsibility to authorize it explicitly. Allowing cases like the ECOWAS intervention to legitimate implied authorization will merely encourage the Security Council to avoid taking stands on difficult issues of when to use force.[42]

---

humanitarian assistance and enforce no-fly zone in Bosnia). The examples of the use of force subsequent to the gulf war against Iraq are not uncontroverted and are dealt with in part III *infra*.

[40] *See, e.g.*, Weston, *supra* note 10, at 523–24 (describing pressures brought to bear on Council members prior to the vote on Resolution 678).

[41] The U.S. constitutional experience with the doctrine of implied authorization of force favors rejection of such a doctrine on the international level. Just as the United States sought to bypass the cumbersome and difficult process of securing Security Council authorization to use force against Iraq by inferring extant Council authority, so post–World War II U.S. Presidents have often avoided seeking explicit congressional authorization and instead construed implied authority to use force from legislative enactments such as appropriations statutes. *See War Powers, Libya, and State-Sponsored Terrorism: Hearings Before the Subcomm. on Arms Control, International Security, and Science of the House Comm. on Foreign Affairs,* 99th Cong., 2d Sess. 5, 10, 29 (1986) (testimony of State Department Legal Adviser Abraham D. Sofaer). *See also* MICHAEL J. GLENNON, CONSTITU-TIONAL DIPLOMACY 100–02 (1990); *War Powers Legislation: Hearings Before the Senate Comm. on Foreign Relations,* 92d Cong., 1st Sess. 103, 587, 650 (1971). Legislative acquiescence in presidential unilateral war making has also been construed by the Executive as constituting implied authorization. The result of all this has been a general decline in the congressional role on the initiation of hostilities.

[42] The question of institutional responsibility fundamentally distinguishes authorization by acquiescence from the problem of Article 27(3) voting. Charter Article 27(3) provides that Security Council action requires "the concurring votes of the permanent members." Despite the apparent clarity of this language, the Organization's consistent practice has been to permit passage of a resolution despite the absence of or abstention by permanent members. *See* Myres S. McDougal & Richard Gardner, *The Veto and the Charter: An Interpretation for Survival,* 60 YALE L.J. 258, 278 (1951); Constantin A. Stavropoulos, *The Practice of Voluntary Abstentions by Permanent Members of the Security Council Under Article 27, Paragraph 3, of the Charter of the United Nations,* 61 AJIL 737, 742 (1967). Both Chayes and Meeker argued during the Cuban missile crisis that, just as political necessity called for treating abstention as meeting the requirement of concurring votes, so acquiescence by the Security Council could constitute the required authorization. *See* Meeker, *supra* note 22, at 522; Chayes, *supra* note 22, at 556.

Apart from the fact that the custom on the meaning of Article 27(3) is based on the *travaux préparatoires* and a continuous and generally accepted practice that does not exist for implied Security Council authorizations of force, *see* Akehurst, *supra* note 24, at 217, a clear difference exists between abstention by a permanent

In addition to promoting the peaceful resolution of disputes and the Security Council's assumption of responsibility, requiring a clear Council authorization is necessary to ensure that the world community affirmatively supports the use of force and does not merely acquiesce in the actions of a powerful state. Allowing ambiguity in the authorization of force enables powerful states to pick and choose which Council resolutions to enforce and more generally to act unilaterally under the guise of multilateral authority. Ambiguity is often the handmaiden of great-power assertiveness. James Madison's insight that government cannot be based on the proposition that men are angels may be appropriately applied to the behavior of states. It is certainly rare for a nation to be motivated not primarily by its own national interest, but in the community's interest. The history of humanitarian intervention is replete with invocations of humanitarian goals by strong powers or multilateral coalitions to justify their own geopolitical interests.[43]

Of course, situations will arise in which most UN members will want the United States or some other state to be able to use force, and China or some other state or bloc of states may be unalterably opposed. But in the extreme case of an ongoing genocide for which the Security Council will not authorize force, perhaps the formal law ought to be violated to achieve the higher goal of saving thousands or millions of lives. In these circumstances, the acting state would have to weigh the risk of universal condemnation and sanctions. Thus, it would have to make a convincing case that the military action is not based on a mere pretext and will be effective and proportionate. Silence by the Security Council might then reflect a community consensus that the legal requirement for its authorization ought to give way to the moral imperative. That extreme case is unusual, however, and certainly does not resemble the recent Iraqi inspection crisis. While the accusation that Iraq is still seeking to develop weapons of mass destruction alleges a serious threat to the peace, no one claims either that Iraq is currently employing such weapons to kill thousands of people, or that it has the capability, opportunity or intention of imminently doing so.[44] Only claims of this magnitude might fit the extreme cases that would possibly justify using force in violation of international law. In dealing with those cases, it is

---

member and acquiescence by the Council as a body. Such abstention presumptively means that despite its concerns or objection to the resolution, the permanent member is willing to allow the measure to pass; no such intent can be presumptively imputed to failure by the Council to condemn a particular use of force. *See id.* Most important, while Security Council members have no responsibility to vote yes or no on a resolution and ought not to be forced to do so, the Council does have a responsibility to act or refuse to act as a body regarding a breach of the peace. Not permitting permanent members' abstention or absence to act as a veto fosters open responsibility on their part, *see* McDougal & Gardner, *supra,* at 286; allowing Council acquiescence to act as authorization fosters abdication.

[43] *See* Thomas M. Franck & Nigel S. Rodley, *After Bangladesh: The Law of Humanitarian Intervention by Military Force,* 67 AJIL 275 (1973). Franck and Rodley examine the historical record of humanitarian interventions and conclude that "[i]n very few, if any, instances has the right [to humanitarian intervention] been asserted under circumstances that appear more humanitarian than self-interested and power-seeking." *Id.* at 290. "[T]he kind of unilateral military intervention which has occurred in the past is usually not to be encouraged . . . those kinds of intervention which it would be desirable to encourage have for reasons of self-interest almost never occurred in the past . . . . " *Id.* at 305. *See also* Falk, *supra* note 10 (summarizing prior U.S. interventions); Marc Trachtenberg, *Intervention in Historical Perspective, in* EMERGING NORMS OF JUSTIFIED INTERVENTION 15 (Laura W. Reed & Carl Kaysen eds., 1993); Oscar Schachter, *The Legality of Pro-Democratic Invasion,* 78 AJIL 645, 650 (1984); Corfu Channel (Merits), 1949 ICJ REP. 4, 35 (Apr. 9) (noting that a right of intervention by force "has, in the past, given rise to most serious abuses . . . . [F]rom the nature of things, it would be reserved for the most powerful States . . .").

[44] That Russia, France, China, a majority of the Security Council, other key members of the 1991 coalition such as Egypt, Syria and Pakistan, many of our Middle East allies such as Turkey, and what undoubtedly was a majority of member states of the United Nations opposed military action demonstrates that the international community did not view the threat posed by Iraq as warranting the use of force. *See* Bruce W. Nelan, *Selling the War Badly,* TIME, Mar. 2, 1998, at 26; Robin Wright, *What a Difference 7 Years Makes in the Gulf,* L.A. TIMES, Feb. 18, 1998, at A10. Usually reliable allies such as Egypt and Pakistan specially attended the Council meeting on Resolution 1154 and strongly advised against the use of force.

preferable to recognize that on the rare occasions when a nation is solely motivated by humane considerations, it must violate the law to save humanity, than to use those cases to dilute the prohibition on the unilateral use of force as a whole.

The observations of Thomas Franck and Nigel Rodley as to the desirability of creating exceptions to the prohibition on unilateral humanitarian intervention apply with equal force to interventions that rely on implied or ambiguous Security Council authorization:

> In exceptional circumstances . . . a large power may indeed go selflessly to the rescue of a foreign people facing oppression. But surely no general law is needed to cover such actions. . . . [I]n human experience it has proven wiser to outlaw absolutely conduct which, in practical experience, is almost invariably harmful, rather than to try to provide general exceptions for rare cases. Cannibalism, given its history and man's propensities, is simply outlawed, while provision is made to mitigate the effect of this law on men adrift in a lifeboat. The hortatory, norm-building effect of a total ban is greater than that of a qualified prohibition, especially at that stage of its legal life when the norm is still struggling for general recognition. This is a question of balance. So long as the preponderant predictable applications of a proposed exception to the prohibition on unilateral force are socially undesirable—and the historical record so indicates—the exception should not be made.[45]

Some scholars and officials argue that UN diplomacy is at times aided by a unilateral threat by powerful states to use force and cite the U.S. threat against Iraq as having been necessary to end the 1998 inspection crisis.[46] But even if the U.S. threat did play a role,[47] that merely suggests that illegal action can at times have useful consequences, at least in the short run. The rule of law requires that we sometimes sacrifice using force to punish people or regimes that are evil so as to secure a more peaceful domestic and world order.

International law, the United Nations and multilateralism require that a nation must accept the limits imposed by law as well as the power endowed by it. That the world community and the Security Council are occasionally more reluctant to use force than our policy makers would like is a restraint imposed by the international legal system. Unless we are prepared to concede that all nations have a right to use force to enforce Security Council resolutions—a result that the United States would not favor—we ought to accept the Charter's legal regime with the clear recognition that it sometimes requires us to forgo policy options we may prefer. Multilateralism obliges nation-states to define their national interest in a manner that does not conflict with the international community's view of its interest. Multilateralism is thus tied to respect for international law. Multilateralism is not a tactic; it is an end that furthers respect for international law.[48]

III. DRAFTING AND INTERPRETING AUTHORIZATIONS TO USE FORCE

The basic principle that the use of force in international relations other than in the exercise of self-defense requires an express authorization by the UN Security Council leaves open the question of how explicit authorizations should be drafted and interpreted. The requirement of explicit authorization implies the corollary that implemen-

---

[45] Franck & Rodley, *supra* note 43, at 290–91.

[46] *See* Ruth Wedgwood, *The Enforcement of Security Council Resolution 687: The Threat of Force against Iraq's Weapons of Mass Destruction,* 92 AJIL 724 (1998).

[47] Secretary-General Annan and French President Chirac both recognized the useful role of the American and British threat to use force in diplomatically ending this crisis. We are not in a position to dispute the accuracy of Annan's observation, but note how often threats of force have failed to secure Hussein's compliance with UN resolutions in the past, most notably in January 1991 and January 1993, when actual force had to be used. We suspect that Annan's personal approach succeeded where the attitude of American diplomats backed by force would not have.

[48] See Madeleine Albright, *The United States and the United Nations: Confrontation or Consensus?* VITAL SPEECHES OF THE DAY, No. 12,354, Apr. 1, 1995, for the view that "multilateralism is a means, not an end."

tation of express authorizations that contain ambiguous language should be confined to objectives that were clearly intended by the Security Council.

The Persian Gulf war and the difficulties attendant on the lengthy process of ensuring Iraqi compliance with the cease-fire agreement highlight the tension between the Security Council's explicit issuance of a broad mandate to states to use force to achieve the Organization's objectives and the pressure those states exerted to interpret that mandate in their own national interests. In November 1990, when Resolution 678 authorized member states to use force to oust Iraq from Kuwait, few, if any, of the Council members could have contemplated that the resolution would authorize the bombing of Iraq to secure compliance with an inspection regime—a requirement imposed only after the war's end and the restoration of Kuwaiti sovereignty. Thus, the recent Iraqi inspection crisis raises an important question regarding Security Council authorizations to use force: how should such resolutions be framed and interpreted so as to achieve the collective-security purposes of the United Nations while limiting the scope and extent of the violence authorized?

Korea and the Gulf War Authorizations

The United Nations experience during the Korean War illustrates the difficulties that arise from broad authorizing language. Resolution 83 of June 27, 1950, authorized "members of the United Nations to furnish such assistance to the Republic of Korea as may be necessary to repel the armed attack and to restore international peace and security in the area."[49] The Security Council's discussion yields little evidence regarding the meaning of "restore international peace and security in the area."[50] Several days after the resolution was adopted, Secretary of State Acheson stated that U.S. actions taken "pursuant to the Security Council resolution" were "solely for the purpose of restoring the Republic of Korea to its status prior to the invasion from the north and of reestablishing the peace broken by that invasion."[51] However, by the end of September 1950, as a result of the successful allied landing in Inchon, which routed the North Koreans, the United States and its allies faced the question whether to pursue the retreating North Koreans into the North and seek their total destruction. That issue had a legal component: was such action authorized by Resolution 83 or did it require new UN authorization?

Initially, President Truman apparently believed that crossing the parallel required a UN decision. However, shortly thereafter, the Department of State asserted that Resolution 83 provided the requisite authority to pursue the retreating North Koreans.[52] The U.S. ambassador to the United Nations argued that "[f]aithful adherence to the United Nations objective of restoring international peace and security in the area counsels the taking of appropriate steps to eliminate the power and ability of the North Korean aggressor to launch future attacks."[53] The Indian Government and several other states believed that further specific authorization was legally necessary, although the majority of UN members did not oppose the U.S. position.[54] Nonetheless, the United States did submit the issue to the General Assembly, which approved the crossing of the 38th

---

[49] SC Res. 83, UN SCOR, 5th Sess., Res. & Dec., at 4, UN Doc. S/INF/5/Rev.1 (1950).
[50] The phrase tracks Article 39 of the Charter.
[51] *See* LELAND M. GOODRICH, KOREA: A STUDY OF U.S. POLICY IN THE UNITED NATIONS 198 (1956).
[52] *Id.* at 127.
[53] 23 DEP'T ST. BULL. 579 (1950).
[54] *See* I. F. STONE, THE HIDDEN HISTORY OF THE KOREAN WAR 133 (1952).

parallel on October 7, 1950, after South Korean forces under General MacArthur's command were already in North Korean territory.[55]

The legal significance of the U.S. decision to seek additional UN authorization is unclear. The U.S. position was that such authorization was unnecessary because military operations required broad and flexible legal authority to deal with changing situations, authority that had been granted by Resolution 83. As a textual matter, the U.S. argument was strong, particularly because the North Koreans had not indicated any desire for a cease-fire and had suggested that they might strike to the south again.[56] Nevertheless, the fact that for policy reasons the United States sought and obtained new authorization is some evidence of state practice that contractee states do seek further authorization when the objectives of the action change.[57]

The Korean example illustrates that where contractee states seek to escalate warfare in a manner that projects a major change in the political or military objectives that the Security Council intended to authorize—in Korea from repelling the North Korean attack on the South to unifying the country—they should seek new authorization and not rely on ambiguous language in the original resolution. Maintaining the control of the Council over the warfare it authorizes requires that, although operational command may be delegated to states, major policy changes in objectives, or major military actions that seriously threaten to widen the war, must be authorized by the United Nations. A change in objectives poses grave risks of widening the war, a risk that eventuated in Korea. Because of those risks, Security Council resolutions must be interpreted to authorize what was clearly intended, not what can conceivably be justified. The Korean case demonstrates that when broad political agreement exists, the necessary authorization can be obtained fairly quickly without compromising the military situation.

Moreover, when the authorized states seek to widen a war to achieve new political and military objectives, the Charter's presumption in favor of peaceful resolution of disputes requires the Council seriously to consider whether a negotiated settlement can be reached. Since the invocation of new objectives often means that the original objectives have by and large been accomplished—as happened in Korea—a request for new authorization would force the United Nations to thoroughly assess the prospects for a peaceful settlement. Unfortunately, the pressure to pursue the military option to total victory propelled Washington to ignore and frustrate the efforts of Secretary-General Trygve Lie and others to achieve a settlement in October 1950, efforts that might have prevented the loss of hundreds of thousands of lives.[58]

As was the case in Korea, the gulf war mandate of Resolution 678 authorized states to use all necessary means to "restore international peace and security in the area." From a purely textual perspective, that authorization seems to have few, if any, limits. "Area" is undefined and could mean Iraq or the entire Middle East.[59] "Restoring

---

[55] GA Res. 376 (V), UN GAOR, 5th Sess., Supp. No. 20, at 9, UN Doc. A/1775 (1950). The United States turned to the General Assembly because the Soviet delegation had returned to the Security Council and would have vetoed any extension of the UN objectives. The Assembly's resolution did not explicitly state that UN forces were authorized to enter North Korea, but everyone involved understood that such was its intent. *See* D. W. BOWETT, UNITED NATIONS FORCES 43 (1964); TRYGVE LIE, IN THE CAUSE OF PEACE 345 (1954).

[56] *See* LIE, *supra* note 55, at 345.

[57] In a similar sense, President Bush's decision to seek congressional approval of the gulf war was claimed to be political, and not legally necessary, but many have viewed it as evidence that the Executive must seek authorization for military operations of substantial magnitude.

[58] *See, e.g.,* LIE, *supra* note 55, at 345 (describing his peace proposal, which he believed had met with considerable interest in October 1950).

[59] A legal opinion of the UN Deputy Legal Counsel, UN Doc. S/AC.25/1991/Note 15 (1991), held that the word "area" in the prior Resolution 665 on Iraq was not defined geographically and that it was therefore necessary to interpret it in accordance with the context and the object and purpose of the text. *See* Helmut

international peace and security" could mean occupying Iraq, removing Saddam Hussein from power, or bombing Iraq's military/industrial capacity.[60] Officially, the United States never made those broad claims during the war. Indeed, shortly after it ended, U.S. officials testified that Resolution 678 had not granted open-ended authority to occupy Iraq, and that the military incursions into Iraq during the war were authorized only because they were "pursuant to the liberation of Kuwait, which was called for in the UN resolution."[61] Moreover, in response to accusations that the coalition's bombing campaign stretched the boundaries of the Security Council's authorization, many states, including those fighting in the gulf war, declared that their sole purpose was to liberate Kuwait.[62] Thus, if Resolution 678 is still extant, it should be interpreted narrowly and consistently with its object and purpose. The clear intent of the Security Council in 1990 was to provide authority to oust Iraq from Kuwait, not to grant a blanket license for any member state to attack Iraq to enforce inspections mandated after the war.[63]

Limiting the legitimate objectives of UN-authorized uses of force does not unduly affect military efficacy, since it does not restrict the military means or tactics that can be employed but, rather, the political goals for which force can be utilized. Authorized states would retain the discretion to determine the military means needed to achieve the goals clearly articulated by the Security Council. They would not, however, be empowered by ambiguous language to escalate the fighting to achieve objectives not clearly mandated. To adopt the contrary position would essentially be to eviscerate Security Council control over authorized uses of force.

Subsequent to the war, the United States and the United Kingdom interpreted Resolution 678 as authorizing force to achieve compliance with the cease-fire. While incorrect but textually plausible, this interpretation illustrates the problems raised by authorizations that do not specify precise objectives.[64] In our view, the essentially boilerplate language "to restore international peace and security" added no clear meaning or objectives to either the 1950 Korean or the 1990 Persian Gulf authorization. It was

---

Freudenschuß, *Between Unilateralism and Collective Security: Authorizations of the Use of Force by the UN Security Council,* 5 EUR. J. INT'L L. 492, 499 n.21 (1994).

[60] *See* Eugene V. Rostow, *United What? Enforcement Action or Collective Self-Defense?* 85 AJIL 506, 516 (1991) (allied occupation might be deemed necessary); Editorial, *Legitimate Aims of the Allies,* INDEPENDENT (London), Jan. 23, 1991, at 18 (removing Hussein from power required).

[61] Testimony of Assistant Secretary of State John Kelley and Assistant Secretary of Defense Henry Rowen before the Europe and Middle East Subcomm. of the House Comm. on Foreign Affairs, Federal News Service, June 26, 1991, at 151, *available in* LEXIS, News Library, Fednew File.

[62] *See* Statements of Sir David Hannay (UK), UN Doc. S/PV.2977 (Part II) (closed) (1991), *reprinted in* IRAQ AND KUWAIT, *supra* note 10, at 39; Mr. Vorontsov (USSR), *id.* at 45; Mr. Wilenski (Australia), *id.* at 51; Mr. Razali (Malaysia), *id.* at 55.

[63] The use of the term "restore" is further textual evidence of this specific intent; restoration means returning to the status quo prior to the Iraqi invasion of Kuwait. Virtually all of the Security Council members stated in voting for Resolution 678 that they were doing so, in the words of Mr. Hurd, the UK representative, to demand "the reversal of the aggression—namely full compliance with previous resolutions." *See* UN Doc. S/PV.2963, at 82 (1990). As Mr. Shevardnadze of the USSR noted, "The purpose of the resolution we have just adopted is to put an end to the aggression and make it clear to the world that aggression cannot be rewarded." *Id.* at 94–95.

[64] An authorizing resolution could contain ambiguous language for several reasons. The first is poor drafting or insufficient attention to particular language, a problem fairly easily cured. More substantively, ambiguous language could reflect compromises in the negotiating process designed to allow Security Council members subsequently to argue for more or less expansive interpretations. We believe that in those situations, the Charter presumptively favors the less expansive view, which could be overcome only by clear intent to the contrary. Division in the Council over objectives suggests that further debate and authorization are necessary prior to the use of force.

unnecessary and invited difficulties. The legitimate objectives of both wars did not require such open-ended language. They ought to have been limited to the recreation of the status quo ante.

Post–Persian Gulf War Authorizations

Many states were concerned about the minimal role that the Security Council played during the gulf war and the perceived lack of accountability to the Organization of the states that took action pursuant to the authorization. This concern led to attempts by members of the Council to rectify these problems in the authorizations to use force adopted after the gulf war. Some of these authorizations in Bosnia, Somalia, Haiti and Rwanda imposed more extensive consulting requirements. Other provisions focused on providing a unified command and control under UN auspices, or at least on authorizing the Secretary-General to exercise more command over military operations.[65] In Bosnia, a dispute between the United States and the Secretary-General arose as to whether air strikes against Bosnian Serb targets had to be authorized by the Secretary-General and approved by the UN commander.[66] When most of its NATO allies supported the Secretary-General, the United States backed down and recognized UN authority. The Somalia authorizations accorded substantial authority to the Secretary-General as well.[67]

The authorizations since the gulf war have also focused on limiting the mandate granted by the Security Council. In both the Bosnia and the Somalia operations, the Security Council, instead of broadly mandating the use of force as in Resolutions 678 and 83, ratcheted up the level and more precisely delineated the purposes of force to be employed. In Bosnia, the Council enacted specific resolutions, first to authorize force to secure the delivery of humanitarian supplies, next to enforce the no-fly zone, and then to protect the safe havens.[68] In Somalia, the initial Resolution 794 authorized "the Secretary-General and Member States . . . to use all necessary means to establish . . . a secure environment for humanitarian relief operations."[69] That generally worded authorization was interpreted broadly by the Secretary-General, who supported the general disarming of the Somalia factions, and more narrowly by the United States. Security Council Resolution 814, adopted on March 26, 1993, over four months later, explicitly authorized the expansion of the mandate of UNOSOM, the UN force in Somalia.[70] After

---

[65] *See* Quigley, *supra* note 10, at 266–67.

[66] *See* Freudenschuß, *supra* note 59, at 510–11.

[67] Resolution 794 authorized "the Secretary-General and the Member States concerned to make the necessary arrangement for the unified command and control of the forces involved" in the Somalia operation. Resolution 814, expanding UNOSOM's role, and Resolution 837 both authorized the Secretary-General to oversee the use of force. Because of the attempts at unified command and control, the Somalia resolutions were unanimously approved by the Security Council. SC Res. 794, UN SCOR, 47th Sess., Res. & Dec., at 63, UN Doc. S/INF/48 (1992); SC Res. 814, UN SCOR, 48th Sess., Res. & Dec., at 80, UN Doc. S/INF/49 (1993); SC Res. 837, *id.* at 83, para. 5.

[68] On August 13, 1992, Resolution 770 was enacted, calling upon states to take all measures necessary to facilitate the delivery of humanitarian assistance to Sarajevo and other parts of Bosnia. While Britain, France and the United States stressed the narrowness of the authorization, India, Zimbabwe and China still objected to the lack of UN control over the operation and abstained. Almost two months later, the Council established a no-fly zone over Bosnia in Resolution 781, but refused to authorize force to enforce it. Not until March 3, 1993, did the Security Council in Resolution 816 authorize the enforcement of the flight ban and on June 4 adopt Resolution 836 to protect the safe havens. See Freudenschuß, *supra* note 59, at 503–09, for the history of these resolutions.

[69] SC Res. 794, *supra* note 67, para. 10.

[70] Nonetheless, controversy continued as to the scope of the UN mandate and an independent commission established by the Security Council to investigate the ambush of the peacekeeping forces accused the UN force of "overstepping" its mandate. *See* SEAN D. MURPHY, HUMANITARIAN INTERVENTION: THE UNITED NATIONS IN AN EVOLVING WORLD ORDER 235 (1996); Paul Lewis, *Report Faults Commanders of U.N. Forces in Somalia*, N.Y. TIMES, May 20, 1994, at A10. The Somalia case demonstrates that the problem of having commanders interpret their

the attacks against the UN troops by the forces of General Aidid, the Security Council explicitly authorized his arrest in Resolution 837. The Council and participating states did not rely on the arguably broad language of Resolution 794, but specifically authorized each escalation of force.

In addition, the Security Council has placed temporal limits on authorizations. France's authorization to intervene in Rwanda was limited to two months.[71] Resolution 940, which permitted member states to use all necessary means to facilitate the military leadership's departure from Haiti, also contained a more general grant of authority "to establish and maintain a secure and stable environment that will permit implementation of the Governors Island Agreement."[72] The broad mandate under this resolution could arguably have been interpreted to be virtually unlimited. To counteract this problem, Resolution 940 required that the Security Council, not the participating states, should determine when a stable and secure environment had been established and the multinational forces' functions terminated.[73] A termination provision was also included in Resolution 1031, which authorized NATO to use force to implement the Dayton Accords with respect to Bosnia. In that resolution the Council terminated all its prior authorizations in that regard and decided, "with a view to terminating the authorization granted" to the NATO force, to review it within one year to determine whether it should be continued.[74] In Somalia, the original authorization in Resolution 794 contained no time limit, but each subsequent resolution authorized UNOSOM II to use force for a limited period of time (usually about six months).[75] That authorization was periodically renewed until finally terminated on March 31, 1995.[76]

This admittedly brief survey suggests that substantive and temporal limitations on Security Council authorizations are possible; that relatively narrow authorizations are workable; and that contractee states can be required to seek new authorizations to undertake expanded uses of force. On the basis of experience in the Korean War, the Persian Gulf war and these later incidents, we suggest several guidelines regarding the promulgation and interpretation of resolutions authorizing the use of force.

First, resolutions should set forth clear, explicit and limited objectives. They should eschew clauses that would appear to grant nations a blank check to employ force to achieve potentially limitless objectives. In most cases, we believe it possible to achieve reasonable clarity of objectives and avoid indeterminate language such as "restore international peace and security." In some cases, it may prove necessary to use language such as "secure a stable environment." If, however, the objectives cannot be defined

---

mandate too broadly is present even where the operation is directed by a UN commander under the supervision of the Secretary-General. The problem is considerably exacerbated, however, by the contracting-out model. *See generally* MURPHY, *supra*, at 241–42.

[71] SC Res. 929, *supra* note 39.

[72] Several governments objected to Resolution 940, criticizing, inter alia, the lack of a time frame for the proposed action (Mexico) and the similarity between its operative paragraph and Resolution 678 on the gulf crisis (Brazil). UN Doc. S/PV.3413, at 5–9 (1994).

[73] SC Res. 940, *supra* note 39, para. 8. In Haiti, the United States defined its mission narrowly, to return Aristide to power and provide the Haitians with a short rebuilding time. In January 1995, the Security Council determined that a sufficiently stable and secure environment was in place to transfer authority to a UN peacekeeping force. *See* MURPHY, *supra* note 70, at 274.

[74] SC Res. 1031, paras. 19, 21 (Dec. 15, 1995), *reprinted in* 35 ILM 251 (1996).

[75] SC Res. 814, *supra* note 67, para. 6 (mandate for expanded UNOSOM authorized for an initial period through Oct. 31, 1993).

[76] SC Res. 954, UN SCOR, 49th Sess., Res. & Dec., *supra* note 39, at 59. For an excellent overview of the post–Persian Gulf war humanitarian interventions, see MURPHY, *supra* note 70, ch. 5.

Collective Security Law

BYPASSING THE SECURITY COUNCIL

clearly, the Council ought to examine whether authorizing the use of force is advisable and evaluate other mechanisms that would enable it to maintain some control over the operation.

Second, resolutions should be temporally limited, either by a renewable set time period or by a provision requiring the Security Council to determine whether the objective has been achieved. To avoid the possibility of a veto that would permit the authorization to remain in force, the Council might provide that it must approve such determinations by majority vote or supermajority, or require an affirmative vote in order to continue the authorization.[77]

Finally, authorizing resolutions should be interpreted narrowly both to minimize violence and to ensure that the Security Council supports the particular use of force. This guideline is consistent with the provisions on the use of force in the Charter, as well as its object and purpose. A liberal interpretation of such authorizations would not be consistent with the Charter.

Several objections could be made to the foregoing analysis. First, such limitations could be viewed as counterproductive, encouraging noncompliance by the nation being penalized by the Council. For example, the limits contained in post–Persian Gulf war authorizations were criticized by some as being too weak and ineffective. While imposing temporal and substantive limitations on the use of force could possibly hinder UN military operations, the alternative of granting contractee states virtually limitless discretion is more dangerous in that it provides no international check on potentially devastating military escalations.[78]

Second, it could be argued that these recent efforts by the Security Council to control the scope and extent of the uses of force add little to our understanding. In contrast to the Korean and gulf wars, they involved relatively small-scale operations in which the major powers were reluctant to employ force. Thus, in the Bosnia crisis, the Western states and Russia were cautious or opposed to the assertive use of force,[79] and often rejected draft resolutions proposed by the nonaligned members of the Security Council seeking broad authorizations.[80] Similarly, in Somalia the United States initially, and at various points thereafter, sought to narrow the objective for which force would be used, while the Secretary-General pushed to widen the mandate. In these situations, the major

---

[77] Several objections could be raised to this proposal. First, just as Congress cannot circumvent the present-ment and bicameral provisions in the U.S. Constitution by providing for a legislative veto, *see* INS v. Chadha, 462 U.S. 919 (1983), so it could be argued that the Security Council cannot circumvent the Charter's grant of a veto power to the permanent members. However, the Charter, unlike the Constitution, is not premised on separation of powers and the proposed Council action would not be circumventing the power of another branch. Moreover, the rationale for providing the veto does not apply to situations of the "reverse veto." David D. Caron, *The Legitimacy of the Collective Authority of the Security Council,* 87 AJIL 552, 576 (1993). As Caron has persuasively argued, the possibility of modified voting clauses supports the objectives of the United Nations, enhances the legitimacy of Security Council decision making, and should be politically feasible. *Id.* at 584–87.

[78] Our claim is not that Security Council decisions regarding the use of force and its objectives are necessarily wiser than such decisions by individual nations. The Charter is not based on such a presumption. However, the Charter does embody the principles, first, that force should be employed in the interest of the international community and not in the national interest of particular states, and, second, that force should be used only as a last resort. The requirement that the Security Council control the use of force aids in ensuring that force is not used solely to promote national interest; and also acts, in the words of Thomas Jefferson written in the U.S. constitutional context, "to chain the dogs of war." 15 THE PAPERS OF THOMAS JEFFERSON 397 (Julian P. Boyd ed., 1958).

[79] *See* PHYLLIS BENNIS, CALLING THE SHOTS 140–49 (1996).

[80] For example, the Non-Aligned Group circulated a draft resolution in April 1993 that would have "authorized Member States, pursuant to Article 51, to provide all necessary assistance to the Government of Bosnia and Herzegovina to enable it to resist and defend the territory of the Republic of Bosnia and Herzegovina against Serbian attacks." The Non-Aligned Group generally criticized the narrow interpretations of the UN force's role in Bosnia. *See* Freudenschuß, *supra* note 59, at 508–09.

powers often willingly accepted temporal and substantive controls on the use of force, restrictions that would have been rejected in a major war in which a permanent member had substantial interests.

We would hope that the post–gulf war practices of calibrating and limiting objectives and imposing temporal limits and Security Council control would be transferable to a major conflict. Unfortunately, past experience and present reality do not make us sanguine about those prospects. More realistically, the momentum toward war, the assertion of national interest and the perceived necessity for military flexibility and power to counteract aggression might once again, as in the Korean and gulf wars, overwhelm other Charter values: Council control, minimizing authorized violence and pursuing peaceful settlement. For these reasons, the Security Council should place strong emphasis on maintaining control over the *initial* decision to authorize the use of force and insist that nations not resort to nondefensive uses absent a clear Council mandate.

IV. CEASE-FIRE AGREEMENTS AND SECURITY COUNCIL AUTHORIZATIONS OF FORCE

The prior two sections dealt with the initiation and contracting out of the use of force: this section concerns problems that occur in terminating contracted-out authorizations. As the Iraqi inspection crisis illustrates, states have claimed the authority to use force subsequent to a permanent cease-fire ending hostilities.

The basic Charter principles that we have outlined—peaceful resolution of disputes and Security Council control over the use of force—require that, even where there is no termination provision in the authorization to use force, that authority expires with a permanent cease-fire unless explicitly continued. Such authorization cannot be revived by the contractees unilaterally; it is for the Security Council to consider whether a breach of that cease-fire justifies a reauthorization of force.

The Effect of the UN Charter

Pre-Charter law permitted a party to a cease-fire to treat its serious violation as a material breach, entitling it to resume fighting.[81] The United States and the United Kingdom rely on this law to argue that Iraqi violations of the inspection regime established during the cease-fire revived the Resolution 678 authorization to use force. This view ignores the prohibition on the use of force under Article 2(4), which, properly understood, "changes a basic legal tenet of the traditional armistice."[82] Post-Charter law holds that UN-imposed cease-fires reaffirm the basic obligation of states to refrain from using force. Therefore, a violation of the cease-fire, even a material breach, is not a ground for the other party to revive hostilities, at least short of an armed attack giving rise to an Article 51 right of self-defense.[83] As one scholar writes, "Although terms of the armistice agreements dealing with important but collateral issues such as verification regimes or implementation mechanisms may fail, the overriding obligation not to resort to force as a means of dispute settlement is deemed severable and continues to be binding."[84]

Strong policy interests make it advisable that Security Council authorizations to use force be terminated by the establishment of a cease-fire unless explicitly and unambig-

---

[81] See Hague Convention [No. IV] Respecting the Laws and Customs of War on Land, Oct. 18, 1907, annexed Regulations, Art. 40, 36 Stat. 2277, 1 Bevans 631.

[82] David Morris, *From War to Peace: A Study of Cease-fire Agreements and the Evolving Role of the United Nations*, 36 VA. J. INT'L L. 802, 822–23 (1996).

[83] See Richard R. Baxter, *Armistices and Other Forms of Suspension of Hostilities*, 149 RECUEIL DES COURS 353, 382–85 (1976 I); Ernest A. Simon, *The Operation of the Korean Armistice Agreement*, MIL. L. REV., Jan. 1970, at 105, 126–27; Morris, *supra* note 82, at 822, 897.

[84] Morris, *supra* note 82, at 822–23.

uously continued by the Council itself. The overall objectives of the Charter and the changes it has wrought in the law on the use of force mandate that disputes be settled by peaceful means, if at all possible. This suggests that the end of hostilities, however that is accomplished, reestablishes the Article 2(4) obligations on all states not to use force, including in implementing cease-fire provisions, and not to do so without a new Council authorization. For example, no one would seriously claim that member states of the UN command would have the authority to bomb North Korea pursuant to the 1950 authorization to use force if in 1999 North Korea flagrantly violated the 1953 armistice.

Moreover, that rule is especially necessary when the Security Council control consists of authorizing member states to use force, a more decentralized approach than envisioned by the Charter's framers. To permit authorizations to continue after a permanent cease-fire ends hostilities would allow individual states to use force indefinitely, a result that would undermine the Council's control[85]—particularly when the authorized states include a permanent member that could veto any Council resolution terminating the authorization. Every authorization to use force thus far has been at the behest of a permanent member of the Security Council. This trend is likely to continue. In such situations the potential use by that permanent member of what has been termed a "reverse veto" to block the Council from terminating an authorization that no longer enjoys the support of the international community undermines the Council's legitimacy and Charter-mandated control over the use of force.[86]

Indeed, the gulf war and its aftermath illustrate the problematic use of the veto threat to reverse the Charter's objective of peaceful settlement. In response to the peace initiatives pursued by the Soviet Union and other nations in the days before the coalition's ground attack, both the United States and the United Kingdom reportedly threatened to veto any resolution that would terminate the UN sanctions and the Resolution 678 authorization of force in return for an Iraqi pullout from Kuwait.[87] More recently, the possibility of a U.S. and UK veto undoubtedly lurked in the background in preventing the Security Council from explicitly stating that the Resolution 678 authorization had terminated and that a new resolution must be adopted before any member state could use force to enforce UN inspections in Iraq. Consequently, the better interpretation of the legal situation regarding the further use of force by member states after a permanent cease-fire has been reached is that a new Council authorization must be obtained. That view is consistent with the law and objectives of the Charter.

Certainly, the use of the veto threat to prevent the repeal of an authorization that the majority of the Council wants terminated could be addressed in other ways. As already discussed in part III, the initial authorization can set a time limit for the use of force or provide for its own termination by majority or supermajority vote of the Council;[88] or it can be narrowly drawn to ensure that force is used only for limited purposes. At times,

---

[85] The U.S. experience with broad legislative delegations of emergency power that did not terminate when the immediate crisis was over ought to make the international community wary of continuing authorizations to use force beyond the termination of hostilities. In the 1970s, Congress and the Executive both recognized that the failure to provide for the termination of broad emergency power had allowed the President to dangerously accumulate unchecked power. For example, the emergency that Truman declared in 1950 in the context of the Korean War continued for over 25 years and formed the legal basis for executive action having nothing to do with the original purpose of the emergency declaration. In response to the concerns over the authorization of emergency power of indefinite duration, Congress enacted the National Emergencies Act, terminating virtually all emergency authority based on the past declaration of emergency. *See* Pub. L. No. 94–412, 90 Stat. 1255 (1976) (codified at 50 U.S.C. §1601 (1994)).

[86] *See* Caron, *supra* note 77, at 552, 576–84.

[87] *Id.* at 577, 583.

[88] See Caron, *supra* note 77, at 584–85, for an argument that the Security Council has the authority to take such action.

however, the Council will not be able to so limit the contractee's mandate because of strong contrary pressure from powerful states or the nature of the operation. Therefore, *at a minimum,* to ensure that Security Council authorizations do not continue in perpetuity, the approach we have argued is correct since it flows from Article 2(4) of the Charter—authorization to use force should cease with the establishment of a permanent cease-fire unless it is explicitly continued by the Security Council.[89]

Allowing authorizations to use force to continue indefinitely would further alienate the smaller UN members, would decrease the legitimacy of such mandates, and could result in more resistance to them. It could be argued that the converse rule would perversely result in the continuation of hostilities by states so authorized, to avoid the extinguishment of their authorization by way of a cease-fire. But hostilities end and cease-fires are signed when the military and political situations converge in that direction, and states would be unlikely to avoid ending hostilities for fear that their UN authorization would lapse.

Practice Prior to the Gulf War

UN practice prior to the gulf war supports this approach to cease-fire law under the Charter. The various Middle East conflicts between Israel and Arab governments led to strong assertions by the Security Council and UN officials that violations of cease-fires or armistices do not legally justify forceful countermeasures by individual states. When the Security Council, on July 15, 1948, imposed a cease-fire on the belligerents, the UN mediator, Count Bernadotte, sent instructions interpreting the Council's resolution to mean that "(1) No party may unilaterally put an end to the truce. (2) No party may take the law into its own hands and decree that it is relieved of its obligations under the resolution of the Security Council because in its opinion the other party has violated the truce."[90] Nonetheless, the Israelis and Arabs continued to violate the cease-fire on the basis of alleged violations by the other party. The Security Council then adopted a resolution reiterating that "[n]o party is permitted to violate the truce on the ground that it is undertaking reprisals or retaliations against the other party."[91]

In 1956, as the Middle East situation deteriorated, the Security Council asked Secretary-General Dag Hammarskjöld to review enforcement of and compliance with the armistice agreement. Both Israel and Egypt desired the armistice to allow—in conformity with pre-Charter customary international law—each party the right to take reprisals in response to the other's violations. The Secretary-General rejected that view, arguing "that [Israeli-Egyptian] compliance [with the armistice] should be unconditional, subject only to resort to the Security Council if attacked and the inherent right to self-defense." Even the right of self-defense was narrowly circumscribed: "only the Security Council could decide that a case of non-compliance was a justification for self-defense [under] Article

---

[89] A distinction should be made between permanent cease-fires designed to end hostilities definitively and a temporary lull in fighting or a provisional cease-fire designed to last only a few days or weeks until a more permanent cessation of fighting is reached. The Korean armistice and gulf war cease-fires were clearly designed to end hostilities permanently, although resolution of some of the underlying political tensions could take years or decades to achieve. Moreover, other forms of a definitive end to hostilities should be subsumed within this proposed rule, such as the situation where the states acting under Security Council authority permanently withdraw their forces after a humanitarian intervention, as happened in Somalia.

[90] *See* Morris, *supra* note 82, at 839. Shabtai Rosenne, the former Legal Adviser to the Israeli Ministry of Foreign Affairs, noted the fundamental change in the law relating to armistice agreements: "our Armistice Agreements are always subordinate to the obligation, contained in the Charter, to refrain from the threat or use of force and to settle international disputes by peaceful means." *Id.* at 849.

[91] 1 SYDNEY D. BAILEY, HOW WARS END 293 (1982). This statement is based on the post-Charter rule that Article 2(4) prohibits reprisals. REISMAN & BAKER, *supra* note 29, at 50–52, 70–71, have questioned whether that purportedly ironclad rule accurately reflects state practice.

51." For Hammarskjöld, the key principle was the binding nature of the cease-fire, irrespective of infringements of other articles of the armistice, a principle that resulted from the basic obligations of all UN members not to use force.[92]

It might be argued that UN-negotiated or imposed cease-fires ending hostilities between individual states are different from a UN cease-fire terminating hostilities between UN-authorized forces and an aggressor state. While there is an obvious factual difference when the United Nations is a party to the conflict, both situations present similar theoretical problems and scholars have not treated them differently.

Most cases of hostilities between nations will involve claims by at least one nation of authorization under Article 51 of the Charter to use force in self-defense. Nonetheless, a UN-imposed or -brokered cease-fire will extinguish that nation's claim of right under Article 51, even if the cease-fire does not fully vindicate its claims. Similarly, nations acting pursuant to a Chapter VII authorization have a valid right to use force, but that right is also extinguished after hostilities end and a permanent cease-fire is promulgated. In both situations the Charter's command that peaceful means be used to settle disputes requires that nations not use force after the imposition of a cease-fire unless either a new aggression occurs, reactivating Article 51, or authorization is given by the Security Council. For example, if Kuwait, with the assistance of the United States and Saudi Arabia, had operated exclusively under Article 51 and successfully reversed its conquest by Iraq, a UN-brokered cease-fire would have extinguished any right of those states to resume fighting in the event of an Iraqi violation of the cease-fire agreement (unless Iraq reinvaded Kuwait, retriggering Article 51). The legal situation should not be different because Resolution 678, and not solely Article 51, authorized the coalition's efforts.

It could still be argued that force used under Security Council authorization ought to be different from wars between individual nations because UN authorizations might be broader than the Article 51 exception and might therefore survive a cease-fire. For example, Resolution 678 and Korean War Resolution 83 both contain broad language authorizing force, not merely to defend Kuwait and South Korea, but "to restore international peace and security in the area." However, the experience under the Korean armistice strongly suggests that Council authorizations to use force end with a cease-fire or armistice. That armistice ended hostilities but did not explicitly extinguish or continue the Resolution 83 authorization to use force.[93] In the negotiations leading to the armistice, the South Korean Government took the position that violations of the armistice by North Korea or failure to achieve Korean unification at the political conference proposed in the armistice should automatically lead to a resumption of hostilities.[94] The United States and the UN coalition rejected that position, although the sixteen UN members with armed forces in Korea stated their commitment to defend South Korea if attacked by the North.[95]

In 1955 and again in 1956, South Korea argued at the United Nations that North Korean and Chinese violations warranted termination of the armistice and the resump-

---

[92] *See* Report of the Secretary-General to the Security Council pursuant to the Council's resolution of 4 April 1956 on the Palestine question, UN SCOR, 11th Sess., Supp. for Apr.–June, at 40, UN Doc. S/3596 (1956).

[93] *See* Agreement concerning a Military Armistice in Korea, July 27, 1953, Art. V, para. 62, 4 UST 234, 261 (providing that the "Agreement shall remain in effect until expressly superseded either by mutually agreeable amendments and additions or by provision in an appropriate agreement for a peaceful settlement at a political level between both sides").

[94] *See* BURTON I. KAUFMAN, THE KOREAN WAR: CHALLENGES IN CRISIS, CREDIBILITY AND COMMAND 200–02 (2d ed. 1997).

[95] *See* Letter dated 7 August 1953 from the Acting U.S.A. Representative to the UN, addressed to the Secretary-General, transmitting a special report of the Unified Command on the armistice in Korea in accordance with the Security Council Resolution of 7 July 1950 (S/1588), UN Doc. S/3079 (1953); *see also* GOODRICH, *supra* note 51.

tion of hostilities, a position that no other country adopted.[96] In 1957 the Unified Command announced that Communist violations of the armistice provision prohibiting the introduction of combat equipment and weapons relieved the Unified Command of its obligation to comply with that provision, but that it would continue to observe the cease-fire and implement all of the other armistice provisions.[97] The Unified Command's position was thus consistent with Hammarskjöld's position in 1956 and Bernadotte's view in 1948.

In 1967 the United States brought the Security Council's attention to serious violations of the armistice, including armed attacks resulting in almost five hundred UN and South Korean casualties. The United States claimed the right to take "appropriate measures in self-defense" to protect "civilians and military personnel" but studiously avoided making any claim or threat to take forceful countermeasures against North Korea.[98] One military analyst of the armistice concludes that in only one incident during the whole period between 1953 and 1967 did the UN forces engage in what might be construed as a reprisal for armed attacks against South Korea,[99] and even that incident could come within the law of hot pursuit.

The Iraqi Cease-Fire and the General Rule on Cease-Fires

The permanent cease-fire that ended the 1991 Persian Gulf war supports, although not completely without doubt, the general rule that Security Council authorizations of force expire with a cease-fire. Resolution 687 is a detailed resolution that sets the terms for a formal cease-fire; it includes provisions on, inter alia, settling the boundary dispute between Iraq and Kuwait; establishing a demilitarized zone; eliminating Iraq's chemical, biological and nuclear weapons capability; continuing economic sanctions; and setting up a compensation fund. The terms of the resolution do not state that force can be employed unilaterally by UN member states to enforce its mandates. Its paragraph 1, however, does affirm that all thirteen prior Security Council resolutions, to the extent not modified by 687, survived the cease-fire, and Secretary-General Boutros Boutros-Ghali believed that Resolution 678 "remained in force" even after the cease-fire.[100] Despite the general terms of paragraph 1, the history and text of the cease-fire resolutions clearly show that the Resolution 678 authorization to use force expired with the conclusion of the permanent cease-fire.

After the suspension of hostilities, a provisional cease-fire, Resolution 686, was adopted. The distinction between a temporary cease-fire that does not terminate an authorization and a permanent one that does is illustrated by these Iraqi resolutions. Resolution 686 explicitly refers to paragraph 2 of Resolution 678, the "all necessary means" authorization, and "recognizes" that it "remain[s] valid" "during the period required for Iraq to comply with" the terms of the provisional cease-fire. Thus, the unilateral use of force provision of Resolution 678 would remain "valid" only temporarily,

---

[96] See Unified Command Report on the Neutral Nations Supervisory Commission in Korea, UN Doc. A/3167 (1956); 1956 U.N.Y.B. 129, 130; see also BAILEY, supra note 91, at 474–75.

[97] BAILEY, supra note 91, at 478.

[98] See United Nations Command Report to the United Nations on the increase in violations by North Korea of the Military Armistice Agreement in Korea, UN Doc. S/8217, at 5–6 (1967).

[99] See Simon, supra note 83, at 126–27.

[100] UN DEP'T OF PUBLIC INFORMATION, THE UNITED NATIONS AND THE IRAQ-KUWAIT CONFLICT, 1990–1996, UN Sales No. E.96.I.3 (1996) (Introduction by Boutros Boutros-Ghali, Secretary-General of the United Nations, at 33) [hereinafter IRAQ-KUWAIT CONFLICT]. It is unclear what "remained in force" meant, because he could not have meant that any member state could continue to attack Iraq despite the formal cease-fire.

pending Iraqi compliance with the provisional cease-fire.[101] Moreover, the Security Council rejected a U.S. effort to authorize force if Iraq failed to comply with all the provisions of the cease-fire.[102]

Resolution 687, in contrast to Resolution 686, did not explicitly state that Resolution 678 would remain valid until Iraq complied with its detailed terms.[103] The crux of Resolution 687 was the transformation of the temporary cessation of hostilities into a permanent cease-fire upon Iraq's *acceptance* of, not compliance with, its terms.[104] Of all the detailed provisions in the cease-fire, only paragraph 4 guaranteeing the inviolability of the Iraq-Kuwait border contains language authorizing the use of force, and then only by the Security Council and not by individual states.[105] That the Council decided to guarantee Kuwait's boundary by force if necessary—a guarantee that is central to both Article 2(4) of the Charter and the 1991 Persian Gulf war—excludes an interpretation of Resolution 687 as continuing the Resolution 678 authorization so as to allow individual nations to use force to rectify other, presumably less central violations. It would be illogical for Resolution 687 to require Security Council action to authorize force against threatened boundary violations, yet dispense with such action if Iraq violated another provision of the resolution.[106]

---

[101] The conditions of the provisional cease-fire required Iraq to rescind its purported annexation of Kuwait; accept in principle its liability for damages suffered by Kuwait; release prisoners and other nationals it held; return Kuwait's property; and provide information on mines and chemical and biological weapons in Kuwait, and in allied occupied Iraqi territory (but not in Iraq generally). Resolution 686 did not include any obligation to submit to inspections. *See* SC Res. 686 (Mar. 2, 1991), *reprinted in* 30 ILM 568 (1991).

[102] The language in Resolution 686 was subject to negotiations in the Council. The U.S. first draft contained a broader authorization that would have affirmed the right of the coalition to "resume offensive combat operations if Iraq does not comply with all demands" in the resolution. *See* Freudenschuß, *supra* note 59, at 499. That would have constituted an explicit authorization of the U.S. right to use force in the event of violations of the provisional cease-fire. The U.S. position was criticized and the resulting language of operative paragraph 4 reiterated the right to use force only in accordance with Resolution 678. *See* SC Res. 686, *supra* note 101.

[103] The difference in language between 686 and 687 in referring to prior resolutions is significant. Resolution 686, *supra* note 101, "*[a]ffirms* that all twelve resolutions noted above *continue to have full force and effect*" (emphasis added). The later Resolution 687 contains no such language; it "*[a]ffirms* all thirteen resolutions noted above, except as expressly changed below to achieve the goals of this resolution, including a formal cease-fire." *See* SC Res. 687 (Apr. 3, 1991), *reprinted in* 30 ILM 846 (1991).

[104] *See* SC Res. 687, *supra* note 103; *see also* UN CHRON., June 1991, at 4. On April 11, Paul Noterdaeme of Belgium, President of the Security Council, formally acknowledged Iraq's acceptance, "adding that Council members had asked him to note that conditions established in the resolution had been met and *that the formal cease-fire was effective.*" *Id.* at 7 (emphasis added). That the permanent cease-fire was declared upon Iraqi *acceptance* of its terms and not compliance with its provisions (as had been the case with Resolution 686's temporary cease-fire) is evidence that Resolution 678's broad authorization of force was extinguished.

[105] The U.S. first draft of Resolution 687 would have authorized the coalition states "to use all necessary means" to guarantee the border. Freudenschuß, *supra* note 59, at 500. That language was rejected as going too far. The statements by supporters of Resolution 687 at the time of its adoption make clear that individual nations were not empowered to use force, even to respond to a boundary violation. (In the case of a boundary violation that constituted an armed attack on Kuwait, Article 51 would authorize self-defense.) India's representative stated that paragraph 4

> does not confer authority on any country to take unilateral action under any of the previous resolutions of the Security Council. Rather, the sponsors have explained to us that in case of any threat or actual violation of the boundary in future the Security Council will meet to take, as appropriate, all necessary measures in accordance with the Charter.

UN Doc. S/PV.2981, at 78 (1991) (remarks of Mr. Ghorekhein, India). Russia explicitly agreed with India's interpretation, which was not contradicted by the sponsors of Resolution 687. *Id.* at 101. Indeed, one sponsor, the United Kingdom, concurred that the provision represented a "guarantee by the Security Council to step in" if the border was violated. *Id.* at 113.

[106] Both India and China abstained on Resolution 686 because they disagreed with its continuation of the Resolution 678 authorization of force. UN Doc. S/PV.2978 (1991), *reprinted in* IRAQ AND KUWAIT, *supra* note 10, at 95, 99. That both countries voted affirmatively for Resolution 687 is further evidence that it was not understood to have continued the authorization under Resolution 678.

Moreover, paragraph 34 of Resolution 687 states the Council's decision "to remain seized of the matter and to take such further steps as may be required for the implementation of the present resolution and to secure peace and security in the area." That provision makes clear that the Council, not individual states, determines not only whether Iraq has violated Resolution 687 but also whether to take "further steps" for its implementation. The express vesting of this authorization in the Security Council is inconsistent with the view that Resolution 678 continues to allow individual states to decide for themselves whether to use force to implement the cease-fire resolution.

Despite the language and history of Resolution 687, U.S. and UK officials have asserted since 1991 that the Resolution 678 authorization to use force remains in effect, and on several occasions they have deployed forces against Iraq.[107] They argue that the traditional material breach doctrine is applicable to UN cease-fires and that an Iraqi breach of the cease-fire therefore reactivates Resolution 678. However, even if the resolution survived the cease-fire and can be reignited under traditional armistice law to address material breaches, the question remains: who decides when a material breach reactivates the authorization to use force—the Security Council or the United States and its coalition partners? The practice since the cease-fire confirms what is central to Resolution 687: that this authority is held by the Security Council alone. Since the Council made the cease-fire with Iraq, it is the party to determine whether Iraq is in breach. Thus, for Council-imposed cease-fires, retaining the material breach doctrine turns out to lead to the same consequences as the Charter rule propounded above: only the Council can decide to resume hostilities.

The question of who determines whether Iraq has materially breached the cease-fire[108] underscores the basic problem with the contracting-out model of UN enforcement: Is this a UN operation for which the threshold decision to employ force is determined by the Security Council? Or once force has been authorized, are all decisions delegated to individual states for the duration of the dispute? Professor Ruth Wedgwood and U.S. officials argue that the "cease-fire on the ground was in fact a decision of coalition forces," not the Council, and that, presumably, any of those forces can therefore declare Iraq in material breach and use force to secure compliance.[109] That coalition forces declared a cessation of hostilities on the ground is not inconsistent with the fact that the formal, legally binding cease-fire was established by the Security Council, not by the United States or any other state. It was declared pursuant to an elaborate Council resolution setting forth its terms and conditions. The Iraqi notification of acceptance, after which the "formal cease-fire is effective," was delivered not to the United States or its coalition partners, but to the Security Council and the Secretary-General. Furthermore, the cease-fire resolution explicitly states that the Council (not individual countries) will "take such further steps as may be required" for its implementation.

The practice since 1991 lends support to the position that a finding by the Security Council of a material breach is necessary before force can be employed. In January 1993,

---

[107] Shortly after the formal cease-fire, President Bush and other U.S. officials asserted that the Resolution 678 authorization was still in effect and threatened force against Iraq to achieve compliance with Resolution 687. *See* Letter from President Bush to the Speaker of the House of Representatives and President Pro-Tem of the Senate, 27 WEEKLY COMP. PRES. DOC. 1284 (Sept. 16, 1991). U.S. officials apparently based this interpretation on paragraph 34 of Resolution 687. John E. Yang & John M. Goshko, *Bush Says Iraq Violates Cease-Fire: Pentagon Preparing Range of Options*, WASH. POST, June 29, 1991, at A1.

[108] That the term material breach is objective under Article 60 of the Vienna Convention on the Law of Treaties and not subjective simply means that when one party to an agreement declares a material breach to exist, its subjective view is not dispositive but must be measured against the objective facts. It does not mean that a third party can declare a cease-fire null and void despite the refusal of both parties to the agreement to declare that a material breach exists. *See* Vienna Convention on the Law of Treaties, *opened for signature* May 23, 1969, Art. 60, 1155 UNTS 331.

[109] *See* Wedgwood, *supra* note 46, at 726.

the United States, the United Kingdom and France launched air strikes against Iraq in response to various Iraqi violations of the cease-fire agreement.[110] Those strikes were undertaken only after the Council found the Iraqi actions to "constitute an unacceptable and material breach of the relevant provisions of resolution 687."[111] While the air strikes do suggest that the Security Council was willing at that time to countenance a use of force pursuant to Resolution 678, they also reaffirm what is central to our discussion: that it is for the Council and not individual states to declare Iraq in "material breach" of the cease-fire and thus to authorize force.[112]

Since June 1996, numerous unsuccessful attempts have been made to persuade the Security Council to determine that Iraq is in material breach of the cease-fire agreement.[113] These attempts reflect the UK view that such a Council finding is necessary to authorize military action,[114] a view informed by the traditional law of cease-fires, the UN Charter, Resolution 687 and past practice.

Finally, the winter 1998 practice with respect to the Iraqi inspection regime confirms the general proposition that authorizations by the Council to use force either terminate with a permanent cease-fire or at least require it to declare a material breach and reauthorize force. After Kofi Annan returned from Baghdad in February 1998 with the

---

[110] In January 1993, Iraqi authorities refused to guarantee the safety and free movement of United Nations aircraft transporting the United Nations Special Commission (UNSCOM) and United Nations Iraq-Kuwait Observation Mission (UNIKOM) personnel into Iraq. Iraq had also crossed the Kuwaiti border without permission and failed to remove its six police posts from the Kuwaiti side of the demilitarized zone. *See* IRAQ-KUWAIT CONFLICT, *supra* note 100, at 86–87.

[111] *See* Statement by the President of the Security Council concerning United Nations flights into Iraqi territory, UN Doc. S/25081 (1993), and Statement by the President of the Security Council concerning various actions by Iraq vis-à-vis UNIKOM and UNSCOM, UN Doc. S/25091 (1993), *reprinted in* IRAQ-KUWAIT CONFLICT, *supra* note 100, at 512–13. The Security Council President's January 11 statement on behalf of the Security Council "reaffirms that the boundary was at the very core of the conflict" and that in Resolutions 687 and 773 the Security Council had guaranteed the inviolability of the border and undertaken to take all necessary measures to that end as appropriate. These raids therefore do not support the argument that the inspection violation, standing alone, would have authorized force.

[112] The presidential statements of January 8 and 11 follow a line of Security Council statements and resolutions, starting with Resolution 707 of August 15, 1991, and continuing with informal presidential statements of February 19 and 28, 1992, and July 6, 1992, that determined Iraq to be in material breach of Resolution 687. *See* UN Docs. S/23609, S/23663 & S/24240, respectively (1992). This practice confirms that the determination of material breach was to be made by the Security Council and not by individual member states.

While clearly it would have been preferable for the Council to determine that Iraq was in material breach of the cease-fire and authorize military action by means of a formal resolution, in recent years the Council has relied heavily on presidential statements reflecting the consensus reached in closed sessions by the members. *See* Kirgis, *supra* note 15, at 519–20.

[113] U.S. officials and at least one scholar have suggested that the United States can deem the cease-fire suspended because the Security Council has found Iraq to be in flagrant or serious violation of prior resolutions. *See* Wedgwood, *supra* note 46, at 726. But serious violations do not necessarily, as a matter of law, constitute a material breach and the Security Council has decided not to find that a material breach has occurred. It has refused to do so aware of the argument that British and American officials make, that such a finding would negate the cease-fire and pave the way for military action. That the Council chooses to use a host of other terms to characterize Iraqi noncompliance is legally significant: it refuses to use the term that in the past has been taken to legally nullify a cease-fire.

[114] *See* UN Council Stops Iraq's Weapons Search Plan, BALTO. SUN, June 15, 1996, at 7A (United States and United Kingdom had urged Council to declare Iraq in "material breach"); James Bone, *Americans Fail to Win UN Consensus on Military Action*, TIMES (London), Nov. 12, 1997; *ABC News This Week* (Nov. 30, 1997) (Annan stating that Council had decided not to declare Iraq in material breach). When the Iraqi-UN crisis involving UNSCOM inspections heated up in the winter of 1998, the Security Council again repeatedly rejected U.S. and UK efforts to obtain either a resolution or a presidential statement declaring Iraq in material breach of Resolution 687. Only after it became apparent that the Council would not do so did the British shift position and argue that such a resolution was unnecessary. Laura Silber, *UN Deeply Divided Over Use of Force*, FIN. TIMES (London), Feb. 6, 1998, at 4. Even after Annan's February 1998 agreement with Iraq, the British urged the passage of a resolution "which would declare Iraq in material breach" if it did not comply with the agreement. *Richardson Discusses Iraq Deal* (morning ed., NPR broadcast, Feb. 25, 1998). Again, Britain and the United States were rebuffed.

agreement with Iraq's President Saddam Hussein, the United States and the United Kingdom lobbied for a Council resolution that would have automatically authorized force if Iraq violated the Annan agreement. Resolution 1154 not only rejected such automaticity,[115] but clarified the view of a majority of the Council that its explicit authorization was required to renew the use of force.[116] As the Russian delegate noted, "No one can ignore the resolution adopted today and attempt to act by bypassing the Security Council." Similarly, France stated that the resolution was designed "to underscore the prerogatives of the Security Council in a way that excludes any question of automaticity. . . . It is the Security Council that must evaluate the behavior of a country, if necessary to determine any possible violations, and to take the appropriate decisions."[117] While U.S. officials still argue that the failure of its members to introduce language explicitly requiring member states to return to the Council leaves individual nations free to employ force if Iraq violates the resolution, the Council's repeated rebuffs to the U.S. and UK effort to obtain authority to use force constitute if not explicit, at least implicit, disapproval of the U.S. claim.

CONCLUSION

The crisis in the fall of 1998 regarding the threat of the United States and NATO to use force against Yugoslavia unless it withdrew its security units and army from Kosovo demonstrates that the problems discussed in this article are likely to recur. The United States, again, was asserting that it and its allies have the authority to use force based upon claimed implicit Security Council authorization: Resolution 1199, while it condemned Yugoslavia's actions in Kosovo, did not explicitly authorize the use of force.[118] As in the Iraqi inspection crisis the previous spring, the United States conflated a Security Council condemnation of a nation's actions with an authorization to use force. That conflation

---

[115] According to members who spoke in the Council, Resolution 1154's sponsors assured other members that the resolution did not automatically authorize nations to use force in the event of an Iraqi violation. As Russia emphasized in the Council, any "hint of automaticity with regard to the application of force has been excluded" and "would have been unacceptable for the majority of the Council." UN Doc. S/PV.3858, *supra* note 4, at 17–18. *See also id.* at 5 (Japan) and 18 (Gambia).

[116] Resolution 1154 warned Iraq that continued violations of its obligations to permit unconditional access to UNSCOM "would have the severest consequences." But this warning did not leave the United States the right to use such force unilaterally in the event of a breach. Paragraph 5 forecloses this possibility. The Security Council does not merely remain seized of the matter, it remains "actively" seized and does so "to ensure implementation of this resolution." SC Res. 1154 (Mar. 2, 1998), *reprinted in* 37 ILM 503 (1998).

[117] UN Doc. S/PV.3858, *supra* note 4, at 15, 18. *See also id.* at 14 (China), 10 (Kenya, Sweden), 9 (Brazil), and 7 (Costa Rica). Other members strongly implied that individual nations could not use force when they stated that in the event of an Iraqi violation, the Security Council would provide an appropriate response. *Id.* at 9, 12–13, 18 (Gabon, Slovenia, Gambia).

[118] SC Res. 1199 (Sept. 23, 1998). Resolution 1199 expressed the Council's grave concern at the "excessive and indiscriminate use of force by Serbian security forces and the Yugoslav Army" in Kosovo, and acted under Chapter VII of the Charter to demand, inter alia, that Yugoslavia "cease all action by the security forces affecting the civilian population and order the withdrawal of security units used for civilian repression." *Id.*, para. 4. The resolution did not mention the use of force, and after the vote Russia explicitly stated that it had voted for it because "no measures of force and no sanctions at this stage are being introduced by the Security Council." Crossette, *supra* note 9, at Al. Moreover, Resolution 1199, in paragraph 16, states that the Security Council "*[d]ecides*, should the concrete measures demanded in this resolution and Resolution 1160 (1998) not be taken, to consider further action and additional measures to maintain or restore peace and stability in the region."

Nonetheless, U.S. officials have argued that Resolution 1199 implicitly gives NATO the authority to use force against Yugoslavia through the invocation of Chapter VII. *See supra* note 9 and Goshko, *supra* note 9. Immediately following a NATO meeting in Brussels on October 8, 1998, Secretary of State Albright stated that she believed Resolution 1199 gave NATO the necessary legal grounds for military action against Serbia. Tim Bucker & Jon Hibbs, *International: Blair Attacks West's Disunity on Kosovo*, DAILY TELEGRAPH (London), Oct. 9, 1998, at 17.

ignored the Charter's requirement that the Council must not only condemn a nation's actions as a threat to the peace, but also decide that force should be employed to counteract the threat.

The grave dangers attendant on a regime of law permitting individual nations or even regional organizations to use nondefensive force without explicit Security Council authorization led all the NATO allies to reject the U.S. position in June 1998.[119] Although NATO has since moved closer to using force without clear Council approval, a number of European nations still appear uneasy about doing so.[120]

When force should be employed to counteract a particular threat to the peace can be difficult to discern, particularly in a world that abounds in dangerous and malevolent actors. Often a real or imagined evil will exert a tremendous centrifugal pull on most of us to support forceful action. Nonetheless, the perils associated with warfare—that great powers can use humanitarian concerns to mask geopolitical interest;[121] that major air strikes such as those threatened against Iraq and Serbia in 1998 have serious consequences in lives lost, destruction caused and the resulting destabilization; that warfare is of limited utility as a means of solving complex, long-standing, underlying problems; that a world order that allows individual or coalitions of nations to deploy offensive military might for what they deem are worthy causes amounts to anarchy—these perils require that force be used only as a last resort as determined by a world body. That principle, inscribed in the UN Charter, stipulates that the Security Council must explicitly approve non-Article 51 uses of force.

During the Cold War, many claimed that the Security Council could not fulfill its first and primary responsibility of ensuring international security. The end of the Cold War and the reversal of Iraq's invasion of Kuwait in 1991 were viewed as reviving the Council's role in collective security. The early 1990s brought fears from some quarters that the United Nations was acquiescing too readily in U.S. uses of force. At times, these fears led to criticisms of explicit UN authorizations of force as illegitimate, unwise, or merely constituting a multilateral veneer for unilateral action. At other times, critics claimed that forceful action was being taken in the name of the United Nations that had not really been authorized by the Security Council.

While it is too early to provide any definitive answer, it may well be that the recent events portend a restoration of the Council's proper role. The world needs a Security

---

[119] The United States was "the only [NATO] country" that during the June discussion took the position that NATO did not need explicit Security Council authorization to use force in Kosovo. Remarks of Secretary of Defense William S. Cohen at Los Angeles Foreign Affairs Council Breakfast, Federal News Service, June 29, 1998, at 10, *available in* LEXIS, News Library, Fednew File. *See also* David Buchan & Ralph Atkins, *Kosovo Crisis Moves into Uneasy Lull*, FIN. TIMES, June 18, 1998, at 2 (German cabinet opposes NATO action without Security Council approval); Paul Koring, *Alliance Rift Weakens Threat of Air Strikes in Kosovo*, GLOBE & MAIL (Toronto), June 24, 1998, at A13 (Canada and France adamant that Council resolution needed); William Drozdiak, *Further NATO Action in Kosovo Now in Doubt*, WASH. POST, June 18, 1998, at A32 (France, Italy, Denmark, Germany will not approve NATO use of force without UN mandate); Susan Blaustein, *End the "Dance of Appeasement,"* L.A. TIMES, June 21, 1998, at 2 (Tony Blair insists on securing Council resolution). Secretary-General Annan openly stated that "[a]ll use of military power by regional groups should be sanctioned by the United Nations." Moreover, "[i]t would set a dangerous precedent . . . —who else are they going to discipline tomorrow? How could they tell other regions or governments not to do the same thing without Council approval?" UN Press Release No. SG/T/2142 (July 6, 1998) ⟨www.un.org/News/Press⟩. European officials also feared that NATO action would set a precedent that would allow other countries to bypass the Security Council in the future. *See* Drozdiak, *supra.*

[120] *See* Roger Cohen, *Americans Rebuke Yugoslav Leaders*, N.Y. TIMES, Oct. 9, 1998, at A1 (naming Germany, Italy and Denmark as having such reservations).

[121] The strong opposition to the proposed U.S. attack may be explained by the fact that many perceived that U.S. geopolitical reasons and not merely enforcing the inspections regime were motivating U.S. saber rattling. *See* Roger Cohen, *The World: War Fever; The Weapons Too Terrible for the Parade of Horribles*, N.Y. TIMES, Feb. 8, 1998, §4, at 1.

Council powerful enough and sufficiently unified to authorize strong countermeasures against aggressors or genocidal regimes and yet not be a mere multilateral rubber stamp for unilateral decision making. It must steadfastly uphold its mandate pursuant to Article 41 to authorize force only as a last resort.

POSTSCRIPT

On December 16, 1998, the United States and the United Kingdom launched four days of air strikes against Iraq, claiming that Iraq had failed to cooperate fully with the UN weapon inspectors. The United States and Great Britain acted without obtaining the Security Council's authorization to use force and, thus, as this article has argued, in violation of the Charter.[122] The United States and Great Britain argued, as they had in February, that they had legal authority to use force to respond to Iraqi cease-fire violations. Other nations again disagreed.[123]

The December 1998 bombing of Iraq suggests that our hopeful prediction of a strengthened role for the Security Council in controlling the use of force must be tempered by the painful reality of superpower unilateralism. The symbolism of the bombs falling on Iraq while the Council debated its response to a report from a UN special commission about Iraqi compliance with UN resolutions starkly illustrates the refusal of the United States to accept limits on its power. The U.S. position is that it will enforce Security Council resolutions by force, whether or not the Council sees fit to do so. In the short run, the Council was rendered impotent. For the long term, the consequences are potentially serious. The Security Council will be reluctant to authorize and contract out force it cannot control; powerful nations will act on their own.

---

[122] On November 5, 1998, at its 3939th meeting, the Security Council adopted Resolution 1205, which condemned Iraq's decision to cease cooperation with UNSCOM as "a flagrant violation of Resolution 687" but did not authorize the use of force. *See* Josh Friedman, *UN Council Scolds Iraq, Condemnation Falls Short of Military Threat*, NEWSDAY, Nov. 6, 1998, at A18. Various members stressed, as they had in February, the "prerogatives" of the Council and argued that its control over international peace and security "must not be circumvented." *See* Security Council Press Release No. SC/6591, at 5 (France), 7 (Sweden, Brazil), 6 (Russia), 8 (Kenya) (Nov. 5, 1998).

[123] Only three Security Council members—Japan, the United States and Britain—spoke in favor of the air strikes. Security Council Press Release No. SC/6611, at 5 (UK), 8 (U.S.) 9 (Japan) (Dec. 16, 1998). The Russians and Chinese accused the United States and the United Kingdom of an "unprovoked act of force" that "violated the principles of international law and the principle of the Charter," *id.* at 4 (Russia). A number of nonpermanent members opposed the use of force and reiterated that force must be authorized by the Security Council, *id.* at 6 (Costa Rica), 8 (Sweden), 9 (Brazil), 10 (Kenya). International reaction was generally negative, although some European and Asian allies supported the military action.

Part IV
Collective Security outside the UN

[17]

NATO, the UN and the Use of Force: Legal Aspects

Bruno Simma*

Abstract

The threat or use of force by NATO without Security Council authorization has assumed importance because of the Kosovo crisis and the debate about a new strategic concept for the Alliance. The October 1998 threat of air strikes against the FRY breached the UN Charter, despite NATO's effort to rely on the doctrines of necessity and humanitarian intervention and to conform with the sense and logic of relevant Council resolutions. But there are 'hard cases' involving terrible dilemmas in which imperative political and moral considerations leave no choice but to act outside the law. The more isolated these instances remain, the less is their potential to erode the rules of international law. The possible boomerang effect of such breaches can never be excluded, but the danger can be reduced by spelling out the factors that make an ad hoc decision distinctive and minimize its precedential significance. In the case of Kosovo, only a thin red line separates NATO's action from international legality. But should such an approach become a regular part of its strategic programme for the future, it would undermine the universal system of collective security. To resort to illegality as an explicit ultima ratio for reasons as convincing as those put forward in the Kosovo case is one thing. To turn such an exception into a general policy is quite another. If the Washington Treaty has a hard legal core which even the most dynamic and innovative (re-)interpretation cannot erode, it is NATO's subordination to the principles of the UN Charter.

1 The Threat or Use of Force in International Law

Contemporary international law establishes beyond any doubt that serious violations of human rights are matters of international concern. Impressive networks of rules and institutions, both at the universal and regional levels, have come into being as a result of this international concern. In the event of human rights violations which

* Professor of International and European Community Law, Institut für Internationales Recht — Völkerrecht, Ludwig-Maximilians-Universität, Professor-Huber-Platz 2, D-805 39 München, Germany: member of the Editorial Board. This article was originally presented at Policy Roundtables organized by the United Nations Association of the U.S.A. in New York and Washington, D.C., on 11 and 12 March 1999. Footnote references have been provided only where considered essential.

2 *EJIL* 10 (1999), 1–22

reach the magnitude of the Kosovo crisis, these developments in international law allow states, acting individually, collectively or through international organizations, to make use of a broad range of peaceful responses. According to the dominant doctrine in the law of state responsibility (developed by the United Nations International Law Commission), the obligation on states to respect and protect the basic rights of all human persons is the concern of all states, that is, they are owed *erga omnes*. Consequently, in the event of material breaches of such obligations, every other state may lawfully consider itself legally 'injured' and is thus entitled to resort to countermeasures (formerly referred to as reprisals) against the perpetrator. Under international law in force since 1945, confirmed in the General Assembly's Declaration on 'Friendly Relations' of 1970,[1] countermeasures must not involve the threat or use of armed force. In the case of Kosovo, pacific countermeasures were employed, for instance, by the European Union last year, with the suspension of landing rights of Yugoslav airlines within the EU. Leaving aside the question of whether this particular measure proved to be effective, it is somewhat surprising that a major Member State of the EU, at least initially, did not regard itself in a position legally to have recourse to this peaceful means of coercing the FRY to respect the human rights of the Kosovar Albanians. Yet this same state expressed no such doubts about the legality of its participation in the NATO threat of armed force which developed just a few weeks later.

The world community, for its part, acting through the United Nations Security Council, resorted to a mandatory arms embargo *vis-à-vis* the FRY, including Kosovo.[2] We do not have the necessary information at hand to be able to give a sound assessment of the impact and effectiveness of these non-military measures.

In the face of genocide, the right of states, or collectivities of states, to counter breaches of human rights most likely becomes an obligation.[3] In Kosovo, however, what the international community is facing (i.e., at the time of writing, early March 1999) are massive violations of human rights and rights of ethnic minorities, but not acts of genocide in the sense of the 1948 Convention.[4]

Turning to the issue of enforcement of respect for human rights by military means, the fundamental rule from which any inquiry must proceed is Article 2(4) of the UN Charter, according to which

> [a]ll Members [of the UN] shall refrain in their international relations from the threat or use of force against the territorial integrity or political independence of any state, or in any other manner inconsistent with the Purposes of the United Nations.

It is clear, on the basis of both a teleological and historical interpretation of Article 2(4), that the prohibition enacted therein was, and is, intended to be of a comprehensive nature. Thus, contrary to certain views expressed during the Cold

---

[1] GA Res. 2625 (XXV) (1970).

[2] Operative para. 8 of SC Res. 1160 (1998).

[3] Cf. the judgment of the International Court of Justice in the *Genocide (Bosnia-Herzegovina v. Yugoslavia)* case (1996).

[4] Convention on the Prevention and Punishment of the Crime of Genocide, 1948.

War years, the phrase '... or in any other manner inconsistent ...' is not designed to allow room for any exceptions from the ban, but rather to make the prohibition watertight. In contemporary international law, as codified in the 1969 Vienna Convention on the Law of Treaties (Articles 53 and 64), the prohibition enunciated in Article 2(4) of the Charter is part of *jus cogens*, i.e., it is accepted and recognized by the international community of states as a whole as a norm from which no derogation is permitted and which can be modified only by a subsequent norm of general international law having the same peremptory character. Hence, universal *jus cogens*, like the prohibition embodied in Article 2(4), cannot be contracted out of at the regional level. Further, the Charter prohibition of the threat or use of armed force is binding on states both individually and as members of international organizations, such as NATO, as well as on those organizations themselves.

Moreover, it is important to draw attention to Article 52 of the just-mentioned Vienna Convention, according to which '[a] treaty is void if its conclusion has been procured by the threat or use of force in violation of the principles of international law embodied in the Charter of the United Nations', paramount among these principles being Article 2(4).

The law of the UN Charter provides two exceptions from the prohibition expressed in Article 2(4) (the mechanism of the so-called 'enemy-state-clauses' (Articles 53 and 107) should be left aside as it is now unanimously considered obsolete). The first exception, embodied in Article 51 of the Charter, is available to states which find themselves to be victims of aggression:

> Nothing in the present Charter shall impair the inherent right of individual or collective self-defence if an armed attack occurs against a Member of the United Nations, until the Security Council has taken measures necessary to maintain international peace and security. Measures taken by Members in the exercise of this right of self-defence shall be immediately reported to the Security Council and shall not in any way affect the authority and responsibility of the Security Council under the present Charter to take at any time such action as it deems necessary in order to maintain or restore international peace and security.

As the Charter reference to collective self-defence, Article 51 constitutes the legal foundation of the Washington Treaty by which NATO was established.[5] Article 5 of the NATO Treaty bases itself expressly on Charter Article 51.

According to the UN Charter, then, individual or collective self-defence through the use of armed force is only permissible in the case of an 'armed attack'. Like Article 2(4), Article 51 has become the subject of certain gross (mis-)interpretations, most of them put forward during the Cold War when the Security Council regularly found itself in a state of paralysis. Against such attempts to turn a clearly defined exception to the comprehensive Charter ban on the threat or use of force into a convenient basis for all sorts of military activities, it should be emphasized once again that Article 51 unequivocally limits whatever farther-reaching right of self-defence might have existed in pre-Charter customary international law to the case of an 'armed attack'. In

---

[5]   North Atlantic Treaty (1949), 34 UNTS 243.

Collective Security Law

4   *EJIL* 10 (1999), 1–22

particular, any offensive self-help by threats or use of armed force without a basis in Chapter VII has been outlawed by the *jus cogens* of the Charter.

With regard to the second exception to the Charter ban on armed force, Chapter VII constitutes the very heart of the global system of collective security. According to its provisions, the Security Council, after having determined that a threat to the peace, breach of the peace, or act of aggression has occurred, may, if necessary, take military enforcement action involving the armed forces of the Member States. In actual UN practice, it is now common for such enforcement action to be carried out on the basis of a mandate to, or more frequently of an authorization of, states which are willing to participate, either individually or in *ad hoc* coalitions or acting through regional or other international organizations, among them prominently NATO. While the implementation of Chapter VII through a 'franchising system' of this kind creates numerous problems of its own, it is universally accepted that a Security Council authorization granted under Chapter VII establishes a sufficient basis for the legality of the use of armed force employed in conformity with the respective Council Resolution(s). Conversely, any threat or use of force that is neither justified as self-defence against an armed attack nor authorized by the Security Council must be regarded as a violation of the UN Charter.

Chapter VIII of the Charter (Regional arrangements) completes the legal regime thus devised. Hence, according to Article 53 para. 1,

> [t]he Security Council shall, where appropriate, utilize such regional arrangements or agencies for enforcement action under its authority.

The UN Secretary-General's 1992 'Agenda for Peace' emphasized the desirability, indeed necessity, of this mechanism of support.[6] However, Article 53 para. 1 then continues:

> But no enforcement action shall be taken under regional arrangements or by regional agencies without the authorization of the Security Council [with the now obsolete exception of the employment of the 'enemy-state-clauses'].

This provision, too, has been subjected to considerable strains, particularly during the Cold War. One especially dubious example is the view that failure of the Council to disapprove regional military action could amount to (tacit) authorization. In view of the veto power of the permanent Council members, this is a specious argument. On the other hand, an interpretation of Article 53 para. 1 does in good faith leave room for the possibility of implicit as well as *ex-post-facto* authorization.

Before concluding this brief *tour d'horizon* of the relevant international law in force, reference must also be made to Article 103 of the Charter, according to which

> [i]n the event of a conflict between the obligations of the Members of the United Nations under the present Charter and their obligations under any other international agreement, their obligations under the present Charter shall prevail.

Prominent among the Charter obligations thus enjoying priority is, of course, the

---

[6]   Boutros Boutros-Ghali, An Agenda for Peace (1992) SC Doc. S/24111, 17 June 1992.

prohibition on the threat or use of force embodied in Article 2(4), in the context of the other provisions of the Charter to which reference is made above (Articles 51 and 53, Chapter VII). Since Article 2(4) reflects a norm of *jus cogens*, any agreements, decisions and obligations conflicting with it are invalid. Hence, Article 103 renders the UN Charter itself, as well as the obligations arising under it from, for instance, binding Security Council decisions, a 'higher law' *vis-à-vis* all other treaty commitments of the UN Member States, among them those stemming from NATO membership.[7]

The question of the legality versus the illegality of so-called 'humanitarian intervention' must be answered in light of the foregoing. Thus, if the Security Council determines that massive violations of human rights occurring within a country constitute a threat to the peace, and then calls for or authorizes an enforcement action to put an end to these violations, a 'humanitarian intervention' by military means is permissible. In the absence of such authorization, military coercion employed to have the target state return to a respect for human rights constitutes a breach of Article 2(4) of the Charter. Further, as long as humanitarian crises do not transcend borders, as it were, and lead to armed attacks against other states, recourse to Article 51 is not available. For instance, a mass exodus of refugees does not qualify as an armed attack. In the absence of any justification unequivocally provided by the Charter 'the use of force could not be the appropriate method to monitor or ensure ... respect [for human rights]', to use the words of the International Court of Justice in its 1986 *Nicaragua* judgment.[8] In the same year, the United Kingdom Foreign Office summed up the problems of unilateral, that is, unauthorized, humanitarian intervention as follows:

> [T]he overwhelming majority of contemporary legal opinion comes down against the existence of a right of humanitarian intervention, for three main reasons: first, the UN Charter and the corpus of modern international law do not seem to specifically incorporate such a right; secondly, State practice in the past two centuries, and especially since 1945, at best provides only a handful of genuine cases of humanitarian intervention, and, on most assessments, none at all; and finally, on prudential grounds, that the scope for abusing such a right argues strongly against its creation ... In essence, therefore, the case against making humanitarian intervention an exception to the principle of non-intervention is that its doubtful benefits would be heavily outweighed by its costs in terms of respect for international law.[9]

The question which arises at this point is, of course, whether the state of the law thus described could have changed in recent years, possibly after the demise of the East–West conflict or under the shock of the genocide and crimes against humanity committed in the former Yugoslavia. Could it not be that 'humanitarian interventions', now undertaken in the spirit of ensuring that Srebrenica does not happen again, as it were, deserve a friendlier reaction also on the part of international lawyers? Do recent or current instances of 'military humanitarianism' show themselves to be uninfected by the less laudable motives that characterized such actions in the past? To what extent will collective decision-making, or the involvement of NATO or the OSCE as such, guarantee that such improper motives are restrained or even eliminated? And, most importantly, how could even the purest

---

[7] Cf. in this regard Art. 7 of the NATO Treaty.

[8] ICJ Reports (1986), at para. 268.

[9] UK Foreign Office Policy Document No. 148, reprinted in 57 *BYbIL* (1986) 614.

6   *EJIL* 10 (1999), 1–22

humanitarian motives behind military intervention overcome the formidable international legal obstacles just described? These obstacles could only be removed by changing the law of the UN Charter. There is no prospect of such a change, however. Thus, 'humanitarian interventions' involving the threat or use of armed force and undertaken without the mandate or the authorization of the Security Council will, as a matter of principle, remain in breach of international law. But such a general statement cannot be the last word. Rather, in any instance of humanitarian intervention a careful assessment will have to be made of how heavily such illegality weighs against all the circumstances of a particular concrete case, and of the efforts, if any, undertaken by the parties involved to get 'as close to the law' as possible. Such analyses will influence not only the moral but also the legal judgment in such cases.

2 Kosovo: A Thin Red Line

In the case of Kosovo, large-scale violence flared up in late 1997/early 1998. At that stage, the international community took steps to involve itself quickly and strongly, at least compared with earlier sad instances. In March 1998 the Security Council, acting under Chapter VII but without expressly determining that the Kosovo crisis amounted to a threat to the peace, adopted Resolution 1160 (1998), in which the Federal Republic of Yugoslavia and the Kosovar Albanians were called upon to work towards a political solution. In the same resolution, as mentioned earlier, the Council imposed a mandatory arms embargo *vis-à-vis* both parties.[10] It emphasized 'that failure to make constructive progress towards the peaceful resolution of the situation in Kosovo will lead to the consideration of additional measures'.[11]

In the days that followed, the situation deteriorated rapidly: fighting intensified and the Serbian security forces as well as the Yugoslav Army used force in an excessive and indiscriminate manner, thus causing numerous civilian casualties, the displacement of hundreds of thousands of innocent persons from their homes, and a massive flow of refugees into neighbouring and more distant countries. In April of 1998, the Contact Group for the Former Yugoslavia agreed, with the exception of the Russian Federation, to impose new sanctions on the FRY. In June, the UN Secretary-General advised NATO of the necessity for a Security Council mandate for any military intervention in Kosovo. However, by that time it had become apparent that the Russian Federation would not agree to such a step.

In September 1998, the Security Council adopted Resolution 1199 (1998) which, also on the basis of Chapter VII, determined that the deterioration of the situation in Kosovo constituted 'a threat to peace and security in the region'.[12] The Council demanded the cessation of hostilities, a ceasefire, as well as immediate steps by both parties to improve the humanitarian situation and enter into negotiations with international involvement. The FRY was requested to implement a series of measures aimed at achieving a peaceful solution to the crisis. In conclusion, the Council '[d]ecide[d], should the concrete measures demanded in this resolution and resolution

---

[10]   SC Res. 1160 of 31 March 1998.
[11]   *Ibid.* para. 19.
[12]   SC Res. 1199 of 23 Sept. 1998.

1160 (1998) not be taken, to consider further action and additional measures to maintain or restore peace and stability in the region'.

During subsequent weeks, however, it became clear that (at least) Russia would veto any Council resolution containing a mandate or an authorization to employ threats or the use of force against the FRY. On the other hand, it was equally clear that the just-quoted reference to eventual further Council action in Resolution 1199 (1998) was not sufficient in itself to provide a legal basis for the threat or use of armed force by UN Member States or international organizations. Thus, the Security Council was in no position to take the 'logical' further step of following up on Resolution 1199 (called a 'spring board resolution' by the then German Foreign Minister Kinkel) and ultimately authorizing enforcement action if the situation did not improve.

At this point NATO took over, as it were. Its members gave the organization the go-ahead for military action if the FRY did not comply with the Council resolutions, and the Alliance prepared for air strikes against the FRY. The principal legal basis for such action was to be the concept of 'humanitarian intervention', linked as closely as possible under the circumstances to the UN Charter in order to further gain legitimacy. The NATO position was summarized in the following terms by Secretary-General Solana on 9 October 1998:

> The relevant main points that have been raised in our discussion yesterday and today are as follows:
>
> - The FRY has not yet complied with the urgent demands of the International Community, despite UNSC Resolution 1160 of 31 March 1998 followed by UNSC Resolution 1199 of 23 September 1998, both acting under Chapter VII of the UN Charter.
> - The very stringent report of the Secretary-General of the United Nations pursuant to both resolutions warned inter alia of the danger of an humanitarian disaster in Kosovo.
> - The continuation of a humanitarian catastrophe, because no concrete measures towards a peaceful solution of the crisis have been taken by the FRY.
> - The fact that another UNSC Resolution containing a clear enforcement action with regard to Kosovo cannot be expected in the foreseeable future.
> - The deterioration of the situation in Kosovo and its magnitude constitute a serious threat to peace and security in the region as explicitly referred to in the UNSC Resolution 1199.
>
> On the basis of this discussion, I conclude that the Allies believe that in the particular circumstances with respect to the present crisis in Kosovo as described in UNSC Resolution 1199, there are legitimate grounds for the Alliance to threaten, and if necessary, to use force.[11]

This announcement appears to have made a certain impression on the FRY. In any case, intensive diplomatic efforts, particularly on the part of US Special Envoy Richard Holbrooke, during the following days led to a ceasefire and the conclusion of two agreements: a first agreement of 16 October 1998 between the FRY and the OSCE, providing for the latter to establish a verification mission in Kosovo, and including an undertaking by the FRY to comply with Resolutions 1160 and 1199; and a second agreement between the FRY and NATO, signed on 15 October 1998, providing for the

---

[11] Letter from Secretary-General Solana, addressed to the permanent representatives to the North Atlantic Council, dated 9 October 1998, document on file with the author.

8   *EJIL* 10 (1999), 1–22

establishment of an air verification mission over Kosovo in order to complement the
OSCE mission. According to the first-mentioned agreement,

> [i]n the event of an emergency situation in Kosovo which in the judgement of the [OSCE]
> Mission Director threatens the safety of members of the Verification Mission, the FRY shall
> permit and cooperate in the evacuation of Verification Mission members [by a NATO
> Extraction Force].[14]

Holbrooke further reached an accord with the FRY, according to which negotiations on a framework for a political settlement were to be completed by 2 November
1998.

On 24 October 1998, the UN Security Council returned to the scene again, reacting
to the conclusion of the Holbrooke agreements with the adoption of Resolution 1203
(1998). Acting under Chapter VII, the Council formally endorsed and supported the
two agreements concluded on 15 and 16 October concerning the verification of
compliance by the FRY and all others concerned in Kosovo with the requirements of
its Resolution 1199, and demanded full and prompt implementation of these
agreements by the FRY. It affirmed that the unresolved situation in Kosovo
constituted a continuing threat to peace and security in the region.

After some time, during which there was an improvement in the humanitarian and
security situation in Kosovo, violence increased again, culminating in the events in
Racak in mid-January 1999. In response, NATO threats of air strikes were resumed.

On 28 January 1999, UN Secretary-General Kofi Annan, he himself a former
special UN envoy to NATO, met with the North Atlantic Council. His statement to the
Council includes the following passages:

> We must build on the remarkable cooperation between the UN and SFOR in Bosnia to further
> refine the combination of force and diplomacy that is the key to peace in the Balkans, as
> everywhere. The success of the NATO-led mission operation under a United Nations mandate
> is surely a model for future endeavours . . . .
>
> Let me conclude by congratulating you on the upcoming 50th anniversary of the alliance,
> and wish you all success in your deliberations on devising a new strategic concept for the next
> century. How you define your role, and where and how you decide to pursue it, is of vital
> interest to the United Nations, given the long tradition of cooperation and coordination
> between NATO and the UN in matters of war and peace. I look forward to hearing your views
> on this matter.[15]

At a press conference in Brussels, the UN Secretary-General, when asked about the
preconditions of military intervention in the FRY/Kosovo, is reported to have said that
'*normally* a UN Security Council Resolution is required'.[16]

On the same day, NATO Secretary-General Solana made a statement to the press on
behalf of the North Atlantic Council, in which he affirmed that NATO fully backed a
new initiative of the Contact Group and was ready to employ its military capabilities if
necessary. He then added: 'You have seen from the visit of the United Nations

---

[14]   38 *ILM* (1999) 24.

[15]   Document on file with the author.

[16]   Document on file with the author (emphasis added).

Secretary-General to NATO earlier today that the United Nations shares our determination and objectives.'[17] On the evening of 29 January 1999, following decisions of the Contact Group taken a few hours earlier aimed at reaching a political settlement between the parties to the Kosovo conflict and establishing a framework and timetable for that purpose, the President of the Security Council made a statement according to which the Council welcomed and supported the decision of the Contact Group and demanded that the parties should accept their responsibilities and comply fully with these decisions as well as the relevant Council resolutions. Further, the Security Council reiterated its full support for international efforts, including those of the Contact Group and the OSCE Verification Mission, to reduce tensions in Kosovo and facilitate a political settlement.[18]

The next day, the North Atlantic Council repeated the threat of air strikes, if the 'requirements of the international community' and all relevant Security Council resolutions were not observed. In this context it welcomed the just-mentioned Presidential Statement.[19] On 1 February 1999, the FRY representative at the UN requested an emergency meeting of the Security Council 'following the NATO threats to the sovereignty of [his] country'. According to the FRY, '[t]he decision by NATO, as a regional agency, to have its Secretary-General authorize air strikes against targets on FRY territory . . . represents an open and clear threat of aggression against the FRY as a sovereign and independent Member State [*sic*] of the United Nations.[20] The FRY letter then drew attention to the requirement of UN authorization of enforcement action to be undertaken by a regional organization.

As of March 1999, the international community is expecting the parties to the Kosovo conflict to return to the negotiating table(s) and hammer out the details of a 'Rambouillet Agreement'. As things currently stand, the Security Council will be requested, in this agreement, to issue a mandate for a NATO-led multinational peace mission (KFOR), involving armed forces of both members and non-members of NATO, to secure the implementation of the 'Rambouillet Agreement', by military means if necessary. However, in view of the fact that the future agreement would embody the consent of the FRY to the deployment of a multinational peace force on its territory, NATO and its member states appear to regard a UN Security Council mandate/ authorization as politically desirable, but not indispensable, should the veto of a permanent member stand in the way. This at least was the viewpoint taken by the German Government in the parliamentary debate in late February 1999, which led to the *Bundestag's* approval of German participation in the military implementation of the future 'Rambouillet Agreement' as well as in NATO operations within the framework of the Extraction Force.[21] A similar view had been expressed earlier on

---

[17] NATO Press Release |99| 11.
[18] S/PRST/1999/5.
[19] NATO Press Release |99| 12.
[20] Document on file with the author.
[21] Cf. *Deutscher Bundestag*, 14. *Wahlperiode*, Docs. 14/397 and 14/414; see further the report of the members of the *Auswärtiger Ausschuß* (foreign relations committee) of the *Bundestag* annexed to the second document, at 5.

10   *EJIL* 10 (1999), 1–22

with regard to the effect of the Holbrooke Agreements on the legality of the presence of the OSCE Verification Mission in Kosovo and on that of the eventual evacuation of OSCE Verification Mission members by the NATO Extraction Force.[22]

In contrast, it is said that the current position of the Russian Federation is to call for a Security Council mandate based on Chapter VI in addition to an agreement with the territorial sovereign. If this condition were met, it appears that Russia would also be willing to participate in a NATO-led multinational peace mission in Kosovo.

Thus stands the chain of events relevant in the present context. In the following, these facts will be assessed in relation to the law set out in Section 1 above.

First, contrary to the standpoint taken in the FRY's request of 1 February for an emergency Council meeting, NATO is not a regional organization in the sense of Chapter VIII of the UN Charter. On the part of NATO, this was expressly clarified years ago in a letter addressed by the organization's former Secretary-General Willy Claes to the UN Secretary-General. Consequently, the requirement enshrined in Article 53 para. 1 of the Charter (cf. text at note 6 *supra*) for an — express or implicit, prior or *ex-post-facto* — authorization of enforcement action under regional arrangements or by regional agencies is not formally applicable in the case of NATO. The Alliance constitutes an international organization on the basis of Article 51 of the Charter; the only 'enforcement action' envisaged in this Article is self-defence. If NATO now widens the scope of its activities beyond 'Article 5 missions',[23] it leaves the area of relative freedom of action granted by Article 51 of the UN Charter and becomes fully subjected to the legal limits established by the 'higher' (cf. Article 103) Charter law intended to contain or prohibit any other, i.e. offensive, kind of coercion or enforcement by military means. Thus, we are back to the basic principle of 'no threat or use of armed force except in self-defense or if called for, respectively authorized, by the Security Council'. In our case, the requirement of such authorization would result (not from Chapter VIII but) from Chapter VII of the Charter. However, as to the modalities of Security Council authorization, the clarifications developed on Article 53 para. 1 will certainly be applicable by way of analogy. The argument could even be made that legal limitations to be applied in cases of interaction between the UN and regional organizations foreseen by the Charter would have even greater weight *vis-à-vis* an organization like NATO which is now venturing into the field of 'enforcement action' against third states (arg. *a minori ad majus*). In concrete terms, NATO could be authorized by the Security Council to threaten or use armed force against the FRY not only expressly and prior to such action but also implicitly *ex post* though not tacitly.

Since, as was shown above, an express authorization of the threat or use of force against the FRY never materialized, the follow-up question would be whether the sequence of Security Council reactions to NATO activities and their results described earlier could be seen as an implicit authorization granted *ex post*. In favour of a positive reply, one could point to the remarkable degree of 'satisfaction', as it were, expressed

---

[22]   Cf. the passage from the agreement of 16 October 1998 quoted *supra* in text at note 14.

[23]   On the internal, 'constitutional' aspects of this development see *infra* Section 3.

by the Council in its Resolution 1203 (1998) as well as in the Presidential Statement of 29 January 1999 with the Holbrooke agreements and the subsequent successes of the Contact Group — results causally linked to the NATO threat of imminent air strikes. These signals of political approval could, at any stage, have been prevented by the opposition of any permanent member of the Council. But the Russian Federation chose to remain silent. On the other hand, however, Russia had made it clear in the fall of 1998 that it was not ready to follow up on Resolutions 1160 and 1199 by agreeing to the ultimate step of unleashing armed force against the FRY. This position appears not to have changed since then. In light of this, the view that the positive reception by the Council of the results of NATO threats of force could be read as an authorization of such force granted implicitly and *ex post* is untenable. But would this not mean that the Security Council has welcomed and endorsed developments brought about in violation of the UN Charter? The question of such illegality *vel non* will have to be looked at, but, independently of a final legal judgment, the fact is that the Security Council, as a political organ entrusted with the maintenance or restoration of peace and security rather than as an enforcer of international law, will in many instances have to accept or build upon facts or situations based on, or involving, illegalities.

In consideration of the foregoing, it may be concluded that the NATO threats of air strikes against the FRY, not having been authorized by the Security Council either expressly or implicitly, are not in conformity with the UN Charter. In this regard, it makes little difference that the threat had not been carried out until the time of writing because Article 2(4) prohibits such threats in precisely the same way as it does the actual use of armed force.

Let us now look at the interaction between the UN and NATO from the other, i.e. the NATO, side. Such a complementary perspective might place the legal deficiency just diagnosed in a mitigating context, so to speak.

Indeed, one is immediately struck by the degree to which the efforts of NATO and its member states follow the 'logic' of, and have been expressly linked to, the treatment of the Kosovo crisis by the Security Council. In an address delivered in Bonn on 4 February 1999, US Deputy Secretary of State Strobe Talbott referred to an 'unprecedented and promising degree of synergy' in the sense that the UN and NATO, among other institutions, had 'pooled their energies and strengths on behalf of an urgent common cause'; as to the specific contribution of the UN, he saw this in the fact that 'the UN has lent its political and moral authority to the Kosovo effort'.[24] Note the silence as to UN legal authority.

Aside from the absence of a formal authorization discussed above, a reading of the relevant Council resolutions together with the respective pronouncements of NATO (members) might lead an observer to conclude that the two sides acted in concert. The most remarkable illustration of this is the way in which SC Resolution 1203 (1998) welcomed and endorsed the agreements between NATO/OSCE and the FRY brought about (or at least, helped along) by the unauthorized NATO threats.

---

[24] Manuscript on file with the author, at 9.

12   *EJIL* 10 (1999), 1–22

If we analyse the reasoning behind the announcement of NATO that armed force would be used if the FRY did not desist from further massive violations of human rights (cf., above all, Secretary-General Solana's letter of 9 October 1998[25]), we see that it follows two lines: first, it evokes elements of the doctrine of 'humanitarian intervention' without calling it by name; but secondly, and much more pronouncedly, it refers to, and bases itself on, the UN Charter and Security Council as well as other UN action concerning Kosovo wherever and in whatever way possible. Above all, it draws attention to SC Resolutions 1160 and 1199 and the fact of the FRY's non-performance of the obligations deriving from them under the Charter. Further, the letter leaves no doubt that it is the United Nations which represents the international community in its concern for the Kosovo crisis and formulates the respective community interests. Thus, NATO tries to convince the outside world that it is acting 'alone' only to the least degree possible, while in essence it is implementing the policy formulated by the international community/United Nations; it is filling the gaps of the Charter, as it were, in a way that is consistent, in substance, with the purposes of the UN. And, as already mentioned, then follows SC Resolution 1203 endorsing and building upon NATO action. Similarly, the Presidential Statement of 29 January 1999 welcomes and supports the achievements of the Contact Group following renewed NATO threats after the massacre at Racak — in the words of US Deputy Secretary of State Strobe Talbott, thus lending 'its political and moral authority to the Kosovo effort'.

Considering this interaction, or 'synergy', between the United Nations and NATO, one can agree with the view of the then German Foreign Minister Kinkel, according to whom NATO, in the state of humanitarian necessity in which the international community found itself in the Kosovo case, acted in conformity with the 'sense and logic' of the resolutions that the Security Council had managed to pass. The NATO threat of force continued and backed the thrust of SC Resolutions 1160 and 1199 and can with all due caution thus be regarded as legitimately, if not legally, following the direction of these UN decisions.

However, despite all this 'synergy', closeness and interrelatedness of NATO and UN engagements in the Kosovo crisis, there is no denying the fact that a requirement of Charter law has been breached.

This deficiency did play a central role in the deliberations of the Parliament of the Federal Republic of Germany (*Bundestag*) in mid-October 1998 in relation to German participation in NATO air strikes. In these debates, the international legal issues involved were discussed at great length and in considerable depth. The respect for UN Charter law demonstrated throughout the debates was remarkable. Such deference became particularly apparent in the critical discussion of the absence of a Security Council authorization. The German Federal Government, while recognizing this legal flaw, argued that the situation in Kosovo was so desperate as to justify the NATO threat, even without UN authorization, in a state of humanitarian necessity leaving no choice of other means. In this regard, differently from the NATO Secretary-General, the Government called a spade a spade and spoke of the NATO threat as an instance of

---

[25]   Reproduced verbatim *supra* text at note 13.

'humanitarian intervention'. The *Bundestag* finally gave its approval to German participation in the NATO action. But it was stressed by all voices in favour of such participation, in particular by the Federal Government, that German agreement with the legal position taken by the Alliance in the specific instance of Kosovo was not to be regarded as a 'green light' for similar NATO interventions in general. To quote Foreign Minister Kinkel before the *Bundestag*:

> The decision of NATO [on air strikes against the FRY] must not become a precedent. As far as the Security Council monopoly on force [*Gewaltmonopol*] is concerned, we must avoid getting on a slippery slope.[26]

This statement will also be relevant for Section 3 of this article. Whether the denial of precedential value expressed in it, which runs like a red thread through the German parliamentary debate, will have the desired effect cannot of course be decided by Germany alone. But what is of great importance is the emphasis on the part of both the German Federal Government and the *Bundestag* on the singularity of the Kosovo case from which no conclusion on a general rule or policy is to be drawn.

To briefly review two more technical issues: to characterize the NATO threat of armed force against the FRY as 'humanitarian intervention' does not fit the standard schema, as it were, of this controversial notion. Within the categories of international legal self-help and enforcement, these threats rather constitute reprisals, or countermeasures, intended to induce the FRY to comply with its obligations arising, in a first phase, from general international law and the relevant Security Council resolutions, and, in a second phase, from the Holbrooke Agreements of October 1998. However, such characterization does not change the result of the legal analysis: as already mentioned at the outset, countermeasures (reprisals) involving the threat or use of armed force are prohibited under international law, irrespective of any good humanitarian intention behind them, except if authorized by the Security Council under Chapters VII or VIII of the Charter.

The second observation relates to the view that, since a 'Rambouillet Agreement' would incorporate the consent of the FRY to the presence of the NATO-led multinational peace force in Kosovo, KFOR would possess a sufficient legal basis even without a Security Council mandate authorizing it. As mentioned earlier, the Russian Federation appears to regard a UN mandate based on Chapter VI as necessary but also as sufficient for the same purpose.

These views seem convincing only in as much as what is envisaged in Kosovo remains within the purview of classic peacekeeping; that is, of a mission not involving the use of armed force. If, however, KFOR is eventually to engage in 'robust' peacekeeping (consider, for instance, the issue of disarming the KLA), a legal basis for the presence and activity of KFOR in the form of FRY consent only appears rather fragile, and a critical departure from former practice. Further, it is not to be expected that in a 'Rambouillet Agreement' the FRY will consent expressly to the use of armed force by KFOR, if necessary, against the Yugoslav army and police (consider the

---

[26] *Deutscher Bundestag, Plenarprotokoll* 13/248, 16 October 1998, at 23129.

14   *EJIL* 10 (1999), 1 22

extremely guarded formula concerning possible action by the NATO Extraction Force within Kosovo in the Holbrooke Agreement of 16 October 1998[27]). In view of the explosive environment in which KFOR is to operate, a Chapter VII mandate in addition to the consent of the territorial sovereign appears highly desirable, to say the least.

By way of conclusion to this section: whether we regard the NATO threat employed in the Kosovo crisis as an *ersatz* Chapter VII measure, 'humanitarian intervention', or as a threat of collective countermeasures involving armed force, any attempt at legal justification will ultimately remain unsatisfactory. Hence, we would be well advised to adhere to the view emphasized and affirmed so strongly in the German debate, and regard the Kosovo crisis as a singular case in which NATO decided to act without Security Council authorization out of overwhelming humanitarian necessity, but from which no general conclusion ought to be drawn. What is involved here is not legalistic hair-splitting versus the pursuit of humanitarian imperatives. Rather, the decisive point is that we should not change the rules simply to follow our humanitarian impulses; we should not set new standards only to do the right thing in a single case. The legal issues presented by the Kosovo crisis are particularly impressive proof that hard cases make bad law.

3 NATO's Future 'Strategic Concept': From 'Out of Area' to 'Out of Treaty'?

At present, NATO is hammering out a new 'strategic concept' to define its role in the 21st century. It is to be adopted on the occasion of the Alliance's 50th Anniversary Summit in Washington in late April 1999. At the time of writing, the negotiating process is still under way. Most documents relating to the issues raised in the present paper are confidential. Nevertheless, the general direction in which the United States in particular wants the Alliance to move in the future is quite clear. For instance, in the address already mentioned above, Deputy Secretary of State Strobe Talbott had, among other things, the following to say about what he referred to as the 'deepening' of NATO:

> In that project [i.e., the transformation of NATO] . . . we must be ambitious. NATO was founded and designed to deal with the Soviet Union and the Warsaw Pact. That state and that alliance are gone, and so is the threat they posed . . . This isn't to say that NATO's original task of collective defense is finished or that collective defense is no longer at the core of the Alliance's mission. NATO must maintain its capability enshrined in Art. V of the Treaty of Washington, to deter and if necessary defeat what might be called classic aggression. Such a threat could arise in the future. But it is less likely to do so if NATO remains robust and ready.
>
> However, that is not enough if NATO is to remain relevant to the times. With the end of the Cold War, new, less spectacular, but more diversified threats have arisen. Disputes over ethnicity, religion or territory, can, as we've already seen, trigger armed conflict, which in turn can generate cross-border political instability, refugee flows and humanitarian crises that endanger European security.

---

[27] See text *supra* at note 14.

NATO must be able to deal with threats like these while maintaining its core function of collective defense.

. . .

[I]n re-inventing NATO, [we] must make hard political choices and a convincing political case with our constituencies. Here, I would submit, is the case we should make about the role and mission of the new NATO: It should start, . . . , with Art. V of the Washington treaty — our commitment to collective defense. But we also need to recognize that most current and foreseeable European security challenges involve non-Art. V missions; therefore we need to be better prepared to deal with them as well.

Furthermore, in this increasingly complex and interdependent world of ours, we face a more diverse and far-flung array of threats than we did in Truman and Adenauer's day. The proliferation of weapons of mass destruction and the scourge of terrorism do not fit neatly into our old slogans and concepts like 'The Free World' and 'The Iron Curtain,' or old geographic simplicities that suggested out-dated geopolitical ones — like 'East versus West.' . . . This means that as we maintain our ability to defend the territorial integrity of all NATO members, we also need forces, doctrines and communication assets that will allow us, when necessary, to address the challenges of ethnic strife and regional conflict that directly affect our security but that lie beyond NATO territory — as we have done, and are doing, in the Balkans. Also, it is mere prudence and common sense, not excessive ambition, to suggest that a truly modernized Alliance should be able to cope effectively with the all-too-modern challenges posed by the spread of ballistic missiles and WMD [weapons of mass destruction].

Some commentators contend that such adaptations require a revision of the North Atlantic Treaty, or believe that we are proposing one. This is untrue. The framers of the Washington Treaty were careful not to impose arbitrary functional or geographical limits on what the Alliance could do to protect its security.

Let me be clear: I am *not* saying there are *no* limiting factors on what NATO can and should do. Of course there are. NATO is a *consensus* organization, and it defines its common interests accordingly — by consensus of its members. We would not go anywhere as an Alliance unless all our members want us to go there. No ally can force others to agree to a NATO action. Under Art. IV of the Treaty of Washington, NATO members will consult when their security is threatened, and together they will determine the appropriate response.

There are also limits implicit in the military capabilities of the Allies themselves. No one is suggesting that we deploy NATO forces, say, to the Spratley Islands.[28]

The Deputy Secretary of State concluded this point by saying:

Nor are we suggesting that NATO act in splendid isolation from — or high-handed defiance of — the United Nations or the OSCE. All NATO Allies are members of both of those organizations. We believe NATO's missions and tasks must always be consistent with the purposes and principles of the UN and the OSCE. We expect NATO and its members will continue to be guided by their obligations under the UN Charter and the Helsinki Final Act.

At the same time, we must be careful not to subordinate NATO to any other international body or compromise the integrity of its command structure. We will try to act in concert with other organizations, and with respect for their principles and purposes. But the Alliance must reserve the right and the freedom to act when its members, by consensus, deem it necessary.[29]

The future role thus envisaged for NATO and the legal-institutional consequences which the proposed new concept implies for the relationship between NATO and the

---

[28] *Supra* note 24.
[29] Manuscript, at 4, 7f.

16   *EJIL* 10 (1999), 1–22

United Nations also became apparent in a 'Resolution on Recasting Euro-Atlantic Security', adopted by the North Atlantic (Parliamentary) Assembly in November 1998. In this document, the Assembly,

> [g]uided by the vision that NATO in the 21st century should be an enduring political-military alliance among sovereign states whose purpose is to apply power and diplomacy to the collective defence and promotion of Allied security, democratic values, the rule of law, and peace,

urged member governments and parliaments of the North Atlantic Alliance

> ...
>
> b. to accelerate progress in developing capabilities to meet emerging security challenges that may demand both Article 5 and non-Article 5 missions, including meeting the threat of the proliferation of weapons of mass destruction and international terrorism and enhancing power projection, surveillance assets, communications, sustainment, information superiority, and interoperability;
>
> ...
>
> d. to seek to ensure the widest international legitimacy for non-Article 5 missions and also to stand ready to act should the UN Security Council be prevented from discharging its purpose of maintaining international peace and security;
>
> e. to affirm that the inherent right of individual or collective self-defence, also enshrined in Article 51 of the UN Charter, must include defence of common interests and values, including when the lattter are threatened by humanitarian catastrophes, crimes against humanity, and war crimes; ...[10]

Certainly, these formulas will not be the last word as to how NATO will define its future legal-institutional relationship with the universal organization of the UN. But the message which these voices carry in our context is clear: if it turns out that a Security Council mandate or authorization for future NATO 'non-Article 5' missions involving armed force cannot be obtained, NATO must still be able to go ahead with such enforcement. That the Alliance is capable of doing so is being demonstrated in the Kosovo crisis. Whether such a course is legally permissible is a different matter. In the November 1998 resolution of the North Atlantic Assembly, two different legal arguments can be identified in this regard. According to the first one, the right of self-defence 'also enshrined' in Article 51 of the UN Charter is to be interpreted so broadly as to include the defence of 'common interests and values'. This text calls for two brief observations: to start with, the wording might create the impression that self-defence in international law has a broader scope than that foreseen in Article 51, i.e., that it is justified not only against armed attacks but beyond that specific instance also against other threats. What other menaces the authors have in mind is then made clear: attacks on 'common [i.e., NATO] interests and values'. To thus widen the scope of self-defence, as a legal institution, is intolerable, indeed absurd, from a legal point of view and does not deserve further comment. What might be mentioned, however, is that 'respect for the obligations arising from treaties and other sources of international law'[11] also counts among the values common to NATO member states.

---

[10]   NATO Doc. AR 295 SA (1998).
[11]   Preamble to the UN Charter.

The second argument, contained in para. d. of the North Atlantic Assembly resolution, reads like a codification of the course that NATO is steering in the Kosovo crisis. Therefore, the legal critique put forward in the preceding part of the present paper is fully applicable. It is probably no coincidence that the wording chosen for para. d. is similar to that of the 'Uniting for Peace' Resolution of the UN General Assembly of 3 November 1950, considering the keenness of NATO to have its actions partake of UN legitimacy, so to speak. But of course, according to 'Uniting for Peace', it was the General Assembly, as a UN organ comprising all Member States, that was to shoulder the burden of maintaining or restoring international peace and security *in lieu* of the Security Council, not an extraneous, regional organization comprising only about 10 per cent of UN membership.

'Uniting for Peace' was an attempt to fill a gap in the Charter system of collective security during the darkest period of the Cold War (and, of course, of the hot war in Korea). As mentioned earlier, during the same period several fundamental Charter provisions, like Articles 2(4), 51 and 53, were subjected to 'realist' reinterpretations in order to allow individual states as well as regional or defence organizations to return to pre-Charter conditions as regards the use of force. Considering the almost permanent stalemate in the Security Council extending over decades, such *ersatz* constructs might have had a certain legitimacy at the time. But today things are different: since the end of the Cold War, the Security Council is functioning precisely in the manner envisaged in 1945. During the decade up to and including 1997, Chapter VII was invoked no less than 112 times; during the same period the number of vetoes cast was extremely small. Considering this state of affairs, to circumvent substantive and, in particular, procedural cornerstones of Charter law is, therefore, much more dangerous to the integrity of the UN peace system than the aberrations of the past.

In view of the Russian position *vis-à-vis* the prospect of NATO 'peace missions' engaging in military enforcement out of area, a new formula has recently been put forward, according to which the necessary legal basis for non-Article 5 missions comprising the use of armed force is, 'as a rule', to be provided either by a mandate of the UN Security Council or by acting 'under the responsibility of the OSCE' (thus the address of German Federal Chancellor Gerhard Schroeder to the Munich Security Forum on 6 February 1999).[12]

The alternative thus offered may possibly appease the Russian Federation, but it cannot satisfy the international lawyer: the OSCE has grown into a regional organization in the sense of Chapter VIII of the Charter. As such, any military enforcement action under its responsibility will require authorization by the UN Security Council according to the rules described earlier. Thus, such peace enforcement under the aegis of the OSCE will not only require the consent of the Russian Federation but also that of the Security Council in accordance with Article 53 para.1 of the UN Charter. From the standpoint of United Nations law, therefore, the issue is not only how to obtain the consent/participation of Russia in peace

---

[12] *Bulletin des Presse- und Informationsamts der Bundesregierung* No. 8, of 22 February 1999, at 91.

18   *EJIL* 10 (1999), 1–22

enforcement but how to achieve this at the regional level in full conformity with the Charter.

Turning to a more subtle, 'linguistic', point, it is interesting to observe how certain, particularly US, voices place the United Nations in the company of regional organizations or similar institutions. For instance, in the Bonn address of Deputy Secretary of State Strobe Talbott repeatedly referred to already, we find the following observation:

> We started [the] process of institutional joint action in Bosnia, and we have built on it in Kosovo. We have seen five bodies — NATO, the EU, the OSCE, the United Nations and the Contact Group develop an unprecedented and promising degree of synergy. By that I mean that these disparate but overlapping organizations have pooled their energies and strengths on behalf of an urgent common cause.[11]

In the current debate, the formula of the UN and relevant Western regional institutions mutually reinforcing each other seems to have gained acceptance. To the present author, this way of describing the relationship of the institutions mentioned is to be treated with great caution. On the one hand, it is undeniably reassuring to see the 'political authority' of the UN emphasized by Mr Talbott relying on and backed up by the muscle of more dynamic regional institutions. But on the other hand, in political as well as legal discourse, this view could (is meant to?) have the effect of putting the United Nations on the same hierarchical level as these institutions, thereby relativizing the legal primacy due to the obligations flowing from the UN Charter.[14] In most quarters of the world, including Germany, it is accepted that the UN Charter is not just one multilateral treaty among others but an instrument of singular legal weight, something akin to a 'constitution' of the international community. This status of the Charter should not be prejudiced by NATO.

In his Bonn address, the US Deputy Secretary of State spoke of the hard political choices to be made 'in re-inventing NATO'.[15] In the same vein, however, he denied that such re-invention would require a revision of the North Atlantic Treaty. In the present paper, focusing as it does on UN law, only a few brief comments can be made in this regard.

If we compare the practices of amendment and revision of the constituent instruments of international organizations in general with the capacity of NATO to absorb, as it were, new roles and missions without any formal changes considered necessary to the original founding treaty, this flexibility is already astonishing at present, even before the imminent 're-invention'. Thus, quite aptly, some members of the German Federal Constitutional Court once spoke of the NATO Treaty as 'a treaty on wheels'.

At the level of international law, the power of member states of international organizations to develop, amend and revise the constitutive instruments of these

---

[11]   Manuscript, at 9.
[14]   Cf. on Charter Art. 103 *supra* Section 1.
[15]   Cf. *supra* text at note 28.

institutions by mutual agreement or subsequent practice is far-reaching. In the case of organizations working on the basis of majority decisions, the legal limits to such changes will be debated, in some instances adjudicated, in terms of doctrines like those of *ultra vires* versus 'implied powers'. These issues will hardly arise in the practice of international organizations which, like NATO, arrive at decisions by unanimous vote or employ a consensus method. Hence, from that point of view almost any transformation of NATO is feasible as long as all members agree, and this without a formal revision of the constituent treaty instrument. In this regard, Mr Talbott's remarks are perfectly correct. However, no unanimity of NATO member states can do away with the limits to which these states are subject under peremptory international law (*jus cogens*) outside the organization, in particular the higher law (cf. Article 103) of the UN Charter on the threat or use of armed force. NATO is allowed to do everything that is legally permissible, but no more. Legally, the Alliance has no greater freedom than its member states. This point has been the main thrust of the present paper.

However, the question of legal limitations to the transformation of NATO leads to a further issue: that of the democratic legitimacy of such 're-invention'. The acuteness and topicality of this question may vary from country to country. In the Federal Republic of Germany it has been at the heart of several great constitutional controversies ultimately resolved by the Federal Constitutional Court (*Bundesverfassungsgericht*). In these cases, one of the decisive issues was the extent to which alterations of existing obligations deriving, *inter alia*, from the NATO Treaty, or the creation of new such obligations, could be affected by way of 'soft law', for instance by decisions of the North Atlantic Council, while still being covered by the *Bundestag's* original approval of the NATO Treaty almost half a century ago. The Court was prepared to go quite far in allowing the dynamic evolution of NATO to escape the prerequisite of new parliamentary approval, but it did indicate certain borderlines, among them, in its 1994 judgment on the constitutionality of German participation in NATO/WEU action against the FRY in the Mediterranean and in UNOSOM II, the conformity of all these activities with the rules and procedures of the UN Charter as the overarching, universal system of collective security. Hence, in view of the strong emphasis placed by the German Government as well as the *Bundestag* on the singular, exceptional character of, and the express denial of precedential value to, the threat of force by NATO against Yugoslavia expressed in the fall of 1998, a general authorization for a 'new' NATO to proceed to military enforcement out of area without UN Security Council assent, if necessary, might well transcend the limits set up by the German Basic Law. The German Constitution provides for several procedures to have this question adjudicated by the Karlsruhe Court. In sum, there is reason for caution here; this is also because the *Bundesverfassungsgericht* has demonstrated its willingness to uphold the constitutional requirements for German participation in international organizations and supranational integration even against heavy political headwinds. [16]

---

[16] Cf. the 1993 *Maastricht* decision, [1994] CMLR 57.

20   *EJIL* 10 (1999), 1–22

As the Background Paper prepared by Jeffrey Laurenti for the United Nations Association of the U.S.A. for the present Roundtables puts it so well, some voices in the current debate fear

> that abandonment of the Security Council's asserted monopoly on determining the lawful use of force against others, except in self-defense, could put the world community on a slippery slope of competing claims of 'rights' to intervene — with the potential consequence of escalating hostilities rather than resolving them. Some see a disquieting historical precedent for alliance self-authorization for use of force in the Warsaw Pact's intervention in Czechoslovakia in 1968 (an intervention that was, to be sure, directed within its own membership). Some warn that such fragmentation of lawful authority on use of force could prompt the emergence of counter-alliances among those fearful of high-handed interventionism by an overweening Western alliance. If the U.N. has too many inhibitions about the use of force, these worry, NATO under U.S. pressure may have too few.[17]

The present author shares these concerns. He feels in good company, in view of the vehemence with which the German Government as well as the *Bundestag* emphasized in the October 1998 debate that the decisions taken by NATO on Kosovo must not be seen as a precedent leading to a general right of the Alliance to intervene militarily out of area without a Security Council mandate/authorization. The genie of NATO 'self-authorization' must not be let out of the bottle. Apparently, this is the opinion of other NATO member governments as well.

The law of nations being a horizontal system, claims to international legality and admissibility put forward by its actors, be they states or organizations, are prone to have a boomerang effect. True, at present NATO is the only regional institution capable of countering (self-defined) security challenges effectively, if necessary by military means. But things might change in the future, and other states or new alliances in Europe or in other parts of the world might then also proclaim to 'stand ready to act' without the Security Council, or affirm to defend certain 'interests and values' by armed force (to use the language of the November 1998 North Atlantic Assembly resolution). Reference to 1968 does not seem to be far-fetched: when the Soviet Union followed up on the Warsaw Pact intervention in Czechoslovakia with the 'Brezhnev doctrine', condemnation by the West, particularly the United States, of both the invasion and the general concept justifying it was resolute and strong; statements about the invalidity of such *inter se* derogations of fundamental Charter precepts abounded. One wishes that some of the respect paid to the UN Charter on that sad occasion would also mark the debate on NATO's strategic concept for the 21st century. The fact also mentioned in the UNA Background Paper, that the Warsaw Pact's intervention in 1968 was directed within its own membership, is not designed to quell legal concerns; on the contrary, the (unauthorized) threat or use of force against a state which is not a member of a certain international organization, and which might therefore not share this organization's 'common interests and values', appears even more indefensible than force employed within the organization's circle of members.

---

[17] J. Laurenti, 'NATO, the U.N., and the Use of Force', background paper prepared for the United Nations Association of U.S.A (1999).

In this regard, the announcement that the new NATO is to become more instrumental in meeting the threat of proliferation of weapons of mass destruction is of a particularly 'extrovert' nature, considering, as the UNA Background Paper does, that, aside from its nuclear-armed members, no country in NATO's own region has programmes for the development of these weapons. As the Background Paper also mentions, the international treaty regimes controlling these weapons all provide for the Security Council to enforce them. In light of this, it is to be hoped that a future role of the Alliance in this field would be linked to the already existing one of the Council by foreseeing the prerequisite of a Security Council mandate for any NATO action which assumes the nature of enforcement.

4 Concluding Remarks

It is disquieting to observe how the UN/NATO relationship has changed within a few years. In 1994, at its Brussels summit, NATO had declared its readiness to cooperate with the United Nations in 'peacekeeping and other operations under the authority of the UN Security Council'. In December 1997, the Final Report of a high-level International Task Force on the Enforcement of UN Security Council Resolutions regarded as 'doubtful that NATO would consider taking enforcement action, at least out of area, without Security Council authorization'.[18]

Less than a year later these doubts were dispelled. In the field under consideration here, NATO action has moved from full collaboration with the UN in both peacekeeping and enforcement in Bosnia to enforcement action in place of the UN, albeit still authorized by the Security Council to implement the Dayton Agreement, and now in the context of Kosovo it has shifted to enforcement in place of the UN without such authorization. For some, this last-mentioned schema is now generally to be embedded in NATO's new 'strategic concept'. According to the UNA Background Paper, this development suggests a shift in the UN/NATO relationship from mutual reinforcement[19] to fundamental competition:

> Under such a scenario, the organization in danger of sliding into irrelevance seems to be not NATO but the United Nations. In a political variant of free-market competition, the U.N. Security Council risks disappearing as a serious security body as the genuinely powerful prefer to work through a more convenient instrument. All that the Security Council can offer is 'legitimacy,' in the view of some Western governments — and NATO may provide the desired multilateral cover, with less obstruction.

Such a development would be deplorable. In the words of UN Secretary-General Kofi Annan:

> [P]eacekeeping is not, and must not become, an arena of rivalry between the United Nations

---

[18] United Nations Association of the U.S.A, *Words to Deeds: Strengthening the U.N.'s Enforcement Capabilities* (1997), at 45.
[19] Cf. on this phrase *supra* text at note 33.

22   *EJIL* 10 (1999), 1–22

and NATO. There is plenty of work for us both to do. We work best when we respect each other's competence and avoid getting in each other's way.[40]

This article has attempted to demonstrate that, while the threat of armed force employed by NATO against the FRY in the Kosovo crisis since the fall of 1998 is illegal due to the lack of a Security Council authorization, the Alliance made every effort to get as close to legality as possible by, first, following the thrust of, and linking its efforts to, the Council resolutions which did exist, and, second, characterizing its action as an urgent measure to avert even greater humanitarian catastrophes in Kosovo, taken in a state of humanitarian necessity.

The lesson which can be drawn from this is that unfortunately there do occur 'hard cases' in which terrible dilemmas must be faced and imperative political and moral considerations may appear to leave no choice but to act outside the law. The more isolated these instances remain, the smaller will be their potential to erode the precepts of international law, in our case the UN Charter. As mentioned earlier, a potential boomerang effect of such breaches can never be excluded, but this danger can at least be reduced by indicating the concrete circumstances that led to a decision *ad hoc* being destined to remain singular. In this regard, NATO has done a rather convincing job. In the present author's view, only a thin red line separates NATO's action on Kosovo from international legality. But should the Alliance now set out to include breaches of the UN Charter as a regular part of its strategic programme for the future, this would have an immeasurably more destructive impact on the universal system of collective security embodied in the Charter. To resort to illegality as an explicit *ultima ratio* for reasons as convincing as those put forward in the Kosovo case is one thing. To turn such an exception into a general policy is quite another. If we agree that the NATO Treaty does have a hard legal core which even the most dynamic and innovative (re-)interpretation cannot erode, it is NATO's subordination to the principles of the United Nations Charter.

To end on a lighter note: all of us leave the path of virtue from time to time. But one should not announce such a dangerous course as a general programme for the future, especially at one's 50th birthday.

---

[40]   Address at Georgetown University on 23 February 1999; UN Doc. SG/SM/6901, PKO 80.

[18]

Security Council Control over Regional Action

Christian Walter

In recent years the participation of regional organizations[1] in the maintenance of international peace and security has been increasing considerably.
The activities of the Economic Community of West African States
(ECOWAS)[2] in Liberia, of the North Atlantic Treaty Organization
(NATO)[3] and the Western European Union (WEU)[4] in former Yugoslavia
as well as of the Organization of American States (OAS)[5] in Haiti are
examples.

To some extent this development is the result of the precarious financial
situation of the United Nations. The financial aspect is exemplified by the
fact that recent Security Council authorizations for action by member
states acting either nationally or through regional organizations were given
"on the understanding that the costs of implementing the offer will be
borne by the Member States concerned"[6]. More important than the financial aspect, however, is the fact that important United Nations missions
failed to achieve their tasks. The replacement of the United Nations
protection force (UNPROFOR) in Bosnia-Herzegovina by a multinational implementation force (IFOR), which is mainly composed of NATO
troops[7], bears a clear political message towards regionalization.

A political reason for inquiring into the relationship between United
Nations and regional organizations may be seen in the Security Council's
hesitation when it dealt with the African civil wars in Burundi, Rwanda

---

1   In the following context "regional organizations" is used for the term
     "regional arrangements and agencies" according to Article 52 para.1 of
     the Charter.
2   UNTS Vol.1010 No.14843; *ILM* 14 (1975), 1200.
3   UNTS Vol.34 No. 541; UNTS Vol.126 No.339.
4   UNTS Vol.19 No. 304; UNTS Vol.211 No.186.
5   The Interamerican System is composed of the Charter of the Organiza-
     tion of American States, UNTS Vol.119 No. 1609; (amended by the
     Protocol of Buenos Aires of 27 February 1967, *ILM* 6 (1967), 310, the
     Protocol of Cartagena de Indias of 26 February 1986, *ILM* 25 (1986), 529,
     the Protocol of Washington of 14 December 1992, *ILM* 33 (1994), 1005
     and the Protocol of Managua of 10 June 1993, *ILM* 33 (1994), 1009), the
     Interamerican Treaty on Reciprocal Assistance of 2 September 1947,
     UNTS Vol.21 No. 324, (amended by the Protocol of San José of 26 July
     1975, *ILM* 14 (1975), 1122) and the American Treaty on Peaceful Settle-
     ment of Disputes of 30 April 1948, UNTS Vol.30 No.449.
6   S/RES/929 (1994) of 22 June 1994, concerning Rwanda and S/RES/940
     (1994) of 31 July 1994 concerning Haiti; see also paragraph 9 of S/RES/
     1080 (1996) of 15 November 1996 concerning Eastern Zaire.
7   See the Reports to the Security Council on IFOR Operations submitted
     by the Secretary-General of NATO, for instance Doc. S/1996/696, Ap-
     pendix.

and Zaire from 1994 onwards. The dilemma is well illustrated by the delayed decisions on an intervention force for Zaire in autumn 1996. It took the Council more than two weeks after pressure for an intervention mounted from international humanitarian organizations and European officials[8] until it decided on a multinational humanitarian relief force[9]. The decisions on the organization of the force took another ten days[10]. However, the force was not set up, since — except for France — possible contributors considered the situation of the refugees to have ameliorated considerably. One may therefore ask under which conditions rapid regional mechanisms may be set up in order to fill the vacuum created on the universal level and thus avoid disastrous consequences of Security Council inaction in civil war situations.

A. Possibilities of Regional Action — An Overview

In Chapter VIII of the Charter its founding fathers tried to integrate regional activities for the maintenance of international peace and security into the universal system of the United Nations. In doing so they intended to avoid some defaults of the system of the League of Nations. In particular, Article 52 paras. 2 to 4 and Article 53 para.1[11] were meant to define the respective competences of the United Nations and of regional organizations. Nevertheless, the scope of application of Chapter VIII of the Charter was to be rather broad. The delegates in San Francisco used the comprehensive formula "regional arrangements or agencies" in Article 52 para.1 in order to make the provisions applicable to a large number of regional organizations[12]. Thus, neither a specific internal structure nor a legally binding treaty under public international law are required. Organizations which are only based on political commitments, like the OSCE, are regional organizations in the sense of Chapter VIII of the Charter[13].

---

8   Calls Mount for Zaire Intervention, International Herald Tribune, Wednesday 30 October 1996, 1.
9   S/RES/ 1080 (1996) of 15 November 1996.
10   Military Leaders Agree on Options for a Zaire Force, International Herald Tribune, Monday, 25 November 1996, 4.
11   Articles mentioned refer to the Charter of the United Nations if not stated otherwise.
12   UNCIO Vol.XII, 701 and 858.
13   This view is largely shared in legal literature, see J.A. Frowein, "Regionale Sicherheitssysteme und nationales Recht", Sitzungsbericht Q zum 60. Deutschen Juristentag, 23 (24 et seq.); D.J. Scheffer, "Commentary on Collective Security", in: L.F. Damrosch/D.J. Scheffer (eds.), *Law and*

Organizations like NATO which were primarily designed to combat aggression from outside the organization may also be considered a regional organization if and when they contribute to the maintenance of international peace and security by means other than collective self-defence[14]. NATO has demonstrated in Bosnia and Herzegovina that organizations of collective self-defence may support the military enforcement of United Nation's non-military sanctions and may contribute to the protection of the civilian population[15].

The recent practice of regional and universal interventions into internal conflicts gives ample material to inquire into the relationship between the United Nations and regional organizations when the maintenance of international peace and security in civil war situations is concerned. The question of whether and to what extent Security Council control over regional organizations was necessary has been a matter of interest for international lawyers since 1945[16]. In most regional interventions the

----

Force in the New International Order, 1991, 101 (107 et seq). This view is confirmed by the practice of the OSCE and United Nations organs. The Security Council mentioned the (then) CSCE in connection with Chapter VIII of the Charter in its resolutions S/RES/743 (1992) of 21 February 1992 and S/RES/795 (1992) of 11 December 1992. In 1993 the General Assembly granted observer status to the OSCE starting with the 49th General Assembly in 1994 (A/RES/48/5 of 13 October 1993), a practice which has been applied to other regional organizations (see A/RES/ 253 (III) of 16 October 1948, concerning the OAS; A/RES/ 477 (V) of 1 November 1950 concerning the League of Arab States and A/RES/ 2011 (XX) of 11 October 1965 concerning the OAU). Furthermore, the OSCE declared itself to be a regional organization in the Helsinki Document of 1992 (para. 25 of the Helsinki Summit Declaration, reprinted in: A. Bloed (ed.), *The Challenges of Change. The Helsinki Summit of the CSCE and its Aftermath*, 1994, 385 (390)).

14   The often mentioned problem of different reporting obligations under Article 51 and Article 54 of the Charter may easily be solved by applying reporting obligations under Article 51 only to measures related to collective self-defence. All other contributions to regional peace and security by regional organizations of collective self-defence have to be reported according to Article 54 of the Charter, see in detail C. Walter, *Vereinte Nationen und Regionalorganisationen*, 1996, 47 et seq. and 347 et seq.

15   This holds true even though the concept of safe areas did not prove to be a successful means of protecting civilian population. The reasons of failure may rather be found in Bosnian Serb blackmailing of the United Nations (by kidnapping United Nations blue-helmets) than in lack of military effectiveness on the part of NATO.

16   The question was intensively dealt with during the cold war, especially with respect to the OAS, see M. Akehurst, "Enforcement Action by

question was not raised by any of the parties to the conflict. Nevertheless, the way regional action was dealt with in the Security Council may cast some light upon the question of control. Before this question is addressed in more detail a short review of the possibilities for regional action under Chapter VIII of the Charter may be useful to highlight the problematic issues.

Regional organizations factually have several means to intervene in a civil war. Apart from methods of peaceful settlement of disputes, which shall not be discussed here[17], non-military sanctions and military interventions are possible reactions. Non-military sanctions may include an arms embargo or economic sanctions. One of the measures taken by the ECOWAS[18] was the imposition of an arms embargo against the National Patriotic Front of Liberia (NPFL), which is one of the opposition groups fighting against the government of the country[19]. When the Government of President Aristide in Haiti was overthrown in a military coup in 1991 the OAS decided to impose economic sanctions against the new military regime[20]. These sanctions included the freezing of Haitian national funds and a trade embargo concerning all goods not destined to meet humanitarian needs.

Apart from such measures not involving the use of military force, regional organizations are capable of intervention by sending troops in order to redress the consequences of civil wars. Such military action is possible in the form of a peace-keeping force, or a regional military intervention against the will of the parties to the civil war may also be envisaged. Regional peace-keeping forces have a tradition which dates back to 1961.

From that year to 1963 the Arab League Security Forces were stationed in Kuwait[21]. From 1976 to 1982 the Arab Security Force (later renamed in Arab Deterrent Force) executed a peace-keeping mission in Lebanon[22] and

---

Regional Agencies, with Special Reference to the Organization of American States", *BYIL* 42 (1967), 175 et seq.

[17] See in this respect, Walter, see note 14, 141 et seq.

[18] See note 2.

[19] Doc. S/24811 of 16 November 1992, Annex I; for general information on the legal issues arising from the Liberian civil war, see G. Nolte, "Restoring Peace by Regional Action: International Legal Aspects of the Liberian Conflict", *ZaöRV* 53 (1993), 603 et seq.

[20] Doc. A/46/550-S/23127 of 9 October 1991, Annex.

[21] For details, see H. Hassouna, *The League of Arab States and Regional Disputes*, 1975, 102 et seq.

[22] For details, see J.P. Isselé, "The Arab Deterrent Force in Lebanon", in: A. Cassese (ed.), *The Current Regulation of the Use of Force*, 1986, 179

in 1982 the OAU sent a peace-keeping force into the civil war in Chad[23]. An example of regional military intervention may be seen in the sending of a ECOWAS cease-fire monitoring group (ECOMOG) into the Liberian civil war. ECOWAS received an invitation to intervene by President Doe but none of the other parties to the conflict consented. It is not quite clear whether such an intervention may be ranged within the scope of peace-keeping[24]. The participation of NATO forces in the protection of the safe areas established by Security Council resolutions 819 (1993) and 824 (1993) has demonstrated that regional military use of force is a means of reaction to civil wars. It is the purpose of this article to inquire into the legal foundations for these reactions by regional organizations. To what extent is Security Council control over regional action necessary and how is it ensured? The starting point for the analysis must be Article 53. This provision requires Security Council authorization for "enforcement action". Hence, the first item to be considered is which regional measures can be considered "enforcement action".

B. The Meaning of "Enforcement Action" in Article 53 Para. 1

I. Military Sanctions as Enforcement Action

It is generally admitted that regional military intervention requires Security Council authorization[25]. It should be noted, however, that during the Cuban missile crisis in 1962 American authors advanced an interpretation of Article 53 which considered as enforcement action measures which were the result of mandatory decisions of the respective regional organization[26].

(203 et seq.).
23 See G.J. Naldi, "Peace-keeping Attempts by the Organization of African Unity", *ICLQ* 34 (1985), 593.
24 See the analysis of Nolte, see note 19, 603 (626 et seq.).
25 G. Ress, "On Article 53", 722 et seq., Mn. 16 and 19, in: B. Simma (ed.), *Charter of the United Nations. A Commentary*, 1994; R. Wolfrum, "Der Beitrag regionaler Abmachungen zur Friedenssicherung: Möglichkeiten und Grenzen", *ZaöRV* 53 (1993), 576, (580 et seq.); see also M. Akehurst, "Enforcement Action by Regional Agencies", *BYIL* 42 (1967), 175, (194 et seq.), where only the question of non-military sanctions is discussed, while the author argues on the assumption that military action requires authorization.
26 See L. C. Meeker, "Defensive Quarantine and the Law", *AJIL* 57 (1963), 515 (520 et seq.) and by A. Chayes, "Law and the Quarantine of Cuba",

Security Council Control over Regional Action 135

According to them all regional measures which were not mandatory for the members of the regional organization did not need Security Council authorization. These authors stress the mandatory character of Security Council decisions under Chapter VII of the Charter as decisive criterion to determine enforcement action[27]. In this respect they refer to the following passage of the Advisory Opinion of the ICJ in the Certain Expenses Case:

> "The Court considers that the kind of action referred to in Article 11, paragraph 2, is coercive or enforcement action. [...] The word "action" must mean such action as is solely within the province of the Security Council. It cannot refer to recommendations which the Security Council might make, as for instance under Article 38 because the General Assembly under Article 11 has a comparable power. The "action" which is solely within the province of the Security Council is that, which is indicated by the title of Chapter VII of the Charter, namely "Action with respect to threats to the peace, breaches of the peace, and acts of aggression"[28].

It is argued that the Court in its Advisory Opinion had refused to qualify recommendations by the General Assembly or the Security Council as enforcement action since these recommendations were not mandatory for the member states[29]. The argument by the Court concerning Article 11 para. 2, is then applied to the interpretation of the term "enforcement action" in Article 53. The result is that only mandatory decisions can be considered to constitute "enforcement action" under Article 53 para. 1. However, this transfer of the Court's arguments concerning Article 11 para. 2, is not possible since Article 53 differs considerably from Article 11 para. 2. In Article 11 para. 2, "action" by the Security Council is contrasted with recommendations by the General Assembly. The only reasonable interpretation of this wording was to distinguish Security Council "action" by its mandatory character as opposed to the non-mandatory recommendations by the General Assembly. Article 53 para. 1, however, does not contain such a contrast between recommendations and Security Council action. Furthermore, the interpretation advanced by Chayes and Meeker does not take into account a second distinctive character of decisions under Chapter VII of the Charter, namely their

---

Foreign Aff. 41 (1962/63), 550 (556) and L. Henkin, "International Law and the Behaviour of Nations", *RdC* 114 (1965), 167 (259 et seq).

27 Cf. Meeker, above.
28 ICJ Reports 1962, 150, (164 et seq.).
29 Meeker, see note 26, 521.

purpose of forcing an aggressor to alter its peace-endangering behaviour[30]. This element, however, is also present in regional sanctions. On a political level the interpretation deserves criticism for it allows for unauthorized use of military force by all regional organizations which merely recommend their members to participate in the action. This would leave it to the discretion of the competent organ of the regional organization whether to recommend and avoid the decision of the Council or to decide on a mandatory basis and seek an authorization. This discretion is not in line with the system of the Charter which concentrates decisions on use of force in the Security Council. In conclusion, it seems preferable to lay the emphasis on the perspective of the target state. From the perspective of that state any action taken against its will has enforcing character, whether mandatory or not. For this reason the proposition by Chayes and Meeker is not convincing[31] and it has not been taken up since it was advanced in the 1960s.

II. Non-Military Sanctions as Enforcement Action?

The question of whether or not non-military sanctions fall within the scope of necessary authorization under Article 53 of the Charter has been a matter of debate since the discussions in the Security Council in the early 1960s when the OAS imposed such sanctions against the Dominican Republic[32]. Following these measures the Soviet Union tried to pass a resolution in the Security Council in which the Council would have authorized the OAS action retrospectively. This resolution was not agreed upon because the Western permanent members of the Council, especially the United States of the OAS, did not want to create a precedent with respect to non-military sanctions. Since then the question was not of practical relevance until the early 1990s when regional organizations increased their peace-keeping and peace-making efforts with respect to civil wars.

---

[30]   See U. Beyerlin, "Regional Arrangements", 1040, Mn. 6, in: R. Wolfrum (ed.), *United Nations: Law, Policies and Practice,* Vol. 2, 1995.

[31]   See also O. Schachter, "Authorized Uses of Force by the United Nations and Regional Organizations", in: L. F. Damrosch/D. J. Scheffer (eds.), *Law and Force in the New International Order,* 1991, 65, (87 et seq.).

[32]   Final Act of the Sixth Meeting of Consultation of Ministers of Foreign Affairs of 21 August 1960, Resolution I, OAS Official Records, OEA/Ser.D/III.12, 7 et seq.; see also M. Akehurst, "Enforcement Action by Regional Agencies, with Special Reference to the Organization of American States", *BYIL* 42 (1967), 175 (188 et seq.).

In the literature on the subject there are mainly three positions as to the question of whether non-military measures are included in the term "enforcement action". A first interpretation requires Security Council authorization for all non-military sanctions. These authors argue that the wording "enforcement action" refers to the wording of Chapter VII and hence all measures possible under Article 40, Article 41 and Article 42 had to be considered enforcement action[33]. Furthermore, it is argued that Article 2 para. 7, required Security Council authorization also for non-military sanctions. Illegal interference was not only possible by use of force but also by non-military measures. The necessary justification required a Chapter VII decision by the Council[34].

A second proposition shares the systematic arguments advanced by those authors who include all non-military sanctions into the requirement of Security Council authorization. However, these lawyers submit that it could not be correct to require an authorization by the Council for measures which are already lawful under general international law[35]. They argue that measures which could be lawfully applied by a single state without a decision of the Council should also be open for regional organizations without seeking an authorization[36]. Therefore regional organizations could enforce *erga omnes* obligations by applying non-military sanctions[37].

The third interpretation restricts the requirement for an authorization to use of military force. This interpretation focuses on the ban on the use of force in Article 2 para. 4, and argues that no corresponding prohibition existed for non-military sanctions[38].

---

[33] R. A. Akindele, *The Organization and Promotion of World Peace*, 1976, 56.

[34] J. M. Ruda, "Relaciones de la O.E.A. y la U.N. en cuanto al mantenimiento de la paz y la seguridad internacionales", *Rev. Jurídica de Buenos Aires*, 1961, 15, (59 et seq.); R. Pernice, *Die Sicherung des Weltfriedens durch regionale Organisationen und die Vereinten Nationen*, 1972, 114.

[35] R. Wolfrum, "Der Beitrag regionaler Abmachungen zur Friedenssicherung: Möglichkeiten und Grenzen", *ZaöRV* 53 (1993), 576, (582).

[36] E. Jiménez de Aréchaga, "La coordination des systèmes de l'ONU et de l'OEA", *RdC* 111 (1964), 419, (481); R. Gerold, *Die Sicherung des Friedens durch die OAS*, 1971, 131.

[37] Wolfrum, see note 35, 581 et seq.

[38] J. A. Frowein, "Zwangsmaßnahmen von Regionalorganisationen", in: U. Beyerlin/ M. Bothe/ R. Hofmann/ E.-U. Petersmann (eds.), *Recht zwischen Umbruch und Bewahrung. Festschrift für Rudolf Bernhardt*, 1995, 57 et seq., (66); J. A. Frowein, "Legal Consequences for International Law Enforcement in Case of Security Council Inaction", in: J. Delbrück (ed.),

Any interpretation should start with the wording of the Charter. However, the use of the term "enforcement action" in Article 53 gives as such no indication as to the question of exactly which kind of measures it covers. From the heading of Chapter VII, in which the term is also used, one might conclude that it comprises both military and non-military measures[39]. This interpretation is supported by systematic considerations. It is argued that the structure of Chapter VIII was parallel to the structure of the Charter as a whole. Article 52 corresponded to Chapter VI in covering peaceful settlement of disputes. In the same way, therefore, Article 53 should apply to all measures possible under Chapter VII[40]. Hence, the authorization requirement also covered non-military sanctions[41]. Additionally, some authors maintain that because of the military force involved in peace-keeping measures, the latter should also be considered to constitute enforcement action in the sense of Article 53 para. 1[42].

1. The San Francisco Discussions

To start the inquiry into the interpretation of Article 53 para.1, a look at the original drafters intentions might prove helpful. The text of the Charter is identical to Chapter VIII, Section C, para. 2, of the Dumbarton Oaks proposals[43]. The provision was dealt with in Subcommittee A of Committee III/4. The discussions in the Subcommittee, however, did not address

---

The Future of International Law Enforcement. New Scenarios — New Law?, 1993, 111, (121 et seq.); M.G. Goldman, "Action by the Organization of American States: When is Security Council Authorization Required under Article 53 of the United Nations Charter?", *UCLA Law Review* 10 (1962/63), 837 et seq., (855).

[39] The heading reads as follows: "Action with Respect to Threats to the Peace, Breaches of the Peace, and Acts of Aggression".

[40] R. Pernice, *Die Sicherung des Weltfriedens durch regionale Organisationen und die Vereinten Nationen*, 1972, 114.

[41] See also F. L. Morrison, "The Role of Regional Organizations in the Enforcement of International Law", in: J. Delbrück (ed.), *Allocation of Law Enforcement Authority in the International System*, 1995, 39 (43 et seq.), who argues that "enforcement action" is action requiring specific justification. According to this proposal measures under Chapter VII would frequently involve specific justification and hence be qualified as "enforcement action".

[42] A. Eide, "Peace-Keeping and Enforcement by Regional Organizations", *JPR* 3 (1966), 125 (141 et seq.); see also O. Kimminich, "Peace-keeping on a Universal or Regional Level", in: R. Wolfrum (ed.), *Strengthening the World Order: Universalism v. Regionalism*, 1990, 37 (47).

[43] UNCIO Vol.XII, 765.

at all the question of which measures were to be considered as "enforcement action". This lack of discussion may be due to the fact that the Subcommittee had to deal with two other important issues. One comprised a number of amendments proposed by different delegations, varying from the request for express authorization[44] over the requirement of a mere notification to the Security Council in case of self-defence[45], to the Australian position of complete independence for regional organizations in case of Security Council inactivity[46]. The second issue of debate in the Subcommittee was the question of the so-called "enemy-state clause" in Article 53 para. 1, in the second part of the second sentence. The amendment issue was solved by the proposition of a new provision dealing with the right to self-defence which became Article 51 in the final version of the Charter. This provision dealt with the concern of many delegations as to what the Charter could foresee in case of Security Council inaction. The wording took into account the proposed French and Turkish amendments and the new provision was agreed upon rather quickly[47]. With the Subcommittee still facing the issue of the enemy state clause, the question of a definition of "enforcement action" does not seem to have caught the attention of the delegates. The records of the San Francisco Conference, therefore, do not contain any guidance for the interpretation.

2. The Use of the Term "Enforcement Action" or "Action" in the Charter

A literal interpretation of the term "enforcement action" remains inconclusive since both military and non-military sanctions are designed to force a state or a faction of a civil war to alter its peace-endangering behaviour. It is interesting to note, however, that the Charter uses the wording "enforcement action" or "action" in some provisions, while others speak of "enforcement measures" or "measures". Article 41 provides for "*measures* not involving the use of armed force"[48]. Article 42 takes up that terminology and continues as follows:

> "Should the Security Council consider that *measures* provided for in Article 41 would be inadequate or have proved to be inadequate, it may

---

44   Bolivia, UNCIO Vol.XII, 767.
45   France, UNCIO Vol.XII, 777; Turkey, UNCIO Vol.XII, 781.
46   UNCIO Vol.XII, 766.
47   See M. Akehurst, "Enforcement Action by Regional Agencies, with Special Reference to the Organization of American States", *BYIL* 42 (1967), 175 (187).
48   Italics added by the author.

take such *action* by air, sea or land forces as may be necessary to maintain or restore international peace and security"[49].

One might be tempted to conclude from the contrast between "measures" and "action" in Article 42 that "action" may be confined to military enforcement. The term "measures" might then apply to both military and non-military sanctions. A look at the other authentic versions of the Charter[50] reveals, however, that the distinction between "measures" and "action" is not maintained consistently. In the Spanish version Article 42 speaks of "medidas" instead of "acción", although generally also the Spanish text distinguishes between "medidas" and "acción". Furthermore Article 2 para. 5, and Article 5 use the term "enforcement action" although both provisions are generally considered to apply to military and non-military measures[51]. In summary, no conclusions may be drawn from the distinction between "action" and "measures", because the wording is not consistently used throughout the Charter[52]. In the light of this result the terms "action" and "measures" do not permit any specific conclusions as to the interpretation of Article 53. Hence the term "enforcement action" in Article 53 has to be interpreted as an autonomous legal term, taking into account the function of the authorization by the Security Council which the provision requires. It may be helpful in this respect to take as a starting point the functions of Security Council decisions under Chapter VII of the Charter.

3. Functions of Decisions by the Security Council under Chapter VII of the Charter

Article 41 foresees measures not involving the use of military force. The measures decided under Article 41 are to be implemented by the member states of the United Nations. Decisions under Article 41 are mandatory for all members. A first function of Article 41, therefore, is to ensure that non-military enforcement measures be implemented by all member states.

A second important function of the provision is to provide a legal basis for the implementation of the measures in cases where otherwise international law would stand against such execution. Non-military sanctions

---

[49]   Italics added by the author.
[50]   See Article 111 of the Charter.
[51]   H. Kelsen, *The Law of the United Nations*, 1950, 92; J. A. Frowein, "On Article 2 (5)", 129 et seq. Mn. 2, in: Simma, see note 25; H.J. Schütz, "On Article 5", 175 et seq., Mn. 12, in: Simma, ibid.
[52]   For further different use of the terms cf. Walter, see note 14, 191 et seq.

may contravene the prohibition of interference into internal affairs[53]. Also, in some cases states are under treaty obligations vis-à-vis the addressee of the measures under Article 41. In both situations Article 41 provides the justification for either enforcing measures in contravention of the prohibition of interference into internal affairs or violating bilateral trade agreements. A second important function of Article 41, therefore, is the justification of non-military sanctions with respect to general international law or bilateral agreements.

Article 42, in the same way as Article 41, allows for decisions which are mandatory for all member states of the United Nations. Also, the decisions under Article 42 provide for justification with respect to the addressee of the measures. By contrast to decisions under Article 41, action according to Article 42 is not only justified with respect to the prohibition of intervention into internal affairs, but, most important, it constitutes a lawful exception to the universal prohibition of the use of force contained in Article 2 para. 4. It is characteristic of the system established by the Charter of the United Nations that — apart from the right to self-defence contained in Article 51 — all decisions on the use of military force are to be concentrated in the Security Council. This distinction between the functions of decisions under Article 41 and Article 42 may prove helpful for the interpretation of Article 53.

4. Consequences for the Interpretation of Article 53

The justification of the use of force which is inherent in Security Council decisions under Article 42 has to be kept in mind when interpreting Article 53. By contrast to the functions of Article 41 of the Charter, the justification with respect to Article 2 para. 4, which is inherent in an Article 42 decision of the Council may not be established in a regional treaty. The functions of decisions under Article 41 could be fulfilled in a regional treaty. The decisions of the competent organ could be mandatory for all members and non-military sanctions could be justified vis-à-vis the addressee if the latter is a member state of the organization[54]. Any use of

---

[53] The possibility of such a violation is not contested. The difficult issue with respect to non-military sanctions and the illegal interference into internal affairs is to determine where legal counter-measures end and where illegal interference begins, see in this respect, R. Jennings/A. Watts, *Oppenheim's International Law*, 9th edition Vol. I/1, 1992, 432 et seq.; W. Kewenig, "Die Anwendung wirtschaftlicher Zwangsmaßnahmen im Völkerrecht", *Reports DGVR* 22 (1982), 7 (15 et seq.); K. Bockslaff, *Das völkerrechtliche Interventionsverbot als Schranke außenpolitisch motivierter Handelsbeschränkungen*, 1987, 82 et seq. and 92 et seq.

military force, however, may only be justified by a decision of the Security Council.

Article 53 has to be interpreted as part of this system of the Charter which concentrates the use of military force within the Security Council. The requirement for authorization must be seen as an instrument to ensure Security Council control over use of military force. It follows from this analysis that it is only military enforcement action which requires Security Council authorization under Article 53. Non-military sanctions do not fall under the same rigid system as military action does. Therefore, an interpretation of the term "enforcement action" in Article 53, which takes into account the system of maintenance of international peace and security established by the Charter and the role of the Security Council within that system, leads to the conclusion that the term only refers to military enforcement action. Non-military sanctions are not subject to an authorization by the Security Council.

5. Recent State Practice

The interpretation of Article 53 which confines the requirement for authorization to regional military action is supported by recent state practice. When the government of President Aristide in Haiti was overthrown the OAS decided to impose economic sanctions on the new military government[55]. The sanctions included a freezing of Haitian funds abroad and an embargo on all goods which were not serving humanitarian needs. These sanctions were considered to be ineffective because of their regional limitation. Therefore, the Security Council was asked to make the sanctions mandatory for all members of the United Nations by imposing them under Article 41[56]. The Council followed that suggestion in resolution 841 of 16 June 1993. In this resolution the previous OAS measures are expressly referred to. The Council stresses that the UN sanctions are consistent with the trade embargo recommended by the OAS[57]. There are no indications in the resolution that the Council had doubts concerning the legality of the previous unauthorized OAS sanctions. Nor, in the debates, 'did any of the delegates question the legality of the regional sanctions. Even the Cuban Government which did not consider the situation in Haiti to constitute a threat to the peace and hence qualified the measures adopted by the Security Council as illegal under the law of the

---

54   The necessity of justification is also stressed by Morrison, see note 41.
55   The decision is reproduced in Doc. A/46/550=S/23127 of 9 October 1991, Annex.
56   Doc S/25958 of 16 June 1993.
57   Resolution 841 (1993), para.3.

Charter, did not criticize the OAS sanctions, but rather qualified them as "imposed by the appropriate regional organization"[58].

A similar procedure had already been applied in the Liberian crisis in 1992. In this case ECOWAS had decided to impose an arms embargo against one of the factions to the civil war[59]. The Security Council was asked by ECOWAS to extend the embargo to the universal level[60]. The Council did that in resolution 788 of 19 November 1992. In the debates preceding the adoption of the resolution, once again, none of the members questioned the previous regional practice[61]. The tacit acceptance of the regional non-military sanctions by the members of the Council may be assessed as expressing their view that non-military sanctions are not subject to an authorization by the Council according to Article 53.

III. Enforcement Action in Civil War Situations

Since the end of the Cold War in 1989/1990 the number of civil wars with ethnic and nationalistic background has been increasing. During the Cold War the question of outside intervention into civil wars was of particular interest since the two superpowers were more or less openly involved as supporters of one of the factions in a specific civil war[62]. With the end of the Cold War the issue of outside intervention into civil wars has lost some of its political relevance. Nevertheless, the question of whether and when Article 2 para.4 applies to internal conflicts remains a difficult legal problem[63], also in the context of regional enforcement action. The main issue is whether Article 2 para.4 prohibits outside intervention into internal

---

58   Doc. S/25942 of 14 June 1993.
59   The decision is reproduced in Doc. S/24811 of 16 November 1992, Annex I.
60   Doc. S/24735 of 29 October 1992.
61   See Doc. S/PV.3138 of 19 November 1992.
62   See J. N. Moore, "The Control of Foreign Intervention in Internal Conflict", *Va.J.Int'l L.* 9 (1968/69), 205 (233 et seq.); see also H. Neuhold, *Internationale Konflikte — Verbotene und erlaubte Mittel ihrer Austragung*, 1977, 96 et seq.
63   As to the question of whether and when Article 2 para.4, may be applied between the different factions in a civil war, see A. Randelzhofer, "On Article 2 (4)", 106 et seq., Mn. 29 - 33, in: Simma, see note 25; D. Rauschning, "Die Geltung des völkerrechtlichen Gewaltverbots in Bürgerkriegssituationen", in: W. Schaumann (ed.), *Völkerrechtliches Gewaltverbot und Friedenssicherung*, 1971, 75 (76 et seq.); see also J.A. Frowein, *Das de-facto Regime im Völkerrecht*, 1968, 35 et seq. and 69.

conflicts. Could the consent of a government[64] overcome the character of enforcement?

Intervention by regional organizations may, to some extent, be comparable to intervention by third states. It is therefore appropriate to analyse the legal regime of unilateral intervention into civil wars. In doing so it is necessary to distinguish between interventions with and without consent of the parties to the conflict. If both parties have consented, the "intervention" acquires the character of a peace-keeping operation and cannot be qualified as enforcement action[65]. It is difficult, however, to assess the current regulations of international law concerning unilateral invitations for intervention into internal conflicts. Such invitations may come from the government or from a rebel group in an internal conflict.

1. Request by the Government for Unilateral Intervention

The traditional position of international law is that the recognized government may invite foreign forces for assistance in combatting rebels[66]. The ICJ referred to this principle in an obiter dictum in its Nicaragua decision:

> "[...] the principle of non-intervention derives from customary international law. It would certainly loose its effectiveness as a principle of law if intervention were to be justified by a mere request of assistance made by an opposition group in another State [...]. Indeed, it is difficult to see what would remain of the principle of non-intervention in international law if intervention, *which is already allowable at the request of the government of a State*, were also to be allowed at the request of the opposition"[67].

An analysis of state practice concerning interventions by invitation faces some difficulties. Firstly, the validity of invitations issued during the Cold War may reasonably be questioned because of the influence of the respective superpower in the situation. With respect to the Soviet Union, the

---

64   See the comprehensive study by A. Tanca, *Foreign Armed Intervention in Internal Conflict*, 1994, 13 et seq.

65   See in detail infra, p. 171 et seq.

66   Jennings/Watts, see note 53, 437 with further references; R. Higgins, "Internal War and International Law", in: C.E. Black/R. Falk, *The Future of International Legal Order*, Vol. III (1971), 81 (94 et seq.); Randelzhofer, see note 63, Mn. 30.

67   Military and Paramilitary Activities in and against Nicaragua, ICJ Reports 1986, 14 (126), para. 246; Italics added by the author.

invitation of Hungary in 1956 may be used as reference[68] and on the American side, the invitation to intervene in the Dominican Republic in 1965 is an example, where even the existence of the invitation was unclear[69]. A second reason for the limited value of state practice is that intervening states tend to give a number of reasons for their action which are sometimes intertwined. Among these justifications the invitation by the government is mentioned. The problem may be illustrated by the American justification for the country's intervention in Lebanon in 1958. President Eisenhower gave the following message to the Congress:

> "On July 14, 1958, I received an urgent request from the President of the Republic of Lebanon that some United States forces be stationed in Lebanon. President Chamoun stated that without immediate showing of United States support, the Government of Lebanon would be unable to survive. This request by President Chamoun was made with the concurrence of all the members of the Lebanese Cabinet. I have replied that we would do this and a contingent of United States marines has now arrived in Lebanon. [...]
>
> After the most detailed consideration, I have concluded that, given the developments in Iraq, the measures taken by the United Nations Security Council are not sufficient to preserve the independence and integrity of Lebanon. I have considered, furthermore, the question of our responsibility to protect and safeguard American citizens in Lebanon of whom there are about 2,500. Pending the taking of adequate measures by the United Nations, the United States will be acting pursuant to what the United Nations Charter recognizes is an inherent right — the right of all nations to work together and to seek help when necessary to preserve their independence"[70].

The statement combines the invitation by President Chamoun with arguments of collective self-defence and a right to protect a country's own nationals in a way that makes it difficult to assess whether each of the given justifications would have been sufficient as sole reason for the intervention. In the same way the French interventions in Northern Africa, which are often quoted as examples for interventions on request[71], are not entirely

---

68   For details see L. Doswald-Beck, "The Legal Validity of Military Intervention by Invitation of the Government", *BYIL* 56 (1985), 189 (222 et seq.).

69   For details see W. Friedman, "United States Policy and the Crisis of International Law", *AJIL* 59 (1965), 857 (868).

70   Department of State Bulletin 39 (1958 II), 182 et seq.

71   Cf. Jennings/ Watts, see note 53, 435 et seq.

conclusive. The intervention in Zaire in 1978 was a reaction to save the lives of European nationals[72] and the French Prime Minister and President justified the intervention in Chad in 1983 expressly by citing Article 51 and the Libyan activities in the border area. The French Minister of Foreign Affairs referred also to previous interventions when he stated in Parliament on 27 September 1978:

> "Si la France a été amenée à intervenir sur le continent africain, elle l'a toujours fait à la demande du gouvernement reconnu du pays intéressé, et en limitant le volume et la durée de son assistance aux nécessités de la situation. Dans chaque cas, il s'est agi de répondre à l'appel d'Etats victimes d'une aggression extérieure"[73].

The statements show that an intervention based solely on the invitation by the government is rare. Rather, additional reasons are invoked and it is the combination of these reasons on which governments rely. It should also be kept in mind that there is a difference between, on the one hand, an invitation by a government which is in overall control over its country and merely requests assistance in a police action and, on the other hand, the desperate cry for help by a government in a situation where it has almost been defeated by opposition forces. While in the first case the pure invitation might suffice, in the second the necessity to give additional reasons, such as foreign intervention on the rebel side, increases.

The Institut de Droit International adopted at its 1975 session in Wiesbaden a resolution in which supporting either side in a civil war was considered illegal[74]. This position is shared to some extent in the literature[75]. The main argument advanced is that third party military intervention was contrary to Article 2 para. 4[76]. The prohibition of the use of force was also protecting the right of a country to solve a civil war without military intervention from outside[77]. Apart from protecting potential

---

[72]   C. Rousseau, "Chronique des faits internationaux", *RGDIP* 83 (1979), 126 (204).

[73]   Quoted from Rousseau, ibid., 171.

[74]   *Annuaire de l'Institut de Droit International* 56 (1975), 544 et seq.

[75]   See the references in Randelzhofer, see note 63, Mn. 31; M. Bothe, "Das Gewaltverbot im allgemeinen", in: W. Schaumann, *Völkerrechtliches Gewaltverbot und Friedenssicherung*, 1971, 11 (26); U. Beyerlin, *Die humanitäre Aktion zur Gewährleistung eines Mindeststandards in nicht-internationalen Konflikten*, 1975, 60 et seq.

[76]   O. Schachter, *Annuaire de l'Institut de Droit International* 56 (1975), 418.

[77]   O. Schachter, "The Right of States to Use Armed Force", *Mich.L.Rev.* 82 (1983/84), 1620 (1641).

victim states, the provision was also designed to ensure international relations which are free from use of force[78]. This was a common interest of the community of states which could not be at the disposal of a single state[79]. The 9th edition of Oppenheim's International Law suggests that the mere fact that a civil war is going on deprives the government of its capacity to issue invitations:

> "So long as the government is in overall control of the state and internal disturbances are essentially limited to matters of local law and order or isolated guerrilla or terrorist activities, it may seek assistance from other states which are entitled to provide it. But when there exists a civil war and control of a state is divided between warring factions, any form of interference or assistance (except probably of a humanitarian character) to any party amounts to intervention contrary to international law. In such a case the authority of any party to the conflict to be the government entitled to speak (and to seek assistance) on behalf of the state will be doubtful; and assistance to any party will prejudice the right of the state to decide for itself its form of government and political system. It is, however, widely accepted that if there is outside interference in favour of one party to the struggle, other states may assist the other party"[80].

The conclusion that governmental power to invite foreign military forces is limited to effective governments is supported by the wording of Article 2 para.4, according to which not only territorial integrity but also political independence are protected. Once the government has lost effective control, any assistance from the outside interferes in the balance of power in that country. The conclusion is further supported by the way in which the United Nations acted during the Congo crisis. Although the Congolese central government had supported direct military action against the rebel province of Katanga, the United Nations did not directly attack the rebel forces. Instead they relied on the concept of "active self-defence" and the Secretary-General declined demands for direct action against Katanga arguing that such action would violate the principle of non-intervention[81]. The Secretary-General's position was shared by a majority in the Security Council against the Soviet and Polish position according to which direct

---

[78]   As to this argument cf.Tanca, see note 64, 19 et seq.

[79]   W. Wengler, *Das völkerrechtliche Gewaltverbot*, 1967, 49 et seq.

[80]   Jennings/ Watts, see note 53, 437 et seq. (footnotes omitted); a similar position is advanced by A. Thomas/A.J. Thomas, *Non-Intervention, the Law and its impact in the Americas*, 1956, 94.

[81]   Doc. S/4417 Add. 6 of 12 August 1960.

action against Katanga would have been possible[82]. With respect to invitations by the government, the prohibition of the use of force and the principle of non-intervention are closely interrelated with the right to self-determination. The latter has an internal protective dimension[83] which prohibits interventions from outside[84]. The interrelation between the principles is expressed in the so called Friendly-Relations Declaration (Declaration on Principles of International Law Concerning Friendly Relations) of the General Assembly of the United Nations.

> "By virtue of the principle of equal rights of and self-determination of peoples enshrined in the Charter, all peoples have the right to freely determine, without external interference, their political status and to pursue their economic, social and cultural development, and every State has the duty to respect this right in accordance with the provisions of the Charter"[85].

The principle of self-determination has mainly been invoked in the context of decolonization[86]. Nevertheless, the wording of the Friendly-Relations Declaration and other international documents reveals that it is a right of all peoples[87]. It is doubtful whether the right to self-determination includes a right to secession[88]. A right to secession would render support for a government which is suppressing a people striving for independence even more difficult. But even, without including a right to secession, the Friendly-Relations Declaration is evidence of the negative attitude of the international community towards unilateral external interference[89].

The Turkish intervention in Cyprus was based on a contractual agreement in the Treaty of Guarantee signed at Nicosia on 16 August 1960[90].

---

[82]   SCOR, 15 Year, 1960,Suppl. July, August, September 1960, 64 et seq.

[83]   M. Pomerance, *Self-Determination in Law and Practice,* 1982, 37 et seq.; J.H. Leurdijk, "Civil War and Intervention in International Law", *NILR* 24 (1977), 143 (150); A. Rosas, "Internal Self-Determination", in: C. Tomuschat (ed.), *The Modern Law of Self-Determination,* 1993, 225 (232 et seq.).

[84]   D. Thürer, *Das Selbstbestimmungsrecht der Völker,* 1976, 184.

[85]   A/RES/2625 (XXV) of 24 October 1970.

[86]   K. J. Partsch, "Self-Determination", in: R. Wolfrum (ed.), *United Nations: Law, Policies and Practice*, 1995, Vol. 2, 1171 et seq.

[87]   C. Tomuschat, "Self-Determination in a Post-Colonial World", in: Tomuschat, see note 83, 1 (2 et seq.) with references of state practice.

[88]   See in this respect D. Murswiek, "The Issue of Secession — Reconsidered", in: Tomuschat, see note 83, 21 (32 et seq.).

[89]   Doswald-Beck, see note 68, 189 (243).

Parties to the treaty are Cyprus on the one part and Greece, Turkey and the United Kingdom of Great Britain and Northern Ireland on the other. The treaty was signed when Cyprus became independent and it contains a clause which reserves for each of the guaranteeing powers the right to intervene in the event of a breach of the treaty[91]. In 1974 the government of Archbishop Makarios was overthrown in a coup. The new government was mainly composed of people who were in favour of a union with Greece and suspicions arose that the Greek government was behind the coup. In this situation Turkey invaded Cyprus and in doing so it relied on the Treaty of Guarantee. The Security Council passed several resolutions on the matter, two of which condemned the Turkish intervention[92].

The Turkish intervention is of interest because it was based on the consent of a government which was not given ad-hoc in a situation of crisis but years before in a treaty. In fact, the Cypriot government at the time of the intervention was opposed to the intervention. Although the previous breach of the treaty was not disputed, the international reactions to the Turkish intervention were largely negative[93]. It has been argued that the negative international reaction to the Turkish intervention created a presumption against the legality of an intervention based upon governmental consent in a treaty[94]. Whether or not this far-reaching conclusion may be drawn is a question which does not have to be answered in this context. With respect to the issue of intervention into civil wars it is sufficient to note that Turkey was not simply relying on a Cypriot violation of the treaty but was accusing Greece of having interfered in the matter. For this reason the case of Cyprus cannot be cited as an example for intervention solely on the grounds of governmental invitation. Apart from that, the negative international reactions cast some doubt on the legality of intervention treaties.

---

90 UNTS Vol.382 No.5475.

91 Article IV: "In the event of a breach of the provisions of the present Treaty, Greece, Turkey and the United Kingdom undertake to consult together with respect to the representations or measures necessary to ensure observance of those provisions.

In so far as common or concerted action may not prove possible, each of the three guaranteeing powers reserves the right to take action with the sole aim of re-establishing the state of affairs created by the present Treaty."

92 S/RES/353 (1974) of 20 July 1974 and S/RES/360 (1974) of 16 August 1974.

93 Cf. the thorough analyis by Doswald-Beck, see note 68, 189 (247 et seq.).

94 Doswald-Beck, ibid., 250.

In summary, the invitation by the government may only be considered as justification for military intervention in situations where the government retains effective control over the country. Interventions based on the consent of an ineffective government — in contrast — violate Article 2 para.4. As for the question of previous consent to military interference on the basis of a treaty the same standard has to be applied. The government may only give a contractual consent to military intervention for situations in which it could give ad-hoc consent, i.e. in situations of effective governmental control. It is not possible to enhance the legalizing effect of requests by the government merely by giving the consent at an earlier stage[95].

2. Consequences for Intervention by Regional Organizations on Request by the Government

The result that an invitation by an ineffective government does not justify military intervention against the prohibition of use of force in Article 2 para.4 may serve as a starting point for discussing invitations for intervention by regional organizations. The main argument when interpreting the meaning of "enforcement action" in Article 53 of the Charter was that authorization by the Security Council was necessary where otherwise a violation of Article 2 para. 4 would occur. This rationale implies that if the request emanates from an ineffective government Security Council authorization would be necessary to justify regional intervention. The following analysis of practice by regional organizations may serve as a test as to whether this tentative conclusion is supported in practice. Relevant practice is the intervention by the Organization of East Caribbean States (OECS)[96] and the United States of America in Grenada in October 1983 and the sending of ECOMOG by ECOWAS into the Liberian Civil War.

In Grenada, which became independent in 1974, the British Crown was Head of State. She was represented by a Governor-General with mainly representative functions, while the executive power was in the hands of a prime minister[97]. In 1979 the Government was overthrown in a coup led by Maurice Bishop. Since then a communist "People's Revolutionary Government" under Bishop had been in charge, which was supported by the communist New Jewel Movement. In 1983 tension arose within the Central Committee of the New Jewel Movement, which led to the killing

---

95   For a different view of the role of self-determination in this context see J. A. Frowein, "Self-Determination as a Limit to Obligations", in: Tomuschat, see note 83, 211 (221 et seq.).

96   *ILM* 20 (1981), 1166.

97   As to the Constitutional Questions, see W. C. Gilmore, *The Grenada Intervention*, 1984, 65 et seq.

of Bishop and military fighting between the different factions. The OECS discussed the matter on 21 October 1983 and decided to intervene with the help of the United States of America[98]. One of the justifications for the intervention was an invitation which the then Governor-General, Sir Paul Scoon, had issued. The exact circumstances of the invitation are unclear. In an interview with the BBC on 31 October Sir Paul said he "thought" that he decided to ask for help on 23 October[99]. On 27 October, the text of a written invitation dated 24 October was presented by the Government of Barbados[100]. In this invitation Sir Paul asks for a peace-keeping force and confirms that he was also seeking help from the United States, Jamaica and the OECS. The circumstances of the invitation are dubious in two respects. Firstly, Sir Paul does not seem to exactly remember in his interview of 31 October 1983 when he decided to ask for help. And secondly, there is some doubt as to when the written request was sent. According to the documentation edited by Gilmore the invitation is undated[101] and there is some suspicion that it was produced after the invasion took place[102].

The United States justified the intervention on three legal grounds: the invitation by the lawful government of Grenada, the 1981 Treaty Establishing the OECS and the protection of United States citizens in Grenada[103]. The reactions of the international community to the intervention were negative. In the Security Council and in the General Assembly of the

---

98 As to the factual background of the events in Grenada, see S. Davidson, *Grenada*, 1987, 17 et seq. and 53 et seq.; see also L. Doswald-Beck, "The Legality of the United States' Intervention in Grenada", *NILR* 31 (1984), 355 (356 et seq.).

99 "I think I decided so on Sunday the 23rd, late Sunday Evening... Later on, as things deteriorated, I thought, because people were scared, you know. I had several calls from responsible people in Grenada that something should be done. "Mr. Governor-General, we are depending on you [that] something be done. People in Grenada cannot do it, you must get help from outside." What I did ask for was not an invasion but help from outside... I asked for help from the OECS countries. I also asked the OECS to ask America whether they can help, and then I confirmed this in writing myself to the President of the U.S.A.", quoted from J.N. Moore, "Grenada and the International Double Standard", *AJIL* 78 (1984), 145 (148).

100 The text of the invitation is reprinted in Moore, ibid.

101 Gilmore, see note 97, 95.

102 S. Davidson, *Grenada*, 1987, 100 et seq.

103 See the statement by Deputy Secretary of State K.W. Dam, reprinted in M.N. Leich, "Contemporary Practice of the United States Relating to International Law", *AJIL* 78 (1984), 200 (203 et seq.).

United Nations most states condemned the action on the grounds that it was contrary to the principle of non-intervention[104]. The intervention by the OECS and the United States therefore provides no arguments that would indicate that interventions by regional organizations be treated differently from unilateral interventions.

The Liberian civil war started at the end of the year 1989. By July 1990 President Doe had lost control over the country except for a small part of Monrovia including the presidential palace[105]. In this situation Doe addressed ECOWAS and asked for an "ECOWAS peace-keeping force". ECOWAS accepted the request and sent a "Cease-Fire Monitoring Group (ECOMOG)". The invitation has been viewed as justifying the intervention by ECOMOG[106]. There seems to be some doubt as to the justifying effect of the request since at the time the invitation was issued Doe was only in control of a small area in Monrovia including the presidential palace and its immediate surroundings. Furthermore the wording of the invitation was not very explicit:

> "It is therefore my sincere hope that in order to avert the wanton destruction of lives and properties and further forestall the reign of terror, I wish to call on your Honorable Body to take note of my personal concerns and the collective wishes of the people of Liberia, and to assist in finding a constitutional and reasonable solution to the crisis in our country as early as possible. Particularly, it would seem most expedient at this time to introduce an ECOWAS Peace-keeping Force into Liberia to forestall increasing terror and tension and to assure a peaceful transitional environment"[107]

Apart from the fact that the letter does not explicitly demand an intervention[108] it is interesting to note that ECOWAS did not invoke the letter as

---

104   SCOR 2489th Mtg. of 26 October 1983; 2491th Mtg. of 27 October 1983; GAOR 1983, 43rd Plenary Mtg. of 2 November 1983, 689 et seq.; see also F.Boyle et al., "International Lawlessness in Grenada", *AJIL* 78 (1984), 172 (174).

105   For details of the developments see Nolte, see note 19, 603 et seq.

106   Nolte, ibid., 633 et seq.

107   The text of the invitation is reprinted in M. Weller (ed.), *Regional Peacekeeping and International Enforcement: The Liberian Crisis*, 1994, 60 et seq.

108   This point is raised by K. O. Kufuor, "The Legality of the Intervention in the Liberian Civil War by the Economic Community of West African States", *Revue africaine de Droit International et Comparé* 5 (1993), 525 (537).

a justification but instead stressed the humanitarian and impartial character of the intervention[109]. The situation in Liberia has been compared to the complete breakdown of governmental authority in Somalia[110]. There may be seen some difference in so far as the number of contenders for government were limited to three factions in the Liberian war. But apart from that difference the analysis is quite correct in that the governmental structures in both states were completely dissolved. Under such circumstances it is difficult to see why the invitation by the President should have more legal value than that of any other faction.

It is interesting to focus on the Somali case in some detail. The first United Nations mission to Somalia (UNOSOM — United Nations Operation in Somalia) was established with S/RES/751 (1992) of 24 April 1992. This resolution is not based on Chapter VII of the Charter, instead the Council refers to the signing of cease-fire agreements in Mogadishu. This mission proved unable to fulfill its task although it was enhanced in size[111]. In S/RES/ 794 (1992) of 3 December 1992 a multinational force under the lead of the United States of America was established and received under Chapter VII the authorization "to establish a secure environment for humanitarian relief operations in Somalia". The multinational force was later replaced by a UNOSOM II mission which was also established under Chapter VII of the Charter[112]. It is interesting to note that the Council did not rely on Chapter VII when the first UNOSOM mission was set up. The most plausible reason for this is that cease-fire agreed on between the factions in Mogadishu was considered to constitute a sufficient legal basis. Only when there was no consent on a cease-fire and a peace-keeping force to monitor it did the Council resort to Chapter VII of the Charter[113]. It is therefore submitted that the reason for applying Chapter VII in the Somali case was not so much that Somalia lacked governmental structures[114], but that when the United Nations forces

---

109 "I must emphasize that the ECOWAS Monitoring Group (ECOMOG) is going to Liberia first and foremost to stop the senseless killing of innocent civilian nationals and foreigners, and to help the Liberian people to restore their democratic institutions. ECOWAS intervention is in no way designed to save one part or punish another." Doc. S/21485 of 10 August 1990 (Annex), 3.

110 T. Farer, "A Paradigm of Legitimate Intervention", in: L. F. Damrosch (ed.), *Enforcing Restraint*, 1993, 316 (336).

111 S/RES/775 (1992) of 28 August 1992.

112 S/RES/814 (1993) of 26 March 1993.

113 S/RES/794 (1992) and S/RES/814 (1993).

114 This fact was stressed very much during the debates in the Security Council, see H. Freudenschuß, "Article 39 of the UN Charter Revisited:

where sent not all of the parties to the conflict consented. This implies that the sending of UNOSOM II had enforcement character in allowing for action against some of the factions to the civil war. The Council considered the Chapter VII mandate necessary in order to overcome the prohibition of use of force in Article 2 para.4. In doing so the Council was not merely substituting a request by a non-existing government, but relied on Chapter VII of the Charter because the measures envisaged had enforcement character.

In conclusion, the standards applicable to regional organizations when intervening into civil wars are very much the same as the standards for unilateral interventions. The civil wars of recent years, especially the atrocities committed in Burundi and Rwanda, and since October 1995 also in the Zairian area bordering these countries, have again raised the question of whether and under which circumstances intervention for humanitarian reasons may be justified.

IV. Humanitarian Intervention as Enforcement Action under Article 53?

Humanitarian interventions may be thought of as taking place unilaterally by single states, as a matter of Security Council decisions under Chapter VII of the Charter and they may also be conceived on a regional collective level, i.e. being planned and executed by regional organizations. The legality of regional humanitarian interventions is a question of Article 53. If they must be considered "enforcement action" in the sense of that provision, a Security Council authorization is required. In search of an answer to this question, it is necessary to analyse the legality of the different forms of humanitarian intervention. If unilateral humanitarian intervention were already possible under the law of the Charter there are no reasons why regional organizations should be barred from similar action. If, on the other hand, even decisions of the Council under Chapter VII could not justify collective humanitarian interventions, then it is difficult to see how an authorization according to Article 53 could justify regional humanitarian interventions. Therefore, a short summary of the

Threats to the Peace and the Recent Practice of the UN Security Council", *Austrian J. Publ. Int. Law* 46 (1993/94), 1 (21); P. C. Szacz, "Centralized and Decentralized Law Enforcement: The Security Council and the General Assembly Acting under Chapters VII and VIII", in: J. Delbrück (ed.), *Allocation of Law Enforcement Authority in the International System*, 1995, 17 (23).

law and practice of unilateral and collective humanitarian interventions by the United Nations is necessary.

1. Illegality of Unilateral Humanitarian Intervention

During the Cold War, American international lawyers in particular argued that, in view of the potential or actual veto dead-lock in the Security Council, a right to unilateral humanitarian intervention had to be acknowledged[115]. The question has been intensely analysed in literature[116]. For the purposes of this article only the main arguments need to be presented.

Those authors who are arguing in favour of a right to humanitarian intervention refer to the wording of Article 2 para.4 of the Charter. According to them, the provision was only prohibiting use of force directed against the territorial integrity or political independence of another state. Neither the political independence nor the territorial integrity of a state were violated in a humanitarian intervention, since it was not directed at changing international borders or questioning the political independence of a state[117]. This argument could only be accepted if the qualification "against the territorial integrity or political independence" in Article 2 para.4 was meant to limit the prohibition of use of force. However, the drafting history shows that the terms were not designed as a limitation but with the intention to stress certain extraordinarily important aspects[118]. Consequently, the provision is understood to constitute a

---

[115] F. R. Tesón, *Humanitarian Intervention*, 1988, 127 and 246 et seq.; R. B. Lillich, "Forcible Self-Help by States to Protect Human Rights", *Iowa L. Rev.* 53 (1967), 325 (344 et seq.); R. B. Lillich, "Intervention to Protect Human Rights", *McGill L. J.* 15 (1969), 205 et seq.; see also A. D'Amato, "The Invasion in Panama was a Lawful Response to Tyranny", *AJIL* 84 (1990), 516 et seq.

[116] A. Pauer, *Die humanitäre Intervention*, 1985; Tesón, see above; P. Malanczuk, *Humanitarian Intervention and the Use of Force*, 1993, with a comprehensive documentation of the existing literature.

[117] M. Reisman/M. S. McDougal, "Humanitarian Intervention to Protect the Ibos", in: R. B. Lillich (ed.), *Humanitarian Intervention and the United Nations*, 1973, 167 (177); Tesón, see note 115, 131; K. Doehring, "Die humanitäre Intervention — Überlegungen zu ihrer Rechtfertigung", in: *The Modern World of Human Rights. Essays in Honour of Thomas Buergenthal*, 1996, 549 et seq., (551).

[118] UNCIO Vol.VI, 304, 335; for further references see I. Brownlie, *International Law and the Use of Force by States*, 1963, 265 et seq.; see also U. Beyerlin, "Humanitarian Intervention", in: R.. Bernhardt (ed.), *EPIL*, 2nd edition, Vol. II, 1995, 926 (927).

comprehensive ban on the use of force in international relations[119]. Additionally, there are good reasons to argue that any humanitarian intervention interferes with the political independence of the state concerned and must therefore be considered to contravene Article 2 para. 4[120]. For these reasons it is not possible to hold that the wording of Article 2 para. 4 allows for humanitarian interventions.

A second argument in favour of unilateral humanitarian intervention is that the collective system established in Chapters VI and VII of the Charter of the United Nations had failed to meet its objectives. It is argued that the comprehensive ban on the use of force in Article 2 para. 4 was subject to a functioning collective system. The failure of the Security Council to meet its tasks under Chapter VII required a search for alternative means of ensuring international peace and security[121]. This argument neglects two important considerations. Firstly, the delegates at the San Francisco Conference had seen the danger of misfunction of the collective system. As a remedy they included the right to individual or collective self-defence in Article 51 [122]. And secondly, the argument presupposes that the mechanism of Chapter VII was designed to be used against internal violations of human rights, since that is the sole purpose of a humanitarian intervention. The application of Chapter VII of the Charter in order to stop violations of human rights is a rather recent development by the practice of the Council in Somalia and Iraq[123]. For this reason the conclusion from the malfunction of the Charter system during the Cold War to a right to humanitarian intervention is not compelling[124].

---

[119] D. W. Bowett, *Self-Defence in International Law*, 1958, 151 et seq.; T. Farer, "The Regulation of Foreign Intervention in Civil Armed Conflict", *RdC* 142 (1974), 291 (388); D. Schindler, "Die Grenzen des völkerrechtlichen Gewaltverbots", *Reports DGVR* 26 (1986), 11 (14); U. Beyerlin, "Die israelische Befreiungsaktion von Entebbe aus völkerrechtlicher Sicht", *ZaöRV* 37 (1977), 213 (217); I. Brownlie, *International Law and the Use of Force by States*, 1963, 265 et seq.; R. M. Derpa, *Das Gewaltverbot der Satzung der Vereinten Nationen und die Anwendung nicht-militärischer Gewalt*, 1970, 30 et seq.; A. Randelzhofer, "Use of Force", in: R. Bernhardt (ed.), *EPIL* 4 (1982), 265 (269 et seq.); A. Randelzhofer, "On Article 2 (4)", 106 et seq., Mn. 34 et seq.; in Simma, see note 25; B. V. Röling, "Aspects of the Ban on Force", *NILR* 24 (1977), 242 (246 et seq.).

[120] M. Akehurst, "Humanitarian Intervention", in: H. Bull (ed.), *Intervention in World Politics*, 1984, 95 (105).

[121] M. Reisman, "Coercion and Self-determination. Construing Charter Article 2 (4)", *AJIL* 78 (1984), 642 et seq. (643).

[122] See UNCIO Vol.XII, 682, 688 (Australia), 777 (France) and 781 (Turkey).

[123] For details see infra, p. 158 et seq.

A third argument for the legality of humanitarian intervention is that it could be considered a customary law exception to the universal prohibition of the use of force[125]. With respect to the customary law argument it is important to note that the pre-Charter practice is of only limited value since the treaty based prohibition of the use of force in Article 2 para. 4 must be given priority over the pre-Charter practice[126]. Furthermore, even for the time before the Charter of the United Nations entered into force, the existence of a customary law foundation for the doctrine of humanitarian intervention was not free from doubts[127]. In any event, under the Charter of the United Nations no cases may be found which would clearly support a customary law exception for humanitarian interventions[128].

The main argument advanced against unilateral humanitarian intervention is the danger of abuse[129]. The opponents to a humanitarian exception to the prohibition of use of force argue that it would be difficult to restrict such an exception to situations where the humanitarian aspect is obvious[130]. The argument of possible abuse is all the more important since it is hard to imagine that potential unilateral intervenors could be bound to the criteria developed by international lawyers in order to limit the scope of a humanitarian exception to the prohibition of the use of force[131]. For

---

[124] As to some modifications to this assessment in the light of the recent practice of the Security Council to protect human rights also under Chapter VII of the Charter, see infra, p. 163 et seq.

[125] J. P. Fonteyne, "The Customary International Law Doctrine of Humanitarian Intervention: Its Current Validity under the UN-Charter", *Cal. W.Int'l L.J.* 4 (1974), 203 (232 et seq.); see also M. Reisman, "Allocating Competences to Use Coercion in the Post-Cold War World: Practices, Conditions and Prospects", in: L.F. Damrosch/D. Scheffer (eds.), *Law and Force in the New International Order*, 1991, 26 (35).

[126] P. Malanczuk, *Humanitarian Intervention*, 1993, 27.

[127] Malanczuk, ibid., 10.

[128] T. Farer, "An Inquiry into the Legitimacy of Humanitarian Intervention", in: Damrosch/Scheffer, see note 125, 185 (193); O. Schachter, *International Law in Theory and Practice*, 1991, 124.

[129] See for instance, J. Zourek, *L'interdiction de l'emploi de la force en droit international*, 1974, 124.

[130] Malanczuk, see note 126, 30; K. Hailbronner, "Die Grenzen des völkerrechtlichen Gewaltverbots", *Reports DGVR* 26 (1986), 49 (100); U. Beyerlin, *Die humanitäre Aktion zur Gewährleistung eines Mindeststandards in nicht-internationalen Konflikten*, 1975, 66.

[131] R. B. Lillich, "Humanitarian Intervention through the United Nations: Towards the Development of Criteria", *ZaöRV* 53 (1993), 557 (562 et seq.); J. P. Fonteyne, "The Customary International Law Doctrine of Humanitarian Intervention: Its Current Validity under the UN-Char-

this reason unilateral humanitarian interventions have to be considered as constituting a violation of Article 2 para.4 and hence illegal under current international law[132].

2. Collective Humanitarian Intervention by the United Nations

On the level of the United Nations, the legal question presented by collective intervention for humanitarian purposes is whether and under which circumstances violations of human rights may be considered to constitute a threat to the peace according to Article 39. There is an older, restrictive interpretation of Article 39 which views the provision closely interrelated with the prohibition of use of force in Article 2 para.4, the prohibition of intervention into internal affairs and with the right to individual and collective self-defence in Article 51. This interpretation comes to the conclusion that only military force with massive cross-border effects can meet the requirement of "threat to the peace"[133]. It is also argued that the term had to be seen in connection with preventing or stopping military hostilities or genocide, otherwise everything could be said to serve the maintenance or restoration of peace[134].

According to most authors, by contrast, the Security Council possesses a large margin of appreciation as far as the conditions laid down in Article 39 are concerned[135]. Following the recent practice[136] of the Council in

---

ter", *Cal. W. Int'l L.J.* 4 (1974), 203 (235); W. D. Verwey, "Humanitarian Intervention", in: A. Cassese (ed.), *The Current Regulation of the Use of Force*, 1986, 57 (74 et seq.); Pauer, see note 116, 197 et seq.

[132] Schachter, see note 128, 123 et seq.; T. Farer, "Human Rights in Law's Empire: The Jurisprudence of War", *AJIL* 85 (1991), 117 (126); Malanczuk, see note 126, 26 et seq.; Beyerlin, see note 130, 64 et seq.

[133] J. Arntz, *Der Begriff der Friedensbedrohung in der Satzung der Vereinten Nationen*, 1975, 64 et seq.; for further references see Pauer, see note 116, 82 (footnote 6).

[134] B. Graefrath, "Iraqi Reparations and the Security Council", *ZaöRV* 55 (1995), 1 (15).

[135] J. A. Frowein,"On Article 39", 605 et seq., Mn. 16 et seq., in: Simma, see note 25; H.Kelsen, *The Law of the United Nations*, 1950, 727 et seq.; R. Higgins, *The Development of International Law through the Political Organs of the United Nations*, 1963, 173 and 176.

[136] For earlier cases see T. M. Franck, "The Security Council and "Threats to the Peace": Some Remarks on Remarkable Recent Developments", in: R.-J. Dupuy (ed.), *Le Développement du rôle du Conseil de Sécurité*, 1993, 83 (89 et seq.).

Iraq[137], Yugoslavia[138], Somalia[139], and Rwanda[140] there seems to be consent that massive internal use of force may fulfill the criterion of "threat to the peace" in cases where such use of force has cross-border effects, for instance where refugees flee to neighbouring countries[141].

A further step towards collective humanitarian intervention may be seen in the actions taken by the Security Council following the coup against President Aristide of Haiti in September 1991[142]. Jean-Bertrand Aristide took over the office as President of Haiti in February 1991. His government was overthrown only eight months later and President Aristide was forced to leave the country[143]. The OAS reacted firstly by imposing a trade embargo[144]. As already mentioned, the trade embargo was later made universally mandatory by the Security Council in S/RES/841 (1993) of 16 June 1993 at the request of the exile government set up by President Aristide[145]. In July 1993 an agreement was reached between the new junta and President Aristide according to which President Aristide would be allowed to return to the country and a government supported by a majority in Parliament would be reinstated[146]. When the military government in Haiti did not implement these commitments the Security Council authorized member states of the United Nations in S/RES/ 940 (1994) of 31 July 1994 to "form a multinational force under unified command and control and, in this framework, to use all necessary

---

137 S/RES/ 688 (1991) of 5 April 1991.
138 Even the first resolution in the Yugoslav crisis, S/RES/ 713 (1991) of 25 September 1991, which was adopted before the declaration of independence by Croatia and Slovenia on 8 October 1991, qualifies the continuation of the situation as a threat to the peace because of its cross-border effects.
139 S/RES/ 794 (1992) of 3 December 1992.
140 S/RES/ 929 (1994) of 22 June 1994.
141 Frowein, see note 135, Mn. 19; R.B. Lillich, "Humanitarian Intervention through the United Nations: Towards the Development of Criteria", *ZaöRV* 53 (1993), 557 et seq. (574); Malanczuk, see note 126, 25.
142 R. B. Lillich, "The Role of the UN Security Council in Protecting Human Rights in Crisis Situations: UN Humanitarian Intervention in the Post-Cold War World", *Tul.J.Int'l & Comp.L.* 3 (1995), 1 (9 et seq.).
143 For details of the events in Haiti, see D. E. Acevedo, "The Haitian Crisis and the OAS response", in: L.F. Damrosch (ed.), *Enforcing Restraint*, 1993, 119 et seq.
144 MRE/RES.1/91 and 2/91, reprinted in Doc. A/47/975=S/26063 of 12 July 1993.
145 Doc. S/25958 of 16 July 1993.
146 Governors Island Agreement, Doc. A/47/975=S/26063 of 12 July 1993, 2 et seq.

means to facilitate the departure from Haiti of the military leadership, consistent with the Governors Island Agreement, the prompt return of the legitimately elected President and the restoration of the legitimate authorities of the Government of Haiti [...]". The situation in Haiti was different from the collective interventions referred to above in so far as the cross-border consequences of the military coup were rather limited and the new military leaders managed to consolidate their power quickly. A difference which is also visible in the wording of resolution 940 where the military government is referred to as "illegal de-facto regime". The main reasons for the intervention therefore have to be seen in the serious violations of human rights committed by the new military rulers. This motivation is evidenced in the text of Resolution 940 :

> "The Security Council,
> Gravely concerned by the significant further deterioration of the humanitarian situation in Haiti, in particular the continuing escalation by the illegal de facto regime of systematic violations of civil liberties, the desperate plight of Haitian refugees and the recent expulsion of the staff of the International Civilian Mission (MICIVIH), which was condemned in its Presidential statement of 12 July 1994 (S/PRST/1994/32)".

It is interesting to note that with the formula "civil liberties" instead of "human rights" the Council not only mentions the basic rights of freedom of the human person, but also includes rights of participation in a democratic society[147]. Furthermore, S/RES/748 (1992) of 31 March 1992 concerning Libya may be referred to in this context. In this resolution the term "threat to the peace" was interpreted in a particularly broad manner[148]. The Council applied under Chapter VII of the Charter non-military sanctions against Libya since the latter did not honour the obligations created in S/RES/731 (1992) of 21 January 1992. Therefore Libya was ordered to extradite two of its nationals who were suspected of being involved in the terrorist bombing of Pan Am flight 103 over Lockerbie (Scotland) on 21 December 1988[149]. In resolution 748 the Council determines the threat to the peace created by the situation in the following way:

---

147 Rather critical towards such an extensive interpretation of the term "threat to the peace", M. Glennon, "Sovereignty and Community after Haiti: Rethinking the Collective Use of Force", *AJIL* 89 (1995), 70 et seq.

148 See Frowein, see note 135, Mn. 19.

149 As to the factual background of the terrorist attack, see the introductory note in K. C. Wellens, *Resolutions and Statements of the United Nations Security Council (1946–1992) — A Thematic Guide*, 1993, 292.

> "Determining, in this context, that the failure by the Libyan Govern-
> ment to demonstrate by concrete actions its renunciation of terrorism
> and in particular its continued failure to respond fully and effectively
> to the requests in resolution 731 (1992) constitute a threat to interna-
> tional peace and security, [...]".

The legality of that resolution is still in dispute before the ICJ in two
parallel proceedings instituted by Libya against the United States of
America and against the United Kingdom, in which Libya asked the
Court, inter alia, to state that it had fully complied with all its obligations
arising out of the Montreal Convention for the Suppression of Unlawful
Acts Against the Safety of Civil Aviation of 23 September 1971[150]. Libya
also asked for the consideration of interim measures in which the United
States and the United Kingdom should have been ordered not to apply
coercive measures against Libya. Libya maintained that there was no threat
to the peace and hence resolution 748, which had been adopted while the
proceedings were pending, was in contravention to the provisions of the
Charter[151]. In its decision on interim measures the Court declined to
consider such an order, arguing that there was prima facie a presumption
that Security Council decisions were lawfully taken under the Charter[152].
While not deciding the question of the legality of the resolution, the
decision may be seen as a tendency to accept the extensive interpretation
of Article 39[153] which is prevailing, not only in the cited practice of the
Council, but also largely accepted in literature[154].

---

150   *ILM* 10 (1971), 1151 et seq.
151   ICJ Reports 1992, 114 et seq. (126), para.39.
152   Ibid., para.41 et seq.
153   T. Franck, "The "Powers of Appreciation": Who is the Ultimate Guard-
      ian of UN Legality?", *AJIL* 86 (1992), 519 (521 et seq.).
154   J. A. Frowein, "On Article 39", 605 et seq., Mn. 19, in: Simma, see note
      25; J. Delbrück," A Fresh Look at Humanitarian Intervention Under the
      Authority of the United Nations", *Ind. L. J.* 67 (1992), 887 (899); J.
      Delbrück, "A More Effective International Law or a New "World Law"?
      — Some Aspects of the Development of International Law in a Changing
      International System", *Ind. L. J.* 68 (1993), 705 (711); A. Roberts, "Hu-
      manitarian war: Military Intervention and Human Rights", *Int'l Aff.* 69
      (1993), 429 (444 et seq.); P. Malanczuk, *Humanitarian Intervention*, 1993,
      25; K.-K. Pease/D. P. Forsythe, "Humanitarian Intervention and Inter-
      national Law", *Austrian J. Publ. Int. Law* 45 (1993), 1 (11 et seq.); D. P.
      Forsythe/K.-K. Pease, "Human rights, Humanitarian Intervention and
      World Politics", *HRQ* 15 (1993), 290 (308); M. R. Hutchinson, "Restor-
      ing Hope: U.N. Security Council Resolutions for Somalia and an Ex-
      panded Doctrine of Humanitarian Intervention", *Harv.Int'l.L J.* 34

Interestingly, in the context of collective humanitarian interventions by the United Nations only few authors raise the argument of danger of abuse which is frequently referred to in respect of unilateral humanitarian intervention[155]. The reason may be seen in the procedural requirements for decisions by the Security Council. For a collective humanitarian intervention by the United Nations unanimity of the permanent members and a majority in the Council are required. This collective decision-making is obviously viewed as presenting a procedural guarantee against abusive interventions by the United Nations. Recent developments are largely seen as establishing a right to collective humanitarian intervention through the United Nations[156].

3. Collective Humanitarian Intervention by Regional Organizations

The practical possibilities of protecting human rights by regional interventions are evidenced by the ECOWAS action in Liberia, which was officially justified by massive violations of human rights which had occurred because of the particularly atrocious civil war in the country[157]. The idea of setting up a regional intervention force (African Crisis Response Force) to cope with the desperate situation of refugees in the Great Lakes Re-

---

(1993), 624 (636 et seq.); O. Corten/P. Klein, "L'autorisation de recourir à la force à des fins humanitaires: droit d'ingérence ou retour au sources?", *EJIL* 4 (1993), 506 (531).

155 But see L. F. Damrosch, "Commentary on Collective Military Intervention to Enforce Human Rights", in: L.F.Damrosch/ D.Scheffer (eds.), *Law and Force in the New International Order*, 1991, 215 (220).

156 R. B. Lillich, "Humanitarian Intervention through the United Nations", *ZaöRV* 53 (1993), 557 et seq. (574); D. Eisner, "Humanitarian Intervention in the Post-Cold War Era", *B.U.Int'l L.J.* 11 (1993), 195 (220); T. Marauhn, "Humanitär motivierte militärische Aktionen", *Humanitäres Völkerrecht — Informationsschriften*, 1993, 20 (21); see also C. Greenwood, "Gibt es ein Recht auf humanitäre Intervention"?, *EA* 4 (1993), 93 et seq.; W. Kühne, "Völkerrecht und Friedenssicherung in einer turbulenten Welt: Eine analytische Zusammenfassung der Grundprobleme und Entwicklungsperspektiven", in: W. Kühne (ed.), *Blauhelme in einer turbulenten* Welt, 1993, 17 et seq.; with some doubts Malanczuk, see note 126, 30; H. Freudenschuß, "The Changing Role of the U.N. Security Council: Trends and Perspectives", in: Kühne, see above, 151 (157 et seq. and 161).

157 D. Wippman, "Enforcing the Peace: ECOWAS and the Liberian Civil War", in: L. F. Damrosch (ed.), *Enforcing Restraint*, 1993, 157 (179 et seq.).

gion[158] may also be seen as a regional approach to humanitarian intervention. Furthermore, the OAS indicated the possibility of regional humanitarian interventions in its Santiago Commitment to Democracy and the Renewal of the Inter-American System[159]. Under the law of the Charter of the United Nations the question has to be answered whether regional humanitarian intervention would constitute "enforcement action" under Article 53 and hence requires Security Council authorization.

First of all, one has to focus on the legality of collective humanitarian intervention through the United Nations. The analysis in the previous section has shown that humanitarian action by the United Nations is based on Chapter VII of the Charter. This legal basis implies that it is the decision under Chapter VII which justifies the collective humanitarian action with respect to the prohibition of the use of force in Article 2 para. 4. The interpretation of the term "enforcement action" in Article 53 resulted in the conclusion that the possible violation of Article 2 para. 4, must be considered as the decisive criterion to qualify regional action as "enforcement action". Hence, all regional measures which need a justification with respect to the prohibition of the use of force must be authorized by the Council[160]. This interpretation of Article 53 leads to the conclusion that a humanitarian intervention by a regional organization is only possible under the condition that it is authorized by the Council under Article 53.

However, the delayed decision on a multinational force for humanitarian purposes in the Great Lakes Region and Eastern Zaire[161] revealed that in cases of urgent need alternative mechanisms are necessary to provide for rapid reaction. Therefore, the question may be asked whether some of

---

158 *Africa Confidential* 37 (1996), 8.

159 This is most explicitly expressed in resolution AG/RES. 1080 (XXI-2/91) of 5 June 1991: "1. Instruir al Secretario General que solicite la convocación inmediata del Consejo Permanente en caso de que produzcan hechos que occasionen una interrupción abrupta o irregular del proceso político institucional democrático o del legítimo ejercicio del poder por un gobierno democráticamente electo en cualquiera de los Estados miembros de la Organización para, en el marco de la Carta, examinar la situación, decidir y convocar una reunión ad hoc de ministros de relaciones exteriores, o un período extraordinario de sesiones de la Asamblea General, todo ello de un plazo de 10 días.
2. Expresar que la reunión ad hoc de ministros de relaciones exteriores o el período extraordinario de sesiones de la Asamblea General tenga por objeto analizar colectivamente los hechos *y adoptar las decisiones que se estime apropriadas, conforme a la Carta y al derecho internacional.*" (Italics added by the author).

160 See supra, p. 141 et seq.

161 S/RES/1080 (1996) of 15 November 1996.

the arguments advanced by the proponents of a unilateral right to humanitarian intervention may be applied to justify collective humanitarian interventions by regional organizations. One of the arguments for the legality of unilateral humanitarian intervention was that the collective system of the Charter might not work properly and alternative solutions for such failure were necessary[162]. The main reason why this argument was considered inconclusive was that Chapter VII of the Charter originally was not designed to ensure international protection of human rights. However, the Council has used Chapter VII for collective humanitarian intervention in recent years and one might ask whether this practice also allows for new arguments in case of inaction by the Council.

If the Security Council is competent to intervene under Chapter VII against violations of human rights, the question arises what the law is if the Council is unable to act because it is blocked by a veto. Is the answer then that no action against massive violation of human rights is lawfully possible? The question may seem somewhat theoretical in a situation where the Council is generally operating reasonably well. But the hesitations on the American side against intervening in the Great Lakes Region and the delay caused by these hesitations show that the question is of practical relevance. Furthermore, it is not self-evident that China and Russia keep their positive or at least neutral position as to humanitarian interventions through the United Nations. In the Haitian case China abstained from the vote but gave a statement which was very critical of collective use of force[163]. In fact, the statement could easily have been used to explain a veto. The Chinese veto in January 1997 when the Council decided on an observer mission for Guatemala further underlines this observation[164].

---

162 See the reference in note 121.

163 "However, we cannot agree to the provision in the draft resolution before us concerning the authorization for Member States to adopt mandatory means under Chapter VII of the United Nations Charter to resolve the problem of Haiti. As always, China advocates a peaceful solution to any international disputes or conflicts through patient negotiations. China does not agree with the adoption of any means of solution based on the resort to pressure at will or even use of force. [...] the practice of the Council's authorizing certain Member States to use force is even more disconcerting because this would obviously create a dangerous precedent.[...]", Doc. S/PV.3413 of 31 July 1994, 10.

164 See the reference in Press Release SC 6314 of 20 January 1997, which was issued when the Council finally decided to establish the mission with S/RES/1094 (1997) of 20 January 1997.

Professor Reisman starts his argument on the premise that the collective mechanism established in Chapter VII of the Charter and the prohibition of the use of force are closely interrelated. According to him, the member states of the United Nations only accepted the ban on the use of force under the condition that the collective system was working[165]. This argument faces the objection that the delegates in San Francisco saw the problem and included the right to individual and collective self-defence into the Charter[166]. The relationship between Article 2 para.4, Article 39 to 42 and Article 51 may be described as follows. The normal reaction to a threat to the peace would be a decision under the collective system under Chapter VII of the Charter. In the absence of collective measures, states may use self-help in accordance with Article 51. It is important to note, however, that the conditions of Article 51 are more difficult to meet than those of Article 39. A "threat to the peace" in the sense of Article 39 is possible without the use of military force, while the "armed attack" necessary under Article 51 requires the cross-border use of military force[167]. In its Nicaragua decision the ICJ even came to the conclusion that not all measures prohibited as use of force under Article 2 para.4 could be qualified as armed attack in the sense of Article 51[168]. It follows from this analysis that the right to individual and collective self-defence has to be understood as a last resort in case of emergency created by Security Council inactivity.

This character of Article 51 is important with respect to the recent Security Council applications of Chapter VII to situations of humanitarian emergencies. When the Charter was framed in 1945 Chapter VII was viewed as allowing for collective measures in classical international conflicts. Hence, the emergency solution of Article 51 was only designed to meet such situations. With the wording "armed attack" it requires a military cross-border activity of some intensity[169]. The situation of a

---

[165] M.Reisman, "Coercion and Self-determination. Construing Charter Article 2 (4)", *AJIL* 78 (1984), 642 et seq. (643).

[166] See the references in note 122.

[167] A. Randelzhofer, "On Article 51", 661 et seq., Mn. 16, in: Simma, see note 25.

[168] "The Court sees no reason to deny that, in customary law, the prohibition of armed attacks may apply to the sending by a State of armed bands to the territory of another State, if such an operation, because of its scale and effects, would have been classified as an armed attack rather than as a mere frontier incident had it been carried out by regular armed forces." Military and Paramilitary Activities in and against Nicaragua, ICJ Reports 1986,14 et seq. (103), para.195.

[169] See the quotation from the Nicaragua-Judgment above.

humanitarian intervention, however, is characterized by the fact that massive violations of human rights, not necessarily with military cross-border effects, constitute the reason for intervening. Sometimes a cross-border effect may be seen in refugee fluxes from one country to another, but these consequences do not amount to an "armed attack". The conclusion is that with respect to the protection of human rights under Chapter VII of the Charter no individual or collective emergency solution is envisaged in the Charter. This lacuna is a result of the extensive practice of the Security Council under Chapter VII of the Charter. With respect to Security Council inaction in case of humanitarian need we are today facing a situation comparable to that of the founding fathers of the Charter before they agreed on the right to self-defence in Article 51. However, we are not framing the Charter but remain subject to its provisions and there is no provision similar to the right of self-defence which could be applied to humanitarian interventions. Hence, the conclusion would be that no humanitarian action is possible if it is not decided on by the Security Council. Nevertheless, the desperate need of the refugees in the Great Lakes Region in October 1996 and the situations in Burundi and Rwanda in 1994 reveal that there is a necessity for alternative action. Could it be possible to develop criteria with which a humanitarian intervention in case of an inactive Security Council might be justified?

A first idea on how to fill the lacuna created by Security Council inaction might be to substitute the decision of the Security Council by a decision of the General Assembly. This would mean applying the "Uniting for Peace" Resolution of the General Assembly[170] to the problem of a blocked humanitarian intervention by the Council. There are good reasons to argue that no enforcement action may be taken following a recommendation by the General Assembly under the Uniting for Peace Resolution[171]. But even apart from these doubts concerning the legality of such

---

[170] A/RES/377 (V) of 3 November 1950.

[171] "Although the Uniting for Peace resolution enables the Assembly to act in situations in which Article 12 would ordinarily prohibit it, so as not to interfere with the Security Council's handling of a situation under consideration by the Council, the Assembly under that resolution can only take the types of actions that are within its normal competence. If the Security Council fails for any reason to take any action that is within its special competence, the Assembly cannot substitue itself — even by adopting a resolution that could be interpreted as granting itself such powers." P. Szacs, "Centralized and Decentralized Law Enforcement: The Security Council and the General Assembly Acting under Chapters VII and VIII", in: J. Delbrück (ed.), *Alllocation of Law Enforcement Authority in the International System. Proceedings of an International*

course of action, it seems obvious from a political point of view that General Assembly decisions are far too difficult to reach and the process would undoubtedly be too slow to be considered as an effective emergency solution. An alternative might be to consider regional organizations as emergency actors[172].

Another possibility might be to take up the idea which may be found behind Article 51[173]. The right to self-defence is designed as an emergency solution in situations where the collective system does not fulfill its peace-preserving or peace-restoring functions. An analogous application of the emergency function of Article 51 would have to take into account the limited applicability of the provision. As already pointed out, the possibilities of the Security Council under Chapter VII of the Charter are much broader than the right to self-defence according to Article 51. The Charter requires states to accept a larger degree of illegal interference before reacting independently of the Security Council. Self-help is limited to the minimum necessary to protect the integrity of the state. This qualification of emergency action under Article 51 would have to be respected when developing an emergency solution for the protection of human rights in cases of Security Council inaction. Hence a regional right to humanitarian intervention would have to face a number of restrictions.

Firstly, it would have to be restricted to situations in which the Security Council is unable to decide on a universal intervention. This is the necessary consequence of the emergency character. Secondly, the conditions under which recourse to the emergency right could be possible would require qualified violations of human rights, just as Article 51 requires a qualified violation of Article 2 para. 4. This raises the question of criteria

---

Symposium of the Kiel Institute of International Law, March 23 to 25 1994, 1995, 17, 34 et seq.; see generally E. Stein/R.C. Morrissey, "Uniting for Peace Resolution", in: R. Bernhardt (ed.), *EPIL* 5 (1983), 379 et seq. (380); M. Akehurst, "Enforcement Action by Regional Agencies, with Special Reference to the Organization of American States", *BYIL* 42 (1967), 175 et seq. (215).

172 See in this respect J. Delbrück, "Wirksameres Völkerrecht oder neues "Weltinnenrecht"? Perspektiven der Völkerrechtsordnung in einem sich wandelnden internationalen System", in: Kühne, see note 156, 101 (26 et seq.).

173 The following suggestion does not mean applying Article 51 to the individuals or groups subject to human rights violations, but rather makes use of the function fulfilled by Article 51 within the system established by the Charter. For an interesting argument on the basis of the rights to self-defence and self-help by the persons concerned, see Doehring, see note 117, 562 et seq.

for the qualified violations of human rights. Such criteria could be developed from the jurisprudence of the ICJ in the Barcelona-Traction Judgment, where the Court qualified "basic rights of the human person" as obligations erga omnes[174]. The Court expressly mentioned in this context the prohibition of genocide and the prohibition of racial discrimination. Apart from that, the question of which rights may be considered as the most basic human rights is difficult to answer. The examples given by the ICJ stress the fact that the core rights of the human person form part of the erga omnes concept[175], while civil liberties of democratic participation, which are also protected in international instruments, would not be included[176]. Another area from which criteria could be adopted is the so-called 1503-procedure of the UN Commission on Human Rights[177]. ECOSOC invented this procedure for dealing with individual communications concerning violations of human rights in Resolution 1503 (XLVIII) of 27 May 1970. The procedure provides for the establishment of a Working Group of the Sub-Commission, which meets for a maximum of ten days immediately before the sessions of the Sub-Commission. Its

---

[174] "In particular, an essential distinction should be drawn between the obligations of a State towards the international community as a whole, and those arising vis-à-vis another State in the field of diplomatic protection. By their very nature the former are the concern of all States. In view of the importance of the rights involved, all States can be held to have a legal interest in their protection; they are obligations erga omnes.
Such obligations derive, for example, in contemporary international law, from the outlawing of acts of aggression, and of genocide, also from the principles and rules concerning the basic rights of the human person, including protection from slavery and racial discrimination. Some of the corresponding rights of protection have entered into the body of general international law (Reservations to the Convention on the Prevention and Punishment of the Crime of Genocide, ICJ Reports 1951, 15 (23)); others are conferred by international instruments of a universal or quasi-universal character." Barcelona Traction, Light and Power Company, Limited, ICJ Reports 1970, 3 et seq. (32, paras. 33 et seq.).

[175] As to the legal structure of erga omnes norms, see C. Annacker, "The Legal Régime of Erga Omnes Obligations in International Law", *Austrian J. Publ. Int. Law* 46 (1993/94); 131 et seq.

[176] See J. A Frowein, "Verpflichtungen erga omnes im Völkerrecht und ihre Durchsetzung", in: R. Bernhardt et al. (eds.), *Völkerrecht als Rechtsordnung — Internationale Gerichtsbarkeit — Menschenrechte. Festschrift für Hermann Mosler*, 1983, 241 (244).

[177] The 1503-procedure is also discussed with respect to humanitarian intervention in: C. Tomuschat, "Gewalt und Gewaltverbot als Bestimmungsfaktoren der Weltordnung", *EA* 36 (1981), 325 (332 et seq.).

Security Council Control over Regional Action 169

task is to determine which communications reveal "a consistent pattern of gross and reliably attested violations of human rights and fundamental freedoms" and to place them before the Sub-Commission. The Sub-Commission has to determine which communications should be referred to the Commission on Human Rights[178].

A combination of the two criteria could allow to formulate conditions for a regional emergency intervention corresponding to the qualification of an "armed attack" in Article 51. A regional humanitarian intervention in case of Security Council inaction would then be possible if the human rights violations may be considered as a "consistent pattern of gross and reliably attested violations of basic rights of the human person". In contrast to the 1503-procedure a regional humanitarian intervention would involve the use of military force. Against this background, and in view of the qualification in Article 51, a further criterion could be seen in the internal use of military force resulting in the violations of human rights. The regional humanitarian intervention, therefore, would require that the above-mentioned consistent pattern of violations was due to massive use of organized military force resulting in numerous losses of human lives[179]. If these criteria are applied to the recent interventions, a regional intervention would not have been possible in a situation comparable to the one in Haiti in 1991/1992. But they could have justified a regional intervention in a situation of genocidal character such as in Rwanda in 1994.

If regional humanitarian intervention was viewed as an emergency solution comparable to the right to individual and collective self-defence in Article 51, the question of structural inability to act in the Security Council would lose its importance. The emphasis then shifts to the existence of an emergency situation. In the same way as collective self-defence under Article 51 does not require a general paralysis of the Council as it occurred during the Cold War, regional humanitarian interventions would not require structural inability to act on the Council's part either. The criteria just developed would simply correspond to the necessity of an "armed attack" in Article 51. If they are fulfilled regional action could be justified, such action would have to cease in analogous application of Article 51 sentence 2 once the Council has taken the necessary measures.

---

178   See C. Tomuschat, "Human Rights, Petitions and Individual Complaints", 619 et seq., (621), Mn. 6, in: R. Wolfrum (ed.), *United Nations: Law, Policies and Practice*, Vol. I, 1995, 619 (621); as to the effectiveness of the procedure see P. Alston, "The Commission on Human Rights", in: P. Alston (ed.), *The United Nations and Human Rights*, 1992, 126 (145 et seq.).

179   See J. N. Moore, "The Control of Foreign Intervention in Internal Conflict", *Va.J.Int'l L.* 9 (1968/69), 205 (264).

A further argument for an emergency right of regional organizations in case of Security Council inaction may be seen in the procedural guarantees against abuse which are ensured by means of the collective decision-making within the regional organization concerned. The necessity to find the majority required in the founding treaty of the organization — in most cases unanimity is necessary[180] — reduces the danger of abusive interventions using humanitarian necessity as a pretext[181].

One should seriously take into account the possible counter-argument that the collective procedure may reduce the danger of abuse but it may not eliminate it. It is obvious that allowing for regional use of military force would create a dangerous loop-hole in the universal prohibition on the use of force. On the other hand, it has to be seen that the question may not be solved by a clear cut answer. What is required is a reasonable balance between the danger of abuse, which is inherent in any transfer of competence, and the urgent need for action in situations where violations of human rights of genocidal character are taking place. In striking this balance a number of factors may be taken into account. Firstly, the character of an emergency solution implies that all other means of peaceful protection of human rights have to be exhausted before a regional organization may resort to the use of force[182]. Secondly, the intervention has to be kept strictly to the minimum necessary to ensure the safety of the population of the country concerned. And thirdly, it should not be overlooked that abuse is also possible on the universal level of the Security Council of the United Nations. The discussions concerning the economic sanctions against Libya because of the failure to extradite the suspected terrorists demonstrate that even the Security Council may be criticized for extensive action. The danger of abuse can only be minimized, it cannot be banned completely.

The consequence of a strict application of the prohibition of the use of force would be that in case of Security Council inactivity no emergency solution would be possible. This would leave the system of the Charter as it was originally established, but in some cases at a high humanitarian price.

---

180   Article 6 para. 2, of the League of Arab States (if the aggressor forms part of the League his vote is not counted); Article V WEU-Treaty; Article 5 NATO-Treaty; Article 20 Inter-American Treaty on Reciprocal Assistance requires a 2/3-majority.

181   This argument is also admitted by those who argue against regional humanitarian intervention, see L. F. Damrosch, "Commentary on Collective Security", in: Damrosch/ Scheffer, see note 155, 215 (221).

182   See in this respect R.B. Lillich, "Humanitarian Intervention through the United Nations: Towards the Development of Criteria", *ZaöRV* 53 (1993), 557 (562 et seq.).

On a line between complete inaction on the one side and unilateral humanitarian intervention on the other, collective regional action under the conditions developed above would seem to present an alternative with some merits. In any case, collective action is preferable to unilateral interventionism.

C. The Question of Control over Regional Action

I. Control over Regional Peace-Keeping

1. The Distinction between Classical Peace-Keeping and Robust Peace-Keeping

In its original concept peace-keeping is designed to provide for neutral forces that were able to assist parties to a conflict in keeping a cease-fire to which they had previously consented[183]. Peace-keeping basically takes place in two forms, either unarmed observers or armed military units are deployed. There is no express legal basis in the Charter for the establishment of peace-keeping forces by the Security Council. However, since a peace-keeping force requires consent by the parties, there is no doubt that it may not be established without the Council deciding under Chapter VII of the Charter if the parties consent to the force[184].

Some doubt has arisen as to the legal basis of peace-keeping forces in situations of civil strife. The question became relevant for the first time during the Congo crisis. While the Opération des Nations Unies au Congo (ONUC) originally was stationed in the rebel province of Katanga with the consent of the local government, the enlargement of ONUC's mandate[185] led to increasing fighting between the peace-keeping force and local military units. The United Nations invoked a right to "active self-defence" which was characterized by military action against anyone trying to dis-

---

183 M. Bothe, "Peace-keeping", 565 et seq. Mn. 58 et seq., in: Simma, see note 25; see also M. Goulding, "The Evolution of United Nations Peacekeeping", *Int.Aff.* 69 (1993), 451 (453 et seq.).

184 Bothe, see above, Mn. 68 et seq.

185 "The Security Council [...],
1. urges that the United Nations take immediately all appropriate measures to prevent the occurrence of civil war in Congo, including arrangements for cease-fires, the halting of all military operations, the prevention of clashes, and the use of force, if necessary in the last resort [...]", S/RES/161 (1961) of 21 February 1961.

turb the force in achieving its mandate[186]. It was conceived as a right to defend the mandate and thus it created a grey zone between peace-keeping and peace-enforcement[187]. The model of active self-defence was also applied in Somalia and Bosnia-Herzegovina where Chapter VII mandates were given to peace-keeping forces which were already in place[188]. These mandates included the use of force, if necessary, to protect the civilian population. In the UNPROFOR case the mandate included the use of force to protect the "safe areas" established by S/RES/824 (1993) of 6 May 1993. In Somalia UNOSOM was given the mandate to "assume responsibility for the consolidation, expansion and maintenance of a secure environment throughout Somalia"[189]. Both mandates conflict with the original concept of peace-keeping forces according to which consent of the parties is the basis of their mission[190]. Since the original concept only includes use of military force in self-defence[191], peace-keeping forces are not equipped with the weapons necessary for enforcement action. With the Chapter VII mandate requiring action against the Bosnian Serbs, UNPROFOR became in turn the target of Bosnian Serb military activities. This resulted in a number of blue-helmets being held hostages at important military points and under humiliating circumstances in May and June 1995[192]. Since a number of these hostages were nationals of NATO-countries, NATO air-strikes, which would have been possible under S/RES/836 (1993) of 4 June 1993, were not used in order to save the lives of the hostages. Thus the attempt to introduce a "robust" peace-keeping prevented effective enforcement action. This negative political record of UNPROFOR is a confirmation of an analysis previously given by the

---

[186] As to the definition of "active self-defence" see Bothe, see note 183, Mn. 65.

[187] See the criticism by O. Schachter, "Authorized Uses of Force by the United Nations and Regional Organizations", in: L.F. Damrosch/ D. Scheffer, (eds.), *Law and Force in the New International Order*, 1991, 65 (84 et seq.).

[188] S/RES/814 (1993) of 26 March 1993, para. 14, and S/RES/837 (1993) of 6 June 1993, para. 5, concerning UNOSOM and S/RES/836 (1993) of 4 June 1993, para. 9 concerning UNPROFOR.

[189] S/RES/814 (1993) of 26 March 1993, para. 14.

[190] See generally Bothe, see note 183, Mn. 58et seq.; E. Suy, "United Nations Peace-Keeping System", in: R. Bernhardt (ed.), *EPIL* 4 (1982), 258 et seq. (261).

[191] R. Siekmann, *National Contingents in United Nations Peace-Keeping Forces*, 1992, 6.

[192] Report of the Secretary-General pursuant to S/RES/ 982 (1995) of 31 March 1995 and S/RES/987 (1995) of 19 April 1995, Doc. S/1995/444 of 30 May 1995, paras. 6, 55, 58, 59 and 62.

Secretary-General in his 1995 Addendum to "An Agenda for Peace"[193]. In this Addendum the Secretary-General criticizes the idea of enforcement mandates for peace-keeping forces. He argues that the "logic of peace-keeping flows from political and military premises that are quite distinct from those of enforcement"[194]. Therefore peace-keeping and peace-enforcement should be treated as distinct concepts[195].

The conclusions drawn by the Secretary-General are compelling from a political point of view. Avoiding the tendency to disguise enforcement action as peace-keeping brings peace-keeping back to its consensual basis and it allows enforcement action to be perceived as what it really is. It also avoids the United Nations being drawn into enforcement operations without being sufficiently equipped. From a legal point of view, the limits of the power of a government to invite foreign troops may also be referred to. If there is only the consent by the government to establish a peace-keeping force the legal issue arising is very much the same as the question of whether a government may invite foreign military forces for its support. This has been answered above in the negative for situations in which the government may not be seen to represent the whole country anymore because of lost authority[196]. The same argument applies for unilateral consent to peace-keeping by the government in situations of civil war. In such situation the consent of the rebel faction or factions is necessary to establish a peace-keeping force in the traditional sense[197].

2. Consequences for the Application of Article 53 Para.1 to Regional Peace-Keeping Missions

Some authors argue that regional peace-keeping generally requires Security Council authorization under Article 53. This would imply a comprehensive control of the Security Council over regional peace-keeping. The main argument for including regional peace-keeping in the term "enforcement action" mentioned in Article 53 is that any use of military force creates a danger of enforcement. According to these authors, the possible escalation which is inherent in the sending of troops, made it necessary that regional peace-keeping be authorized by the Security Council. Bear-

---

193 Doc. A/47/277=S/24111 of 17 June 1992.
194 Doc. A/50/60=S/1995/1 of 3 January 1995, para. 35.
195 Doc. A/50/60=S/1995/1 of 3 January 1995, para.33 et seq.
196 See supra, p. 149 et seq.
197 See M. Bothe, *Streitkräfte internationaler Organisationen*, 1968, 122 et seq., arguing that in civil wars the consent of factions with consolidated control over part of the territory was necessary to render an intervening force a peace-keeping force.

ing in mind the experiences of the United Nations "peace-keeping" forces in Somalia and Bosnia-Herzegovina it is indeed important to stress the potential danger that goes along with military involvement, especially in internal conflicts. Nevertheless, the principle "volenti non fit iniuria" remains applicable in this context. For classical regional peace-keeping missions which are carried out with the consent of the parties a Security Council authorization, therefore, is not necessary. Measures to which all parties consented lack the character of enforcement. This interpretation is supported by a number of regional peace-keeping missions which were carried out without Security Council authorization[198]. Furthermore the CSCE in its Helsinki Document of 1992 "The Challenges of Change" considered peace-keeping not to constitute enforcement action[199]. The CSCE/OSCE carries out several observer missions in Eastern Europe without Security Council authorization[200].

If traditional peace-keeping does not constitute enforcement action in the sense of Article 53 one may raise the question whether this conclusion also applies to regional "robust peace-keeping". Does the enforcement character which may be seen in the lack of consent by at least one of the parties to the civil war render such operations "enforcement action"? Up to now "robust peace-keeping" has been limited to civil wars. In that particular context "robust peace-keeping" is linked with the question of the legality of invitations by the government. Where the government may lawfully invite foreign forces to combat internal rebellion the consent by the government deprives the action of its enforcement character and hence in such a situation no authorization by the Security Council is required.

For those situations in which the consent by the government cannot justify the regional military measures because the government lacks effective control the question of "enforcement action" arises. The "robust peace-keeping" missions established by the United Nations were under-

---

[198] Reference may be made to the Arab League Security Forces in Kuwait (for details see H. A. Hassouna, *The League of Arab States and Regional Disputes*, 1975, 102 et seq. and Doc. A/37/536 of 25 October 1982, 20), the Arab Security Force in Lebanon (for details see I. Pogany, "The Arab League and Regional Peacekeeping", *NILR* 34 (1987), 54 (61 et seq.)), and the OAU force in Chad (for details see, G. J. Naldi, "Peace-keeping attempts by the Organization of African Unity", *ICLQ* 34 (1985), 593 (593)).

[199] Helsinki Decisions, paragraph III.22 and 23, reprinted in: A. Bloed (ed.), *The Challenges of Change. The Helsinki Summit of the CSCE and its Aftermath*, 1994, 385 (400).

[200] See G. Scheltema, "CSCE Peacekeeping Operations", in: Bloed, above, 23, (41 et seq.).

taken with a Chapter VII mandate[201]. Even the new humanitarian mission to Eastern Zaire, the task of which is to facilitate the immediate return of humanitarian organizations to the region, is authorized under Chapter VII of the Charter[202]. This qualification of the use of military force by the Council is indicative for the application of Article 53 para. 1, to such measures. If the Council considers it necessary to decide under Chapter VII in order to adopt a United Nations "robust peace-keeping" mandate then regional "robust peace-keeping" has to be qualified as enforcement action under Article 53 para. 1, and hence requires Security Council authorization.

This conclusion is of particular relevance for the new Statute on Collective Peace-keeping Forces in the Commonwealth of Independent States, which was adopted on 19 January 1996[203]. The previous 1992 Peacekeeping Agreement[204] stressed the necessity of consent by all conflicting parties and required the adoption of a cease-fire agreement as well as the cessation of hostilities before the arrival of the peace-keeping force. However, apart from excluding participation in "combat action" the 1992 Agreement did not address the question of under which circumstances CIS peace-keeping forces may use their weapons. In this respect the new 1996 Statute contains the following interesting provision:

"28. When performing their functions, the personnel of the Collective Peace-keeping Forces shall, by way of exception, have the right to use weapons:
– To ensure their security and protection against any endangerment of their life and health in exercise of their inalienable right to self-defence;
– In the event of attempts to prevent them by force from carrying out the functions entrusted to them;
– To repel an overt armed attack by groups or bands of terrorists or saboteurs, and also in order to arrest them;
– To protect the civilian population from violent endangerment of their

---

201 For Somalia S/RES/814 (1993) of 26 March 1993, for Yugoslavia S/RES/807 (1993) of 19 February 1993 was already adopted under Chapter VII of the Charter; the creation of the "safe areas" in S/RES/824 (1993) of 6 May 1993 and their protection by use of military force in S/RES/836 (1993) of 4 June 1993 were also decided under Chapter VII of the Charter.
202 S/RES/1080 (1996) of 15 November 1996.
203 *ILM* 35 (1996), 783 et seq.; Kazakstan, Turkmenistan and the Ukraine are not parties to that Statute.
204 The Agreement is reproduced in a non-official English translation in *International Peacekeeping* 1 (1994), 23 et seq.

life and health. Weapons may also be used to give an alarm signal or call for assistance".

In allowing the use of force for the protection of the civilian population and in order to repel attempts to prevent the peace-keeping force from carrying out its mandate the Statute corresponds to the concept of "robust peace-keeping" applied by the United Nations in Somalia and Bosnia and Herzegovina. The quoted provision of the 1996 CIS Statute must therefore be viewed as envisaging "robust peace-keeping" by CIS forces. According to the conclusions drawn above the CIS needs a Security Council authorization under Article 53 for this kind of peace-keeping.

In para. 3 the CIS Statute on peace-keeping forces mentions itself the possibility of taking action under an authorization by the Security Council. However, it does not specify under which circumstances the CIS would seek such an authorization. The CIS Statute could be brought in line with the requirements of the Charter if para. 3 was interpreted as foreseeing Security Council authorizations for peace-keeping measures which go beyond the traditional concept of peace-keeping and imply the use of armed force in situations other than self-defence. Hence, the reference to Security Council authorization in para. 3 of the CIS Peace-keeping Statute should be interpreted as envisaging such authorization for "robust peace-keeping" by CIS forces.

II. Control over Regional Military Enforcement Action

Military action by regional organizations is envisaged with two alternatives in Article 53 : The Security Council may utilize regional organizations for enforcement action under its authority (Article 53 para.1, clause 1) or it may authorize regional enforcement action according to Article 53 para.1 clause 2 first part. The two alternatives lead to the same result, namely that military action is taken by a regional organization. But they differ with respect to the political initiative. While with the first alternative the Security Council initiates the action and the regional organization merely constitutes an executive organ, with the second alternative political initiative and execution remain with the regional organization. The Security Council's role is reduced to the authorization of the action. It should be noted, however, that this theoretically clear distinction may lose its preciseness in practice. The Security Council may require certain changes in the concept proposed by the regional organization before the authorization is given. Furthermore, it is quite probable that some states are members both of the Security Council and of the regional organization concerned. This leads to early coordination in and with the Council.

Security Council control over regional enforcement action is guaranteed with both alternatives. With the first one, the action is taken under the authority of the Council which implies its control. With the second alternative, the control is exercised through the authorization. In this respect one may ask how the authorization has to be given. Need it be explicit and prior to the enforcement action or may the Security Council authorize regional enforcement action implicitly and/or ex post?

1. Prior and Explicit Authorization

The Charter envisages prior and explicit authorization as a rule[205]. Under the aspect of Security Council control over regional action a prior and explicit authorization would constitute the most effective way of ensuring such control. The regional organization would present its concept to the Security Council and receive the authorization before using military force. The wording of Article 53, however, seems to be indifferent as to the form of the authorization[206]. The wording "authorization" does not exclude at first sight that an authorization be given ex-post or implicitly. Are there other reasons why the authorization should be given explicitly and prior to the action? Viewed from the purpose of the requirement for an authorization, it must be asked whether an implicit or ex-post authorization could ensure Security Council control over regional action. For both, implicit and ex-post authorizations there is little state practice.

2. Authorization Ex-Post

The issue of ex post authorizations arose in the 1960s when the Security Council dealt with OAS sanctions against the Dominican Republic. The OAS had decided to break off diplomatic relations with the Dominican Republic and to impose economic sanctions on the country[207]. Following this decision the Soviet Union presented a draft resolution in the Security Council which had the following wording:

---

[205] J.A. Frowein, *Das Verhältnis zwischen den Vereinten Nationen und Regionalorganisationen bei der Friedenssicherung und Friedenserhaltung*, 1996, 17.

[206] A. Verdross, *Völkerrecht*, 5th edition, 1964, 654.

[207] Final Act of the Sixth Meeting of Consultation of Ministers of Foreign Affairs of 21 August 1960, Resolution I, OAS Official Records, OEA/Ser.C/II.6.; see also the report according to Article 54 of the Charter in Doc. S/4476 of 1 September 1960.

"The Security Council,
Being guided by Article 53 of the Charter of the United Nations,
Approves the said resolution of the Meeting of Consultation of Minis-
ters of Foreign Affairs of the American States, dated 20 August 1960
[...]".

When interpreting these developments it should be kept in mind that the
main concern of the Soviet Union was to create a precedent with respect
to the necessity of authorizing non-military sanctions[208]. Since the other
members of the Council wanted to avoid such a precedent, the Council
did not adopt the Soviet draft but decided only to take note of the
measures[209]. The draft resolution shows that the Soviet Union and Poland[210], for whatever political reasons, considered ex-post authorizations
to be possible under Article 53. It should also be noted that the Soviet draft
was not rejected because it gave an ex-post authorization but only because
the other members did not want non-military sanctions to be qualified as
enforcement action requiring authorization under Article 53[211].

The main argument advanced against ex-post authorizations is that the
Security Council would lose control over regional actions. The Council
would be faced with faits accomplis[212] and regional organizations would
start enforcement action hoping for approval by the Council[213]. This could
lead to increased regional military actions without Security Council con-

---

[208] See supra.

[209] S/RES/156 (1960) of 9 September 1960: "The Security Council, Having
received the report from the Secretary General of the Organization of
American States transmitting the Final Act of the Sixth meeting of
Consultation of Ministers of Foreign Affairs of the American Republics,
takes note of that report and especially of resolution I approved at the
aforesaid Meeting, whereby agreement was reached on the application of
measures regarding the Dominican Republic." The resolution was adopted by nine votes to none with two abstentions (Soviet Union and Poland).

[210] See the debates preceding the resolution, SCOR, 894th Mtg. of 9 September 1960, 6 et seq.

[211] The French delegate, however, argued that the authorization had to be
given in advance (SCOR 15th Year 893rd Mtg. of 8 September 1960, 15).
But even this statement may be seen as part of the Western States' interest
not to include non-military sanctions into the scope of Article 53.

[212] L. Henkin, "International Law and the Behaviour of Nations", RdC 114
(1965), 167 et seq., 261.

[213] M. Akehurst, "Enforcement Action by Regional Agencies with Special
Reference to the Organization of American States", BYIL 42 (1967), 175,
214.

trol. Hence, ex-post authorization could not be accepted under Article 53. Are these reasons really convincing?

In looking for an answer one has to bear in mind the function of an authorization under Article 53. Its main task certainly is to ensure Security Council control over regional military action. As already mentioned the authorization forms part of the system of the Charter which concentrates the decision on lawful use of force within the Security Council. An authorization is necessary to ensure that it is the Security Council, which — leaving apart the right to self-defence under Article 51 — decides on the legality of using military force. Nevertheless, the interpretation of Article 53 has also to consider that the control by authorization is rather limited. In fact the necessity of an authorization cannot prevent the actual use of military force without such an authorization. This consideration reveals that Article 53 is the procedural solution of a problem to which material criteria are difficult to formulate and to enforce. In other words, since states may not easily be bound to certain criteria under which the use of force may be considered lawful, the Charter requires a Security Council authorization in order to legalize the use of force. The Charter thus vests the power to authorize use of force in the Security Council and in doing so it avoids the necessity to define lawful use of force in an abstract manner. Instead, it is up to the Security Council to decide on a case by case basis on the legality of the use of military force. It is hard to see why this function of the authorization should not be fulfilled in an ex-post authorization. Without approval the regional use of military force would remain illegal from the beginning. Hence the Security Council would still maintain the decision on the lawfulness of use of force.

Furthermore, in case of an approval by the Security Council it seems hard to imagine that such a decision of the Council should remain without legal consequences. Surely the Council itself would be estopped from invoking the illegality of the use of force[214]. Even if the matter was brought before the ICJ it does not seem possible that the latter would be able to decide on the legality of the use of force in question without taking into account the fact that the Security Council gave its approval[215].

Nevertheless, the argument of a danger of increased regional interventionism should be seriously taken into account. It cannot be neglected that the possibility of an ex post authorization might be a motivation to act first and ask later for an approval. A second function of the authorization

---

214 J.A. Frowein, "Zwangsmaßnahmen von Regionalorganisationen", in: U. Beyerlin et al. (eds.), *Recht zwischen Umbruch und Bewahrung, Festschrift für Rudolf Bernhardt*, 1995, 57 (65).

215 Frowein, see note 205, 20.

might, therefore, be seen in helping to reduce the number of military interventions. Without prior Security Council consent their illegality would be manifest. However, the deterring effect of the consequences of intervention without authorization is already put into question by the number of regional interventions during the Cold War, none of which was authorized by the Council. But more important is to keep in mind that the emphasis which has been put into that argument was largely due to the specific danger of outside interventions into internal conflicts during the Cold War. It has already been pointed out that the political circumstances of civil wars have changed considerably. Of course it is still necessary to ensure Security Council control over regional use of military force. But the emphasis has been moving from containing super-power dominated regional hyperactivity to opening possibilities for a controlled but rapid redress for the devastating consequences of civil wars on the civilian population.

The way in which the Security Council dealt with the Liberian crisis may illustrate the practical advantages of ex-post authorizations. As already described, the Liberian civil war started at the end of the year 1989 and by July 1990 President Doe had lost control over the country except for a small part of Monrovia including the presidential palace[216]. ECOWAS accepted President Doe's request for an "ECOWAS peace-keeping force" and sent a Cease-Fire Monitoring Group (ECOMOG). One of the rebel groups, the National Patriotic Front of Liberia (NPFL), which controlled most parts of the country including Monrovia, did not accept ECOMOG as impartial and "declared war" on the force[217]. It was only after several weeks of fighting that ECOMOG gained control over Monrovia[218].

The Security Council did not immediately react to the sending of ECOMOG. The first reaction is a statement by the President of the Council dated 22 January 1991[219] in which the members of the Council "commend the efforts made by the ECOWAS heads of State and Government to promote peace and normalcy in Liberia". A second statement, quite similar in wording, is dated 7 May 1992[220]. These statements have been read as falling within the Council's power of appreciation to determine whether or not an authorization is necessary[221]. It is argued that the

---

[216] For details of the developments see G. Nolte, "Restoring Peace by Regional Action", *ZaöRV* 53 (1993), 603 et seq.

[217] Nolte, see above, 603 (608).

[218] Ibid., 608 et seq.

[219] Doc. S/22133 of 22 January 1991.

[220] Doc. S/23886 of 7 May 1992.

[221] Nolte, see note 216, 633; Frowein, see note 205, 17.

statements express the Council's view that the intervention did not require an authorization under Article 53. Since the statements do not give any indication as to the reason why an authorization was not necessary this question has to be answered in view of the circumstances of the Liberian crisis. Two possibilities are mentioned: either the intervention could be legally based on the invitation by President Doe[222] or an authorization was unnecessary because ECOMOG could be qualified as a peace-keeping force[223]. However, both alternatives are not entirely convincing. The qualification as a peace-keeping force faces the objection that ECOMOG was to a large extent involved in combat operations against the NPFL[224] and the validity of the invitation must be questioned with respect to the limited effectiveness of President Doe's government[225].

In view of doubts which remain with respect to the legality of ECO-MOG's intervention a third possibility may be taken into account. The reactions by the Security Council may be considered as an ex-post authorization. Before analyzing these reactions the further developments of the crisis have to be taken into account. The two presidential statements of 22 January 1991 and 7 May 1992 were issued during a phase of relative stability in Liberia. On 24 October 1990 an armistice came into force[226] and on 31 October 1991 the Agreement Yamoussoukro IV[227] was concluded. By summer 1992 the situation had deteriorated considerably. Although the NPFL signed the Yamoussoukro IV Agreement it did not honour its commitments. ECOWAS reacted by imposing an arms embargo[228]. Heavy fighting was the consequence of an attack on Monrovia by NPFL rebels in October 1992[229].

Following these events, the Security Council for the first time during the crisis, reacted by adopting a formal resolution. In it the Council commended ECOWAS "for its efforts to restore peace, security and stability in Liberia"[230]. Similar wording was used in the following resolu-

---

222 Nolte, see note 216, 633 et seq.
223 Frowein, see note 205, 15; Frowein, see note 214, 63 et seq.
224 See the detailed descriptions by Nolte, see note 216, 608 et seq. and 611 et seq.
225 See supra, p. 152.
226 Conference of Banjul, Doc. A/45/984=S/22025 of 20 December 1990, Annex.
227 Doc. S/24815 of 17 November 1991 (Annex).
228 Doc. S/24811 of 16 November 1992, Annex I; see also the report of the Secretary-General of the United Nations, Doc. S/25402 of 12 March 1993, 7.
229 For details see Nolte, see note 216, 611.
230 S/RES/788 (1992) of 19 November 1992 .

tions S/RES/813 (1993) of 26 March 1993, S/RES/856 (1993) of 10 August 1993 and S/RES/866 (1993) of 22 September 1993. When analyzing this wording one should keep in mind the wording of resolution 678 (1990) which authorized the use of force to drive the Iraqi forces out of Kuwait. In this resolution the Council inter alia authorized member states to "use all necessary means *to restore international peace and security in the area*" (italics added by the author). This authorization clearly implied enforcement action against the Iraqi forces in Kuwait. For this reason the difference in wording in the resolution dealing with the Liberian conflict compared to the relevant presidential statements is significant. While the statements commended efforts to "promote" peace, the resolutions commend efforts to "restore" peace and in doing so used the wording of the Kuwait resolution. While the statements applied to a situation of consent on all sides in the civil war, the resolutions refer to the use of force against one rebel group. Against this background it seems hard to argue that the Security Council was not in favour of the enforcement measures taken[231].

Admittedly, the reactions by the Security Council in the Liberian case are no clear example for an ex post authorization. But they demonstrate that the political circumstances within the Council, as well as in a particular region of the world, may create conditions in which an ex post authorization can help the Security Council in fulfilling its task to maintain international peace and security. The example also underlines a further political advantage of an ex post authorization. ECOMOG had intervened without authorization, but — as the reactions of the Council reveal — the members of the Security Council considered the intervention as a positive element in a process towards the restoration of peace. The way the Council reacted allowed it to commend the intervention and to remain actively engaged in the matter by sending its own observer mission. Had it condemned the intervention for lack of authorization it is difficult to see how further peace-keeping contributions of the United Nations in collaboration with ECOMOG could have been possible.

3. Implicit Authorization

Closely linked to the discussion of an ex-post authorization in the Liberian case arises the question of implicit or tacit authorizations. Again the discussions in the Security Council on the sanctions of the OAS against

---

231   The enforcement character of ECOMOG's tasks is further underlined in the Abuja-Agreement of 19 August 1995 which supplements the Cotonou Agreement. The Abuja-Agreement contains a provision (Art. 8) which is headed "Peace enforcement powers" and which refers to ECOMOG's responsibilities under the Cotonou-Agreement.

the Dominican Republic in 1960 may be a useful starting point. The Council had two draft resolutions to consider: the already mentioned Soviet draft with an ex-post approval of the sanctions and a three-power draft in which the breach of diplomatic relations was merely taken note of. During the discussions the delegate of Ceylon gave the following statement:

> "My point is that, in reality, I find very little difference, except in wording between the draft resolution submitted by the Soviet Union and the draft resolution submitted by Argentina, Ecuador and the United States of America, because the meaning one attaches to the three-power draft is that we are asked to take note of the resolution which had been adopted at the Sixth Meeting of Consultation of Ministers of Foreign Affairs of the American Republics. If we take note of the acceptance of a resolution and take note of it in the very terms of that resolution, it implies that we are not opposed to it. It is not difficult to argue that if one is not opposed to a thing, one more or less concurs in that position"[232].

The statement suggests the possibility of an implicit authorization. Where the question of an implicit authorization is discussed in the literature on Article 53 this notion is mostly rejected[233]. It is feared that unclear resolutions or statements by the Council may be abused as justification for interventions the Council did not intend to authorize. However, the dangers inherent in implicit authorizations may be reduced to some extent if the procedural rules concerning voting and majorities in the Council are transferred to implicit authorizations. A first important clarification should be made with respect to the notion of tacit authorization, i.e. the idea that silence on part of the Council could be interpreted as an authorization. This view, which was presented by American authors in the 1960s[234], has to be rejected. It overruns the checks which are inherent in the voting rights, especially in the veto right of the five permanent mem-

---

232 SCOR 894th Mtg. of 9 September 1960, 5.
233 C. Schreuer, "Regionalism v. Universalism", *EJIL* 6 (1995), 477 (492); C. Schreuer, "Comment", in: J. Delbrück (ed.), *The Future of International Law Enforcement. New Scenarios — New Law?*, 1993, 147 (151); R. Pernice, *Die Sicherung des Weltfriedens durch regionale Organisationen und die Vereinten Nationen. Eine Untersuchung zur Kompetenzverteilung nach Kapitel VIII der UN-Charta*, 1972, 135.
234 L. C. Meeker, "Defensive Quarantine and the Law", *AJIL* 57 (1963), 515 (522); A. Chayes, "Law and the Quarantine of Cuba", *Foreign Aff.* 41 (1962/63), 550 (556 et seq.).

bers of the Council. According to the Charter a majority decision including the permanent members is necessary to render the use of military force lawful. A tacit authorization would amount to the requirement of a majority decision including the five permanent members in order to render a specific use of force illegal. This shift of the burden of finding a majority in the Council runs against the wording of Article 27 para. 3, and cannot be accepted. But the requirements of the Charter may be met if the voting procedure in the Council is transferred to implicit authorizations. An implicit authorization would then require a positive decision in the Council on the use of force in question. This positive decision would have to be supported by a majority of the members of the Council including all permanent members.

If these principles are applied to the statement of the delegate of Ceylon, one has to come to the conclusion that the fact that the Council took note of the sanctions cannot be interpreted as a positive decision on the sanctions. Taking note does not include any qualification of the measures whatsoever. They are neither viewed positively nor negatively. Therefore the resolution submitted by the three American powers cannot be seen as an implicit authorization of the diplomatic sanctions applied by the OAS. In the Liberian case, however, the situation is fundamentally different. Apart from the wording of the resolutions which commended ECOWAS for its efforts to "restore" peace, resolution 866 (1993) of 22 September 1993 provides for further indications that the Council was in fact authorizing the use of force by ECOMOG. Resolution 866 established a United Nations Observer Mission in Liberia (UNOMIL). In doing so the Council for the first time sent parallel to a regional peace-keeping mission a United Nations observer mission[235]. The respective competences of the two missions had to be defined. The ideas of the parties as to the distribution of competences were included in the Cotonou-Agreement of 25 July 1993[236]:

"1. It is also agreed that ECOMOG shall have the right to self-defence where it has been physically attacked by any warring faction thereto.

2. There shall be established, upon deployment of ECOMOG and the full contingent of the United Nations Observer Mission, a Violation Committee consisting of one person from each of the parties hereto and

---

[235] For a detailed analysis see G. Nolte, "Combined Peace-keeping: ECO-MOG and UNOMIL in Liberia", *International Peacekeeping* 1 (1994), 42 et seq.

[236] Doc. S/26272 of 9 August 1993 (Annex).

Security Council Control over Regional Action 185

ECOMOG and the United Nations Observer Mission, chaired by a member of the United Nations Observer Mission.

3. All violations of the cease-fire shall be reported to the United Nations observer mission/observers who shall, immediately upon receipt of the information of violation, commence an investigation and make findings thereof. In the event the violations can be cured by the United Nations observers, they shall pursue such a course. However, should such a course not be possible, the United Nations observers shall submit their findings to the Violation Committee. The Violation Committee shall invite the violating party/(ies) for the purpose of having such a party/(ies) take corrective measures to cure the violations within such time frame as may be stipulated by the Committee. Should the violating party not take the required corrective measures, *ECOMOG shall be informed thereof and shall thereupon resort to the use of its peace-enforcement powers against the violator*"[237].

In resolution 866 the Council defined the respective competences of ECOMOG and UNOMIL as follows:

"UNOMIL shall have the following mandate:
[...] h) *without participation in enforcement operation*, to coordinate with ECOMOG in the discharge of ECOMOG's separate responsibilities, [...]"[238].

This part of the resolution refers to a report by the Secretary-General in which the separate responsibilities are set out more in detail:

"It was agreed that the following elements would underlie the relationship between UNOMIL and ECOMOG: [...] d) should *ECOMOG enter into planned peace enforcement involving combat operations*, UNOMIL observers would not participate in such actions and would, along with other United Nations staff, be temporarily withdrawn from the area"[239].

It seems to result quite clearly from these references to the use of force by ECOMOG in resolution 866 and in the Secretary-General's report that the Security Council was well aware of the fact that the mechanism set up for managing the Liberian crisis included use of force by ECOMOG.

---

237 Italics added by the author.
238 Italics added by the author.
239 Doc. S/26422 of 9 September 1993 (Italics added by the author).

There are two solutions as to the justification of such use of force. One could be seen in the consent of the parties to the Cotonou-Agreement, which provided for peace-enforcement against a violator of the cease-fire. This raises the question of limits of party consent to use of military force; the second interpretation could be that the Council was implicitly authorizing use of force by ECOMOG for the purposes defined in the resolution and the Cotonou-Agreement.

4. General Authorization

The American delegation to the San Francisco Conference discussed the question of a general authorization with respect to the OAS. Most delegates were of the opinion that a general authorization would be possible[240]. There are no indications in the practice of the United Nations that a general authorization would be in line with Article 53. In the literature the question of a general authorization has only recently been addressed. The notion is rejected[241]. It is argued that the Security Council would be unable to keep control over regional enforcement action if a general authorization were given to a regional organization, because the Council would not be in a position to block specific decisions of the organization since the latter could rely on the general authorization.

The problem about a general authorization is that it would shift the burden to find a majority in the Council. Presumably, the Council as the organ carrying primary responsibility for the maintenance of international peace and security (Article 24) could decide that a specific decision under the general authorization should not be executed. Such a decision would require a decision in the Council to block the regional action and hence be subject to the veto of the five permanent members. It can easily be seen that the consequence of a general authorization would be that the majority in the Council would not be necessary to render a specific use of force legal, but rather to render illegal in a specific case a use of force which in principle would be legal under the general authorization.

One might ask the question whether the fact that the state, against which the military action is executed, consented to such action in the founding treaty of the regional organization, can be seen as an equivalent for the loss of control which is implied in the shift of the veto effect. While the

---

240 Foreign Relations of the United States, Diplomatic Papers, 1945, Vol. I, General: The United Nations, 305.

241 J. A. Frowein, "Legal Consequences for International Law Enforcement in Case of Security Council Inaction", in: Delbrück, see note 233, 119; R. Wolfrum, "Der Beitrag regionaler Abmachungen zur Friedenssicherung", ZaöRV 53 (1993), 576 (580).

argument of consent has some merit, it should be kept in mind that the consent to enforcement action in the treaty establishing the regional organization is a necessary prerequisite for any regional measures, irrespective whether they are authorized generally or individually. For this reason the consent is no additional equivalent for the control lost by the shifted veto effect in case of a general authorization. Another way of ensuring control might be to include precise descriptions into the general authorization, defining specific cases in which regional military enforcement action is possible. Whether or not such descriptions are possible in practice remains doubtful. Until now there is no practice of the Council which might point in that direction. From a political point of view it is preferable to keep the action, as far as possible, in the hands of the Council. This is ensured by the possibility of implicit and ex-post authorizations. In cases of inactivity of the Security Council where action is needed for urgent humanitarian reasons there is the possibility of a regional humanitarian intervention, subject to the conditions developed above. In view of the lacking practice by the Council, and the difficulty to abstractly define cases in which enforcement action may be generally authorized, it is preferable to restrict authorizations under Article 53 to specific cases.

The necessity to clearly define the conditions of the authorization may also be illustrated by the authorization in the Kuwait crisis. When Saddam Hussein, after the invasion of Kuwait, did not comply with the demands by the Council to withdraw immediately from the country[242], the Security Council authorized the member states of the United Nations in resolution 678 (1990) "to use all necessary means to uphold and implement resolution 660 (1990) and all subsequent relevant resolutions and to restore international peace and Security in the area". When the Iraqi forces were driven out of Kuwait the question arose whether and to what extent the resolution allowed for military actions on Iraqi territory. Could it be read as justifying military action to remove Saddam Hussein from office? The allied forces stopped their actions at a point where they could be sure that a second invasion of Kuwait shortly afterwards was excluded. The authorization was criticized for its imprecision in literature[243]. The reasoning of the criticism also applies to authorizations for regional organizations. It is hard

---

242 S/RES/660 (1990) of 2 August 1990.
243 B. H. Weston, "Security Council Resolution 678 and Persian Gulf Decision Making: Precarious Legitimacy", *AJIL* 85 (1991), 516 (525 et seq.); Y. Le Bouthillier/M. Morin, "Réflexions sur la validité des opérations entreprises contre l'Iraq en regard de la Charte des Nations Unies et du droit canadien", *CYIL* 29 (1991), 142 (155 et seq.); H. Freudenschuß, "Between Unilateralism and Collective Security: Authorizations of the Use of Force by the UN Security Council", *EJIL* 5 (1994), 492 (524).

to imagine that a general authorization could be drafted in a way that misunderstandings are excluded and the authorization remains applicable to an indefinite number of different cases without the Security Council losing control over the possible actions.

5. Control on the Field

The above-mentioned example of the authorization in the second Gulf War also raises the question of United Nations control on the field. Chapter VIII does not explicitly require such control. It could be argued that control in this respect is exercised through the necessity of reporting all measures to the United Nations under Article 54. However, it is obvious that these reports may not provide first-hand information. They are presented by the regional organization concerned and hence questions as to their objectivity might arise. In this respect the combined approach taken by the United Nations and ECOWAS in Liberia[244] might serve as a new model of ensuring control on the field. On 25 July 1993 the parties had agreed to a new peace agreement (Cotonou Peace Agreement[245]) in which earlier agreements were reaffirmed and a peace-keeping operation by the United Nations was asked for[246]. This United Nations Mission was to be charged with supervising the application of the agreement not only by the parties but also by ECOMOG[247]. In resolution 866 of 22 September 1993 the Security Council inter alia gave the following mandate to UNOMIL:

> "b) to monitor compliance with other elements of the Peace Agreement, [...] and to verify its impartial application".

The reference to impartial application contains the control of UNOMIL over the actions taken by ECOMOG. The combined approach taken in Liberia allows for United Nations monitoring of regional action on the field. This provides the Council with first-hand information on the developments and may be viewed as a new means of United Nations controlling regional organizations.

Since the sending of UNOMIL into the Liberian civil war in 1993, in Georgia and in Tajikistan parallel missions of United Nations and the Commonwealth of Independent States (CIS) are in place. While the

---

244   See in detail, Nolte, see note 235, 42 et seq.
245   Doc. S/26272 of 9 August 1993.
246   The Cotonou Agreement was supplemented by the Abuja Agreement of 19 August 1995, Doc. S/1995/742 of 28 August 1995.
247   Nolte, see note 244, 44.

mandate of UNMOT[248] does not contain any reference to monitoring the CIS forces in Tajikistan[249], the UN Mission UNOMIG in Georgia was expressly given the mandate to control the CIS peace-keeping force in resolution 937 (1994) of 21 July 1994:

> "The Security Council, [...]
> decides also that the mandate of an expanded UNOMIG, based upon the recommendations in the Secretary-General's report, shall be as follows: [...] b) to observe the operation of the CIS peace-keeping force within the framework of the Agreement [...]".

Reports of the Secretary-General in the time after the resolution reveal that UNOMIG was fulfilling the task of control. In a report of 6 January 1995 the Secretary-General reported the following results of UNOMIG's observations of the CIS-Forces:

> "37. The CIS peace-keeping force has been conducting its operations within the framework of implementation of the 14 May agreement. Any variation from its agreed tasks has been made in consultation with the parties"[250].

UNOMIG has witnessed difficult developments which endanger the proper fulfillment of its monitoring functions. Its freedom of movement is restricted by dangerous landmines. Because of its limited demining capacity UNOMIG is compelled to use only roads which have previously been declared to be mine-free by the CIS peace-keeping force[251]. It is obvious that this dependence on the CIS force limits UNOMIG's ability to control that force. Nevertheless, the developments demonstrate that United Nations observers may serve as a useful source of information for controlling regional action on the field. In both cases, in Liberia as well as in Georgia, they are perceived as a parallel sending of peace-keeping forces by the United Nations and a regional organization. But the Liberian example, in particular, where the regional force fulfills peace-enforcement functions reveals that a transfer of the combined approach to enforcement

---

[248] S/RES/968 (1994) of 16 December 1994.

[249] See in this respect the critical statement by the representative of the Czech Republic in the Security Council, Doc. S/PV. 3482 of 16 December 1994, 8.

[250] Doc. S/1995/10 of 6 January 1995, para. 37.

[251] See the report of the Secretary-General of 15 April 1996, Doc. S/1996/284.

action might provide the United Nations with a new means of control over regional peace enforcement.

III. Control over Regional Non-Military Measures

Following the interpretation of "enforcement action" in Article 53 para.1, developed above, the term does not comprise non-military measures. Hence, such measures do not require an authorization by the Council. But how are such measures then controlled by the Council. At first sight it is not obvious how universal and regional non-military sanctions might conflict with each other. But the issue is of potential practical relevance. This may be demonstrated by the following hypothetical example.

In contrast to the current practice of unlimited non-military sanctions there is good cause to assume that in future non-military sanctions under Article 41 might be limited in time. Those members of the Council which accepted such sanctions rather hesitatingly might realize that their influence increases with a time limit. A precedent of a limitation in time has already been set with respect to military measures in resolution 929 of 22 June 1994 concerning Rwanda. In this resolution the Security Council authorized the member states cooperating with the Secretary-General to use all necessary means to achieve the humanitarian objectives set out in the resolution. This authorization, however, was limited to a period of two months following the adoption of the resolution[252]. Furthermore, the General Assembly is putting pressure on the Council to set time limits on Chapter VII decisions. A time limit would require a majority in the Council to prolong the measures once the date of expiration approaches. Could it be legally possible that in a given case, where the majority for prolonging the universal measures is not reached in the Council, a regional organization decides to apply similar or even identical sanctions?

A second example where a regional organization might be tempted to substitute universal measures by regional sanctions could be seen in a case where the Council lifted its sanctions under Article 41 stating expressly that the conditions of Article 39 where not met any more. Could, in such a situation, a regional organization decide to apply sanctions because, in the understanding of its members, there was still a threat to the peace in the region?

In both cases the interpretation of "enforcement action" in Article 53 leads to the conclusion that the regional measures are lawful under the Charter of the United Nations. For the first example of expiring universal

---

[252] S/RES/ 929 (1994), para. 4.

sanctions the result is rather obvious. The Council did not decide on the legality of regional sanctions and hence the situation is quite similar to one where no universal sanctions had been applied before the regional measures came into force. It is in the logic of the restrictive interpretation of "enforcement action" in Article 53 that regional organizations may decide on regional sanctions if the Council is unable to decide on universal measures, irrespective of whether or not such universal measures had been in place before.

The second example, where the universal sanctions are lifted because the Council considered the threat to the peace to have ceased, is more difficult to argue. Can it be correct that regional sanctions may be applied where no threat to the peace exists? This points to the relationship between Article 53 and the conditions for the application of Chapter VII laid down in Article 39. Article 53 does not contain any conditions under which regional enforcement action may take place. Therefore, the preconditions of Chapter VII have to be applied to activities under Article 53[253]. Such an interpretation is all the more conclusive since it is difficult to see how the authorization by the Council which is required in Article 53 should be obtained in the absence of at least a threat to the peace. However, the interpretation of Article 53 resulted in excluding non-military-enforcement action from its scope of application. Hence, for such measures the reference to Article 39 is not applicable.

Does this solution imply that there is no Security Council control over regional non-military sanctions? A certain control can be seen in the possibility that the regional measures might themselves be qualified as threat to the peace by the Council. This would open the possibility for the Security Council to enforce the lifting of the regional sanctions under Chapter VII. However, such a way of controlling regional non-military measures will be difficult to proceed in a case where one of the permanent members of the Council is also member of the regional organization concerned. The veto would seem inevitable in such a case.

The result may seem somewhat surprising at first sight. However, it fits perfectly well into the general principles applicable to non-military sanctions. Non-military sanctions are not subject to the same rigid system as military enforcement action is. Customary international law is applicable to non-military measures even when they are applied by regional organizations. The result underlines the distinction between measures according to Article 41 and action under Article 42. Military action has to stop when the Council so decides. In contrast to this no member of the United Nations is under an obligation to restart bilateral trade with the addressee

---

[253] G. Ress, "On Art. 53", 722 et seq., Mn. 10, in: Simma, see note 25.

of a trade embargo once the Security Council has lifted that embargo. In conclusion, measures under Article 41 may be applied unilaterally after the embargo has ended. Even in cases where bilateral or multilateral trade agreements are in place and the refusal to restart trade violates these treaties there is no competence of the Security Council to enforce those obligations. An exception may again be made when the Council considers the unilateral measures to constitute a threat to the peace and requires that they be lifted.

D. Conclusion

The end of the Cold War allowed the reopening of Chapter VIII of the Charter, the provisions of which had remained without application for a considerable period of time. The practice since the beginning of the 1990s shows several possibilities of sharing the burden of maintenance of international peace and security between the universal and the regional level.

1. The activities of NATO in the Yugoslav crisis could be described in management terms as "outsourcing". While the overall crisis management rests with the Security Council the military part is given to a regional organization. From a political point of view this describes the "utilization" of regional organizations envisaged by Article 53 para. 1. Legally speaking, the mandate for NATO may rather be seen as an application of Chapter VII, especially of Article 48, since neither the former Yugoslavia nor the successor republics were members of NATO[254]. But the case may be viewed as an example for leaving the military part of an operation to a regional organization.

2. The Yugoslav experience may also be interpreted as an example for substituting an unsuccessful universal mission by a regional operation. The political implications of the failure of UNPROFOR certainly included that a new United Nations mission would have faced serious problems of authority. The regional option provided for a new start and IFOR was therefore able to act without the political handicap which a direct United Nations successor operation to UNPROFOR would have faced.

3. The cooperation between the United Nations and ECOWAS in Liberia may be seen to represent a slightly different type of burden sharing. In the eyes of some factions to the civil war in Liberia the regional intervention through ECOMOG cast some doubt on the neutrality of ECOWAS. Therefore, the parties to the conflict asked for a United

---

[254] For further references as to Article 48 as a basis for IFOR, see C. Walter, *Vereinte Nationen und Regionalorganisationen*, 1996, 278 et seq.

Nations observer mission which had inter alia the task to monitor the activities of ECOMOG. In doing so, enforcement operations (if they were necessary) could be left to ECOMOG, while the United Nations mission was charged with monitoring that ECOMOG did not use its enforcement competences excessively. In addition to that both missions jointly were asked to supervise the maintenance of the Cotonou-Agreement[255]. The possibility of combined peace-keeping with the United Nations mission, not only monitoring the activities of the parties to the conflict, but also those of the respective regional organization is also evidenced by the UN observers in Georgia and in Tajikistan.

4. Finally, the Liberian civil war highlights the dilemma which may be created by an inactive Security Council. Had ECOWAS not intervened in the civil war, the disastrous situation for the civilian population would certainly have continued since action on part of the Council was not very probable. After an active phase in the beginning 1990s the Council seems to become more and more reluctant towards military involvement in civil wars. The option of filling a possible lacuna created by Security Council inaction by collective regional humanitarian action should be taken into serious consideration as an alternative.

---

[255] Supplemented by the Abuja Agreement of 19 August 1995, Doc. S/1995/742 of 28 August 1995.

[19]

The Search for Subsidiarity:
The UN, African Regional Organizations
and Humanitarian Action

DAVID O'BRIEN

This article focuses on the subsidiarity debate on restructuring the operational relationship for humanitarian action between the UN and regional intergovernmental organizations. The principle of subsidiarity favours decentralized control within a tiered governance system. In light of financial and political pressures to regionalize humanitarian action, this article explores the competencies of prominent African regional organizations. This comparative examination illustrates that while the call for subsidiarity is alluring, the search for a working model endures. Should signs of Western disengagement continue, the regional mechanisms for peace and security operations or humanitarian assistance would be unable to cope. An effective architecture for humanitarian action is feasible but this will require rethinking current patterns of international assistance and collaboration.

This article examines current efforts to revive and bring into action the principle of subsidiarity in the 'tiered regime'[1] of the UN, regional and subregional intergovernmental organizations. It is motivated in part by recent UN Secretary-General reports that call for such a re-examination and a concern that political pressures to regionalize humanitarian action may weaken international efforts to prevent and respond to crises. In the new context where peace and security operations and relief assistance are increasingly integrated, it is important that the future debate on subsidiarity incorporates a broad understanding of humanitarian action.[2] To date, however, attention has largely concentrated on reworking the division of responsibility and resources in the peace and security sector. The humanitarian assistance field has been largely overlooked. It is equally critical that the current debate be informed by an empirical grounding of the capacities of regional and subregional intergovernmental organizations. As this article demonstrates in the case of African organizations, many lack the

David O'Brien, Center on International Cooperation, New York.

International Peacekeeping, Vol.7, No.3, Autumn 2000, pp.57–83
PUBLISHED BY FRANK CASS, LONDON

requisite mandates, financial and organizational capacity to go it alone. If these organizations are to be bolstered in the name of subsidiarity, a careful balance needs to be struck between their military and civilian roles. Furthermore, donor efforts to increase the operational capacity of regional organizations should be clear about how responsibility is to be shared between member states, regional organizations and the UN system.

Subsidiarity, a principle of power allocation, favours delegating power to a lower tier of authority.[3] For W. Andy Knight and others who employ the concept pragmatically, subsidiarity is an elastic concept that can legitimize 'both the expansion and restriction of authority by linking governance to the issue of competencies'.[4] A related term, burden-sharing, is frequently evoked in management and financial policy debates. Burden-sharing and subsidiarity are often used synonymously but this obfuscates an important distinction: burden-sharing is concerned with the exchange of resources among authorities to realize common objectives whereas subsidiarity refers to the site of decision making authority within a tiered governance system.

Two agendas appear to be competing in the search for subsidiarity. One variant is based on burden-*sharing* which seeks to build a new cooperative and complementary division of labour between the UN and regional organizations. The coupling of external financial assistance and logistical support to strengthen regional and subregional organizations could over time enhance international collaboration for humanitarian action. This assumes of course that governments and intergovernmental organizations in the affected regions are committed to preventing and responding to emergencies.[5] Burden-*shifting*, on the other hand, has the opposite intent. It seeks to devolve responsibility for humanitarian response without due concern for whether the capacity exists to respond effectively. Transferring the burden of action to countries or regions affected by humanitarian emergencies appeals to Western governments that either are reluctant to commit military or civilian personnel to politically volatile and physically dangerous situations, or are unwilling to underwrite the costs of assistance in regions where their narrowly defined national interests do not lie. Shifting the burden of action in this manner will not result in effective humanitarian action.

This article is organized into four sections. The first section highlights several previous efforts and criteria to structure responsibility in tiered international regimes. In the section that follows, the financial and political forces driving the subsidiarity debate are illustrated. In light of pressure to regionalize humanitarian action, section three presents a comparative survey of Africa's principal regional and subregional organizations. This section reports several encouraging initiatives to widen and deepen regional cooperation. Nevertheless, the current institutional mechanisms and financial resources in Africa are insufficient to meet current and projected humanitarian needs without international assistance. The following section examines different approaches by the international community to enhance African institutional capacities for humanitarian action. This review finds considerable effort devoted to developing Africa's peacekeeping role to the neglect of instruments for humanitarian assistance. In the final analysis, a burden-sharing approach could strengthen international cooperation for humanitarian action. The burden-shifting option, on the other hand, represents an affront to humanitarian principles and an abrogation of global responsibility.

Subsidiarity

Arguably, the first formal and consensual attempt to allocate political authority in a tiered regime comprising sovereign states and an intergovernmental body dates to the creation of the Central Commission for the Navigation of the Rhine in 1815. Its 'principle of local control' placed primary authority for determining trade and transport rules among adjacent states. However, a small secretariat was charged with overall coordination and standard setting.[6]

More recently, the Treaty of Rome establishing the European Community invoked the principle of subsidiarity. Article 3b determined that decision-making power should be assigned according to the following criteria:

> In areas which do not fall within its exclusive competence, the Community shall take action, in accordance with the principle of subsidiarity, only if and in so far as the objectives of the proposed action cannot be sufficiently achieved by the Member States and can therefore, by reason of the scale or effects of the proposed action, be better achieved by the Community.[7]

The subsidiarity debate in Europe has since centred on which tier of government, from local to supranational, represents the appropriate site of authority in a given issue area.

In contrast, the tiered regimes envisioned by the League of Nations Covenant and the UN Charter are more formulaic by design. For example, Article 24 of the Covenant of the League of Nations states that all then existing international bodies be placed under its direction.[8] Likewise, the architects of the UN Charter sought to order international relations but in contrast to the League's direct control, the UN sought ultimate authority in a more decentralized framework.

This preference is evident in both Chapters VI (Pacific Settlement of Disputes) and VIII (Regional Arrangements) of the UN Charter. In the former, the parties to any dispute threatening international peace and security 'shall, first of all, seek a solution...[and]...resort to regional agencies or arrangements, or other peaceful means of their own choice'.[9] Failure to resolve the dispute would then justify action by the Security Council as per Article 37(2). Again in Chapter VIII the bottom-tier approach to conflict prevention is highlighted: 'Such agencies shall make every effort to achieve pacific settlement of local disputes through such regional arrangements or by such regional agencies before referring them to the Security Council.'[10] As if to remove any doubt of the preference for a lower-tier approach, the Charter stipulates that the Security Council should actively promote regional solutions to regional problems.[11] In practice, member states of the UN and regional organizations have not lived up to the Charter's anticipated response sequence. However, unfolding events in the 1990s brought the role of regional organizations back into focus. Increasingly, the donor community and member states of regional organizations are promoting the role of regional organizations as crisis managers.

Subsidiarity, Why Now? Why African Organizations?

Renewed interest in redefining relations with regional organizations signals the UN's midlife crisis brought on in part by the stress resulting from African conflicts. Increasingly, permanent Security Council members appear intent on retiring the UN's role as peacemaker in Africa.[12] In the presence of repeated humanitarian crises there are mounting political and financial reasons why donors are calling for greater participation of regional organizations. The one glimmering sign of hope radiates not from New York or Geneva but from Africa under the rubric of the African renaissance. While there is some evidence of greater regional cooperation in Africa, applying subsidiarity to humanitarian action will require an enhancement of African intergovernmental capacities and strengthened operational and political cooperation with the UN system.

To better understand the current context, the principal drivers behind the subsidiarity debate are examined. On the one hand, recent events have clearly illustrated the limits of global multilateral commitment to Africa and the decline of Western engagement. On the other hand, there is renewed interest within Africa in addressing the causes and consequences of humanitarian crises on that continent.

Peace and Security Operations

Simply stated, the UN agencies responsible for peace and security and humanitarian affairs are currently overstretched. When UN Secretary-General Javier Perez de Cuéllar began his two-term tenure (1982–91), the

Cold War had severely rusted the UN's peace and security machinery. The spheres of influence carved by the US and the USSR impinged on the UN's security mandate and its ability to cooperate with regional organizations. At the time of Boutros Boutros-Ghali's Secretary-General appointment (1991–95), the Reagan Doctrine's anti-communist offensive and the East–West ideological conflict had abated, but lamentably, it was followed by a new generation of conflicts the international community was ill-prepared (or unwilling) to address.

Evan Luard describes the implication of the Cold War transition in the following terms: 'The concept of a network of regional organizations complementing the work of the UN was somewhat hypothetical for Perez de Cuéllar, [but] it assumed a practical urgency for Boutros Boutros-Ghali.'[13] This urgency was caused by state collapse and armed conflict in Yugoslavia, Somalia, Mozambique, Angola, the Great Lakes, and tragically, in numerous other areas. The increasing number of intrastate conflicts, their destabilizing regional consequences, and the escalating expense of deploying Blue Helmets to more places for larger, costlier missions brought into focus burden-sharing between the UN and regional organizations.

The financial imperative of sharing the costs of the UN's burgeoning peacekeeping operations was only partly alluded to in Boutros-Ghali's influential *Agenda for Peace*. He acknowledged in 1992 that 'regional action as a matter of decentralization, delegation and cooperation with United Nations efforts could...lighten the burden of the Council', but emphasized a more laudable motivating factor – to 'contribute to a deeper sense of participation, consensus and democratization in international affairs'.[14] Six years following the publication of *Agenda for Peace*, Kofi Annan still held to Boutros-Ghali's democratizing intentions but the UN's burgeoning peacekeeping burden created an even greater sense of urgency – cooperation with regional arrangements was by now 'necessary'. In Annan's words, 'providing support for regional and subregional initiatives in Africa is both necessary and desirable. Such support is necessary because the United Nations lacks the capacity, resources and expertise to address all problems that may arise in Africa.'[15] As the next section demonstrates, the search for alternative resources and partnerships also pertains to humanitarian assistance.

Humanitarian Assistance

The numerous civil and interstate wars of the 1990s created a humanitarian crisis that overwhelmed the humanitarian community. Not only did the principal humanitarian actors have to alter their operating guidelines from one based on a natural disaster model to one informed by the complexities of operating in a theatre of war, they also experienced increasing difficulty reaching the numbers of people in need. For the major donors and humanitarian agencies responding to ever more refugees, displaced persons and shattered communities, funding became a pressing issue. Many UN operational agencies explored new burden-sharing arrangements. For instance, the 1998 UNHCR Annual Executive Committee meeting specifically examined burden-sharing.[16] Meanwhile UNICEF, UNHCR and the UNDP all began to probe private sector support.[17]

Three trends in humanitarian relief illustrate the deficiencies of multilateral cooperation. First, there is insufficient financial commitment to meet current and projected humanitarian needs. The UN Office for the Coordination of Humanitarian Affairs (OCHA) reports that global humanitarian needs decreased gradually from their peak in 1994 to 1997 but rebounded sharply in 1998. Meanwhile, funding declined continually.[18] According to OCHA data, the percentage of global estimated needs met through the UN inter-agency appeals process deteriorated steadily, from 75.8 per cent in 1994, to 64 per cent in 1997, and to just 32.9 per cent mid-way in 1998.[19]

Second, when international assistance is provided, its distribution is uneven. This is owed to the fact that agencies are unlikely to recoup operational expenses from the donors if there is media and political disinterest.[20] Sudan, a country that has continually been the subject of UN agency appeals, receives the African average, with 32 per cent of projected needs covered mid-way through 1998. Appeal responses for Sierra Leone, Liberia and Guinea-Bissau fell below this average while the 1997 appeal for the Republic of Congo received only 7.9 per cent of estimated requirements.

Third, there is an imbalance among humanitarian contributors. In 1995–96, ten donors accounted for 92 per cent of total funds coordinated by OCHA's funding mechanism; the top 20 (all OECD countries, plus the European Commission) contributed 99 per cent. Within the regions in which crises occur, on the other hand, only a few governments have responded to CAP appeals. In Africa, only Libya, South Africa, Tunisia, and Mauritius reported making financial contributions in 1995 and 1996, amounting to 0.02 per cent of total donor funding for those years. In the same time period, emergencies in Africa consumed almost 50 per cent of donor assistance. African countries do contribute by other means (such as resettling refugees and bilateral support) but the depth and extent of recent humanitarian tragedies in Africa are immense and survival for many is dangerously dependent on the uncertain flow and direction of external funds.

African Renaissance and Western Retrenchment

The scope of humanitarian emergencies and the decline of resources makes a pressing case for renewed international commitment. One hope for

THE UN, AFRICAN REGIONS AND HUMANITARIAN ACTION   63

realigning responsibility for humanitarian action is couched in South African President Thabo Mbeki's notion of an 'African renaissance'. More of a rallying call than a current reflection of reality, the renaissance message seeks to inspire African leaders to create the conditions for peace, security and development. President Mbeki argues that the response to Africa's challenges must be pan-African in character because of 'the fact that none of our countries is an island which can isolate itself from the rest, and that none of us can truly succeed if the rest fail'.[21] Secretary-General Salim Ahmed Salim of the Organization of African Unity (OAU) has similarly urged African governments to work within the context of the OAU and increase their efforts to prevent and respond to emergencies.[22]

How the African renaissance message resonates in African capitals is important, but so too is its interpretation in the West. In the view of a former Mauritanian foreign minister, 'African solutions for African problems' has been used as 'a pretext for western military disengagement'.[23] One close observer of US policy in Africa concurs with this assessment, arguing that the 'new mantra' in US foreign policy towards Africa is informed by the belief that the US does not wield influence there and therefore should disengage.[24] In the words of then Deputy Secretary of State Strobe Talbott, the UN, too, cannot bring peace to Africa 'even with every imaginable reform and improvement'.[25] This cultivated view of waning UN and US influence clearly provides a rationale for greater African involvement. While the US, as illustrated below, provides military training to enhance African peacekeeping, it has been a reluctant supporter of UN intervention in Africa,[26] and it has not leveraged its considerable resources to nurture greater UN–regional partnerships. Such actions reflect a position intent on shifting the burden of responsibility to Africa.

Burden-shifting represents a conundrum to multilateral efforts to uphold international peace and security. The voice of Sir Kieran Prendergast, UN Under-Secretary-General for Political Affairs, is one among many in the UN diplomatic community that is quick to point out that the African renaissance message signals a window of opportunity to build new cooperative partnerships between the UN system and African organizations.[27] However, the UN does not have the resources to develop operational ties with regional organizations, and African governments cannot afford to wait. As an OCHA report candidly observes, the lesson of Rwanda for African leaders was that they 'should no longer wait for action by the international community or the Security Council.'[28] Either taking a cue from Salim Salim or Thabo Mbeki, or preparing for Western disengagement, some African governments are coordinating their actions within regional organizations to develop new, or re-invigorate old institutional arrangements.

Collective Security Law

As the next section illustrates, however, intergovernmental capacities to prevent and respond to the causes and consequences of humanitarian emergencies vary significantly among Africa's subregional organizations. There is a need to strengthen intergovernmental competence and authority within the subregions and link subregion arrangements in a working partnership with the OAU and the UN system. While this represents an ideal framework of subsidiarity, this framework for international cooperation is a distant reality.

Regional Responses to Regional Problems

A working model of subsidiarity requires greater participation of African governments and their intergovernmental organizations in addressing the causes and consequences of humanitarian crises. Historically, the involvement of African intergovernmental organizations has been on an *ad hoc* basis and reliant on extra-regional resources. This section explores the institutional capacities of several prominent regional arrangements to create a baseline survey of what exists and to draw attention to emerging developments and subregional variations.

The focus on regional organizations as opposed to national or local government stems from the recognition that both peace and security and relief operations are frequently transnational in character. Even when this is not the case, successful prevention, preparation, reaction and rehabilitation initiatives often require, or benefit from, intergovernmental cooperation. Finally, regional organizations have the potential ability to pool resources and to coordinate action with a regional outlook. These elements are required to respond to large-scale humanitarian emergencies.[29]

The following analysis concentrates on existing and emerging humanitarian mechanisms at the regional and subregional level. This survey brings peace and security and humanitarian assistance within a single framework. Separate treatments of these two forms of assistance or subsuming one under the other is problematic. As Adam Roberts observes, 'many peace-keeping operations in the 1990s have had as central tasks assistance to, and protection of, humanitarian action'.[30] Considering this convergence, it is surprising that UN documents calling for subsidiarity do not address the conceptual link between peace and security operations and humanitarian assistance.[31] For African intergovernmental organizations to play a constructive role in the future they will require greater policy making, coordination and operational capacity in both these sectors.

Regional Capacity Profiles for Humanitarian Action

The OAU is Africa's principal political forum. It is also Africa's only intergovernmental organization with an existing mandate for both peace and security operations and humanitarian assistance. Since its founding in 1963, the OAU has upheld its Charter's principle of non-interference in the domestic affairs of member states and respect of their territorial integrity. Consequently, the OAU's peace and security mandate has been primarily restricted to peacemaking and peacebuilding initiatives in interstate conflicts. The OAU's 1981 Inter-African Force to Chad was its first military response to an intrastate conflict. The financial, legal and political problems resulting from this mission cast serious doubt on the organization's capacity for such action.[32] And yet, insufficient international response to subsequent African crises has forced the OAU's hand to act. Recent examples include the OAU peacekeeping missions to Rwanda following the Arusha Agreement, and the OAU Military Observer Mission to Burundi (OMIB). Although the OMIB has been cited as a success story, the OAU's inability to carry the financial burden for this mission and other initiatives indicates its limits for independent action.[33]

Seeking to improve upon its *ad hoc* and crisis-driven reaction to regional crises, in 1993 the OAU established the Mechanism for Conflict Prevention, Management and Resolution. The draft declaration founding the Mechanism emphasized its conflict early warning and preventive role in the hope that this would 'obviate the need to resort to the complex and resource demanding peace-keeping operations, which our countries will find difficult to finance'.[34] Latterly, and largely due to external pressure, the OAU has debated developing a standing peacekeeping force. The second meeting of the OAU Chief of Defence Staff recommended that a force should be composed of a brigade-size contingent from each of the five African subregions. The feasibility of creating this regionally representative force was cast quickly in doubt because 'not all sub-regional organizations are in a position to conduct Peace Support Operations'.[35] The Chiefs of Defence Staff agreed to pursue this idea but ruled out the OAU's involvement in peace-enforcement operations. For these, the OAU would continue to defer to subregional initiatives, following the precedent set by ECOWAS' Military Observer Group (ECOMOG).

The OAU's machinery for humanitarian assistance was revamped twice in the 1990s. Prior to these reforms, humanitarian assistance was restricted to refugees which involved three bodies, the Commission on Refugees, the Coordinating Committee on Assistance to Refugees and the Bureau for Refugees. Currently, responsibility for refugees and displaced persons is placed with the Humanitarian Affairs, Refugees and Displaced Persons Division.

The Commission on Refugees was established in 1964 to examine Africa's refugee problem and make recommendations to the Council of

Ministers, the OAU's policy making body. The Commission provides assistance to refugees and conducts fact-finding missions. Together with the Coordinating Committee, the Commission coordinates relief assistance among other OAU member states, UN agencies and NGOs and develops capacity building projects. The principal duties of the Humanitarian Affairs, Refugees and Displaced Persons Division include upholding the OAU refugee convention, undertaking education and training activities, and keeping the international community informed on Africa's refugee situation. While this framework represents the most comprehensive arrangement for humanitarian action, it has been largely ineffective in rising to the challenge of civil wars and large-scale humanitarian crises.

In contrast to the OAU's overarching mandate, the majority of Africa's subregional organizations were created to promote economic development. The maxim that peace and stability are the *sine qua non* of economic development was belatedly accepted as a justification by some subregional arrangements to expand their scope of cooperation. To date, only the Economic Community of West African States (ECOWAS) and the Southern African Development Community (SADC) are in the process of developing a basic structure to undertake humanitarian action. Subregional organizations in north, central and east Africa, such as the Arab Maghreb Union, the Entente Council, the Central African Customs and Economic Union, the Economic Community of Central African States[36] or the Common Market for Eastern and Southern Africa[37] have neither the mechanisms in place for humanitarian action nor have they indicated a move in this direction.

The Intergovernmental Authority on Development (IGAD)[38] represents the most recent subregional effort to develop regional capacity for humanitarian action. IGAD was founded in 1986 to counter famine and coordinate international development initiatives. This initial focus was revived and expanded in 1996 to include political and humanitarian affairs and economic cooperation.

Member states have displayed a genuine interest in moving beyond political dialogue to address the sources of conflict and humanitarian needs. IGAD presently operates the Early Warning Food Information System for Food Security and acts as a contact point for information on desertification control. IGAD's Division of Political and Humanitarian Affairs promotes regional dialogue to prevent and mediate regional conflicts. This Division is developing a Program on Conflict Prevention, Resolution and Management that seeks to institutionalize consultations and decision-making processes, create a conflict early-warning mechanism and coordinate peace-building efforts.[39] Support for this and other operational projects is reliant on external aid. An important source of financial assistance comes from the IGAD

Partnership Forum, which was established in 1997 by 15 OECD countries and multilateral development agencies.

On an *ad hoc* basis IGAD has become increasingly active in mediating interstate and intrastate conflicts, such as in Sudan and Somalia conflicts. It has yet to play an operational role by either providing or coordinating humanitarian relief.[40] In Sudan or Somalia relief assistance has been dominated by international agencies. The scale of these relief operations, such as Operation Lifeline Sudan or coping with the approximately 600,000 refugees of the Ethiopian-Eritrean war, greatly exceed IGAD's operational and financial capacity. It is unrealistic to suggest that IGAD would be able to mount a multi-million dollar relief operation in the medium to long term. Despite its lack of resources, its recent creation, long standing rivalries among its members and recent armed conflicts, Sudan, Ethiopia and Eritrea, and Somali factional rulers have called on IGAD to mediate their disputes.

In comparison, ECOWAS[41] and SADC[42] have relatively advanced capabilities for humanitarian action. The ECOWAS treaty, signed in 1975, had the primary objective of creating an economic and monetary union although its activities extend to agriculture, industry, natural resource management, health and social programmes. Interestingly, its original treaty was silent on the issue of regional security. The 1981 Protocol on Mutual Assistance on Defence (MAD) changed this, calling for collective action in the event of interstate and domestic conflicts. The MAD Protocol entered into force in 1986. Twelve years following, ECOWAS members established concrete guidelines for the development of a conflict prevention and peacekeeping mechanism.

In October 1998, ECOWAS Heads of State endorsed a proposal to create the ECOWAS Mechanism for Conflict Prevention, Management, Resolution, Peace-Keeping and Security. Among its recommendations was the transformation of the *ad hoc* ECOWAS Military Observer Group (ECOMOG) into a permanent stand-by force. In creating the Mechanism, the authors drew attention explicitly to the importance of relief assistance as a prevention and conflict-management tool. For this reason, the Mechanism makes a direct link between peace and security operations and humanitarian assistance. The decision making authority for humanitarian assistance will come under the mandate of the new Department of Operations, Peace-Keeping and Humanitarian Affairs. Pending the full implementation of the provisions of the Protocol of Non-Aggression (1978), MAD (1981), and Article 58 of the ECOWAS Revised Treaty, the ECOWAS Mechanism's implementation date is scheduled for late 2000. On 9 December 1999, ECOWAS members agreed to protocols on a security and mediation council, four observation bureaux and a council of wise men. Implementing what has been agreed to, arguably ECOWAS' weak point, remains.[43]

The absence of a permanent mechanism with conferred powers and procedures has not prevented ECOWAS from undertaking peace and security operations in the interim. Led by Nigeria, ECOMOG undertook peace-enforcement and peacekeeping operations in Liberia and Sierra Leone. ECOWAS was also called upon by the government of Guinea Bissau to stop a rebellion and, most recently, to restore Cote d'Ivoire's President Bedie to power after he was dethroned by a bloodless military coup on 24 December 1999. ECOWAS did not respond to President Bedie's call but ECOMOG was re-deployed to Sierra Leone.

ECOMOG is receiving considerable attention because it is the first sizeable force to be controlled and financed by an African subregional organization. On humanitarian grounds, there was a clear need to intervene in Liberia and Sierra Leone, but some member states, particularly Francophone ones, were concerned by Nigeria's dominant role and its motives for military intervention. Additionally, the draft document proposing the ECOWAS Mechanism cited these critical shortcomings: the use of force was not legally authorized; ECOMOG was not sufficiently multinational; and the ECOWAS Secretariat did not have proper command and control over the operation.[44] Implementing the Mechanism might enhance regional security but it is too early to state whether it will advance international and humanitarian law in the process. Moreover, the return to democratic politics in Nigeria might have a significant impact on ECOMOG's future. As Adekeye Adebajo and Chris Landsberg have recently noted, President Obasanjo is responding to parliamentary pressures to scale down Nigeria's financial contribution to ECOMOG. Their prediction that 'it is unlikely that Nigeria will continue its sub-regional fire-fighting role unless the burden is more equitably shared with other regional and extra-regional actors', does not bode well for ECOMOG's future.[45]

SADC has taken the opposite approach to ECOWAS. It first created programmes on and infrastructure for enhancing food security and then it initiated dialogue on creating a peace and security arrangement. SADC's initial mandate advanced regional economic cooperation among southern African states while simultaneously solidifying a political bloc against the then-apartheid regime in South Africa. In the early 1990s, the political context in South Africa changed and in 1992, the 'frontline states' adopted a new vision for regional cooperation that took into account South Africa's transition and the new challenges facing the region. It then reorganized to distribute the gains from economic, social and political cooperation and moved away from a security alliance.

SADC has several agricultural and environmental agencies that develop and promote sustainable agricultural practices. These agencies are not geared towards responding to emergencies; rather they emphasize preventive action and promote agricultural production. The Food Security Technical and Administrative Unit (FSTAU) and the Regional Early Warning Unit have considerable technical experience in food security and early warning systems. They work with government agencies to monitor climatic conditions and food reserves to predict food shortages. This information is disseminated widely to member states, external governments and international organizations by SADC's communication centre. Despite discussions following the 1992 southern African drought to create a regional disaster-management system and emergency fund, SADC members have not given it serious attention. The folly of eight years of inaction on this matter was tragically demonstrated by SADC's non-action during the massive flooding in Mozambique beginning February 2000.[46]

SADC's Organ on Politics, Defence and Security was established in June 1996 after several failed efforts to create a common security regime. The Organ is responsible for mediating conflicts and coordinating diplomatic negotiations.[47] More recently the Organ revisited plans to develop a regional peacekeeping force. Building on regional peacekeeping training exercises, delegates to the 20th Inter-state Defence and Security Committee recommended that SADC should develop a permanent SADC multinational peacekeeping force.[48] The planned inauguration date of the SADC peace force is January 2001. The March 1999 announcement followed a year-long feasibility study that examined operational and legal issues relating to the use of force. Alert to the sensitive nature of establishing a peacekeeping force, the agreement calls for a joint UN-OAU monitoring role. This check on SADC's deployment echoed a 1998 South African government White Paper proposing a legislative framework for potential peacekeeping deployment elsewhere in Africa.[49]

Even before the creation of the proposed SADC peace army, member states debated whether it should intervene collectively to back the Democratic Republic of Congo in repelling armed incursions from Rwanda and Uganda. No consensus was reached during the 1999 SADC Summit but some members backed Kabila's regime after the OAU was unsuccessful in securing a ceasefire agreement and unwilling to launch a peace-enforcement operation. The division in SADC pits the hawkish position of President Mugabe of Zimbabwe (current chair of the Organ) against the more diplomatic track of South Africa. Under President Mandela, South Africa proceeded very cautiously in dealing with regional conflicts. Under the new leadership of Thabo Mbeki, he is taking a more activist position that twins diplomacy backed by the potential use of military assets. Coverage of the ANC's 88th birthday celebration quoted ANC Chairman Moiuoa Lekota telling assembled guests not to be surprised if 'the President sends our forces abroad'.[50] A South Africa taking a lead in addressing conflicts that threaten international peace and security would begin to narrow the gulf between its position and that of Zimbabwe's. Like ECOWAS' first military deployment, selected SADC member state intervention in the Congo remains a source of internal disagreement. The new role South Africa carves for itself, the speed that South Africa and Zimbabwe settle their differences, the tenor of public opinion (a variable that arguably applies only to SADC's democratic states) are several determinants that will influence the operational future of SADC's Organ on Politics, Defence, and Security.

Financing Regional Responses to Regional Problems

For regional organizations to assume a greater responsibility for humanitarian action, member states will have to address the seemingly endemic condition of under-funded core budgets. ECOWAS members, for example, have a relatively strong tradition of regional cooperation but after two and a half decades the executive-secretary still finds it necessary to chide government leaders for their partial financial support. Exact budgetary details are unknown but one recent account estimates that member states owe $30 million in arrears, approximately three times the organization's annual operating budget.[51]

Financial liquidity can be met by launching successful appeals for particular purposes. This practice is characteristic of nearly all international relief assistance. In circumstances where implementing capacity of the agency is low, this method of financing can be of limited use. The principal reason is the difficulty agencies face of scaling-up their operational capacity or being able to coordinate multinational efforts without prior investment in standby arrangements.

Earmarked emergency funds are another method to finance humanitarian action. When response systems are in place, earmarked funds can improve reaction times. Over the last 25 years several development banks and regional organizations (in the North and South) have established emergency funds. To highlight several examples, the Caribbean Development Bank disbursed over $50 million for disaster rehabilitation (1974–97). It has created two additional funding windows for emergency relief. The Asian Development Bank has two earmarked emergency rehabilitation assistance windows, one for small island states and the other open to all borrowing member states. In 1988, the South Asian Association for Regional Cooperation (SAARC) created a Food Security Reserve for emergencies, and the South Pacific Forum Secretariat's Regional Natural Disaster Relief Fund provides immediate financial assistance in the wake of natural disasters. In addition to these geographically defined sources of financing, a few inter-regional funds exist, such as the Islamic Development Bank's Special Assistance Account and OPEC's Fund for International Development.

In Africa, IGAD and SADC have contemplated developing a disaster relief fund but currently only the African Development Bank (ADB) and the OAU have dedicated funds for humanitarian assistance. In 1973, the ADB, then wholly African in its membership, created the Special Relief Fund (later renamed the Special Relief Fund for African Countries Affected by Drought). As of June 1998, the Fund's cumulative contributions total $34 million. In 1984 the OAU created the Special Emergency Assistance Fund for Drought and Famine (SEADF). The SEADF provides loans and grants, typically not exceeding $1 million for relief assistance and food production. As of June 1998, it disbursed close to $25 million, the majority generated on a voluntary basis by African governments. Also at its discretion is the OAU's Special Contingency Fund for Assistance to African Refugees (SCFAR). This Fund finances the operations of the Bureau of Refugees, Displaced Persons and Humanitarian Affairs. The SCFAR has a $600,000 annual operating budget provided by a two per cent allocation of the OAU regular budget. Like the majority of financial arrangements, it is open to voluntary contributions and international contributions.

Compared to humanitarian assistance funds, peacekeeping has attracted more external support. Shortly after the OAU established the Mechanism for Conflict Prevention, Management and Resolution, it created the Peace Fund to finance the Mechanism's operational activities. Although the Mechanism and the Peace Fund met with considerable enthusiasm from some member and non-member states, the Peace Fund relies increasingly on non-African support and has had difficulty keeping a positive balance. From its inception in 1993 until March 1996, the Peace Fund received approximately $11.5 million but had a deficit. As of that time, half of the Peace Fund's resources came directly from the OAU's budget, and voluntary contributions, non-African states contributed the remaining half.[52] Following Salim Salim's appeal for support at the 1996 OAU Summit, the Fund attracted considerable resources. As of March 1998, the Peace Fund had approximately $6 million in reserves, raising close to $26 million to date. This cumulative total includes: $1.5 million from African voluntary contributions, $6.6 million from the 6 per cent annual contribution from the OAU's regular budget, and $17.6 million from outside of Africa.[53] The Peace Fund collected more money in four years than the OAU's SEADF fund did over the course of its 14 year existence.

Non-African contributions to the Peace Fund rose sharply from 50 per cent in 1996 to 68 per cent by 1998. This presents two related problems. First it creates the perception that African countries are less committed to sustaining the Peace Fund than donors despite the fact that OAU member states have set an important precedent by supporting the OAU Peace Fund directly from the OAU's regular budget. In contrast, UN humanitarian assistance is voluntary. The second related problem, to quote Salim Salim, is the ownership of initiatives which will 'become questionable if non-African resources...outstrip African ones for conflict management activities'.[54] In mirror fashion, IGAD created its Peace Fund, but unlike the OAU Peace Fund, it solely depends on external contributions. IGAD members do raise sufficient funds to cover secretariat overheads but project funding remains reliant on external donors. In sum, African organizations require more resources but the source of this funding and its reliability will continue to limit the ability of regional organizations to assume a direct operational role.

This section has illustrated important regional and subregional developments that deepen and widen the humanitarian capacities of several African intergovernmental organizations. At present the OAU offers the most comprehensive institutional framework for managing and mobilizing resources for humanitarian action. Importantly, some OAU member states have begun, however tentatively, to endorse the view that intrastate conflict represents a threat to regional security and economic growth and in turn appear willing to prioritize human security over national sovereignty. Also significant are initiatives within SADC and ECOWAS to build on their *ad hoc* responses to humanitarian emergencies. Once the ECOWAS Mechanism and SADC peace force are operational, west and southern Africa will have the basis of a complementary system for preventing and reacting to humanitarian emergencies. Similar developments have yet to materialize in north and central Africa but there is hope among donors that IGAD will play a more significant role in the Horn.

Assisting the Development of Subsidiarity

This section investigates multilateral and bilateral assistance designed to enhance regional capacity for peace and security operations and humanitarian assistance. This survey is representative of emerging trends – it is not a comprehensive list of donor projects. As noted earlier, funding for international humanitarian assistance rose sharply in the 1990s, and most of this assistance was reflexive in nature. During the same period, a chorus of international efforts sought to influence donors to adopt a preventive rather than a palliative approach.[55] Responding to critics and experimenting with new modalities, some donors developed institution-building projects to enhance government and intergovernmental capacities for humanitarian action. Several features of these approaches stand out. In the humanitarian assistance field, prevention is stressed, whereas for peace and security, donors tended to emphasize response mechanisms. Moreover, little attention is paid to promoting each within an integrated regional framework.

Finally, the bilateral nature of most programmes side-steps the issue of clarifying lines of responsibility among the UN agencies, regional and subregional organizations and governments.

Capacity Development for Peace and Security Operations

As mentioned earlier, the model of subsidiarity envisioned in the UN Charter did not materialize during the Cold War period. When Boutros-Ghali revisited the working of the tiered relationship between the UN and regional organization in his *Agenda for Peace*, he trumpeted the virtues of a subsidiarity model, not least because of its potential to 'lighten the burden of the [Security] Council'. While that model is conceptually appealing, making cooperation work will test the commitment of the international community. As one recent UN document underscores, the international community will have to invest 'significantly' to develop an African peacekeeping capacity before the burden on the Security Council is lifted.[56]

Following the consultative process initiated by Boutros Boutros-Ghali in July 1998, Kofi Annan convened the third high-level meeting with secretaries-general of regional organizations to rethink cooperative strategies in the field of peace and security. In keeping with the meeting's focus, the UN Security Council subsequently passed Resolution 1197 recommending financial and technical assistance to strengthen African regional and subregional arrangements for conflict prevention.[57] The UN Department of Peacekeeping Operations' (DPKO) contribution to this dialogue has in certain respects shifted the emphasis of debate from conflict prevention to peacekeeping. DPKO's review of principles and precedents in the field of joint UN-regional organization peacekeeping operations began to channel the debate into programme activities.[58] The peace and security agenda it forwards returns to the Charter wherein the UN maintains its control and command authority. At the same time, regional organizations are to take a lead diplomatic role and, in the event of armed conflict, mount a peacekeeping operation.

Concretely, the UN has lent political, material and financial support to several regional and subregional organizations for preventive action, but it lacks sufficient resources to contribute to the development and maintenance of a peacekeeping force in the region. The primary UN funding mechanism is its Trust Fund for Improving Preparedness for Conflict Prevention and Peacekeeping in Africa. The Fund's sole supporter is the UK, and from its establishment in July 1996 to February 1999 the trust fund received a paltry $266,561, of which $151,105 has been spent.[59] Cognizant of its limited resources, the UN is proceeding modestly. In April 1998, the UN established a political liaison office at OAU headquarters. The UN has also proposed several other capacity-building exercises: a scholarship programme; a system of secondment, placing UN liaison officers with regional organizations and officers of regional organizations to the UN; developing standby arrangements; improving systems for exchanging information; and training African police units to increase the civilian composition of peacekeeping operations.[60] All of this indicates a desire to build regional capacity and competencies – a crucial link of a subsidiary strategy.

In the few circumstances where regional organizations have launched peacekeeping and peace-enforcement operations, leadership control and accountability problems were evidenced.[61] There remains, however, considerable interest in increasing the role of regional organizations. The main backing for bolstering African peace and security capacity comes from France, Britain and the US, three of the five permanent members of the Security Council. Their motives have been criticized in light of their Security Council voting records in delaying or preventing the authorization of preventive or reactive UN action. Yet at the same time, these governments are providing bilateral military training to selective African militaries to enhance their peacekeeping capacities.

'Guidimakha 98' was a pilot peacekeeping training exercise hosted by France. The February 1998 exercise brought together 3,000 west African soldiers and involved the US and the UK. This was the beginning of what is known as the 'Strengthening of African Peace-keeping Capacity' (RECAMP) programme. A follow-on training operation took place in January 2000 in Gabon where eight central African military contingents were involved. The British Army and the Foreign Office are also providing peacekeeping training and material to military colleges in Ghana and Zimbabwe under their African Peace-keeping Training Support Programme.

The US programme, the African Crisis Response Initiative (ACRI), aims to train ten peacekeeping battalions. The ACRI project began in 1997, and by March 1998 Senegal, Uganda, Malawi and Mali had completed the first stage. Ghana and Ethiopia were scheduled for joint training exercises in 1998, each receiving approximately $1.2 million to cover training and equipment costs. During US Secretary of State Madeleine Albright's 1998 six-country trip to Africa, she enlisted the support of Kenya. The decision to participate by President Moi, whose democratic credentials to participate in the ACRI programme are highly questionable, represents a reversal of his earlier opposition to ACRI. He had held the opinion that ACRI was a means to absolve UN obligation to respond to Africa's international conflicts. In addition to US military training, the Pentagon launched in Dakar in 1999 a strategic studies centre to promote thinking on security in the continent. The US Defence Department has set aside $42 million to fund the centre, a sum that is higher than the entire annual operating budget of the OAU and 14 times the amount which the UNDP was able to raise to support the OAU Mechanism.[62]

Salim Salim's 1998 Annual Report to the 34th OAU Summit argued that external peacekeeping support needs to be channelled through the OAU's Mechanism for Conflict Prevention, Management and Resolution. In addition, African peacekeeping needs to be embedded within an overall multinational peacekeeping framework spearheaded by the UN Security Council.[63] For the US at least, the authority issue is not a central concern. The US coordinator for ACRI described the logic of US efforts in these words: 'What we are doing and others are doing [is] training units that would be able to respond to a crisis. ...*The political legitimacy of a particular operation would come from the structure of the operation. We are not dealing with that at this point.*'[64] Salim Salim and the Chief of Defence Staff have also criticized US, French and British military support on the basis of its selectivity which introduced a destabilizing dynamic among neighbouring countries.[65] Despite donor interest and the receptiveness among participating African militaries for training, the scale of these exercises will not significantly alter the peacekeeping burden. Meanwhile the political controversy and future costs of maintaining the foreseen standing peacekeeping force argues for an alternative approach – one that enhances the coordinating role of regional organizations in conflicts threatening international security and de-emphasizes, for the time being, their direct military role.

The appropriateness and effectiveness of regional organizations in maintaining regional peace and security is a contested subject. Mark Zacher's early study of regional arrangements finds the OAU effective only during its first three years in defusing regional conflicts. Nevertheless he accredits the organization with propagating the norm of non-interference.[66] Keeping in mind this contribution, it is relevant to question the merits of transferring military response capacity to Africa. MacFarlane and Weiss, in their study of regional security mechanisms elsewhere, debunk the notion that regional organizations are more adept at managing regional conflicts on the grounds of their nuanced perspective, greater self-interest and ability to accommodate sovereignty issues. They observe that these attributes are likely more than offset by the disadvantages resulting from partisanship and inability to mobilize political and financial resources. Consequently, they recommend that the UN maintains its pre-eminent role in security issues.[67] A few examples supporting their thesis are the political divisions evident in SADC resulting from its Congo intervention, contested land claims and border disputes affecting all Maghreb countries, and the Francophone–Anglophone division within ECOWAS.

The partisanship and local rivalries that MacFarlane and Weiss refer to in the military field have parallels in other aspects, including the management and delivery of humanitarian assistance. There is, however, a

76   INTERNATIONAL PEACEKEEPING

need for a regional relief response capacity in Africa. Such capacity would have several merits, not least of which would be the ability to respond if timely and adequate external assistance is not forthcoming. Currently, though, international assistance seems more inclined to finance and support regional peace and security operations than to build capacities for humanitarian assistance.[68]

Capacity Development for Humanitarian Assistance

Existing initiatives to enhance African capacity to undertake relief operations (prevention, relief, rehabilitation and mitigation) are predominately bilateral efforts between governments. To date, regional arrangements have been largely overlooked as potential collaborators. In a context where national relief systems are weak, easily overwhelmed, and the causes and consequences of humanitarian emergencies are shared there is a strong case for developing a regional humanitarian system.

The few partnerships that have emerged focus on prevention, including famine prevention projects, food security initiatives and early warning systems. In the UN system, the operational agencies (for example, WFP, FAO and UNDP) have taken the lead in collaborating with regional organizations. OCHA, with its responsibility for humanitarian coordination, has not taken an active role in integrating humanitarian issues into the peace and security agenda pursued by DPA and DPKO. OCHA's collaboration with regional organizations is limited in scope. As expressed in its 1999 workplan, OCHA seeks to 'promote the participation of African institutions in the development policy on humanitarian issues by organizing three workshops in regional centres in Africa during 1999 with specific recommendations for resulting follow-up action'.[69] In light of the few regional organizations that have existing humanitarian instruments, OCHA, with its limited resources, is not well positioned to promote or coordinate capacity development. The recently established UN liaison office at OAU headquarters will hopefully create an opening for OCHA to enhance regional humanitarian coordination.

The peripheral role of regional organizations in planning, implementing or coordinating relief assistance is partly the consequence of bilateral aid that reinforces the centrality of national and non-governmental institutions. Two notable exceptions are the Club du Sahel's assistance to the Permanent Inter-State Committee for Drought Control in the Sahel (CILSS) in west Africa, and the US Greater Horn of Africa Initiative (GHAI) programme which involves IGAD. GHAI, launched in 1994, represents a considerable investment in supporting the development of a regional humanitarian system. GHAI seeks to coordinate various US government agencies working with IGAD, its member states and civil society organizations in the region. Interestingly, this programme is premised on the synergistic benefits of an integrated regional network.

The promotion of IGAD as a regional instrument mirrors a long-running partnership between the CILSS and the Club du Sahel, a forum of OECD donors. CILSS was founded by the Francophone members of ECOWAS after the 1972–73 Sahel drought and is now one of the most developed institutions of its kind in Africa. It has developed operational and research capabilities in food security, natural resource management and agricultural development. When CILSS was established it was in a similar position to IGAD today with uncertain political and financial support. In the case of CILSS, the Club du Sahel provided ongoing technical and financial assistance. CILSS' contribution to reducing food insecurity gradually improved but it was ill-prepared to respond to the 1985 Sahelian drought. The emphasis had been on prevention but when an international response was required, both CILSS and the international community failed to coordinate relief assistance with a regional perspective. Left undirected, donor food aid was not coordinated, it arrived late and undermined grain markets the following year.

As a result of the 1985 failures and at the request of CILSS Ministers, a Network for the Prevention of Food Crisis in the Sahel was created. The Network is a permanent but informal mechanism for information exchange between CILSS and the Club du Sahel. The Network links CILSS' specialized agencies with Club du Sahel members and their multilateral relief and development agencies to exchange food security projections, discuss mitigation strategies, and coordinate relief assistance. The Network is recognized by the World Food Program as a model of institutional cooperation for strengthening humanitarian action. The evolving partnership arrangement between CILSS and Club du Sahel demonstrates that strengthening CILSS' own technical capacity is as important as nurturing collaborative ties among governments and other organizations. It also points to the danger of relying too heavily on prevention mechanisms and the peril of not having a follow-up strategy for emergency assistance should prevention and early warning systems fail.

The donor emphasis on strengthening prevention strategies is logical. In theory, early-warning systems can provide timely and accurate information on potential or actual disasters that, in turn, can improve the reaction time and the overall response. This is the motivation behind FAO's Global Information and Early Warning System on Food and Agriculture (GIEWS)[70] and OCHA's Integrated Regional Information Network (IRIN).[71] OCHA describes its network as a humanitarian information system that updates and alerts actors and institutions on a wide range of humanitarian, political, economic and social issues from a regional perspective. While regional, these networks are

Collective Security Law

not embedded in the structures of existing regional and subregional organizations. Miskel and Norton argue that early-warning systems are conceptually sound but their case studies of the Rwanda, Burundi and Zaire crises of 1996 indicate that early warning is not sufficient.[72] In light of the tragic repercussions of the international community's belated response to the Great Lakes crisis and recognizing that early warning systems do fail as evidenced in the 1985 Sahelian famine, partnership arrangements should ensure that regional organizations have at a minimum the capacity to coordinate efforts with local and international agencies.

The ability of regional organizations to prevent or respond to humanitarian needs, either independently or in concert with the UN, would be enhanced if they had the capacity for peace and security and relief operations. This balanced approach recognizes the current interdependence and potential complementarity of military and civilian assets. However, donors are not pursuing this approach. Rather, the major bilateral donors are supporting regional peacekeeping arrangements, which is expensive, politically divisive within subregional groupings and may aggravate tensions between regional clubs. While armed conflict is a source of grave human suffering and death, natural disasters affect even more people in Africa.[73] Thus, donor assistance could make a lasting impact by increasing their support to existing and emerging humanitarian instruments in CILSS, IGAD, SADC and within the humanitarian component of ECOWAS' Mechanism for Conflict Prevention, Management, Resolution, Peace-Keeping and Security. While the donor community should build on these promising developments, subregional mechanisms in north and central Africa present a more complicated problem. It is one thing for an organization to widen its mandate but it is quite another when no mandate exists and those that do are not supported by member states.

Conclusions

Realigning responsibility within the tiered regime of the UN and regional organizations holds many consequences for regional organizations and their member states. Principally, they will be under increasing pressure to provide more leadership, personnel and financial resources. Movement in this direction is congruent with recent African leadership statements calling on Africans and African organizations to assume greater responsibility for meeting humanitarian needs and achieving development objectives. However, the forces driving the subsidiarity debate do not indicate that the major actors are committed to burden-sharing so as to create the requisite competencies among African intergovernmental organizations.

The survey of Africa's regional and subregional organizations demonstrates that the principal ones have neither the institutional mechanisms nor sufficient financial resources to undertake humanitarian action at the level recent emergencies have required. Some organizations have developed particular niches, however, and several others are seeking to expand their capabilities. In an encouraging development, crisis-driven *ad hoc* responses are being replaced by more institutionalized humanitarian mechanisms. The response of the donor community and UN agencies has been mixed. There have been some innovative and longstanding partnerships to prevent and respond to the multidimensional causes and consequences of humanitarian emergencies. On balance, however, the track record of major bilateral donors (and the US in particular) demonstrates that they are intent on leaving Africa to its own resources. To date, African militaries have received support to groom them for their future peacekeeping role. Many important issues remain outstanding, such as whether or not regional arrangements will adhere to international law governing the use of force; the need to clarify governance issues at the regional level concerning authorization and control over the use of force; and, what role, if any, regional instruments will have in coordinating regional and international humanitarian action.

The call for subsidiarity foresees an increased involvement of regional organizations in humanitarian affairs. Whether the regionalization of humanitarian action results in more effective action will depend on whether the' burden-sharing or burden-shifting approach prevails. Noting the resources currently available at the regional level, it is not overstating the influence of bilateral and multilateral donors to claim that they could play a significant part in fortifying Africa's emerging instruments. The burden-shifting option would lift what is a very small financial contribution for OECD countries and relocate it to the emerging humanitarian efforts in Africa with potentially disastrous effect. If the burden is shifted in this manner, the international humanitarian system will be dealt an additional setback that it can ill afford. In that framework, burden-shifting would be an affront to humanitarian principles and an abrogation of global responsibility.

ACKNOWLEDGEMENTS

The author benefited from comments on an earlier version of this article from Dylan Hendrickson, W. Andy Knight, Shepard Forman, Cesare Romano, Barnett Rubin, Stewart Patrick and from a conversion with Adekeye Adebajo. The views expressed here do not necessarily reflect theirs or the Center on International Cooperation's. The author acknowledges the partial support of the John D. and Catherine T. MacArthur Foundation.

80   INTERNATIONAL PEACEKEEPING

NOTES

1. This term is borrowed from Cary Coglianese and Kalypso Nicolaïdis, 'Securing Subsidiarity: Legitimacy and the Allocation of Governing Authority', *Working Papers*, Harvard: John F. Kennedy School of Government, 1997.

2. Humanitarian action is defined as consisting of peace and security operations and humanitarian assistance. The former encompasses the following elements: (i) peacemaking (ii) peace-enforcement (iii) peacekeeping, and (iv) peacebuilding. The latter involves the following components: (i) preparedness planning (ii) mitigation (iii) relief assistance, and (iv) rehabilitation.

3. See, for example, CEPR, *Making Sense of Subsidiarity: How Much Centralization for Europe*. Monitoring European Integration 4, London: Centre for Economic Policy Research, 1993.

4. W. Andy Knight, 'Towards a Subsidiarity Model for Peacemaking and Preventive Diplomacy: Making Chapter VIII of the UN Charter Operational', *Third World Quarterly*, Vol.17, No.1, 1996, p.49.

5. Unfortunately, this condition cannot be taken for granted. In both war-torn environments and natural disasters, humanitarian assistance has been manipulated by governments for political gain and personal profit. See for example, Alex DeWaal, *Famine Crimes: Politics and the Disaster Relief Industry in Africa*, Oxford: James Curry, 1997, Chapters 5 and 8; and, David Keen, *The Benefits of Famine: A Political Economy of Famine in South-Western Sudan, 1983–1989,* Princeton N.J.: Princeton University Press, 1994.

6. See Genevieve Peterson, 'Political Inequality at the Congress of Vienna', *Political Science Quarterly*, Vol.60, No.4, 1945, pp.544–7; and, Harold Jacobson, *Networks of Interdependence: International Organizations and the Global Political System*, New York: Alfred A. Knopf, 2nd edition, 1984, pp.8–9.

7. Treaty Establishing the European Community (signed in Rome on 25 Mar. 1957), available at <http://www.europa.eu.int/abc/obj/treaties/en/entr6b.htm#Article_3b> (visited 10 July 1999). The principle was then reinserted in the Treaty on European Union (TITLE I, Common provisions, Article G(5), signed in Maastricht 1992).

8. *The Covenant of the League of Nations* (signed 28 June 1919), available at <http://ac.acusd.edu/History/text/versaillestreaty/all440.html> (visited 2 Aug. 1999).

9. UN Charter, Chapter VI: Pacific Settlement of Disputes, Article 33 (1).

10. *UN Charter*, Chapter VIII: Regional Arrangements, Article 52 (2). The only restriction placed on regional action is the use of force where the Security Council reserves ultimate authority (Article 53 (1)).

11. Chapter VIII, Article 52 (3) reads: 'The Security Council shall encourage the development of pacific settlement of local disputes through such regional arrangements or by such regional agencies either on the initiative of the states concerned or by reference from the Security Council'.

12. A recent exception is the Security Council approval of the UN Mission in the Democratic Republic of the Congo (MONUC) on 30 Nov. 1999, to monitor the Lusaka Ceasefire Agreement of July 1999. The Security Council authorized the deployment of 5,537 military officers, including up to 500 military observers. As of 29 Feb. 2000, there are 83 military, 28 international civilian and 28 local staff currently active.

13. Evan Luard, *The United Nations*, New York: St. Martin's Press, 1994, p.186.

14. Boutros Boutros-Ghali, *Agenda for Peace: Preventive Diplomacy, Peace Making and Peacekeeping* (A/47/277-S/24111), 17 June 1992, para.64.

15. Kofi Annan, *The Causes of Conflict and the Promotion of Durable Peace and Sustainable Development in Africa*, New York: United Nations, July 1998, para.41.

16. UNHCR, *International Solidarity and Burden-sharing in All its Aspects: National, Regional and International Responsibilities for Refugees* (A/AC.96/904), 31 August 1998. Also see, 'UN Regular Budget Should Fund Humanitarian Affairs Coordination, Economic and Social Council is Told', *Press Release*, ECOSOC/5777, 15 July 1998.

17. 'UN Looks to Donors for Aid', *Chronicle of Philanthropy*, Vol.11, No.22, 9 September 1999.

18. The difference between the UN inter-agency appeal and government contribution represents

the funding gap. For more information and supportive data, see *The Financial Tracking Database For Complex Emergencies,* available at <http://www.reliefweb.int/fts/index.html>.

19. Bilateral and government support to NGOs are not included here, nor are all humanitarian emergencies. For more on OCHA data as a measure of aggregate funding, and a more detailed analysis of the shortcomings of current funding arrangements, see Shepard Forman and Rita Parhad, 'Paying for Essentials: Resources for Humanitarian Assistance', *Journal of Humanitarian Assistance,* <http://www.nyu.edu/pages/cic/pubs/humanassist_bg.html>, 1997; and United Nations, *Strengthening of the Coordination of Humanitarian and Disaster Relief Assistance of the United Nations, Including Special Economic Assistance: Strengthening of the Coordination of Emergency Humanitarian Assistance of the United Nations* (A/53/139-E/1998/67), 12 June 1998.

20. On the role of the media see, Larry Minear, Colin Scott and Thomas G. Weiss, *The News Media, Civil War, and Humanitarian Action,* Boulder, Colo.: Lynne Rienner, 1996.

21. 'The African Renaissance, South Africa and the World', Speech by Deputy President Thabo Mbeki at United Nations University, 9 Apr. 1998.

22. Salim Ahmed Salim, *Introductory Note to the Report to the 68th Ordinary Session of the Council of Ministers and to the 34th Ordinary Session of the Assembly of Heads of State and Government,* Addis Ababa, 22 May 1998.

23. Ahmedou Ould Abdallah, quoted in *Le Monde Diplomatique,* April 1999, p.9. As a footnote to this, the UN General Assembly has insisted that 'measures aimed at helping Africa should not become a justification for reduced engagement in the continent by the international community'. UN, *Enhancement of African Peacekeeping Capacity* (General Assembly, A/54/63), 12 February 1999, para.7.

24. Chester Crocker, former US Assistant Secretary of State for Africa, quoted in 'US Seen Leaving Africa to Solve its Own Crises', *The Boston Globe,* 19 Feb. 1999, A2.

25. 'The Increasing Role of Regional Organizations in Africa', *Dispatch Magazine,* Bureau of Public Affairs, US Department of State, Vol.5, No.45, 1994.

26. According to European and UN diplomats quoted in the *Boston Globe* (n.24 above), 'In some cases, as in Sierra Leone, the United States has actively thwarted efforts by the United Nations to take on peacekeeping operations that might have prevented some of Africa's wars.' The article also mentions Washington's reluctance to back a British proposal to deploy peacekeepers in Sierra Leone in the winter of 1997. By the spring of 1997 guerrilla forces had ousted the elected president. Similarly, the Angolan army invaded the Republic of Congo in 1998 after the Clinton administration refused to back a UN proposal to deploy a UN peacekeeping mission. The article suggests that the real motivation behind the lack of US engagement in Africa is its reticence to finance UN missions in Africa.

27. Sir Kieran Prendergast, interview with Joe Sills, Annual Meeting of the Academic Council of the United Nations System, New York, 17 June 1999.

28. OCHA, *Humanitarian Coordination: Lessons Learned,* 1998, p.3.

28. NGOs are important actors but they rarely have the capacity to undertake, in a coherent and coordinated manner, the range of humanitarian actions at a national or regional level. Furthermore, most NGOs do not have an independent funding base. While the private and corporate sector make humanitarian contributions, their contributions have been episodic and therefore unreliable.

30. Adam Roberts, 'The Role of Humanitarian Issues in International Politics in the 1990s', *International Review of the Red Cross,* No.833, 1999, pp.19–43. Boutros Boutros-Ghali popularized this expansion of current activities as multifunctional peacekeeping. See Boutros Boutros-Ghali, *Supplement to an Agenda for Peace* (A/50/60–S/1995/1), 3 Jan. 1995, para.8–22.

31. See for example, Boutros-Ghali (n.14 and 30 above); DPKO, *Cooperation Between the United Nations and Regional Organizations in Peacekeeping and Peace Support Operations,* New York: DPKO, Lessons Learned Unit, Mar. 1999; and OCHA, *OCHA in 1999,* New York and Geneva: Office for the Coordination of Humanitarian Affairs, 1999. Compare with, Kofi Annan (n.15 above), para.46–62.

32. Roy May and Gerry Cleaver, 'The OAU Intervention in Chad: Mission Impossible or Mission Evaded', *International Peacekeeping,* Vol.5, No.1, 1998.

33. Cedric De Coning, 'The Role of the OAU in Conflict Management in Africa', *Conflict Management, Peacekeeping and Peacebuilding: Lessons for Africa from a Seminar Past*, Monograph No.10, South Africa: Halfway House, Institute for Security Studies, 1997, p.7.
34. Quoted in Connie Peck, *Sustainable Peace*, New York: Rowman & Littlefield, 1998, p.163.
35. *Recommendations of the Chiefs of Defence Staff Adopted in the Second Meeting in Harare Concerning the Peace Support Operations*, Addis Ababa: OAU.
36. ECCAS member states all participate in the UN Standing Advisory Committee on Security Questions in Africa, which meets twice a year to discuss ways to reduce small arms trade, but the organization itself does not have an established security arrangement.
37. COMESA's treaty calls on member states to maintain an atmosphere conducive to peace and security 'with a view to preventing, better managing and resolving inter-State or intra-State conflicts', Article 163, Chapter 27.
38. IGAD member states include: Djibouti, Eritrea, Ethiopia, Kenya, Somalia, Sudan and Uganda.
39. Intergovernmental Authority on Development, *Programme on Conflict Resolution and Management: Terms of Reference for the Elaboration of a Strategy for the IGAD Region*, Djibouti, 1997.
40. IGAD's 1998 'Sub-regional Disaster Preparedness Strategy' outlines an action plan to become more involved in disaster management. The study was supported by the Food and Agriculture Organization of the United Nations. It represents a widening of previous work in the food security field.
41. ECOWAS member states include: Benin, Burkina Faso, Cape Verde, Côte d'Ivoire, Gambia, Ghana, Guinea, Guinea-Bissau, Liberia, Mali, Mauritania, Niger, Nigeria, Senegal, Sierra Leone and Togo. In Dec. 1999, Mauritania announced its intention to leave ECOWAS.
42. SADC member states include: Angola, Botswana, Congo DR, Lesotho, Malawi, Mauritius, Mozambique, Namibia, Seychelles, South Africa, Swaziland, Tanzania, Zambia and Zimbabwe.
43. *Africa Research Bulletin*, Dec. 1999, p.13789.
44. ECOWAS Executive Secretariat, *ECOWAS Mechanism for Conflict Prevention Management Resolution Peace-Keeping and Security: Draft Mechanism*, Meeting of the Ministers of Defence, Internal Affairs and Security, Banjul, 23–24 July 1998.
45. Adekeye Adebajo and Chris Landsberg, '*Pax Africana* in the Age of Extremes', *South African Journal of International Affairs*, Vol.7, No.1, 2000, p.16.
46. A ministerial coordination meeting on the flood disaster in Southern Africa took place on 3 Mar. 2000. One medium to long term issue discussed was the possibility of creating a SADC Disaster Management Unit.
47. For a complete list of tasks and organization of the Organ, see Gavin Cawthra, 'Sub-Regional Security Cooperation: The Southern African Development Community in Comparative Perspective', *Working Paper*, Copenhagen Peace Research Institute, 1996.
48. Henry Ludski, 'The Force Will Be With Us, Go-ahead for SADC Peace Army', *Sunday Times* (S. Africa), 21 Mar. 1999.
49. *Africa Research Bulletin*, Dec. 1998, p.13350.
50. *Africa Research Bulletin*, Jan. 2000, p.13821.
51. Paul Ejime, 'ECOWAS New Chief Outlines Priorities', *Pan African News Agency*, 24 Nov. 1997.
52. De Coning (n.33 above), pp.8–9; Paul Ejime, 'Burundi Conflict Gulps Lion's Share of OAU Peace Fund,' *Pan African News Agency*, 25 Feb. 1997.
53. OAU, *Report of the Secretary General on the OAU Peace Fund, June 1993–March 1998*, Addis Ababa: OAU, 1998.
54. Ibid.
55. Perhaps the most ambitious initiative dedicated to influencing bilateral and multilateral approaches to conflict is the Carnegie Commission on Preventing Deadly Conflict. See their flag ship report, *Preventing Deadly Conflict: Final Report*, Washington D.C.: Carnegie Commission of New York, 1997.
56. UN (n.23 above).
57. UN Security Council Resolution 1197, 1998.

58. DPKO (n.31 above).
59. UN (n.23 above), Annex 1.
60. Ibid., para.43.
61. For supportive evidence see, Eric G. Berman, 'The Security Council's Increasing Reliance on Burden-Sharing: Collaboration or Abrogation?', *International Peacekeeping*, Vol.4, No.1, 1998, pp.1–21.
62. *Africa Research Bulletin*, Nov. 1999, p.13779.
63. Salim Ahmed Salim (n. 22 above), para.109–11.
64. Ambassador Marshall McCallie and Col. David E. McCracken, *On-the-Record Briefing, African Crisis Response Initiative*, US Dept. of State: Washington D.C., 28 July 1998, emphasis added.
65. Nigerian Foreign Minister Tom Ikimi called these bilateral initiatives 'an attempt to divide Africa and weaken its efforts to take care of its own security', *Panafrican News Agency*, 1 June 1998.
66. Mark Zacher, *International Conflicts and Collective Security, 1946–77*, New York: Praeger, 1979, p.155.
67. Neil S. MacFarlane and Thomas G. Weiss, 'The UN, Regional Organizations and Human Security', *Third World Quarterly*, Vol.2, No.1, 1994. Also see OECD, *Conflict, Peace and Development Cooperation on the Threshold of the 21st Century*, Paris: OECD, Development Assistance Committee, 1998, p.103.
68. It is significant in this respect that Security Council Resolution 1208 (19 November 1998) 'requests...the establishment of a new category within the...Trust Fund for Improving Preparedness for Conflict Prevention and Peacekeeping in Africa to support...the security and civilian and humanitarian character of refugee camps and settlements'.
69. OCHA (n.31 above), para.116.
70. See, <http://www.fao.org/waicent/faoinfo/economic/giews/english/giewse.htm>, for a fuller description.
71. OCHA has established three networks in Africa covering central and east Africa, west Africa, and southern Africa. All three regional networks are under-funded. OCHA (n.31 above), para.37.
72. James Miskel and Richard Norton, 'Humanitarian Early-Warning Systems', *Global Governance*, Vol.4, No.3, 1998, pp.317–29.
73. According to 1993–97 data compiled by the Centre de recherche sur l'épidémiologie des déastres (CRED), 44 million people in Sub-Saharan Africa were 'affected' by natural disasters whereas conflict affected 28 million, available at <www.md.ucl.ac.be/entities/esp/epid/mission/table4.htm> (visited Sept. 1998).

Name Index